MICROSOFT°
VISUAL C# .NET 2003
UNLEASHED

Kevin Hoffman
Lonny Kruger

SAMS

Sams Publishing, 800 East 96th St., Indianapolis, Indiana, 46240 USA

Microsoft Visual C# .NET 2003 Unleashed

Copyright © 2005 by Sams Publishing

International Standard Book Number: 0-672-32676-0

Library of Congress Catalog Card Number: 2004095069

Printed in the United States of America

First Printing: December 2004

07 06 05 04   4 3 2 1

Trademarks

Warning and Disclaimer

Bulk Sales

Sams Publishing offers excellent discounts on this book when ordered in quantity for bulk purchases or special sales. For more information, please contact

> **U.S. Corporate and Government Sales**
> 1-800-382-3419
> corpsales@pearsontechgroup.com

For sales outside of the U.S., please contact

> **International Sales**
> international@pearsoned.com

Associate Publisher
Michael Stephens

Acquisitions Editor
Neil Rowe

Development Editor
Mark Renfrow

Managing Editor
Charlotte Clapp

Project Editor
Andy Beaster

Copy Editor
Mike Henry

Indexer
Ginny Bess

Proofreader
Tracy Donhardt

Technical Editor
Dimitry Ivonov
Doug Holland
Christian Kenyeres

Publishing Coordinator
Cindy Teeters

Multimedia Developer
Dan Scherf

Designer
Gary Adair

Page Layout
Susan Geiselman

Contents at a Glance

Introduction 1

Part I: Introduction to the Visual Studio .NET IDE

1 The Visual Studio .NET IDE 6

Part II: Language Fundamentals

2 Introduction to C# 36
3 Expressions and Control Structures 52
4 Strings and Regular Expressions 74
5 Arrays and Collections 92
6 Objects and Classes 112
7 File and Stream I/O and Object Persistence 128
8 XML Fundamentals 154
9 Multithreaded Programming 184
10 Events and Delegates 210
11 Reflection and Code Attributes 228
12 Assemblies and AppDomains 242
13 COM and Windows Interoperability 274
14 High-Performance Programming 294

Part III: Windows Applications

15 Introduction to Windows Forms 314
16 Windows Forms User Interface Controls 330
17 Creating Visually Compelling Windows Forms Applications 350
18 Consuming Web Services 372
19 Smart Clients 390
20 Deploying Windows Applications 402

Part IV: Web Applications

21 Introduction to Web Forms and ASP.NET 424
22 Web UI Controls 440
23 State Management in ASP.NET 456
24 Caching 484
25 Advanced ASP.NET 498
26 Deploying ASP.NET Applications 520

Part V: Data Access

27 Using .NET Data Providers 536

28 Creating a Custom ADO.NET Data Provider 554

29 Typed DataSets and XSD 588

30 Windows Forms Data Binding 612

31 Web Forms Data Binding 634

Part VI: Web Services

32 Introduction to Web Services 662

33 Using WSE 2.0 678

Part VII: Secure Applications

34 Code Access Security 694

35 Securing Sensitive Data 710

36 Securing ASP.NET Web Applications 734

37 Licensing and Intellectual Property 754

Part VIII: Enterprise and Connected Applications

38 Interface Programming 774

39 Remoting 792

40 COM+ Enterprise Services 808

41 Enterprise Templates 828

Part IX: Debugging and Testing

42 Debugging Your Applications 850

43 Monitoring Your Applications 872

44 Instrumenting Your Application 890

45 The Future of C# 908

Index 918

Table of Contents

Introduction   1

Part I: Introduction to the Visual Studio .NET IDE   5

CHAPTER 1: The Visual Studio .NET IDE   6

Window Management and Customization 7

    Customized Interfaces with Visual Studio .NET's "Developer Profiles" 7

    Configuring Keyboard Shortcuts 8

    Filtering the MSDN Help 9

    Maximizing Your Viewable Area 9

    Using Visual Studio .NET 2003's Dockable Windows 10

Understanding Visual Studio .NET 2003's Tool Windows 14

Working with Documents 18

    Enhancing the Text Editor 18

    Finding Help Where You Need It 22

    Editing HTML 26

    Editing XML 29

    Editing Binary Files 30

Using External Tools 30

    Defining Your Own Tools 31

Summary 32

Further Reading 32

Part II: Language Fundamentals   35

CHAPTER 2: Introduction to C#   36

Why Learn Yet Another Language? 37

Learning Common Types 38

    Understanding Value Types 38

    Understanding Reference Types 39

    Reference Versus Value Types 40

What Is the Common Language Runtime? 40

    Multiple Languages, One Runtime 42

    Isolation 42

Platform Invoke 42

Code Access Security 42

The JIT Compiler 43

Code Execution 43

COM Interoperability 43

Rotor: Microsoft's Shared Source Common Language Infrastructure 44

Take Out the Trash: Theory of Garbage Collection 44

Reference Counting 44

Generations 44

Collection 45

Partial Collection 45

Nondeterministic Finalization 45

Using IDisposable to Create Well-Behaved Objects 46

Introduction to the Base Class Library 48

The Canonical "Hello World" Example 49

Summary 51

Further Reading 51

CHAPTER 3: Expressions and Control Structures   **52**

Expressions and Control Structures 53

Basic Expressions 53

Legal Variable Names 53

Using C# Operators 54

Pre/Post Operators 60

Program Flow Control: Control Structures 60

The Program Execution Path 60

Conditional Statements 60

The if Control Structure 61

The if/else Control Structure Combination 61

Short Circuit Evaluation 62

Using the Ternary Operator 64

The switch Statement 65

Looping 68

The for Loop 68

Using the for Statement 69

The foreach Statement 69

The while Loop 70

The do..while Loop 72

Summary 73

Further Reading 73

CHAPTER 4: Strings and Regular Expressions   **74**

String Basics 75

Understanding the Immutability of Strings 75

Applying Formatting to Strings 75

Using Escape Sequences 79

Locating Substrings 80

Adding Padding 80

Trimming Characters 81

Replacing Characters 81

Splitting Strings 82

Modifying Case 82

The StringBuilder 83

Appending Values 83

Using AppendFormat 83

Inserting Strings 83

Replacing Strings and Characters 84

Removing Substrings 84

Using Regular Expressions 85

Understanding Expression Syntax 85

How to Use Matching 85

Validating Data with Regular Expressions 89

Grouping Matches 89

Replacing Matched Strings 90

Summary 91

Further Reading 91

CHAPTER 5: Arrays and Collections   **92**

Using Arrays 93

Understanding Single-Dimensional and
Multidimensional Arrays 93

Explaining Jagged Arrays 95

Passing Arrays as Parameters 96

Collection Basics 98
   Understanding the Basic Collection Interfaces 98
   Iterating Through Collections 98
Collections Provided by the Base
Class Libraries 99
   Using an `ArrayList` 100
   Using a `Stack` 101
   Using a `Hashtable` 102
   Using a `BitArray` 103
   Using the `Queue` 104
   Using a `SortedList` 106
Creating Custom Collections 107
   Implementing the `CollectionBase` Class 107
   Creating a `AddressList` Collection 107
Summary 109
Further Reading 110

CHAPTER 6: Objects and Classes   **112**
Objects and Classes 112
   Class Attributes 113
   Operations in Object-Oriented Design and Programming 114
   Classes 116
   Objects 117
   Object State Maintenance 118
Advanced Topics in Classes and Objects 118
   Inheriting from Base Classes 119
   Introduction to Polymorphism 122
Summary 125
Further Reading 126

CHAPTER 7: File and Stream I/O and Object Persistence   **128**
File and Stream I/O 128
   Understanding File and Stream I/O 129
   Using Streams: `FileStream`, `MemoryStream`, `StringReader`, and
   `StringWriter` 132
   Using the `FileSystemWatcher` 138
Object Persistence 142
   Serializing Objects 143
   Extending Standard Serialization 149

Summary 152

Further Reading 152

CHAPTER 8: XML Fundamentals   **154**

Working with the DOM 155

    Creating an XML Document 161

    Working with XML Nodes, Elements, and Attributes 162

    Persisting the DOM 163

Using the XmlReader Classes 163

    What Is an XmlReader? 164

    Using the XmlTextReader 164

    Using the XmlValidatingReader 166

    Using the XmlNodeReader 167

    Making Use of XmlConvert 167

Exploring XPath 168

    Learning the Syntax 169

    Filtering Nodes 170

Introduction to the XPathDocument 171

    Introduction to XSLT 175

    Transforming XML Documents 175

Serialization XML Style 179

    Using Basic XML Serialization 179

    Customizing XML Serialization 181

Summary 183

Further Reading 183

CHAPTER 9: Multithreaded Programming   **184**

Thread Basics 185

    Understanding the Key Thread Properties and Methods 185

    Explaining the ThreadStart Delegate 187

    Creating a Thread 188

    Running a Thread 188

    Terminating a Thread 188

    Suspending a Thread 191

    Creating a Pause by "Sleeping" a Thread 191

    Joining a Thread 191

Synchronization 192
    Understanding the Different Types of Synchronization 193
Applying the lock Keyword 193
    Raising Thread Events 194
    Using the Mutex Class 196
    Using the Monitor Class 198
    Safeguarding Variables (Interlocked Increment/Decrement) 203
    Reading Without Waiting (ReaderWriterLock) 203
Using the Thread Pool for Asynchronous Programming 206
    Explaining the WaitCallback Delegate 206
    Queuing a Work Item 207
    Passing Data to Threads 208
Further Reading 209

CHAPTER 10: Events and Delegates   210
What Is a Delegate? 210
    Types of Delegates 215
    Delegates Inside 218
    Combined Delegates 219
    Events 221
Summary 226
Further Reading 226

CHAPTER 11: Reflection and Code Attributes   228
Working with Reflection 228
    Introduction to Reflection 229
    How Reflection Works 229
    Discovering Type Information at Runtime 229
Using Code Attributes 234
    Introduction to Code Attributes 234
    Using Code Attributes 235
    Creating Custom Attributes 236
    Querying Custom Attributes 238
Summary 241
Further Reading 241

CHAPTER 12: Assemblies and AppDomains   **242**

Assemblies 243

Introduction to Assemblies 243

Assembly Building Blocks 243

   Introducing the Assembly Manifest 244

   Metadata 246

   Inside the Assembly—MSIL Code 247

   Assembly Resources 247

Creating Assemblies 247

Embedding Content and
Resources in Assemblies 251

Localization and Satellite Assemblies 255

   Satellite Assemblies 256

AppDomains 259

   Introduction to AppDomains 259

   Programming with AppDomains 260

Putting It Together—A Real-World Example 264

   Building Application Plug-Ins 264

Summary 273

CHAPTER 13: COM and Windows Interoperability   **274**

Using .NET Code to Interact with COM 275

   Introduction to COM Interop 275

   The Runtime Callable Wrapper 275

   .NET to COM Marshalling 276

   Code Interoperability Example: .NET Code
   Invoking COM Code 278

COM to .NET 281

   The COM Callable Wrapper 281

   .NET Code Attributes for COM Interop Programming 281

   Marshalling Data from COM to .NET 282

   Interop Programming Example: COM Code Utilizing .NET Components 283

   When to Use Interop 285

Primary Interop Assemblies 286

   Overview of Primary Interop Assemblies 286

   Working with PIAs 286

   Producing and Deploying PIAs 287

Platform Invoke (P/Invoke) 288

    Introduction to Platform Invoke 288

    Consuming Unmanaged DLLs 288

    Platform Invoke—Data Marshalling 289

    Platform Invoke Sample—The Win32 API 290

    When to Use Platform Invoke 292

Summary 292

Further Reading 292

CHAPTER 14: High-Performance Programming   **294**

Introduction to Garbage Collection 295

    Garbage Collection Internals—Generations 295

    Coding with the Garbage Collector in Mind 296

    Caveat: Nondeterministic Finalization Versus Deconstruction 297

Memory and Class Management in the Common Language Runtime 300

    Boxing and Unboxing 300

    Collections and Boxing 302

    Using the `StringBuilder` Class 303

High-Performance Code: Best Practices 305

    Using Exceptions 305

    Chunky API Calls 305

    Value Versus Reference Types 306

    Tip: Using `AddRange` on Collections 307

    Jagged Versus Rectangular Arrays 307

    `For` Versus `Foreach` 308

    Utilizing Asynchronous I/O 310

Summary 310

Further Reading 310

Part III: Windows Applications   **313**

CHAPTER 15: Introduction to Windows Forms   **314**

Windows Forms Basics 314

    Introducing the `Main` Method 315

    Understanding the Forms Designer 316

Hello World 318

   Creating an Application Using the Windows
   Application Wizard 319

   Setting the Properties 321

   Compiling and Running the Application 322

   Responding to a Button Click 324

Summary 329

Further Reading 329

CHAPTER 16: Windows Forms User Interface Controls   **330**

Standard Windows Forms User Interface Controls 330

   Performing Actions with Controls 330

   Storing and Changing Values with Controls 334

   Maintaining Lists with Controls 337

User Controls 347

Summary 349

Further Reading 349

CHAPTER 17: Creating Visually Compelling Windows Forms Applications   **350**

Visual Inheritance 351

   Using Inherited Forms 351

   WinForms Visual Inheritance in Action 352

   Visual Inheritance Best Practices 358

Creating and Using Dynamic Context Menus 359

   Introduction to Contextual, Adaptive User Interfaces 360

   A Sample Dynamic Context Menu in Action 360

Drawing Custom List Elements 363

Using the DrawMode Property 363

   Creating a Custom ListBox 363

   Creating Custom Menu Items 365

Shaped Forms 368

   Introduction to Shaped Forms 368

   Creating a Sample Shaped Form 368

Summary 370

Further Reading 370

CHAPTER 18: Consuming Web Services   **372**

   Adding Web References 373

      Adding References in Visual Studio .NET 373

      Using `WSDL.EXE` 377

   Supporting Dynamic URLs 378

      Storing URLs in `app.config` 379

      Storing URLs in Isolated Storage 379

      Dynamic URLs via UDDI Consumption 382

   Consuming Web Services Asynchronously 383

      Multithreaded Service Consumption Sample 384

      Web Service Client Reliability 385

      Testing for Network Connection 386

      Handling Web Service Errors 387

      Supporting Offline Actions 387

   Summary 388

   Further Reading 388

CHAPTER 19: Smart Clients   **390**

   Smart Clients 390

      Understanding the Smart Client 391

      Deploying Smart Client Updates from a Centralized Server 392

      Make Use of Web Services for Smart Client
      Back-End Support 396

      Deciding Whether to Process on the Server Side or Client Side for Efficiency 400

      Make Use of Online and Offline Functionality 400

   Summary 401

   Further Reading 401

CHAPTER 20: Deploying Windows Applications   **402**

   Installing .NET Applications 402

      Understanding Assembly Deployment 403

      Placing Assemblies in the Global Assembly Cache 404

      Private Installations 409

   Web Installations 410

      Deploying from a URL 410

      Deploying Smart Client Applications 412

MSI/Project Installations 415

    Creating an Installation Project 415

Summary 421

Further Reading 421

Part IV: Web Applications   423

CHAPTER 21: Introduction to Web Forms and ASP.NET   424

Understanding the Web Forms Designer 424

Creating an ASP.NET "Hello World" Application 426

Basic Event Handling 433

Summary 438

Further Reading 438

CHAPTER 22: Web UI Controls   440

Server Controls 440

    User Controls 444

Summary 455

Further Reading 455

CHAPTER 23: State Management in ASP.NET   456

Client-Side State Management 456

    Understanding View State 456

    Using Hidden Form Fields 463

    Explaining Cookies 467

    Understanding Query Strings 471

    Passing Server Control Values Between Forms 474

Server-Side State Management 479

    Explaining Application State 480

    Understanding Session State 481

Summary 482

Further Reading 483

CHAPTER 24: Caching   484

Caching 484

    Introduction to ASP.NET Caching 485

    `OutputCache` Directive 486

Using `HttpCachePolicy` 489

Using the `Cache` Object 491

Summary 496

Further Reading 496

CHAPTER 25: Advanced ASP.NET   **498**

Creating ASP.NET Applications in a Web Farm 499

ViewState in a Web Farm 499

Session State Maintenance in a Web Farm 501

Application State in a Web Farm 503

Web Farm Configuration and Deployment 504

Web Farm Best Practices, Recommendations,
and Caveats 505

Localization and Globalization in ASP.NET 506

Using Localized Resources 506

Displaying Localized Content 507

"Out of the Box" Localization Functionality 511

Creating Custom HttpModules 513

Understanding the ASP.NET Application Events 513

Creating a Custom HttpModule 513

Creating Custom HttpHandlers 516

Building a Synchronous HttpHandler 516

Summary 518

Further Reading 519

CHAPTER 26: Deploying ASP.NET Applications   **520**

Manually Deploying an ASP.NET Application 521

Deploying via "Copy Project" 521

XCopy Deployment 522

When to XCopy 522

Automated Deployment 523

Creating a Setup Project 523

Deploying a Setup Project 529

Advanced ASP.NET Deployment 529

Web Farm Considerations 530

Firewalls, DMZs, Routers, and Security Constraints 530

Hosted Environment Considerations 532

Summary 533

Further Reading 533

Part V: Data Access   535

CHAPTER 27: Using .NET Data Providers   536

SQL Server Data Provider 537

    Introduction to the SQL Server Data Provider 537

    Using the `SqlConnection` Class 537

    Using Database Connection Strings with a `SqlConnection` 539

    The `SqlCommand` Class 540

    The `SqlDataReader` Class 542

    The `SqlDataAdapter` Class 542

Working with the OLEDB Data Provider 544

    Overview of the OLEDB Data Provider 545

    Using the `OleDbConnection` 545

    Using the `OleDbCommand` 545

    Using the `OleDbDataReader` 546

    Using the `OleDbDataAdapter` 546

Additional Data Providers 547

    The Oracle .NET Data Provider (ODP.NET) 547

    The Microsoft .NET Data Provider for Oracle 547

    The .NET ODBC Data Provider 548

    The mySQL .NET Data Provider 548

`DataSet` and `DataAdapter` Binding 548

    `DataSet` Review 548

    Associating a DataSet with a `DataAdapter` 549

    Sample: Hooking Up a `DataSet` to a Live Data Source 549

Summary 552

Further Reading 552

CHAPTER 28: Creating a Custom ADO.NET Data Provider   554

Custom Data Providers 555

    When to Create a Data Provider 555

    Steps for Implementing a Custom Data Provider 556

    Sample Data Provider Scenario 556

    Overview of the Remote Data Provider 557

Implementing `IDataParameter` and `IDataParameterCollection` 558
    The `IDataParameter` Interface 558
    The `IDataParameterCollection` Interface 559
    The `RDPParameter` Class 559
    The `RDPParameterCollection` Class 563
Implementing a Custom Connection 565
    The `IDbConnection` Interface 566
    The `RDPConnection` Class 566
Implementing a Custom Command 569
    The `IDbCommand` Interface 569
    The `RDPCommand` Class 570
Implementing a Custom DataReader 575
    The `IDataReader` Interface 575
    The `RDPDataReader` Class 576
Implementing a Custom DataAdapter 582
    The `IDbDataAdapter` Interface 582
    The `RDPDataAdapter` Class 582
Summary 587

CHAPTER 29: Typed DataSets and XSD   **588**
XML Schema Definition 589
    Introduction to XSD 589
    Primitive Data Types in XSD 591
    Derived Data Types 591
    Complex Data Types 592
    Grouping Elements 593
    Annotating XML Schemas 593
    XML Schema Facets 594
    Programming XML Schemas—The `XmlSchema` Class 595
Structuring DataSets with Schema 599
    Defining Tables and Columns Using XML Schema 599
    Defining DataSet Keys and Constraints with XML Schema 600
Typed DataSets 603
    Creating Typed DataSets in Visual Studio .NET 606
    Building Typed DataSets Using XSD.EXE 607
    Using Typed DataSets 607
    Annotating Typed DataSets 609

Summary 611

Further Reading 611

CHAPTER 30: Windows Forms Data Binding   **612**

Data Binding Overview 613

    Introduction to Windows Forms Data Binding 613

    Simple Data Binding 613

    Complex Data Binding 616

    One-Way and Two-Way Data Binding 616

Data Binding Mechanics 616

    The `BindingContext` Class 617

    The `CurrencyManager` Class 617

    The `PropertyManager` Class 620

Data Binding Samples 621

    Simple Binding 621

    Binding to a `ComboBox` 622

    `DataGrid` Binding 622

Advanced Binding Samples 625

    Header/Detail Forms 625

    Cascading Header/Detail 628

Summary 632

CHAPTER 31: Web Forms Data Binding   **634**

Data Binding Overview 635

    Introduction to Web Forms Data Binding 635

    `<%# %>` Binding Syntax 635

    Simple Data Binding 636

    Complex Data Binding 638

    The `DataBind()` Methods 638

Data Binding Mechanics 639

    `Container.DataItem` 639

    `DataBinder.Eval` 639

    The `ItemDataBound` Event 640

Data Binding Samples 641

    Simple Binding 641

    `Repeater` Binding 641

DataList Binding 645

DataGrid Binding 647

Advanced Binding Samples 647

Header and Detail Forms 648

Cascading Header and Detail 652

Summary 657

Further Reading 658

Part VI: Web Services   661

CHAPTER 32: Introduction to Web Services   662

Introduction to Web Services 663

Defining Web Services 663

Overview of SOAP 663

Overview of WSDL 665

Building Web Services 665

Hello World 665

Complex Serialization 669

Using Transactions with a Web Service 673

Maintaining State with a Web Service 673

Contract-First Programming with Web Services 674

Review of Web Service Consumption 674

Creating a Client Proxy for a Web Service 674

Making Synchronous Calls 674

Making Asynchronous Calls 675

Summary 676

Further Reading 676

CHAPTER 33: Introduction to WSE 2.0   678

Introduction to WSE 2.0 679

Overview of GXA 679

Evolution of WSE 679

TCP Messaging 679

SOAP over TCP 680

SoapSender and SoapReceiver 680

The SoapService Class 683

The SoapClient Class 686

Security 687

   Introduction to WSE Security 687

   `UsernameTokens` 688

   X.509 Certificates 689

   Signing Messages 690

Messaging with Attachments Using WSE 2.0 690

   Introduction to DIME 690

   Transferring Files Via WSE 691

Summary 691

Further Reading 691

Part VII: Secure Applications   693

CHAPTER 34: Code Access Security   694

Introduction to CAS 695

   Using Code Access Security Permissions 696

   Code Access Permissions 696

   Identity Permissions 697

   Role-Based Security Permissions 698

CAS Administration 698

   Modifying CAS Policy 698

   Policy Administration Tools 699

   Increasing Assembly Trust Levels 700

   Adjust Zone Security 701

   Evaluate Assembly 701

   Creating a Deployment Package 703

Writing CAS-Aware Code 704

   Using Imperative Security Syntax 704

   Using Declarative Security Syntax 705

   Blocking Unwanted Clients 706

Summary 708

Further Reading 709

CHAPTER 35: Securing Sensitive Data   710

Secret Key (Symmetric) Encryption 711

   `DESCryptoServiceProvider` 711

   `RC2CryptoServiceProvider` 712

`RijndaelManaged` 713

`TripleDESCryptoServiceProvider` 713

Using Hashes to Protect Data 716

`MACTripleDES` 716

`SHA1Managed` 718

`MD5CryptoServiceProvider` 719

Public Key Encryption and Signatures 720

`DSACryptoServiceProvider` 721

`RSACryptoServiceProvider` 723

Windows Data Protection API 723

Using DPAPI 724

Creating a DPAPI Wrapper 726

Protecting Data in .NET with DPAPI 732

Summary 733

CHAPTER 36: Securing ASP.NET Web Applications   **734**

User Security 734

Authenticating Users 735

Authorizing Users with Roles 740

Implementing `IIdentity` and `IPrincipal` 740

Data Security in ASP.NET Applications 748

Protecting Connection Strings and `Web.config` Data 748

Protecting User Passwords 748

Deciding When to Use SSL 751

Data Security with ViewState Encryption 751

Summary 752

Further Reading 752

CHAPTER 37: Licensing and Intellectual Property   **754**

Licensing Overview 755

Licensing Defined 755

When to License and Protect 755

Types of Licensing and Verification 756

Implementing Custom Licensing 757

Introduction to the License Provider and License Manager 757

Creating a License 759

Creating a License Provider 760

Building Licensed Controls 764

Licensed Web Controls Versus Windows Forms Controls 768

Licensing Implementation Strategies 768

Deciding on a Licensing Deployment Method 768

Deciding on a Licensing Verification Method 768

Deciding on a License Purchase Method 768

Deciding on a Licensing Method 769

Protecting Your Intellectual Property 769

Protecting Intellectual Property by Hiding Your
Licensing Algorithm 769

Protecting Intellectual Property Through Obfuscation 770

Protecting Intellectual Property with Alternative
Back-Ends 770

Summary 771

Further Reading 771

Part VIII: Enterprise and Connected Applications   773

CHAPTER 38: Interface Programming   **774**

Interface Programming 774

Understanding the Interface 774

Declaring the Interface Implicitly 778

Declaring the Interface Explicitly 784

Mapping the Interface 786

Inheriting the Interface 789

Summary 790

Further Reading 790

CHAPTER 39: Remoting   **792**

Remoting Architecture 792

Introduction to Remoting 792

Explaining Application Domains 793

Understanding the Context 795

Choosing a Channel 796

Life and Death of the Remote Object 797

Building the Remoting Server Application 803

Building the Client 805

IIS and Remoting 806

Summary 807

Further Reading 807

CHAPTER 40: COM+ Enterprise Services   **808**

Overview of COM+ 809

    Transactions 809

    JIT Activation in COM+ 810

    Object Pooling 810

    Construction Strings 811

    Role-Based Security 811

    Queued Components 812

    Events 812

Building COM+ Components 813

    Transactions 813

    Construction Strings 815

    JIT Activation Sample 817

    Object Pooling 817

    Shared Properties 818

Security in COM+ 820

    Object and Security Contexts 820

    Role-Based Security 821

Advanced COM+ 823

    Events 823

    Queued Components 826

Summary 827

Further Reading 827

CHAPTER 41: Enterprise Templates   **828**

Enterprise Templates 828

    Introducing the Enterprise Template 829

    Static and Dynamic Content 830

    Static Prototypes 831

    Subproject Wizards 831

    Custom Wizards 831

Policy Files 831

    TDL Elements 832

Teaching by Example 834

    Setting Up the Prerequisites 834

    Laying Out the Template 835

    Creating the Template Structure 836

    Assigning a Policy to the Template 839

    Making the Template 840

    Making the Template Available to Users 844

    Testing the Template 845

Summary 846

Further Reading 847

Part IX: Debugging and Testing   **849**

CHAPTER 42: Debugging Your Applications   **850**

The Visual Studio .NET Debugging Environment 850

    Setting Up the Application for Debugging 850

    Understanding Syntax and Error Messages 852

    Understanding the Debugging Tool Windows 854

    Navigating the Application 858

    Setting and Using Breakpoints 859

Debugging with Visual Studio .NET 861

    Debugging an Application 861

CHAPTER 43: Monitoring Your Applications   **872**

Debugging and Tracing Statements 872

    Trace Listeners 876

    Trace Switches 882

    Custom Trace Listeners 885

Summary 888

CHAPTER 44: Instrumenting Your Application   **890**

Instrumenting Applications 890

    Introduction to Instrumenting an Application 891

    Methods of Instrumentation 892

    Windows Event Log 892

Examining the `Debug` and `Trace` Classes 895

Windows Management Instrumentation 897

Enterprise Instrumentation Framework 902

Introducing the EIF 902

Enterprise Instrumentation Framework Requirements 903

Elements of the EIF 903

Request Tracing 906

Configuring EIF 906

Summary 907

Further Reading 907

CHAPTER 45: The Future of C#   **908**

The Future of C# 908

Generics 909

Anonymous Methods 912

Nullable Types at Last 913

List Management with Iterators 913

Partial Types 914

Static Classes 915

Summary 916

Further Reading 916

Index   **918**

About the Authors

Kevin Hoffman started programming on a Commodore VIC-20 donated by his grandfather. Ever since then, he has been hopelessly addicted to programming. Instead of spending time outside, absorbing rays from that big yellow thing (he's not even sure what it's called), he spent most of his time as a kid and up through high school and college learning as many programming languages as he could get his hands on. At one time or another, he has written applications in ADA, Assembly, Scheme, LISP, Perl, Java, Python, Tcl/Tk, C, C#, Visual Basic .NET, C++, Pascal, Delphi, Visual Basic, VAX/VMS Pascal, BASIC, dozens of proprietary scripting languages, PL/SQL, and probably a few more that he couldn't remember. He's even written a few programs for OS/2 and Mac OS X.

He started out working for a company that produces scientific instruments. He wrote code that interfaced PCs with data logging and gathering tools as well as real-time data analysis programs. From there he moved on to working technical support for Unix systems, PCs, SQL databases, and client/server applications. After that he made the infamous jump to a dot-com, where he wrote an extensive amount of Visual Basic, VBScript, and ASP code. After an additional job working with another *n*-tier, COM-based ASP application, he moved to Houston, where he now endures the heat with his wife, dog, and two cats.

Lonny Kruger has more than 18 years of experience in developing C/C++, C#, Pascal, Delphi, Java, JavaScript, and Prolog programs, specializing in real-time applications and user interface design. Mr. Kruger has served as Systems Engineering Manager, Development Manager, Senior Architect, Project Manager, Principal Investigator, and Senior Programmer for many projects including NASA's Next Grade Project, a tool for the rapid assembly and analysis of satellites, and was responsible for the development of hurricane tracking and prediction software using the CIA's world database. In addition to his programming experience, Mr. Kruger served six years in the United States Marine Corps, including a tour of duty in Saudi Arabia and Kuwait during the first Gulf War.

Dedication

I would like to dedicate this book to my wife, Connie. I often complain about the difficulties of dealing with writer's block, dealing with code that doesn't compile, and much more. Creating a book for programmers, written by a programmer, is a difficult task. However, regardless of how hard I think it might be to write books like this, nothing is harder than putting up with me while I'm writing. I want to dedicate this book to her and thank her for having more patience and understanding than I have myself.

—Kevin Hoffman

I dedicate this book to my wife Leah, my son Joshua, and my soon to be born little girl, Megan Leah. To my wife, thank you for putting up with me for the past twelve years. When I think that everyone else is wrong, because I am always right, it is comforting to know that you will always be there to show me that I am mistaken. To my son Joshua, nothing is more special than to spend time playing with you and I am sorry that this book took so much of it away from us. Thank you for allowing me the time to write this book. To my soon to be born little girl, I have waited a long time for you and I can't wait to meet you. Leah, Joshua, and Megan, thank you for putting up with me and I love you all.

—Lonny Kruger

We Want to Hear from You!

As the reader of this book, *you* are our most important critic and commentator. We value your opinion and want to know what we're doing right, what we could do better, what areas you'd like to see us publish in, and any other words of wisdom you're willing to pass our way.

As an associate publisher for Sams Publishing, I welcome your comments. You can email or write me directly to let me know what you did or didn't like about this book—as well as what we can do to make our books better.

Please note that I cannot help you with technical problems related to the topic of this book. We do have a User Services group, however, where I will forward specific technical questions related to the book.

When you write, please be sure to include this book's title and author, as well as your name, email address, and phone number. I will carefully review your comments and share them with the author and editors who worked on the book.

Email: feedback@samspublishing.com

Mail: Michael Stephens
            Associate Publisher
            Sams Publishing
            800 East 96th Street
            Indianapolis, IN 46240 USA

For more information about this book or another Sams Publishing title, visit our website at www.samspublishing.com. Type the ISBN (0672326760) or the title of a book in the Search field to find the page you're looking for.

INTRODUCTION

Welcome to Visual C# .NET 2003

Today, people are living in a busy time. Gone are the days when it took two to three weeks to get a decision on a credit application for a car. We live in a time where we need what we want, and we want what we need, right now.

Wanting information right now is a common theme in today's environment. Having it right now is today's challenge. Whether it's while driving in the car, flying in an airplane, working, or while watching television at home, we all want it now. To solve this dilemma, IBM introduced the world to personal computers. For a time this was great, but personal computers were too expensive for the average person to have at home, so other companies introduced the portable computer. Don't let the term *portable* confuse you, this computer was everything but portable. The portable computer eventually became small enough to actually carry around and everything seemed right with the world, at least for a time. However, as time passed, so did the fad of starting up your laptop to find the phone number or address of the person you were trying to contact. So, along came mobile devices. With time, mobile devices such as personal digital assistants (PDAs), cellular phones, and cellular phones that thought they were PDAs became more advanced and brought us to the brink of having everything that we wanted at our fingertips...but not quite.

The great thing about the world is that everyone has his own ideas. Some ideas are great, and some...well, some are not so great. The problem with this is that most people have a bias toward their own ideas and think that their way is the right way. This causes companies to develop technologies to handle tasks in their own image and makes communication between similar devices, made by different manufacturers, difficult if not impossible. Imagine this: You are tasked with gathering stock prices from different vendors of stock quotes. One source requires that you query its database with a proprietary protocol. Another has a file that is reproduced every minute and requires you to download it and parse the file for all the information that is needed. And finally, the third source does not have a published interface and therefore requires that you perform *screen scraping* to produce the information required. Without the presence of a standard method of accessing the information, retrieving the required data is, at the very least, complicated.

Along Came .NET

Fortunately, our friends in Redmond thought about this problem for quite a while and came up with a solution they call *.NET*. Microsoft took the time necessary to come up with an end-to-end solution for such areas as cross-language interoperability, runtime management of system stability, web services that use a standard protocol such as *SOAP (Simple Object Access Protocol),* and seamless communication of distributed components, just to name a few.

In writing this book, we have first and foremost tried to give you the information necessary to understand the technology and be able to apply this knowledge to your future projects. Secondly, we want you to understand not only how it works, but also why it works. Too many programmers today are content with knowing that making a call to function A will cause the system to perform a certain task. That's fine, but if you don't know how function A performs the task, how are you going to know why or if it breaks function B when used in a certain context? If you don't know how it works, you won't know how you can make your code faster, more efficient, more scalable, and more reliable. This book will take you into the internals of the .NET Framework. You will learn not only how to use attributes in C#, you'll also learn what they actually do, so that if something breaks, you will have a little insight into the framework to help you quantify the issue and quickly create a solution.

What's New in Visual Studio .NET

The first time you open Visual Studio .NET, you will notice that there have been many changes from previous versions. Visual Studio .NET and the .NET Framework will change the way you view and create software. Some of the differences between Visual Studio .NET and its predecessors like Visual C++ 6.0 include

- ▸ **Redesigned user interface**: The Visual Studio .NET user interface is a combination of the best features found in the previous versions of Visual C++, Visual Basic, and Visual InterDev.

- ▸ **Advanced Help system**: Help is literally at your fingertips. With the new Dynamic Help system, links to help documentation are *context aware*; that is, they are displayed based on what you are currently working on. Also, Microsoft Developers Network (MSDN) is now incorporated into the integrated development environment (IDE) without having to use an external help application.

- ▸ **Vastly improved debugger**: By incorporating multiple languages into Visual Studio .NET, they support cross-language debugging. You now have the ability to easily step from Visual Basic .NET to Visual C# code.

▶ **Deployment support**: Visual Studio .NET now contains the necessary toolset to deploy your finished application to its final destination. Using Microsoft Installer technology, you can create merge modules or entire installations within the Visual Studio .NET IDE.

▶ **Automatic code documentation**: By using a combination of Extensible Markup Language (XML) tags, you can create well-formatted documentation for your code without relying on third-party utilities.

▶ **.NET**: .NET is a technology that can't really be summed up in one succinct phrase. Needless to say, .NET is more than just a framework. Included within the .NET umbrella are such things as Windows Forms, web services and, of course, the new Microsoft programming language, C#.

The changes that come with Visual Studio .NET are enormous. Trying to understand all of these changes can seem overwhelming. However, upon completion of this book, you will know how, and be able to use all the features of the .NET Framework. If you need to create several objects that must communicate with each other across process or even the Internet, you will apply what you learn in Chapter 39, "Remoting." If you need to create an object that can persist itself after the program has terminated, you will use the knowledge from Chapter 7, "File and Stream I/O and Object Persistence." In all, you will benefit from the beginning from informed design decisions.

Part I

Introduction to the Visual Studio .NET IDE

CHAPTER 1 The Visual Studio .NET IDE

1

The Visual Studio .NET IDE

IN BRIEF

This chapter explains and demonstrates the features and capabilities of the Visual Studio .NET integrated development environment (IDE). The first section talks about the basics of the IDE. You will learn how to customize the Help system, lay out the keyboard according to your preferences, maximize your viewable area, and get a basic understanding of developer profiles. In addition, we will explore the different tool windows within the IDE.

In the next section, we will discuss how to work with different document types. You will learn how to enhance the text editor, edit HTML files, binary files, Extensible Markup Language (XML) files, and how to find help where you need it.

Finally, the chapter will explain how to use external tools within the Visual Studio .NET environment. You will learn how to define your own tools and launch them from within the IDE.

WHAT YOU NEED

RECOMMENDED SOFTWARE	Visual Studio .NET
RECOMMENDED HARDWARE	.NET-enabled desktop client
SKILLS REQUIRED	Basic computer operation

THE VISUAL STUDIO .NET IDE AT A GLANCE

Window Management and Customization   7

  Customized Interfaces with Visual Studio .NET's "Developer Profiles"   7
  Configuring Keyboard Shortcuts   8
  Filtering the MSDN Help   9

  Maximizing Your Viewable Area   9
  Using Visual Studio .NET 2003's Dockable Windows   10

Understanding Visual Studio .NET 2003's Tool Windows   14

Working with Documents   18

  Enhancing the Text Editor   18
  Finding Help Where You Need It   22
  Editing HTML   26

  Editing XML   29
  Editing Binary Files   30

Using External Tools   30

  Defining Your Own Tools   31

Summary   32

Further Reading   32

Window Management and Customization

Before Visual Studio .NET, Visual Basic developers had a drastically different editing environment than Visual C++ developers. Add to that the different environments included within Visual InterDev, and you can see that combining all of these languages into a single IDE would be difficult. This is a primary reason why Visual Studio .NET employs developer profiles.

Customized Interfaces with Visual Studio .NET's "Developer Profiles"

Immediately afterinstalling Visual Studio .NET, you are presented with the developer profile page within the embedded browser of the IDE, as shown in Figure 1.1. The profile page enables you to choose from a list of preset window layouts based on the type of developer you are.

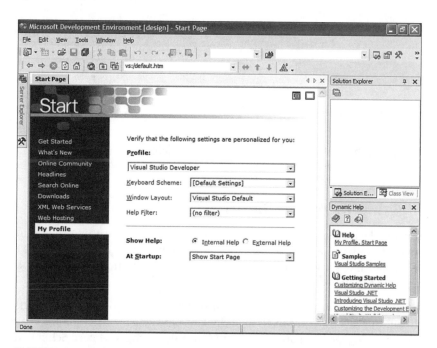

FIGURE 1.1   You can choose the developer profile you are most comfortable with by changing settings on the Profile page.

By choosing the Visual C# Developer profile, the window layout will be organized in a way that is most common for C# developers, as shown in Figure 1.2. I, however, will be using the default Visual Studio Developer profile throughout this

Window Management and Customization

book. You are free to change what you use; just keep in mind that what you see in the book and what you see within your IDE will be different, although the terminology will be the same.

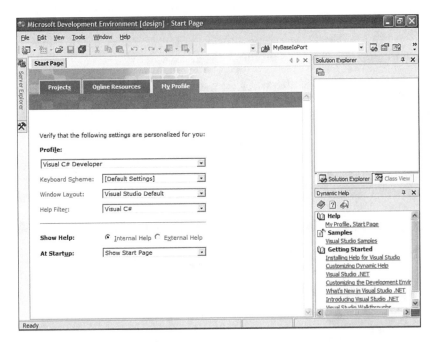

FIGURE 1.2   If you prefer the same window layout as Visual C#, you can easily customize Visual Studio .NET to suit your needs.

Configuring Keyboard Shortcuts

When many developers first install Visual Studio .NET, the first thing they want to do is make sure that the keyboard shortcuts and menus work in a way they're familiar with. One thing some Visual C++ 6.0 developers may notice is that the F7 key doesn't build the project.

If you really can't get used to the new keyboard layout, but still want to retain the default window layout, you can change the keyboard scheme by selecting Visual C++ 6 (or the language you are comfortable with) from the Keyboard Scheme drop-down list. Likewise, if you prefer the default keyboard scheme but would like to revert back to the window layout from your previous language's IDE, you can choose the window layout you prefer from the corresponding drop-down list.

Filtering the MSDN Help

MSDN documentation is a vast library of knowledge, samples, articles, and reference materials. Sifting through this huge collection of information can sometimes be a daunting task. Documentation is extremely helpful, but too much can make searching extremely difficult and unproductive.

Help filters can remove documentation from your view so that you minimize and false positive search results. You can specify the Help filter that you might need, but my advice is to not use any filters, at least not yet. You can think of the MSDN documentation as a mini–World Wide Web on your computer. It comprises hundreds of hyperlinked documents, forming a relationally and hierarchically organized collection of knowledge. What happens when you sit down to look something up on the Internet? You open your browser and immediately a hyperlink to an unrelated story catches your interest. You follow and after skimming it over quickly, another link catches your eye. By the time you know it, you're reading stories about Brazilian cockroaches when all you really wanted to know was the current prices of stocks in your portfolio.

Although you won't read about Brazilian cockroaches in MSDN, you will occasionally skim a document that you weren't intending to look for. In doing so, you will learn about some unrelated technology you weren't familiar with before.

TIP

You can choose to leave the MSDN help filter enabled so that only the exact type of information you are looking for will appear in your results. However, leaving the filter off might prove more useful than you think. While you are looking for a reference to a particular keyword, you might find some information that you will find useful in the future. If you have the spare time to do it, randomly sifting through the MSDN documentation can be enlightening.

Maximizing Your Viewable Area

Many developers prefer to have the resolution of their monitor set very high. They do this for one real reason: screen real estate. If you're like many other programmers, you typically have many programs running at one time and continually switch back and forth between them. With a high monitor resolution, you can arrange many windows in a way that enables you to easily view each one; but at lower resolutions, you are usually limited to working with one program at a time.

Visual Studio .NET contains many useful features that enable you to effectively organize the child windows of the IDE in such a way that it is possible for you to work efficiently and still have convenient access to the necessary development tools contained within those windows. The source code window is the most important window within the IDE and as such should not be obscured by any supporting tools. If you've ever programmed with Visual C++ 6.0 and entered a debugging session that required the use of many debugging windows, you would almost lose all sight of

Window Management and Customization

your source window—especially on monitors with low resolutions. To solve this problem, Visual Studio .NET employs the use of docking and auto-hiding windows.

Using Visual Studio .NET 2003's Dockable Windows

There are two types of windows within the Visual Studio .NET IDE. The first type is a document window and is considered the centerpiece of your current project. This includes such things as your source code or the current resource that you are editing. The other type of window is used for support and is known as a tool window. It is this type of window that allows docking to the IDE. A window is docked when it fits within a certain area of the IDE like a puzzle piece and does not obscure your current document window. A tool window can be docked on any side of the document window.

Open Visual Studio .NET and locate the Solution Explorer window that is currently docked to the right side of the IDE (if your developer profile is currently set to Visual Studio Developer). Right-click on the Solution Explorer window and select the Floating item from the contextual menu, as shown in Figure 1.3. By doing this, you have disabled the docking feature for that window and can now move the window to any location. Note, however, that a floating window can obscure any windows underneath it—such as your current document window.

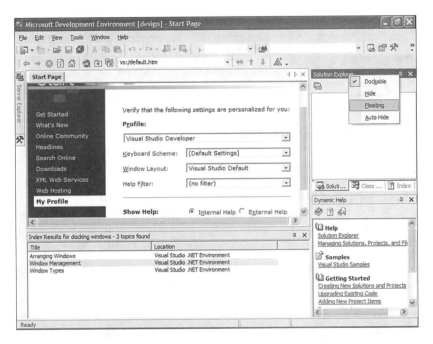

FIGURE 1.3   You can change the behavior of windows by right-clicking on the tool window's title bar.

Window Management and Customization

Right-click on the Solution Explorer tool window's title bar again, but this time select the Dockable menu item. You'll notice that even though you changed that window to dockable, it still floats above the other windows. A tool window can be dockable, but that doesn't necessarily mean that it has to be docked to a certain location on the IDE. To dock a tool window, you must drag that window to the location that you want to dock it to. Click on the title bar of the Solution Explorer window and drag it to the right side of the screen again. When you do this, you can see various gray frames that signify where the window will be docked after you've released the mouse button.

There are different places within the IDE that a window can be docked. You can dock a tool window to another tool window as shown in Figure 1.4. In that figure, you can see three tool windows docked side by side. You might notice that some tool windows enter into a tabbed layout when they are docked, which is the default docking layout for the Solution Explorer and Class View windows. To add another tool window to a group of tabbed tool windows, drag the title bar of the tool window you want to dock onto the tabs of the group; you will see a new tab created as you do this. You can then drag that tab to specify which location you want the tabbed tool window to occupy when the mouse button is released.

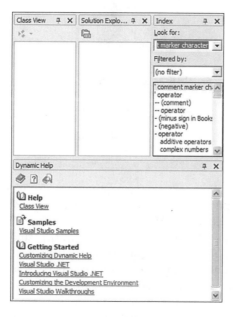

FIGURE 1.4   Visual Studio .NET enables you to dock tool windows in a variety of ways to suit your style.

Window Management and Customization

Auto-Hiding Windows

The ability to dock windows is a great feature and will help in maximizing your view of the current document window. However, you can achieve more screen real estate by auto-hiding the docked tool windows within the IDE.

Auto-hiding works by minimizing a tool window to the edge of the screen when you are not using it. After the tool window has been minimized, it is replaced by a tab with the name of the window and the document window is subsequently expanded to take advantage of the extra space that is available. By default, Visual Studio .NET contains two tool windows that are auto-hidden. If you look at the left side of the IDE, you can see two tabs labeled Server Explorer and Toolbox, as shown in Figure 1.5. If you move your mouse cursor over one of the tabs, the corresponding tool window will be maximized and the document window will adjust accordingly.

FIGURE 1.5   Auto-hidden tool windows increase screen real estate by hiding the window until you need to use it.

To auto-hide a tool window, click the push pin located in the upper-right corner of the tool window. Locate the Server Explorer tool window and if it is not docked to the edge of the IDE, dock it now. When you click on the push pin in the right corner of that window, a couple of things will happen with the window layout. First, the Solution Explorer window is enlarged and fills the entire height of the IDE. Because the window is auto-hidden, it can use that space when it is maximized because that space will normally be used for something else when the tool window is minimized. So, not only do you maximize the document window when a tool window is auto-hidden, you also maximize the space that the tool window occupies when it is active and viewable.

TIP

You can auto-hide all the current tool windows with just a few clicks. Select Window, Auto Hide All to make all the current tool windows auto-hidden. Take note, however, that there is no corresponding Unhide All feature; you will have to manually unhide each of the tool windows separately.

Another action that occurs when you auto-hide a tool window happens if the tool window was part of a tabbed group of docked windows. After you've turned on the auto-hide feature of a tool window within a tabbed group of docked tool windows, the entire group becomes auto-hidden, as shown in Figure 1.6. This might not be what you expected, but you can customize this behavior.

FIGURE 1.6   Auto-hiding a single tool window contained within a group of tabbed docked tool windows auto-hides the entire group.

To change the behavior of auto-hiding a group of tabbed and docked tool windows so that only a single window is auto-hidden, select Tools, Options from the main menu. In the General settings item, which should be selected by default, check the check box labeled Auto Hide Button Affects Active Tab Only, as shown in Figure 1.7. By changing this setting, only the currently active tab will be auto-hidden, rather than the entire group.

Window Management and Customization

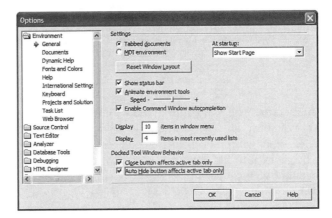

FIGURE 1.7   You can change the behavior of auto-hidden windows contained within tabbed groups by changing IDE settings.

Understanding Visual Studio .NET 2003's Tool Windows

As you begin working with Visual Studio .NET, you'll use several of the supporting tool windows to help you design and develop your project. Furthermore, as you work through the projects and read the discussions contained within this book, the functionality of certain tool windows will be discussed in depth.

This section briefly discusses each of the tool windows and what each window's function is within Visual Studio .NET. Note that some windows are specific to a certain language or technology and might not be discussed within this book other than in this section.

By default, many of these tool windows are not visible. To view a specific tool window, select the View main menu item. Note that some windows might also be contained within the View, Other Windows menu group.

TABLE 1.1

Visual Studio .NET 2003's Tool Windows

Window	Description
Class View	The Class View window is a view into a solution that is organized based on similar type properties. For instance, all the classes within your C# project will be placed within the Classes tree view item. You can also browse your project's struct declarations, defined macros, global variables and functions, and even base classes and interfaces.

TABLE 1.1

Continued

Command Window	The Command Window is used to control the Visual Studio .NET IDE by invoking the objects and methods of its automation object model by using a command-line interface.
Contents	The Contents window is a tree-view–based window that displays the contents of MSDN documentation. This is a departure from Visual C++ 6.0, which required the use of an external application to view documentation.
Document Outline	The Document Outline tool window is used to view the organization of the tags contained within an HTML document.
Dynamic Help	Dynamic Help, which is discussed later in this chapter, is a smart context-aware Help window that displays links to Help documentation relevant to the current task you are working on.
Favorites	The Favorites tool window displays the contents of your Internet Explorer Favorites folder. Selecting a link within this window will open the corresponding website within the integrated browser window contained within the Visual Studio .NET IDE.
Find Results	The Find Results window displays the results of a search operation. The search may be within the current document, the current solution, or within the file system of the operating system. Clicking an item within the Find Results window will open that document to the location where the search found the item it was looking for.
Find Symbol Results	The Find Symbol Results window is similar to the Find Results window, but is the result of searching for symbols such as namespaces, class names, and variables within your current project.
Index	The Index tool window contains the index view of the MSDN documentation. Typing a partial name within the Look For field will scroll the index window to the appropriate index result.
Index Results	Some links within the Index window might point to multiple documentation links. The Index Results window displays each of these documents as well as the section where each is included in the documentation.
Macro Explorer	The Macro Explorer window is a tree view that contains the defined Visual Studio .NET macros. By selecting a macro within the tool window, you can run, edit, rename, or delete that macro.
Object Browser	The Object Browser should be familiar to Visual Basic developers. This window is actually a document window due to its complex feature set. It enables you to view not only the different objects contained within your current project, but also the objects defined within the current operating system, such as the various installed COM components and .NET assemblies.
Output	The Output window displays the output that is generated from running various command-line tools within the IDE. This window would, for example, display the results of running the compiler on a source file or the output of the linker as you link several object files.
Pending Checkins	This window is used for the source code control integration feature of Visual Studio .NET. The Pending Checkins window displays any files that are currently checked out in source code control and are contained within your current solution.

Understanding Visual Studio .NET 2003's Tool Windows

TABLE 1.1

Continued

Properties	The Properties window displays the properties of the object you are currently working on. In the past, this was usually reserved for dialog or ActiveX control properties, but has been expanded to include the properties for such things as a source code file and even the properties for the current project you are working on.
Resource View	The Resource View window displays a hierarchical collection of resources that are used within your solution. Resources can include such things as bitmap files, assembly manifests, icons, and string tables, to name a few.
Search Results	This window displays the results of doing a search within the documentation. Each item that appears within the Search Results window contains the name of the document where the item being searched for was found as well as which section of the documentation that item was found in.
Server Explorer	The Server Explorer is an exciting addition to Visual Studio .NET. This tool window enables you to browse not only the local machine you are working on but remote servers as well. With this tool, you can navigate and edit databases, explore system services, view event logs, interact with the message queue, and query performance counters.
Solution Explorer	The Solution Explorer replaces the File View window that was present in Visual C++ 6.0. You can view all the projects contained within your solution as well as each of the associated files within that project. Furthermore, you can organize the files within this view by creating folders and dragging files into those folders. By default, several folders are created and their subsequent files are organized automatically for you.
Task List	The Task List serves many purposes. First, it enables you to create to-do items to remind you to complete certain tasks. You can also associate an importance level with the task. Second, the IDE scans your source code and places any comments that begin with certain keywords, such as TODO, as an item in the task list. It also includes the file and line number for that task so that you can double-click the item to open the file at the appropriate location.
Toolbox	The Toolbox window contains all the controls necessary for graphical user interface design. The included controls consist of HTML controls, ActiveX controls, Windows Forms controls, XML schema elements. A clipboard history is maintained within the Clipboard Ring tab.

The following tool windows are used to support the debugging process. To view these windows, you must be actively debugging a project. When you are debugging, you can access these windows by selecting Debug, Windows from the main menu.

TABLE 1.2

Visual Studio .NET 2003's Debugging Tool Windows

Window	Description
Autos	The Autos window displays information about the variables currently within scope of your executing application, and only those contained within the current or previous executable statement. Displayed information includes the name of the variable, its current value, and the variable's data type.
Breakpoints	The Breakpoints tool window is used to control the management of the various breakpoints that you have set within your application. This window contains many features, such as being able to specify conditional breakpoints and the ability to disable or remove breakpoints. The list view of the window also includes rich information contained in columns.
Call Stack	The Call Stack window displays the current contents of the call stack as you debug your application. Items at the top of the window are the most recently called functions, whereas the bottom items represent the beginning of the call stack. Each function also includes parameter information, such as its current value and data type.
Disassembly	The Disassembly window contains the disassembled machine code and its associated source code, and is not for the uninitiated developer. You might find yourself inadvertently entering this window as breakpoints within operating system code are hit inadvertently, usually as a result of incorrect source code within your project.
Immediate	The Immediate window is one of the most useful, but perhaps least used, debugging windows. This tool window enables you to evaluate expressions, execute statements, get and set variable values, and print various pieces of information The Locals window is similar to the Autos window. However, the Locals window contains variables within the current scope and is not limited to just the current or previous executable statement.
Memory	The Memory window enables you to view memory contents contained within your application's allocated memory space. I have found this window useful when performing such tasks as file and string parsing and various bit-manipulation tasks.
Modules	The Modules window displays the modules, DLLs, or EXEs, currently loaded by your application. You can choose to display various pieces of information such as the module's filename, path, version information, and memory location.
Registers	As with the Disassembly window, the Registers window is definitely not for a beginning developer unless that developer is actively working with assembly language. This window displays the current contents of each of the processors registers. Furthermore, this window also enables you to change the values within the registers, although this is something that should be done only if you know what you are doing. In most cases I don't, so I don't touch the registers' values.
This	The This window is convenient if your application uses classes. This window displays the data members within the active this pointer. For Visual Basic .NET developers, it points to the Me object.
Threads	The Threads window enables you to view all the threads created by your application. It also enables you to control which threads are active and makes it possible for you to freeze or thaw threads.

TABLE 1.2

Continued

Watch	You can think of the Watch window as a variable bookmark window. The Watch window enables you to place any variable in it, and displays the current variable's value at all times (unless the variable is not within scope of the current executing context). Furthermore, the Watch variables will be retained between debugging sessions.

Working with Documents

Although it seems that wizards and their corresponding automatic code generation capabilities decrease the amount of code that you write, they obviously can't write all the code for you. Visual Studio .NET contains many features that enhance the code-writing process. With various code-viewing features placed at your fingertips, writing code has been improved with Visual Studio .NET. In the following sections, you will learn how to enhance the text editors, how to find help where you need it, and how to edit HTML, XML, and binary files.

Enhancing the Text Editor

The old adage that states "Time is money" definitely rings true within the software engineering field. Anything that can remove the tedium and nuances of editing source code and enable you to concentrate on the actual code itself will prove helpful. This being the case, the Visual Studio .NET IDE contains several features that aid in writing C# code.

Code Outlining in the IDE

Large projects can contain large source files. As a file grows, so does the frustration that occurs when you have to navigate to different parts within that file. Outlining helps alleviate this frustration. The structure of a C# source code file is organized based on functional blocks of code. Outlining takes advantage of this by enabling you to contract these blocks in a tree-view fashion, leaving either the first line of the code block (in the case of a conditional block of code), or a block of code containing either a data type declaration or function definition. Figure 1.8 shows a source code file with outlining turned on. As you can see from this figure, outlining enables you to easily view and navigate through your source code. Clicking the plus sign within the tree view expands the block, and clicking the subsequent minus sign for an expanded code block collapses that block.

By default, outlining is turned on for Visual C# .NET source code. To disable outlining for a single file within a single editing session, click Edit, Outlining from the main menu and select an outlining option. If you would rather turn off outlining for all C# source code files, click Tools, Options from the main menu. Expand the Text Editor item located on the left of the Options dialog. Select the C# item and then click on the Formatting option, as shown in Figure 1.9. To turn off outlining, clear the check box labeled Enter Outlining Mode When Files Open.

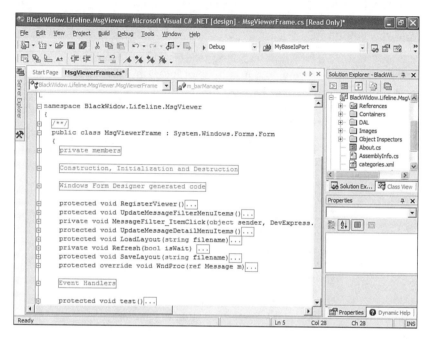

FIGURE 1.8   Outlining improves your ability to efficiently navigate through large source code files.

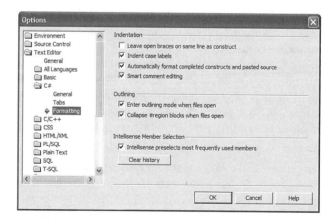

FIGURE 1.9   Turn on outlining by default by changing Visual Studio .NET options.

Working with Documents

Backward/Forward Navigation Within the IDE

If the Back button on a web browser were a physical button, it would probably have to be replaced more often than you change the oil in your car. Visual Studio .NET takes a feature found within web browsers and applies it to source code editing. As a developer, you have to jump to different places within a source code file. In some instances, you just need to view a small piece of code and then return to the last place you were editing.

Backward and forward navigation was designed to support instances like the one just mentioned. When you move your current cursor location within a source file or into a different source file altogether, the place you jumped from is saved into the Visual Studio .NET history buffer. If you need to jump back to the position you came from, you can click the Navigate Backward toolbar button. If you want to jump back several history positions, you can use the drop-down list that is displayed when you click the arrow on the Navigate Backward button, as shown in Figure 1.10.

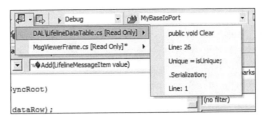

FIGURE 1.10   Use the Navigate Backward toolbar button to jump to previous positions within your source code.

Using Bookmarks

Backward and forward navigation is useful, but you might need a little more control and organization when you jump through your source code. Bookmarks enable you to mark a line of code to make it easier to jump back to that location later. Visual C++ 6.0 contained bookmarks, but that implementation was missing one feature that has prevented me from ever using a bookmark. Whenever a bookmark was set, it was immediately lost whenever you closed the source file that the bookmark was set in. Visual Studio .NET has expanded the bookmark feature by adding several new bookmark types as well as adding support for bookmark management via the Task List tool window.

Unnamed, or temporary, bookmarks enable you to set a bookmark in a file but only as long as the file is open. As was just mentioned, when an unnamed bookmark is set, it will be removed when the file is closed. There are several ways to set an unnamed bookmark. The easiest way is to make sure that the Text Editor toolbar is visible. The last four icons on that toolbar are used to manage unnamed bookmarks, as shown in Figure 1.11. To enable an unnamed bookmark, click on the solid blue flag icon, which is the first unnamed bookmark icon on the left of the Text Editor toolbar by default. To remove an unnamed bookmark, position your text cursor on the line containing the bookmark and click on the blue flag icon that contains the red X. After an unnamed bookmark has been set, a cyan-colored rounded rectangle appears in the left margin of the source code window, as shown in Figure 1.12.

FIGURE 1.11   You can work with unnamed bookmarks quickly using the Text Editor toolbar.

A named bookmark persists even when the source code file that contains the bookmark is closed. The reason that these are referred to as *named bookmarks* is because of their integration with the Task List tool window. After a named bookmark has been set, it is displayed in the Task List tool window containing the text of the line as the name, the source file the bookmark resides in, and the line number within that source file. Furthermore, the left margin of the source code window displays a blue arrow, as shown in Figure 1.12. To jump to a named bookmark, double-click the Task List entry for that bookmark. If the line of text for a named bookmark isn't descriptive enough, you can click on the item and change the text to better suit your needs, as shown in the second Task List item in Figure 1.12.

The last type of bookmark is something that many people will use quite often. In fact, there will probably be times when they use it without even realizing that they're doing so. Many people used to create to-do messages in their code so that they could keep track of tasks in a large project. In C++, the following code snippet illustrates how to create a TODO message:

```
// To use: #pragma TODO("Message")
#define __LINE ( __LINE__ )
#define __GETLINE(x) "(" #x ")"
#define GETLINE __GETLINE __LINE
#define TODO(msg) message ( __FILE__ GETLINE " : TODO: " #msg " " )
```

Although this is an extremely useful piece of code, there is one glaring problem with it: The TODO message is displayed only when your project is built. TODO messaging has become so standard that it's now integrated into the Visual Studio .NET IDE. However, rather than showing up only when your project is built, it shows up dynamically within the Task List tool window whenever the IDE finds a comment that begins with TODO. Furthermore, you can use several other defined messages, such as HACK and UNDONE.

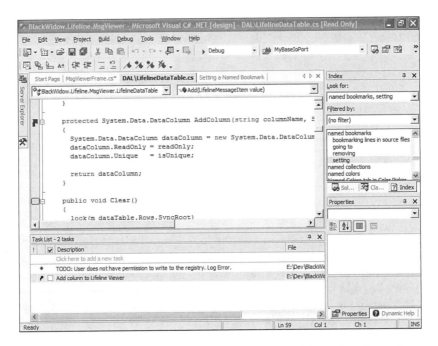

FIGURE 1.12 Named bookmarks enable you to mark important lines of code so that you can easily jump to that location later even if the source file is closed.

There might be times when you need to add to the list of TODO messages. Thankfully, you can edit the Visual Studio .NET options to add new keywords, which are formally known as *comment tokens* that the task list will recognize. To add a new token, click on Tools, Options from the main menu. Select Environment, Task List from the list of option headings, as shown in Figure 1.13. To add a new comment token, type the word you want to use in the Name field and click the Add button. You also have the option of setting a priority field. If you set this field, a corresponding icon is placed immediately before the entry within the task list. A high priority item is preceded by a red exclamation point and a low priority item is preceded by a blue down arrow. Normal priority items do not have a corresponding icon.

Finding Help Where You Need It

Could you imagine developing an application from scratch without any form of documentation or help from the application programming interface (API) you're working with? Developers need good documentation to get the job done. In fact, when learning a new technology, most programmers turn to sample code, books, magazine articles, and API documentation before they start writing code. This book is a prime example. Visual Studio .NET contains an abundance of useful tools that provide documentation literally at your fingertips.

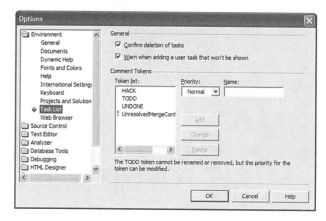

FIGURE 1.13   You can add new comment tokens by editing the Visual Studio .NET IDE options for the task list.

Dynamic Help

Dynamic Help is a new feature introduced with Visual Studio .NET that provides context-aware help as you work on your project. By default, the Dynamic Help tool window is located at the bottom right of the IDE, as shown in Figure 1.14. As you work within the IDE using the various tool windows, Dynamic Help constantly changes and provides links to the documentation based on the tool you are currently using. As you work within your source code, the Dynamic Help engine parses the code surrounding the cursor location and provides links to such things as current function calls, parameter information, and relevant samples.

TIP

Because it is constantly searching for help every time you press a key on the keyboard, using Dynamic Help requires a PC with a lot of horsepower. Unless you have a machine that is up to the challenge, think twice before leaving the Dynamic Help tab displayed. In fact, even on a machine with a great deal of horsepower, Dynamic Help consumes a lot of memory. Consider not using it all, and for maximum performance, use the MSDN documentation externally.

To see Dynamic Help in action, select the Class View tab contained in the docked tabbed group located on the right side of the IDE. As you do this, the Dynamic Help window displays links to information on how to use Class View as you saw in Figure 1.14.

Working with Documents

FIGURE 1.14   Dynamic Help displays links that are relevant to what you are working on within the IDE.

Code Comment Reports

As developers, you are busy writing code and making sure that your program works the way it's supposed to in all environments that it supports. When you're done with a project, it's time to start looking at and adding new features so that your application evolves over time. With all that programming, there's no time to document your modules or custom APIs. However that is not the mindset that you should take. Reading another developer's code can sometimes be difficult, to say the least. What is needed is a way to automatically generate documentation.

Automatically generated documentation has generally been provided by third-party vendors, but using and learning the process to hook up these tools can sometimes be complicated. Visual Studio .NET contains a built-in documentation generator that can parse your source code and create documentation in HTML format. You can further enhance this document by using XML style tags within your source code. For instance, to create a description for a function, you can use a `<summary>` tag immediately before the function name, as shown in the following snippet:

```
// <summary> Method for performing a task on a Test Form. </summary>
public void TestForm.PerformTask()
{
  // do something
}
```

To generate a code comment report, click Tools, Build Comment Web Pages from the main menu. In the dialog that is shown, you can choose to build documentation for the entire solution or for individual projects within the solution. The page shown in Figure 1.15 was generated for the function in the code snippet you just saw.

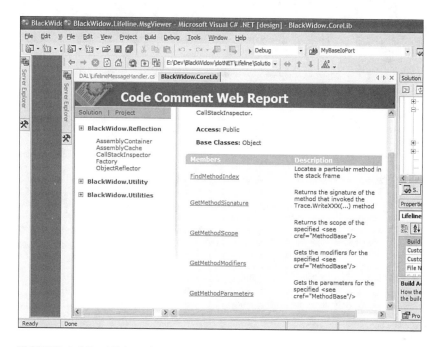

FIGURE 1.15   With code comment reports, there's really no excuse not to create documentation for your code now.

Intellisense

Visual C++ developers really got excited about Intellisense. There was no more endless pouring through documentation looking for the correct parameters for a function call. You no longer had to tirelessly examine header files for functions contained within code that wasn't documented.

Intellisense, by parsing all the source code you work with, creates a database that it uses to resolve references to a variety of coding constructs, such as functions, classes, structs, defined macros, and even interface methods and properties. Whenever you use one of these constructs, Intellisense kicks in as you're editing your source code and displays a small ToolTip containing the correct information for the context you are working in. For example, when you type in a left parenthesis signifying the beginning of a function parameter list, Intellisense displays the function declaration, as shown in Figure 1.16.

Working with Documents

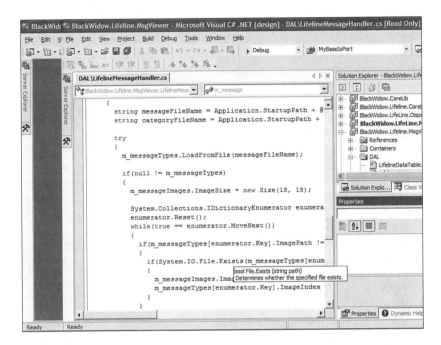

FIGURE 1.16   Intellisense can display function parameter lists, class methods, and variables while you're editing your source code so that you don't have to constantly refer to documentation.

ToolTips for parameter lists aren't the only thing Intellisense can do, however. Typing in a variable that is a class causes the IDE to drop down a combo box listing all the member variables and functions contained within that class. When you type in the name of a class's member variable, you can place and hold your mouse cursor over that variable and a ToolTip describing the data type of that variable will be displayed after a short period.

Editing HTML

One thing you'll realize, especially when working with the projects in the Internet Programming section, is that the Visual Studio .NET IDE contains an extremely well-done HTML editor. This is no doubt due to the apparent push to web-enable projects of all types. As a Visual C# .NET developer, you will use the HTML editor for a variety of projects, some of which include web services and ASP.NET projects.

Before Visual Studio .NET, you had to rely on an external editor to create HTML files. You could open an HTML file within the Visual Studio IDE, but you had to resort to plain text editing with no supporting toolset to help you get the job done. That was fine for developers who claim that Notepad is the best HTML editor. But for people like me, Visual Studio .NET provides tools that enable me to easily work with HTML files. To get a quick feel for HTML editing within the IDE, click File, New, File from the main menu. When the New File dialog is displayed, click on the General category and then select HTML Page from the list of file types contained in the right-side list box.

Web Page Design Using the Design View

There are two ways to work with an HTML page. You can switch between these two views by clicking the Design and HTML buttons on the bottom right of the HTML view window, as shown in Figure 1.17. Design view enables you to visually construct your HTML page using the web controls found within the toolbox tool window. To create a new control, click the control you want to add from the toolbox and then drag and drop that control onto the HTML page. When the control appears, you can change its properties by using the Properties tool window, which by default is located at the bottom right of the IDE. You can easily select the current HTML page's controls by clicking them with your mouse or by using the Document Outline tool window, as shown in Figure 1.18. If the Document Outline tool window is not visible, click View, Other Windows, Document Outline from the main menu.

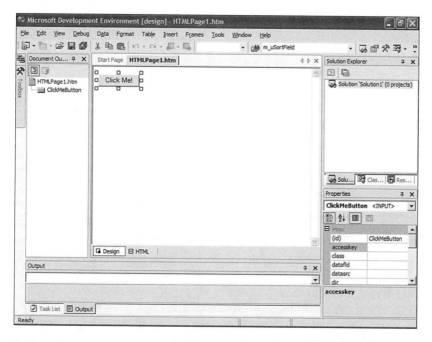

FIGURE 1.17   Visual Studio .NET's HTML editor contains many features, such as auto-completion, validation, and event handler script generation for objects.

Working with Documents

HTML View

After you have finished designing the layout of your HTML page, you can switch to HTML view to work with the HTML text of your web page by clicking the HTML button located at the bottom left of the HTML view window. If the Document Outline tool window is still open, its contents will change from listing only the HTML controls to listing a full tree view of all the document's tags in a hierarchical fashion. Furthermore, the Script Outline button will be enabled. It is located at the top of the Document Outline tool window, as shown in Figure 1.18. The Script Outline view of the Document Outline tool window enables you to easily add event handlers to your document for any of the objects the page refers to.

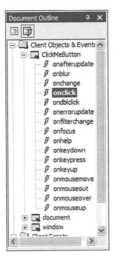

FIGURE 1.18   The Document Outline tool window enables you to look at your HTML page in a hierarchical fashion. It also supports adding event handlers to the HTML page's controls quickly.

Ensuring HTML Correctness

The HTML editor contains several features that assist you in editing the HTML source directly. Whenever you type in the left bracket that signifies the beginning of an HTML tag, a drop-down list displays a listing all the tags that are valid within the context you are working in. Selecting one of these tags will then create the beginning and ending tags and your text cursor will be inserted in between the two. Furthermore, a drop-down list is displayed whenever you start adding attributes to a tag. This list also is context aware and will display a list of valid attributes for only the tag currently being edited.

As you're working with the HTML code, the HTML editor is constantly checking your document for correctness. Whenever the editor notices that the document is incorrect, it places a red squiggly line underneath the offending portion of code, as shown in Figure 1.19. When you hover your mouse cursor over that piece of code, a ToolTip displays an error message to explain the error.

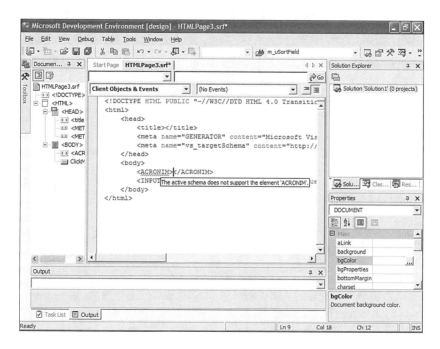

FIGURE 1.19   The HTML editor helps you easily spot errors in HTML code by marking the offending code with a red squiggly line and displaying a ToolTip containing an error message when the mouse cursor hovers over it.

Editing XML

A few years ago, Extensible Markup Language (XML) was virtually unheard of to the average developer. However, in recent years, it has become one of the most-adopted technologies to date. When working with the various .NET technologies, you will run into many places where XML plays a pivotal role. Everything from data sources and web services to configuration files contains XML as the underlying data mechanism.

Just as the HTML editor supported a Design view and an HTML view, the XML editor for Visual Studio .NET contains a Design view and an XML view. When a new XML file is created, however, you will be presented with only the XML view because the editor doesn't know how to visually display the XML data without some extra help. This extra help comes in the form of an XML schema. Visual Studio .NET also contains a schema editor that enables you to both visually create the schema as well as hand-code the schema, if you so desire. In fact, when visually creating the schema, the Toolbox tool window contains all the valid schema design elements that you would need. Adding the schema design elements to your file is a simple matter of dragging and dropping them.

Editing Binary Files

If you've ever had to create your own file format, you no doubt used a binary editor, sometimes known as a *hex editor*, to view a sample file your application produced. Or if you've ever worked with pointers, especially in the area of string parsing, you stepped through code to see what effect certain lines would have on the contents of your Memory debug window.

When viewing binary data, you had to use an external third-party tool to view the data in hexadecimal format. Visual Studio .NET now contains a binary editor that enables you to view any type of binary file and even makes it possible for you to change the values within that file.

Using External Tools

Even though the Visual Studio .NET IDE contains so many features that you might even start to think it can read your mind and write your code for you, it unfortunately can't. There are some things that are either not built into the IDE by design or are better left to external tools.

Many tools are available for your use that are either installed with Visual Studio .NET or are available through third-party developers. It wouldn't be that nice if I devoted large amounts of material talking about a third-party developer tool, so this book will focus on the tools that ship with Visual Studio .NET where appropriate.

External tools are only somewhat integrated within the IDE, in that the IDE simply provides a mechanism to launch them using the main menu. You can find a list of installed tools by clicking Tools from the main menu. What you see in that list is only a partial list of the many tools that are provided with Visual Studio .NET. If you're the curious type like me, you've already gone through all the Visual Studio .NET folders and launched every executable file you found to see what it does. If not, you might want to think about doing so. Not only is it useful because you might find a tool that could potentially help you with a project, but it's also extremely fun (don't ask me why).

Defining Your Own Tools

One of the very first things I do whenever I install Visual Studio .NET on a computer is create an Explore Here tool. The Visual Studio .NET IDE enables you to add to the Tools menu by defining external tools. To create an external tool definition—in this case we'll create the Explore Here tool—click Tools, External Tools from the main menu. The External Tools dialog will be displayed as shown in Figure 1.20. You can click on each of the tools listed under the Menu Contents entry to see how it is defined. To create a new tool, click on the Add button. For the Title field, enter **Explore Here**. In the Command field, simply type in **explorer.exe**, which is the executable that you want the IDE to launch when the tool is selected from the Tools menu. Click the button containing the right-facing arrow and select Project Directory for the Arguments field. The Initial Directory field also should point to Project Directory, as shown in Figure 1.20. When you are finished, click OK to close the dialog. Now when you select Tools, Explore Here from the main menu, an explorer window will open to the location where your project is located.

FIGURE 1.20   The Tools menu enables you to launch external tools directly from the IDE. You can also add new tools to the menu by selecting External Tools from the Tools main menu item.

1

Summary

In this chapter, you took a brief look at all the exciting features of the Visual Studio .NET IDE. Visual Studio .NET contains many more enhancements and features from its predecessors, but still retains some of the features included in previous Visual Studio products. Window management and customization is an important topic and it is one you should master as soon as possible. When you get past learning how to use the tools provided within Visual Studio .NET, you are free to concentrate on your main priority: the source code.

As you work through the various projects and discussions in this book, you will take a closer look at some of the many tools that can help you develop your applications. If you need information that you can't find in the context of the chapter you are reading, remember that Visual Studio .NET contains links to many of the topics discussed in this book.

Further Reading

Programming C#, Third Edition by Jesse Liberty, O'Reilly. ISBN: 0596004893.

The Applied Microsoft .NET Framework Programming in C# Collection, Microsoft Press. ISBN: 0735619751.

Part II

Language Fundamentals

CHAPTER 2 Introduction to C#

CHAPTER 3 Expressions and Control Structures

CHAPTER 4 Strings and Regular Expressions

CHAPTER 5 Arrays and Collections

CHAPTER 6 Objects and Classes

CHAPTER 7 File and Stream I/O and Object Persistence

CHAPTER 8 XML Fundamentals

CHAPTER 9 Multithreaded Programming

CHAPTER 10 Events and Delegates

CHAPTER 11 Reflection and Code Attributes

CHAPTER 12 Assemblies and AppDomains

CHAPTER 13 COM and Windows Interoperability

CHAPTER 14 High-Performance Programming

2 Introduction to C#

IN BRIEF

In this chapter, you will be introduced to various aspects of the .NET Framework, including data types, the Common Language Runtime, and garbage collection. The goal of this chapter is to give you a basic understanding of the .NET Framework, how it works, and how C# is an integral part of that framework. You don't have to have any previous exposure to C# to read this book. Some background and experience with programming in general would be helpful, but is also not necessary.

WHAT YOU NEED

RECOMMENDED SOFTWARE	.NET Framework Visual Studio .NET
RECOMMENDED HARDWARE	.NET-enabled desktop client
SKILLS REQUIRED	Basic programming skills

INTRODUCTION TO C# AT A GLANCE

Why Learn Yet Another Language?	37

Learning Common Types	**38**		
Understanding Value Types	38	Reference Versus Value Types	40
Understanding Reference Types	39		

What Is the Common Language Runtime?	**40**		
Multiple Languages, One Runtime	42	The JIT Compiler	43
Isolation	42	Code Execution	43
Platform Invoke	42	COM Interoperability	43
Code Access Security	42	Rotor: Microsoft's Shared Source Common Language Infrastructure	44

Take Out the Trash: Theory of Garbage Collection	**44**		
Reference Counting	44	Partial Collection	45
Generations	44	Nondeterministic Finalization	45
Collection	45	Using `IDisposable` to Create Well-Behaved Objects	46

Introduction to the Base Class Library	48

The Canonical "Hello World" Example	49

Welcome to the .NET Framework. One of the main goals of the .NET Framework is to provide a universal, safe type system through which any language can communicate with managed code written in any other language. By defining a common set of data types, such as int, char, string, and the like, it also provides the ability for an object written in one language to be used and accessed in another language. As a result of the .NET Framework effort, C# was developed to harness the power of the platform. In addition, C# represents an evolution in language design.

C# features many object-oriented features, such as properties for data encapsulation, polymorphic behavior, inheritance, and interface implementation. In addition, C# allows for a developer to tap into unsafe code (discussed later) when performance is at a premium. C# was developed to provide the best aspects of C++, Java, SmallTalk, and Modula2. Elements from each of the languages can be seen in C# and in the Common Language Runtime itself.

Why Learn Yet Another Language?

It seems that all too often someone comes up with a new and improved tool to solve the crisis of the day, when in fact it's the same crisis everyone has been dealing with for years and a plethora of existing tools to choose from already exists. The current crisis of the day is developing a software application that is network aware, database connected, web service–enabled, and any other advanced feature that clients, customers, and management alike need for the next generation of software applications.

So, why create a new language? After all, there are so many languages out there to choose from; surely one of them would suffice to do the job. We have Visual Basic for high-level abstraction and C++ for expressiveness and raw power. Although these languages are great and fill a vital role, the real need for a new language is not so much the language itself, but the idea behind a new platform for software development in general.

In the same way that some people like the city life but others prefer the quiet countryside, the choice of languages is also a personal preference. Of course, language wars are often debates over language semantics, the expressive power and performance versus ease of use and high-level constructs such as object-oriented features. However, one thing has always remained constant: the need to reach the Holy Grail of software engineering, code reuse. Or, better yet, component-based development. The ability to create a component and use it in a software application that is written in another programming language is what developers have been searching for. Many attempts and standards have been created to address this very issue. This includes CORBA, COM, DCOM, Win32 libraries, and so on. However, each solution has had a single unavoidable roadblock: a common type system that unifies all languages and allows them to pass information back and forth in a consistent well-defined format.

Learning Common Types

Take an integer for example. Simple things such as the size of an integer are often taken for granted. Integers might not necessarily be the same size (or even in the same byte-order) on two different machines and operating systems. If you said 32 bits, you'd be somewhat correct. An integer on a 32-bit processor is in fact 32 bits in size. However, some languages such as C++ do not specify the size of an integer. They merely state that an integer is the size that can be handled by a single processing cycle for the target CPU. Okay. That's good for cross-platform languages such as C and C++. However, it makes it difficult for interoperability with other languages, such as Visual Basic.

The common type system does more than just define the size of an integer. The common type system provides three major functions:

▶ Provides a framework for cross-language integration, type safety, and high-performance code.

▶ Provides an object-oriented model that supports the complete implementation of many programming languages.

▶ Defines rules that languages must follow. This ensures that objects written in different languages can interact with each other.

The common type system has two classifications of types: value types and reference types.

Understanding Value Types

Value types contain their data directly. In addition, value types are allocated on the runtime stack; this will become important during the discussion of the garbage collection system. Value types can be built-in, such as a char or int type, or user-defined via the `struct` keyword. Table 2.1 provides a listing of the value types in the Framework Class Library, hereafter referred to as the FCL.

TABLE 2.1

Value Types Defined by the .NET FCL

Category	Class Name	Description	C# Data Type
Integer	Byte	An 8-bit unsigned integer	byte
	SByte	An 8-bit signed integer*	Sbyte
	Int16	A 16-bit signed integer	short
	Int32	A 32-bit signed integer	int
	Int64	A 64-bit signed integer	long
	UInt16	A 16-bit unsigned integer*	ushort
	UInt32	A 32-bit unsigned integer*	uint
	UInt64	A 64-bit unsigned integer*	ulong

TABLE 2.1

Continued

Category	Class Name	Description	C# Data Type
Floating point	Single	A single-precision (32-bit) floating-point number	float
	Double	A double-precision (64-bit) floating-point number	double
Logical	Boolean	True or false Boolean value	bool
Other	Char	A Unicode (16-bit) character	char
	Decimal	A 96-bit decimal value	decimal
	IntPtr	A signed integer whose size depends on the target platform	IntPtr
	UIntPtr	An unsigned integer whose size depends on the target platform	UIntPtr

NOTE

Value types with an asterisk in the description are not compliant with the common language specification (CLS). That means those particular types are not required or supported by all .NET-targeted languages. All Microsoft languages, such as VB .NET, C#, Managed C++, and JScript support the types listed in Table 2.1.

Table source: msdn.microsoft.com/library/default.asp?url=/library/en-us/cpguide/html/cpconthenetframeworkclasslibrary.asp

Value types created within the scope of a method exist only for the duration of that method. After the method has returned, its call stack is reclaimed and the value type no longer exists. Classes can also contain value types. In this case, the data for the value type exists for the duration of the existence of the object.

Understanding Reference Types

Reference types are objects that are allocated and managed by the garbage collector. Reference types are instances of classes created using the new keyword. An example would be the following:

```
MyClass myClass = new MyClass( );
```

The myClass instance is created on the heap and managed by the garbage collector. Reference types do not disappear when they go out of scope the way that value types do. Rather, as the name implies, when all references to a reference type are gone, the garbage collector will reclaim the memory. More about the garbage collector will be discussed later.

Reference Versus Value Types

The key difference between value type and reference type is the way they are passed to methods. Depending on what language you're coming from, this might take some getting used to. For instance, in Visual Basic, not VB .NET, parameters default to pass by reference. That means that if a method (sub/procedure) modifies the parameter, the caller will see that modification. This is not the case with value types. Value types are passed to a method via a copy. A copy of the value is created on the call stack to the method. Sometimes it's just easier to see it in code, as in Listing 2.1.

LISTING 2.1
Passing a Value Type to a Method

```
class MyClass {
    static public void ByValue( int i ) {
        i = 20;
    }
}

int i = 10;
Console.WriteLine( "Value of i := {0}", i );
MyClass.ByValue( i );
Console.WriteLine( "Value of i := {0}", i );
```

In Listing 2.1, a local variable i is declared and set to an initial value of 10. The WriteLine method displays the value to the output window. Next, the code passes the local variable i to the ByValue method of MyClass. In reality, a copy of i is placed on the call stack and not the actual variable i. This point is crucial. The code within the ByValue method is free to change the value of the parameter that was passed in; however, after the method has returned, any modifications made by the method to the parameter are lost. Therefore, the last WriteLine method will display the following message: Value of i := 10.

Armed with some basic knowledge of the .NET type system, the next step is to understand how the runtime system supports these types.

What Is the Common Language Runtime?

The first misnomer to point out is that code compiled for .NET is not interpreted as it is with Java and the Java Virtual Machine. (Java code using the latest version of J2SE or J2EE can now, in fact, be JIT-compiled.) Rather, all compilers for .NET emit special code known as Intermediate Language or IL. The Common Language Runtime performs just-in-time compilation to native code as needed. This allows for increased code performance and the ability to verify the managed code. Figure 2.1 depicts a visual representation of layers that make up the Common Language Runtime.

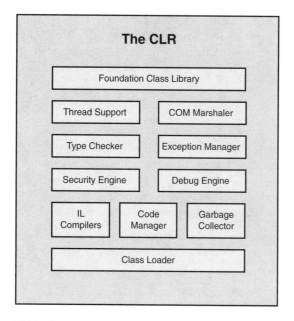

FIGURE 2.1   Layers of the Common Language Runtime.

The Common Language Runtime provides several benefits over traditional unmanaged code. A subset of these benefits includes the following:

- Performance improvements including memory management, code optimization, and security

- The ability to reuse components developed in other languages

- Cross language inheritance of classes

- Garbage collection

- Allow for compiler writers to target IL rather than a specific CPU or operating system

- Metadata for assemblies

- Unified threading model

- Relief from DLL hell

Multiple Languages, One Runtime

Because the runtime understands only IL, any language can be targeted to execute on the .NET platform. As long as a target language complies with the common language specification (CLS), cross-language development is not hindered by data types, object references, memory management, or threading models. The Common Language Runtime provides the infrastructure for which all languages can take advantage of. Currently, there are more than 20 languages for .NET.

Isolation

Another major advantage that the Common Language Runtime offers is application isolation. This isolation allows for security and stability. Through the use of AppDomains (isolated execution apartments), if a .NET application becomes unstable, it will not have any effect on other applications executing within the Common Language Runtime or on the operating system itself. This protection has been a long sought-after need for Windows applications.

AppDomains also protect applications from each other by preventing memory over-writes and malicious attacks on executing applications. The AppDomain provides a boundary that protects the executing application from outside interference.

As you will see in an upcoming chapter, AppDomains are also valuable for many other reasons, including hosting plug-in DLLs that can extend the functionality of your application.

Platform Invoke

Another benefit of the Common Language Runtime is the concept of PInvoke, which is the ability of .NET applications to invoke the Win32 API when necessary. The Common Language Runtime provides a type-marshalling system for converting between .NET types (such as string) to Win32-native types (such as char* [a character pointer]). Any Win32 API method can be imported with a simple declaration such as the following:

```
using System.Runtime.InteropServices;

public class MyWin32Wrapper {
    [DllImport( "User32.dll" )]
    static public extern void Beep( int frequency, int duration );
}
```

Code Access Security

To protect OS resources, access permissions, and execution security, the Common Language Runtime implements artifact-based security. Not only can permissions be limited to users, but an *assembly* (a compiled .NET component), can be restricted based on metadata held within it. This allows for restrictions to be placed on the execution of the assembly regardless of the user's system privileges.

The security system also examines the source of the IL. Code from the local machine has a higher security privilege than code being executed from a remote share. Such security prevents remote execution of nontrusted application code.

Security was built into .NET from the ground up. In Windows XP and beyond, even the application loader recognizes .NET applications and performs preliminary security validations to ensure that the assembly was not modified before handing over execution to the Common Language Runtime itself.

The JIT Compiler

Traditional compiler implementers were left to handle code optimization based on target CPU, execution prediction, register allocation, code unwinding, and so on. With .NET and the Common Language Runtime, compilers that target the .NET platform need to be concerned only with emitting IL. The Common Language Runtime invokes a JIT (just-in-time) compiler as needed for the execution of the IL. The JIT compiler is optimized to handle loop unrolling, caching nonvolatile variables, and optimizing execution flow among other things.

Code Execution

Execution of IL works by first determining whether the method/code to be executed has already been compiled; if not, the IL is JIT compiled, cached, and executed. If the IL segment has already been compiled, the cached native code is executed. In essence, an application will execute faster the second time a section of code is executed.

COM Interoperability

The ability to leverage components is key to the .NET Framework. Before .NET, COM was the *lingua franca* of component development and reuse. The Common Language Runtime supports COM component use via an interop layer in which a runtime-callable wrapper is created. This managed wrapper hides the complexities of dealing with traditional COM development and component usage. No longer do developers need to know about GUIDs, IUnknown, IDispatcher, and the ambiguous VARIANT type. The managed wrapper handles type conversion, interface querying, and connection points and translates them to .NET types, interfaces, and events. All the grunt work is taken care of for the developer.

Along with the ability to consume classic COM components, the Common Language Runtime also provides a mechanism to expose a newly created .NET component as a classic COM object. COM clients such as VB 6 can consume these .NET components in the same manner as a classic COM object. To accomplish this task, a COM-callable wrapper is created. This wrapper handles intercepting calls to IUnknown and IDispatch. In addition, the type marshaller is used to convert .NET types to COM types. It's important to note that not all .NET constructs have a COM equivalent.

COM does not support static methods, polymorphism, or data types not specified by the COM standard.

Rotor: Microsoft's Shared Source Common Language Infrastructure

To round out the discussion about the Common Language Runtime, the ultimate reference is Rotor. Rotor is a shared source implementation of the common language infrastructure (CLI). Its goal is to provide students, professors, and professionals with an insight into the development of tools targeted at .NET. Rotor can be downloaded from the Microsoft website.

Take Out the Trash: Theory of Garbage Collection

Memory management used to be a painful exercise in application development, not to mention a source of security flaws. Applications that have poor memory management continue to consume system resources and eventually bring down the operating system. .NET solves this problem by making use of a generational garbage collector to manage all allocated memory within the application's process. This frees the developer from the tedious task of ensuring that allocated memory is properly release backed to the system.

Reference Counting

When an object is created, the garbage collector allocates memory from the existing application memory pool or, if necessary, increases the memory pool to accommodate the memory allocation. When the object is created, there is a single reference to it. During execution of code, the garbage collector keeps track of the number of references to the object. With each additional reference, a counter is incremented. When references go out of scope, the reference counter is decremented. When the reference counter reaches zero, the object and the memory it occupies are tagged for collection.

Generations

To provide efficient memory management, the garbage collector (GC) is based on the idea that newly created objects will have a short lifetime. These objects are created lower in the managed heap. Figure 2.2 shows a simplified view of the managed heap.

As objects age, they are moved up in the generation ladder. The garbage collector scans the generations from lowest to highest when looking to reclaim objects. The lower generation, generation 0, is scanned most frequently while generation 2 is scanned least.

Take Out the Trash: Theory of Garbage Collection

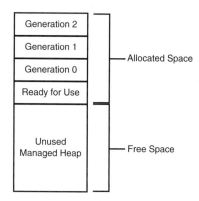

FIGURE 2.2   Basic view of the managed heap and generations.

Collection

The GC implements both full and partial collections. In a full collection cycle, the program execution is stopped. By stopping the execution, the GC is free to move memory and fix up the addresses without affecting the executing program. During a full collection cycle, the GC locates all live and dead objects. The live objects are pushed up a generation and the dead objects are reclaimed. A full collection is very expensive and, as such, the GC implements a partial collection algorithm to provide optimal performance.

Partial Collection

Partial collection works under the premise that objects in generation 0 are more likely to be short-lived than in generation 1, and so on up the generation ladder. The GC scans for *roots* (pointers to objects) and determines which objects can be reached and which cannot be reached. In a perfect world, objects in generation 0 would be reclaimed more often than objects in generation 1. Therefore, the GC scan rate for generation 0 would be higher than that of generation 1 and 2.

Nondeterministic Finalization

An often heated discussion about the GC revolves around the topic of nondeterministic finalization. Essentially, *nondeterministic finalization* is not knowing exactly when an object is going to be reclaimed. At first sight, this might not seem like such an important topic. However, when you consider dealing with expensive resources such as database connections, socket connections, and graphics resources, this quickly becomes a big deal. Consider the code in Listing 2.2.

LISTING 2.2

Potential Resource Leak in .NET

```
public class MyDataLayer {
  private SqlConnection connection;

  public void DoDBWorkA( ) {
    if( connection == null || connection.State != ConnectionState.Open ) {
      OpenConnection( ); //opens connection to the database
    }
    ...rest of code...  }
  public void DoDBWorkB( ) {
    if( connection == null || connection.State != ConnectionState.Open ) {
      OpenConnection( ); //opens connection to the database
    }
    ...rest of code...  }

}
//else where in code
MyDataLayer dataLayer = new MyDataLayer( );
dataLayer.DoDBWorkA( );
dataLayer.DoDBWorkB( );
```

With nondeterministic finalization, you never know exactly when the
SqlConnection might get disposed of and its underlying resources are reclaimed.
This is really not a resource leak as much as it is poor coding and a lack of understanding how nondeterministic finalization works. When creating objects that
contain expensive resources, such as the database connection, .NET provides the
design pattern or concept of IDisposable.

NOTE

An interface defines a contract specifying methods and/or properties that a class agrees to implement. Although the introduction of an interface might seem a bit premature, it is necessary in order
to understand how a developer can interact with the GC.

Using IDisposable to Create Well-Behaved Objects

By implementing IDisposable, a class says two things. First, it says, "I use expensive resources
that need to be released when you've finished with me." Second, "the GC will call the Dispose
method upon collection of the object if you forget to." To create a better .NET citizen, the
MyDataLayer class has been updated to implement the IDisposable interface and the
calling code uses the C# keyword using to ensure that the Dispose method will be invoked
when it's done with the object. Look at the updated code for the MyDataLayer class in
Listing 2.3.

LISTING 2.3
Creating a Better .NET Citizen

```csharp
public class MyDataLayer : IDisposable {
    private SqlConnection        connection;

    public void Dispose( ) {
        if( connection != null )
            connection.Dispose( );
        connection ==null;
    }
    public void DoDBWorkA( ) {
        if( connection == null || connection.State != ConnectionState.Open ) {
            OpenConnection( ); //opens connection to the database
        }
        ...rest of code...
    }
    public void DoDBWorkB( ) {
        if( connection == null || connection.State != ConnectionState.Open ) {
            OpenConnection( ); //opens connection to the database
        }
        ...rest of code...
    }
    ...rest of code for MyDataLayer
}
//Working with the MyDataLayer class
using( MyDataLayer dataLayer = new MyDataLayer( )) {
    dataLayer.DoDBWorkA( );
    dataLayer.DoDBWorkB( );
}
```

There are a couple of key points to cover from Listing 2.3. First is the implementation of the IDisposable interface. By implementing the IDisposable interface, the MyDataLayer class is making a statement that it contains one or more expensive resources that should be released as soon as possible. When you encounter a class that implements this interface, be sure to invoke the Dispose method when you're done with it. Second, the use of the using keyword ensures that the Dispose method will be invoked automatically upon exiting the using scope.

The using keyword ensures that when execution exits, the execution block, the Dispose method of the MyDataLayer object, will be invoked. Doing so ensures that the underlying SqlConnection is disposed thereby returning that expensive resource back to the connection pool.

Take Out the Trash: Theory of Garbage Collection

There are other practices that you should employ to write memory efficient code in .NET. The following is a basic to-do list for efficient memory usage and faster generation 0 collection:

- ▶ Limit object allocation.

- ▶ Keep objects as small as necessary. Don't create bloated code.

- ▶ Keep object references to a minimum.

That's the basic tour of the GC provided by .NET. For more detailed information, see the Rotor shared source. Next, we'll look at the class framework provided by .NET.

Introduction to the Base Class Library

The Base Class Library (BCL), provides a ton of code that you as a developer can leverage to build your applications. The BCL is extensive in terms of the number of classes it provides, and an exhaustive coverage of all that it offers would require a tome all to itself. It is interesting to note that the BCL was developed almost entirely in C#. Table 2.2 provides a basic listing of the FCL namespaces and a partial listing of what can be found under that namespace.

TABLE 2.2

An FCL Overview

Namespace	Key Classes
System	Basic types (`int`, `char`, `string`) Console class for console I/O Standard exceptions
System.Diagnostics	Debugging class Trace listeners Performance counters
System.Drawing	Image support Graphics support for both 2D/3D
System.IO	File I/O Streams
System.Reflection	Metadata classes; used for dynamic discovery of methods, properties, and fields
System.Text	Text manipulation classes `StringBuilder`
System.Text.RegularExpression	Support for full regular expression
System.Web	Base web core classes `HttpHandlers`

TABLE 2.2

Continued

`System.Web.UI`	Core web UI classes
`System.Web.UI.HtmlControls`	Standard HTML control classes
`System.Web.UI.WebControls`	.NET versions of standard HTML controls, such as button, radio button, table, and so on
`System.Windows.Forms`	Windows development UI controls

Table 2.2 does not give a complete namespace listing, but instead lists some of the most commonly used namespaces.

The Canonical "Hello World" Example

I'm fairly certain that by law it is required for every programming book to provide the famous "Hello World" example. So, rather than face potential criminal charges, a walkthrough for creating a Console C# "Hello World" application follows.

Begin by staring Visual Studio .NET and selecting File, New Project. Next, select a C# console application and name it Hello World as shown in Figure 2.3.

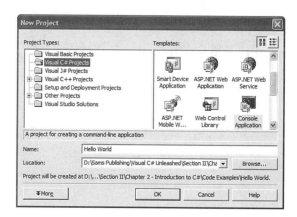

FIGURE 2.3   Creating a .NET console application for Hello World.

Visual Studio .NET will create a default source file, `Class1.cs`, and provide some basic boilerplate code as shown in Listing 2.4.

The Canonical "Hello World" Example

LISTING 2.4
Generated Boilerplate Code for a C# Console Application

```
using System;

namespace Hello_World
{
    /// <summary>
    /// Hello World example
    /// </summary>
    class Class1
    {
        /// <summary>
        /// The main entry point for the application.
        /// </summary>
        [STAThread]
        static void Main(string[] args)
        {
            //
            // TODO: Add code to start application here
            //
        }
    }
}
```

Replace lines 16 though 18 **1** with the following line of code:

```
Console.WriteLine( "Hello World" );
```

The Main method should now look like Listing 2.5.

LISTING 2.5
Updated Main Method Replacing Comments with Code

```
1: static void Main(string[] args)
2: {
3:     Console.WriteLine( "Hello World" );
4: }
```

The Console.WriteLine method will print the string Hello World to a console window. Figure 2.3 shows the results from executing the code. To execute the code, select Debug, Start Without Debugging or simply press Ctrl+F5 to launch the application.

Summary

In this chapter, we explored the underpinnings of the .NET platform. This tour included topics covering the built-in security provided by the Common Language Runtime, along with the cross-language support and common data types. In addition, you've seen your first C# example in this book.

Further Reading

Programming C#, Third Edition by Jesse Liberty, O'Reilly. ISBN: 0596004893.

The Applied Microsoft .NET Framework Programming in C# Collection, Microsoft Press. ISBN: 0735619751.

3

Expressions and Control Structures

IN BRIEF

In this chapter, we will explore the basic control structures provided by C#. Each of these constructs will be explored and discussed in terms of syntax and proper usage.

WHAT YOU NEED

RECOMMENDED SOFTWARE	.NET Framework
	Visual Studio .NET
RECOMMENDED HARDWARE	.NET-enabled desktop client
SKILLS REQUIRED	C# coding

EXPRESSIONS AND CONTROL STRUCTURES AT A GLANCE

Expressions and Control Structures	53
Basic Expressions	53
Legal Variable Names	53
Using C# Operators	54
Pre/Post Operators	60
Program Flow Control: Control Structures	60

The Program Execution Path	60	Short Circuit Evaluation	62
Conditional Statements	60	Using the Ternary Operator	64
The if Control Structure	61	The switch Statement	65
The if/else Control Structure Combination	61		

Looping	68		
The for Loop	68	The while Loop	70
Using the for Statement	68	The do..while Loop	72
The foreach Statement	69		

Expressions and Control Structures

The goal with any programming language is to implement application logic in order to achieve the desired functionality. C# is a modern language that offers traditional expressions and control structures along with a few new ones to simplify the development process. In addition, C# is a type-safe language and enforces type safety at various levels. Such adherence to type safety is both a blessing and a curse. Depending on the language you're familiar with, some of your old habits will cause you a lot of frustration with C# because it enforces correct code and type safety. The purpose of this chapter is to explore the type safety offered by C# while delving into the expression syntax and control structures offered by the language.

3

Basic Expressions

An *expression* is defined as a syntactically correct program statement. However, for the purpose of this chapter, the expressions we're most interested in revolve around assignment and evaluation, and true/false determination. An assignment expression has at least one variable and one value to be assigned to that variable. Such is the case of declaring an integer value and assigning it the default value of 10. All variables must be initialized before use; otherwise, the C# compiler will bitterly complain about the usage of an uninitialized variable. So, what does this mean exactly? Take a look at the following C# statements **1** :

```
int i;         //C# complains about the uninitialized variable
int j = 10;    //variable j has the initial value of 10
int k;
k = 10;        //okay as long as done before usage of k
```
1

C# requires all variables to be initialized before usage. The variable can be initialized during declaration or before its first usage. However, it's best to initialize a default value during its declaration; doing so will aid in future debugging attempts.

Legal Variable Names

Before moving too far into C# syntax, it's important to understand variable naming in C#. C# is a case-sensitive language. Variable names that differ only by case are considered two different entities. The following declarations illustrate this point:

```
int wholePart = 10;
int WholePart = 20;
```

Legal Variable Names

The first declaration of an integer named wholePart is considered unique based on case and does not conflict with the second declaration of WholePart. Although each variable is spelled the same, because they differ in case, C# considers them two separate entities. This is important to note if you are coming from a language such as Microsoft Visual Basic where case sensitivity is not an issue. In addition, C# specifies rules for how variables can be named. Legal names start with a letter or underscore followed by one or more letters, underscores, or digits. Listing 3.1 shows some legal and illegal variable declarations to illustrate the C# rules for variable names.

LISTING 3.1

C# Variable Naming Rules

```
int 9abc;        //illegal. Starts with an integer
int _abc;        //legal starts with an underscore
int _9abc;       //legal starts with an underscore
int #myAge;      //illegal. Starts with an illegal character
int myAge_1;     //legal. Starts with a char followed by
```

Using C# Operators

C# provides several operators for arithmetic, logical, increment, decrement, and other operations. C# also provides for shorthand notations for common situations such as adding an amount to a variable. In addition, most of the C# operators can be overloaded by the developer. Overloading enables the developer to specify the behavior for the operator when applied to a specific type. Overloading will be covered later in this chapter. Table 3.1 provides a listing of all operators for C#.

TABLE 3.1

C# Operators

Category	Operator	Description	Can Overload?
Arithmetic	+	Addition	Yes
	–	Subtraction	Yes
	*	Multiplication	Yes
	/	Division	Yes
	%	Modulus remainder	Yes
Logical	&	Bitwise AND	Yes
	|	Bitwise OR	Yes
	^	Bitwise exclusive OR	Yes
	!	Logical negation	Yes
	~	Bitwise complement	Yes
	&&	Logical AND	Not directly
	||	Logical OR	Not directly

TABLE 3.1

Continued

Category	Operator	Description	Can Overload?
Increment/decrement	++	Pre/post increment	Yes
	--	Pre/post decrement	Yes
Shift	<<	Binary left shift	Yes
	>>	Binary right shift	Yes
Relational	==	Equality	Yes
	!=	Not equal	Yes
	<	Less than	Yes
	>	Greater than	Yes
	<=	Less than or equal	Yes
	>=	Greater than or equal	Yes
Assignment	=	Assign	No
	+=	Add assign	Not directly
	-=	Subtract assign	Not directly
	*=	Multiply assign	Not directly
	/=	Divide assign	Not directly
	%=	Modulus assign	Not directly
	&=	Bitwise AND assign	Not directly
	|=	Bitwise OR assign	Not directly
	<<=	Left-shift assign	Not directly
	>>=	Right-shift assign	Not directly
Member access	.	Member access	No
Indexing	[]	Indexing	No, but indexers can be defined
Cast	()	Casting	No, but cast operators can be defined
Conditional	?:	Ternary if statement	No
Object creation	new	Creates an instance of an object	No
Type information	as	Safe cast to specified type	No
	is	Used to determine whether a type is of a specified type	No
Overflow	checked	Controls overflow checking context	No
	unchecked	Controls overflow checking context	No
Indirection and address	*	Pointer dereference	No
	->	Pointer member access	No
	[]	Pointer indexing	No
	&	Address of	No

3

Using C# Operators

It's important to note the operators for which overloading cannot be performed directly. This category of operators is really shorthand notations for an extended syntax. For example, the expression x += y gets expanded and evaluated as x = x + y; therefore, if the addition operator + is overloaded, that operator will be used in the evaluation of the += operator. Operator overloading is a powerful feature of C# that offers the flexibility to allow for user-defined types to be manipulated as if they were built-in C# types. To explore the power of C# operators, create a new C# console application and name it Operators. Then copy the code from Listing 3.2 into the project. Build and run the project without debugging (Ctrl+F5) to see the output.

LISTING 3.2
C# Operator Overloading in Action

```
//////////////////////////////////////////////////////
///This project demonstrates operator overloading
///in C#
//////////////////////////////////////////////////////
using System;

namespace Operators {


    /// <summary>
    /// Mile class will define operators for increment/decrement
    /// </summary>
    public class Mile {

        private int      m_wholePart   = 0;
        private int      m_tenthPart   = 0;

        public int WholePart { get { return m_wholePart; } set { m_wholePart =
        value; } }
        public int Tenths    { get { return m_tenthPart; } set { m_tenthPart =
        value; } }

        public Mile( ) { }


        //operators

        /// <summary>
        /// Increment the tenths of a mile
        /// </summary>
        static public Mile operator++( Mile mile ) {
            mile.m_tenthPart++;
```

LISTING 3.2
Continued

```csharp
        if( mile.m_tenthPart >= 10 ) {
            mile.m_wholePart++;
            mile.m_tenthPart -= 10;
        }
        return mile;
    }

    /// <summary>
    /// Decrement the number of tenths in the mile
    /// </summary>
    static public Mile operator--( Mile mile ) {
        mile.m_tenthPart--;
        if( mile.m_tenthPart < 0 ) {
            mile.m_wholePart--;
            mile.m_tenthPart = 10 + mile.m_tenthPart;
        }
        return mile;
    }

    /// <summary>
    /// Add two mile objects together
    /// </summary>
    static public Mile operator+( Mile a, Mile b ) {
        int tenthPart    = a.m_tenthPart + b.m_tenthPart;
        int wholePart = a.m_wholePart + b.m_wholePart;
        if( tenthPart >= 10 ) {
            tenthPart = tenthPart - 10;
            wholePart++;
        }
        Mile result = new Mile( );
        result.m_tenthPart    = tenthPart;
        result.m_wholePart    = wholePart;
        return result;
    }

    /// <summary>
    /// Subtract two different Mile objects
    /// </summary>
    static public Mile operator-( Mile a, Mile b ) {
        Mile result = new Mile( );
        result.m_tenthPart    = a.m_tenthPart - b.m_tenthPart;
```

Using C# Operators

LISTING 3.2
Continued

```csharp
        if( result.Tenths < 0 ) {
            result.m_tenthPart              = 10 - result.m_tenthPart;
            result.m_wholePart              = a.m_wholePart - b.m_wholePart -
1;
        } else {
            result.m_wholePart              = a.m_wholePart - b.m_wholePart;
        }
        return result;
    }


    /// <summary>
    /// Returns the number of feet in a mile when casted to an float value
    /// </summary>
    static public explicit operator float( Mile mile ) {
        float feet = 5280 * mile.m_wholePart;
        feet *= ( (float)mile.m_tenthPart / 10.0f );
        return feet;
    }

    /// <summary>
    /// override the ToString method and return WholePart.TenthPart
    /// </summary>
    public override string ToString() {
        return string.Format( "{0}.{1}", m_wholePart, m_tenthPart );
    }

}


/// <summary>
/// Test harness for operators
/// </summary>
class OperatorTest {

    /// <summary>
    /// Defines the entry point for the application
    /// </summary>
    static void Main( ) {
        Mile mile = new Mile( );
```

LISTING 3.2
Continued

```
            mile.WholePart    = 5;          //5 miles
            mile.Tenths       = 1;          //5.1 miles

            mile++;                         //5.2 miles                              2
            Console.WriteLine( mile );      //the ToString //method will be invoked
                                            on the Mile class
            mile++;                         //5.3 miles
            Console.WriteLine( mile );

            float feet     = (float)mile;   //get the //number of feet in 5.3 miles

            //Display the number of feet in 5.3 miles
            Console.WriteLine( "Number of feet in {0} miles is {1}", mile, feet );


            Mile mile2     = new Mile( );
            mile2.WholePart    = 2;

            Mile result = mile - mile2;       //result should equal 3.3 miles
            Console.WriteLine( "{0} - {1} = {2}", mile, mile2, result );
        }
    }
}
```

3

Listing 3.2 begins by defining a class called Mile. The Mile class keeps track of whole miles and tenths of a mile. By overloading various operators such as increment, decrement, and addition, and a casting operator, the Mile class acts as if it were a built-in C# type. Walking through the code with the debugger will help to gain an insight as to what is happening during the execution of the code. Place a breakpoint on the shaded line **2** at line 114 of Listing 3.2. This is the first place where one of the overloaded operators will be invoked. It's important to realize that operators are just syntactic sugar for method calls. The literal translation of line 114 is mile = Mile.operator++(mile). For now, ignore everything in the listing expect for the operator-overloading code **3**. The rest, such as the properties WholePart and Tenths, and the fields m_wholePart and m_tenths, will be covered in Chapter 6, "Objects and Classes." Right now, just focus on the operators. From line 114, the code executes the overloaded increment operator found on line 29. From there, the m_tenths value is incremented with the same ++ operator that is defined for integer types.

Pre/Post Operators

The increment (++) and decrement (--) operators have two usages. That is, they can be used for both pre-operation and post-operation evaluation. When the operators appear before the variable, the operation takes place before the variable is evaluated. When they follow the variable, the operation takes place after the variable has been evaluated. Take a look at the following statements:

```
int i = 10;
Console.WriteLine( i++ ); //prints 10, then increments i to 11
Console.WriteLine( ++i ); //increments i to 12 and prints 12
```

When the value of i is sent to the WriteLine method the first time, i is evaluated to 10 and that value is passed to the WriteLine method. The variable i is then incremented to 11. On the next line, because the increment operator is before the variable (and therefore a pre-operation operator), i is incremented before its value is evaluated and passed to the WriteLine method.

Program Flow Control: Control Structures

An application simply cannot function without control structures. The following sections will show you how programs written in C# execute code and in what order, as well as how you can change the way code executes with loops, conditionals, and more.

The Program Execution Path

Building an application requires the translation of business requirements into code. To implement business rules and application logic, it's necessary to have the ability to handle various conditions such as Hourly Wage > 50 and take the appropriate action. The next section is a guide through the control structures that C# offers to implement application logic, conditional processing, and looping. Most of what follows should be familiar to anyone with previous programming knowledge. However, there are some twists that you might not be aware of.

Conditional Statements

Conditional statements form the heart of decision-making logic. They allow for business logic such as "If customer order is greater than 100 dollars, offer 10% discount; else, offer 5% discount." C# offers several mechanisms to implement such logic. Something that needs to be pointed out before venturing too far is that C# requires conditional expressions to be boolean; that is, they evaluate to true or false.

Languages such as C/C++ are not as strict and allow for expressions to merely evaluate to zero/nonzero in order to determine the process flow. This is *not* the case with C#. The C# compiler will quickly issue an error message if the expression does not evaluate to a type-safe boolean expression.

The `if` Control Structure

The `if` conditional statement represents the most basic of program flow control structures. The `if` statement evaluates a boolean expression to determine whether to execute one or more statements. By default, the `if` statement controls the execution of the very next statement. However, the use of code blocks allows the `if` statement to control several statements. Code blocks are statements contained within the { and } characters. The following code snippets illustrate this concept.

Controlling a single statement:

```
if( boolean expression is true )
   someStatement( );              //Controlled by the if statement
thisStatementAlwaysExecutes( );
```

or

```
if( boolean expression is true )
//controls the execution of code between { and } brackets
{
 statement_1();
 statement_2();
}
```

The `if/else` Control Structure Combination

The extension of the `if` statement is the `if/else` combination, which allows for the `if` statement to control two code blocks. When the condition being evaluated is true, the first control statement(s) is executed; otherwise, the `else` block is executed. This allows for the statement "If customer order is greater than 100 dollars, offer 10% discount; else, offer 5% discount" to be easily implemented as follows:

```
if( customerOrderTotal > 100 )
   discount = .10; //10% discount
else
   discount = .05; //5% discount
```

In addition, the `if/else` statement can make use of code blocks to control the execution of multiple statements:

```
if( customerOrderTotal > 100 ) {
```

Program Flow Control: Control Structures

```
Console.WriteLine( "Applying a 10% discount" );
discount = .10; //10% discount
} else {
Console.WriteLine( "Applying a 5% discount" );
discount = .05; //5% discount
}
```

Short Circuit Evaluation

Many times the expression being evaluated is a compound expression. A compound expression is two or more conditions to be evaluated such as "Customer is a preferred customer and order amount > 1000, apply a 15% discount." In this case, two different conditions must evaluate to true for the specified action to occur. C# takes a shortcut approach to evaluate the need to perform a full evaluation of every expression. For instance, if there are two expressions to evaluate and both must be true for the full statement to be true, C# evaluates the first statement. If the first statement is false, there is no need to even evaluate the second statement because the entire expression will be false regardless. Table 3.2 provides a basic truth table that further illustrates this point.

TABLE 3.2

Truth Table for Short Circuit Evaluations

Value	Operator	Value	Result
True	AND	True	True
True	AND	False	False
True	OR	True	True
True	OR	False	True

Such short-circuit evaluations save processing cycles and improve code performance by eliminating unnecessary code execution. The code in Listing 3.3 shows various short circuit evaluations in action.

LISTING 3.3

Understanding How Short Circuit Evaluations Work

```
using System;

namespace ShortCircuitEvaluation
{

   /// <summary>
   /// Summary description for Class1.
   /// </summary>
```

LISTING 3.3
Continued

```csharp
class Class1   {

    static bool ReturnsTrue( ) {
        Console.WriteLine( "*********[ EXECUTING ReturnsTrue ]***********" );
        return true;
    }

    static bool ReturnsFalse( ) {
        Console.WriteLine( "*********[ EXECUTING ReturnsFalse ]***********" );
        return false;
    }
    /// <summary>
    /// C# short Circuit evaluation example
    /// </summary>
    [STAThread]
    static void Main(string[] args)    {


        Console.WriteLine( "true AND ReturnsTrue( )" );
        if( true && ReturnsTrue( ) ) {
            Console.WriteLine( "Evaluated trueExpression " +
                "and executed ReturnsTrue( )" );
        }


        Console.WriteLine( System.Environment.NewLine );

        Console.WriteLine( "true AND ReturnsFalse( )" );
        if( true && ReturnsFalse( ) ) {
            Console.WriteLine( "This won't execute" );
        } else {
            Console.WriteLine( "Evaluated trueExpression " +
                "and executed ReturnsFalse( )" );
        }


        Console.WriteLine( System.Environment.NewLine );

        Console.WriteLine( "true OR True evaluation" );
        if( true || ReturnsTrue( ) ) {
            Console.WriteLine( "Evaluated only trueExpression " +
                "then short circuit. ReturnsTrue( ) was not executed" );
        }
```

Program Flow Control: Control Structures

LISTING 3.3
Continued

```
            Console.WriteLine( System.Environment.NewLine );

            Console.WriteLine( "true OR ReturnsFalse( )" );
            if( true || ReturnsFalse( ) ) {
                Console.WriteLine( "Evaluated only trueExpression "+
                    "then short circuit. ReturnsFalse( ) was not executed" );
            }

            Console.WriteLine( System.Environment.NewLine );

            Console.WriteLine( "false AND ReturnsTrue( )" );
            if( false && ReturnsTrue( ) ) {
                Console.WriteLine( "This won't execute" );
            } else {
                Console.WriteLine( "Evaluated only falseExpression. "+
                    "ReturnsTrue( ) was not executed" );
            }

            Console.WriteLine( System.Environment.NewLine );

            Console.WriteLine( "false OR ReturnsTrue( )" );
            if( false || ReturnsTrue( ) ) {
                Console.WriteLine( "Evaluated both false and ReturnsTrue()" );
            }
        }
    }
}
```

The code in Listing 3.3 exercises the short-circuit evaluation feature of C#. The best way to understand what is happening in the code is to set a breakpoint on line 27 **4** and begin stepping through the code. Remember, to set a breakpoint, place the cursor on the source line and press F9 or left-click in the channel for the line. To single step the execution, press F11, which allows for stepping into method calls.

Using the Ternary Operator

The ternary operator is a very compact version of an `if/else` statement. Although a handy shortcut, overuse of the ternary operator can lead to very terse code and should be used only when really needed for very simple expressions. The syntax for the ternary operator is as follows:

```
result = <expression> ? <statement 1> : <statement 2>;
```

When the expression is true, statement 1 is executed; otherwise, statement 2 is executed. Notice that the ternary operator expects to return a result. So, for implementing "if order total > 1000, apply 10% discount; else 5% discount" would be implemented as follows:

```
double discount = orderTotal > 1000 ? .10 : .5;
```

I suggest that using the ternary operator should not create expressions any more complex than the previous example. After all, the statements being executed can in fact be as complex as another nested ternary operator. For instance, consider the following:

```
double discount = preferredCustomer ? orderTotal > 1000 ? .10 : .05 : orderTotal >
2000 "+" ? .1 : .025;
```

Any idea what that snippet of code does? Create a small project and type in the code to see what it does. Again, the key point is to develop readable code, not cryptic code.

The `switch` Statement

The idea of the `switch` statement is to alleviate excessive `if` statements and to offer a clean approach to handling multiple conditions for a given expression. The `switch` statement can be thought of as a multiple-choice-style statement. The syntax for the `switch` statement is as follows:

```
switch( expression ) {
  case const-expression-1:
        one or more statements;
        break;
  case const-expression-2:
        one or more statements;
         break;
  case const-expression-3:
        one or more statements;
        break;
  .

  .

  .

  default:
     one or more statements;
     break;
}
```

Program Flow Control: Control Structures

The expression to be evaluated can be an integer, character, string, or enum. Each case statement expression must be a const value, meaning that it is defined at compile time and not runtime. For instance, the case expression cannot be the result of a method call or a variable that can change its value.

The switch statement evaluates each case statement until a match is found. If no match is found, the default case is used. The default case is not required, but allows for a catch-all case for evaluation. There are a few things about the switch statement to keep in mind:

▶ Each case statement that contains statements must have a break statement. This includes the default case.

▶ Cases can fall through only if the case is empty, meaning that it does not have statements within its body.

▶ To jump from one case statement to another, the dreaded goto statement is used.

NOTE

The statements within each case block can be any valid C# statement, including method calls and return statements. However, it is best to keep the code within each case short and simple by keeping the number of statements to a minimum.

Again, the main purpose of the switch statement is to provide a cleaner mechanism than using multiple if-else-if combinations. Consider the following two listings. Listing 3.4 uses multiple if-else-if statements for evaluation, whereas Listing 3.5 uses the switch statement to accomplish the same task.

LISTING 3.4

Unnecessary Clutter with if-else-if Statement

```
using System;

namespace ifelseif {
    /// <summary>
    /// Cluttered ifelseif sample
    /// </summary>
    class Class1 {
        /// <summary>
        /// The main entry point for the application.
        /// </summary>
        [STAThread]
        static void Main(string[] args) {
            Console.Write( "Enter the type of pet " +" you own: (example dog, cat,
            fish, bird)" );
```

LISTING 3.4
Continued

```
            string animal = Console.ReadLine( );

            if( animal.ToLower( ).Equals( "dog" ) ) {
               Console.WriteLine( "Bark Bark" );
            } else if( animal.ToLower( ).Equals( "cat" ) ) {
               Console.WriteLine( "Meow" );
            } else if( animal.ToLower( ).Equals( "fish" ) ) {
               Console.WriteLine( "swim" );
            } else if( animal.ToLower( ).Equals( "bird" ) ) {
                Console.WriteLine( "Poly want a cracker" );
            } else {
                  Console.WriteLine( "Nice pet" );
            }
        }
    }
}
```

3

LISTING 3.5
Using the `switch` Statement to Improve Readability

```
using System;
namespace SwitchStatement {

    class Class1 {

        /// <summary>
        ///Demonstrates the usage of the switch statement
        /// </summary>
        [STAThread]
        static void Main(string[] args) {
            Console.Write( "Enter the type of pet" +" you own: (example dog, cat,
            fish, bird)" );
            string animal = Console.ReadLine( );

            switch( animal.ToLower( ) ) {
                case "dog":
                    Console.WriteLine( "Bark Bark" );
                    break;
                case "cat":
                    Console.WriteLine( "Meow" );
                    break;
                case "fish":
```

LISTING 3.5
Continued

```
                Console.WriteLine( "swim" );
                break;
            case "bird":
                Console.WriteLine( "Poly want a cracker" );
                break;
            default:
                Console.WriteLine( "Nice pet" );
                break;
        }
      }
    }
}
```

Although Listings 3.4 and 3.5 both implement the same overall functionality, the switch statement provides several advantages for this type of situation. First, the readability of the code is improved. Second, the animal.ToLower( ).Equals( ) method that was used in Listing 3.4 is reduced to a single use rather than five. This is a performance gain, as will be discussed in Chapter 4, "Strings and Regular Expressions."

Looping

Looping provides the ability to perform a task one or more times until a larger task is complete. This is a reoccurring theme in development. Tasks such as computing the total payroll for a division within a company require looping through each employee's salary information and summing the total value. Rather than hard-coding the necessary statements for *N* number of employees, a loop can be used to process each employee until all employee salary information has been processed.

C# offers various looping constructs that can be used to perform repetitive tasks. Each has benefits and a time and place for its use. There is no such thing as one-size-fits-all, and this is the reason why there are so many ways to accomplish a particular task.

The for Loop

The for statement is the most common looping construct and is found in most languages. Although its syntax differs from language to language, its overall purpose is still the same: to iterate over a set of statements for a fixed number of cycles. At least, that's the way it should be used. The for statement has the following syntax:

```
for( initial value; test; increment/decrement value )
    single-statement;
```

or

```
for( initial value; test; increment/decrement value )
{
   One or more statements;
}
```

The `for` statement controls the very next C# statement. For multiple statements to be under control of the `for` statement, it's necessary to use code blocks { } to enclose the statements.

Using the `for` Statement

The `for` loop is basically a block of code that executes a set number of times, performing some repetitive task, enabling the programmer to write the code only once even though it executes multiple times. Loops are at the core of the set of skills required of every programming.

Using the `for` statement to accomplish a repetitive task is as simple as the following:

```
for( int i = 0; i < 50; i++ )
   Console.WriteLine( "I will not chew gum in school");
```

Notice that the value i goes from 0 to less than 50. This equates to the loop executing 50 times—the range from 0 to 49, inclusive. This is a common place for error because it is easy to test for i <= 50; which, of course, would result in 51 executions of the loop rather than 50 as intended.

The real value of the `for` statement is the ability to loop though items in an array or collection. Because of this, we'll put off further exploration of the `for` statement until Chapter 5, "Arrays and Collections."

The `foreach` Statement

The `foreach` statement is new to modern languages. It allows for traversal over containers that implement the `IEnumerable` interface and provide an enumerator that implements the `IEnumerator` interface. That might seem confusing, but it will become clearer in Chapter 5. Only in the context of Chapter 5 will the `foreach` statement make more sense. However, just to give you something to ponder, the syntax looks like this:

```
foreach( Type T in myCollection ) {
   T is now in scope for use and represents the current item
}
```

The `while` Loop

Like the `for` statement, the `while` statement allows for one or more statements to be executed until a test condition evaluates to true. Unlike the `for` statement, the purpose of the `while` statement is to execute for an unspecified number of iterations. This comes in handy for operations such as reading data from a database where the number of rows returned is not known at the time of processing or when parsing a string into tokens. The format of the `while` statement is very simple. The syntax is

```
while( expression )
{
statement1;
statement2;
   .
   .
   .
statementN;
}
```

Like the `for` statement, the `while` statement controls the next C# statement. To control a group of statements, the statements must be grouped within the code block { }.

To demonstrate the basic use of the `while` statement, Listing 3.6 creates a very simple calculator. This calculator will handle expressions only in the format of "digit operator digit," where the operator is one of the following: +, -, *, /.

LISTING 3.6
Using the `while` Statement to Parse an Input String

```
using System;
namespace WhileStatement {

    class Class1 {
        /// <summary>
        ///Evaluates a simple math expression such as 25 + 30
        ///Does not handle complex expressions ///like 20 + 30 * 2 - 5.
        /// </summary>
        [STAThread]
        static void Main(string[] args) {

            Console.Write( "Enter a simple math expression: " );
            string expression = Console.ReadLine( );

            float result      = 0;
            int idx           = 0;
```

LISTING 3.6
Continued

```
//eat white space
while( char.IsWhiteSpace( expression[ idx ] ) )
    idx++;

//parse the 1st digit
string digit    = string.Empty;
char c = expression[ idx++ ];
while( char.IsDigit( c ) ) {
    digit = digit + c;
    c = expression[ idx++ ];
}
int digit1 = Int32.Parse( digit );

//eat white space
while( char.IsWhiteSpace( expression[ idx ] ) )
    idx++;

//parse the operator
char op = expression[idx++];

//eat white space
while( char.IsWhiteSpace( expression[ idx ] ) )
    idx++;

//parse the 2nd digit
digit    = string.Empty;
c = expression[ idx++ ];
while( char.IsDigit( c ) ) {
    digit = digit + c;
    if( idx < expression.Length )
        c = expression[ idx++ ];
    else
        break;    //exits the while loop
}
int digit2 = Int32.Parse( digit );

//what was the operator?
switch( op ) {
    case '+':
        result = (float)(digit1 + digit2);
        break;
```

3

LISTING 3.6
Continued

```
            case '-':
                result = (float)(digit1 + digit2);
                break;
            case '*':
                result = (float)(digit1 * digit2);
                break;
            case '/':
                result = (float)digit1 / (float)digit2;
                break;

        }

        //display the result
        Console.WriteLine( "The result of " + expression
            + " is " + result.ToString( ) );
    }
  }
}
```

Listing 3.5 shows the basic use of the while statement to perform parsing of a string into tokens: namely, digits and the operator. Notice line 50 and the use of the break statement. The break statement is not only used within the switch control statement, but also can be used within the for and while statements to exit the loop. The counterpart to the break statement is the continue statement.

The continue statement skips the remaining body of the loop statement and transfers control back to the next iteration of the enclosing loop statement. It's worth noting that the continue statement is rarely used, and chances are that you will find a use for it only once every few years.

The do..while Loop

The final looping control structure is the do..while statement. The do..while statement works in the same fashion as the while statement, with one key difference: The do..while statement is guaranteed to execute at least once. This is due to the fact that the control expression is evaluated at the *end* of each iteration rather than at the *start* of each iteration. The while statement, on the other hand, evaluates the control expression before proceeding and therefore might not execute at all.

The syntax for the do..while statement is merely an upside-down while statement as such:

```
do {
    statement1;
    statement2;
    statement3;
} while( control-expression );
```

To contrast the difference between the two statements, create a new console application and copy the code statements in Listing 3.7 into the Main method.

LISTING 3.7

Difference Between while and do..while

```
do {
    Console.WriteLine( "do..while executes at least once" );
} while( false );

while( false ) {
    Console.WriteLine( "while statement does not even have to execute" );
}
```

Summary

This chapter covered the basic control structures provided by C# to implement flow control logic within an application. You've seen the syntax and the usage for each of these control structures as well as learned when each of them should be used. In addition, we touched on the foreach statement that will be covered in Chapter 5.

Further Reading

Programming C#, Third Edition by Jesse Liberty, O'Reilly. ISBN: 0596004893.

The Applied Microsoft .NET Framework Programming in C# Collection, Microsoft Press. ISBN: 0735619751.

4

Strings and Regular Expressions

IN BRIEF

This chapter covers .NET strings and their manipulation, along with the very powerful feature of regular expressions. The first section deals with the .NET String class. You will learn about the workings of .NET strings, formatting, and manipulation of .NET strings.

The second section deals with the `StringBuilder` class. You will learn efficient ways to handle string concatenation and manipulation.

The final section deals with regular expressions. You will learn to apply this powerful engine for matching, grouping, validating, and replacing strings.

WHAT YOU NEED

RECOMMENDED SOFTWARE	.NET Framework Visual Studio .NET
RECOMMENDED HARDWARE	.NET-enabled desktop client
SKILLS REQUIRED	C# coding

STRINGS AND REGULAR EXPRESSIONS AT A GLANCE

String Basics	75		
Understanding the Immutability of Strings	75	Splitting Strings	82
Applying Formatting to Strings	75	Modifying Case	82
Using Escape Sequences	79	The `StringBuilder`	83
Locating Substrings	80	Appending Values	83
Adding Padding	80	Using `AppendFormat`	83
Trimming Characters	81	Inserting Strings	83
Replacing Characters	81	Replacing Strings and Characters	84
		Removing Substrings	84

Using Regular Expressions	85
Understanding Expression Syntax	85

How to Use Matching	85		
Validating Data with Regular Expressions	89	Grouping Matches	89
		Replacing Matched Strings	90

Summary	91

Further Reading	91

String Basics

The .NET Framework finally brings a unified string definition to the multiple languages targeted at .NET. A *string*, as far as the Common Type System (CTS) is concerned, is just an array of Unicode characters. The .NET `String` class provides several methods that allow for easy comparison, concatenation, formatting, and general manipulation of strings.

Understanding the Immutability of Strings

The `String` class in .NET is immutable; in other words, the string itself is never modified. When characters or other strings are appended to a string, a new string is created as a result. The original string and the string to append are used to generate an entirely new string. Such immutability can cause a performance degradation for applications in which heavy string manipulation is performed. To avoid this reduction in performance, you should make use of the `StringBuilder` class, which is discussed in the following section, for all heavy-duty string manipulation.

> **TIP**
>
> Actually, there are very few cases in which you would not want to use a `StringBuilder`. As a general rule, if you perform more than one string concatenation within a scope block (method, `for` loop, and so on), or even a single very large concatenation, you should remove the standard concatenation and replace it with the use of a `StringBuilder`.

Applying Formatting to Strings

After declaring a string, the next task is to format data for presentation. This area of string formatting is not well documented and few examples exist to fully illustrate how rich the string-formatting features are within .NET.

Basic string formatting allows for data to be inserted to locations within a string. These insertion locations are denoted by using placeholders along with an ordinal value that corresponds to the sequence of the item to be inserted. For example, consider inserting an integer value within a string **1**. Listing 4.1 shows how to insert values into a string.

LISTING 4.1
Simple String Formatting Example

```
using System;
namespace Listing_4_1 {
    class Class1 {

    static void Main(string[] args) {
```

String Basics

LISTING 4.1
Continued

```
          int a    = 1;
          int b    = 2;
          int c    = 3;
          string OneItem    = string.Format( "Value of a = {0}", a );
          string TwoItems   = string.Format( "Value of a = {0}, b = {1}", a, b );
          string ThreeItems = string.Format( "Value of a = {0},
b = {1}, c = {2}", a, b, c );
          Console.WriteLine( OneItem );
          Console.WriteLine( TwoItems );
          Console.WriteLine( ThreeItems );


        }
      }
    }
```

Each placeholder represents the zero-based index of the item in the argument list to insert into the string. This is the most basic type of formatting available and also the most often used.

There also exists the ability to align values either left or right within a padded region of the insertion point. The padding ensures that the width of the inserted item with is at least *N* character spaces wide and the alignment determines whether the inserted string is aligned to the left or right of the area. Listing 4.2 demonstrates how to make use of padding and alignment **2**.

LISTING 4.2
Padding and Alignment in String Formatting

```
using System;

namespace Listing_4_2 {

  class Class1 {

    static void Main(string[] args)    {
      string rightAlign = string.Format( "[{0,20}]","Right Aligned");
      string leftAlign  = string.Format( "[{0,-20}]","Left Aligned" );

      Console.WriteLine( rightAlign );
      Console.WriteLine( leftAlign );
    }
  }
}
```

Beyond basic insertion and padding of values into a string, string formatting also offers the ability to format data such as currency, dates, and hexadecimal values. The list of formatting options can be separated into two categories: basic and custom. Basic and custom formatting applies to both integer values and date values. Tables 4.1 through 4.4 list the formatting for integers and dates for both basic and custom formatting.

TABLE 4.1

Basic Integer Formatting

Specifier	Type	Format	Input	Output
c	Currency	{0:c}	250.25	$250.25
			-250.25	-$250.25
d	Decimal (whole number)	{0:d}	250	250
			-250	-250
e	Scientific	{0:e}	3.14	3.140000e+000
			-3.14	-3.140000e+000
f	Fixed point	{0:f}	3.14	3.14
			-3.14	-3.14
g	General	{0:g}	3.14	3.14
			-3.14	-3.14
n	Number with commas for thousands	{0:n}	25000	25,000
			-25000	-25,000
p	Percent	{0:p}	.25	25.00%
		{0,2:p}	.25555	25.56%
X	Uppercase hexadecimal	{0:X}	15	F
x	Lowercase hexadecimal	{0:x}	15	F

TABLE 4.2

Custom Integer Formatting

Specifier	Type	Format	Input	Output
0	Zero placeholder	{0:00.0000}	3.14	3.1400
#	Digit placeholder	{0:(#).##}	3.14	(3).14
.	Decimal point	{0:0.0}	3.14	3.1
,	Thousand separator	{0:0,0}	2500.25	2,500
, .	Number scaling	{0:0,.}	2000	2
				(Note: Scales by 1000)
%	Percent	{0:0%}	25	2500%
				Multiplies by 100 and adds percent sign
;	Group separator	{Positive-*Format*};{Negative-*Format*};{Zero-*format*}		

String Basics

With the exception of the group separator, custom integer formatting is obvious at first glance. The group separator allows for multiple format options based on the integer value to be formatted. Essentially, the group separator allows for three different format specifications, based on the value of the integer to be formatted. Those specifications apply to a positive value, and then a negative value, and finally a zero value. For instance, if you want negative floating point values to appear in parentheses, the following formatting could be used:

```
string result = string.Format("{0:$##,###.00;$(##,###.00);$-.--}", amount);
```

The next common data type for formatting is the `DateTime` struct within .NET. There are many options when it comes to formatting dates, and Tables 4.3 and 4.4 list the various formatting specifiers and outcomes for date formatting.

TABLE 4.3

Basic Date Formatting

Specifier	Description	Format	Result Using `System.DateTime.Now`
d	Short date	{0:d}	4/17/2004
D	Long date	{0:D}	April 17, 2004
t	Short time	{0:t}	11:50 AM
T	Long time	{0:T}	11:50:30: AM
f	Full date and time	{0:f}	April 17, 2004 11:51 AM
F	Long full date and time	{0:F}	April 17, 2004 11:51:45 AM
g	Default date and time	{0:g}	4/17/2004 11:53 AM
G	Long default date and time	{0:G}	4/17/2004 11:53:45 AM
M or m	Month day	{0:M}	April 17
R or r	RFC1123 date string	{0:r}	Sat, 17 Apr 2004 11:55:17 GMT
s	Sortable date string ISO 8601	{0:s}	2004-04-17T11:56:22
u	Universal sortable date pattern	{0:u}	2004-04-17 11:58:11Z
U	Universal sortable full date pattern	{0:U}	Saturday, April 17, 2004 3:58:32 PM
Y or y	Year month pattern	{0:Y}	April, 2004

TABLE 4.4

Custom Date Formatting

Specifier	Description	Format
d	Displays the day of the week as a number	{0:d}
dd	Displays the day of the month as a leading zero integer	{0:dd}

TABLE 4.4

Continued

Specifier	Description	Format
ddd	Displays the abbreviated day of the week	{0:ddd}
dddd	Displays the full name of the day of the week	{0:dddd}
f,ff,fff,ffff...	Displays seconds fractions in one or more digits	{0:f} or {0:ff}
g or gg	Displays the era, such as B.C. or A.D.	{0:g}
h	Displays the hour from 1–12	{0:h}
hh	Displays the hour from 1–12 with leading zero	{0:hh}
H	Displays the hour in military format 0–23	{0:H}
HH	Displays the hour in military format 0–23 with leading zero for single-digit hours	{0:HH}
m	Displays the minute as an integer	{0:m}
mm	Displays the minute as an integer with leading zero for single-digit minute values	{0:mm}
M	Displays the month as an integer	{0:M}
MM	Displays the month as an integer with leading zero for single-digit month values	{0:MM}
MMM	Displays the abbreviated month name	{0:MMM}
MMMM	Displays the full name of the month	{0:MMMM}
s	Displays the seconds as a integer	{0:s}
ss	Displays the seconds as an integer with a leading zero for single-digit second values	{0:ss}
t	Displays the first character of A.M. or P.M.	{0:t}
tt	Displays the full A.M. or P.M.	{0:tt}
y	Displays two-digit year, with no preceding 0 for values 0–9.	{0:y}
yy	Displays two-digit year	{0:yy}
yyyy	Displays four-digit year	{0:yyyy}
zz	Displays the time zone offset	{0:zz}
:	Time separator	{0:hh:mm:tt}
/	Date separator	{0:MM/dd/yyyy}

Using Escape Sequences

It is often necessary to include in a string special characters such as tab, newline, or even the \ character. To insert such formatting, it is necessary to use the escape character (\), which tells the formatting parser to treat the next character as a literal character to be inserted into the resulting string. To insert the escape character, it is necessary to escape it with the escape character. The following code illustrates this:

```
string escapeMe = string.Format( "C:\\SAMS\\Code" );
```

With the escape character in place, the value of escapeMe is "C:\SAMS\CODE".

FORMATTING NOTES

If you don't want to use the double-backslash (\ \) syntax, C# provides a special shortcut that you can use. By preceding any string literal with the @ symbol, it acts as an escape for the entire string, enabling you to write code that looks like this:

```
string myFile = @"C:\SAMS\Code\File.txt";
```

As a special note, the { character can also cause difficulty when attempting to use it in a string that contains other formatting characters. To display the { character itself, use { { to escape it. This comes into play only during the following:

```
string myString = string.Format( "{{x}} = {0}", x );
```

Otherwise, if no other formatting is taking place, just use a single { character.

Locating Substrings

One of the most common string-processing requirements is the locating of substrings within a string. The System.String class provides several methods for locating substrings and each method in turn provides several overloaded versions of itself. Table 4.5 details the methods for locating substrings.

TABLE 4.5

Substring Methods of the System.String Class

Method	Description
EndsWith	Used to determine whether a string ends with a specific substring. Returns true or false.
IndexOf	Returns the first index (zero-based) location of the supplied substring or character. Returns –1 if the substring is not found.
IndexOfAny	Returns the first index (zero-based) location of the supplied substring or partial match. Returns –1 if the substring is not found.
LastIndexOf	Returns the last index of the specified substring. Returns –1 if the substring is not found.
LastIndexOfAny	Returns the last index of the specified substring or partial math. Returns –1 if the substring is not found.
StartsWith	Returns true if the string starts with the specified substring or character.

Adding Padding

Just as with format specifiers and padding, the String class provides a set of padding methods that pad a string with a space or specified character. Padding can be used to pad spaces or characters to the left or right of the target string. The code in Listing 4.3 shows how to pad a string to 20 characters in length with leading spaces.

LISTING 4.3
20 Characters Wide String Left Padded with Spaces

```
string leftPadded     = "Left Padded";
Console.WriteLine("123456789*123456789*123456789*");
Console.WriteLine( leftPadded.PadLeft(20, ' ' ) );
```

The output of the code in Listing 4.3 is as follows:

```
123456789*123456789*
         Left Padded
```

Trimming Characters

Sometimes it is necessary to remove characters from a string and this is the purpose of trimming. The `Trim` method allows for the removal of spaces or characters from either the start or end of a string. By default, the `Trim` method removes leading and trailing spaces from a string.

In addition, there are two other trimming methods. `TrimStart` removes spaces or a list of specified characters from the beginning of a string. `TrimEnd` removes spaces or a list of specified characters from the end of a string.

You can access the `Trim` method and others like it on any string variable, as shown here:

```
string myTrimmedString = myString.Trim();
```

Replacing Characters

To replace characters or substrings in a string, use the `Replace` method. For instance, to remove display formatting from a phone number such as (919) 555-1212, the following code can be used:

```
string phoneNumber = "(919) 555-1212";
string fixedPhoneNumber =
  phoneNumber.Replace( "(", "" ).  Replace( ")", "" ).Replace( "-", "" )
  .Replace( " ", "" );
Console.WriteLine( fixedPhoneNumber );
```

Notice how the `Replace` method is used. Each time `Replace` is called, a new string is created. Thus, the cascading use of the `Replace` method to remove all unwanted strings is necessary.

REPLACING WITH EMPTY STRINGS

When you want to remove a character and replace it with nothing, you must use the string version rather than the empty character '' notation; otherwise, the compiler will issue a warning about empty character declarations.

Splitting Strings

String splitting comes in handy for parsing comma-separated values or any other string with noted separated characters. The Split method requires nothing more than a character parameter that denotes how to split up the string. The result of this operation is an array of strings where each element is a substring of the original string. To separate or spilt a comma-separated list such as apple,orange,banana, merely invoke the Split method passing in the comma as the split token. The following code demonstrates the result:

```
string fruit = "apple,orange,banana";
string[] fruits= fruit.Split( ',' );
foreach (string fruitName in fruits)
    Console.WriteLine(fruitName);
//Result
//fruits[0] -> apple
//fruits[1] -> orange
//fruits[2] -> banana
```

Modifying Case

The last two major methods of the String class involve changing the case of a string. The case can be changed to uppercase or lowercase and results in a new string of the specified case. Remember that strings are immutable and any action that modifies a string results in a new string. Therefore, the following takes place:

```
string attemptToUpper  = "attempt to upper";
attemptToUpper.ToUpper( );
//attemptToUpper is still all lower case
```

To see the effect of the ToUpper() method, the result string has to be assigned to a variable. The following illustrates the proper use of ToUpper():

```
string allLower = "all lower";
string ALL_UPPER = allLower.ToUpper( );
//ALL_UPPER -< "ALL LOWER";
```

The `StringBuilder`

To improve performance, the `StringBuilder` class is designed to manage an array of characters via direct manipulation. Such an implementation eliminates the need to constantly allocate new strings. This improves performance by saving the garbage collector from tracking and reclaiming small chunks of memory, as would be the case using standard string functions and concatenation. The `StringBuilder` class is located in the `System.Text` namespace.

Appending Values

The most basic use of the `StringBuilder` class is to perform string concatenation, which is the process of building a result string from various other strings and values until the final string is complete. The `StringBuilder` class provides an `Append` method. The `Append` method is used to append values to the end of the current string. Values can be integer, boolean, char, string, DateTime, and a list of others. In fact, the `Append` method has 19 overloads in order to accommodate any value you need to append to a string.

Using `AppendFormat`

In addition to appending values to the current string, `StringBuilder` also provides the ability to append formatted strings. The format specifiers are the same specifiers listed in the previous section. The `AppendFormat` method is provided in order to avoid calls to `string.Format(...)` and the unnecessary creation of additional strings.

Inserting Strings

The insertion of strings is another useful method provided by the `StringBuilder` class. The `Insert` method takes two parameters. The first parameter specifies the zero-based index at which to begin the insertion. The second parameter is the value to insert at the specified location. Similar to the `Append` method, the `Insert` method provides 18 different overloads in order to support various data types for insertion into the string. Listing 4.4 shows the usage of the `Insert` method.

LISTING 4.4
Using the `Insert` Method to Create a SQL Statement

```
using System;
using System.Text;

namespace Listing_4_4 {
```

LISTING 4.4
Continued

```
class Class1 {

  [STAThread]
  static void Main(string[] args) {
    StringBuilder stmtBuilder    = new StringBuilder( "SELECT FROM MYTABLE" );

    Console.Write( "Enter Columns to select from MYTABLE: ");
    string columns = Console.ReadLine( );                //FirstName, LastName

    stmtBuilder.Insert( 7, columns );
    //insert a space after the column names
    stmtBuilder.Insert( 7 + columns.Length, " " );
    //SELECT FirstName, LastName FROM MYTABLE
    Console.WriteLine( stmtBuilder.ToString( ) );
    }
  }
}
```

Replacing Strings and Characters

You might run across a need to generate strings based on templates where certain
tokens (substrings) are later replaced with values. In fact, this is how Visual Studio
.NET works. There is a template file from which each project is created. The new
source file that is created is generated from a template and various tokens are
replaced based on the type of project, the name of the project, and other options.
You can achieve this same effect using the Replace method provided by
StringBuilder.

Using the Replace method, it is possible to create template strings, such as SQL
statements, and replace tokens with actual values as demonstrated by the following
code:

```
StringBuilder selectStmtTemplate = string StringBuilder();
selectStmtTemplate.Append( "SELECT $FIELDS FROM $TABLE" );

selectStmtTemplate.Replace( "$FIELDS", fieldList );
selectStmtTemplate.Replace( "$TABLE", tableName );
```

Removing Substrings

The Remove method allows for sections of the underlying string to be completely
removed from the StringBuilder object. The Remove method takes two

parameters. The first parameter specifies the zero-based index of the position denoting the starting point. The second parameter specifies the length or number of characters to remove.

Using Regular Expressions

The .NET Framework provides rich regular expression support and functionality within the base class library. Previously, regular expressions were only supported via third-party libraries for languages such as C++ and Visual Basic. In .NET, the regular expression syntax is fully supported and there are a number of classes in the `System.Text.RegularExpressions` namespace geared to leveraging this powerful string processing language.

Understanding Expression Syntax

The hardest part of using regular expressions in .NET is to first gain an understanding of the language. Unlike C#, the syntax for regular expressions is somewhat cryptic and takes time and practice to understand and apply it correctly.

The language itself is based on a set of escape sequences. These escape sequences translate into patterns that are applied to recognizing items within a source string. Each escape sequence has a particular meaning and often works in combination with other elements to create the overall expression. The best way to learn the language of regular expressions is to jump in with both feet.

How to Use Matching

The most basic use of regular expressions is that of matching substrings within a string. Matching can be for words, characters, or any other conceivable sequence required. For example, given the string "Angie called Albert" we could begin by locating the capital letter A only if it begins a word. The following regular expression would do just that:

```
\bA
```

Translated, it means "begin on a word boundary and find the letter A." The matches produced would be two matches for the letter A: the first letter of Angie and Albert. No other characters would be included in the match result. We could extend this pattern to locate all words that begin with the letter A. The regular expression to accomplish this would be as follows:

```
\bA\w+
```

How to Use Matching

This expression translates to "begin at word boundaries, and locate the letter A followed by one or more characters or digits." This expression again produces two matches. This time the matches are Angie and Albert.

If we want to find words that do not begin with the letter A, but rather contain the letter A or a, the following expression could be used:

```
\b[^aA\s]\w*[aA]\w+
```

This expression reads, "find words that do not begin with a or A or a space, that begin with letters or digits and contain either a or A, and are followed by one or more letters or digits." Table 4.6 lists the basic escape sequences for regular expressions.

TABLE 4.6

Regular Expression Single-Character Escape Sequences

Escape Sequence	Description
\a	Matches the ASCII character 7 (system bell)
\b	Matches the ASCII character 8 if inside []; otherwise, represents a word boundary
\d	Matches a decimal digit 0–9
\D	Matches any nondecimal digit
\e	Matches the escape character 0x1B
\f	Matches the form feed
\n	Matches the newline
\r	Matches the carriage return
\t	Matches the tab character
\040	Matches ASCII characters as octal representations; 040 matches the space
\x20	Matches ASCII characters expressed in hexadecimal; only two digits
\cC	Matches control sequences such as Control+F
\u0020	Matches Unicode characters using hexadecimal representation; four digits
\	When not followed by a control character, the following character is the match character

The items in Table 4.6 are included for completeness and are probably not going to be part of normal usage. Table 4.7 lists the standard character classes for regular expressions.

TABLE 4.7

Regular Expression Character Classes

Character Class	Description
.	Matches all characters except for the newline character, \n
[abc]	Matches any character contained in the set
[^abc]	Matches any character not in the set
[0-9a-zA-Z]	Matches the range of characters denoted with the hyphen
\p{*name*}	Matches any character in the named character class specified by name
\P{*name*}	Matches any character not in the named character class specified by name
\w	Matches any word character; ECMAScript-compliant behavior is equivalent to [a-zA-Z0-9]
\W	Matches any nonword character; [^a-zA-Z0-9]
\s	Matches any whitespace
\S	Matches any nonwhitespace character
\d	Matches any decimal digit
\D	Matches any nondecimal digit : [^0-9]

At this point, you have seen the basic character classes and escape sequences as well as some regular expressions. Next, you'll make use of the .NET RegEx class to match input and display the results. Listing 4.5 matches various phone number input types and shows how to test and match for multiple formats.

LISTING 4.5

Using the Regex Class for String Matching

```
using System;
using System.Text;                  //StringBuilder
using System.Text.RegularExpressions;  //Regular Expression classes

namespace Listing_4_5
{
    class Class1
    {
        static void Main(string[] args)    {

            string phoneNumber1          = "555-1212";
            string phoneNumber2          = "919-555-1212";
            string phoneNumber3          = "(919) 555-1212";
            string invalidPhoneNumberFormat = "919.555.1212";

            //Match the phone number for the following formats
            //1: 555-1212
```

4

How to Use Matching

LISTING 4.5
Continued

```
//2: 919-555-1212
//3: (919) 555-1212

StringBuilder  expressionBuilder = new StringBuilder( );

//The @ symbol is used so the \ is ignored as a C# escape sequence
//start at beginning of line (^), 3 digits hyphen 4 digits
expressionBuilder.Append( @"^\d{3}-\d{4}" );
//or, another expression to follow
expressionBuilder.Append( "|" );
//start at beginning of line (^), 3 digits hyphen 3 digits hyphen 4
// digits
expressionBuilder.Append( @"^\d{3}-\d{3}-\d{4}" );
//or last expression to meet the criteria
expressionBuilder.Append( "|" );
//start at beginning of line (^), open paren ( //3 digits close paren )
//space 3 digits hyphen 4 digits
//Note: the open and close parens must be //escaped with the \
//character.
expressionBuilder.Append( @"^\(\d{3}\)\s\d{3}-\d{4}" );

//Now we have the regular expression, create the RegEx object
Regex phoneMatchExpression = new Regex( expressionBuilder.ToString( ) );

//Match the phone numbers
if( phoneMatchExpression.Match( phoneNumber1 ).Success )
    Console.WriteLine( "phoneNumber1 matches" );
else
    Console.WriteLine( "phoneNumber1 has invalid format" );

if( phoneMatchExpression.Match( phoneNumber2 ).Success )
    Console.WriteLine( "phoneNumber2 matches" );
else
    Console.WriteLine( "phoneNumber2 has invalid format" );

if( phoneMatchExpression.Match( phoneNumber3 ).Success )
    Console.WriteLine( "phoneNumber3 matches" );
else
    Console.WriteLine( "phoneNumber3 has invalid format" );

if( phoneMatchExpression.Match( invalidPhoneNumberFormat ).Success )
```

LISTING 4.5
Continued

```
            Console.WriteLine( "invalidPhoneNumberFormat matches" );
        else
            Console.WriteLine( "invalidPhoneNumberFormat has invalid format" );


    }
  }
}
```

Validating Data with Regular Expressions

Whenever you hear the phrase *data validation*, think of applying regular expressions. By using regular expressions, you can validate character ranges, length, and format. A useful example of this is validating passwords for standards compliance; for example, if the password must be alphanumeric with at least one uppercase letter and one digit. To handle such validation, it is necessary to understand and apply regular expression assertions. Table 4.8 lists the assertions and their descriptions.

TABLE 4.8

Regular Expression Assertions

Assertion	Description
(?=pattern)	Specifies that the pattern follows this location
(?!pattern)	Specifies that the pattern does not follow this location
(?<=pattern)	Specifies that the pattern precedes this location
(?<!pattern)	Specifies that the pattern does not precede this location

Armed with assertions, it is now possible to validate a password whose length is 8 to 12 characters and must include at least 1 uppercase character and 1 digit. The following expression uses assertions to implement this validation:

`^(?=.*\d+)(?=.*[a-z]+)(?=.*[A-Z]+).{4,8}$`

Grouping Matches

When parsing strings, the ability to locate substrings and quickly access them can be difficult with the `System.String` and `System.StringBuilder`. However, the regular expression grouping support allows for quick access to matched substrings. By creating a named group, you can quickly access the captured data for the expressed pattern. Such grouping makes a task such as parsing and accessing web query string parameters very simple to do.

How to Use Matching

Grouping is accomplished by creating a named or unnamed group using the following syntax:

```
(?<group-name>pattern)
```

With the group name specified, a returned `Match` object contains a `Groups` collection that can be indexed by the name of the captured group. Listing 4.6 shows how to use grouping to parse and capture data from the web query string `param1=data1&param2=data2`.

LISTING 4.6

Grouping with Regular Expressions

```csharp
using System;
using System.Text.RegularExpressions;

namespace Listing_4_6 {

  class Class1    {

    static void Main(string[] args)    {

      string queryString = "param1=data1&param2=data2";

      Regex queryStringExpression = new Regex( @"param1=(?<param1>\w+[^&])
&param2=(?<param2>\w+[^&])" );

      Match match = queryStringExpression.Match( queryString );

      if( match.Success ) {
       //display the group data
       Console.WriteLine( "param1 := {0}", match.Groups[ "param1" ].Value );
       Console.WriteLine( "param2 := {0}", match.Groups[ "param2" ].Value );
      }
    }
  }
}
```

Replacing Matched Strings

One of the more useful features of regular expression is the ability to implement search-and-replace-style functionality with a very powerful language—that language of course being regular expressions. The replacement works for both named and unnamed groups and allows for a new string to be created based on the matched pattern and supplied replacement expression.

> **TIP**
>
> Unnamed groups are created whenever a pattern is enclosed in parentheses. These unnamed groups have a one-based ordinal number assigned to them and can be referenced as $1, $2, $3, ...

Looking back at the phone number validation example, if the phone number is 9195551212 and you want to display it as (919) 555-1212, you could use a matching expression in combination with a replacement expression. The code necessary to create the desired result is as follows:

```
string match = @"(\d{3})(\d{3})(\d{4})";
string replace = @"($1) $2-$3";
string result = Regex.Replace( match, replace );
```

After executing the `Replace` method, the result string would contain the newly formatted phone number.

Summary

This chapter covered the `System.String` class in detail: It is used to create formatted strings and locate substrings. You gained an understanding of the inefficiencies of multiple string creation due to the immutability of managed strings. These inefficiencies lead to the usage of the `StringBuilder` class for more efficient string construction. Finally, you explored the very powerful features of regular expressions and the varied use for which they can be applied.

Further Reading

Programming C#, Third Edition by Jesse Liberty, O'Reilly. ISBN: 0596004893.

The Applied Microsoft .NET Framework Programming in C# Collection, Microsoft Press. ISBN: 0735619751.

Mastering Regular Expressions, Second Edition by Jeffrey Friedl, O'Reilly. ISBN: 0596002890.

Regular Expression Pocket Reference by Tony Stubblebine, O'Reilly. ISBN: 059600415X.

5 ARRAYS AND COLLECTIONS

IN BRIEF

This chapter explains and demonstrates the different types of arrays and collections that are available in the .NET Framework. In the first section, you will learn about the different `Array` types and how to use each one. Next, you will learn the basics of the .NET `Collection` classes and how to iterate through the collections. Finally, you will learn how to create you own collection by descending from `System.Collections.CollectionBase`.

WHAT YOU NEED

RECOMMENDED SOFTWARE	.NET Framework C# .NET environment
RECOMMENDED HARDWARE	.NET-enabled desktop client
SKILLS REQUIRED	C# coding

ARRAYS AND COLLECTIONS AT A GLANCE

Using Arrays	**93**		
Understanding Single-Dimensional and Multidimensional Arrays	93	Explaining Jagged Arrays	95
		Passing Arrays as Parameters	96
Collection Basics	**98**		
Understanding the Basic Collection Interfaces	98	Iterating Through Collections	98
Collections Provided by the Base Class Libraries	**99**		
Using an ArrayList	100	Using a BitArray	103
Using a Stack	101	Using the Queue	104
Using a Hashtable	102	Using a SortedList	106
Creating Custom Collections	**107**		
Implementing the CollectionBase Class	107	Creating a AddressList Collection	107
Summary	**109**		
Further Reading	**110**		

Using Arrays

An *array* is simply a list or collection of items. Every array in the Common Language Runtime inherits from the `System.Array` class. Table 5.1 lists the terminology commonly used when talking about arrays.

TABLE 5.1

Array Terminology

Term	Definition
Element	An item stored in the array
Length	The number of elements the array can hold
Rank	The number of dimensions of the array
Lower bound	The starting index for the array

In the following sections, you will learn how to create single-dimensional and multidimensional arrays. Then you will learn how to create and use a *jagged* array (array of arrays). Finally, you will learn how to pass an array as a parameter.

Understanding Single-Dimensional and Multidimensional Arrays

Single-dimensional and multidimensional arrays are exactly what their names imply. They have a rank of either 1 or *N* and take one of the following forms:

Single-Dimensional Array

```
variable-type[] variableName = new variable-type[length]
```

For multidimensional arrays, the form is only slightly different. You simply add a comma (,) in the declaration. One comma declares it as a two-dimensional array. Two commas declare it as a three-dimensional array, and so on.

Two-Dimensional Array

```
variable-type[,] variableName = new variable-type[length, length]
```

If you want to create an array using late binding, the static method `System.Array.CreateInstance` is the correct choice. The following code snippet declares and allocates an integer array of rank 1 and a length of 10; in other words, it declares a single-dimension array that can hold 10 integers:

```
int[] intArray = new int[10];
```

Using Arrays

In the preceding example, you will notice that the brackets ([]) are placed after the type and not after the variable. For those of you who come from a C++ background, this will be a hard thing to remember, but it makes sense and you will eventually get used to it. Also, even though `System.Array` provides a method named `System.Array.GetLowerBounds` that provides the lower bound of the array, arrays in C# have a zero-based index. The code in Listing 5.1 demonstrates how to create a single dimensional array of strings to hold the months of the year.

LISTING 5.1
Storing the Months of the Year in a Single-Dimensional Array

```
using System;

namespace SimpleArrays
{
  class SimpleArray
  {
    static private string[] months =
      new string[12] { "Jan", "Feb", "Mar", "Apr",
        "May", "Jun", "Jul", "Aug", "Sep", "Oct", "Nov", "Dec" };

    /// <summary>
    /// The main entry point for the application.
    /// </summary>
    [STAThread]
    static void Main(string[] args)
    {
      //
      // TODO: Add code to start application here
      //
      foreach(string month in months)
      {
        System.Console.WriteLine(month);
      }
      System.Console.ReadLine();
    }
  }
}
```

Listing 5.2 presents the same array with a slight modification ▪1▪. The days in the month are added to the array. Also, to print out the contents of the array, the logic is changed to use a `for` loop instead of a `foreach`. In the following example, we know the exact lengths of the dimensions of the array. However, there are many instances when this information is not known. In such cases, you need to use the methods and properties provided by the `System.Array` class to determine these values:

```
System.Array.GetLowerBound(int dimension)
System.Array.GetUpperBound(int dimension)
System.Array.Rank
```

By adding the `System.Array.GetUpperBound` method call to the `for` loop, you can determine the length of the specified dimension and iterate through all items in that dimension.

LISTING 5.2

Storing the Months of the Year Along with the Days in the Month in a Two-Dimensional Array

```
using System;

namespace TwoDimensionalArrayExample
{
    /// <summary>
    /// Summary description for Class1.
    /// </summary>
    class SimpleArray
    {
        static private string[,] months =
            new string[12,2]
            { {"Jan", "31"}, {"Feb", "28"}, {"Mar", "31"},
              {"Apr", "30"}, {"May", "31"}, {"Jun", "30"},
              {"Jul", "31"}, {"Aug", "31"}, {"Sep", "30"},
              {"Oct", "31"}, {"Nov", "30"}, {"Dec", "31"} };

        /// <summary>
        /// The main entry point for the application.
        /// </summary>
        [STAThread]
        static void Main(string[] args)
        {
            for(int i=months.GetLowerBound(0); i<=months.GetUpperBound(0); i++)
            {
                System.Console.WriteLine(months[i, 0] + " has " + months[i, 1] + " days.");
            }
            System.Console.ReadLine();
        }
    }
}
```

1

5

Explaining Jagged Arrays

A *jagged array* is simply an array of arrays. It takes a little different form from that of a two-dimensional array in that the dimensions are no longer separated by a comma. Think of a standard two-dimensional array as rectangular and a jagged array as having an inconsistent shape, with each element of the array containing a

Using Arrays

different number of sub-elements. Now each dimension has its own set of brackets. The following code snippet demonstrates how to declare and initialize a jagged array of integers:

```
int[][] intArray=new int[][] { new int[] {1,3,7,9},
                               new int[] {2,4,6,8,10}
                             }
```

Listing 5.3 modifies the example introduced in the multidimensional array to use a jagged array instead of a two-dimensional array.

LISTING 5.3
Jagged Array Example

```
using System;

namespace JaggedArrayExample
{
  class JaggedArray
  {
    static private string[][] months = new string[2][];

    [STAThread]
    static void Main(string[] args)
    {
      months[0] = new string[12]
          {"Jan", "Feb", "Mar", "Apr", "May", "Jun", "Jul", "Aug", "Sep",
          "Oct", "Nov", "Dec"};
      months[1] = new string[12]
          {"31", "28", "31", "30", "31", "30", "31", "31", "30",
          "31", "30", "31" };

      for(int i=0; i<12; i++)
      {
        System.Console.WriteLine(months[0][i] + " has " + months[1][i] + " days.");
      }

      System.Console.ReadLine();
    }
  }
}
```

Passing Arrays as Parameters

Passing arrays as parameters can be accomplished in the same manner as all out and ref parameters. That is, all out parameters do not have to be initialized before calling the function to which you are calling. However, the function that you are calling must assign the array type before returning. In addition, all `ref` parameters must be assigned before calling the function. Listing 5.4 demonstrates the proper way to pass an Array using `out` and `ref`.

LISTING 5.4
Passing Arrays as Parameters

```csharp
using System;

namespace PassingArraysAsParameters
{
  class ArraysAsParameters
  {
    static public void InitializeArray(out string[][] months)
    {
      months = new string[2][];
    }

    static public void ModifyArray(ref string[][] months)
    {
      months[0] =
        new string[12] { "Jan", "Feb", "Mar", "Apr", "May", "Jun",
          "Jul", "Aug", "Sep", "Oct", "Nov", "Dec"};
      months[1] =
        new string[12] { "31", "28", "31", "30", "31", "30", "31",
          "31", "30", "31", "30", "31" };
    }

    [STAThread]
    static void Main(string[] args)
    {
      string[][] months;
      InitializeArray(out months);
      ModifyArray(ref months);

      for(int i=0; i<12; i++)
      {
        System.Console.WriteLine(months[0][i] + " has " + months[1][i] + " days.");
      }

      System.Console.ReadLine();
    }
  }
}
```

5

Collection Basics

Collections are groups of items or as in C#, objects. In C# .NET, each built-in collection implements the `ICollection` interface. Because the `ICollection` interface inherits from the `IEnumerable` interface, each built-in collection also implements the `IEnumerable` interface. In the following sections, you will gain a basic knowledge of what collections are and how they operate.

Understanding the Basic Collection Interfaces

These are collections that are provided with C#, out of the box; they all reside in the `System.Collections` namespace. Each implements the `ICollection` interface. Table 5.2 shows the members of the `ICollection` interface.

TABLE 5.2

`ICollection` **Members**

Member	Description
GetEnumerator	This method returns an `Enumerator` that can be used to iterate over a collection. This method is inherited from the `IEnumerable` interface.
Count	This property gets the number of elements contained in the collection.
IsSynchronized	This property indicates whether the class is thread safe.
SyncRoot	This property can be used to get an object to synchronize the collection.
CopyTo	This method copies the elements of the collection to an array.

Table 5.3 lists the collection interfaces.

TABLE 5.3

Collection Interfaces

Interface	Description
ICollection	Provides a standard interface for all collections implemented in C#
IComparer	Provides the ability for a collection to sort the items contained within its collection
IDictionary	Represents a collection that contains key/value pairs
IDictionaryEnumerator	Provides the ability for a key/value collection to sort the items contained within its collection
IEnumerable	Provides the ability for a collection to iterate over the items contained within its collection
IList	Provides the ability for a collection to be accessed by an index

Iterating Through Collections

Because the `ICollection` interface inherits from the `IEnumerable` interface, collections provide the ability to iterate over the items that the collection contains.

Iterating through a collection can be done in a few different ways. Because all collections implement the IEnumerable interface, you can use the IEnumberable.GetEnumerator to return an enumerator that is capable of iterating through the collection.

ENUMERATORS

An *enumerator* is an object that enables you to iterate through the items contained within a collection. An enumerator can be used only to read the values of a collection; it cannot be used to change the contents of the collection. When an enumerator is first instantiated, it is positioned before the first element of the collection. If you try to access the first element, using Current, before calling the MoveNext method, an exception will be thrown. Call MoveNext to move the enumerator to the next element of the collection. When the enumerator reaches the end of the collection, it will be positioned after the last element of the collection and will return false. Again, if you call Current when the enumerator is positioned after the last element in the collection, an exception will be thrown.

TABLE 5.4

Methods and Properties of an Enumerator

Name	Description
Current	This property returns the current object in the collection.
MoveNext	This method moves the enumerator to the next item in the collection.
Reset	This method moves the enumerator to its initial position.

The following code fragment demonstrates how to iterate through a collection:

```
protected void PrintList(System.Collections.ArrayList list)
{
  IEnumerator enumerator = list.GetEnumerator();
  while(enumerator.MoveNext())
  {
    System.Console.WriteLine((string) enumerator.Current);
  }
}
```

Collections Provided by the Base Class Libraries

Out of the box, C# contains several useful collections. Each of them is slightly different from the other and has its own advantages and disadvantages. This next section gives small examples of how to use each one.

Collections Provided by the Base Class Libraries

Using an `ArrayList`

Like an array, an `ArrayList` is a collection that can be accessed through an index. Listing 5.5 demonstrates how to create, add items to, remove, and iterate through an `ArrayList`.

LISTING 5.5

An `ArrayList` Example

```
using System;
using System.Collections;

namespace ArrayListCollection
{
      class Class1
      {
   static protected ArrayList list = new ArrayList();

   protected static void PrintList(System.Collections.ArrayList list)
   {
     IEnumerator enumerator = list.GetEnumerator();
     while(enumerator.MoveNext())
     {
       System.Console.WriteLine((string) enumerator.Current);
     }
   }

   [STAThread]
   static void Main(string[] args)
   {
     // Add items to list
     for(int i=0; i<10; i++)
     {
       list.Add("Item " + i.ToString());
     }

     // Iterate through the list.
     PrintList(list);

     System.Console.WriteLine("*************");

     // Remove an Item
     list.Remove("Item 7");

     PrintList(list);
```

LISTING 5.5
Continued

```
      System.Console.ReadLine();
    }
  }
}
```

Using a `Stack`

A `Stack` is a simple LIFO (Last In First Out) collection. It introduces three new methods: `Push`, `Pop`, and `Peek`. Listing 5.6 demonstrates how to create, add items to, remove, and iterate through a `Stack`.

LISTING 5.6
A `Stack` Example

```
using System;
using System.Collections;

namespace StackExample
{
  class Class1
  {
    static protected Stack list = new Stack();

    protected static void PrintList(System.Collections.Stack list)
    {
      IEnumerator enumerator = list.GetEnumerator();
      while(enumerator.MoveNext())
      {
        System.Console.WriteLine((string) enumerator.Current);
      }
    }

    [STAThread]
    static void Main(string[] args)
    {
      // Add items to list
      for(int i=0; i<10; i++)
      {
        list.Push("Item " + i.ToString());
      }

      // Iterate through the list.
```

Collections Provided by the Base Class Libraries

LISTING 5.6
Continued

```
        PrintList(list);

        System.Console.WriteLine("*************");

        // Remove an Item
        list.Pop();

        PrintList(list);

        System.Console.ReadLine();
    }
  }
}
```

Using a Hashtable

A Hashtable is a dictionary collection. In other words, it is a collection of key/value pairs. To enumerate through this list, you should use IDictionaryEnumerator. The following example, Listing 5.7, demonstrates how to create, add items to, remove, and iterate through a Hashtable.

LISTING 5.7
A Hashtable Example

```
using System;
using System.Collections;

namespace HashtableExample
{
  class Class1
  {
    static protected Hashtable list = new Hashtable();

    protected static void PrintList(System.Collections.Hashtable list)
    {
      IDictionaryEnumerator enumerator = list.GetEnumerator();
      while(enumerator.MoveNext())
      {
        System.Console.WriteLine((string) enumerator.Value);
      }
    }
```

LISTING 5.7
Continued

```
[STAThread]
static void Main(string[] args)
{
  // Add items to list
  for(int i=0; i<10; i++)
  {
    list.Add("Item " + i.ToString(), "Item " + i.ToString());
  }

  // Iterate through the list.
  PrintList(list);

  System.Console.WriteLine("*************");

  // Print a item from the index
  System.Console.WriteLine((string) list["Item 7"]);


  System.Console.ReadLine();
  }
 }
}
```

Using a `BitArray`

A `BitArray` is a collection of bits (true/false) values. Listing 5.8 demonstrates how to create, modify, and iterate through a `BitArray`.

BITMASKING AND `BitArrays`

A `BitArray` is, as mentioned, an array of true/false values. There are many cases in software development today when you need to store a list of true/false values that might or might not be of finite length.

In the past, programmers have solved this problem by using integers to do the work of a `BitArray`. For example, a 32-bit `Integer` can be used to store 32 individual Boolean values. It creates a very memory- and storage-efficient way of managing lists of Booleans. Getting and setting individual bit values was done with *bitwise operators*. If you ever find yourself in a situation where you think you need to use bitmasking and bitwise operators for a list of Booleans, consider using the `BitArray` instead.

Collections Provided by the Base Class Libraries

LISTING 5.8

A `BitArray` Example

```
using System;
using System.Collections;

namespace BitArrayExample
{
  class Class1
  {
    static protected BitArray list = new BitArray(12);

    protected static void PrintList(System.Collections.BitArray list)
    {
      IEnumerator enumerator = list.GetEnumerator();
      while(enumerator.MoveNext())
      {
        System.Console.WriteLine((bool) enumerator.Current);
      }
    }

    [STAThread]
    static void Main(string[] args)
    {
      // Add items to list
      for(int i=0; i<10; i++)
      {
        list.Set(i, (i/2==0));
      }

      // Iterate through the list.
      PrintList(list);

      System.Console.ReadLine();
    }
  }
}
```

Using the Queue

A Queue is a simple FIFO (First In First Out) collection. The following example, Listing 5.9, demonstrates how to create, add items to, remove, and iterate through a Queue.

LISTING 5.9
A Queue Example

```
using System;
using System.Collections;

namespace QueueExample
{
  class Class1
  {
    static protected Queue list = new Queue();

    protected static void PrintList(System.Collections.Queue list)
    {
      IEnumerator enumerator = list.GetEnumerator();
      while(enumerator.MoveNext())
      {
        System.Console.WriteLine((string) enumerator.Current);
      }
    }

    [STAThread]
    static void Main(string[] args)
    {
      // Add items to list
      for(int i=0; i<10; i++)
      {
        list.Enqueue("Item " + i.ToString());
      }

      // Iterate through the list.
      PrintList(list);

      System.Console.WriteLine("*************");

      // Remove an Item
      list.Dequeue();

      PrintList(list);

      System.Console.ReadLine();
    }
  }
}
```

5

Collections Provided by the Base Class Libraries

Using a `SortedList`

A `SortedList` is a hybrid collection. It is a mixture of an `ArrayList` and a `Hashtable`. The following example, Listing 5.10, demonstrates how to create, add items to, remove, and iterate through a `SortedList` **2**.

LISTING 5.10

A `SortedList` Example

```csharp
using System;
using System.Collections;

namespace SortedListExample
{
  class Class1
  {
    static protected SortedList list = new SortedList();

    protected static void PrintList(System.Collections.SortedList list)
    {
      IDictionaryEnumerator enumerator = list.GetEnumerator();
      while(enumerator.MoveNext())
      {
        System.Console.WriteLine((string) enumerator.Value);
      }
    }

    [STAThread]
    static void Main(string[] args)
    {
      // Add items to list
      for(int i=0; i<10; i++)
      {
        list.Add("Item " + i.ToString(), "Item " + i.ToString());
      }

      // Iterate through the list.
      PrintList(list);

      System.Console.WriteLine("*************");

      // Print a item from the index (Access Like a Hashtable)
      System.Console.WriteLine((string) list["Item 7"]);

      // Print a item from the index (Access Like a Arraylist)
      System.Console.WriteLine((string) list.GetByIndex(7));
```

LISTING 5.10
Continued

```
        System.Console.ReadLine();
    }
  }
}
```

Creating Custom Collections

Creating custom collections is a relatively simple, if not tedious, task. To create a
`Collection`, simply create a class that implements the `ICollection` interface.
However, to implement the `ICollection` interface, you must also implement the
`IEnumerable` interface. If the custom collection that you plan to implement does
not use a list of some sort that already implements this interface, you will have to
implement it yourself.

Implementing the `CollectionBase` Class

To make the task of creating a custom collection easier, the .NET Framework provides
a base class called `CollectionBase`. The `CollectionBase` class is an abstract base
class for providing strongly typed collections. Instead of writing your own base class,
it is easier and recommended that you extend this class.

Creating a `AddressList` Collection

Using the knowledge you gained in the previous sections, you will now create a
custom collection of addresses. To do this, we will create a class that descends from
the `CollectionBase` class. You will override a few methods so that the collection
returns a concrete type of `Address`, instead of the `Object` type returned by all out-
of-the-box collections. Listing 5.11 demonstrates how to extend the
`CollectionBase` class to provide a strongly typed collection of addresses.

LISTING 5.11
AddressCollection

```
using System;

namespace AddressCollection
{
  public class CustomAddress
  {
    protected string m_id;
    protected string m_city;
```

Creating Custom Collections

LISTING 5.11
Continued

```
protected string m_country;
protected string m_postalCode;
protected string m_state;
protected string m_streetAddress1;
protected string m_streetAddress2;
protected string m_suite;

public void Copy(CustomAddress address)
{
  if(null != address)
  {
    m_id                          = address.m_id;
    m_city                        = address.m_city;
    m_country                     = address.m_country;
    m_postalCode                  = address.m_postalCode;
    m_state                       = address.m_state;
    m_streetAddress1              = address.m_streetAddress1;
    m_streetAddress2              = address.m_streetAddress2;
  }
}

public CustomAddress()
{
}
}

/// <summary>
/// Address:
/// </summary>
public class Address : CustomAddress
{

  public Address() : base()
  {
  }

  public string Country {get { return m_country; } set { m_country = value; } }
  public string Id { get { return m_id; } set { m_id = value; } }
  public string PostalCode
```

LISTING 5.11
Continued

```
      { get { return m_postalCode; } set { m_postalCode = value; } }
   public string State { get { return m_state; } set { m_state = value; } }
   public string City { get { return m_city; } set { m_city = value; } }
   public string StreetAddress1
      { get { return m_streetAddress1; } set { m_streetAddress1 = value; } }
   public string StreetAddress2
      { get { return m_streetAddress2; } set { m_streetAddress2 = value; } }
}

public class AddressCollection : System.Collections.CollectionBase
{
   public AddressCollection() : base()
   {
   }

   public virtual int Add(Address value)
   {
     return base.InnerList.Add(value);
   }

   public Address GetItem(int index)
   {
     return (Address) List[index];
   }
   public void SetItem(int index, Address value)
   {
     List[index] = value;
   }
  }
}
```

Summary

In this chapter, you learned the different types of arrays and collections that are provided in the .NET Framework. You also learned how to create your own strongly typed collection of addresses. You can now apply the knowledge that you learned to determine which array or collection to use and, if necessary, create your own custom collection.

Further Reading

Programming C#, Third Edition by Jesse Liberty, O'Reilly. ISBN: 0596004893.

The Applied Microsoft .NET Framework Programming in C# Collection, Microsoft Press. ISBN: 0735619751.

5

6 Objects and Classes

IN BRIEF

This chapter will explain and demonstrate the fundamentals of object-oriented programming. You'll learn the terminology used in object-oriented programming and how that terminology and information is applied to design in a class diagram. The chapter will then progress to a discussion of the fundamentals behind classes and objects, and how they relate to each other. Finally, you will take a look at advanced object-oriented programming by using inheritance and polymorphism.

WHAT YOU NEED

RECOMMENDED SOFTWARE	.NET Framework
	Visual Studio .NET
	C# .NET environment
RECOMMENDED HARDWARE	.NET-enabled desktop client
SKILLS REQUIRED	C# coding

OBJECTS AND CLASSES AT A GLANCE

Objects and Classes	**112**		
Class Attributes	113	Classes	116
Operations in Object-Oriented Design and Programming	114	Objects	117
		Object State Maintenance	122
Advanced Topics in Classes and Objects	**118**		
Inheriting from Base Classes	119	Introduction to Polymorphism	122
Summary	**125**		
Further Reading	**126**		

Objects and Classes

It might not seem like it, but object-oriented concepts have been around for nearly 30 years. In the next few sections of this chapter, you will learn the basics of object-oriented programming and its terminology. You will start by defining the terms *object, class, attribute, operation,* and *state.* From there, you will learn the specifics of each term and how it is applied in Visual C# .NET. Finally, you will create a straightforward sample application using the techniques you just learned.

OOP BASIC GUIDELINES

When first entering the world of object-oriented programming, it can seem overwhelming. Several questions inevitably come to mind: What deserves to be an object? How should I abstract the problem domain? Is this object too big and does it do too much? Should I break it up further? All of these questions are valid and should have specific answers.

The easy answer is that an object should do its intended job—no more and no less. The problem arises when you're deciding what the object's intended job involves. This is when many programmers get lost. They code the solution one way, and then go back and do it another way. This continues until they decide that the solution is acceptable. Although refactoring is a good thing (see Martin Fowler's book on the subject), this way of designing is a bit ridiculous, not to mention time-consuming.

Fortunately, there is an easier way to create this design. Although many programmers like to dive in, it is more beneficial to take the time to do some upfront design. This can involve a white board, paper, Microsoft Visio, IBM's Rational Rose, or any other tool. The point is to create the design first. This enables you to easily scrap what you have and start over. It doesn't matter how good you are, you will change your design many times. If you don't, there's something suspicious and you should rethink your position.

Class Attributes

6

This next section will show you what attributes are, and how they carry over from the design board into code as properties and fields.

Definition

The definition of *attribute* varies slightly depending on whether you consult a dictionary or whether you consult the MSDN documentation. A dictionary definition says that an attribute is a quality or characteristic inherent in someone or something. This applies to classes when you are designing. When designing classes, you ascribe to those classes attributes that fit the model being designed. When you get to the coding phase, attributes (qualities or characteristics) become properties and fields of a class or object.

Description of an Attribute

An *attribute* is a physical characteristic of a class or object (the terms *class* and *object* are defined later in this section). That characteristic can be something as simple as the color of the object or as complex as a contained object or class. Unlike a class or object, an attribute has no identity outside of the class or object that contains it. For example, the color red, outside of a representation of a bicycle, does not have an identity. However, as part of an instance of a bicycle, the color red makes up an essential part of the object's state (object state is described later in this section).

Design and UML Notation of Attributes

In UML, an attribute begins with a lowercase letter. This type of capitalization is sometimes referred to as *camel case*. An attribute is also prefaced by a scope indicator:

Objects and Classes

+, -, or #. Each symbol corresponds to an appropriate scoping type: public, private, and protected, respectively. Figure 6.1 shows four private attributes inside a class definition. Although public is a valid scoping operator for attributes, it is considered extremely bad object-oriented programming practice to use it because doing so violates encapsulation.

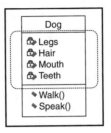

FIGURE 6.1   In UML, attributes are listed in the second compartment of a class.

6

Examples of Attributes

The examples in Table 6.1 show attributes and their corresponding declarations in Visual C#.

TABLE 6.1

UML Attribute Design Versus Code

UML Notation	Visual C# Declaration
-birthDate	private DateTime m_birthDate;
-hairColor	private string hairColor = "blue";
#lastName	protected string m_lastName = "Kruger";
#firstName	protected string m_firstName = "Lonny";
+badAttribute	public string m_badAttribute = "should never use public attributes";

Operations in Object-Oriented Design and Programming

Where you can think of attributes as characteristics that can be represented with nouns (age, height, weight, sex, and so on), operations are actions that an object performs, and can therefore be represented by verbs (run, walk, jump, calculate, and the like).

An operation is a service exposed by a class or object. When an object receives a message from another object, the receiving object knows exactly which operation corresponds to that message and it invokes the desired action. This is possible because each class definition contains operation signatures. An operation signature consists of its name, return type, and any parameters that may be passed to it. Because of the information that makes up a signature, one class definition can contain multiple operations with the same name. However, it is not possible to have multiple operations with the same signature.

UML Notation for Operations

In UML, an operation follows the following form and is listed in the third compartment of a class as shown in Figure 6.2:

```
Name(argument : ArgumentType = DefaultValue, ...):
  ReturnType {PropertyValues} {Constraints}
```

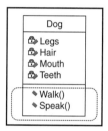

FIGURE 6.2   In UML, operations are listed in the third compartment of a class.

In Visual C# .NET, an operation takes the following form:

```
Attributes Modifiers ReturnType Name(ParameterList)
{
}
```

Examples of Operations

The examples in Table 6.2 show attributes and their corresponding declarations in Visual C# .NET.

TABLE 6.2

Operations (Design) Versus Methods (Code)

UML Notation	Visual C# .NET Declaration
-InternalOpen()	private void InternalOpen()
#SetFirstName(firstName:string)	protected void SetFirstName (string firstName)

TABLE 6.2

Continued

#GetLastName():string	protected string GetLastName()
+Open()	public void Open()

Classes

Looking at the real world, it is difficult to think of anything that cannot be represented as a class. Everywhere you look is an instance of a class. For example, a bird, a dog, a cat, a cow, and a person can all be modeled as a class. Each of them has a basic definition that all members of that class must share.

There are three main things that make up a class definition: attributes, operations, and constraints. As defined earlier, attributes are characteristics of a class or object; operations are actions that class or object can perform; and constraints are parameters to which the class or object must conform. For example, a dog can be represented as a class with certain attributes, such as legs, hair, mouth, and teeth. It can also have operations, such as walk and speak. Finally, it can also have a constraint, which states that if a person calls the dog, it must go to that person.

UML Notation for Classes

In UML, a class is depicted by a rectangle, as shown in Figure 6.3. An object has three compartments: name, attributes, and operations. The first compartment is for the object's name and stereotype. A stereotype is generally used to describe the use of a class. For example, you could create a class definition that serves as a storage container for a collection of objects. Depending on the intended implementation of that class, you could give that class a stereotype of <<container>> or <<collection>>.

FIGURE 6.3   In UML, a class is indicated by a rectangle.

Examples of Classes

Figure 6.4 shows the class definition for Door. It can be read as a Door has attributes of color, doorType (interior or exterior), and isClosed (opened or closed). In addition, the operations Open and Close can be performed.

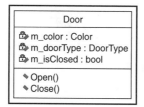

FIGURE 6.4   A class representation
of a door.

Objects

An object is an instance of a class. However, it is easier to think of an object as a real-world thing, such as an apple, a person, a cow, and so on. An object contains state information that is defined in the class structure. For example, in the case of the Door class described in the class example, an object representation would be the actual door that you step through. It has a clearly defined state, such as brown, open, and exterior. An object knows which messages it receives have a corresponding operation and appropriately invokes that operation when received.

UML Notation for Objects

Similar to the class representation, an object is depicted by a rectangle, as shown in Figure 6.5. The rectangle contains either the name of the object or the name of the object and the corresponding class name. The name of the object usually begins with a lowercase letter and is underlined.

When attributes are displayed, the rectangle is divided into two separate compartments. They are displayed with the attribute name followed by a sample value or the value of that attribute in the current context. Because operations are not contextual, they are not shown in the object representation.

FIGURE 6.5   Similar to a class
representation, an
object is depicted
by a rectangle.

Examples

Figure 6.6 shows an instance of class Point named aPoint. It has two attributes: X and Y. In the current context, the values of X and Y are 200 and 100, respectively.

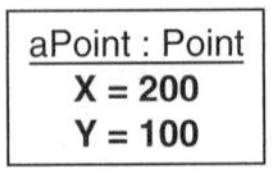

Objects and Classes

FIGURE 6.6   The object `aPoint`,
which is an instance
of the class `Point`.

Object State Maintenance

Each object or instance of a class that has at least one attribute is said to have state. The *state* of an object is the value of the attributes of an object at any one time. For example, in the example presented in the "Objects" section, the state of the object `aPoint` is X=200 and Y=100.

State Notation

Because it is useful to model the state of an object only when it is necessary to perform some action based on the state of that object, state is generally not shown on design models. However, if you need to indicate the state of an object, there are two ways to do so. The first way is to use the object symbol, as in Figure 6.5, and show the attributes section along with the state values. The second way is to use a state diagram. Although a state diagram is useful, the creation of one is beyond the scope of this chapter.

Examples of State

In Figure 6.7, the state of the object `jimmy` is `hair=red`, `height=6'0''`, and `position=prone`.

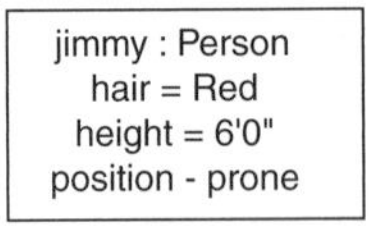

FIGURE 6.7   Illustrating the state
of the `Person`
object, `jimmy`.

Advanced Topics in Classes and Objects

So far, this chapter has provided a basic introduction to object-oriented programming by taking a glimpse at classes, objects, attributes, and operations. This next section will illustrate some of the more advanced topics. In object-oriented programming, advanced topics include inheritance and polymorphism. Although inheritance and polymorphism are basic necessities in any object-oriented language, they are some of the more difficult things to understand for beginners. In the next few sections, you will take a look at inheritance and polymorphism, and their uses.

Inheriting from Base Classes

When applied to object-oriented programming, inheritance means that if a class inherits from a base class, it inherits all the operations, attributes, properties, events, and their implementations from that base class. The only exceptions are that the class does not inherit instance constructors, destructors, and static constructors, nor does it inherit those things to which it explicitly has been denied access.

Although the derived class inherits its methods, attributes, and so forth from a base class, scoping might not allow the derived class to access the inherited items. For example, if a method is marked as private, no descendants will be able to call this method.

Figure 6.8 shows a class diagram for the inheritance example program in Listing 6.1. The diagram shows a base class, appropriately named BaseClass, with a method named SomeMethod. It also shows a derived class named DerivedClass that inherits from the base class BaseClass. This means that when the DerivedClass class is instantiated, as shown in Listing 6.1, you can invoke the SomeMethod operation from the instance of DerivedClass.

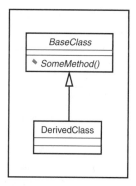

FIGURE 6.8 Class diagram for the inheritance example in Listing 6.1.

LISTING 6.1
Inheritance Example

```
using System;

namespace SAMS.VisualCSharpDotNetUnleashed.Chapter6
{
```

Advanced Topics in Classes and Objects

LISTING 6.1
Continued

```csharp
public class BaseClass
{
  public void SomeMethod()
  {
    System.Console.WriteLine("Hello from the base class.");
  }
}

public class DerivedClass : BaseClass
{
}

class InheritanceExample
{
  [STAThread]
  static void Main(string[] args)
  {
    DerivedClass dc = new DerivedClass();
    dc.SomeMethod();

    System.Console.WriteLine("*** Press the enter key to continue ***");
    System.Console.ReadLine();
  }
}
```

When using inheritance, it is important to understand that inheritance extends its base class and is transitive. This means that if you have a class C that inherits from class B, which inherits from class A, class C inherits everything from class B and class A. In addition, it is possible for a derived class to hide inherited members by declaring new operations with the same name or signature. The following code snippet demonstrates this principle:

```csharp
public class BaseClass
{
  public void SomeMethod()
  {
    System.Console.WriteLine("Hello from the base class.");
  }
}
```

```
public class DerivedClass : BaseClass
{
  new public void SomeMethod()
  {
    System.Console.WriteLine("Hiding the inherited method.");
  }
}
```

Because an instance of a class contains all the instance attributes declared in that class as well as all the instance attributes that it inherits, an implicit conversion or cast exists from a derived class type to any of its base class types. For example, if class C inherits from class B and class B inherits from class A, class C could be converted or cast to either class B or class A. Listing 6.2 shows how this could be useful.

LISTING 6.2
Inheritance Example 2

```
using System;

namespace SAMS.VisualCSharpDotNetUnleashed.Chapter6
{
  public class BaseClass
  {
    public void SomeMethod()
    {
      System.Console.WriteLine("Hello from the base class.");
    }
  }

  public class DerivedClass : BaseClass
  {
  }

  class InheritanceExample
  {
    protected static void InvokeSomeMethod(BaseClass bc)
    {
      bc.SomeMethod();
    }

    [STAThread]
    static void Main(string[] args)
    {
      BaseClass bc = new BaseClass();
```

6

Advanced Topics in Classes and Objects

LISTING 6.2

Continued

```
DerivedClass dc = new DerivedClass();
InvokeSomeMethod(bc);
```
1
```
InvokeSomeMethod(dc);

        System.Console.WriteLine("*** Press the enter key to continue ***");
        System.Console.ReadLine();
    }
  }
}
```

Listing 6.2 instantiates two classes: BaseClass and DerivedClass. Because DerivedClass inherits from the base class BaseClass, you can implicitly cast this instance to the type BaseClass **1** and therefore pass it as a parameter to the InvokeSomeMethod method, whose only parameter is of type BaseClass.

Introduction to Polymorphism

6

Polymorphism is the capability to appear in many forms. In object-oriented languages, *polymorphism* is the capability to process objects differently, depending on the class or data type. In other words, it is the capability to provide different implementations for a method or property with the same signature. For example, the class structure in Figure 6.9 contains four classes: Shape, Rectangle, Triangle, and Circle.

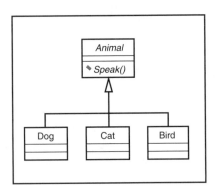

FIGURE 6.9 The class diagram of the Shape class and its descendents.

The first class, or base class, is Shape. Inside the Shape class is a method named CalculateArea. For the Rectangle class, the calculation of the area is area =

length × width. For the `Triangle` class, area = 1/2 × base × height. Finally, for the `Circle` class, area = $\Pi \times$ radius^2. Without polymorphism, this method would be impossible to implement. It becomes a problem when you have a reference to the base type, `Shape`, and need to calculate the area of that shape.

Fortunately, there is polymorphism. Polymorphism guarantees that the correct method will be called, regardless of the data type. In Visual C# .NET, there are three types of polymorphism: interface polymorphism, inheritance polymorphism, and abstract class polymorphism.

> ▶ Interface polymorphism—In Visual C# .NET, many classes can implement the same interface, and one class can implement many interfaces. For more information on interfaces, please see Chapter 38, "Interface Programming."

> ▶ Inheritance polymorphism—Inheritance polymorphism is the most often form of polymorphism. It enables you to provide different implementations of methods by using the `virtual` keyword. When you inherit from a base class, you inherit all of the attributes, methods, properties, and events that go along with the base class. In addition, you inherit the implementation of those items. Unfortunately, there are times that you do not want to inherit that functionality; or, at the very least, you want to alter it. By marking the method or property `virtual` (in the base class), you can override the functionality in descendant classes.

> ▶ Abstract class polymorphism—An abstract class is one that is marked with a type modifier of `abstract`. Because an abstract class usually has abstract methods (an *abstract method* is one that is defined, but does not have an implementation), it cannot be instantiated.

> Implementing polymorphism through an abstract class is similar to doing so with inheritance polymorphism. The difference is the method is not marked `virtual`, but `abstract`. An abstract method provides no implementation and is completely reliant on descendant classes to provide functionality. An abstract method is also similar to a method defined in an interface because it provides a contract stating that this method will be implemented in a descendant class.

Making Methods Virtual

When a method is modified by the keyword `virtual`, it allows descendant classes to override the implementation that it provides. This is an essential part of any object-oriented language. When declaring a method virtual, you assert that you expect this method to be overridden in a descendant class. If you do not expect this to happen, you should not declare a method virtual because it comes with additional overhead.

The overhead comes in the form of checking the runtime type of the object for an overriding method. When this occurs, the overriding method in the most descended class will be called. If this class is the base class, the virtual method in the base class will be called and all the resources expended checking for the type and looking for an overriding method would be wasted. Because the method in the descendant class overrides that in the base class, you must declare the method with the same signature as the virtual method that it overrides. Listing 6.3 shows a sample program that demonstrates the power of polymorphism.

LISTING 6.3

Polymorphism in Action

```
using System;

namespace SAMS.VisualCSharpDotNetUnleashed.Chapter6
{
    public class Animal
    {
        public virtual void Speak()
        {
        }
    }
    public class Dog : Animal
    {
        public override void Speak()
        {
            System.Console.WriteLine("Bark.. Bark");
        }
    }
    public class Cat : Animal
    {
        public override void Speak()
        {
            System.Console.WriteLine("ummmmm... I see a bird!");
        }
    }
    public class Bird : Animal
    {
        public override void Speak()
        {
            System.Console.WriteLine("Please don't eat me mister cat!");
        }
    }
    class PolymorphismExample
    {
        static protected void MakeTheAnimalSpeak(Animal animal)
        {
```

LISTING 6.3
Continued

```
      animal.Speak();
  }

  [STAThread]
  static void Main(string[] args)
  {
    Dog dog = new Dog();
    Cat cat = new Cat();
    Bird bird = new Bird();

    MakeTheAnimalSpeak(dog);
    MakeTheAnimalSpeak(cat);
    MakeTheAnimalSpeak(bird);

    System.Console.WriteLine("*** Press the enter key to continue ***");
    System.Console.ReadLine();
  }
 }
}
```

In the sample program shown in Listing 6.3, there are four classes: `Animal` **2**, `Dog` **3**, `Cat` **4**, and `Bird` **5**. The class diagram for this listing is depicted in Figure 6.9.

When the application is started, the program instantiates three classes: `Dog`, `Cat`, and `Bird`. After the classes have been instantiated, the program passes the objects to a method named `MakeTheAnimalSpeak`. This method takes as its only parameter a reference to type `Animal`. When this method is called, the method asks the animal to speak. Because of polymorphism, the program is able to determine the correct implementation and the animal speaks appropriately.

Summary

In this chapter, you gained an understanding of the basic terminology used in object-oriented programming. This gave you a foundation from which to move forward in the basics of classes and objects. From there you learned how to add attributes, operations, and properties to a class. Finally, you looked at advanced object-oriented programming by learning about inheritance and polymorphism. These advanced subjects gave you an understanding of how object-oriented programming differs from procedural programming.

Further Reading

C# Design Patterns: A Tutorial, Chapter 4, by James W. Cooper, Addison Wesley. ISBN: 0201844532.

C# for Experienced Programmers, Chapter 5, by H. M. Deitel, et al, Prentice Hall. ISBN: 0130461334.

UML Distilled: A Brief Guide to the Standard Object Modeling Language, Third Edition by Martin Fowler, Addison-Wesley Professional. ISBN: 0321193687.

6

IN BRIEF

This chapter explains and demonstrates the proper use of file and stream I/O, as well as the related and equally important topic of object persistence.

▶ The first section gives you a basic understanding of file I/O and an introduction to the different `Stream` classes provided in the .NET Framework.

▶ The final section gives you an introduction to object persistence.

WHAT YOU NEED

RECOMMENDED SOFTWARE	.NET Framework C# .NET environment
RECOMMENDED HARDWARE	.NET-enabled desktop client
SKILLS REQUIRED	C# coding

FILE AND STREAM I/O AND OBJECT PERSISTENCE AT A GLANCE

File and Stream I/O	128		
Understanding File and Stream I/O	129	Using the `FileSystemWatcher`	138
Using Streams: `FileStream`, `MemoryStream`, `StringReader`, and `StringWriter`	132		
Object Persistence	**142**		
Serializing Objects	143	Extending Standard Serialization	149
Summary	**152**		
Further Reading	**152**		

File and Stream I/O

Computers would essentially be useless without I/O (input and output). Users must have ways of getting information to the computer (keyboard, disk, network, and so on). After the data is in the computer and has been processed, users need a way to get it out (monitor, disk, network, email, and so on). In previous chapters in this book, you saw some examples that used the `System.Console.WriteLine` and `System.Console.ReadlLine` commands. Those are basic implementations of input and output streams. In the following sections, you will learn to use and understand file I/O and streams.

Understanding File and Stream I/O

A file is a collection of data, generally stored on some sort of storage media or disk. File I/O is just that: the input and output of data from files.

As defined at www.dictionary.com, a stream is "a steady flow or succession." In C#, the definition of a stream is similar. It is a flow or succession of data or bytes from a pool of data or storage device. A stream provides for the reading and or writing of data from the current position of the stream. A stream also enables you to jump from one point in the stream to another.

The `File` Class

The `File` object is a class that provides high-level functions to make copying, moving, deleting, and opening files easier. In addition, it provides some methods to aid in the creation of `FileStreams`. To make single calls easier, all the methods provided in the `File` class are static. Listing 7.1 demonstrates some of the features available in the `File` class and shows how to create a file using the `File` class **1**.

LISTING 7.1
File Example

```
using System;
using System.IO;

namespace SAMS.VisualCSharpUnleashed.Chapter7
{
  class FileExample
  {
    [STAThread]
    static void Main(string[] args)
    {
      // Create a new file
      string filePath = @"test.txt";

      // Delete the file if it already exists                    1
      if(File.Exists(filePath))
        File.Delete(filePath);

      // Create the file
      File.Create(filePath);

      System.Console.WriteLine("The file was created.");
      System.Console.ReadLine();
    }
  }
}
```

7

File and Stream I/O

The `FileInfo` Class

The `FileInfo` object is another class that provides high-level functions to make copying, moving, deleting, and opening files easier. In addition, it provides some methods to aid in the creation of streams. Unlike the `File` class, the `FileInfo` class is made up entirely of instance methods. Listing 7.2 demonstrates how to use the `FileInfo` class to list information about a particular file.

TIP

Security checks are made on each call of the static methods in the `File` class. Because the `FileInfo` class is an instance class, the security checks need to be performed only once. A general rule of thumb to use when deciding which class to use is this: If you are performing a single operation on a file, the `File` class might be the right choice. If, however, you are performing multiple operations on a file, the `FileInfo` class is probably the most efficient choice.

LISTING 7.2

`FileInfo` Example

```
using System;
using System.IO;

namespace SAMS.VisualCSharpUnleashed.Chapter7
{
    class Class1
    {
[STAThread]
static void Main(string[] args)
{
  // Create a new file
  string filePath = @"c:\test.txt";

  FileInfo fi = new FileInfo(filePath);

  // Print out the information if the file exists
  if(fi.Exists)
  {
    System.Console.WriteLine(
      "The file: {0} was last accessed on {1} " +
      " and contains {2} bytes of data.", filePath,
      fi.LastAccessTime, fi.Length);
  }
  else
    System.Console.WriteLine("The file: {0} does not exist.", filePath);
```

LISTING 7.2
Continued

```
    System.Console.ReadLine();
  }
 }
}
```

The Directory Class

Whereas the File and FileInfo classes work on individual files, the Directory class provides methods to copy, move, rename, create, and delete directories **2**. Like the File class, the Directory class provides all static methods. Listing 7.3 demonstrates how to create, rename, and move a directory.

LISTING 7.3
Using the Directory Class

```
using System;
using System.IO;

namespace SAMS.VisualCSharpUnleashed.Chapter7
{
    class DirectoryExample
    {
[STAThread]
    static void Main(string[] args)
    {
        string initialDirectory  = @"c:\InitialDirectory";
        string moveDirectoryHere  = @"c:\DirectoryMovedHere";

        if(Directory.Exists(initialDirectory))
        {
            // Delete directory if it exists
            Directory.Delete(initialDirectory, true);
        }

        // Create Directory
        Directory.CreateDirectory(initialDirectory);

        if(Directory.Exists(moveDirectoryHere))
        {
            // Delete directory if it exists
            Directory.Delete(moveDirectoryHere, true);
        }
```

File and Stream I/O

LISTING 7.3
Continued

```
        // Move Directory
        Directory.Move(initialDirectory, moveDirectoryHere);

        // Create 10 Files in the directory
        for(int i=0; i<10; i++)
        {
          string filePath = moveDirectoryHere + @"\Test" + i.ToString();
          File.Create(filePath);
        }

        // Get all of the files in this directory and list them.
        string[] fileList = Directory.GetFiles(moveDirectoryHere, "*.*");
        for(int i=0; i<fileList.Length; i++)
        {
          System.Console.WriteLine(
            "File: {0} exists in Directory: {1}",
            fileList[i], moveDirectoryHere);
        }

        System.Console.ReadLine();
      }
    }
}
```

Using Streams: `FileStream`, `MemoryStream`, `StringReader`, and `StringWriter`

All stream classes perform essentially the same functions. They enable you to create, read, write, and close streams of data from some storage medium. The storage medium can be a disk, memory, pipe, or anything else that allows for the temporary of persistent storage of data. In the following sections, you will learn the purpose and how to use a few of these stream classes.

The `FileStream` Class

The `FileStream` class is a class that provides methods for opening, closing, reading, and writing to files, pipes, and standard input and output streams. In addition, the `FileStream` class provides methods to read and write data synchronously and asynchronously. The main benefit to using the `FileStream` class is that it provides improved performance by buffering input and output. Buffered I/O provides the ability to deal with extremely large files without slowing down or halting the system.

Listing 7.4 demonstrates how to use the `FileStream` class to print out the contents of a file **3**. This program is similar to the `Type` command used in DOS. To use this program, type the name of the program and pass it a command-line argument of the file that you want to list.

```
Example:  FileStreamExample autoexec.bat
```

To enter a command-line argument for a program in Visual Studio.NET, simply right-click on the project (in the Solution Explorer) and click the Properties menu item. Next add the parameter to the Command-Line Arguments item in the Configuration Properties, Debugging section, as shown in Figure 7.1.

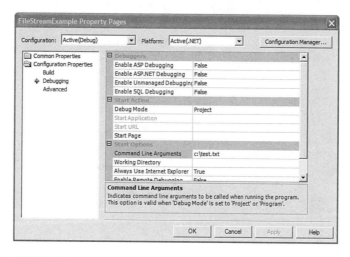

FIGURE 7.1   Add the command-line argument here when testing the application.

LISTING 7.4
Using the `FileStream` Class

```csharp
using System;
using System.IO;

namespace SAMS.VisualCSharpUnleashed.Chapter7
{
  class FileStreamExample
  {
    static public void OutputFile(string filePath)
    {
      FileInfo fileInfo = new FileInfo(filePath);
```

File and Stream I/O

LISTING 7.4
Continued

```
        if(fileInfo.Exists)
        {
            using(FileStream fileStream = fileInfo.OpenRead())
            {
                byte[] byteArray = new byte[fileInfo.Length];

                System.Text.UTF8Encoding temp = new System.Text.UTF8Encoding(true);
                while(fileStream.Read(byteArray, 0, byteArray.Length) > 0)
                {
                    Console.WriteLine(temp.GetString(byteArray));
                }
            }
        }
    }

    [STAThread]
    static void Main(string[] args)
    {
        if(args.Length<1)
            System.Console.WriteLine("usage FileStreamExample {filename}");
        else
            OutputFile(args[0]);
    }
    }
}
```

The MemoryStream Class
The MemoryStream class enables you to read and write data not from disk, but from memory. A memory stream is simply an array of unsigned bytes. Because they are stored in memory, memory streams are generally faster than streams that are stored on disk.

TIP

If you initialize the memory stream in the constructor with any data, you will not be able to increase the size past the initial length of the stream. Any attempt to do so will result in an Exception being thrown. Therefore, if you aren't 100% sure of the size of the stream at construction time, you'd be better served leaving the size dynamically allocated.

Listing 7.5 demonstrates the simple usage of a memory stream.

LISTING 7.5

MemoryStreamExample

```
using System;
using System.IO;

namespace SAMS.VisualCSharpUnleashed.Chapter7
{
  class MemoryStreamExample
  {
    static protected void AddToStream(Stream stream, string stringMessage)
    {
      char[] message = stringMessage.ToCharArray();
      for(int i=0; i<message.Length; i++)
        stream.WriteByte((byte) message[i]);
    }

    [STAThread]
    static void Main(string[] args)
    {
      string message = "This is a message from the Visual C#.NET Book.";
      using(MemoryStream ms = new MemoryStream())
      {
        AddToStream(ms, message);

        ms.Position = 0;
        for(; ms.Position<ms.Length; )
          System.Console.Write((char) ms.ReadByte());
      }

      System.Console.ReadLine();
    }
  }
}
```

The StringReader and StringWriter Classes

The StringReader class enables you to read from a stream that has a storage medium of a string. The StringWriter classes make it possible for you to write to a stream that uses a StringBuilder as its storage medium. Listing 7.6 demonstrates how to use a StringReader and StringWriter.

File and Stream I/O

LISTING 7.6
StringReaderWriterExample

```csharp
using System;
using System.IO;
using System.Text;

namespace SAMS.VisualCSharpUnleashed.Chapter7
{
  class StringReaderWriterExample
  {
    [STAThread]
    static void Main(string[] args)
    {
      string message     = "This is a message from the Visual C#.NET Book.";
      StringBuilder sb  = new StringBuilder(message);

      using(StringWriter sw = new StringWriter(sb))
      {
        sw.Write(" This text was added dynamically.");
      }

      using(StringReader sr = new StringReader(sb.ToString()))
      {
        int ch;

        while((ch = sr.Read()) != -1)
          System.Console.Write((char) ch);
      }

      System.Console.ReadLine();
    }
  }
}
```

Using StreamReader and StreamWriter

The StreamReader and StreamWriter classes are provided to read characters from stream using a specific encoding. Unlike the Stream class, which is used for byte input and output, the StreamReader and StreamWriter classes are used for character input and output. By default, these classes use UTF-8 encoding and are not thread safe. Listing 7.7 demonstrates how to read and write to a file **4** using the StreamReader and StreamWriter classes.

LISTING 7.7
StreamReaderWriterExample

```
using System;
using System.IO;

namespace SAMS.VisualCSharpUnleashed.Chapter7
{
  class StreamReaderWriterExample
  {
    static public void CreateFile(string filePath)
    {
      using(StreamWriter sw = new StreamWriter(filePath))
      {
        sw.WriteLine("This is Line One.");
        sw.WriteLine("This is Line Two.");
        sw.WriteLine("This is Line Three.");
        sw.WriteLine("This is Line Four.");
        sw.WriteLine("Just to be different Line Five.");
      }
      System.Console.WriteLine("File created with data using the StreamWriter
class.");
    }

    static public void OutputFile(string filePath)
    {
      using(StreamReader sr = new StreamReader(filePath))
      {
        while(sr.Peek() > 0)
        {
          string lineOfText = sr.ReadLine();
          Console.WriteLine(lineOfText);
        }
      }
    }

    [STAThread]
    static void Main(string[] args)
    {
      if(args.Length<1)
        System.Console.WriteLine("usage FileStreamExample {filename}");
      else
      {
        if(File.Exists(args[0]))
          OutputFile(args[0]);
```

7

File and Stream I/O

LISTING 7.7
Continued

```
        else
          CreateFile(args[0]);

        System.Console.ReadLine();
      }
    }
  }
}
```

Using the `FileSystemWatcher`

Until now, you have learned about and how to use the `File`, `Directory`, and `Stream` classes that are provided in .NET. This enabled you to create, delete, read, and write to and from these objects. This is a very useful thing to know, but what if you need to perform some actions based on these events and you are not the one performing these actions? Fortunately, .NET provides the `FileSystemWatcher` class. By setting the `FileSystemWatcher.NotifyFilter` property to one or more of the notification filters, this class enables you to receive a notification when a change occurs to a file or directory. Table 7.1, which is found in the .NET Framework 1.1 MSDN Library, describes the different filters available to you through the `FileSystemWatcher` class.

TABLE 7.1
Notification Filters

Member Name	Description
`Attributes`	The attributes of the file or folder
`CreationTime`	The time the file or folder was created
`DirectoryName`	The name of the directory
`FileName`	The name of the file
`LastAccess`	The date the file or folder was last opened
`LastWriteu`	The date the file or folder last had anything written to it
`Security`	The security settings of the file or folder
`Size`	The size of the file or folder

When a file or directory is created, renamed, deleted, or updated, the `FileSystemWatcher` class generates an event to notify you of the change. However, it is important to realize that more then one notification can be generated for one event. For example, when you create a file and write to that file, you could receive the CreationTime, FileName, LastAccess, and LastWrite notifications. Listing 7.8 demonstrates how to use the FileSystemWatcher class to monitor a directory for added files **5** and then move them to another directory. This enables you to use a directory as sort of an inbox. When a file is received, you can perform some sort of processing and then move it to an archive directory when complete.

LISTING 7.8
FileSystemWatcher Example

```csharp
using System;
using System.IO;

namespace SAMS.VisualCSharpUnleashed.Chapter7
{
  class FileSystemWatcherExample
  {
    protected string                 m_importDir   = string.Empty;
    protected string                 m_archiveDir  = string.Empty;
    protected FileSystemWatcher      m_watcher     = null;
    protected System.Threading.Thread  m_watchThread = null;

    public FileSystemWatcherExample(string importDir, string archiveDir)
    {
      m_importDir  = importDir;
      m_archiveDir = archiveDir;

      if(!Directory.Exists(m_importDir))
        Directory.CreateDirectory(m_importDir);
      if(!Directory.Exists(m_archiveDir))
        Directory.CreateDirectory(m_archiveDir);

      m_watchThread = new System.Threading.Thread(
          new System.Threading.ThreadStart(ThreadStart));
      m_watchThread.Start();
    }

    public void Shutdown()
    {
      m_watcher.EnableRaisingEvents = false;
      m_watcher      = null;
      m_watchThread = null;
    }

    protected void Initialize()
```

5

File and Stream I/O

LISTING 7.8
Continued

```
  {
      string[] files = System.IO.Directory.GetFiles(m_importDir, "*.*");

     for(int i=0; i<files.Length; i++)
     {
        ProcessFile(files[i]);
     }
  }

  protected void WatchFiles(string directory)
  {
     if(System.IO.Directory.Exists(directory))
     {
        m_watcher = new FileSystemWatcher();
        m_watcher.Path           = directory;
        m_watcher.NotifyFilter =
           NotifyFilters.FileName | NotifyFilters.Attributes |
           NotifyFilters.LastAccess | NotifyFilters.LastWrite |
           NotifyFilters.Security | NotifyFilters.Size;
        m_watcher.Changed += new FileSystemEventHandler(OnChanged);
        m_watcher.EnableRaisingEvents = true;
     }
  }


  protected void ThreadStart()
  {
     try
     {
        // Notifications will not occur if files already exist,
        // so process the ones// already in the directory.
        Initialize();

        // Monitor the Import Directory.
        WatchFiles(m_importDir);
     }
     catch(Exception e)
     {
        System.Diagnostics.Debug.WriteLine(e.Message);
     }
  }
```

LISTING 7.8
Continued

```
protected void ProcessFile(string filePath)
{
  try
  {
    // Because of multiple notifications, we might have already processed the
    //file.
    // Check to see if it still exists.
    if(System.IO.File.Exists(filePath))
    {
      string newFileName = filePath;
      newFileName = newFileName.Replace(m_importDir, m_archiveDir);

      if(!System.IO.File.Exists(newFileName))
      {
        // Perform some processing on the file here.
        System.Console.WriteLine("Moving {0} to the archive directory.",
filePath);

        // Now move the file.
        System.IO.File.Move(filePath, newFileName);
      }
      else
      {
        System.Diagnostics.Debug.WriteLine("Could not process the file " +
filePath +
" because it already exists in the archive directory.");
      }
    }
  }
  catch(Exception e)
  {
    System.Diagnostics.Debug.WriteLine(e.Message);
  }
}

public void OnChanged(object source, FileSystemEventArgs e)
{
  // The file has changed, so process it now.
  ProcessFile(e.FullPath);
}
```

7

File and Stream I/O

LISTING 7.8
Continued

```
[STAThread]
static void Main(string[] args)
{
    FileSystemWatcherExample fwe =
      new FileSystemWatcherExample(@"c:\import", @"c:\archive");
    // Wait until the user presses the return key before exiting.
    System.Console.ReadLine();
    fwe.Shutdown();
}
}
}
```

> **TIP**
>
> In most situations, the `FileSystemWatcher` is an extremely powerful and useful tool, enabling you to monitor events that occur in the file system. However, depending on the environment being monitored, various factors and other third-party software packages can cause this component to delay notifications, or even completely fail to receive notifications. If you need mission-critical, accurate timing notifications, you might find that the `FileSystemWatcher` doesn't perform as well as needed.

Object Persistence

Object persistence is the ability to persist an object's state to some sort of storage medium. This enables an object to save itself in a particular format, to be either persisted or transported and restored at a convenient point in time.

The .NET Framework enables you to persist objects to disk, memory, or other storage mediums through serialization. It also provides you with some default serializers to accomplish this task. The .NET Framework provides two basic forms of serialization: binary and XML. Although there are more differences, as described in Table 7.2, the basic difference is that XML is a readable and open standard, whereas binary is not.

TABLE 7.2

Binary and XML Serialization

Serialization Form	Description
Binary	Binary serialization serializes all fields and properties of a class. It provides type fidelity and is used by Remoting to transfer objects to another computer by value.
XML	XML serialization serializes only the public fields and properties in a class. It does not preserve type fidelity.

In the following sections, you will learn how to serialize (store) objects to disk and then deserialize (restore) them.

Serializing Objects

To serialize an object, it is necessary to make that object serializable. To do this you can either mark the object as serializable by using the `Serializable` attribute or by implementing the `ISerializable` interface in your object and serializing the desired fields yourself.

Marking the object as serializable by using the `Serializable` attribute is by far the easier of the two approaches to implement. The following code snippet demonstrates how to do this:

```
[Serializable]
class SomeObject
{
  ...
}
```

Using the `ISerializable` interface takes a little more effort. It will be described in the next section, "Extending Standard Serialization."

Listing 7.9 demonstrates how to use a `BinaryFormatter` to serialize and deserialize an object from disk.

LISTING 7.9
SerializationDeSerializationExample

```
using System;
using System.Xml;
using System.Xml.Serialization;
using System.Runtime.Serialization.Formatters.Binary;
using System.Runtime.Serialization;
using System.IO;
using System.Collections;

namespace SAMS.VisualCSharpUnleashed.Chapter7
{
  public enum serialize { Binary, XML };

  [Serializable]
  public class CustomAddress
  {
    protected string m_id;
    protected string m_city;
```

7

Object Persistence

LISTING 7.9
Continued

```
protected string m_country;
protected string m_postalCode;
protected string m_state;
protected string m_streetAddress1;
protected string m_streetAddress2;
protected string m_suite;

public void Copy(CustomAddress address)
{
  if(null != address)
  {
    m_id                                          = address.m_id;
    m_city                                        = address.m_city;
    m_country                                     = address.m_country;
    m_postalCode                                  = address.m_postalCode;
    m_state                                       = address.m_state;
    m_streetAddress1                              = address.m_streetAddress1;
    m_streetAddress2                              = address.m_streetAddress2;
  }
}

public CustomAddress()
{
}
}

/// <summary>
/// Address:
/// </summary>
[Serializable]
public class Address : CustomAddress
{

  public Address() : base()
  {
  }

  public Address(string address, string city, string state, string zip) : base()
  {
    StreetAddress1 = address;
```

LISTING 7.9
Continued

```
      City          = city;
      State         = state;
      PostalCode    = zip;
    }

  public string Country {get { return m_country; } set { m_country = value; } }
  public string Id { get { return m_id; } set { m_id = value; } }
  public string PostalCode
    { get { return m_postalCode; } set { m_postalCode = value; } }
  public string State { get { return m_state; } set { m_state = value; } }
  public string City { get { return m_city; } set { m_city = value; } }
  public string StreetAddress1
    { get { return m_streetAddress1; } set { m_streetAddress1= value; } }
  public string StreetAddress2
    { get { return m_streetAddress2; } set { m_streetAddress2= value; } }
}


[Serializable]
public class User : Address
{
  protected string m_userName;

  public User() : base()
  {
  }

  public User(string userName, string address,
    string city, string state, string zip) : base(address, city, state, zip)
  {
    m_userName = userName;
  }

  public string UserName { get {return m_userName; } set { m_userName = value; } }
}

// Generic class to serialize objects using the XML serializer.
public class GenericXMLSerializer
{
  protected GenericXMLSerializer()
  {
  }
```

7

Object Persistence

LISTING 7.9
Continued

```csharp
public static void SerializeObject(string filename, object value, Type type)
{
  System.Xml.XmlTextWriter xmlWriter =
    new XmlTextWriter(
    new System.IO.StreamWriter(
      System.IO.File.Open( filename, System.IO.FileMode.Create ) ) );
  try
  {
    System.Xml.Serialization.XmlSerializer serializer =
      new System.Xml.Serialization.XmlSerializer( type );
    xmlWriter.Formatting = Formatting.Indented;
    serializer.Serialize(xmlWriter, value);
  }
  finally
  {
    xmlWriter.Close();
  }
}

public static object DeserializeObject(string filename, Type type)
{
  object result = null;

  XmlTextReader reader = new XmlTextReader(filename);
  try
  {
    System.Xml.Serialization.XmlSerializer serializer =
      new System.Xml.Serialization.XmlSerializer(type);

    result = serializer.Deserialize(reader);
  }
  finally
  {
    reader.Close();
  }

  return result;
}

// Generic class to serialize objects using the Binary Formatter.
public class GenericBinarySerializer
```

LISTING 7.9
Continued

```
{
  protected GenericBinarySerializer()
  {
  }

  public static void SerializeObject(string filename, object value)
  {
    BinaryFormatter binaryWriter = new BinaryFormatter();

    using(FileStream fs =
      new System.IO.FileStream(filename, System.IO.FileMode.Create))
    {
      binaryWriter.Serialize(fs, value);
    }
  }

  public static object DeserializeObject(string filename)
  {
    object result = null;

    BinaryFormatter binaryWriter = new BinaryFormatter();

    using(FileStream fs =
      new System.IO.FileStream(filename, System.IO.FileMode.Open))
    {
      result = binaryWriter.Deserialize(fs);
    }

    return result;
  }
}

class SerializationDeserializationExample
    {

  public static void SerializeObject(
    string filename, object value, Type type, serialize serializationType)
  {
    switch(serializationType)
    {
      case serialize.Binary:
        GenericBinarySerializer.SerializeObject(filename, value);
```

Object Persistence

LISTING 7.9
Continued

```csharp
        break;
      case serialize.XML:
        GenericXMLSerializer.SerializeObject(filename, value, type);
        break;
    }
  }

  public static object DeserializeObject(string filename,
    Type type, serialize serializationType)
  {
    object result = null;

    switch(serializationType)
    {
      case serialize.Binary:
        result = GenericBinarySerializer.DeserializeObject(filename);
        break;
      case serialize.XML:
        result = GenericXMLSerializer.DeserializeObject(filename, type);
        break;
    }

    return result;
  }

  [STAThread]
  static void Main(string[] args)
  {
    string filePath      = @"c:\user.object";

    // To change the storage mechanism, simply change the
    // following variable to the desired method.
    // Note:  If you change the storage mechanism,
    // you will have to manually delete the file (If it exists).
    serialize serializationType = serialize.Binary;

    if(!File.Exists(filePath))
    {
      User newUser =
        new User("Lonny",  "123 Nowhere Street",
          "Raleigh",    "NC", "27615");
      SerializeObject(filePath, newUser, typeof(User), serializationType);
```

LISTING 7.9
Continued

```
    }

    User user =
      (User) DeserializeObject(filePath, typeof(User), serializationType);
    System.Console.WriteLine("{0} lives at {1} in {2}, {3} {4}",
      user.UserName, user.StreetAddress1,
      user.City, user.State, user.PostalCode);
    System.Console.ReadLine();
  }
    }
}
```

Extending Standard Serialization

To do this, you must first realize the interface and then implement the
`ISerializable.GetObjectData` method. The following code snippet demonstrates the minimum information required to implement this method:

```
void ISerializable.GetObjectData(SerializationInfo info,
  StreamingContext context)
{
  info.SetType(typeof(int));
  context = m_value;
}
```

In the following example, Listing 7.10, you will see how to take a class that is
normally serializable and limit the fields that are actually persisted to disk. This
listing is a good example of how to extend the standard serialization that is provide
with the .NET Framework.

LISTING 7.10
ExtendingSerialization Example

```
using System;
using System.Runtime.Serialization.Formatters.Binary;
using System.Runtime.Serialization;
using System.IO;

namespace SAMS.VisualCSharpUnleashed.Chapter7
{
  [Serializable()]
  public class UselessInformation : ISerializable
```

7

Object Persistence

LISTING 7.10
Continued

```csharp
{
  private string m_doNotStoreThis = string.Empty;
  private string m_storeThis       = string.Empty;

  public UselessInformation()
  {
  }

  private UselessInformation(SerializationInfo info, StreamingContext context)
  {
    m_storeThis = (string) info.GetValue("StoreThis Here", m_storeThis.GetType());
  }

  public string DoNotStore
  {
    get { return m_doNotStoreThis; }
    set { m_doNotStoreThis = value; }
  }

  public string StoreThis
  {
    get { return m_storeThis; }
    set { m_storeThis = value; }
  }

  public void GetObjectData(SerializationInfo info, StreamingContext context)
  {
    info.AddValue("StoreThis Here", m_storeThis);
  }
}

// Generic class to serialize objects using the Binary Formatter.
public class GenericBinarySerializer
{
  protected GenericBinarySerializer()
  {
  }

  public static void SerializeObject(string filename, object value)
  {
    BinaryFormatter binaryWriter = new BinaryFormatter();
```

LISTING 7.10
Continued

```
    using(FileStream fs =
      new System.IO.FileStream(filename, System.IO.FileMode.Create))
    {
      binaryWriter.Serialize(fs, value);
    }
  }

  public static object DeserializeObject(string filename)
  {
    object result = null;

    BinaryFormatter binaryWriter = new BinaryFormatter();

    using(FileStream fs =
      new System.IO.FileStream(filename, System.IO.FileMode.Open))
    {
      result = binaryWriter.Deserialize(fs);
    }

    return result;
  }
}

class ExtedingSerializationExample
{
  [STAThread]
  static void Main(string[] args)
  {
    string filePath      = @"c:\user.object";

    File.Delete(filePath);
    if(!File.Exists(filePath))
    {
      UselessInformation info = new UselessInformation();
      info.DoNotStore = "Should not be stored.";
      info.StoreThis  = "Needs to be stored.";

      GenericBinarySerializer.SerializeObject(filePath, info);
    }


    UselessInformation info2 =
```

7

Object Persistence

LISTING 7.10
Continued

```
        (UselessInformation) GenericBinarySerializer.DeserializeObject(filePath);
        string doNotStoreResult =
        ((info2.DoNotStore == string.Empty) ? "** NO VALUE **" : "Something is
broke");
        System.Console.WriteLine(
        "Value stored in 'StoreThis': {0} \r\nValue Stored in DoNotStoreThis: {1}",
        info2.StoreThis, doNotStoreResult);
        System.Console.ReadLine();
    }
  }
}
```

Summary

In this chapter, you learned the functions and the proper usage of file and stream I/O and object persistence. You also got a basic understanding of the different `Stream` classes that the .NET Framework provides. Finally, you learned about object persistence and how it is used by the .NET Framework. The lessons that you learned in this chapter will prove invaluable in your endeavors with C# and other .NET languages.

Further Reading

Programming C#, Third Edition by Jesse Liberty, O'Reilly. ISBN: 0596004893.

The Applied Microsoft .NET Framework Programming in C# Collection, Microsoft Press. ISBN: 0735619751.

8 XML Fundamentals

IN BRIEF

In this chapter you will explore the various XML support provided by the .NET Framework. This chapter is divided into five sections with each section discussing a particular area of support for XML.

In the first section, you will explore the basic XML DOM. This includes loading, storing, adding nodes, elements, and attributes. The second section deals with the various `XmlReader`-derived classes along with conversion of XML types. The third section is about the use of XPath to location elements within an XML document. XPath is a very powerful search feature and we'll cover its varied usage. The fourth section introduces the `XPathDocument` and XSLT transformations. The ability to transform data from one XML document to another is a need commonly encountered in B2B applications. Finally, in the last section, you will learn about the rules and requirements when using XML Serialization.

WHAT YOU NEED

RECOMMENDED SOFTWARE	.NET Framework Visual Studio .NET
RECOMMENDED HARDWARE	.NET-enabled desktop client
SKILLS REQUIRED	C# coding

XML FUNDAMENTALS AT A GLANCE

Working with the DOM	**155**		
Creating an XML Document	161	Persisting the DOM	163
Working with XML Nodes, Elements, and Attributes	162		
Using the `XmlReader` Classes	**163**		
What Is an `XmlReader`?	164	Using the `XmlNodeReader`	167
Using the `XmlTextReader`	164	Making Use of `XmlConvert`	167
Using the `XmlValidatingReader`	166		
Exploring XPath	**168**		
Learning the Syntax	169	Filtering Nodes	170
Introduction to the XPathDocument	**171**		
Introduction to XSLT	175	Transforming XML Documents	175
Serialization XML Style	**179**		
Using Basic XML Serialization	179	Customizing XML Serialization	181
Summary	**183**		
Further Reading	**183**		

Working with the DOM

The XML Document Object Model (DOM) is a programming interface for XML documents. It defines the way an XML document can be accessed and manipulated and is designed to be used with any programming language or operating system. The XML DOM enables you to create and navigate an XML document. In addition, it makes it possible for you to add, modify, and delete elements from the document.

> **TIP**
>
> Because the XML DOM stores documents in memory, it can consume a lot of resources when manipulating a large XML document. In addition, you should persist this document after creating it.

The Microsoft XML DOM implementation supports all the necessary functions needed to traverse the node tree, access nodes and their attributes, insert and delete nodes, and convert from the node tree back to XML. In addition, it includes the following classes for building and representing XML: XmlDocument, XmlElement, XmlAttribute, XmlNode, XmlNodeList, and XmlComment. All these classes are located in the System.Xml namespace.

> **TIP**
>
> There are two main classes that make up the core of the XML DOM implementation: XmlNode and XmlNodeList. The first class, XmlNode, is an abstract class that represents an XML document. The second class, XmlModeList, is an ordered list of nodes. All other classes, such as the XmlDocument, XmlElement, XmlAttribute, XmlComment, and XmlDocumentFragment, are inherited from the XmlNode class.

8

> **NOTE**
>
> Although this chapter shows the primary ways in which to use the XML DOM in .NET, it does not contain detailed information about every class that is declared in the System.Xml namespace. However, many resources that contain this information are available on the Internet and should be used to gain more knowledge on the implementation of the XML DOM.

Listing 8.1 shows you how to create an XML document, work with XML nodes, elements, attributes, and store a document.

Working with the DOM

LISTING 8.1
XML DOM Demonstration Sample

```csharp
using System;
using System.Xml;
using System.Collections;

namespace SAMS.VisualCSharpDotNetUnleashed.Chapter8
{
        public abstract class CustomFactory
        {
                public static XmlDocument GetDocument(ICustomElement customElement)
                {
                        XmlDocument document = new XmlDocument();
                        document.AppendChild(GetNodeInternal(customElement, document));
                        return document;
                }

                private static XmlNode GetNodeInternal(
                                ICustomElement customElement,
                                XmlDocument document)
                {
                        if (customElement != null)
                        {
                                XmlNode node = GetElementInternal(customElement, document);
                                for (int i = 0; i < customElement.GetChildren().Count;
i++)
                                {
                                        XmlNode childNode =
                                                GetNodeInternal(
                                                        customElement.GetChildren()[i] as
ICustomElement, document
                                                );

                                        if (childNode != null)
                                        {
                                                node.AppendChild(document.
CreateWhitespace("\r\n"));
                                                node.AppendChild(childNode);
                                                node.AppendChild(document.
CreateWhitespace("\r\n"));
                                        }
                                }
```

LISTING 8.1
Continued

```
                            return node;
            }
            else
            {
                        return null;
            }
    }

        private static XmlElement GetElementInternal(
ICustomElement customElement,
XmlDocument document)
            {
                XmlElement element =
                        document.CreateElement(customElement.GetElementName());

                if (customElement.GetElementAttributes() != null)
                {
                        IEnumerator e =
                            customElement.GetElementAttributes().Keys.GetEnumerator();
                        while (e.MoveNext())
                        {
                                XmlAttribute attribute =
document.CreateAttribute(e.Current.ToString());
                                        attribute.Value =
        customElement.GetElementAttributes()[e.Current].ToString();
                                        element.Attributes.Append(attribute);
                        }
                }
                if (customElement.GetElementInnerText() != "")
                {
                        element.InnerText = customElement.GetElementInnerText();
                }
                return element;
            }
    }

    public interface ICustomElement
    {
```

8

Working with the DOM

LISTING 8.1
Continued

```
            string GetElementName();
            IDictionary GetElementAttributes();
            string GetElementInnerText();
            IList GetChildren ();
            void AddChild (ICustomElement customElement);
    }

    public abstract class CustomElement : ICustomElement
    {
            public abstract string GetElementName();
            public virtual IDictionary GetElementAttributes()
            {
                    return null;
            }
            public virtual string GetElementInnerText()
            {
                    return "";
            }
            public IList GetChildren ()
            {
                    return _customElements;
            }
            public void AddChild (ICustomElement customElement)
            {
                    if (customElement != null)
                    {
                            _customElements.Add(customElement);
                    }
            }
            private IList _customElements = new ArrayList();
    }

    public class Companies : CustomElement, ICustomElement
    {
            public override string GetElementName()
            {
                    return "companies";
            }
    }

    public class Company : CustomElement, ICustomElement
    {
```

8

LISTING 8.1
Continued

```csharp
        public Company (string name)
        {
                _name = name;
        }


        public override string GetElementName()
        {
                return "company";
        }


        public override IDictionary GetElementAttributes()
        {
                IDictionary attributes = new Hashtable();
                attributes.Add("name", _name);
                return attributes;
        }


        private string _name;
}


public class CellPhones : CustomElement, ICustomElement
{
        public override string GetElementName()
        {
                return "cell-phones";
        }
}


public class CellPhone : CustomElement, ICustomElement
{
        public CellPhone (string name, int year) : this(name, year, "")
        {
        }


        public CellPhone (string name, int year, string description)
        {
                _name = name;
                _year = year;
                _description = description;
        }


        public override string GetElementName()
```

Working with the DOM

LISTING 8.1
Continued

```
                    {
                            return "cell-phone";
                    }

                    public override IDictionary GetElementAttributes()
                    {
                            IDictionary attributes = new Hashtable();
                            attributes.Add("name", _name);
                            attributes.Add("year", _year);
                            return attributes;
                    }

                    public override string GetElementInnerText()
                    {
                            return _description;
                    }

                    private string _name, _description;
                    private int _year;
            }

            public class DOMSample
            {
                    [STAThread]
                    static void Main(string[] args)
                    {
                            XmlDocument document = CustomFactory.GetDocument(GetCompanies());
                            Console.WriteLine(document.OuterXml);
                    }

                    private static ICustomElement GetCompanies ()
                    {
                            Companies companies = new Companies();
                            Company company = new Company("Siemens");
                            CellPhones cellPhones = new CellPhones();
                            CellPhone cellPhone =
                                    new CellPhone("MC-60", 2003, "Some Description of
MC-60 cell phone");
                            cellPhones.AddChild(cellPhone);
```

LISTING 8.1
Continued

```
                company.AddChild(cellPhones);
                companies.AddChild(company);
                return companies;
            }
        }
}
```

The preceding example is based on the XML structure shown in Listing 8.2, which enables you to build XML structures that contain only four tags: companies, company, cell-phones, and cell-phone. This XML structure defines a set of companies that sell different models of cell phones. (The company and cell-phone tags have additional attributes, such as name, year, and so forth.)

LISTING 8.2
XML Sample

```
<companies>
        <company name = "Siemens">
                <cell-phones>
                        <cell-phone name="MC60" year="2003">Some description of phone
                </cell-phone>
                </cell-phones>
        </company>
</companies>
```

8

Creating an XML Document

As you can see, all XML elements (such as comments, nodes, attributes, and so on) can be created only in the context of the XML document. For example, you cannot create an instance of the XmlAttribute class by using its constructor. Instead, you must use the CreateAttribute method of the XmlDocument class and pass to it the name of the attribute. Because this attribute is available only in the context of the document that created it, it is not possible to add this attribute to an element that has been created in another document.

The following code snippet demonstrates how to create an XML document:

```
XmlDocument document = new XmlDocument();
```

Working with the DOM

After the XML document has been created, you can populate it manually (as shown in Listing 8.1) or load a prepared XML from a string or file. The following list shows the most commonly used methods that can be used to create XML manually.

- ▸ `CreateAttribute`—Creates an `XmlAttribute` with the specified name

- ▸ `CreateComment`—Creates an `XmlComment` containing the specified data

- ▸ `CreateElement`—Creates an element with the specified name

- ▸ `CreateNode`—Creates an `XmlNode` with the specified node type, `Name`, and `NamespaceURI`

- ▸ `CreateCDataSection`—Creates an `XmlCDataSection` containing the specified data

- ▸ `CreateWhitespace`—Creates an `XmlWhitespace` node

After you have created one of these XML elements, you can assign it to another element (add it to the children list). By using the `Create()` and `AppendChild()` methods, you can create XML that is located in memory. After this XML has been created, you could browse this XML, search for elements, or remove elements. In addition, you could also save this XML to a file or any other data storage medium.

To load XML into `XmlDocument` from a string, you should use the `XmlDocument.LoadXml()` method. This method takes as its only parameter the string containing the XML. By default, the `LoadXml()` method does not preserve either white space or significant white space. Also, this method does not perform data type definition (DTD) or schema validation. If you need this validation to occur, use the `Load` method and pass it an `XmlValidatingReader`.

By using the `XmlDocument.Load()` method, you can load an XML document from a file, stream, URL, `TextReader`, or `XmlReader` and always preserve significant white space.

Working with XML Nodes, Elements, and Attributes

The `XmlNode`, `XmlElement`, and `XmlAttribute` classes are some of the most important in the XML DOM. Both the `XmlElement` and `XmlAttribute` classes are inherited from the `XmlNode` class. The `XmlElement` class can contain the following child node types: `Element`, `Text`, `Comment`, `ProcessingInstruction`, `CDATA`, and `EntityReference`. In addition, it can be the child of a `Document`, `DocumentFragment`, `EntityReference`, or `Element` nodes. This class enables you to add and remove children and attributes, traverse and search child nodes, get and set inner text, and more.

The `XmlAttribute` class can contain either the `Text` or `EntityReference` nodes. Because it is not considered a child node, the `Attribute` node does not appear as the child node of any other node type. The XmlAttribute node enables you to perform all actions defined in the XmlNode class; however, with only a limited set of node types. For example, you cannot add XmlDeclaration as a child to the attribute.

Earlier in this chapter, Listing 8.1 showed you how to work with the XmlAttribute, XmlNode, and XmlElement classes. This was demonstrated in the methods CustomFactory.GetNodeInternal and CustomFactory.GetElementInternal.

Persisting the DOM

The simplest way to persist XML is to save it to a file on a disk. You can accomplish this by invoking the XmlDocument.Save() method. For example:

```
document.Save("c:\some.xml");
```

You can also use both the WriteTo() and WriteContentTo() methods to store XML. The main difference between these methods is that the WriteTo() method saves the whole element into the destination, whereas the WriteContentTo() method saves only the children of the element for which the WriteContentTo() method was invoked.

Both of these methods enable you to store XML into an instance of an XmlWriter, which allows you to store information into a file, TextWriter, or stream. The following code snippet demonstrates how to use the WriteTo() method:

```
XmlDocument document = new XmlDocument();
XmlTextWriter writer = new XmlTextWriter(Console.Out);
document.WriteTo(writer);
```

8

> **NOTE**
>
> Because the WriteTo() method is defined in the XmlNode class, it is supported by all XML elements. In contrast, the Save() method is available only in the XmlDocument class.

Using the XmlReader Classes

Classes for reading XML documents encapsulate functionalities used by applications for connecting to and reading data from XML documents. The functionalities work very similarly to those that retrieve data from a database (the database server returns a pointer of the cursor's object, which contains all requested data and allows access to this data). Clients of XML readers take a pointer to the reader's instance that is independent from the structure of the data stream that should be processed. The reader encapsulates the processed stream as an XML tree. Methods of the reader's classes enable you to move through nodes of XML (instead of moving from byte to byte, as it implemented in the simple streams). From the XML reader's point of view, the XML document is not just a simple text file. Rather, the XML document is a serialized set of nodes that are structured as a tree view. XML readers allow us to traverse forward only; we could not move to the parent node or neighbor node of the current node.

What Is an XmlReader?

The XmlReader is an abstract class that is used for building concrete functionality for reading XML. The .NET Framework contains three XML reader classes: XmlTextReader, XmlValidatingReader, and XmlNodeReader. Each class has a common set of properties and methods that are derived from the XmlReader class.

NOTE

Notice that the value returned by a property sometimes depends on the class in which the property is declared. For example, the CanResolveEntity property makes sense only in the XmlValidatingReader class and returns true. In other classes, the property returns false and is not used in the application.

Using the XmlTextReader

The XmlTextReader class allows quick read-only and forward-only access to XML data streams. It checks the reasonableness of an XML document and generates exceptions in order of the mistakes it finds. This class also checks whether there are described links on the DTD in the XML. But XmlTextReader doesn't check the accordance of XML to DTD.

This class has been populated for quick processing of tolerant XML documents that are available in files, by URLs, or in streams. If you need to check an XML document's accordance to the DTD, you should use the XmlValidatingReader class.

You could create an instance of XmlTextReader class by using one of its constructors. All of them require a data source—a stream, file, and so on. The default XmlTextReader class's constructor is marked as protected, so you are not allowed to use it directly.

Listing 8.3 illustrates a simple example of using the XmlTextReader class. This example reads the XML file and outputs to the console all the names of nodes of this one and the count attributes in each node. The example is based on the XML shown in Listing 8.4. The results of the example's processing are shown in the Listing 8.5.

LISTING 8.3

XmlTextReader Source Code Sample

```
using System;
using System.Xml;
namespace XmlTextReaderSample
{
  class XmlTextReaderSample
  {
    [STAThread]
    static void Main(string[] args)
    {
      XmlTextReader xmlTextReader = new XmlTextReader("sample.xml");
      Console.Out.WriteLine("Set of element in the 'sample.xml' document:");
      while (xmlTextReader.Read())
      {
        if (xmlTextReader.NodeType == XmlNodeType.Element)
        {
          Console.Out.WriteLine((new String(' ', xmlTextReader.Depth * 3)) + "Name:
<" +
            xmlTextReader.Name +  ">; Depth: " + xmlTextReader.Depth.ToString() +
            "; Attributes count: " + xmlTextReader.AttributeCount.ToString() + ";");
        }
      }
    }
  }
}
```

8

LISTING 8.4

XML Document Processed in Listing 8.3

```
<?xml version="1.0" encoding="utf-8" ?>
<companies>
        <company name="BMW">
                <cars>
                        <car name="X3" year="2003"/>
                        <car name="X5" year="2004"/>
                </cars>
        </company>
        <company name="Daewoo">
                <cars>
                        <car name="Lanos" year="1999"/>
                        <car name="Nubira" year="2000"/>
                        <car name="Leganza" year="2000"/>
```

Using the XmlReader Classes

LISTING 8.4
Continued

```
            </cars>
        </company>
</companies>
```

LISTING 8.5
Results of Processing Listing 8.3

```
Set of element in the 'sample.xml' document:
Name: <companies>; Depth: 0; Attributes count: 0;
   Name: <company>; Depth: 1; Attributes count: 1;
      Name: <cars>; Depth: 2; Attributes count: 0;
         Name: <car>; Depth: 3; Attributes count: 2;
         Name: <car>; Depth: 3; Attributes count: 2;
   Name: <company>; Depth: 1; Attributes count: 1;
      Name: <cars>; Depth: 2; Attributes count: 0;
         Name: <car>; Depth: 3; Attributes count: 2;
         Name: <car>; Depth: 3; Attributes count: 2;
         Name: <car>; Depth: 3; Attributes count: 2;
```

Using the XmlValidatingReader

The XmlValidatingReader class is inherited from the XmlReader class and enables you to verify the XML document according to the DTD, the XDR (*XML-Data Reduced*) schema, and the XSD schema. The DTD and XSD are official recommendations of W3C and XDR is the Microsoft implementation of the XML schema.

The XmlValidatingReader class is a wrapper class that is used for validating both whole XML documents and XML fragments and usually works in tandem with the XmlTextReader class. In such cases, the XmlTextReader class is used to traverse the XML document. In addition, it is used for validation.

Almost all custom logic of this class is implemented in the Read, Skip, and ReadTypedValue methods.

The Skip method ignores child elements of the current node of the XML document or fragment. (Notice that you could not skip an incorrect XML fragment. In such a case, an exception will be thrown.)

The ReadTypedValue method returns the value of node that is coerced to one of the Common Language Runtime's data types. If the method can find a correspondence between the XSD type and Common Language Runtime type, the value with Common Language Runtime type will be returned. Otherwise, the value in the string format will be returned.

Using the XmlNodeReader

The main purpose of the XmlNodeReader class is to traverse XML documents that are represented as a DOM model, but not as a stream of text. It works similarly to the XmlTextReader class with the following difference: XmlTextReader browses nodes of the XML stream, but XmlNodeReader browses XML DOM (it should be initialized by this XML DOM during constructor executing).

The set of methods presented in the XmlNodeReader class is the same as in XmlTextReader class. Also, you could use XmlValidatingReader in tandem with XmlNodeReader as well as with XmlTextReader.

Making Use of XmlConvert

The value of XML attributes commonly contains just a string entity. Occasionally, you will need to process this not as a string but as another type such as Date, Boolean, and so on. This value can be converted from a string to another type by using the static class XmlConvert or System.Convert. Although these classes are similar, the XmlConvert works according to the XSD specification and ignores the current regional settings presented on the local computer.

Consider the following example: An attribute has a value of 2-5-1980 and because of the current regional setting on the local machine, this value could be interpreted as February 5, 1980. In this case, if you were to use the System.Convert class, the sting will be correctly converted into a Date instance. However, if you use the XmlConvert class, an exception will be thrown because the XML specification declares the format of dates as YYYY-MM-DD. Therefore, you should transform the 2-5-1980 string into 1980-2-5. Because the XmlConvert class guarantees a correct transformation of data between Common Language Runtime and XSD types, it should be used when working with XML attributes' values.

The XmlConvert class can be used in another way. Sometimes there is a necessity to pass some characters that are not supported by XML specification into XML data stream. The XmlConvert class enables you to transfer and process XML with those characters. For this purpose, you could use the EncodeName and DecodeName methods. For example, some applications generate XML documents that contain tag names with characters that are not supported by the XML specification (for example, spaces). Such a name is not supported by XML, so you should use the EncodeName method to correct it. For example, assume that a tag has the name Some Tag. By invoking the EncodeName method, you will receive the following result: Some_0x0020_Tag.

> **NOTE**
>
> The following characters are also equated to a space in XML specification: ASCII 0x0D (caret return), ASCII 0x0A (new line), ASCII 0x09 (tabulation).

8

As you can see, the space has been replaced with _0x0020_, which is the hexadecimal representation of a space. A sequence of characters with the format _0xHHHH_ is interpreted by the XmlConvert class as a special character that should be replaced after the DecodeName method's invocation. The following example shows the sequence of these methods' invocation (with results):

```
XmlConvert.EncodeName("Some Tag"); //Result: Some_0x0020_Tag
XmlConvert.DecodeName("Some_0x0020_Tag "); //Result: Some Tag
```

> **NOTE**
>
> Notice that the sequence of characters should have a format that exactly coincides with the _0xHHHH_ format. For example, if the tag name contains the string _0x020_, it will be ignored by the XmlConvert class.

Exploring XPath

XML Path Language (or XPath) is a W3C standard that primarily allows identifying parts of an XML document. In other words, with the help of XPath, you can locate one or several nodes in the XML document. In addition, XPath is used for numerical calculations, string manipulations, testing Boolean conditions, and more. XPath is used by various other W3C specifications, such as XSLT, XQuery, XPointer, and XML Schema. Due to this, XPath technology is one of the more important things that every XML developer should know.

The Microsoft .NET Framework works with the XPath 1.0 W3C recommendation. The classes in System.Xml and System.Xml.XPath namespaces allow the execution of XPath queries and working with the result sets.

The XPath specification broadly covers the following topics:

▸ Data model—This section describes the general concepts and terms used in XPath. There are seven defined types of nodes in XPath: root node, element node, attribute node, text node, namespace node, processing instruction node, and comment node.

▸ Location paths—This section details the constructs and syntax used for addressing parts of an XML document. A location path is used to address a certain node set of a document. The location path syntax is very similar to other hierarchical notations used in computer applications, such as URIs, file/folder paths, and so on. The location path can be either absolute or relative (for example, /companies/company/cell-phones/phone[position()=2]).

▸ Expressions—This section describes the most basic XPath construct: an expression. Location paths (explained earlier) are a special case of XPath expressions. Expressions are made up of operands and operators. By using expressions, you could take a *node set* (an unordered collection of nodes without duplicates), a Boolean value, a floating-point number, or a string.

▶ Functions—This section discusses 27 functions that are divided into four categories: node set functions, string functions, Boolean functions, and number functions. Each function takes zero or more arguments and returns a single result. Function example: `concat(A, B)`.

All classes that encapsulate XPath functionality in .NET are located in the `System.XML.XPath` namespace. They provide the XPath parser and evaluation engine that is described in the W3C XML Path Language Version 1.0 Recommendation.

Learning the Syntax

This section discusses the most commonly used XPath syntax constructions. You can find more detailed information about each XPath technology on the Internet (for example, www.w3schools.com/xpath/xpath_syntax.asp).

The main term in XPath is the path of a node in the XML tree. A simple example of a path is `companies/company/cell-phones/cell-phone` (this example is based on the XML example in Listing 8.2).

An XPath query returns all the nodes that are located by a particular path and can contain wildcards in the path's definition. For example, by using the path `companies/*/cell-phones` in an XPath query, it would return all nodes that are located in the `companies` node and all children of this one. Branches in XPath can be defined by using square brackets. The following query returns all `cell-phones` nodes from the `companies` node and the child node of this one called `company`: `companies/company[cell-phones]`.

In addition, you can use the equals operator in a query; for example, `companies/company/cell-phones[cell-phones='Some Description']`. This query returns all cell phones that have a description equal to 'Some Description'.

NOTE
Notice that comparison operators can be used only inside square brackets.

Attributes in the query should be defined with the @ character before the name of the attribute. The following example returns all cell phones with the name `MC60`: `companies/company/cell-phones/cell-phone[@name='MC60']`.

8

The following list contains all of the operators and wildcards that are predefined in XPath:

- ▶ / Selects child nodes from the collection that is located at the left side of it. If using it at the beginning of the query, the search will be performed from the root node.

- ▶ // Recursive search. It selects a node in any depth. If using it at the beginning of query, the recursive search will be performed from the root node.

- ▶ . The current context.

- ▶ * Wildcard that selects all elements (ignores the name of element).

- ▶ @ Attribute (prefix of attribute's name). If the name of the attribute is not set, the search will return all attributes.

- ▶ : Namespaces separator. It separates namespace's prefix from the name of the element or attribute.

- ▶ ( ) Groups operation for obvious setting of sequence.

- ▶ [ ] Applies a filter. Also used as an index of collections.

- ▶ + Addition.

- ▶ - Subtraction.

- ▶ Div Division (according to IEEE 754).

- ▶ * Multiplication.

- ▶ Mod Returns remainder from division.

8

Filtering Nodes

As previously described, square brackets can be used for filtering nodes: `[pattern]`. The `pattern` located inside the brackets is very similar to the SQL statement WHERE. The filter could be applied to all elements in the collection and return only nodes that correspond to it. You could apply several filters on one level of query. You are not allowed to use empty filters. Filters are always applied for the node in the current context. So, the following example returns all companies with the child node `cell-phones`: `/companies/company[cell-phones]`. Also you could use `.` instead of the name of the context node: `/companies/company/cell-phones/cell-phone[.='Some Value']`.

If the filter should return not only one element, you could use the keyword `any` or `all`. If you are not using it, the filter will return only the first element that corresponds to the filter.

Filters could contain Boolean expressions, comparison expressions, and appellation expressions. The following list contains the set of operators that can be used in filters:

- ► and   Logical AND
- ► or   Logical OR
- ► not()   Negation
- ► =   Equality
- ► !=   Inequality
- ► <   Less than
- ► <=   Less than or equal to
- ► >   Greater than
- ► >=   Greater than or equal to
- ► | Union; returns the union of two sets of nodes

The following is the order of priority for each operator:

1. ()   Grouping
2. []   Filtering
3. / and //   path
4. <, <=, >, >=   Comparison
5. =, != Comparison
6. | union
7. not()   Boolean negation
8. and   Boolean AND
9. or   Boolean OR

> **NOTE**
>
> Notice that all operators are case sensitive. This means that each operator is very similar to its meaning in SQL.

Introduction to the XPathDocument

In the previous sections, you received an overview of the basics of XPath. This section shows you how to use XPath in .NET.

Introduction to the `XPathDocument`

As previously described, the .NET framework presents a set of classes for working with XPath. Serving as a gateway into the .NET Framework's XPath world, the `XPathDocument` class is similar to the `XmlDocument` class. However, it doesn't build a tree of XML nodes in memory, but rather processes them one node at a time building XML nodes only when you require them. The main purpose of the `XPathDocument` class is to perform XPath queries and XSL transformations.

Listing 8.7 presents an example that utilizes the `XPathDocument` and `XPathNavigator` classes. The following XML snippet is used by Listing 8.7:

```xml
<?xml version="1.0" encoding="utf-8" ?>
<companies>
        <company name="Siemens">
                <cell-phones>
                        <cell-phone name="C35" year="2000">Cell phone C35</cell-phone>
                        <cell-phone name="MC60" year="2003">Cell phone MC60</cell-phone>
                </cell-phones>
        </company>
        <company name="Motorola">
                <cell-phones>
                        <cell-phone name="C350" year="2001">Cell phone C350</cell-phone>
                        <cell-phone name="T205" year="2000">Cell phone T205</cell-phone>
                </cell-phones>
        </company>
</companies>
```

LISTING 8.7

Using `XPathDocument` and `XPathNavigator`

```csharp
using System;
using System.Xml.XPath;
namespace XPathSample {
        class XPathSample {
                [STAThread]
                static void Main(string[] args) {
                    XPathDocument xpathDocument = new XPathDocument("../../sample.xml");
                    XPathNavigator xpathNavigator = xpathDocument.CreateNavigator();
                    xpathNavigator.MoveToRoot();
                    NavigateTree(xpathNavigator, 0);
                }
```

LISTING 8.7
Continued

```
private static void NavigateTree (
                XPathNavigator xpathNavigator, int depth) {
    if (xpathNavigator.HasChildren) {
        xpathNavigator.MoveToFirstChild();
        DisplayNode(xpathNavigator, depth);
        depth ++;
        NavigateTree(xpathNavigator, depth);
        depth --;
        while (xpathNavigator.MoveToNext()) {
            DisplayNode(xpathNavigator, depth);
            depth ++;
            NavigateTree(xpathNavigator, depth);
            depth --;
        }
        xpathNavigator.MoveToParent();
    }
}
private static void DisplayNode(
                XPathNavigator xpathNavigator, int depth) {
    string prefix = new String(' ', depth * 3);
    if (xpathNavigator.NodeType == XPathNodeType.Text) {
        Console.Out.WriteLine(prefix + "Node: " + xpathNavigator.Value + ".
");
    } else {
        Console.Out.Write(prefix + "Node: <" + xpathNavigator.Name
+ ">. ");

        if (xpathNavigator.HasAttributes) {
            int attributesCount = 1;
            while (xpathNavigator.MoveToNextAttribute()) {
                attributesCount ++;
            }
            Console.Out.Write("Count of attributes: " + attributesCount + ".");
            if (attributesCount != 1) {
                xpathNavigator.MoveToParent();
            }
        }
        Console.Out.WriteLine();
    }
}
}
}
```

8

Introduction to the XPathDocument

In Listing 8.7, we've created an instance of the XPathDocument class that allows us only to create an instance of the XPathNavigator instance. This class is mostly used for collaboration with XPathDocument. It allows us to navigate through the XML document and perform XPath queries.

After that, we've created an XPathNavigator instance by invocation of the CreateNavigator() method of the XPathDocument class.

The last step is an invocation of the custom method NavigateTree(). This one is recursive and navigates through all nodes (beginning from root) of the XML document.

As soon as we review the use of the XPathNavigator and XPathDocument classes, we can start a discussion of how to perform XPath queries. The following example shows how to execute XPath queries by using XPathNavigator and how to navigate the result set through XPathNodeIterator. Listing 8.8 shows how to search all last cell phones in each node located by path: companies/company/cell-phones.

LISTING 8.8
XPathNodeIterator **Using Sample**

```
using System;
using System.Xml.XPath;
namespace XPathSample
{

  class XPathNodeIteratorSample
  {
    [STAThread]
    static void Main(string[] args)
    {
      XPathDocument xpathDocument = new XPathDocument("../../sample.xml");
      XPathNavigator xpathNavigator = xpathDocument.CreateNavigator();
      XPathNodeIterator xpathNodeIterator =
        xpathNavigator.Select("//companies/company/cell-phones/cell-phone[last()]");
      int i = 0;
      Console.Out.WriteLine("Count of nodes that match to XPath query: " +
xpathNodeIterator.Count);
      while (xpathNodeIterator.MoveNext())
      {
        Console.Out.WriteLine((++i) + ". Name: <" +
          xpathNodeIterator.Current.Name + ">. Value: " +
xpathNodeIterator.Current.Value + ".");
      }
    }
  }
}
```

Introduction to XSLT

XSLT stands for *eXtensible Stylesheet Language: Transformations*. It is a language which, according to the very first sentence in the specification (found at www.w3.org/TR/xslt), is primarily designed for transforming one XML document into another. However, XSLT is more than capable of transforming XML to HTML and many other text-based formats, so a more general definition might be as follows: *XSLT is a language for transforming the structure of an XML document*. Now we are going to discuss why we might need to transform XML.

XML is a simple, standard way to interchange structured textual data between computer programs. Part of its success comes because it is also readable and writable by humans using nothing more complicated than a text editor, but this doesn't alter the fact that it is primarily intended for communication between software systems. As such, XML satisfies two compelling requirements:

- ▸ Separating data from presentation
- ▸ Transmitting data between applications

Another of the key benefits of XML is that it unifies the worlds of documents and data, providing a single way of representing structure regardless of whether the information is intended for human or machine consumption. The main point is that whether the XML data is ultimately used by people or by a software application, it will very rarely be used directly in the form it arrives in; it must first be transformed into "something else." To communicate with a human reader, that something else might be a document that can be displayed or printed: for example, an HTML file, a PDF file, or even audible sound. Converting XML to HTML for display is probably the most common application of XSLT today. After you have the data in HTML format, it can be displayed on any browser.

To transfer data between different applications, you need to be able to transform data from the data model used by one application to the model used in another. To load the data into an application, the required format might be a comma-separated-values file, a SQL script, an HTTP message, or a sequence of calls on a particular programming interface. Alternatively, it might be another XML file using a different vocabulary from the original. As XML-based electronic commerce becomes widespread, so the role of XSLT in data conversion between applications also becomes ever more important. Just because everyone is using XML does not mean the need for data conversion will disappear. There will always be multiple standards in use. So, XSLT is an ideal tool for transforming an XML document of one format to an XML document with another format.

Transforming XML Documents

Let's discuss how we can use XSLT in .NET. All XSL instructions are performed by an XSL processor. As input data, the XSL processor requires an XML document that

Introduction to the `XPathDocument`

should be formatted and an XSL document. After processing, it could return another XML document (that is based on the input XML), HTML document, or another structured document (for example, PDF).

All classes required for XSL transformations are located in the following namespaces: `System.Xml` (`XmlTextWriter` class), `System.Xml.Xsl` (`XslTransform` class), and `System.Xml.XPath` (`XPathDocument` class).

Before we create an example, we should create the XML file that should be transformed (Listing 8.9) and the XSLT file that contains the transformation template (Listing 8.10).

LISTING 8.9
XML File That Should Be Transformed

```xml
<?xml version="1.0" encoding="utf-8" ?>
<cell-phones>
        <cell-phone name="C35" year="2000" company="Siemens"/>
        <cell-phone name="MC60" year="2003" company="Siemens"/>
        <cell-phone name="C350" year="2001" company="Motorola"/>
        <cell-phone name="T205" year="2000" company="Motorola"/>
</cell-phones>
```

As you can see, the XML file defines a set of cell phones (`cell-phones/cell-phone` tag) with the attributes `name`, `year`, and `company`.

LISTING 8.10
XSL File That Contains Transformation Template

```xml
<xsl:stylesheet xmlns:xsl="http://www.w3.org/1999/XSL/Transform" version="1.0">
<xsl:output method="html" />
 <xsl:template match="/">
   <html>
     <body>
       <table width="100%">
         <tr>
           <td width="30%"><b>Cell Phone's Name</b></td>
           <td width="30%"><b>Company</b></td>
           <td width="40%"><b>Creation Date</b></td>
         </tr>
         <tr>
           <td colspan="3">
             <hr width="100%"/>
           </td>
```

LISTING 8.10
Continued

```
          </tr>
          <xsl:for-each select="/cell-phones/cell-phone">
            <tr>
              <td width="30%"><xsl:value-of select="@name"/></td>
              <td width="30%"><xsl:value-of select="@company"/></td>
              <td width="40%"><xsl:value-of select="@year"/></td>
            </tr>
          </xsl:for-each>
        </table>
      </body>
    </html>
  </xsl:template>
</xsl:stylesheet>
```

In looking at the XML file in Listing 8.10, you will see a tag containing the following element: <xsl:stylesheet>. This is a mandatory element in every XSL stylesheet. The second tag (<xsl:output>) indicates the output type and the next tag (<xsl:template>) is used to define the processing of the sample.xml file.

From there, the example uses a simple XPath selection query to get the data and insert it in into HTML tags.

NOTE

You should understand that this chapter doesn't cover the syntax of XSL technology and doesn't explain the structure of stylesheets and rules of XSL documents creation. For more information on the structure and syntax of stylesheets, visit the www.w2.org/tr/xslt website.

Listing 8.11 presents a simple example that performs XSL transformations.

LISTING 8.11
XSL Transformation Sample Source Code

```
using System;
using System.Xml;
using System.Xml.Xsl;
using System.Xml.XPath;
namespace XSLTSample
```

8

Introduction to the XPathDocument

LISTING 8.11
Continued

```
{
  class XSLTSample
  {
    [STAThread]
    static void Main(string[] args)
    {
      XslTransform xslTransform = new XslTransform();
      XPathDocument xpathDocument = new XPathDocument("../../sample.xml");
      XmlTextWriter xmlTextWriter = new XmlTextWriter("../../sample.html", null);
      xslTransform.Load("../../sample.xslt");
      xslTransform.Transform(xpathDocument, null, xmlTextWriter);
    }
  }
}
```

Let's discuss it step by step:

- First, we created an instance of the XslTransform class (System.Xml.Xsl namespace).

- Following that we created XPathDocument and initialized it with our XML document (sample.xml). XPathDocument will be used during the transformation process as source for the Transform() method.

- The next step is instantiation of the XmlTextWriter class. We've initialized it with the filename of the location where resulting HTML should be written (sample.html).

- In the next step, we initialized an instance of the XslTransform class with the file that contains the XSLT template (sample.xslt).

- Finally, we invoked the Transform() method of XslTransform class and passed to it the XPathDocument class's instance and the XmlTextWriter class's instance that were created earlier.

After the example has been executed, we can view the HTML file generated as a result of the transformation (see Figure 8.1).

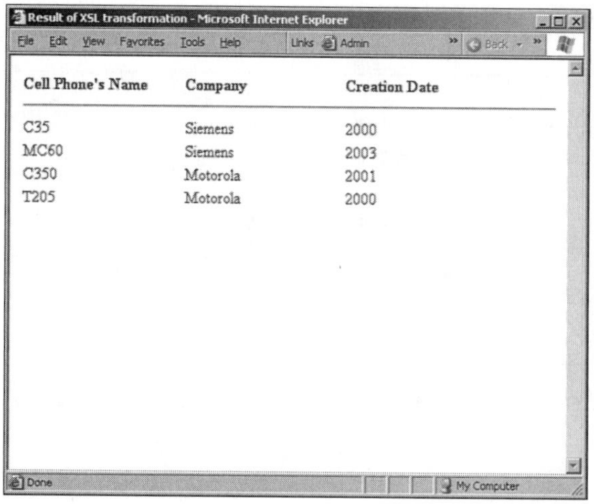

FIGURE 8.1   The generated HTML file.

Serialization XML Style

XML serialization enables us to transform an instance of some class to XML and vice versa. Developers often need to perform XML serialization.

Using Basic XML Serialization

Listing 8.12 presents an example of XML serialization. In this example, there is a simple class that needs to be serialized: CellPhone. The first step is to create an instance of the class XmlSerializer and initialize is with the type XMLSerializationSample.CellPhone. Next, the CellPhone class is instantiated and the properties set to the desired values. Finally, the Serialize method is invoked and the CellPhone is serialized.

LISTING 8.12
XML Serialization Example

```
using System;
using System.Xml.Serialization;
namespace XMLSerializationSample
{
  public class CellPhone
  {
    public CellPhone ()
    {
```

8

Serialization XML Style

LISTING 8.12
Continued

```
        }
        public string Name
        {
                get {return this._name;}
                set {this._name = value;}
        }
        public int Year
        {
                get {return this._year;}
                set {this._year = value;}
        }
        public string Description
        {
                get {return this._description;}
                set {this._description = value;}
        }
        private string _name = "";
        private int _year = 2000;
        private string _description = "";
    }
    class XMLSerializationSample
    {
      [STAThread]
      static void Main(string[] args)
      {
        XmlSerializer serializer = new
Xmlizer(Type.GetType("XMLSerializationSample.CellPhone"));
        CellPhone cellPhone = new CellPhone();
        cellPhone.Description = "Some description";
        cellPhone.Name = "MC60";
        serializer.Serialize(Console.Out, cellPhone);
      }
    }
}
```

The result of the example's run is shown in Listing 8.13.

LISTING 8.13
Generated XML Document Based on Listing 8.12

```
<?xml version="1.0" encoding="cp866"?>
<CellPhone xmlns:xsd=
```

LISTING 8.13
Continued

```
"http://www.w3.org/2001/XMLSchema" xmlns:xsi="http://www.w3.org/2001/XMLSchema-
instance">
  <Name>MC60</Name>
  <Year>2000</Year>
  <Description>Some description</Description>
</CellPhone>
```

The following lines show us how to deserialize XML by using `Deserialize()` method:

```
XmlSerializer serializer =
  new XmlSerializer(Type.GetType("XMLSerializationSample.CellPhone"));
CellPhone anotherCellPhone =
  (CellPhone) serializer.Deserialize(new XmlTextReader("cellphone.xml"));
Console.WriteLine(anotherCellPhone.Description);
```

Customizing XML Serialization

In the preceding section, you learned how to serialize an object by using `XmlSerialization`. This section shows you how to customize this class. For example, suppose that you need to represent a public property of a class not as an XML element, but as an XML attribute. However, the standard serialization process converts public properties into XML elements only. Therefore, you will need to customize the serialization process to accomplish your goal.

There are several predefined metadata attributes in .NET that enable us to customize serialization. They control how classes are mapped to XML and contain auxiliary information for `Serialize()` and `Deserialize()` methods of the `XmlSerializer` class. Each attribute customizes how `XmlSerializer` maps a class, field, or property to an XML document. The attributes can also declare types that are not explicitly referenced in a source file.

Now let's tune the source code defined in Listing 8.12 by adding serialization attributes to the class and properties definitions (Listing 8.14).

LISTING 8.14
Using Attributes for Customizing XML Serialization

```
using System;

using System.Xml.Serialization;
namespace XMLSerializationSample {
  [XmlRoot("cell-phone")]
```

8

Serialization XML Style

LISTING 8.14
Continued

```
public class CellPhone {
  public CellPhone () {
  }
  [XmlAttribute("name")]
  public string Name {
        get {return this._name;}
        set {this._name = value;}
  }
  [XmlAttribute("year")]
  public int Year {
        get {return this._year;}
        set {this._year = value;}
  }
  [XmlElement("description")]
  public string Description {
        get {return this._description;}
        set {this._description = value;}
  }
  private string _name = "";
  private int _year = 2000;
  private string _description = "";
}
class XMLSerializationSample {
  [STAThread]
  static void Main(string[] args) {
    XmlSerializer serializer =
      new XmlSerializer(Type.GetType("XMLSerializationSample.CellPhone"));
    CellPhone cellPhone = new CellPhone();
    cellPhone.Description = "Some description";
    cellPhone.Name = "MC60";
    serializer.Serialize(Console.Out, cellPhone);
  }
}
}
```

As you can see, the definition of the CellPhone class has changed in the following way:

▶ The XmlRoot attribute was added ([XmlRoot("cell-phone")]) before the class declaration; now the root element of XML will be cell-phone.

▶ The XmlAttribute attributes were added before the Name and Year properties ([XmlAttribute("name")], [XmlAttribute("year")]). They will be defined in the XML as attributes of the cell-phone node.

- ▶ The Description property has been declared with the attribute XmlElement ([XmlElement("description")]). In the resulting XML document, the description node will be presented inside the cell-phone node.

Listing 8.15 shows the result of running the example described in Listing 8.14.

LISTING 8.15
XML Generated After Customizing XML Serialization

```
<?xml version="1.0" encoding="cp866"?>
<cell-phone xmlns:xsd="http://www.w3.org/2001/XMLSchema"
  xmlns:xsi="http://www.w3.org/2001/XMLSchema-instance" name="MC60" year="2000">
  <description>Some description</description>
</cell-phone>
```

Summary

In this chapter, you learned that the .NET Framework is a very powerful toolkit for working with XML documents. In addition, you learned the main rules for working with XML DOM technology. You also reviewed the following questions: What is XML DOM? What does XML DOM stand for? And how do you work with XML nodes by using XML DOM classes?

From these discussions, you could draw the conclusion that the XML DOM technology enables you to read, edit, and create XML documents and save them into memory. In addition, the XML DOM helped you to traverse an XML document and locate its attributes, nodes, and other elements with different types.

The next topic discussed in this chapter was XPath. XPath enables you to build queries for searching an XML document's nodes. Finally, you learned how to use the built-in XML serialization functionality as well as how to customize the way in which the document is serialized.

Further Reading

XML Unleashed by Michael Morrison, Sams Publishing. ISBN: 0-672-31514-9.

XML By Example by Benoît Marchal, Que Publishing. ISBN: 0-7897-2242-9.

Inside XML by Steven Holzner, New Riders Publishing. ISBN: 0-7357-1020-1.

9 Multithreaded Programming

IN BRIEF

This chapter illustrates the benefits of multithreaded programming, as well as the technical details involved in using threads in your applications. The first section talks about the basics of multithreaded programming. You will learn how to create, pause, join, stop, and terminate threads. Next, the chapter illustrates thread synchronization in depth. You will learn why you need to synchronize threads and the various methods of doing so. Finally, you will see examples of the use of the thread pool class. You will learn how to create worker threads and post work items to a thread pool.

WHAT YOU NEED

RECOMMENDED SOFTWARE	.NET Framework C#.NET environment
RECOMMENDED HARDWARE	.NET-enabled desktop client
SKILLS REQUIRED	C# coding

MULTITHREADED PROGRAMMING AT A GLANCE

Thread Basics   **185**

Understanding the Key Thread Properties and Methods	185
Explaining the `ThreadStart` Delegate	187
Creating a Thread	188
Running a Thread	188

Terminating a Thread	188
Suspending a Thread	191
Creating a Pause by "Sleeping" a Thread	191
Joining a Thread	191

Synchronization   **192**

| Understanding the Different Types of Synchronization | 193 |

Applying the `lock` Keyword   **193**

Raising Thread Events	194
Using the `Mutex` Class	196
Using the `Monitor` Class	198

| Safeguarding Variables (`Interlocked` Increment/Decrement) | 203 |
| Reading Without Waiting (`ReaderWriterLock`) | 203 |

Using the Thread Pool for Asynchronous Programming   **206**

| Explaining the `WaitCallback` Delegate | 206 |

| Queuing a Work Item | 207 |
| Passing Data to Threads | 208 |

Further Reading   **209**

Thread Basics

A *thread* is a logical unit of execution for a program. The use of multiple threads in an application enables the programmer to create a more pleasurable experience for the user. Before getting into the details of how to employ the use of threads, you will learn some of the more important properties and methods of the thread class. In the following sections, you will learn how to create, run, join, stop, suspend, and pause a thread.

Understanding the Key Thread Properties and Methods

The thread class has several key properties. These properties enable you to control the basic makeup of a thread class. Table 9.1 is a list of some of the more important properties.

TABLE 9.1

Notable Members of the `Thread` class

Property	Description
ApartmentState	This property indicates whether the thread runs in a single-threaded (STA) or multi-threaded (MTA) apartment.
CurrentThread	This is a static read-only property that returns the currently active or running thread.
IsAlive	This property returns true if the thread has not been terminated or aborted; otherwise, it returns false.
IsBackground	This property returns true if the thread is a background thread; otherwise, it returns false.
IsThreadPoolThread	This method returns true if the thread is a member of a managed thread pool; otherwise, it returns false.
Name	This property enables the user to either get or set the name of the thread. This is a write-once field.
Priority	This property enables the user to set the priority of a thread. It can be one of the following values: ThreadPriority.Highest, ThreadPriority.AboveNormal, ThreadPriority.Normal, ThreadPriority.BelowNormal, or ThreadPriority.Lowest.
ThreadState	This property enables the user to get the state of the thread.

TIP

A background thread is essentially the same thing as a foreground thread, but with one exception: An active foreground thread prevents a process from closing, whereas a background thread does not. When a process terminates, it waits for all foreground threads to terminate and then issues an abort to all background threads.

Thread Basics

TIP

Setting the name of a thread can be very useful when debugging a multithreaded application so that you can distinguish one thread from another. For example, if you issue `Debug.WriteLine` statements, providing the name of the thread from which the debug statement originated can be invaluable while stepping through an application.

TIP

Because this property has a `Flags` attribute, it can contain multiple values. To see whether a specific value is contained in this field, perform a bitwise comparison.

Table 9.2 contains a listing of `ThreadState` values.

TABLE 9.2

`ThreadState` Listing

State	Description	Value
Aborted	The thread has been aborted and is currently in the stopped state.	256
AbortRequested	A request to have this thread aborted has been made, but has not yet been processed.	128
Background	The thread is marked as a background thread.	4
Running	The thread is in the started state.	0
Stopped	The thread has been stopped.	16
StopRequested	**This is for internal use only.** A stop request has been issued to the thread.	1
Suspended	The thread is suspended.	64
SuspendRequested	A request has been made to suspend the thread.	2
Unstarted	The thread has not yet been started. The processor has not been requested to schedule the thread for execution.	8
WaitSleepJoin	The thread is being blocked as a result of a call to one of the following methods: `Wait`, `Sleep`, or `Join`.	32

In addition to these properties, several key methods are used to control the flow of threads. Those methods are listed here:

▶ Abort—This method raises a `ThreadAbortException` exception to cause the thread to terminate.

9

> **TIP**
>
> Although it is possible to catch a `ThreadAbortException` exception and perform some logging or other functions, it cannot be suppressed. The system will automatically raise the exception again at the end of the catch. The only way to cancel this exception is to use the `Thread.ResetAbort` method.

- ▶ `Interrupt`—This method causes a thread that is in a `WaitSleepJoin` state to be interrupted; otherwise, it waits for the thread to be placed in this state before interrupting it.

- ▶ `Join`—This method blocks the calling thread indefinitely until it terminates. This method cannot be used on a thread that is in the `ThreadState.Unstarted` state.

- ▶ `ResetAbort`—This method cancels a pending `Thread.Abort` command on the current thread.

- ▶ `Resume`—This method causes a suspended thread to resume execution.

- ▶ `Sleep`—This method causes the thread to be blocked for a specified period of time. A value of `0` indicates that the thread should be suspended to allow other threads to process. A value of `Infinite` suspends the thread indefinitely.

- ▶ `SpinWait`—This method causes a thread to wait *n* number of cycles before resuming.

- ▶ `Start`—This method causes a thread to be placed in the `ThreadState.Running` state and allows the processor to schedule it for execution. This method will not restart a thread that has been terminated.

- ▶ `Suspend`—This method suspends the thread from execution. It does not have any effect on a thread that is already suspended.

- ▶ `VolatileRead`—This method reads the latest value of a field regardless of how many processors are used. This method affects only single memory access.

- ▶ `VolatileWrite`—This method writes the value of a field immediately. This is done to make sure that it is not cached and is available to all processors.

Explaining the `ThreadStart` Delegate

A `ThreadStart` delegate is a wrapper around the program code that is to be executed by the thread. It is used as the only parameter passed during the creation of an instance of the `Thread` object. As with all delegates, it must contain the same parameters as the delegate declaration. You can create a `ThreadStart` delegate like this:

```
ThreadStart workerThreadStart = new ThreadStart(SimpleWorkerThreadMethod);
```

Thread Basics

Creating a Thread

You can use a Thread object to create a new instance of a thread to run a portion of the code associated with a process. However, before running a thread, you must first gain an instance of a Thread. Obtaining an instance of a thread can be accomplished in two ways. The first way is by creating a new instance of the thread class and passing in the ThreadStart delegate:

```
Thread workerThread = new Thread(workerThreadStart);
```

The second way is to use the static property CurrentThread from the thread class:

```
Thread workerThread = Thread.CurrentThread;
```

Running a Thread

Running a thread is done by calling the Start method on an instance of a Thread object:

```
workerThread.Start();
```

This causes the operating system to place the thread into a running state. When the thread is in a running state, the operating system can schedule it for execution.

Terminating a Thread

There are two ways that a thread can terminate. The first way is for the method that is wrapped by the ThreadStart delegate to finish its execution. This is demonstrated in the following code fragment:

```
public static void SimpleWorkerThreadMethod()
{
  Console.WriteLine("Hello from the worker thread.");
}
```

In this case, the thread will terminate immediately after the call to Console.WriteLine. The second case is when a thread receives a ThreadAbortException exception. In this case, a thread will always terminate. As you can see, there is an infinite loop in the following code sample:

```
public static void SimpleWorkerThreadMethod()
{
  for(int i=0; ; i++)
  {
    Console.WriteLine("Hello from the worker thread.");
```

```
  }
}
```

Under normal circumstances, this thread would never terminate. If you were to call this method from your main thread, the program would never terminate and you would have to kill the process. However, if you were to call this method from a separate thread, you could call the `Thread.Abort` method, which would cause the thread to terminate by throwing a `ThreadAbortException` ■1 exception and thereby breaking out of the loop. This is demonstrated in Listing 9.1.

LISTING 9.1
Sample Thread Application

```
using System;
using System.Threading;

namespace SimpleThreadSample
{
  /// <summary>
  /// This class demonstrates the basic use of threads.
  /// </summary>
  class SimpleAbortThreadClass
  {
    [STAThread]
    static void Main(string[] args)
    {
      // Create the ThreadStart delegate.
      Console.WriteLine("{Main Thread} Creating the thread start delegate.");
      ThreadStart workerThreadStart = new ThreadStart(SimpleWorkerThreadMethod);
      // Pass the ThreadStart delegate to the Thread in the Thread constructor.
      Console.WriteLine("{Main Thread} Creating the worker thread.");
      Thread workerThread = new Thread(workerThreadStart);
      // Start the thread.
      Console.WriteLine("{Main Thread} Starting the worker thread.");
      workerThread.Start();
      Console.ReadLine();
      workerThread.Abort();
      Console.WriteLine("{Main Thread} Aborting worker thread.");
      workerThread.Join();
      Console.WriteLine("{Main Thread} Worker Thread Terminated.");
      Console.ReadLine();
    }

    public static void SimpleWorkerThreadMethod()
    {
```

9

Thread Basics

LISTING 9.1
Continued

```
    for(int i=0; ; i++)
    {
      try
      {
        Console.WriteLine("Hello from the worker thread.");
      }
      catch(Exception e)
      {
        Console.WriteLine(e.ToString() + " Exception caught.");
      }
    }
  }
}
```

Notice that in the `SimpleWorkerThreadMethod` method, the inside of the infinite loop is wrapped in an exception handler that catches all exceptions. This would typically catch any exception that occurs and suppress this error. But because the `ThreadAbortException` exception is a special case that cannot be suppressed, the exception is automatically rethrown after the exception handler. This causes the thread to terminate. The only way that this exception can be suppressed is to catch it and then call the `Thread.AbortReset` method. This is demonstrated by the following code sample:

```
public static void SimpleWorkerThreadMethod()
{
  for(int i=0; ; i++)
  {
    try
    {
      Console.WriteLine("Hello from the worker thread.");
    }
    catch(Exception e)
    {
      Console.WriteLine(e.ToString() + " Exception caught.");
      Thread.AbortReset();
    }
  }
}
```

Suspending a Thread

When a thread is suspended, it is no longer scheduled by the processor for execution. It is simply waiting to be reawakened by some outside force. A thread can be suspended by simply calling the `Thread.Suspend` method.

```
workerThread.Suspend();
```

When the `Thread.Suspend` method is called, the thread is suspended and no longer executing. To cause the thread to continue again, the `Thread.Resume` method must be called:

```
workerThread.Resume();
```

Creating a Pause by "Sleeping" a Thread

When a thread is sleeping, it is simply blocked from execution for a specified period of time and is said to be in a `WaitSleepJoin` state. The `WaitSleepJoin` state will be explained in further detail in the next section. To place a thread in a sleeping state, simply call the `Thread.Sleep` method and pass the time for the thread to sleep, in milliseconds, to the method as its only parameter:

```
workerThread.Sleep(1000);
```

Passing in a 0 as the timeout causes the thread to be suspended, which allows other threads time to execute. Passing the keyword `Infinite` causes the thread to be blocked indefinitely. After the specified period of time, the thread is released and processing continues.

Joining a Thread

Calling the `Thread.Join` method causes the calling thread to enter the `WaitSleepJoin` state and to be blocked until the thread instance (shown in the example that follows as *workerThread*) is terminated. If the thread does not terminate, the calling thread will be blocked indefinitely. To join a thread, simply call the `Thread.Join` method:

```
workerThread.Join();
```

This method should be used when it is necessary to wait for a thread to terminate before continuing to process **2**. Listing 9.2 demonstrates waiting for a thread to terminate before allowing the program to finish:

9

Thread Basics

LISTING 9.2
A Simple Thread Class

```csharp
using System;
using System.Threading;

namespace SimpleThreadSample
{
  /// <summary>
  // This class demonstrates the basic use of threads.
  /// </summary>
  class SimpleThreadClass
  {
    [STAThread]
    static void Main(string[] args)
    {
      // Create the ThreadStart delegate.
      Console.WriteLine("{Main Thread} Creating the thread start delegate.");
      ThreadStart workerThreadStart = new ThreadStart(SimpleWorkerThreadMethod);

      // Pass the ThreadStart delegate to the Thread in the Thread constructor.
      Console.WriteLine("{Main Thread} Creating the worker thread.");
      Thread workerThread = new Thread(workerThreadStart);

      // Start the thread.
      Console.WriteLine("{Main Thread} Starting the worker thread.");
      workerThread.Start();
      workerThread.Join();
    }

    public static void SimpleWorkerThreadMethod()
    {
      Console.WriteLine("Hello from the worker thread.");
    }
  }
}
```

Synchronization

With the introduction of Win32 came preemptive multitasking. *Preemptive multitasking* means that a thread may be interrupted at any time to allow another thread to process. This happens without regard to the state of the thread. This also means that if one thread is trying to write to a variable and another thread is trying to read that same variable, the outcome can be indeterminate. Imagine raising an apple to eat it and at the same time you begin to take a bite, someone else shoves his head in there and takes a bite first. Besides potentially getting an unexpected taste of human hair, the result is that you don't get what you wanted or expected. If you don't employ some sort of synchronization scheme in your multithreaded applications, this is essentially the same problem that can occur. In this section, you will see and use the different synchronization types and the ways that they are implemented in .NET.

Understanding the Different Types of Synchronization

As with everything, there are many ways to accomplish the same task. Each way takes a different approach, and with each approach comes some advantages and disadvantages. The same holds true with the different synchronization schemes. Table 9.3 lists the four basic types of synchronization and the corresponding .NET class that uses each scheme.

TABLE 9.3

Win32 Basic Synchronization Types

Synchronization Type	Description	Corresponding .NET Class(es)
Mutex	A `mutex` synchronization prevents more then one thread from accessing a shared resource at a time.	`Mutex`
Critical Section	A critical section synchronization does the same thing as a `mutex`, but with one exception: It does not work across processes.	`lock`, `Monitor`, `Interlocked`, `ReaderWriterLock`
Semaphore	A semaphore synchronization limits the number of threads that can access the same shared resource.	None
Event	An event synchronization can signal other threads to perform specific actions.	`AutoResetEvent`, `ManualResetEvent`, `WaitHandle`

9

Applying the `lock` Keyword

One of the simpler synchronization techniques to employ is the `lock` keyword, which offers an easy way to protect a resource. Similar to the `Monitor` class, the `lock` keyword employs the critical section technique to protect a resource. The `lock` keyword takes one parameter:

```
lock(object obj)
```

Applying the lock Keyword

This parameter is an object and as such must be a reference type, not a value type. To protect a resource using the lock keyword, simply wrap the code in a lock block. The following code demonstrates how to lock a section of code:

```
lock(this)
{
  // Resource Protected Code
  counterVariable++;
}
```

Raising Thread Events

Introduced in Win32, events were used to synchronize threads by signaling other threads that it was okay to proceed with processing. This scheme is typically used when one thread needs to wait on another one to complete its task before proceeding. In .NET, two classes have been introduced to handle events: AutoResetEvent and ManualResetEvent. Both classes do exactly the same thing, with one exception. AutoResetEvent resets the signaled state of the event to unsignaled when another waiting thread is released. In contrast, ManualResetEvent does exactly what its name implies: It waits until the event is manually reset before changing the signaled state to unsignaled. To wait for the event to be signaled, either the WaitOne, WaitAny, or WaitAll method must be called. After any one of these methods has been called, the calling thread is placed in the WaitSleepJoin state and is blocked until the event is signaled or a timeout occurs. Listing 9.3 demonstrates how to wait on an event to occur before proceeding **3**.

LISTING 9.3
Waiting for an Event

```
using System;
using System.Threading;

namespace EventClass
{
  public class ClassCounter
  {
    protected int m_iCounter = 0;

    public void Increment()
    {
      m_iCounter++;
    }

    public int Counter
    {
```

LISTING 9.3
Continued

```
      get
      {
        return m_iCounter;
      }
    }
  }

  public class EventClass
  {
    protected ClassCounter m_protectedResource = new ClassCounter();
    protected ManualResetEvent m_manualResetEvent = new ManualResetEvent(false);
    protected void ThreadOneMethod()                                         3
    {
      m_manualResetEvent.WaitOne();
      m_protectedResource.Increment();
      int iValue = m_protectedResource.Counter;
      System.Console.WriteLine(
        "{Thread One} - Current value of counter: " + iValue.ToString());
    }

    protected void ThreadTwoMethod()
    {
      int iValue = m_protectedResource.Counter;
      System.Console.WriteLine(
        "{Thread Two} - Current value of counter: " + iValue.ToString());
      m_manualResetEvent.Set();
    }

    [STAThread]
    static void Main(string[] args)
    {
      EventClass exampleClass = new EventClass();

      Thread threadOne = new Thread(new ThreadStart(exampleClass.ThreadOneMethod));
      Thread threadTwo = new Thread(new ThreadStart(exampleClass.ThreadTwoMethod));

      threadOne.Start();
      threadTwo.Start();
      System.Console.ReadLine();
    }
  }
}
```

9

Applying the `lock` Keyword

You should run the code in Listing 9.3 to get a good idea for how it works. In short, the first thread will wait for the second thread to signal once (using `WaitOne`) manually before it continues. Therefore, the second thread will report a lower value than the first thread.

Using the `Mutex` Class

`Mutex` is a special synchronization class that not only allows threads to synchronize, but also allows synchronization to take place across processes. Like most synchronization schemes, it allows only one thread to access a resource at a time. `Mutex` has four constructors:

```
Mutex aMutex = new Mutex();
Mutex aMutex = new Mutex(bool initiallyOwned);
Mutex aMutex = new Mutex(bool initiallyOwned, string name);
Mutex aMutex = new Mutex(bool initiallyOwned, string name, out bool createdNew);
```

Each successive constructor builds upon the previous constructor's parameters. The first constructor does not take any parameters and creates an unnamed mutex that does not acquire ownership to that mutex. The second constructor adds a Boolean parameter that indicates whether or not the mutex should acquire ownership upon construction. The third constructor introduces the concept of naming a mutex. This is useful when creating a mutex for interprocess synchronization. Finally, the fourth constructor adds a Boolean parameter that indicates whether or not ownership of the mutex was successfully acquired after construction. This parameter is an out parameter and, as such, is passed uninitialized. The following example demonstrates how to use a mutex to guarantee that only one instance of an application can exist at a time. To create a single-instance application, we must first create a mutex:

```
Mutex singleInstanceMutex = new Mutex(true, "Single Instance Application", out
isOwned);
```

After the mutex has been created, the code must check whether the `isOwned` property is set to true. If it is set to true, you know that there are no other instances of this application running and you can continue to start the application. If the `isOwned` property is set to false, you know that another instance is running and you must therefore terminate this new instance. Listing 9.4 demonstrates how to create a single-instance application by placing the mutex construction in the `Main` section of the code.

LISTING 9.4
Single Instance Application Using a `Mutex` Class

```
[STAThread]
static void Main()
{
```

LISTING 9.4
Continued

```
bool isOwned;
// The next line assumes that System.Threading is declared in the using section.
Mutex singleInstanceMutex =
  new Mutex(true, "Single Instance Application", out isOwned);
try
{
  if(isOwned)
    Application.Run(new Form1());
}
finally
{
  if(isOwned)
    singleInstanceMutex.ReleaseMutex();
}
}
```

As shown in the previous example, the mutex can be used to determine whether another thread or process owns the given mutex. If another thread or process owns the mutex, the code can assume that the mutex is already being used. You might be wondering what your code would do if it needs to wait for mutex ownership to be released. Fortunately, .NET adds a method named `Mutex.WaitOne` to the `Mutex` class. `Mutex.WaitOne` is an overloaded method that has three forms:

```
public virtual void Mutex.WaitOne();
```

```
public virtual bool Mutex.WaitOne(int millisecondTimeout, bool exitContext);
```

```
public virtual bool Mutex.WaitOne(TimeSpan timeout, bool exitContext);
```

The `millisecondTimeout` parameter specifies the time the thread should wait to receive a signal. The `exitContext` parameter specifies whether the thread should first exit a synchronization context before trying to reacquire it. This essentially means that if the thread currently owns the context, it should release it first, which could allow another thread to take ownership, and then wait until it can reacquire ownership before proceeding. The `timeout` parameter is the same as `millisecondTimeout`, except it uses a TimeSpan class instead of raw milliseconds, making for easier-to-read code. Listing 9.5 demonstrates how to wait **4** until it is safe to access a mutex-protected resource.

Applying the `lock` Keyword

LISTING 9.5
Waiting on a Mutex

```
Mutex testMutex = new Mutex(false, "Test Mutex");
try
{
    // Wait until a signal is received before moving on.
    testMutex.WaitOne();
}
finally
{
//   We own the Mutex, so we must release it.
    testMutex.ReleaseMutex();
}
```

Using the `Monitor` Class

The capability for a process to restrict or lock access to a section of code is commonly known as a *critical section*. The `Monitor` class gives you the ability to use critical sections to control access to a section of code by granting a lock to a single thread. Similar to the `lock` keyword, the `Monitor` class provides a simple mechanism to lock a section of code. Simply wrap the code to be protected in a `Monitor.Enter` / `Monitor.Exit` code block, as illustrated in Listing 9.6. Both the `Monitor.Enter` and the `Monitor.Exit` methods take one parameter.

```
Monitor.Enter(object obj);
Monitor.Exit(object obj);
```

This parameter is the object in which to acquire the `Monitor` lock. Because the `Monitor` class is used to lock objects, this parameter must be a reference type, not a value type.

LISTING 9.6
Using the `Monitor` Class

```
using System;
using System.Threading;

namespace SimpleMonitorClass
{
  public class ClassCounter
  {
    protected int m_iCounter = 0;

    public void Increment()
```

LISTING 9.6
Continued

```
      {
        m_iCounter++;
      }

      public int Counter
      {
        get
        {
          return m_iCounter;
        }
      }
    }

    public class SimpleMonitorClass
    {
      protected ClassCounter m_protectedResource = new ClassCounter();

      protected void IncrementProtectedResourceMethod()
      {
        Monitor.Enter(m_protectedResource);
        try
        {
          m_protectedResource.Increment();
        }
        finally
        {
          Monitor.Exit(m_protectedResource);
        }
      }

      [STAThread]
      static void Main(string[] args)
      {
        SimpleMonitorClass exampleClass = new SimpleMonitorClass();
        exampleClass.IncrementProtectedResourceMethod();
      }
    }
}
```

Using the Monitor class in the fashion illustrated in Listing 9.6 **5** is essentially the same thing as using the lock keyword. However, unlike the lock keyword, the Monitor class also employs the TryEnter, Wait, Pulse, and PulseAll methods.

Applying the lock Keyword

The difference between the TryEnter and the Enter methods is simple: The Enter method waits indefinitely for the lock to the protected section to be released before returning, whereas the TryEnter method returns immediately, regardless of whether the lock was acquired. The Monitor.TryEnter method is an overloaded function that has three forms:

```
static bool Monitor.TryEnter(object obj);


static bool Monitor.TryEnter(object obj, int millisecondTimeout);


static bool Monitor.TryEnter(object obj, TimeSpan timeout);
```

The obj parameter is the same as the one used in the Monitor.Enter method. millisecondTimeout is the time in milliseconds to wait to acquire the lock before returning. The same holds true for the timeout parameter, except that it is the time specified by the TimeSpan object. On all three methods, the Boolean return value indicates whether the lock was acquired before returning. The following code fragment illustrates the use of the Monitor.TryEnter method:

```
protected void IncrementProtectedResourceMethod()
{
    if(Monitor.TryEnter(m_protectedResource) == true)
    {
        try
        {
            m_protectedResource.Increment();
        }
        finally
        {
            Monitor.Exit(m_protectedResource);
        }
    }
}
```

Both the Monitor.Pulse and the Monitor.PulseAll methods take threads that are waiting on the protected resource and are in the WaitSleepJoin state and place them in the Started state. This allows those threads to prepare to continue executing after the lock has been acquired. Along with the Monitor.Pulse and Monitor.PulseAll methods is the Monitor.Wait method. This method allows a thread to release a lock, if one has already been acquired, and to wait until another thread signals that it has completed its processing using the protected resource. The Monitor.Wait method has five overloaded methods:

```
static bool Monitor.Wait(object obj);


static bool Monitor.Wait (object obj, int millisecondTimeout);


static bool Monitor.Wait (object obj, TimeSpan timeout);


static bool Monitor.Wait (object obj, int millisecondTimeout, bool exitContext);


static bool Monitor.Wait (object obj, TimeSpan timeout, bool exitContext);
```

The first three methods have identical parameters to the Monitor.TryEnter method and function the same way. The last two methods take an additional Boolean parameter called exitContext. This parameter indicates whether to exit the synchronization context before attempting to reacquire it. Listing 9.7 demonstrates how to properly use the Monitor.Wait and Monitor.PulseAll methods.

LISTING 9.7
Waiting and Pulsing Using the Monitor Class

```
using System;
using System.Threading;

namespace MonitorPulseClass
{
  public class ClassCounter
  {
    protected int m_iCounter = 0;

    public void Increment()
    {
      m_iCounter++;
    }

    public int Counter
    {
      get
      {
        return m_iCounter;
      }
    }
  }

  public class MonitorPulseClass
```

Applying the lock Keyword

LISTING 9.7
Continued

```
{
  protected ClassCounter m_protectedResource = new ClassCounter();

  protected void ThreadOneMethod()
  {
    lock(m_protectedResource)
    {
      Monitor.Wait(m_protectedResource);
      m_protectedResource.Increment();
      int iValue = m_protectedResource.Counter;
      System.Console.WriteLine(
        "{Thread One} - Current value of counter: " + iValue.ToString());
    }
  }

  protected void ThreadTwoMethod()
  {
    lock(m_protectedResource)
    {
      int iValue = m_protectedResource.Counter;
      System.Console.WriteLine(
        "{Thread Two} - Current value of counter: " + iValue.ToString());
      Monitor.PulseAll(m_protectedResource);
    }
  }

  [STAThread]
  static void Main(string[] args)
  {
    MonitorPulseClass exampleClass = new MonitorPulseClass();

    Thread threadOne = new Thread(new ThreadStart(exampleClass.ThreadOneMethod));
    Thread threadTwo = new Thread(new ThreadStart(exampleClass.ThreadTwoMethod));

    threadOne.Start();
    threadTwo.Start();
    System.Console.ReadLine();
  }
}
}
```

As shown in Listing 9.7, the Monitor.Wait and Monitor.PulseAll methods are wrapped in a lock block. This is necessary because these methods, along with the Monitor.Pulse method, must be called from a synchronized section of code or an exception will be thrown.

Safeguarding Variables (Interlocked Increment/Decrement)

For simple operations such as incrementing, decrementing, or exchanging values of a variable, .NET introduces the Interlocked class. This class prevents synchronization problems by allowing these operations to take place as an atomic operation. It is also a handy shortcut and cuts down on the amount of synchronized code that you have to write if all you need to do is perform simple operations in a synchronized context. The following code fragment demonstrates how to use this class:

```
public void DemonstrateInterlocked()
{
    // Increment value 1
    Interlocked.Increment(ref m_integerValue1);
    // Decrement value 2
    Interlocked.Decrement(ref m_integerValue2);
    // Sets variable 1 to the value of variable 2 and returns the original value.
    int orignalValue = Interlocked.Exchange(ref m_integerValue1, m_integerValue2);
}
```

To check whether a value is the same before exchanging, use the Interlocked.CompareExchange method instead.

Reading Without Waiting (ReaderWriterLock)

Synchronization problems arise when one thread is in the process of changing a variable's value at the same time that another thread is either trying to do the same or is reading the value. This can cause unpredictable results and is generally a bad thing. Most of the other synchronization techniques discussed in this chapter prevent this by blocking a thread from performing an operation while another thread is executing the section of code that is being protected. If all these threads are simply reading the protected values, the code is blocking the other threads needlessly. To overcome this challenge, .NET uses the ReaderWriterLock class. This enables us to block other threads only when a protected variable is being updated. Listing 9.8 demonstrates the use of the ReaderWriterLock class.

9

Applying the lock Keyword

LISTING 9.8
Reading a Value Without Waiting

```
using System;
using System.Threading;

namespace ReaderWriterClass
{
  public class ReaderWriterClass
  {
    protected ReaderWriterLock m_rwLock = new ReaderWriterLock();
    protected int m_counter = 0;
    protected int m_readerBlocks = 0;
    protected int m_writerBlocks = 0;

    protected void ThreadOneMethod()
    {
      for(int i=0; i<200; i++)
      {
        try
        {
          m_rwLock.AcquireReaderLock(0);
          try
          {
            System.Console.WriteLine(m_counter);
          }
          finally
          {
            m_rwLock.ReleaseReaderLock();
          }
        }
        catch(Exception)
        {
          Interlocked.Increment(ref m_readerBlocks);
        }
      }
    }

    protected void ThreadTwoMethod()
    {
      for(int i=0; i<100; i++)
      {
        try
        {
          m_rwLock.AcquireWriterLock(0);
```

LISTING 9.8
Continued

```
        try
        {
          Interlocked.Increment(ref m_counter);
        }
        finally
        {
          m_rwLock.ReleaseWriterLock();
        }
      }
      catch(Exception)
      {
        Interlocked.Increment(ref m_writerBlocks);
      }

      Thread.Sleep(1);
    }
  }

  public int ReaderBlocks
  {
    get
    {
      return m_readerBlocks;
    }
  }

  public int WriterBlocks
  {
    get
    {
      return m_writerBlocks;
    }
  }

  [STAThread]
  static void Main(string[] args)
  {
    ReaderWriterClass exampleClass = new ReaderWriterClass();

    Thread threadOne = new Thread(new ThreadStart(exampleClass.ThreadOneMethod));
    Thread threadTwo = new Thread(new ThreadStart(exampleClass.ThreadTwoMethod));
```

Applying the `lock` Keyword

LISTING 9.8
Continued

```
        threadOne.Start();
        threadTwo.Start();

        // Wait for both threads to finish before proceeding.
        threadOne.Join();
        threadTwo.Join();
        // Print out the results
        System.Console.WriteLine(
          "Reader Blocks {0}, Writer Blocks {1}" ,
          exampleClass.ReaderBlocks, exampleClass.WriterBlocks);
        System.Console.ReadLine();
      }
    }
}
```

Using the Thread Pool for Asynchronous Programming

Many applications spend a lot of time doing nothing. Nothing, that is, except waiting for some kind of events or special circumstances to occur. After these events or circumstances have occurred, the application awakens, processes the events and then goes back to sleep. To make these tasks more efficient, .NET uses a thread pool. The following section explores the ThreadPool class and how to use it.

Explaining the `WaitCallback` Delegate

Similar to the `ThreadStart` delegate, `WaitCallback` is a wrapper around the program code that is to be executed by a thread pool:

```
WaitCallback workerThreadCallback = new WaitCallback(ThreadPoolWorkerThreadMethod);
```

Unlike the `ThreadStart` delegate, the `WaitCallback` delegate takes one parameter:

```
static void ThreadPoolWorkerThreadMethod(Object stateObject)
{
...
}
```

This parameter is a state object that can be used to pass information to the worker thread.

Queuing a Work Item

In order to use a thread pool, you have to queue work items. To do so, simply call the method `ThreadPool.QueueUserWorkItem` and pass an instantiated `WaitCallback` delegate to this method:

```
ThreadPool.QueueUserWorkItem(new WaitCallback(ThreadPoolThreadMethod));
```

If you need to pass data or state information to a work item, use the overloaded form of the `QueueWorkItem` to pass in the extra information as an object:

```
ThreadPool.QueueUserWorkItem(new WaitCallback(ThreadPoolThreadMethod), stateInforma-
tion);
```

Listing 9.9 demonstrates the use of a simple thread pool. It queues a work item and then waits for the user to press the Enter key before exiting the program. Because the thread pool uses background threads, removing the line of code that waits for the Enter key to be pressed would cause the program to exit before running the thread pool task. This is what is known as a *race condition*.

TIP

Just as bad as synchronization issues, race conditions can wreak havoc on your application. Any time you have a thread executing in the background, you need to make sure that one of two things is possible:

> ► If your application attempts to terminate, your thread will force the application to wait until the thread has completed its task successfully.

> ► If the application terminates, your background thread process can trap the `ThreadAbort` exception and properly dispose of any in-progress work by rolling it back or whatever else needs to be done.

If the background thread fails to handle either of these two cases, your application will be unstable while that thread is running, and will produce inconsistent results every time the application terminates during that thread.

LISTING 9.9
Queuing a Work Item

```
using System;
using System.Threading;

namespace SimpleThreadSample
{
```

Using the Thread Pool for Asynchronous Programming

LISTING 9.9
Continued

```csharp
public class SimpleThreadPool
{
  [STAThread]
  static void Main(string[] args)
  {
    Console.WriteLine("{Main Thread} Queing the work item.");
    ThreadPool.QueueUserWorkItem(new WaitCallback(ThreadPoolThreadMethod));

    Console.WriteLine("{Main Thread} Press the 'Enter' key to exit the process.");
    Console.ReadLine();
    Console.WriteLine("{Main Thread} Exiting the process.");
  }

  static void ThreadPoolThreadMethod(Object stateObject)
  {
    Console.WriteLine("{Thread Pool} Hello Thread Pool.");
  }
}
}
```

Passing Data to Threads

Occasionally, there is a need for a thread to use data or state from an outside section of code. You could use properties or methods to set the values of class-scope variables, but suppose that the thread method is a static method. If this is the case, the method does not have a pointer to the this variable and therefore does not have access to any class-scope variables. To solve this problem, the ThreadPool constructor takes a WaitCallback delegate as a parameter. As you learned earlier in this section, the WaitCallback delegate takes an object as its only parameter. This enables you to pass any information or state to the ThreadPool as an object that will in turn be passed to the thread method. Listing 9.10 demonstrates how to pass a variable to a ThreadPool worker thread **6**.

LISTING 9.10
Passing Data to a Worker Thread

```csharp
using System;
using System.Threading;

namespace SimpleThreadSample
{
  public class SimpleThreadPool
```

LISTING 9.10
Continued

```
{
  [STAThread]
  static void Main(string[] args)
  {
    Console.WriteLine("{Main Thread} Queuing the work item.");
    ThreadPool.QueueUserWorkItem(                                          6
      new WaitCallback(ThreadPoolThreadMethod), "This is a state message");

    Console.WriteLine("{Main Thread} Press the 'Enter' key to exit the process.");
    Console.ReadLine();
    Console.WriteLine("{Main Thread} Exiting the process.");
  }

  static void ThreadPoolThreadMethod(Object stateObject)
  {
    Console.WriteLine(
      "{Thread Pool} The data passed in is '" + stateObject.ToString() + "'");
  }
}
}
```

Summary

This chapter started you off with an introduction to the Thread class and the basic
concepts behind multithreaded programming and how the various Windows operating systems use pre-emptive multitasking. Building on this knowledge, this chapter
covered the core issues surrounding multithreaded programming: synchronization
and thread-safe data. You saw how to use the lock keyword, the Monitor class, and
the Mutex class to provide thread safety for your processes. Finally, this chapter
examined the thread pool as a simplified way of queuing work items.

Further Reading

C# Threading Handbook by Tobin Titus, et al, Wrox Press. ISBN: 1861008295.
(Possibly out of print.)

9

10 Events and Delegates

When developers made the switch from functional programming to object-oriented programming, many things became easier. The Win32 development model relies heavily on the concepts of function pointers and callbacks. In other unmanaged languages, the use of function pointers can be fraught with errors caused by type conversions. Most developers who are familiar with pointer programming are also familiar with the fact that type conversions are always a source of pain and stress.

One of the advantages of C# is how operations related to type conversion can be protected. C# doesn't support pointers to functions, but it does enable developers to use delegates and events for the implementation of callbacks and notifications. A *delegate* is a mechanism of the .NET Framework that is, in a nutshell, a type-safe, managed function pointer.

This chapter explains what delegates are and how to use them in C# applications. The chapter also describes the internal structure of delegates and many of the features related to building event-based systems in C#.

WHAT YOU NEED

RECOMMENDED SOFTWARE	.NET Framework Visual Studio .NET
RECOMMENDED HARDWARE	.NET-enabled desktop client
SKILLS REQUIRED	C# coding

EVENTS AND DELEGATES AT A GLANCE

What Is a Delegate?	210		
Types of Delegates	215	Combined Delegates	219
Delegates Inside	218	Events	221
Summary	226		
Further Reading	226		

What Is a Delegate?

The Common Type System provides the .NET Framework with a standardized way of describing and manipulating data types in a language-agnostic manner. In addition to common types such as integers, strings, dates, bytes and more, the CTS also defines a delegate, making delegates available to C#, Visual Basic .NET, and any other .NET language.

All delegates in the .NET Framework are descendants of the System.Delegate class. A delegate serves as a placeholder for information about a specific method call. As mentioned earlier, a delegate also is a type-safe, managed function pointer.

The following is a list of the steps required to implement delegates in your application. The first step is the declaration of the delegate. You should use the predefined C# keyword `delegate`. The following is an example of declaring a delegate:

```
delegate string SomeDelegate(string someStringValue);
```

This code defines only the new class named `SomeDelegate`. This class declaration defines the method signature for which the delegate will be used. The signature of a method, with respect to declaring delegates, includes the method's return type and its argument list.

> **TIP**
>
> Remember that the delegate is really just a placeholder for an actual method, not a method itself. As such, the name of the delegate can be anything, and doesn't have to match the name of any real method. A recommended guideline is to postfix the name of the delegate with the word `Delegate`.

In this case, the method described by the `SomeDelegate` delegate should return a string value and take one string input parameter (`someStringValue`).

Because a delegate is a class, it can be declared in both the namespace and in some other class. So, both of the code examples in Listing 10.1 are correct.

LISTING 10.1
Declaration of Delegates

```
//Example #1
using System;
        delegate string SomeDelegate(string someStringValue);
        class SomeApplication {
                public static void Main() {
                    ...
                }
}


//Example #2
using System;
class SomeApplication {
        delegate string SomeDelegate (string someStringValue);
        public static void Main() {
                ...
        }
}
```

10

What Is a Delegate?

The second example in Listing 10.1 declares the delegate `SomeDelegate` as a subclass of the other class (`SomeApplication`).

> **NOTE**
>
> In the delegate's declaration (before the keyword `delegate`), you could use an access modifier (`private`, `public`, and so on) in the same way that you can for any other class declaration.

After defining the delegate, the second step is the declaration of a variable that is of the delegate's type. An instance of a delegate works just like any other managed object, so its creation is similar to the creation of any other class:

```
SomeDelegate someDelegate;
```

The preceding code declared the `someDelegate` variable of the type `SomeDelegate`.

The third step is initialization of the delegate's instance. Initialization of the delegate's instance can be performed in the same way as the initialization of an ordinary class; that is, by using the new operator with the delegate's constructor:

```
SomeDelegate someDelegate;
someDelegate = new SomeDelegate([Some Method Name]);
```

Let's discuss the second line of the preceding example. As you can see, we've passed an identifier of the method (`[Some Method Name]`) to the delegate's constructor. So, our delegate's instance will be some kind of pointer to the passed method. The signature of the passed method should be the same as the signature declared by the delegate. In our case, we should pass to the delegate's constructor method with one string input parameter. Also, this method should return a string value.

> **NOTE**
>
> If you are trying to pass a method's identifier to the constructor of an ordinary class, the compiler will return an error of the following format:
>
> ```
> [SomeFile.cs(10:10)]: error CS0654: Method
> "Delegates.SomeApplication.SomeMethod(string)" referenced without parentheses
> ```
>
> The error can be explained in this way: The concept of delegates is supported at the C# syntax level, and this enables us to pass to the delegate's constructors only an identifier for the method (without parameters). But for nondelegate classes, this feature is unavailable.

An instance of the `Delegate` class can be bound both to static and nonstatic methods. When you're trying to bind a `Delegate` with a static method, use the class's name before the method's name. If the name of a class is missing, the compiler uses the name of the class in which the `Delegate` is initialized. When you're trying to bind a `Delegate` with a nonstatic method, you use an instance of a class as the identifier. If the name of an object is missing, the compiler uses the current instance (`this`):

```
someDelegate =
   new SomeDelegate(SomeClassName.SomeStaticMethodName);//static method


someDelegate =
   new SomeDelegate(someInstance.SomeNonStaticMethodName);//non static method
```

The final step in the process of using delegates is an invocation of the method to which the delegate is bound. You can perform this operation by using the name of the delegate's instance with parameters (it looks like an invocation of an ordinary method). For an example, examine the following sample source code:

```
string someResult = someDelegate("Some string value");
```

We've passed a set of input parameters in parentheses.

Listing 10.2 illustrates the simple use of delegates.

LISTING 10.2
Sample Source Code Using Delegates

```
using System;

namespace Delegates {
    delegate string SomeDelegate (string someStringValue);
    delegate void AnotherDelegate ();

    class SomeClass {
                public void SomeMethod () {
                        Console.WriteLine("SomeClass.SomeMethod non static
method has been invoked ...");
                }
    }

    public class SomeApplication {
            private static string SomeMethod (string someStringValue) {
                    Console.WriteLine("SomeApplication.SomeMethod static method has
```

10

What Is a Delegate?

LISTING 10.2
Continued

```
been invoked with " +
                " parameter [" + someStringValue + "] ...");
                return "[" + someStringValue + "] was passed to SomeMethod ...";
        }


        [STAThread]
        static void Main(string[] args) {
                Console.WriteLine("Invocation of the non static
SomeClass.SomeMethod
 method through "+
                "AnotherDelegate example [in]");
                SomeClass someClass = new SomeClass();
                AnotherDelegate anotherDelegate = new
AnotherDelegate(someClass.SomeMethod);
                anotherDelegate();
                Console.WriteLine("Invocation of the non static
SomeClass.SomeMethod
method through" +
                "AnotherDelegate example [out]");
                Console.WriteLine();


                Console.WriteLine("Invocation of the static
SomeApplication.SomeMethod
method "+
                "SomeDelegate example [in]");
                SomeDelegate someDelegate = new SomeDelegate(SomeMethod);
                string someResult = someDelegate("Some string value");
                Console.WriteLine(someResult);
                Console.WriteLine("Invocation of the static SomeApplication.
SomeMethod method through+
        "SomeDelegate example [out]");
            }
        }
}
```

Listing 10.3 presents the next trace.

LISTING 10.3
Trace of Delegates Using Sample Code

```
Invocation of the non static SomeClass.SomeMethod method through
    AnotherDelegate example [in]
```

LISTING 10.3
Continued

```
SomeClass.SomeMethod non static method has been invoked ...
Invocation of the non static SomeClass.SomeMethod method through
  AnotherDelegate example [out]

Invocation of the static SomeApplication.SomeMethod method through
  SomeDelegate example [in]
SomeApplication.SomeMethod static method has been invoked with
  parameter [Some string value] .
[Some string value] was passed to SomeMethod ...
Invocation of the static SomeApplication.SomeMethod method through
  SomeDelegate example [out]
```

Now we can begin a review of the types of delegates.

Types of Delegates

There are two types of delegates in .NET: singlecast and multicast. An example of using a singlecast delegate was reviewed earlier. With the help of this type of delegate, only one method can be invoked per one delegate's invocation. A singlecast delegate (shown in the preceding code **1**) is a one-to-one ratio between delegate and referenced method. A multicast delegate enables us to invoke either one or several methods simultaneously.

The main difference between a singlecast and a multicast delegate is in the delegate's signature. A delegate that does not return any data (return type void) is considered multicast. Such a delegate can be used to invoke multiple methods with the same signature. You might recognize this model as the event publisher/subscriber model from Windows and event-based programming.

You are allowed to create multicast delegates by inheriting your custom delegate's class from System.MulticastDelegate.

10

> **NOTE**
>
> If you create a delegate with a return type that is not equal to void, your delegate will be singlecast.

In Listing 10.2, AnotherDelegate was declared as multicast delegate. In Listing 10.4, we modify the previous example by adding one method, AnotherMethod, to SomeClass with a signature that corresponds to the signature of the AnotherDelegate delegate. Also change the invocation format of AnotherDelegate by using a combination of delegates.

What Is a Delegate?

LISTING 10.4
Sample Source Code of Using Singlecast and Multicast Delegates

```
using System;

namespace Delegates {
        delegate string SomeDelegate (string someStringValue);
        delegate void AnotherDelegate ();

        class SomeClass {
            public void SomeMethod () {
                    Console.WriteLine("SomeClass.SomeMethod non static method has
been invoked ...");
                }

            public void AnotherMethod () {
                    Console.WriteLine("SomeClass.AnotherMethod non static method
has been invoked ...");
                }
        }

    public class SomeApplication {
            private static string SomeMethod (string someStringValue) {
                    Console.WriteLine("SomeApplication.SomeMethod static method has
been invoked with "+
  "parameter [" + someStringValue + "] ...");
                    return "[" + someStringValue + "] was passed to SomeMethod ...";
            }

            [STAThread]
            static void Main(string[] args) {
                    Console.WriteLine("Invocation of the non static
SomeClass.SomeMethod method through AnotherDelegate example [in]");
                    SomeClass someClass = new SomeClass();
                    AnotherDelegate anotherDelegate1 =
  new AnotherDelegate(someClass.SomeMethod);
                    AnotherDelegate anotherDelegate2 =
  new AnotherDelegate(someClass.AnotherMethod);
                    AnotherDelegate
anotherDelegatesCombination =
  (AnotherDelegate) Delegate.Combine(anotherDelegate1, anotherDelegate2);
                    anotherDelegatesCombination();
                    Console.WriteLine("Invocation of the non static SomeClass.
```

10

LISTING 10.4
Continued

```
SomeMethod and"+
   "SomeClass.AnotherMethod methods through AnotherDelegate Combination example
[out]");
                    Console.WriteLine();

                    Console.WriteLine("Invocation of the static
 SomeApplication.SomeMethod method "+
"through SomeDelegate example [in]");
                    SomeDelegate someDelegate = new SomeDelegate(SomeMethod);
                    string someResult = someDelegate("Some string value");
                    Console.WriteLine(someResult);
                    Console.WriteLine("Invocation of the static SomeApplication.
SomeMethod method "+
   "SomeDelegate example [out]");
            }
    }
}
```

The code in Listing 10.5 is returned by the next trace.

LISTING 10.5
Trace of Singlecast and Multicast Delegates Using Code

```
Invocation of the non static SomeClass.SomeMethod method through
   AnotherDelegate example [in]
SomeClass.SomeMethod non static method has been invoked ...
SomeClass.AnotherMethod non static method has been invoked ...
Invocation of the non static SomeClass.SomeMethod and
   SomeClass.AnotherMethod methods through AnotherDelegate Combination example
[out]

Invocation of the static SomeApplication.SomeMethod
   method through SomeDelegate example [in]
SomeApplication.SomeMethod static method has been invoked
   with parameter [Some string value] ...
[Some string value] was passed to SomeMethod ...
Invocation of the static SomeApplication.SomeMethod method
   through SomeDelegate example [out]
```

10

A more detailed use of multicast delegates will be discussed later.

Delegates Inside

So far, you have seen the simplest example of using delegates. Now you will look deeper into delegates. Let's start from singlecast delegates because multicast delegates are extensions of these.

The following is a declaration of both the `Delegate` and `MulticastDelegate` classes:

```
public abstract class Delegate : ICloneable, Iserializable
public abstract class MulticastDelegate : Delegate
```

Both of these are abstract classes. Their implementations are located in the library `mscorlib.dll` (namespace `System`).

As mentioned earlier, all singlecast delegates should be inherited from the `System.Delegate` class. You can find a detailed specification of it on the MSDN site. At the moment, we are interested in only two properties of this class:

```
public object Target {get;}
public MethodInfo Method {get;}
```

If a delegate is bound to a nonstatic method, the `Target` property will be set as a pointer to the concrete instance of some class—the object's context. If the delegate is associated with a static method, the value of the `Target` property will be null. The second property (`Method`) contains all data related to the delegate-associated method. This value can't be null. Both these properties are read-only. So, the values of these properties are set during the process of the delegate's initialization.

Let's review the Delegate's constructor. The class `System.Delegate` has two constructors:

```
protected Delegate(Type target, string method);
```

```
protected Delegate(object target, string method);
```

The first constructor is used for initialization of delegates that are associated with a static method. The first parameter defines the type (class) where a static method is located. The second parameter contains the name of the method for association with the delegate.

The second constructor initializes delegates, which should be bound with a nonstatic method. The first parameter defines the object's context where the bound method is

10

located. The purpose of the second parameter is the same as in the first delegate's constructor.

However, you will use neither the first nor second constructor because C# has language shortcuts that hide some of the underlying plumbing required to implement delegates. The actual usage of delegate declaration and instantiation varies slightly from the .NET constructors.

Now we will discuss how a delegate's associated method could be invoked. Let's discuss code mentioned in the earlier examples.

```
string someResult = someDelegate("Some string value");
```

The compiler will recognize that someDelegate is an instance inherited from the System.Delegate class, and will pass all input parameters to the method indicated by the delegate. After this, the compiler will try to invoke the method to which the delegate is bound.

Invocation of the method is performed with help of Reflection. Reflection is a toolkit for working with types at runtime. Reflection enables us to read information about some type, invoke methods, and take the values of properties and many others (see Chapter 11, "Reflection and Code Attributes").

As mentioned earlier, each delegate has the property Method. The type of this property is MethodInfo. This contains the Invoke method, which enables us to perform some method at runtime. The compiler uses data from the Target property of the delegate and the Method property to prepare code for performing methods associated with the delegate.

As input parameters, this method takes the parameter passed to the delegate. In our case, there is only one string parameter, someStringValue, with the value "Some string value".

Combined Delegates

In Listing 10.4, the code declared the AnotherDelegate delegate with a returned type of void. A delegate that has void as its returned type is called a *multicast delegate*. The main feature of multicast delegates is the possibility to call several methods simultaneously. You could do so by using the static method Combine of the System.Delegate class:

```
public static Delegate Combine(Delegate[])
public static Delegate Combine(Delegate, Delegate)
```

What Is a Delegate?

Let's discuss how to use this method. The following source code lines are from Listing 10.4:

```
AnotherDelegate anotherDelegate1 = new AnotherDelegate(someClass.SomeMethod);
AnotherDelegate anotherDelegate2 = new AnotherDelegate(someClass.AnotherMethod);
AnotherDelegate anotherDelegatesCombination =
   (AnotherDelegate) Delegate.Combine(anotherDelegate1, anotherDelegate2);
anotherDelegatesCombination();
```

In this code, we've created two multicast delegates of type `AnotherDelegate`. Each instance of `AnotherDelegate` in our example is bound to its own method, which has the same signature as the signature of `AnotherDelegate`.

After creating the delegates, we create the `anotherDelegatesCombination` instance of the `AnotherDelegate` class. We perform this operation by an invocation of the `Combine` method of the `System.Delegate` class. This method takes collections of delegates, or two delegates, as input data and returns a combination of delegates of the same type. (It returns an instance of the first delegate from the list of delegates and links it with the next delegate in the list.) When combined, the delegate is invoked and all delegates included in the combination also will be invoked.

Let's discuss how the multicast delegate is implemented. Actually, it is very similar to the singlecast delegate. The main difference is this: The class `System.MulticastDelegate` contains the private field _prev that is a pointer to the other delegate in the combination. With the help of this field, delegates can be linked in the combination.

There are several other useful methods in the `System.MulticastDelegate` class:

```
public static Delegate Remove(Delegate source, Delegate value);
```

This method removes the delegate described in the parameter `value` from the delegates' combination described in the parameter `source`.

The second method is `GetInvocationList`:

```
public virtual Delegate[] GetInvocationList();
```

This line returns an array of singlecast delegates. If the method is invoked for a multicast delegate, all elements from the delegates list will be returned in an array. In the case of a singlecast delegate, the array will include only one delegate.

10

Events

The official definition of an event is the following:

An event in C# is a way for a class to provide notifications to clients of that class when some interesting thing happens to an object. The most familiar use for events is in graphical user interfaces; typically, the classes that represent controls in the interface have events that are fired when the user does something to the control (for example, click a button).

Declaring an event is directly dependent on delegates. A delegate object encapsulates a method so that it can be called anonymously.

An event is a mechanism by which a client class can pass in delegates to methods that need to be invoked whenever something happens. When something does happen, the delegate(s) given to the method by its clients are invoked.

To declare an event in C#, we could use the syntax like the following:

```
public delegate void SomeDelegate(string sender);
public event SomeDelegate SomeEvent;
```

After an event has been declared, it must be associated with one or more event handlers before it can be raised. An event handler is nothing more than a method that is called using a delegate. You could use the += operator to associate an event with an instance of a delegate that already exists.

Let's look at another example:

```
someClass.SomeEvent += new SomeDelegate(someClass.SomeEventHandler);
```

You can also associate an event with a set of handlers (instances of a delegate). You can do so like this:

```
someClass.SomeEvent += new SomeDelegate(someClass.SomeEventHandler);
someClass.SomeEvent += new SomeDelegate(anotherClass.SomeEventHandler);
```

In the preceding example, the SomeEvent event of SomeClass has two handlers. One of them is located in SomeClass and the other is in AnotherClass. You can also assign some static method as a handler to an event.

An event handler can also be detached, as follows:

```
someClass.SomeEvent -= new SomeDelegate(someClass.SomeEventHandler);
```

In C#, events may be fired by calling them by a name similar to method invocation (for example, SomeEvent ("Some Sender")). The next example will help you to better understand events.

10

What Is a Delegate?

NOTE

Just a few words about compiler behavior related to events processing.

Whenever an event is defined for a class, the compiler generates three methods that are used to manage the underlying delegate:

▶ add_<*EventName*>—This is a public method that calls the static `Combine` method of `System.Delegate` in order to add another method to its internal invocation list. However, this method is not used explicitly. The same effect can be achieved by using the `+=` operator as specified earlier.

▶ remove_<*EventName*>—This is a public method that calls the static `Remove` method of `System.Delegate` in order to remove a receiver from the event's invocation list. This method is not called directly. Its job is performed by the `-=` operator.

▶ raise_<*EventName*>—This is a protected method that calls the compiler-generated `Invoke` method of the delegate in order to call each method in the invocation list.

Let's discuss the following example. It will clarify all potential event-related questions for you:

```
using System;
namespace Events {
      delegate void SomeDelegate (string sender);

      interface ISomeInterface {
            event SomeDelegate SomeEvent;
            void PerformSomeEvent ();
            void SomeEventHandler (string sender);
      }

      abstract class AbstractClass : ISomeInterface {
            public virtual event SomeDelegate SomeEvent;

            public abstract void SomeEventHandler (string sender);

            public abstract void PerformSomeEvent();

            protected void PerformSomeEventInternal (string sender) {
                  if (null != SomeEvent) {
                        SomeEvent(sender);
                  }
            }
```

10

```
        protected void SomeEventHandlerInternal
          (string sender, string receiver) {
                Console.WriteLine("Some Event has been handled.");
                Console.WriteLine("Sender is: [" + sender + "]");
                Console.WriteLine("Receiver is: [" + receiver + "]");
                Console.WriteLine("------------------------------");
          }
    }


class SomeClass : AbstractClass, ISomeInterface {
      public override void PerformSomeEvent() {
            PerformSomeEventInternal("Some class");
      }


      public override void SomeEventHandler (string sender) {
            SomeEventHandlerInternal (sender, "Some Class");
      }
}


class AnotherClass : AbstractClass, ISomeInterface {
      public override void PerformSomeEvent() {
            PerformSomeEventInternal("Another class");
      }


      public override void SomeEventHandler (string sender) {
            SomeEventHandlerInternal (sender, "Another Class");
      }
}



class SomeApplication {
      public static void SomeEventStaticHandler (string sender) {
            Console.WriteLine("Some Event has been handled.");
            Console.WriteLine("Sender is: [" + sender + "]");
            Console.WriteLine("Receiver is: [Some Application]");
            Console.WriteLine("------------------------------");
      }


      [STAThread]
      static void Main(string[] args) {
            SomeClass someClass = new SomeClass();
            AnotherClass anotherClass = new AnotherClass();
            someClass.SomeEvent +=
new SomeDelegate(someClass.SomeEventHandler);
```

10

What Is a Delegate?

```
                    someClass.SomeEvent +=
    new SomeDelegate(anotherClass.SomeEventHandler);
                    someClass.SomeEvent +=
    new SomeDelegate(SomeApplication.SomeEventStaticHandler);
                    someClass.PerformSomeEvent();
            }
        }
}
```

Before working with events, we should first define the delegate:

```
delegate void SomeDelegate (string sender);
```

The second step is a declaration of a class with a public event:

```
interface ISomeInterface {
        event SomeDelegate SomeEvent;
        ...
    }

abstract class AbstractClass : ISomeInterface {
        public virtual event SomeDelegate SomeEvent;
        ...
}
```

The next step is that all event handlers in all classes should be notified of the event. The signature of the event's handler should be the same as the signature of the delegate on which this event depends. In our case, the SomeEvent event is based on the SomeDelegate delegate, so all handlers for some event should have the following signature:

```
void SomeHandler (string someStringParameter);
```

All handlers should implement custom logic for each class that should be performed when the event is raised.

After performing all the previous steps, you can declare the method in the class where the event is declared—that will raise the event:

```
protected void PerformSomeEventInternal (string sender) {
        if (null != SomeEvent) {
                SomeEvent(sender);
        }
}
```

Note that we should compare the event with null before we raise it. Otherwise, if the event doesn't have any handlers assigned to it, the application will cause an exception like the following:

```
Unhandled Exception: System.NullReferenceException:
Object reference not set to an instance of an object.
   at Events.AbstractClass.PerformSomeEventInternal(String sender)
  in c:\chapter 10 -
  events and delegates\code example\events and delegates\events\main.cs:line 20
   at Events.SomeClass.PerformSomeEvent() in c:\chapter 10 -
   events and delegates\code example\events and
 delegates\events\main.cs:line 33
   at Events.SomeApplication.Main(String[] args) in c:\chapter 10 -
   events and delegates\code example\events and delegates\events\main.cs:line 67
```

After all these steps have been performed, you should assign handlers to the event. You could do so like this:

```
someClass.SomeEvent += new SomeDelegate(someClass.SomeEventHandler);
someClass.SomeEvent += new SomeDelegate(anotherClass.SomeEventHandler);
someClass.SomeEvent += new SomeDelegate(SomeApplication.SomeEventStaticHandler);
```

Note that you are allowed to assign static handler methods (`SomeApplication.SomeEventStatisHandler`) as well as nonstatic methods to an event.

After this, you could raise the event by using the event method mentioned earlier:

```
someClass.PerformSomeEvent();
```

The result of running the test application is shown in the following trace:

```
Some Event has been handled.
Sender is: [Some class]
Receiver is: [Some Class]
-------------------------------
Some Event has been handled.
Sender is: [Some class]
Receiver is: [Another Class]
-------------------------------
Some Event has been handled.
Sender is: [Some class]
Receiver is: [Some Application]
-------------------------------
```

10

Three handlers were assigned to the event, so three trace blocks are shown onscreen. Each block shows us the name of raised event, the name of the event's sender, and the name of event's receiver.

Summary

In this chapter, we discussed delegates and events. A *delegate* is an object that encapsulates some anonymous method by itself. To use a delegate, you should declare it, instantiate it with some method that should be associated with delegate, and then invoke it.

We also discussed what multicast and singlecast delegates are, their internal structure, and the common rules of their use. *Multicast* delegates are lists of linked delegates that are invoked by turn.

An *event* is a way for a class to provide notifications to clients of that class when some interesting thing happens to an object. We discussed the step-by-step process of creating and using events. The process comprises the following steps:

- Delegate declaration
- Event declaration
- Declaration of event handlers
- Event-raising method declaration
- Registration of event handlers
- Event raising

Finally, we took a look at the most typical example of event use.

Further Reading

Programming Windows with C# (Core Reference) by Microsoft Press. ISBN: 0735613702.

10

11 Reflection and Code Attributes

IN BRIEF

Managed code written for the .NET Framework is always accompanied by various kinds of metadata. This metadata controls everything from defining the list of referenced assemblies that an application needs to run properly, to simpler information such as the product version, product name, and so on.

This metadata is stored on disk, but it is also available to managed code at runtime. While the managed code is running, it can, at any time, make queries against the metadata associated with it. In addition to this metadata, type information including class definitions, members, properties, attributes, and instance data is also available.

The mechanism that makes all of this available is called *reflection*. Reflection allows managed code to not only inspect metadata about itself, but also about any other code that might be running at the same time. This chapter will show you how to use reflection to discover type and metadata information at runtime, and how to use custom code attributes to create your own runtime-discoverable metadata about your code.

WHAT YOU NEED

RECOMMENDED SOFTWARE	.NET Framework SDK v1.1 Visual Studio .NET 2003 with C# installed
RECOMMENDED HARDWARE	PC that meets .NET SDK minimum requirements
SKILLS REQUIRED	C# and .NET familiarity

REFLECTION AND CODE ATTRIBUTES AT A GLANCE

Working with Reflection	228		
Introduction to Reflection	229	Discovering Type Information at Runtime	229
How Reflection Works	229		
Using Code Attributes	**234**		
Introduction to Code Attributes	234	Creating Custom Attributes	236
Using Code Attributes	235	Querying Custom Attributes	238
Summary	**241**		
Further Reading	**241**		

Working with Reflection

This next section provides an overview of reflection and how it works. In addition, this section provides examples of using reflection to query information at runtime.

Introduction to Reflection

As mentioned in this chapter's introduction, reflection is a technology that allows managed code to inspect various aspects of the code and metadata at runtime. This allows managed code to do simple things such as obtaining a list of the properties belonging to an object instance, or even more complex things such as querying custom attributes or obtaining an image from a resource embedded within an assembly.

How Reflection Works

One of the main keys to making reflection work is understanding that data types are objects. Understanding this point is crucial to understanding reflection. Managed code can obtain an object instance that is a System.Type. Because you can treat a data type as an object, you can execute methods and query properties of that data type. Methods on the System.Type class enable you to query the list of members belonging to that type or a list of attributes, methods, and so on.

One of the main differences between a managed environment and an unmanaged environment is that the .NET managed environment not only manages the in-memory instances, but the Common Language Runtime actually knows the data type information about each instance it is managing.

With a traditional, unmanaged language, data is stored in memory. If your code creates an array of 16-bit integers that is two elements long, there could be a sequential set of four bytes that represents that array. With this unmanaged language, there is no real information about what kind of data is represented by that array; the only information about the code is contained in the code itself. With a managed environment, like the .NET Framework, not only would the array data be stored, but the data type of the array would also be stored.

For example, when you create an instance of a class Porsche, the Common Language Runtime is managing that class. At runtime, without having access to the source code that generated that class, managed code can inspect Porsche and determine that it inherits from SportsCar, which in turn inherits from Car. If the only information maintained in the Porsche class is a simple integer, then, in an unmanaged environment, a Porsche that inherited from SportsCar that inherited from Car would look identical to an integer representing a simple loop counter.

By maintaining reflection information at runtime, managed code becomes extremely powerful and has several advantages over its unmanaged counterparts.

11

Discovering Type Information at Runtime

You probably do some things in your code quite often without realizing that you are using reflection or capabilities provided by reflection. Take a look at the following code snippet **1** :

Working with Reflection

```
1   if (theCar is Porsche)
    {
        // do something
    }
```

This code performs some action if the variable `theCar` is of the type `Porsche`. The is keyword not only checks the instantiation type, but also checks the types of all inherited ancestors.

THE is OPERATOR

The is operator checks the entire lineage of an object hierarchy. It returns true if the variable can be cast to the destination type without exception. This means that it returns true for the object's instantiation type, the type of its parent, and its ancestors. To make an explicit check on the instantiation type, use the typeof operator and get the type's fully qualified name.

The typeof operator is another keyword that you might have used in reflection and not known that you were doing so. When applied to an object instance, typeof returns the System.Type corresponding to that object, as shown in the following code line:

```
System.Type carType = typeof(myPorsche);
```

As you can see, the typeof operator returns an instance of the System.Type class. After you have obtained an instance of the System.Type class using any of several different methods, you can accomplish quite a few things. Table 11.1 lists some of the more commonly used methods and properties of the System.Type class.

TABLE 11.1

Commonly Used Methods and Properties of System.Type

Method / Property	Description
Assembly	Gets the assembly to which the type belongs
Attributes	Gets the attributes associated with the type (discussed later)
BaseType	Gets the type from which the class inherits as a direct parent
FullName	Gets the fully qualified name of the data type
IsAbstract	Indicates whether the type is an abstract type
IsClass	Indicates whether the type is a class
IsInterface	Indicates whether the type is an interface
Namespace	Gets the namespace of the data type
GetConstructors()	Returns a list of constructors for this type
GetEvents()	Gets a list of events declared or inherited by the type
GetMember()	Gets a specified member of the type
GetMembers()	Gets all the members defined by the type

11

TABLE 11.1

Continued

Method / Property	Description
GetProperty()	Gets a specific property of the type
GetProperties()	Gets all the properties defined by the type

Read the code in Listing 11.1 and the explanation that follows. Listing 11.1 provides a sample of using reflection to obtain information about a class at runtime.

LISTING 11.1
Reflection Example

```csharp
using System;

namespace ReflectionSample
{
public class Car
{
    private int numWheels = 4;

    public Car()
    {
    }

    public int NumWheels
    {
    get
    {
        return numWheels;
    }
    set
    {
        numWheels = value;
    }
    }

    public void PrintWheels()
    {
    Console.WriteLine(numWheels);
    }
}

public class SportsCar : Car
{
    private string color = string.Empty;
```

11

Working with Reflection

LISTING 11.1
Continued

```csharp
    public SportsCar()
    {

    }

    public string Color
    {
      get
      {
        return color;
      }
      set
      {
        color = value;
      }
    }

    public void PrintColor()
    {
      Console.WriteLine(color);
    }
  }

  public class Porsche : SportsCar
  {
    private int someValue = 12;
    public Porsche()
    {
    }

    public int SomeValue
    {
      get
      {
        return someValue;
      }
      set
      {
        someValue = value;
      }
    }
```

LISTING 11.1
Continued

```
    public void PrintValue()
    {
        Console.WriteLine(someValue);
    }
}

class Class1
{

  [STAThread]
  static void Main(string[] args)
  {
    Porsche myPorsche = new Porsche();

    Type carType = myPorsche.GetType();

    // list all the methods of carType                          3
    MethodInfo[] methods = carType.GetMethods();
    foreach (MethodInfo method in methods)
    {
        Console.WriteLine(method.Name);
    }

    Console.WriteLine("--");
    // list all the properties                                  4
    PropertyInfo[] properties = carType.GetProperties();
    foreach (PropertyInfo property in properties)
    {
        Console.WriteLine(property.Name);
    }
    Console.WriteLine("--");

    // get the inheritance tree                                 5
    Type parent = carType.BaseType;
    Console.Write(carType.Name + " ->");
    while (parent != null )
    {
        Console.Write(" -> " + parent.Name);
        parent = parent.BaseType;
    }
```

11

Working with Reflection

LISTING 11.1
Continued

```
    Console.ReadLine();


    }
  }
}
```

This sample starts by creating a hierarchy of classes **2**, a `Porsche` class that inherits from `SportsCar`, which in turn inherits from `Car`. Each of these classes defines a property and a method. By now, having covered the basics of object-oriented programming in C#, you should be familiar with these types.

The first thing the example does with Reflection is to list all the different methods **3** of the `carType` object. If you run the example, you will see that there are some methods you might not have expected—these are methods that belong to the `System.Object` class.

The second piece of code **4** illustrates how to get a list of all the properties that belong to a given type using the `GetProperties()` method. This method has some optional parameters that enable you to filter the list of properties, just as there are optional parameters to the `GetMembers()` **3** method.

Finally, code that many programmers find the most interesting **5** shows how to traverse an object's hierarchy and obtain all of its parents and ancestors. This section of code produces the following output:

```
Porsche -> SportsCar -> Car -> Object
```

This output further reinforces the notion that all classes in the .NET Framework inherit from `System.Object`.

Using Code Attributes

This next section illustrates the concepts surrounding code attributes, including an overview of attributes and how they work, and finally a sample showing you how to create and consume custom code attributes.

Introduction to Code Attributes

The .NET Framework allows for many kinds of metadata to be stored with code. You can store resources embedded in assemblies, and assemblies have metadata that describes things such as product name, product version, and the list of required and referenced assemblies.

In addition to the standard metadata, there are code attributes that can be used to "decorate" code. These attributes provide extremely useful information about the code, and can even dictate how the code is executed by its environment.

Using Code Attributes

You might have seen code attributes in action but not noticed that you were using them. For example, when you create a method that is exposed to web service clients via WSDL, you decorate that method with the `WebMethodAttribute` attribute, as shown here:

```
[WebMethod()]
public string HelloWebServiceWorld()
{
    return "Hello World";
}
```

There are other attributes that control transaction behavior within COM+, attributes that control object serialization and XML serialization formats, and much more.

By convention, code attributes in the .NET Framework all have an `Attribute` postfix. Thankfully, C# recognizes this and enables you a shortcut of leaving off the postfix when declaring the attribute.

You saw earlier that data types actually inherit from `System.Object`, just like every other class in the .NET Framework. Similarly, code attributes are actually classes. When you decorate a class, member, or assembly with a code attribute, you are actually creating an instance of that class at runtime using either a default or a parameterized constructor.

The following code snippet shows a brief example of what a class decorated with your own custom attributes might look like:

```
[MyClassAttribute("Hello")]
public class MyClass
{
    private int my_Val;

    public MyClass() { }

    [MyPropertyAttribute(42)]
    public int MyValue { get { return my_Val; }
      set { my_Val = value; } }
}
```

As mentioned previously, you can leave off the `Attribute` postfix to make things more readable.

11

Creating Custom Attributes

It is important to recognize the difference between code attributes and comments. Code attributes provide additional details and information to runtime facilities. Code comments provide information to people reading the code at design-time.

WHEN TO ATTRIBUTE AND WHEN TO COMMENT

When deciding whether you should put information in an attribute or a comment, make sure that you put in attributes only information that must be available to the code at runtime. For example, people often use attributes to create object-relational database mappings by mapping members to stored procedure parameters or table columns. Developers use attributes for many other purposes as well. However, for simple comments that are useful only to people reading the code while it is not being executed, use comments—attributes add slight overhead to the application while running.

In the next section, you will see how to create your own custom attribute. For the purposes of demonstration, consider the following scenario:

You have developed a high-availability solution. A requirement of this solution is that administrators are notified the instant an exception is trapped within the application. In addition, the programmer who created the method in which the exception was thrown must be notified as well.

At design-time, it's fairly easy to tell who is responsible for writing a specific class or method. You can look at comments or source control reports or just ask around the office. At runtime, it's an entirely different situation. The only way for the code to know who developed a method at runtime is to decorate that method with an attribute.

As mentioned earlier, code attributes are nothing more than special classes. When you decorate code with an attribute, you are informing the Common Language Runtime to create an instance of that attribute class and make it available throughout the lifetime of that application.

The code in Listing 11.2 creates a custom code attribute class responsible for maintaining the name and email address of the author of a section of code.

LISTING 11.2
A Sample Code Attribute Class

```
using System;

namespace AttributeDemo
{
    [AttributeUsage(AttributeTargets.Method | AttributeTargets.Class)]
    public class CodeAuthorAttribute : System.Attribute
    {
        private string authorName = string.Empty;
```

LISTING 11.2
Continued

```
    private string authorEmail = string.Empty;

    public CodeAuthorAttribute( string initAuthorName, string initAuthorEmail )
    {
      authorName = initAuthorName;
      authorEmail = initAuthorEmail;
    }

    public string AuthorName
    {
     get
     {
       return authorName;
     }
     set
     {
       authorName = value;
     }
    }

    public string AuthorEmail
    {
      get
      {
        return authorEmail;
      }
      set
      {
        authorEmail = value;
      }
    }
  }
}
```

For the most part, it's a pretty simple class. It has a property that represents the name of the code author, and another property that represents the email address of the code author. The two lines that stand out **6** are the line with the `AttributeUsageAttribute` declaration, and the line that indicates that the class inherits from the `System.Attribute` class.

Something interesting happens when you apply this code attribute to some other class **7**, as shown in Listing 11.3.

Using Code Attributes

LISTING 11.3
A Class Decorated with a Custom Attribute

```
using System;

namespace AttributeDemo
{
  public class ClassWithError
  {
    public ClassWithError()
    {
    }
```

7   `    [CodeAuthor("Kevin Hoffman", "someemail@someaddress.com")]`

```
    public void DoSomething()
    {
      try
      {
        // a little chicanery to get
        // a divide-by-zero error to compile
        int x = 12;
        int y = 4;
        int z = y-4;
        int aa = x/z;
      }
      catch (Exception e)
      {
        Console.WriteLine("Something went wrong!");
        Console.WriteLine(e.ToString());
      }
    }
  }
}
```

Querying Custom Attributes

The code in the previous section showed you how to create your own
custom attribute. That code showed you how to decorate a class with your
own custom attribute. In this next section, you'll see how to use Reflection to find
out what attributes are associated with a piece of code, and how to get at the values
within those attributes.

In this next sample, you'll take some of the code from the previous sample and build
on it. In the previous code, there was a simple exception handler to trap the

division-by-zero error. In Listing 11.4, you'll add some code to display the name and email address of the author who wrote the code.

The first thing to do is create a method that will take a method as an argument, and return the method's author. Listing 11.4 shows a class with a static method that does just that.

LISTING 11.4
A Utility Class to Find A Method's Author Using a Custom Code Attribute

```
using System;
using System.Reflection;
using System.Diagnostics;

namespace AttributeDemo
{
  /// <summary>
  /// Summary description for AttributeTool.
  /// </summary>
  public class AttributeTool
  {
    public AttributeTool()
    {

    }

    public static CodeAuthorAttribute GetMethodAuthor(MethodBase method)
    {
      object[] attributes =
        method.GetCustomAttributes( typeof(CodeAuthorAttribute), true );
      return (CodeAuthorAttribute)attributes[0];
    }
  }
}
```

The preceding code returns the first `CodeAuthorAttribute` found by calling the `GetCustomAttributes` method. This is a sample, so it doesn't handle the case in which no such attributes are found. In production code, you would want to handle such a situation.

With this method in place, you can modify the code in Listing 11.3 to obtain the author of the method and display that information to the console in the event of an unexpected exception. Listing 11.5 shows the modified class.

11

Using Code Attributes

LISTING 11.5
Code That Displays the Author of a Method After an Error

```
using System;
using System.Reflection;

namespace AttributeDemo
{
  public class ClassWithError
  {
    public ClassWithError()
    {
    }


    [CodeAuthor("Kevin Hoffman", "someemail@someaddress.com")]
    public void DoSomething()
    {
      try
      {
        // a little chicanery to get
        // a divide-by-zero error to compile
        int x = 12;
        int y = 4;
        int z = y-4;
        int aa = x/z;
      }
      catch
      {
        Console.WriteLine("Something went wrong!");
        CodeAuthorAttribute caa = AttributeTool.GetMethodAuthor
( MethodBase.GetCurrentMethod() );
        Console.WriteLine("The person you need to blame is {0} @ {1}",
          caa.AuthorName, caa.AuthorEmail);
      }
    }
  }
}
```

This code invokes the utility class that was created in Listing 11.4 to get an instance of the `CodeAuthorAttribute`. When the preceding code is executed, you should see output that looks like the following lines:

```
Something went wrong!
```

```
The person you need to blame is Kevin Hoffman @
someemail@someaddress.com
```

The code threw a division-by-zero exception, and then trapped it. The exception handler then used a utility class to retrieve information on the author of the method. Using the hypothetical scenario defined at the beginning of this section, you could expand the sample to send that programmer an email that contains a serialization of the exception thrown.

Summary

This chapter provided an overview of reflection and code attributes and how they work together to provide extremely powerful functionality. The chapter started off with a discussion of what reflection is, how it works, and how it is an embedded, core part of the Common Language Runtime. Following that, the chapter went into a discussion of code attributes. Finally, you saw an example of how to create your own custom attributes and how to use reflection to query the values within that custom attribute.

After having read this chapter and followed along with the samples contained within it, you should have a more thorough understanding of both reflection and code attributes.

Further Reading

Pro .NET 1.1 Remoting, Reflection and Threading: From Professional to Expert by Tobin Titus, et al, aPress. ISBN: 1590594525.

Mastering Visual C# .NET by Jason Price and Mike Gunderloy, Sybex. ISBN: 0782129110.

11

12 Assemblies and AppDomains

IN BRIEF

This chapter will take you on a tour of assemblies and AppDomains, two of the most important core pieces of the .NET Framework. To learn any part of the .NET Framework, from the most simple application development techniques to advanced programming, you must have a thorough understanding of AppDomains and assemblies.

The first half of this chapter is dedicated to the *assembly*, a logical storage unit used by the .NET Framework for multiple purposes. The latter half of this chapter introduces you to the AppDomain and gives you enough information that you can progress to dealing with the innermost workings of AppDomains by writing code that makes use of both assemblies and AppDomains.

WHAT YOU NEED

RECOMMENDED SOFTWARE	.NET Framework SDK v1.1 Visual Studio .NET 2003 with C# installed
RECOMMENDED HARDWARE	PC that meets .NET SDK minimum requirements
SKILLS REQUIRED	C# and .NET familiarity

ASSEMBLIES AND APPDOMAINS AT A GLANCE

Assemblies	243		
Introduction to Assemblies	243		
Assembly Building Blocks	243		
Introducing the Assembly Manifest	244	Inside the Assembly—MSIL Code	247
Metadata	246	Assembly Resources	247
Creating Assemblies	247		
Embedding Content and Resources in Assemblies	251		
Localization and Satellite Assemblies	255		
Satellite Assemblies	256		
AppDomains	259		
Introduction to AppDomains	259	Programming with AppDomains	260
Putting It Together—A Real-World Example	264		
Building Application Plug-Ins	273		

Assemblies

As I mentioned in this chapter's introduction, assemblies are one of the most essential things that must be learned by everyone who plans on writing any code using the .NET Framework SDK. It doesn't make any difference whether you're planning to create web, Windows, console, or service applications; a thorough understanding of the assembly is essential to the success of any project.

Introduction to Assemblies

An assembly is a logical grouping of metadata, code, and resources. You cannot create any functional code on the .NET Framework without using assemblies. Before this chapter gets into the structure and components of an assembly, it will examine a list of all the things that assemblies are responsible for:

- Provides a container for code that can be executed by the Common Language Runtime.

- Creates a secured entity. When permissions are assigned to .NET Framework code, they are assigned at the assembly level.

- Supplies a container for type definitions. When you create a class, the assembly in which that class resides is a permanent part of that class definition. You cannot separate the containing assembly from data types contained within.

- Provides a target for versioning. The assembly is the lowest denominator for containing versions in the .NET Framework. Every type and resource in a given assembly has exactly the same version.

- Supplies a logical unit of deployment. Applications in the .NET Framework load only the types they need at runtime. These types are loaded from assemblies deployed with the application or even from locations on a network or the Internet.

This might seem a bit overwhelming at first, but it becomes clearer as you start to work with assemblies and see them in action.

Assembly Building Blocks

There is a very common misconception surrounding assemblies. When people learning .NET for the first time approach veterans, they often ask the question, "What is an assembly?" Unfortunately, most of the time, the response is incorrect. If you've asked that question and been told that an assembly is essentially just a DLL or an EXE file, you've been given only part of the story.

12

Assembly Building Blocks

You might remember that I earlier referred to an assembly as a *logical* unit of storage and deployment. I did not say that it was a *physical* unit of storage and deployment. This difference might seem like semantics, but it makes quite a big difference when you begin working with larger, more complex applications that have many deployment files.

In most cases, an assembly is actually just one DLL or EXE file. This is what is called a *single-file* assembly. This is the most common type of assembly and is sufficient for a majority of programming tasks that you might need to accomplish with the .NET Framework.

However, some programming tasks require the use of an assembly that is actually more than one file. Such assemblies are referred to as *multifile assemblies*. When you build an application that will be used internationally, or an application that uses various logically grouped resources such as images, text files, XML files, or strings that appear in different languages depending on the location of the user, you will be making use of multifile assemblies.

Before you get your hands dirty with some code involving assemblies, there is one other aspect of assemblies that is often overlooked in introductory texts. There are two different kinds of assemblies (regardless of whether it is multifile or single file): static and dynamic.

A *static* assembly is one that exists on disk. This assembly can be a single file or a grouping of files. You'll see how that grouping of files is stored later in the chapter. You can copy a static assembly from one location to another so long as all the files that are part of the assembly are copied with it.

The other kind of assembly is a dynamic assembly. A *dynamic* assembly is one that exists only in memory. Through some fairly complex reflection code, you can actually emit code directly into memory, compile it (creating a dynamic assembly), and execute it without ever having placed a file on disk. It might sound obscure, but there are quite a few very good uses for technology like this.

Figure 12.1 is an illustration of a complex multifile assembly. Each component of the assembly is discussed in the text following the figure.

Introducing the Assembly Manifest

The assembly manifest is a collection of data information. This information describes the assembly itself, as well as all the various components of the assembly and how they relate to each other. The manifest contains the assembly metadata (discussed in the next section) and can be stored in what is called a *portable executable (PE) file*. A PE file is either a DLL or an EXE. Many people confuse the term *assembly* with a PE file. Although the two are related, they are definitely not the same thing.

Example Multi-File Assembly

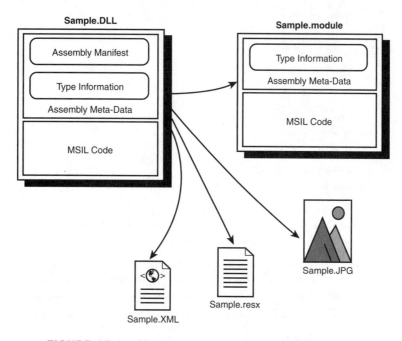

FIGURE 12.1   Illustration of a complex multifile assembly.

No discussion of assemblies or assembly manifests would be complete without discussing an incredibly useful tool that comes with the .NET Framework SDK: ILDASM.EXE.

To examine an assembly manifest, run the ILDASM tool. You can either browse to its location, or open a Visual Studio .NET 2003 Command Prompt and type **ILDASM** at the command prompt. A small Windows Forms application will open up.

With ILDASM running, open the file \Windows\Microsoft.NET\Framework\v1.1.4322\System.Data.dll. After the file has opened, you should see an organized tree list of the assembly's contents. Double-click the Manifest section (indicated with a red triangle facing right). You will be confronted with a window that should look similar to the one in Figure 12.2.

TIP

The information presented here might seem a bit overwhelming at first. It isn't necessary to completely grasp everything shown so far. However, understanding that something called the assembly manifest exists, and that it is part of every .NET assembly (whether single-file or multifile) will certainly make learning some advanced .NET topics much easier.

12

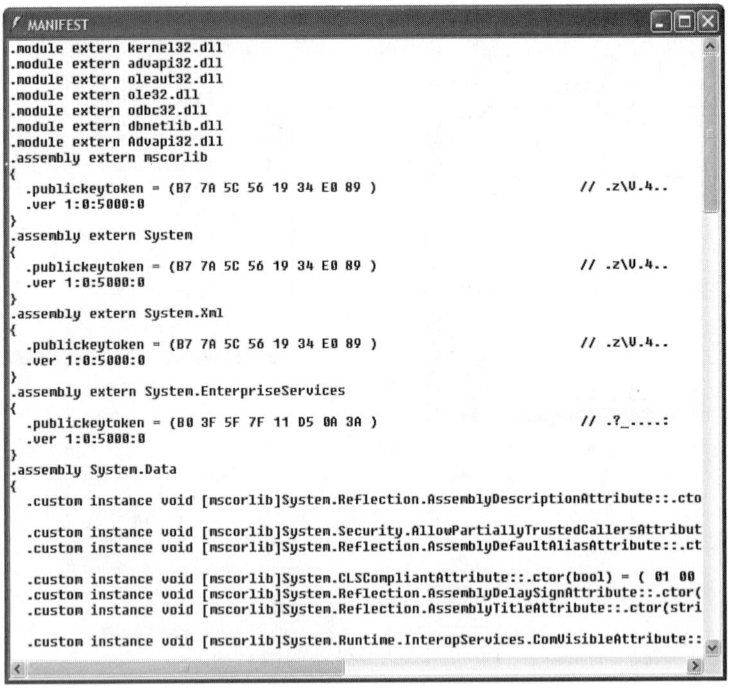

Assembly Building Blocks

FIGURE 12.2   The assembly manifest for the
System.Data assembly.

Metadata

With the manifest still open, take a look at what looks like lines of code in an odd
language. You can see statements like the following:

```
.assembly extern mscorlib
```

These statements are metadata. They are pieces of data that describe the functionality, contents, and references of the assembly. This particular statement indicates to
the Common Language Runtime that this assembly makes use of the mscorlib
library. In the preceding chapter, you saw how to create and use code attributes.
Attributes are also metadata, and assembly-scope attributes are stored in the manifest. If you scroll down somewhat in the Manifest window, you can see some custom
code attributes and their associated values (displayed in a hexadecimal ASCII string).

When an assembly is loaded at runtime, the Common Language Runtime uses the
manifest to determine what must be done to properly handle that assembly, including locating all the assemblies that are required by the assembly being loaded, its
components, embedded files, and linked external files.

12

Inside the Assembly—MSIL Code

In addition to all the information contained in the manifest, an assembly can contain code. When you compile your C# assembly, the C# is converted into Microsoft Intermediate Language (MSIL). This is the language that the Common Language Runtime understands and executes when your application is running. Unlike traditional C or C++ programs, which compile directly to machine code, .NET code is compiled into MSIL. When the MSIL is loaded at runtime, it is JIT (just-in-Time) compiled into machine code and then cached for future use. This extra degree of separation from the machine code is what allows code written for the .NET Framework to claim (limited) portability.

To take a look at some MSIL, close the Manifest window and then use the tree navigation structure to drill down to `System.Data.AcceptRejectRule.Cascade`. Double-click the `Cascade` line (indicated by a teal diamond with an S in the middle). The following text appears in a new window:

```
.field public static literal valuetype
System.Data.AcceptRejectRule Cascade = int32(0x00000001)
```

This text indicates to the Common Language Runtime that the enumeration called `AcceptRejectRule` has a public static enumerated value called `Cascade` that has the value of 1. You don't need to know MSIL in order to write effective code targeting the .NET Framework. However, knowing that high-level language code written in C# or Visual Basic .NET (or any other .NET language) is converted into MSIL at compile time and then converted into machine code at runtime is essential to gaining a full understanding of .NET.

Assembly Resources

Another thing that you can store in an assembly is a resource. Resources can be a table of multilingual strings, a bitmap, a text file, an XML file, a JPG file, or virtually anything. Resources in an assembly can either be embedded directly in the body of the assembly itself or they can be linked externally. An externally linked resource will be listed in the assembly manifest. When the Common Language Runtime loads the assembly, it will see the reference in the manifest and attempt to load the file indicated as a resource. A very important thing to remember is that regardless of where an assembly resource is located, the location is transparent to a programmer consuming the resource. As you'll see in code later in this chapter, the method calls to obtain resources are the same whether the resource is physically stored inside a .DLL or linked externally.

12

Creating Assemblies

There are many ways that you can create assemblies. If you are one of the many programmers who prefer a command-line over point-and-click, you can simply open

Creating Assemblies

a command prompt and make use of the AL.EXE command-line utility. This is the Assembly Linker tool, and is used to link precompiled modules and resources into assemblies.

If you are creating a dynamic assembly, you will probably be using reflection to emit the assembly directly into memory. There are some situations in which this type of code is necessary, but it is by no means the most common way of creating assemblies.

Most developers will be creating assemblies with Visual Studio .NET (or another IDE if you don't use Visual Studio .NET). You create an assembly whenever you build a project that creates either a .DLL or an .EXE output file.

The following section will illustrate how to create a new assembly. It won't do much to start with, but you'll add to it later in the chapter. To start with, open Visual Studio .NET and create a new C# Class Library project. Call the project AssemblyIntro.

TIP

A useful habit that many have developed is to delete the Class1.cs file that comes with a new Class Library project. This is done because most developers never use the default namespace. The routine is this: Delete Class1.cs, set the default namespace and assembly name, and then add your new class. The new class will automatically have the correct namespace.

Open the Project Properties dialog and set the default namespace to SAMS.CSharpUnleashed.Chapter12.AssemblyIntro. Make sure that you also set the assembly name to the same value. It will create an assembly called SAMS.CSharpUnleashed.Chapter12.AssemblyIntro.dll. It looks like a long namespace name, but many developers like descriptive namespaces, and there will be a lot of work with namespaces later in the chapter.

Double-click the AssemblyInfo.cs file and fill in the blanks however you like. Set the assembly description to whatever you like. When you're done filling that in, add a new class to the project and call it AssemblyTool.

Set the code for the AssemblyTool class to the code contained in Listing 12.1.

LISTING 12.1
The Code for the AssemblyTool Class

```
using System;
using System.Reflection;
using System.Text;

namespace SAMS.CSharpUnleashed.Chapter12.AssemblyIntro
```

12

LISTING 12.1
Continued

```csharp
{
  /// <summary>
  /// This is the AssemblyTool sample class
  /// </summary>
  public class AssemblyTool
  {
    public AssemblyTool()
    {

    }

    public static string GetAssemblyInfo()
    {
      // gets the Assembly in which this code is executing, not
      // necessarily the Assembly of the main executable (EXE)
      Assembly thisAssembly = Assembly.GetExecutingAssembly();
      AssemblyName thisName = thisAssembly.GetName();
      StringBuilder sb = new StringBuilder();
      sb.AppendFormat("Assembly Name: {0}\n", thisAssembly.FullName);
      sb.AppendFormat("Assembly Version: {0}\n", thisName.Version.ToString());
      sb.AppendFormat("Assembly Culture: {0}\n", thisName.CultureInfo.ToString());
      return sb.ToString();
    }
  }
}
```

The preceding code uses some reflection methods to get access to the current assembly. The `Assembly` class exposes a lot of methods for obtaining information about any assembly, whether the assembly was loaded from disk, from a URL, by execution, or by being dynamically created in memory.

So, we have an assembly and a class inside that assembly. Let's take a look at it in ILDASM; doing so will be a good exercise in learning what actions in Visual Studio .NET look like as results in an assembly manifest.

Figure 12.3 shows the new assembly manifest from the newly created `SAMS.CSharpUnleashed.Chapter12.AssemblyIntro.dll`.

To test this code and see what the output looks like, add a new Console Application project to the `AssemblyIntro` solution called `Harness`. Add a reference from the Harness project to the `AssemblyIntro` project. Now define the `Class1.cs` class as shown in Listing 12.2.

12

Creating Assemblies

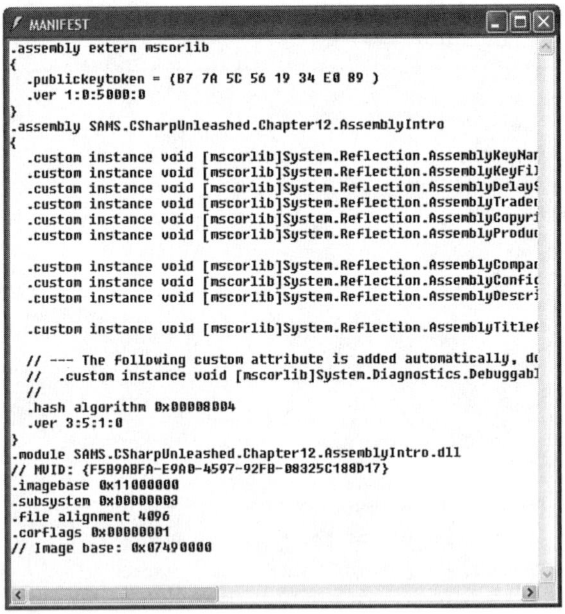

```
MANIFEST
.assembly extern mscorlib
{
  .publickeytoken = (B7 7A 5C 56 19 34 E0 89 )
  .ver 1:0:5000:0
}
.assembly SAMS.CSharpUnleashed.Chapter12.AssemblyIntro
{
  .custom instance void [mscorlib]System.Reflection.AssemblyKeyNar
  .custom instance void [mscorlib]System.Reflection.AssemblyKeyFil
  .custom instance void [mscorlib]System.Reflection.AssemblyDelay$
  .custom instance void [mscorlib]System.Reflection.AssemblyTrader
  .custom instance void [mscorlib]System.Reflection.AssemblyCopyri
  .custom instance void [mscorlib]System.Reflection.AssemblyProdu(

  .custom instance void [mscorlib]System.Reflection.AssemblyCompar
  .custom instance void [mscorlib]System.Reflection.AssemblyConfi(
  .custom instance void [mscorlib]System.Reflection.AssemblyDescri

  .custom instance void [mscorlib]System.Reflection.AssemblyTitle(

  // --- The following custom attribute is added automatically, d(
  //   .custom instance void [mscorlib]System.Diagnostics.Debuggabl
  //
  .hash algorithm 0x00008004
  .ver 3:5:1:0
}
.module SAMS.CSharpUnleashed.Chapter12.AssemblyIntro.dll
// MVID: {F5B9ABFA-E9AD-4597-92FB-08325C188D17}
.imagebase 0x11000000
.subsystem 0x00000003
.file alignment 4096
.corflags 0x00000001
// Image base: 0x07490000
```

FIGURE 12.3   Assembly manifest from
SAMS.CSharpUnleashed.
Chapter12.AssemblyIntro.
dll.

LISTING 12.2
The Test Harness Console Application

```
using System;

using SAMS.CSharpUnleashed.Chapter12.AssemblyIntro;

namespace Harness
{
  /// <summary>
  /// Summary description for Class1.
  /// </summary>
  class Class1
  {
    /// <summary>
    /// The main entry point for the application.
    /// </summary>
    [STAThread]
    static void Main(string[] args)
```

LISTING 12.2
Continued

```
    {
      Console.WriteLine( AssemblyTool.GetAssemblyInfo() );
      Console.ReadLine();
    }
  }
}
```

When you run this application, you'll get a console window with the following output:

```
Assembly Name: SAMS.CSharpUnleashed.Chapter12.AssemblyIntro, Version=3.5.1.0,
    Culture=neutral, PublicKeyToken=null
Assembly Version: 3.5.1.0
Assembly Culture:
```

You should now have a fairly good idea of what the components of an assembly are. You've seen what assembly manifests look like, how they're structured and used by the Common Language Runtime, and the previous exercise showed you what it looks like to create and make use of a single-file assembly.

Before you go on, remember that assemblies are a logical unit of deployment, security, and functionality. Security can be specified using an assembly as a target. Assemblies are the unit of deployment for the .NET Framework, and code, content, and resources can be either embedded in or linked with an assembly. Security is a topic for another chapter, but you'll get an overview of resources and embedded content next.

Embedding Content and Resources in Assemblies

The previous section discussed embedded and linked files. When you create an assembly, the manifest informs the Common Language Runtime of all dependent files. If you want to make sure that a specific icon, image, text file, or whatever file you need, is considered a necessary part of your application, you can make it a part of your assembly.

There are two ways to make a file part of your assembly. You can either embed the file directly into the assembly, or you can make the assembly refer to the file via the manifest. When using Visual Studio .NET, it is actually quite easy to create embedded resources, so that's what will be covered in this next section.

12

Embedding Content and Resources in Assemblies

Keep in mind that you can store absolutely anything as an embedded resource. Neither Visual Studio .NET nor the Common Language Runtime cares what information you're storing. Whenever you get a resource out of a loaded assembly, you get it as a stream (part of System.IO). This stream can contain any kind of data, including binary data for images, text data for XML, culture-specific string tables, and much more.

For this example, assume that you've decided that you want to add some kind of read-only set of data to your assembly. Perhaps you want to store a table of ZIP Code and county lookups, state names, or any other kind of large set of read-only data that you want to distribute with your application but you don't want to expose in some accessible format, such as Access or Excel.

Add a new item to the AssemblyIntro project, select XML File, and call it EmbeddedData.xml. Set its contents to the following:

```xml
<?xml version="1.0" encoding="utf-8" ?>
  <EmbeddedData>
    <DataNode id="21">
      <DataValue>This is a data value</DataValue>
    </DataNode>
    <DataNode id="35">
      <DataValue>This is another data value</DataValue>
    </DataNode>
  </EmbeddedData>
```

In that file's properties panel, set the build action to Embedded Resource. This instructs Visual Studio .NET to compile the file directly into the assembly. This is extremely important because if the file is not marked as an embedded resource, it will not be linked and will not appear in the compiled assembly.

To get at the embedded data, you need to make use of some more reflection. Listing 12.3 shows the new AssemblyTool class and a new method, GetDataNodeValue, to retrieve data nodes from the preceding XML.

LISTING 12.3
The New AssemblyTool Class, Modified for Embedded Resources

```csharp
using System;
using System.IO;
using System.Xml;
using System.Reflection;
using System.Text;

namespace SAMS.CSharpUnleashed.Chapter12.AssemblyIntro
{
```

LISTING 12.3
Continued

```csharp
/// <summary>
/// This is the AssemblyTool sample class
/// </summary>
public class AssemblyTool
{
  private static XmlDocument doc = null;

  public AssemblyTool()
  {

  }

  public static string GetAssemblyInfo()
  {
    // gets the Assembly in which this code is executing, not
    // necessarily the Assembly of the main executable (EX
    Assembly thisAssembly = Assembly.GetExecutingAssembly();
    AssemblyName thisName = thisAssembly.GetName();
    StringBuilder sb = new StringBuilder();
    sb.AppendFormat("Assembly Name: {0}\n", thisAssembly.FullName);
    sb.AppendFormat("Assembly Version: {0}\n", thisName.Version.ToString());
    sb.AppendFormat("Assembly Culture: {0}\n", thisName.CultureInfo.ToString());
    return sb.ToString();
  }

  private static void LoadEmbeddedDoc()
  {
    Assembly thisAssembly = Assembly.GetExecutingAssembly();
    Stream s = thisAssembly.GetManifestResourceStream(
      "SAMS.CSharpUnleashed.Chapter12.AssemblyIntro.EmbeddedData.xml");
    doc = new XmlDocument();
    doc.Load( s );
  }

  public static string GetDataNodeValue( int nodeId )
  {
    if (doc == null)
      LoadEmbeddedDoc();

    XmlNode node = doc.SelectSingleNode(
    string.Format("//DataNode[@id='{0}']", nodeId ) );
    if (node != null)
```

12

Embedding Content and Resources in Assemblies

LISTING 12.3
Continued

```
        return node.InnerText;
    else
        return "No node found";


    }
  }
}
```

The first new method, `LoadEmbeddedDoc`, uses `GetManifestResourceStream` to obtain a stream for the embedded XML document. Remember this method because you'll use it nearly every time you try to grab embedded data from an assembly. The second method, `GetDataNodeValue`, first checks to see whether `XmlDocument` is null.

TIP

Reflection operations are typically very costly in terms of time and processor consumption. If at all possible, store the results of reflection operations to avoid repetitive and redundant calls. In this case, the XML document is cached so that throughout the lifetime of the application process, the reflection operation is performed only once.

If the document is null, the `LoadEmbeddedDoc` method is invoked. Then some XPath is used to find the appropriate `DataNode` element and return its value.

Add the following few lines of test code to the main class to exercise the new code sections:

```
Console.WriteLine( AssemblyTool.GetDataNodeValue(21) );
Console.WriteLine( AssemblyTool.GetDataNodeValue(35) );
Console.WriteLine( AssemblyTool.GetDataNodeValue(50) );
```

Build the application again and run it, and you should see the following three new lines of text:

```
This is a data value
This is another data value
No node found
```

12

You might be wondering how this might actually be useful for you. If you are thinking about monolithic applications or large installs on DVD-ROMs, it might not seem all that useful. However, the situation changes if you think modular. In a situation in which your application relies on data embedded in an assembly and your application is configured for dynamic updates from the Internet, you can easily imagine a scenario where you could simply make changes to the embedded XML (or text files, or images, or language-specific strings, and so on) and they would propagate to your application (be it web-based or Windows-based) seamlessly. XML resources can also expose to other applications complex data structures to allow for in-depth processing, such as exposing an identity to an application that supports plug-ins (creating plug-ins will be covered at the end of this chapter).

Localization and Satellite Assemblies

At this point, you should have a good idea of how to create an assembly, what an assembly is, and how to program against it. In addition, you've seen how to embed resources such as XML files or images into the assembly and use the GetManifestResourceStream method to obtain a stream that can be used to view the resource. The next section of this chapter takes a look at what Visual Studio .NET calls *assembly resource files*.

An *assembly resource file* is essentially an XML file that contains resources. These resources can be strings, bitmaps, images, XML—whatever you like. To retrieve data from a resource file, you must supply a string identifier. When Visual Studio .NET has a .resx file, you can double-click it to pull up an editor that enables you to edit it in either an XML view or a data view. Every resource has a name that is used to retrieve it. That name is given to an instance of the ResourceManager class to obtain a resource. Here is an example of retrieving an integer from an assembly resource file that is part of a project:

```
ResourceManager rm = new ResourceManager("MyApp.MyResources",
    Assembly.GetExecutingAssembly());
int myint = (int)rm.GetObject("mynumber");
```

This should look pretty similar to the code to retrieve the embedded XML stream. The difference between the assembly resource file and doing it manually (as we did earlier) is that the assembly resource file supports *localization*. In other words, in addition to each resource being identifiable by name, it is also identifiable by *culture*.

The logic for finding a resource is actually fairly complex, but also extremely helpful. It works in a hierarchy, starting from most-specific culture to least-specific culture. For example, if your application defines strings in the neutral French culture, but someone's application is running in a location that speaks French but is not in France, the ResourceManager will still be able to find the appropriate French strings. If your application defines French resources as well as resources for the neutral (empty string) culture, people who are in non-French locations will still be able to locate the neutral resources and use those.

12

Satellite Assemblies

A *satellite assembly* is one that contains nothing but resources. It is usually created automatically for you by Visual Studio .NET, but you can do it manually using the command-line compilation tools. There are quite a few benefits of satellite assemblies, some of which are as follows:

▶ Resources can be added dynamically to the application after deployment.

▶ Modification of localized resources in satellite assemblies does not require recompilation of the application.

▶ Only those assemblies for the current culture are loaded, reducing memory overhead.

The model by which the Common Language Runtime locates localized resources is referred to as the *spoke-and-hub* model. As I said, it is a recursive descending hierarchy to locate the most appropriate resources given the current thread's culture. Figure 12.4 illustrates the spoke-and-hub model for resource location. When Visual Studio .NET creates satellite assemblies, they are placed in directories corresponding to spokes in the model shown in Figure 12.4.

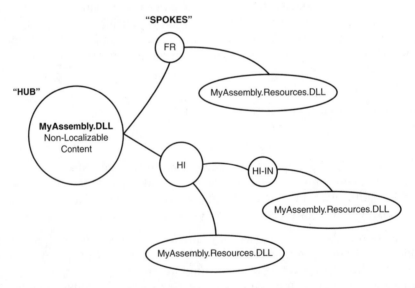

"HUB and SPOKE" Model for Resource Localization

FIGURE 12.4   The spoke-and-hub model for resource localization.

Now that you know how satellite assemblies work and what they do, you can create some. To do this, you'll create three separate assembly resource files. Right-click the

AssemblyIntro project and add a new item of type Assembly Resource File. Call these three files `Strings.resx`, `Strings.hi.resx`, and `Strings.fr.resx`. For the first file, add a resource string called `greeting`, with a value of `Hello` and a type of `System.String`. Make sure that you move the cursor off the current row before you save it, or the IDE will erase the entry. Table 12.1 shows how you should set up the various strings in each file.

TABLE 12.1

Multilingual Greetings in a `.resx` File

File	Name	Value	Type
Strings.resx	greeting	Hello	System.String
Strings.hi.resx	greeting	Namaste	System.String
Strings.fr.resx	greeting	Bonjour	System.String

It is vitally important that the string have the same name across all the different cultures. If you've followed Table 12.1, you should now have a greeting text in English, Hindi, and French.

Now write some code that accesses these strings. First, add the following method to the `AssemblyTool` class:

```
public static string GetResourceString( string id )
{
  ResourceManager rm =
    new ResourceManager(
      "SAMS.CSharpUnleashed.Chapter12.AssemblyIntro.Strings",
      Assembly.GetExecutingAssembly());
  return rm.GetString( id );
}
```

Note how the entire namespace is used as the first argument to the `ResourceManager`. Also note that the code didn't specify the culture. If no culture is specified manually, the `ResourceManager` class will use the current thread's culture.

Now add the following lines of code to the `Class1` class in the `Harness` console application as shown in Listing 12.4 (the additions have been highlighted).

LISTING 12.4
The Revised `Class1` Class

```
using System;
using System.Threading;
using System.Globalization;
```

12

Localization and Satellite Assemblies

LISTING 12.4
Continued

```
using SAMS.CSharpUnleashed.Chapter12.AssemblyIntro;

namespace Harness
{
  /// <summary>
  /// Summary description for Class1.
  /// </summary>
  class Class1
  {
    /// <summary>
    /// The main entry point for the application.
    /// </summary>
    [STAThread]
    static void Main(string[] args)
    {
      Console.WriteLine( AssemblyTool.GetAssemblyInfo() );
      Console.WriteLine("--");
      Console.WriteLine( AssemblyTool.GetDataNodeValue(21) );
      Console.WriteLine( AssemblyTool.GetDataNodeValue(35) );
      Console.WriteLine( AssemblyTool.GetDataNodeValue(50) );
      Console.WriteLine("--");
      Console.WriteLine( AssemblyTool.GetResourceString( "greeting" ) );

      CultureInfo ci = new CultureInfo("hi-IN");
      Thread.CurrentThread.CurrentCulture = ci;
      Thread.CurrentThread.CurrentUICulture = ci;
      Console.WriteLine( AssemblyTool.GetResourceString( "greeting" ) );

      ci = new CultureInfo("fr-FR");
      Thread.CurrentThread.CurrentCulture = ci;
      Thread.CurrentThread.CurrentUICulture = ci;
      Console.WriteLine( AssemblyTool.GetResourceString( "greeting" ) );

      Console.ReadLine();
    }
  }
}
```

12

As expected, you see a greeting in three different languages when you run the application. Before moving on to AppDomains, take a look at the bin\debug directory of the application. Figure 12.5 shows that the French and Hindi satellite assemblies have actually been stored in separate directories.

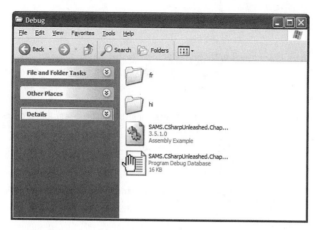

FIGURE 12.5 The debug directory, showing the directories for satellite assemblies.

AppDomains

This section of the chapter deals with AppDomains. AppDomains are essentially
Common Language Runtime sandboxes; that is, separated memory spaces within a
runtime host. Quite a few things can be done with AppDomains. Most of the time,
programmers are unaware of the fact that their code is executing within an
AppDomain and as such miss out on some very powerful features of the .NET
Framework.

Introduction to AppDomains

An AppDomain is both an in-memory construct used by the Common Language
Runtime for isolating applications from each other, as well as a class provided by the
.NET Framework. Tables 12.2 and 12.3 describe some of the more notable and useful
methods and properties belonging to the AppDomain class.

TABLE 12.2

Methods of the AppDomain Class

Method	Description
CreateDomain	This static method creates a new AppDomain in memory within the current Common Language Runtime host process. It accepts various arguments that serve to uniquely identify the new AppDomain.
CreateInstanceFrom	This method creates an instance of a type from within the given AppDomain. When you use the new operator, you create instances within the current AppDomain. To create instances in other AppDomains, use this method.

12

Localization and Satellite Assemblies

TABLE 12.2

Continued

Load	Loads an assembly into the given AppDomain.
Unload	Unloads the given AppDomain. Note that you cannot remove individual assemblies from an AppDomain; you must unload the entire domain.
GetAssemblies	This method gets a list of all the assemblies currently loaded into the AppDomain.
GetData	You can store name/value pairs in the AppDomain itself just as you can with CallContexts. This method retrieves a named value from the AppDomain.
SetData	This method sets a named value within the AppDomain.

TABLE 12.3

Properties of the AppDomain Class

Property	Description
BaseDirectory	Gets the base directory from which assemblies will be searched when being loaded.
CurrentDomain	This static method gets an instance of the currently active AppDomain in which the code is running.
Evidence	Contains the evidence and identity information for the current AppDomain.
FriendlyName	Indicates the FriendlyName of the AppDomain. In most cases, this is the name of the executable or application.
SetupInformation	This property is of type AppDomainSetup and contains assembly-binding data, including information on cache downloads, base directories, search paths, and more.

Programming with AppDomains

With that information in hand, you can now take a look at an example of programming with AppDomains. This next sample will show you how to use GetData and SetData to store and retrieve values that have the same scope as the AppDomain. In addition, you'll see how to create new AppDomains and load instances of classes into domains other than the default.

The first thing to do is to add a new method to the AssemblyTool class. It is shown highlighted in Listing 12.5. Note the addition of the new namespaces and the fact that AssemblyTool now inherits from MarshalByRefObject. Don't worry about this class; you'll see plenty of it in this book's coverage of remoting. For now, think of it as a marker that tells the Common Language Runtime to share the same object between AppDomains instead of creating a serialized copy. If the AssemblyTool class didn't have this marker, the method in Listing 12.5 would not work properly.

LISTING 12.5
The Modified `AssemblyTool` Class

```
using System;
using System.Runtime.Remoting;
using System.Resources;
using System.IO;
using System.Xml;
using System.Reflection;
using System.Text;

namespace SAMS.CSharpUnleashed.Chapter12.AssemblyIntro
{
  /// <summary>
  /// This is the AssemblyTool sample class
  /// </summary>
  public class AssemblyTool : MarshalByRefObject
  {
    private static XmlDocument doc = null;

    public AssemblyTool()
    {

    }

    public static string GetAssemblyInfo()
    {
      // gets the Assembly in which this code is executing, not
      // necessarily the Assembly of the main executable (EX
      Assembly thisAssembly = Assembly.GetExecutingAssembly();
      AssemblyName thisName = thisAssembly.GetName();
      StringBuilder sb = new StringBuilder();
      sb.AppendFormat("Assembly Name: {0}\n", thisAssembly.FullName);
      sb.AppendFormat("Assembly Version: {0}\n", thisName.Version.ToString());
      sb.AppendFormat("Assembly Culture: {0}\n", thisName.CultureInfo.ToString());
      return sb.ToString();
    }

    private static void LoadEmbeddedDoc()
    {
      Assembly thisAssembly = Assembly.GetExecutingAssembly();
      Stream s = thisAssembly.GetManifestResourceStream(
        "SAMS.CSharpUnleashed.Chapter12.AssemblyIntro.EmbeddedData.xml");
      doc = new XmlDocument();
      doc.Load( s );
```

12

LISTING 12.5
Continued

```csharp
    }

    public static string GetDataNodeValue( int nodeId )
    {
      if (doc == null)
      LoadEmbeddedDoc();

      XmlNode node = doc.SelectSingleNode(
      string.Format("//DataNode[@id='{0}']", nodeId ) );
      if (node != null)
        return node.InnerText;
      else
        return "No node found";
    }

    public static string GetResourceString( string id )
    {
      ResourceManager rm =
       new ResourceManager(
         "SAMS.CSharpUnleashed.Chapter12.AssemblyIntro.Strings",
         Assembly.GetExecutingAssembly());
      return rm.GetString( id );
    }


    public string GetAppDomainInfo()
    {
      AppDomain ad = AppDomain.CurrentDomain;
      StringBuilder sb = new StringBuilder();
      sb.AppendFormat("------\nAppDomain: {0}\n", ad.FriendlyName);
      sb.AppendFormat("\tHash Code: {0}\n", ad.GetHashCode());
      if (ad.GetData("MYVALUE") != null)
        sb.AppendFormat("\tStored Value: {0}\n", ad.GetData("MYVALUE"));
      foreach (Assembly asm in ad.GetAssemblies())
      {
        sb.AppendFormat("\tLoaded Assembly: {0}\n", asm.GetName().Name);
      }
      return sb.ToString();
    }
  }
}
```

12

The key piece here is the `GetAppDomainInfo` method. It uses some reflection methods to obtain information about the current AppDomain, including its name, hashcode, and even the list of all assemblies currently loaded into that AppDomain. Also note the use of `GetData` to retrieve a named value. We'll be using `SetData` to set that value in the `Harness` project next.

Make sure that the `AssemblyIntro` project compiles, add a using statement for System.Runtime.Remoting at the top of Class1.cs, and then add the following code to the end of `Class1` in the `Harness` project:

```
// experiment with an AppDomain
AssemblyTool at = new AssemblyTool();
AppDomain.CurrentDomain.SetData("MYVALUE", 1024);
Console.WriteLine( at.GetAppDomainInfo());

AppDomain ad = AppDomain.CreateDomain("SecondDomain",
                null, (AppDomainSetup)null);
Console.WriteLine("New domain has {0} Assemblies loaded.",
                ad.GetAssemblies().Length);
ad.SetData("MYVALUE", 42);

ObjectHandle handle = ad.CreateInstance(
  "SAMS.CSharpUnleashed.Chapter12.AssemblyIntro",
  "SAMS.CSharpUnleashed.Chapter12.AssemblyIntro.AssemblyTool");

AssemblyTool at2 = (AssemblyTool)handle.Unwrap();
Console.WriteLine( at2.GetAppDomainInfo());

Console.WriteLine("New domain has {0} Assemblies loaded.",
                ad.GetAssemblies().Length);
```

In the preceding code, an instance of `AssemblyTool` is created in the current AppDomain. Then, using the new method, the AppDomain information is displayed. Then a new AppDomain is created and the `CreateInstance` method is used to create a new instance of the `AssemblyTool` class in the new AppDomain. Finally, the instance from the second domain is used to display the AppDomain information.

If everything works properly, you should see very clearly that the two AppDomains are very distinct. They each have their own list of loaded assemblies, and therefore have their own unique lists of loaded types. Here is the output from the new section of code added to the test `Harness` application:

```
AppDomain: Harness.exe
        Hash Code: 2
        Stored Value: 1024
        Loaded Assembly: mscorlib
```

12

```
        Loaded Assembly: Harness
        Loaded Assembly: SAMS.CSharpUnleashed.Chapter12.AssemblyIntro
        Loaded Assembly: System.Xml
        Loaded Assembly: System
        Loaded Assembly: SAMS.CSharpUnleashed.Chapter12.AssemblyIntro.resources
        Loaded Assembly: SAMS.CSharpUnleashed.Chapter12.AssemblyIntro.resources


New domain has 1 Assemblies loaded.
------
AppDomain: SecondDomain
        Hash Code: 8
        Stored Value: 42
        Loaded Assembly: mscorlib
        Loaded Assembly: SAMS.CSharpUnleashed.Chapter12.AssemblyIntro
        Loaded Assembly: System.Xml


New domain has 3 Assemblies loaded.
```

There is quite a bit of interesting information available here. The default domain (named `Harness.exe`) has several assemblies loaded; in addition, you can see two `.resources` assemblies loaded. These are the satellite assemblies built in the previous section of this chapter.

When the new domain is created, it contains only one loaded assembly: `mscorlib`. After the code loads the `AssemblyTool` type into the new AppDomain, you can see that it loads `SAMS.CSharpUnleaded.Chapter12.AssemblyIntro` (the assembly in which the `AssemblyTool` class resides) and `System.Xml`. This is because for the Common Language Runtime to be able to properly handle the `AssemblyTool` type, it needs metadata from the `System.Xml` assembly.

Putting It Together—A Real-World Example

This next section will take you through the process of creating a rudimentary framework for building applications that can be extended via plug-ins. These applications can be web applications or Windows applications; it doesn't make any difference except how you present the user interface to your users. In this section, you will be putting to use your newly acquired knowledge of assemblies and AppDomains to create a real-world example and to do something fun with the new technology.

Building Application Plug-Ins

This next section will show you how to take all the techniques that you've learned throughout this chapter and put them to use in a real-world application: plug-ins.

If you've been using any computer over the past few years, you probably know about plug-ins. They enable you to play games with your friends over an instant messenger application; they make it possible for you to change the look and feel of your favorite media player; and they expand the functionality of existing applications by adding new menu items, tools, features, windows, and more. Users love plug-ins because they get to have access to the core features of an application, and they are in control over which extras they put in their application. In addition to being great for end users, plug-ins provide developers with the ability to create add-ins to the other applications with shortened development time. An application that supports plug-ins will probably have a much stronger chance of building a thriving user community than applications that don't.

To create your plug-in application, create a new Visual Studio .NET solution called `Plugins`. In this solution, create a class library called `PluginAPI`, a console application called `PluginTester`, and another class library called `SamplePlugin`. To make the console application the startup project, you can create that one first.

Most plug-in applications work on the assumption that when a third-party developer creates a plug-in, that developer abides by some pre-established rules. In most languages, those rules are defined by interfaces. Our plug-in application will be no different.

Every plug-in produced for the sample application will implement the `IPlugin` interface. This allows the *host* application (the application that locates and launches plug-in modules) to easily identify plug-ins and treat them all identically, regardless of who created the plug-in or what functionality it provides.

Vendors often produce a suite of plug-ins that provide some logically related functionality and want to bundle them all in the same assembly. This example will allow for this as well, assuming that a given assembly can contain one or more plug-in classes.

The code here won't get too complex; otherwise the details of the code might bog you down and prevent you from learning the key points of the chapter. As a result, this plug-in is going to do only one thing: identify itself. After you've learned how this plug-in framework functions, you can easily add your own functionality that suits your application.

Every plug-in framework should start with the development API or SDK. Application vendors that support plug-ins will typically distribute code that enables the creation of plug-ins. In this case, all we need is the `IPlugin` interface. Go ahead and create the `IPlugin` interface in the `PluginAPI` project shown in Listing 12.6.

12

Putting It Together—A Real-World Example

LISTING 12.6
The `IPlugin` Interface

```
using System;

namespace SAMS.CSharpUnleashed.Plugins.API
{
  /// <summary>
  /// Summary description for IPlugin.
  /// </summary>
  public interface IPlugin
  {
    string PluginName { get; }
  }
}
```

Pretty simple, right? All that's been done is indicate that every plug-in that implements the `IPlugin` interface must have a property called `PluginName` that supports at least a get-accessor.

The next step on the way to creating a plug-in application is to create the plug-in itself. Given the simple interface just shown, the plug-ins should be fairly short. To make sure that the solution can support multiple plug-ins, create two: a blue plug-in and a red plug-in.

Add a reference to the `PluginAPI` project from the `SamplePlugin` project. This is what a third-party developer would do when creating a plug-in for your application.

Now take a look at the code in Listing 12.7 for the `BluePlugin` and `RedPlugin` classes (`BluePlugin.cs` and `RedPlugin.cs`, respectively).

LISTING 12.7
The `RedPlugin` and `BluePlugin` Sample Plug-In Classes

```
using System;
using System.Runtime.Remoting;
using System.Reflection;

using SAMS.CSharpUnleashed.Plugins.API;

namespace SAMS.CSharpUnleashed.SamplePlugin
{
  /// <summary>
  /// Summary description for BluePlugin.
  /// </summary>
  public class BluePlugin : MarshalByRefObject, IPlugin
  {
```

LISTING 12.7
Continued

```csharp
    public BluePlugin()
    {

    }

    #region IPlugin Members

    public string PluginName
    {
      get
      {
       return PluginTool.GetResourceString( "BluePlugin" );
      }
    }

    #endregion
  }
}


using System;
using System.Runtime.Remoting;
using System.Reflection;

using SAMS.CSharpUnleashed.Plugins.API;

namespace SAMS.CSharpUnleashed.SamplePlugin
{
  /// <summary>
  /// Summary description for RedPlugin.
  /// </summary>
  public class RedPlugin : MarshalByRefObject, IPlugin
  {
    public RedPlugin()
    {

    }
    #region IPlugin Members

    public string PluginName
    {
      get
```

Putting It Together—A Real-World Example

LISTING 12.7
Continued

```
    {
      return PluginTool.GetResourceString( "RedPlugin" );
    }
  }


  #endregion
  }
}
```

Obviously these won't compile yet because you haven't yet written the `PluginTool` class. Given the previous examples in this chapter involving resources, you can probably guess what the `GetResourceString` method does. The `PluginTool` class (also part of the `SamplePlugin` project) is shown in Listing 12.8.

LISTING 12.8
The `PluginTool` Class

```
using System;
using System.Reflection;
using System.Resources;

namespace SAMS.CSharpUnleashed.SamplePlugin
{
  /// <summary>
  /// Summary description for PluginTool.
  /// </summary>
  internal class PluginTool
  {
    internal static string GetResourceString( string id )
    {
      ResourceManager rm = new ResourceManager(
        "SAMS.CSharpUnleashed.SamplePlugin.Strings",
        Assembly.GetExecutingAssembly());
      return rm.GetString( id );
    }
  }
}
```

Create the `Strings.resx` file by adding it to the `SamplePlugin` project and create two named strings: `RedPlugin` and `BluePlugin`. The values used in this sample were `This is the Red Plugin` and `This is the Blue Plugin`, respectively, but you can use anything you like. Feel free to get more complicated and make your plug-in identify itself in more than one language using code from earlier in the chapter as a reference.

Now you should be ready to write the code that would appear in the host application. This code will iterate through all the files in a given directory (probably a directory called `Plugins` or something similar) and retrieve a list of all the plug-ins available in all the files in that directory.

Before you write that code, there is a small lesson to be learned. Earlier in the chapter, it was mentioned that after you've loaded an assembly, it cannot be unloaded until its containing AppDomain is unloaded. For applications that have only one AppDomain, this means that the assembly will remain loaded until the application is shut down.

For many applications, this isn't a problem. However, a plug-in application needs to iterate through many, many assemblies to obtain the list of available plug-ins, and over the course of an execution can launch many of those plug-ins. If the application could not release the memory associated with iterating through the available plug-ins or with launched plug-in modules, it would become bloated very quickly and would be operating very inefficiently.

One way around this is to do all the work of assembly loading related to plug-ins in a completely separate AppDomain. You've already seen how to create a new AppDomain and instantiate a type into that AppDomain. In that case, the type will have a method that loads a list of identified plug-ins from a given directory. When that method is done, the calling code can simply unload the temporary AppDomain and the memory associated with the search operation will be released.

Add a new class called `PluginLoader` to the `PluginTester` console application. It is shown in Listing 12.9.

LISTING 12.9
The `PluginLoader` Class

```
using System;
using System.Runtime.Remoting;
using System.Reflection;
using System.IO;
using System.Collections;

using SAMS.CSharpUnleashed.Plugins.API;

namespace PluginTester
{
    /// <summary>
    /// Summary description for PluginLoader.
```

Putting It Together—A Real-World Example

LISTING 12.9
Continued

```
/// </summary>
public class PluginLoader : MarshalByRefObject
{
  public ArrayList GetPluginsFromDirectory( string dir )
  {
    Console.WriteLine(
      "About to search for Plugins from within the AppDomain {0}\n",
      AppDomain.CurrentDomain.FriendlyName);
    ArrayList pluginNames = new ArrayList();
    string[] files = System.IO.Directory.GetFiles( dir, "*.dll");
    foreach (string filename in files)
    {
      Assembly pluginModule = Assembly.LoadFrom(filename);

      foreach (Type t in pluginModule.GetTypes())
      {
        Type iface =
          t.GetInterface("SAMS.CSharpUnleashed.Plugins.API.IPlugin");
        if (iface != null)
        {
          IPlugin plug =
            (IPlugin)pluginModule.CreateInstance( t.FullName );
          pluginNames.Add( plug.PluginName );
        }
      }

    }
    return pluginNames;
  }
 }
}
```

There's quite a bit going on in the preceding code. The first step is to grab the list of all the DLL files in the directory and iterate through them.

TIP

Although the code used a file that ends with the .DLL extension, you can rename the file anything you like, such as `SamplePlugin.plg` or `SamplePlugin.plugin`. An advantage to that naming convention is that with a unique file extension, you can associate an action and an icon with it, allowing your application to be launched when someone double-clicks or downloads a plug-in module.

With the filename in hand, the code can create an assembly from that filename. Remember that `Assembly.LoadFrom` not only creates an assembly, but it also loads that assembly into the *current* AppDomain. With the `Assembly` reference, the code then iterates through all the types stored in that assembly, looking for any type that implements the `IPlugin` interface. Your code has to iterate through because the programmers can call their classes anything they like, with any namespace they like. Because of that, you have to explicitly search for classes that implement `IPlugin`. It might be a little extra effort, but the result is an extremely flexible and reliable plug-in solution.

Finally, after the code has found a class that implements `IPlugin`, it creates an instance of that class *in the current domain* and then simply adds the plug-in module's name to the output `ArrayList`.

The last thing you need to do is wrap the `GetPluginsFromDirectory` method call in its own AppDomain to enable the application to control the allocation of memory. You can do this in your own class if you like or you can even do it with an overload of `GetPluginsFromDirectory` that asks for the name of an AppDomain as well as a directory. For this sample, the code was just put in `Class1.cs` in `PluginTester` as shown in Listing 12.10.

LISTING 12.10
The `PluginTester` Console Application

```
using System;
using System.Runtime.Remoting;
using System.Collections;
using System.Reflection;

using SAMS.CSharpUnleashed.Plugins.API;

namespace PluginTester
{
  /// <summary>
  /// Summary description for Class1.
  /// </summary>
  class Class1
  {
    /// <summary>
    /// The main entry point for the application.
    /// </summary>
    [STAThread]
    static void Main(string[] args)
    {
      AppDomain ad = AppDomain.CreateDomain("PluginLoader");
```

12

Putting It Together—A Real-World Example

LISTING 12.10
Continued

```
ObjectHandle handle = ad.CreateInstance("PluginTester",
  "PluginTester.PluginLoader");
PluginLoader pl = (PluginLoader)handle.Unwrap();
ArrayList pluginNames = pl.GetPluginsFromDirectory(@"C:\Plugins");
AppDomain.Unload(ad);
foreach (string name in pluginNames)
{
  Console.WriteLine("Plugin Located: {0}", name );
}

Console.ReadLine();
    }
  }
}
```

The preceding code creates a new AppDomain called `PluginLoader`. Then, just as was done earlier, it creates an `ObjectHandle` from a type within an assembly and unwraps it to create an instance of the `PluginLoader` class in the secondary AppDomain. After the `PluginLoader` has been instantiated in the other domain (it must be a `MarshalByRefObject` due to remoting, which you'll learn about later in the book), you can simply invoke the method and then dispose of the domain via `AppDomain.Unload()`.

The output of running this console application looks something like the following:

```
About to search for Plugins from within the AppDomain PluginLoader

Plugin Located: The Blue Plugin
Plugin Located: The Red Plugin
```

It might look like a lot of work, but creating a framework like this has quite a few places where you can build very reusable and scalable code and use it for multiple projects. The benefit of enabling your application to work with third-party plug-ins can easily outweigh any complexity in creating the host application and the plug-in API.

12

Summary

This chapter started with a discussion of the assembly, a logical unit of storage, deployment, and security within the .NET Framework. You saw how important it is and what a core part of the Framework it is. After that you got a taste of programming with assemblies.

From there, the chapter went into a discussion of AppDomains and AppDomain programming, illustrating some of the incredible power that you can add to your application simply by being aware of their existence.

Finally, all the new information was summed up by building a rudimentary plug-in system, including a host application responsible for locating and identifying plug-in modules. The goal of this chapter is to show you some things you might not ordinarily get a chance to use. Although you could easily spend your entire .NET experience without using an AppDomain or an assembly, perhaps you now see what you would be missing without them.

12

13 COM and Windows Interoperability

IN BRIEF

Anyone who has ever done a significant amount of work with COM (Component Object Model) knows that the intentions of the standard were great, but the implementation fell short of the desired solution.

The goal of COM was to create a solution that would enable developers to create separate, self-contained components that could then be employed by developers using different programming languages in other environments. The actual solution did indeed provide that framework, but that framework has many limitations. The .NET Framework removes quite a few of those limitations.

It would be extremely easy for us to assume that COM is dead and that we don't need to concern ourselves with it. Unfortunately, COM is still alive and kicking, and must be dealt with whether we like it or not. A considerably large number of COM objects are still active and in use, so one goal of this chapter is to show you how to interact with those COM components.

In addition to interacting with COM, you must be able to interact with the underlying operating system as well as other DLLs that are not COM libraries (yes, they do actually exist). This chapter will take you through an examination of OS and DLL interoperability through a feature of .NET called *platform invoke*.

The topic of COM interoperability is one that can consume a book on its own. The information contained in this chapter should be enough to get you going, but will skip some of the low-level implementation details to avoid bogging you down and diluting the big picture.

WHAT YOU NEED

RECOMMENDED SOFTWARE	.NET Framework SDK v1.1 Visual Studio .NET 2003 with C# installed Visual Basic 6.0 (for COM Interop)
RECOMMENDED HARDWARE	PC that meets .NET SDK minimum requirements
SKILLS REQUIRED	C# and .NET familiarity Familiarity with COM

COM AND WINDOWS INTEROPERABILITY AT A GLANCE

Using .NET Code to Interact with COM	**275**		
Introduction to COM Interop	275	Code Interoperability Example: .NET	
The Runtime Callable Wrapper	275	Code Invoking COM Code	278
.NET to COM Marshalling	276		

COM to .NET	**281**		
The COM Callable Wrapper	281	Interop Programming Example: COM	
.NET Code Attributes for COM Interop Programming	281	Code Utilizing NET Components	283
		When to Use Interop	285
Marshalling Data from COM to .NET	282		

Primary Interop Assemblies	**286**		
Overview of Primary Interop Assemblies	286	Working with PIAs	286
		Producing and Deploying PIAs	287
Platform Invoke (P/Invoke)	**288**		
Introduction to Platform Invoke	288	Platform Invoke Sample—	
Consuming Unmanaged DLLs	288	The Win32 API	290
Platform Invoke—Data Marshalling	289	When to Use Platform Invoke	292
Summary	**292**		
Further Reading	**292**		

Using .NET Code to Interact with COM

.NET to COM, refers to the use of a managed .NET class to interact with an unmanaged COM component. The next section will show you how COM Interop works, what it looks like under the hood, and how to write code that makes use of COM objects from inside managed code.

Introduction to COM Interop

The Component Object Model (COM) gives developers the ability to expose functionality to other applications, components, and host applications through a binary standard to which all COM components must comply.

The .NET Framework provides several enhancements to the features and functionality made available through the COM standard. Until the day when the last COM component is replaced with a .NET component, you need to learn how to write .NET code that makes use of these COM components.

The main unit of deployment in the .NET Framework is the assembly. An assembly can be comprised of one or more files, and is described by metadata. Metadata allows any .NET assembly to determine enough information about other assemblies to communicate and instantiate other classes.

COM objects aren't described by metadata in the way that you might think of .NET metadata. Instead, COM objects are described by binary data stored in a type library. You can think of a type library as the COM equivalent of an assembly manifest.

The Runtime Callable Wrapper

For a managed .NET component to communicate with a COM object, the Common Language Runtime's process boundary must be crossed. Every time you cross a

13

process boundary from managed code, you need to perform marshalling to translate the information. If developers had to implement all of that marshalling themselves every time they wanted to use a COM object, none of them would ever use a COM object.

Using information obtained from a type library, the .NET Framework constructs a special proxy called the *runtime callable wrapper (RCW)*. This proxy looks like a standard managed object to anyone using it, but it has a special capability to send information across process boundaries to COM objects and to receive information back from those COM objects.

For each COM object, one and only one proxy is generated. That might not seem significant now, but it makes quite a bit of difference to multithreaded programs. If you have multiple threads accessing what might ordinarily be a multithreaded COM object through an RCW, all threads will be stacked up and waiting in line at the RCW itself.

Take a look at Figure 13.1, which illustrates the interaction between managed components and the runtime callable wrapper. There is always one RCW per COM object, even though you can have more than one .NET object instance per COM object (and therefore more than one instance per RCW).

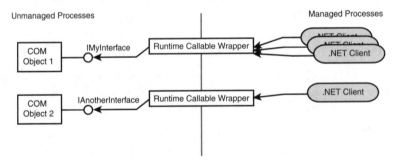

FIGURE 13.1   Interaction of managed and unmanaged COM code via the RCW.

In addition to providing the basic communication between managed components and COM components, the RCW provides marshalling between data types supported by the Common Language Runtime and data types supported by COM. The COM standard defines a strict set of data types to which all method arguments and return values must conform.

.NET to COM Marshalling

As mentioned earlier, the RCW takes care of translating information between managed components and COM components for method arguments and return values. It has several other features that allow it to make accessing a COM object from .NET appear to be as seamless and integrated as accessing a managed component from .NET.

Table 13.1 gives you a listing of each COM type and its corresponding .NET Framework type. Although a lot of this is automated for you, it is always extremely handy to know how the stock RCW will translate your data. If you don't like how the data is being marshaled, you can actually write your own custom marshal code, but that topic is beyond the scope of this book.

TABLE 13.1

COM Interop Data Marshalling Table

COM Value Type	COM Reference Type	C# Data Type
Bool	bool *	int
char, small	char *, small *	sbyte
Short	short *	int16
long, int	long *, int *	int
Hyper	hyper *	long
unsigned char, byte	Unsigned char *, byte *	byte
wchar_t, unsigned short	wchar_t *, unsigned short *	ushort
unsigned long, unsigned int	Unsigned long *, unsigned int *	uint
unsigned hyper	Unsigned hyper *	ulong
Float	float *	float
Double	double *	double
VARIANT_BOOL	VARIANT_BOOL *	bool
void *	void **	IntPtr
HRESULT	HRESULT *	Int16 or IntPtr
SCODE	SCODE *	int
BSTR	BSTR *	string
LPSTR or [string, ...] char *	LPSTR *	string
LPWSTR or [string, ...] wchar_t *	LPWSTR *	System.String
VARIANT	VARIANT *	object
DECIMAL	DECIMAL *	decimal
DATE	DATE *	System.DateTime
GUID	GUID *	System.Guid
CURRENCY	CURRENCY *	decimal
IUnknown *	IUnknown **	Object
IDispatch *	IDispatch **	Object
SAFEARRAY(type)	SAFEARRAY(**type**) *	type[]

13

Although this table of marshalling values was introduced in the .NET to COM section, it applies equally to data traveling in the other direction: COM to .NET. The next section will show you how to put this knowledge to use in an example of COM Interop code.

Code Interoperability Example: .NET Code Invoking COM Code

At this point, you're probably itching to get your hands dirty and start writing some Interop code. To create an Interop scenario in which you are making use of a COM object from the .NET Framework, you need the following things:

▶ A registered COM object—A COM object installed by a developer or vendor's installation software

▶ A type library—Obtained from the vendor's COM object

▶ An RCW—Generated at runtime on your behalf by the Common Language Runtime

The first thing you need to do is figure out what COM component you're going to make use of. If you've been contemplating COM Interop as a solution to your problems, you probably already have a good idea of which object you want to make use of.

When giving an example of Interop using an existing COM object, it often becomes more of a struggle of finding the right way to consume the vendor's API and less of an instructional exercise. This time you'll write some VB6 code to act as a mock-up of some fully functional COM object.

Open VB6. Struggle through the IDE enough to create an ActiveX DLL. This is going to create the first of the three things you need: a type library. Listing 13.1 shows the code for the COMHello ActiveX DLL with a class called HelloWorld.cls.

LISTING 13.1
The HelloWorld Class (Part of the COMHello ActiveX DLL)

```
Public Function GetMyData() As String
    Dim phonyData As String

    phonyData = "<tempDataSet>" & _
        "<customers customerid=""ALFKI""" & _
        " companyname=""Alfreds Futterkiste"" " & _
        "contactname=""Maria Anders""/></tempDataSet>"

    GetMyData = phonyData

End Function
```

13

As you can see, this is a pretty basic method that simulates some data retrieval. Rather than forcing you to look at old ADODB code to retrieve some data, I faked the retrieval of a few columns of the Northwind customer table in an XML representation of a DataSet. When you do a `Make` on this ActiveX DLL from within Visual Basic, the IDE will automatically register this as a COM component.

The first thing you need is the type library. You can get it by one of two methods: using a utility called `TlbImp.exe` or using Visual Studio .NET. Because there's a lot of material to cover, this chapter discusses only the use of the Visual Studio .NET method.

Now you can get back to modern technology and open Visual Studio .NET 2003. Create a new console application; you can call it anything you like. Right-click the References node and choose Add Reference. When the references dialog appears, click the COM tab and scroll down until you find `COMHello`. Double-click it and click OK to add the reference.

Behind the scenes, Visual Studio .NET is using the same code that `TlbImp.exe` uses in order to extract the type library from the COM DLL. After it has the type library, Visual Studio .NET creates a managed proxy class that enables you to access the `COMHello` ActiveX DLL as if it were managed **1**. The code in Listing 13.2 shows the code for the console application that invokes the `COMHello.HelloWorld` COM object.

LISTING 13.2
The Console Application Code That Utilizes a VB6 COM Object

```
using System;
using System.IO;
using System.Data;

namespace DotNet2COM
{
  /// <summary>
  /// Summary description for Class1.
  /// </summary>
  class Class1
  {
    /// <summary>
    /// The main entry point for the application.
    /// </summary>
    [STAThread]
    static void Main(string[] args)
    {
```

Using .NET Code to Interact with COM

13

LISTING 13.2
Continued

```
COMHello.HelloWorldClass helloWorld = new
 COMHello.HelloWorldClass();
DataSet ds = new DataSet();
StringReader sr = new StringReader( helloWorld.GetMyData() );
      ds.ReadXml( sr );
      sr.Close();
      Console.WriteLine(ds.GetXml());
      Console.WriteLine(
      string.Format(
        "Data from COM object returned {0} tables, " +
        "first table named {1} with {2} rows.\n",
        ds.Tables.Count.ToString(),
        ds.Tables[0].TableName,
        ds.Tables[0].Rows.Count.ToString()));
      Console.WriteLine(
      string.Format("First customer: {0}, Company {1}",
      ds.Tables[0].Rows[0]["customerid"].ToString(),
      ds.Tables[0].Rows[0]["companyname"].ToString()));
      Console.ReadLine();
    }
  }
}
```

The beauty of COM Interop is that, at first glance, nothing in this code gives you any impression that you are making COM Interop calls; you are insulated from all of that. The line

```
COMHello.HelloWorldClass helloWorld = new COMHello.HelloWorldClass();
```

might look a little awkward because of the naming convention, but it certainly doesn't indicate that it is a COM Interop call. The rest of the code deals with loading the XML returned by the method call into a DataSet and displaying it. Figure 13.2 shows the output of the preceding code.

Although this sample was overly simplistic, it should give you an idea of how to quickly invoke a COM object from .NET. The .NET Framework type library import process takes all the hard work out of creating a COM object wrapper and gives you an easy-to-use managed interface. This shouldn't fool you, however. There is a lot of code under the hood that makes it all possible. You can even write all the code that wraps the COM object yourself if you are into doing things the long way.

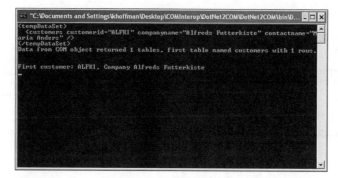

FIGURE 13.2 Output of the console application invoking a VB6 COM object.

COM to .NET

Exposing a .NET managed object as a COM object for consumption by·COM clients follows a similar process as exposing a COM object for consumption by managed clients. This next section will show you the ins and outs of getting started with .NET and COM Interop by exposing a .NET managed component as a COM component.

The COM Callable Wrapper

Just as .NET components need a runtime callable wrapper in order to communicate across process boundaries with COM objects, COM objects need a COM callable wrapper (CCW) in order to communicate with .NET components. Unable to communicate directly with managed code, the CCW acts as a proxy that both provides access to the exposed component and handles the default marshalling behavior (refer to Table 13.1 for a list of data type marshalling).

Figure 13.3 illustrates the relative position of the COM callable wrapper in a typical communication process.

.NET Code Attributes for COM Interop Programming

Even with the help of the CCW, it can be quite complicated to expose a .NET component to the COM world. One of the main reasons for that is because there are settings governing component behavior that are normally configured by developers within their COM components. Although you can create simple components that don't need any custom settings, it certainly helps to know what you can and can't modify. To get access to the various behavior modification properties of a COM component, the .NET Framework has created several code attributes that mark classes and assemblies for various levels of COM Interop.

13

COM to .NET

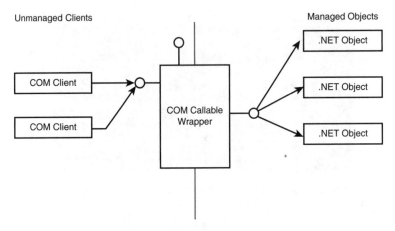

FIGURE 13.3   Illustration of the CCW.

Marshalling Data from COM to .NET

Table 13.2 contains a listing of some of the most common attributes used in COM Interop programming (a few of the less common attributes have been deliberately omitted). Although you might be able to avoid many of these by doing everything from within Visual Studio .NET, they're still good to know. This list is available in the MSDN library. If you are an old hand at COM programming, many of these attributes will make perfect sense to you. If you get more confused after seeing these attributes, you might benefit from curling up with a good book on COM. (Don Box's *Essential COM* is just that: essential.)

TABLE 13.2

COM Interop Programming Code Attributes

Attribute	Description
AutomationProxyAttribute	Indicates whether the type should be marshaled using the default automation marshaler or a custom proxy.
ClassInterfaceAttribute	Controls the type of class interface produced by the class: AutoDispatch, AutoDual, None.
CoClassAttribute	Identifies the original CLSID of a type imported from a type library. This is usually generated automatically by a tool, such as TlbImp.exe.
ComImportAttribute	If true, indicates that the coclass or interface was imported from a COM type library. This is usually applied automatically by tools.
ComRegisterFunctionAttribute	When used, this attribute indicates that the method should be called when the assembly is registered with COM, allowing developer-defined code to be executed.

TABLE 13.2

Continued

ComUnregisterFunctionAttribute	Like `ComRegisterFunctionAttribute`, but this attribute allows the developer's code to be executed when the assembly is unregistered from the COM system.
ComVisibleAttribute	By default, every public managed types is visible once it has registered with COM. Applying this attribute will make a type invisible from COM.
GuidAttribute	Indicates the globally unique identifier for a given type or interface, or the entire assembly (type library when exposed via COM).
InAttribute	Indicates that data should be marshaled in. Can be used to indicate input parameters via attributes.
OutAttribute	Indicates outbound marshaling to the COM system. Can be used to attribute parameters.
InterfaceTypeAttribute	Controls how a managed interface is exposed to COM (`Dual`, `IUnknown`, or `Dispatch` only). Affects compatibility with non-C++ COM implementations such as VB6.
MarshalAsAttribute	Forces the marshaling system to use a particular data type when marshaling the indicated field or parameter.
OptionalAttribute	Indicates an optional parameter.
ProgIdAttribute	Contains the ProgID of the associated .NET class.
StructLayoutAttribute	Manually controls the physical size and position of class members. Often applied by a Interop tool, such as `TlbImp.exe`.

Interop Programming Example: COM Code Utilizing .NET Components

To consume a .NET component via COM from a COM client, there are a few things you need to do. First, you have to create the .NET component. Second, you have to expose or register that component with COM. Third, you need to write the COM client in an unmanaged language, such as VB6 or C++.

To get started with the .NET component, create a new C# class library called COMtoDotNet. Then create a single class called DataGrabber. Here you're going to simulate the activity of some kind of data-driven component by querying data out of the Northwind database **2**. The code in Listing 13.3 shows the listing for DataGrabber.

COM to .NET

LISTING 13.3
The `DataGrabber` Class to Be Exposed to COM Clients

```
using System;
using System.Data;
using System.Data.SqlClient;

namespace COMtoDotNet
{
  /// <summary>
  /// Summary description for Class1.
  /// </summary>
  public class DataGrabber
  {
    public DataGrabber()
    {

    }

    public string GetData()
    {
      SqlConnection conn = new SqlConnection(
        @"(set to your connection)");
      SqlDataAdapter da = new SqlDataAdapter(
        "SELECT * FROM Customers", conn );
      DataSet ds = new DataSet();
      da.Fill(ds, "Customers");
      return ds.GetXml();
    }
  }
}
```

This code doesn't look too complicated. All you're doing is returning a string that contains the XML representation of the entire `Customers` table in the Northwind database.

Right-click the project and open the Properties window. Select the Configuration Properties node; on the Build tab, change the Register for COM Interop setting to true. This will allow Visual Studio .NET to automatically register your assembly with COM. If you want to register your assembly manually, you can open a command prompt and use the `regasm` utility.

After making sure that your `DataGrabber` class builds without error in the class library, it's time to move on to creating the COM client. You could use C++ to create a COM client, but VB6 is much easier to read and takes up much less room.

Open the VB6 IDE and create a new Windows application. Now you can add a reference to your newly created COM object. Open the Project menu and choose References. You'll see a check box list of various program IDs. Somewhere near the top, you will see a COM object called COMtoDotNet. Check that box and then click OK.

With the reference to the .NET component exposed via COM in place, you can write code that makes use of that component's methods. To get started, drop a button onto the form's surface; that button will be used to trigger the invocation of the managed COM component. The code for the form is shown in Listing 13.4.

LISTING 13.4
The VB6 Client Consuming the .NET COM Object

```
Private Sub Command1_Click()
    Dim c2d As COMtoDotNet.DataGrabber
    Dim data As String

    Set c2d = New COMtoDotNet.DataGrabber
    data = c2d.GetData()
    Text1.Text = data
End Sub
```

It all looks remarkably easy. This fact is actually a source of contention among many programmers. As you'll see in the next section, COM Interop isn't always a good thing. And even when COM Interop is a good thing, it is always more complicated than the tools make it seem.

When to Use Interop

So far you've seen the simplest ways that you can make use of COM Interop. These methods will actually work for a majority of the situations you'll come across. However, you might encounter some situations in which you have to get deep down into the attributes and type libraries and write custom marshalling to get things working.

With that aside, you need to be able to decide when you should use COM Interop. The first thing that you should know is that COM Interop is slow. Each time a .NET component makes a call to a COM object or a COM object makes a call to a .NET component, a significant amount of latency and overhead occurs. If you find yourself in a situation in which you need to make many repeated calls to the same object on the other side of a callable wrapper, you might want to reconsider the use of COM Interop.

Another question that often comes up is whether you should rewrite your existing COM objects in .NET or use Interop to reuse the existing components. Obviously if

13

those objects have to stay alive for backward compatibility, you will need to use Interop. However, if you can spare the time and effort to rewrite the components to take full advantage of not only the Framework itself but also the additional architectural structure available, it will be well worth your trouble to do so.

Primary Interop Assemblies

You've seen how to quickly create a COM object that can then have its type library imported and made available to .NET via Visual Studio .NET or the TlbImp.exe processor. When vendors want to make their components available to .NET programmers, they produce what is called a *primary Interop assembly (PIA)*. The next section of this chapter deals with what PIAs are, how they work, and how you can make and consume them in your own code.

Overview of Primary Interop Assemblies

PIAs are unique assemblies that contain COM proxies that are ready to be used by managed code. What happens all too often is that, without a PIA, every developer creates his own Interop assembly with TlbImp or Visual Studio .NET and is free to make changes and distribute that component with the application.

A PIA is made unique by virtue of being signed with a key pair file. Key pairs are generated using the sn.exe utility that is part of the Framework SDK. Rather than every developer creating their own COM wrappers around a vendor's COM components, the vendor can supply a single unique assembly that contains the vendor-approved COM wrappers that might be optimized to work with the vendor's product.

Working with PIAs

Primary Interop assemblies can be distributed with the application that contains the related COM components or they can be distributed as separate downloads from the vendor's website. If you aren't sure whether a particular COM component has a PIA, contact the component's vendor to double-check. If you create your own library and sign those types with your own key pair, your components could end up having compatibility issues with the vendor's PIA should the vendor produce one.

To write code that utilizes a PIA, all you have to do is add a reference to the PIA from your managed code project and use the classes and methods contained within the PIA as if they were managed. Typically any marshaling and COM compatibility issues will have been taken care of by the vendor, so most PIAs provide clean, easy-to-use implementations.

Producing and Deploying PIAs

Producing a PIA involves several steps. There are both suggested guidelines for features that a PIA should provide, and hard requirements that are enforced by the Framework itself. The following is the list of requirements that Microsoft lists as conditions that must be met for an assembly to be considered a valid primary Interop assembly:

▶ Includes all the COM types from the original type library, and the GUID for each type remains the same.

▶ The PIA must be signed with a strong name using the standard .NET Framework key pair signing mechanisms.

▶ The assembly must contain the `PrimaryInterOpAssembly` attribute.

▶ (Guideline) Should avoid redefining external COM types or types outside the control of the original publisher.

▶ For all external COM dependencies, the PIA should reference only other PIAs. In other words, it should not use an untrusted source of COM Interop for external COM component usage.

There are a few other suggestions and guidelines available for creating primary Interop assemblies. One of the suggestions that I strongly agree with is that all PIAs should have a namespace that ends with `Interop`. This would prevent future conflicts with a pure managed solution published by the same vendor.

The physical generation of a primary Interop assembly can be done one of two ways. The hard way involves manually writing the C# code that contains all the appropriate COM attributes (refer to Table 13.2 earlier in the chapter for some common COM attributes) to expose the types to COM. The second method involves using `TlbImp.exe` to create a managed assembly based on the information contained in a COM type library. Because `TlbImp` is the most common and the easiest to use, that's the method that will be discussed here.

To create a primary Interop assembly, it must be signed with public key encryption in the same way you sign your own assemblies for which you are providing a strong name.

To create a managed wrapper around a COM component, provide a signature key, and indicate that the assembly will be a primary Interop assembly, you can use the following syntax:

```
TlbImp filename /primary /keyfile:keyfilename /out:assemblyfilename
```

This code will create a new assembly called *assemblyfilename* that is marked as a PIA, signed with the key pair found in the file *keyfilename*. If you want to change

13

the namespace to reflect that the assembly is a PIA, you can use the /namespace option, as shown in this sample execution:

```
TlbImp ComComponent.tlb /primary /keyfile:ComComponent.snk
 /namespace:COMCompany.ComComponent.InterOp
 /out:COMCompany.ComComponent.InterOp.dll
```

The preceding command creates a new primary Interop assembly that is a managed wrapper for the functionality contained in the ComComponent type library, and changes the namespace of the managed classes to COMCompany.ComComponent.InterOp.dll.

Platform Invoke (P/Invoke)

So far, this chapter has covered how to communicate between COM DLLs and managed DLLs in both directions. This next section will discuss how to use managed code to invoke code that exists in unmanaged DLLs that are not registered with COM. Sometimes I feel like an old man describing 8-track tapes to teenagers when I explain to programmers that there are DLLs that have exposed functions but that don't have a visible object hierarchy, nor are they registered with COM or managed by the .NET Framework. I have actually heard people say, "You can actually do that?" Yes. You can indeed do that. In fact, the entire low-level Win32 API does that. The next section of this chapter is all about platform invoke: what it is, how to use it, and when to use it.

Introduction to Platform Invoke

Platform invoke is a concept rather than a method call. The idea behind platform invoke is that you can declare a method in C# that is external, as indicated by the keyword extern. This keyword tells the Common Language Runtime that the actual source for that method is stored elsewhere. When combined with enough attributes to identify the unmanaged DLL and unmanaged method name and parameters, the Common Language Runtime is able to marshal (see earlier sections for information about marshalling) between your managed code and the unmanaged library.

Consuming Unmanaged DLLs

When you want to make use of a method in an unmanaged DLL, you need to provide the Common Language Runtime with enough information to do the appropriate marshalling for you. First and foremost, the Common Language Runtime needs to know *where* to find the code for the method you're invoking. Secondly, the Common Language Runtime needs to know *what* the data types are of all the arguments and return values. Finally, you can also specify *how* you want those methods invoked for maximum compatibility with languages such as C and Delphi, which pass parameters differently and store strings differently.

Platform Invoke—Data Marshalling

Data marshalling with platform invocations takes place in much the same manner as with COM marshalling. The main difference is that there is no callable wrapper. The method calls are marshaled directly to the operating system (hence the term *platform*). Table 13.3 lists the data type translation and marshalling between C# and the operating system data types found in the Win32 API header file `wtypes.h`. You can find a similar chart in the MSDN library.

TABLE 13.3

Platform Invoke Marshalling Overview

Unmanaged Type (`wtypes.h`)	Unmanaged C Type	C# Type	Size
HANDLE	Void*	IntPtr	32 bits
BYTE	Unsigned char	byte	8 bits
SHORT	Short	short	16 bits
WORD	Unsigned short	ushort	16 bits
INT	Int	int	32 bits
UINT	Unsigned int	uint	32 bits
LONG	Long	int	32 bits
BOOL	Long	int	32 bits
DWORD	Unsigned long	uint	32 bits
ULONG	Unsigned long	uint	32 bits
CHAR	Char	char	Varies
LPSTR	Char*	string or StringBuilder	Varies
LPCSTR	Const char*	string or StringBuilder	Varies
LPWSTR	Wchar_t*	string or StringBuilder	Varies
LPCWSTR	Const wchar_t*	string or StringBuilder	Varies (Unicode sizing)
FLOAT	Float	single	32 bits
DOUBLE	Double	double	64 bits

When you find yourself looking at various unmanaged DLLs (including the Win32 API), and you need to figure out how to decorate your method wrappers with the right attributes and how to declare your parameters and return values, the Table 13.3 will help you determine the data types. Just find the unmanaged data type in the left two columns and then locate the appropriate C# type and size, and you should be able to create a proper platform invoke `extern` method.

Platform Invoke (P/Invoke)

Everything that you do rests on the use of one main attribute: `DllImportAttribute`. You use this attribute to decorate an `extern` method in C# so that it will match up with an unmanaged function in an unmanaged DLL. Provided the match is appropriate, you will then be able to call the declared method as if it were a purely managed method, leaving the details of marshalling to and from the OS neatly tucked behind the Common Language Runtime curtains. Table 13.4 contains a list of the properties you can set on the `DllImportAttribute` attribute.

TABLE 13.4

`DllImportAttribute` **Public Fields**

Property	Description
BestFitMapping	Indicates whether to use best-fit mapping between ANSI and Unicode characters.
CallingConvention	Sets or gets the calling convention of an entry point (Cdecl, Fastcall, StdCall, ThisCall, Winapi). Winapi isn't a calling convention, but a flag to use the default for the OS on which the method is running.
CharSet	Controls the marshalling of string parameters.
EntryPoint	This is the name or the ordinal value of the entry point (function) to be called. If omitted, the Common Language Runtime will use the name of the C# method marked with the DllImportAttribute attribute.
ExactSpelling	Controls whether the Common Language Runtime will search the DLL for alternate entry points.
PreserveSig	If set, indicates that the managed signature is a pure translation of the unmanaged signature.
SetLastError	If set, the callee uses the SetLastError Win32 API method before returning from the attribute-decorated method.
ThrowOnUnmappableChar	If set, indicates that an exception should be thrown when a Unicode character is mapped to an unknown ANSI character (appears as a ?).
dllName	This is not a public field. It is set in the constructor of the DllImportAttribute attribute only and indicates the name of the DLL in which the unmanaged code resides.

Platform Invoke Sample—The Win32 API

The following is an example of consuming an unmanaged DLL from within managed code. The problem with a lot of unmanaged DLL consumption is that the method signatures are difficult and hard to use. As a result, the following code is a quick example using one of the more simple methods in the Win32 API, `sndPlaySoundA` **3** (you could also use the corresponding `W` function for Unicode support).

13

LISTING 13.5
A Platform Invoke Sample

```csharp
using System;
using System.Runtime.InteropServices;

namespace SAMS.Evolution.CSharpUnleashed.Chapter13.Pinvoke
{
  /// <summary>
  /// Summary description for Class1.
  /// </summary>
  class Class1
  {
    /// <summary>
    /// The main entry point for the application.
    /// </summary>
    [STAThread]
    static void Main(string[] args)
    {
      sndPlaySoundA(@"C:\windows\media\Windows XP Startup.wav", 0);
    }

    [DllImport(@"c:\windows\system32\winmm.dll", EntryPoint="sndPlaySoundA",
        CallingConvention=CallingConvention.StdCall, SetLastError=true)]
    public static extern unsafe int sndPlaySoundA(string pszSound, uint fuSound);
  }
}
```

3

In Listing 13.5, I used the `DllImportAttribute` attribute to make use of a function in the `winmm.dll` library. The entry point (function name) is called `sndPlaySoundA` (ANSI convention, the Win32 API uses methods that end in W for wide string [Unicode] methods). The method will use the `stdcall` format for passing parameters on the stack. After the method has executed, it plays the Windows XP startup sound once in synchronous mode (indicated by the 0 parameter value).

The beauty of `DllImportAttribute` is that after you've declared the `extern` method, you can call it as if the method were pure managed code and you have to worry about setting up marshalling conventions only once.

It might seem daunting trying to manually figure out how all of these methods are supposed to be called and what the parameters are supposed to be. The good news is that a lot of the hard work has already been done for you. There are various sources for previously generated Win32 API declarations, such as the user samples area on www.gotdotnet.com and others.

13

When to Use Platform Invoke

When you are using languages such as C# or Visual Basic .NET, the line between when to use P/Invoke and when not to use it is pretty clearly drawn. If the particular task you want to perform is already provided for you by the .NET Base Class Library, there is no need to use Interop and platform invoke. However, if you are using Visual C++ .NET, the line is a bit more clouded. There are times when invoking the method call using native, unmanaged code from within C++ .NET will actually function faster than some of the code provided by the .NET Framework. For everyone except the most hard-core Win32 API experts, I suggest using the BCL classes whenever available, and resorting to using P/Invoke only when the task you need to perform cannot be done within managed code.

Summary

This chapter has been packed full of some interesting information. First, you looked at a few different ways to communicate with COM components. You saw sample code for invoking COM components from within managed code, and the reverse where your COM components (or in this case, VB6 Windows application) invoke managed .NET code. Wrapping up the discussion on interoperability, you looked at co-existing happily with the operating system and the functionality that it provides via unmanaged DLLs and how to access that functionality using platform invoke and the DllImport attribute.

Further Reading

Essential COM by Don Box, Addison-Wesley Professional. ISBN: 0201634465.

Programming .NET Components by Juval Löwy, O'Reilly. ISBN: 0596003471.

COM and .NET Component Services by Juval Löwy, O'Reilly. ISBN: 0596001037.

14 High-Performance Programming

IN BRIEF

Throughout the rest of this book, you will see how to improve the performance of your ASP.NET web applications and speed up your Windows Forms applications, your Web Services, and much more.

You can learn all the performance techniques in the world for each application type, but they won't help you very much if the code you write at the lowest level doesn't run as fast or use memory as efficiently as it could.

This chapter will demonstrate how to create high-performance C# code by showing you valuable techniques for memory management, dealing with the Garbage Collector, and speed techniques to improve the basic code that will be used in web applications and Windows applications alike.

WHAT YOU NEED

REQUIRED SOFTWARE	.NET Framework SDK v1.1 Visual Studio .NET 2003 with C# installed
RECOMMENDED HARDWARE	PC that meets .NET SDK minimum requirements
SKILLS REQUIRED	C# and .NET familiarity

HIGH-PERFORMANCE PROGRAMMING AT A GLANCE

Introduction to Garbage Collection	**295**		
Garbage Collection Internals—Generations	295	Caveat: Nondeterministic Finalization Versus Deconstruction	297
Coding with the Garbage Collector in Mind	296		
Memory and Class Management in the Common Language Runtime	**300**		
Boxing and Unboxing	300	Using the StringBuilder Class	303
Collections and Boxing	302		
High-Performance Code: Best Practices	**305**		
Using Exceptions	305	Tip: Using AddRange on Collections	307
Chunky API Calls	305	Jagged Versus Rectangular Arrays	308
Value Versus Reference Types	306	For Versus Foreach	308
		Utilizing Asynchronous I/O	310
Summary	**310**		
Further Reading	**310**		

Introduction to Garbage Collection

Garbage-collected environments are systems that provide for high-speed memory allocation, automatic disposal of unused allocations, and automatic fragmentation management. This really means that unlike languages such as C, where you must manage your own memory allocations with functions like `malloc()`, Garbage Collectors (GCs) enable you to allocate what you need, when you need it, and the rest is managed for you.

Unfortunately, this often leads to a hands-off attitude by many programmers. They assume that because the GC is running in the background, nothing needs to be done with their code. The truth is that the GC can be your best friend and worst enemy, depending on how you write your code.

Garbage Collection Internals—Generations

Generations are used to partition up the managed heap. The *managed heap* is the storage area where all memory allocations by your Common Language Runtime application are performed. Figure 14.1 shows the managed heap and the three generations. We will talk more about what all of this means shortly.

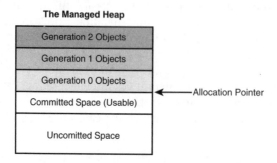

FIGURE 14.1   Managed heap model showing three generations.

Throughout the lifetime of a .NET application, two types of garbage collections can occur: full collections and partial collections. A *full collection* stops the execution of your program in order to scan through the entire managed heap looking for roots. Roots can be a number of things, but most of the time roots consist of stack variables and global objects that contain references into the managed heap (such as class instances that have global scope throughout your application). During a full collection, the collector goes through all the roots and tags each reachable, or *live*, object. When the full collection finishes, the list of reachable objects is preserved and all

unreachable objects become *condemned* and are destined to be thrown in the trash by the Garbage Collector. Part of the final collection process involves compacting and defragmenting the managed heap.

Because full collections have an incredible effect on the performance of your application (your application will stop responding until the full collection is complete), there is a need to be able to do something faster to decrease the consequences to your application. This is the job of a partial collection. Partial collections involve the use of generations (shown in Figure 14.1). The more recently an object has been allocated, the lower its generation number. So, you can assume that Generation 0 (often referred to as *Gen0* or *G0*) contains the newly allocated objects.

When a partial collection occurs, the roots are traversed just as in a full collection. However, the old objects are temporarily ignored (they are in Gen1 or Gen2) and only the roots for Gen0 are examined and collected. This shortcut scenario allows the work of a full collection to be postponed by assuming that all the older objects are still *live*. Through research and profiling applications, Microsoft determined that the highest degree of churn (quick allocation and deallocation) occurs in short-term objects such as temporary variables, temporary strings, placeholders, and small utility classes. In short, Generation 0 objects are collected most frequently and collecting Generation 0 objects takes the shortest amount of time.

This works only if the assumption that old objects are still live. To accurately determine when the collector needs to work on Generation 1 or 2, we need to know which objects in the older generations have been modified. Storing this "dirty" flag is accomplished by a data structure called the *card table*. The card table is an array of bits, with each bit representing a specific segment of memory. (The size of memory monitored by each bit varies with different GC implementations on different operating systems.) When an object written to that is in a memory segment monitored by the card table, the bit flag is switched, which indicates that piece of memory has been modified.

The real partial collection in the GC occurs just as mentioned earlier, but with one new twist. After the collection of G0 takes place, the all older objects that have been modified (as indicated by the card table) are then treated as roots. Those roots are then traversed as if they were G0 roots and a collection is performed.

Coding with the Garbage Collector in Mind

Now that you have a basic idea of how the Garbage Collector works, you can think about how to make sure that your code doesn't work in such a way that it slows down the GC. Entire books have been written about the Common Language Runtime and the code that drives it, including the Garbage Collector, so this overview will just talk about how to avoid some common GC pitfalls in your code.

If you know how the Garbage Collector works, you know how it can slow down. One of the most common ways in which the GC can be slowed down is through having

too many things allocated. The more roots there are to traverse, the slower each collection will be. You can't even count on a partial collection to save time, particularly if the high number of allocations is in Generation 0 objects. When you are writing code, always keep in mind how many allocations you are performing. Array creation usually generates quite a few allocations that might or might not be necessary, depending on your code.

Keep in mind that the GC needs to walk the roots in order to find unused objects. The more roots there are to examine, the longer it takes the collector to run. If you create a large structure that contains a large number of references (pointers), the collector has to follow each of those references to determine which objects are live and which objects aren't live each time it runs.

If a large structure with a large number of pointers (or any other structure that is time-consuming for the GC to examine) is long-lived, garbage collection will be handled by a full collection. If a large structure is short-lived, continually collecting that same structure slows down the GC and could also slow down the application.

You should also avoid deeply recursive methods that have many object pointers within each method. Such methods create a large number of roots (remember, roots are stack variables and global object pointers) to deal with on a G0 collection. You might notice that your deeply recursive method takes too long to execute because the GC is struggling to keep up with the root allocations.

Here are some Microsoft guidelines for keeping the number of roots low and the G1 size from expanding quickly:

▸ Allocate only the objects you need, and only when you need them.

▸ When creating objects that will be live for a long period of time, keep their size as small as possible.

▸ Keep as few object pointers on the stack as possible.

The best things that you can do for your code are to run it through a profiler that shows Garbage Collector activity, and to use the preceding advice to tune your code to be more GC-friendly.

Caveat: Nondeterministic Finalization Versus Deconstruction

One fundamental difference between objects in C# (and the .NET Framework in general) and objects in languages like C++ is the distinction between destructors and finalizers. A *destructor* is a method that is called on an object at the instant it is destroyed with a keyword such as `delete` in C++. A *finalizer* is a method that is called by the Garbage Collector during a collection process.

Introduction to Garbage Collection

There is a cost to finalization that you should be aware of. If you implement a finalizer on your class, it will *not* be called when you set the object to null or when the object goes out of scope. It will be called during the next appropriate stage of collection.

When the GC encounters an object that has a finalizer, it has to stop collecting that object. The GC puts the object in a list to deal with later. The problem occurs because any object references inside the finalizer must remain valid until collection time. Everything that the object with a finalizer references, either directly or indirectly, continues to live until the object is collected. If the object manages to get into G2, it could take a very long time to collect. In fact, depending on how long the application runs, there's a good chance that the object won't be collected until your application exits.

There is a way out. If your object absolutely must make use of a finalizer, you can tell the GC to skip the normal collection process for that object if the object implements the `IDisposable` interface and the code invokes the `Dispose` method. In essence, this allows your object to finalize itself and does not put the burden on the GC. Listing 14.1 shows a simple class that implements the `IDisposable` interface.

LISTING 14.1
The Code for a Simple `IDisposable` Implementation

```csharp
using System;

namespace Disposable
{
    /// <summary>
    /// Summary description for DisposableObject.
    /// </summary>
    public class DisposableObject : IDisposable
    {
        private int memberData;

        public DisposableObject()
        {
            // obtain resources to support object
        }

        public int SomeProperty
        {
            get
            {
                return memberData;
            }
```

LISTING 14.1
Continued

```
    set
    {
      memberData = value;
    }
  }

  private void Cleanup()
  {
    // get rid of resources used to support object
  }

  #region IDisposable Members

  public void Dispose()
  {
    Cleanup();
    //tell the GC that it doesn't need to take care of this object, we're done
    //with it.
    System.GC.SuppressFinalize(this);
  }

  #endregion
  }
}
```

There are a couple of good things about IDisposable. The first is that implementing it in a class that requires finalization enables you to do it on your own without slowing down the GC to take care of it. The second is that C# contains the using keyword, which makes blocks of code using the IDisposable object easier to create and to read. After the code inside a using block has completed, anything declared within the using statement automatically has its Dispose method called, even if an exception occurred during the block. The following is a demonstration of employing the using keyword on the class from Listing 14.1:

```
using (DisposableObject dispObject = new DisposableObject())
{
  // do something with the object
  dispObject.SomeProperty = 42;
}
```

This section on the Garbage Collector won't make you an expert on the GC overnight, but at least you will be aware of what the GC is, how it works, and some of the things you can do to speed up your code. The biggest step toward improving your code's GC performance is simply acknowledging that the GC is there to begin with.

Memory and Class Management in the Common Language Runtime

This section of the chapter deals with how the Common Language Runtime manages memory, and how you can make some adjustments in your code to be more accommodating of the Common Language Runtime's memory manager. You will be introduced to the concepts of boxing and unboxing and how those concepts apply when dealing with collections and arrays. In addition, this section discusses string management, how the Common Language Runtime deals with strings, and what you can do to increase string performance.

Boxing and Unboxing

Boxing and *unboxing* refer to the ability to convert between value types and reference types. A *value type* is a simple type such as an integer or a decimal or a float. A value type can also be a struct, which is a simple value version of a class. A *reference type* is a type whose value is not contained in the variable; rather, the variable contains a reference that points into a location on the managed heap for the actual data. Such types are class instances and strings.

Boxing

Boxing is the process by which a value type is treated as an object. Many people think that when a value type is boxed, a dynamic reference is created. For example, assume that you box an integer variable that contains the value 10,000. Then you change the original integer value to 452. Interestingly, the boxed object will not recognize the change. When you box a value type, a copy of it is placed on the managed heap (as opposed to the stack, where normal value types reside) and a reference to that value type is placed in the object variable. After the boxing operation, there is no relation between the original value and the boxed value. Listing 14.2 is a demonstration of boxing a value, and how the boxed value and original value are not linked in any way.

LISTING 14.2
A Boxing Demonstration

```
using System;

namespace Boxing
{
```

LISTING 14.2
Continued

```
/// <summary>
/// Summary description for Class1.
/// </summary>
class Class1
{
  /// <summary>
  /// The main entry point for the application.
  /// </summary>
  [STAThread]
  static void Main(string[] args)
  {
    int x = 10000;
    object ob = x;

    Console.WriteLine("Value of X = {0}", x );
    Console.WriteLine("Value of Ob = {0}", ob );

    x = 452;
    Console.WriteLine("Value of X after change = {0}", x );
    Console.WriteLine("Value of Ob after change = {0}", ob );
    Console.ReadLine();
  }
}
}
```

Here is the output of the code in Listing 14.2:

```
Value of X = 10000

Value of Ob = 10000

Value of X after change = 452

Value of Ob after change = 10000
```

Remember that excessive numbers of allocations are among the things that slow down the GC. Every time a value type is boxed, it is a new allocation. The difficult part is that you never see the allocation. Boxing itself also incurs a performance penalty. You should be aware of when your code is boxing, and avoid it if you can.

Memory and Class Management in the Common Language Runtime

Unboxing

Unboxing is the opposite of boxing. When a reference type is unboxed, it is converted from a reference type to a value type; its value is copied from the managed heap onto the stack.

When a value is unboxed, the object instance is checked to make sure that it is indeed a boxed value of the right type. If this check succeeds, the value is copied from the heap onto the stack and assigned to the appropriate value type variable. As with boxing, unboxing a variable incurs some performance overhead. Whereas boxing creates a new allocation on the managed heap to store the new reference value, unboxing creates a new allocation on the stack to store the unboxed value. The following few lines of code, taken from Listing 14.1, show an unboxing operation:

```
int x = 10000;
object ob = x;


Console.WriteLine("Value of X = {0}", x );
Console.WriteLine("Value of Ob = {0}", ob );


x = 452;
Console.WriteLine("Value of X after change = {0}", x );
Console.WriteLine("Value of Ob after change = {0}", ob );
Console.WriteLine("Value of Ob unboxed to int = {0}", (int)ob);
```

The output of the preceding code is as follows:

```
Value of X = 10000


Value of Ob = 10000


Value of X after change = 452


Value of Ob after change = 10000


Value of Ob unboxed to int = 10000
```

Collections and Boxing

Collections (and other weakly typed classes such as DataSets) through their nature and use perform a large amount of boxing and unboxing. For example, assume that you are using an ArrayList to store integers, as in the following code:

```
ArrayList al = new ArrayList();

// load arraylist from some source

foreach (int x in al)
{
    // do something with integer
}
```

14

There are a few issues with the loop in the preceding code. The first issue is that each iteration through the loop causes an unboxing operation to occur. This could become very slow and very costly, depending on the size of the `ArrayList`. Another issue is that the use of `foreach` causes some generalization code to occur that might be slower than using a number-based `for` loop. Eventually `foreach` will be optimized to work just as fast as a regular `for` loop. Although the `foreach` loop is easier to read, it might not always be the fastest solution.

The bottom line is that the performance penalties for boxing and unboxing are multiplied by the size of a collection whenever you perform a boxing or unboxing operation within an iteration through a collection. The next time you find yourself writing a `for` loop, double-check the contents of the loop to see whether you might be doing something expensive during each iteration.

Using the `StringBuilder` Class

One thing that seems to take people a while to grasp fully is that the .NET Framework treats strings as immutable. In other unmanaged languages, you typically allocate a contiguous block of memory in which to store a string. You can continue along in your code, making changes to the string at will as long as you don't exceed its allocated space.

Consider the following few lines of code:

```
string sample = "This is a sample string";
sample = "This is another sample string";
sample = sample.Replace("sample", "cool");
Console.WriteLine(sample);
```

If this were an unmanaged language, the preceding code would have allocated enough memory to store the phrase "This is a sample string". Then, on the second line, it would have modified the same piece of memory and extended the allocation. The third line would have modified the same area of memory yet again.

.NET, however, treats strings as immutable. When a string has been defined, it cannot be changed or modified. This might make you think that an operation such as

Memory and Class Management in the Common Language Runtime

`Replace` would be impossible to perform on strings. When you modify strings in C#, you are actually creating additional strings that represent the changed values. For example, when you execute the preceding code, the following strings are allocated and stored on the heap:

```
This is a sample string
```

```
This is another sample string
```

```
This is another cool string
```

In the preceding code, each concatenation of a single variable was actually creating a new string in memory. Consider the following `for` loop:

```
string myString = "Hello, ";
for (int i=0; i < 500; i++)
{
   myString += i.ToString();
}
```

The preceding `for` loop contains a few mistakes that might not be immediately obvious. The first mistake is that the `i` variable is intentionally boxed during each iteration, which can cause performance problems. The second mistake is that a string is concatenated with the `+=` operator. As you now know, you cannot modify existing strings in C#; you can only create new strings on the heap. When you iterate through a loop 500 times, concatenating strings to an existing string, you end up with 501 allocated strings on the heap, only one of which is live (that is, only one has a valid reference pointing to it). That means 500 collections must take place on unused strings during the next Garbage Collection process.

There is a way around this performance problem. Whenever you construct a string through concatenation or modify an already allocated string, you can use the `StringBuilder` class instead of simple concatenation. Because of the way the `StringBuilder` class manages its internal data, you can perform all the concatenations you like using `StringBuilder` and you will not have the performance problems that come with standard concatenation. The following code shows you a more efficient way to perform repeated concatenations:

```
StringBuilder sb = new StringBuilder();
sb.Append("Hello ");
for (int x=0; x < 500; x++)
{
    sb.AppendFormat("{0}", x);
}
```

The preceding code has a boxing issue, but at least you don't have 500 unused strings sitting on the heap after the loop.

High-Performance Code: Best Practices

Unfortunately, many people assume that their code is working as fast as it can because it runs fine in the environment in which it is being tested. This leads to an attitude that ignores coding with performance in mind because the application runs fast, with no noticeable drop in performance, regardless of how it is coded.

The next section will show you some ways to write code that preempts a large number of the performance problems that you might experience, but without having to run a lot of complex performance analysis tests.

Using Exceptions

If you've been programming with .NET for a while, you're familiar with the sound of your hard drive grinding and screeching when an unhandled exception is thrown. In fact, the exception sometimes consumes so many resources that you know it's about to happen even before the error dialog appears. The bottom line is that throwing exceptions is extremely expensive for any .NET application, whether it is an ASP .NET web application, a Windows application, or a Windows service.

Keep in mind that the cost involved with exceptions occurs only when exceptions are thrown, not every time you enclose code in a `try/catch` block. Exceptions should be used to handle only unexpected conditions. Never use an exception to deal with something like user interface or input validation, validation of function parameters, and so forth. Exceptions should be reserved for only those circumstances where something went so wrong that the current context could no longer complete its task properly.

To get a good idea for how many exceptions your application generates, you can look at your application in the Performance Monitor (also called *perfmon*). One of the counters that you can examine is the number of exceptions generated. The Framework itself could be throwing exceptions without your knowledge, so it is always a good idea to examine your application's exception performance.

Chunky API Calls

There are two different schools of thought with regard to designing an API. One style is called *chatty*, which refers to very small and frequently invoked methods. The other style is *chunky*, which refers to less frequent, larger method calls. When a method call is referred to as *large*, the word *large* typically indicates the amount of work performed and the time it takes to complete the task.

High-Performance Code: Best Practices

The reason for the debate about chatty versus chunky APIs is that some method calls incur performance overhead simply by invoking them. Such calls include COM Interop, Platform Invoke (P/Invoke), web service, Remoting, and any other call that crosses a process boundary or requires additional effort to marshal information to the called method.

> **TIP**
>
> If you have to choose between whether to perform a task via COM InterOp or via Platform Invoke, consider this: The overhead for creating a P/Invoke call can be as few as 31 instructions, whereas the overhead for making a COM method call can be more than 65 instructions.

There is a vanishing point at which the overhead cost becomes greater than the cost of performing the method call itself. This is when you know that your API has become far too chatty, and you need to combine tasks to create method calls where the overhead cost is minimal compared to the tasks performed by those methods.

Value Versus Reference Types

As you saw earlier in the chapter, value types that are treated as object types incur a boxing performance penalty. Value types are stored on the stack and are not stored on the managed heap. These facts mean that, by default, value types perform slightly better than reference types so long as the value type is small enough.

One way in which you can easily gain some advantage in regard to memory and speed is by examining your code for classes that are nothing more than property containers. You could be using a class to contain some information, but the class doesn't have very many methods (if any at all). If the memory size of the class is also pretty small, you might want to consider turning that class into a `struct`.

Consider the following class:

```
class MyClass
{
    public Myclass() { MyData = 21; }

    public int MyData;
    public int OtherData;
    public string SomeMoreData;
}
```

If you are passing instances of this class as parameters to method calls (reference type), you can definitely get some performance improvement by converting the class into a `struct`, as shown here:

```
struct MyClass
{
    public Myclass() { MyData = 21; }

    public int MyData;
    public int OtherData;
    public string SomeMoreData;
}
```

14

Tip: Using `AddRange` on Collections

When you need to add items to a collection, you should consider using AddRange instead of Add. The reason for doing so is that when you're adding multiple items, using Add within a loop is considerably slower than using AddRange. The AddRange method enables you to add a collection of items to an existing collection. If you find yourself in a situation in which you are looping through a collection, adding values to another collection, it is an ideal time to switch methods and use AddRange.

Jagged Versus Rectangular Arrays

A jagged array is slightly different from a multidimensional array. You can think of a standard multidimensional array as a rectangular array. Jagged arrays are arrays of arrays. When you provide an index into a jagged array, you are referencing an array. But with a multidimensional array, you are referencing one dimension. To make it obvious, the following code shows how you would declare a jagged array as compared to a rectangular array:

```
[STAThread]
static void Main(string[] args)
{

  // declare a jagged array
  string[][] jaggedArray = {
    new string[] { "One", "Two", "Three" },
    new string[] { "One", "Two" },
    new string[] {"One", "Two", "Three", "Four" } };

  // declare a two-dimensional array
  string[,] twoDArray = {  { "One", "Two" },
    { "One", "Two" },
    { "One", "Two" } };
}
```

High-Performance Code: Best Practices

The reason the comparison between rectangular and jagged arrays is mentioned is that the Common Language Runtime can optimize access to jagged arrays much better than it can optimize access to rectangular arrays. If you can figure out a way to accomplish your task with a jagged array, the code's performance will be better if you implement the jagged array to start with, and you won't have to worry about optimizing arrays when your application is complete.

For **Versus** Foreach

It was discussed earlier that using a foreach loop typically results in slower code than using a for loop. This is because the code created to deal with the foreach loop uses generalized objects, whereas you have more specific control over the for loop.

When you use a foreach loop, the .NET Framework automatically builds a try/finally block and uses the IEnumerable interface. The following code iterates through an ArrayList of the days of the week in C# using both a foreach loop and a for loop:

```
foreach (string x in al)
{
  Console.WriteLine(x);
}


for (int i=0; i < al.Count; i++)
{
  Console.WriteLine(al[i].ToString());
}
```

Here is the IL code generated by a foreach loop (word wrap in the code is for clarity only):

```
.try
  {
    IL_0061:  br.s        IL_0075
    IL_0063:  ldloc.3
    IL_0064:  callvirt
      instance object [mscorlib]System.Collections.IEnumerator::get_Current()
    IL_0069:  castclass   [mscorlib]System.String
    IL_006e:  stloc.1
    IL_006f:  ldloc.1
    IL_0070:  call        void [mscorlib]System.Console::WriteLine(string)
    IL_0075:  ldloc.3
    IL_0076:  callvirt
```

```
     instance bool [mscorlib]System.Collections.IEnumerator::MoveNext()
  IL_007b:  brtrue.s    IL_0063
  IL_007d:  leave.s     IL_0093
} // end .try
finally
{
  IL_007f:  ldloc.3
  IL_0080:  isinst      [mscorlib]System.IDisposable
  IL_0085:  stloc.s     CS$00000002$00000001
  IL_0087:  ldloc.s     CS$00000002$00000001
  IL_0089:  brfalse.s   IL_0092
  IL_008b:  ldloc.s     CS$00000002$00000001
  IL_008d:  callvirt    instance void [mscorlib]System.IDisposable::Dispose()
  IL_0092:  endfinally
} // end handler
```

14

Here is the code generated by a simple `for` loop:

```
IL_0093:  ldc.i4.0
  IL_0094:  stloc.2
  IL_0095:  br.s        IL_00ac
  IL_0097:  ldloc.0
  IL_0098:  ldloc.2
  IL_0099:  callvirt
    instance object [mscorlib]System.Collections.ArrayList::get_Item(int32)
  IL_009e:  callvirt    instance string [mscorlib]System.Object::ToString()
  IL_00a3:  call        void [mscorlib]System.Console::WriteLine(string)
  IL_00a8:  ldloc.2
  IL_00a9:  ldc.i4.1
  IL_00aa:  add
  IL_00ab:  stloc.2
  IL_00ac:  ldloc.2
  IL_00ad:  ldloc.0
  IL_00ae:  callvirt
    instance int32 [mscorlib]System.Collections.ArrayList::get_Count()
  IL_00b3:  blt.s       IL_0097
```

You don't have to be able to understand much MSIL to understand that the code for a `foreach` iteration is going to be slower and more time-consuming than the code for a regular `for` loop. If you are running through a potentially large collection, you should consider using a standard `for` loop instead of a `foreach` loop. In the future, the code for `foreach` might be as optimized as the code for a regular `for` loop. However, for now, you should definitely consider the speed of a `for` loop as an advantage over the readability of a `foreach` loop.

14

Utilizing Asynchronous I/O

Another best practice that you can adopt is that of asynchronous I/O. In most cases, you can get away with synchronous I/O whether you are reading from a file on disk or a file indicated by a URL. However, there are times when the information being read from disk (or any other location) is so time-consuming, or the processing of the information being read is so time-consuming, that you can't perform the operation without blocking the user.

The key to asynchronous I/O is the use of `BeginRead`, `EndRead`, `BeginWrite`, and `EndWrite`. You will see plenty of I/O code throughout this book, and a great deal of asynchronous code.

The purpose of this section is to get you to design your application around the concept of asynchronous I/O. Instead of thinking of reading to or writing from a file as something that the user has to wait for, think of it as something that can happen behind the scenes. If you are working on a WinForms application, you can think of using progress bars and status bars to indicate the status of asynchronous operations. You could use some kind of iconographic treatment, such as green, red, and yellow lights in the status bar, to indicate file I/O operations.

The bottom line is that if a user has to sit, unproductive, and wait for an application to do *anything*—whether it is I/O or anything else—that user will be displeased. Anytime you find yourself waiting for your application to finish a task, consider making that task asynchronous so that it can complete in the background while the user can interact with the application.

Summary

After reading this chapter, you should have a better idea of some of the fundamental things you can do in your day-to-day coding—whether it be for a web application or a Windows application—to increase your application's speed and efficiency. This chapter discussed various aspects of the Garbage Collector and how you can structure your code to reduce the effect that the GC has on your application's performance. Also discussed were dealing with things such as boxing and unboxing, value types and reference types, string building and collections, and much more. The point of this chapter is to encourage you to build good habits that will reduce the amount of performance tuning you have to do after your application has been built.

Further Reading

For more information about Common Language Runtime internals and high-performance coding, you can always consult the MSDN .NET Developer's center. This website is constantly being updated with new and relevant articles to .NET developers about performance, security, data access, and much more. The developer's center can be reached at msdn.microsoft.com/netframework. Also keep an eye on the .NET newsgroups (also hosted by Microsoft) and .NET websites such as www.gotdotnet.com and www.asp.net.

A book that takes you deep inside the Common Language Runtime with far more detail than this chapter is *Essential .NET, Volume I: The Common Language Runtime* by Don Box (Addison-Wesley 0201734117).

14

Part III

Windows Applications

CHAPTER 15 Introduction to Windows Forms

CHAPTER 16 Windows Forms User Interface Controls

CHAPTER 17 Creating Visually Compelling Windows Forms Applications

CHAPTER 18 Consuming Web Services

CHAPTER 19 Smart Clients

CHAPTER 20 Deploying Windows Applications

15 Introduction to Windows Forms

IN BRIEF

This chapter explains and demonstrates how to use Windows Forms.

▶ First, you are introduced to the basics of Windows Forms programming.

▶ Next, you learn how to construct and run a simple Hello World application.

▶ Finally, you modify the Hello World application to respond to a button click.

WHAT YOU NEED

RECOMMENDED SOFTWARE	.NET Framework C#.NET environment
RECOMMENDED HARDWARE	.NET-enabled desktop client
SKILLS REQUIRED	C# coding

INTRODUCTION TO WINDOWS FORMS AT A GLANCE

Windows Forms Basics	**314**	Introducing the Main Method	315
Understanding the Forms Designer	316		
Hello World	**318**	Windows Application Wizard	319
		Setting the Properties	321
Creating an Application Using the		Compiling and Running the Application	322
Responding to a Button Click	324		
Summary	**329**		
Further Reading	**329**		

Windows Forms Basics

Windows Forms is the framework for building Windows applications. It enables you to construct an application from scratch in a relatively short period of time. For those who started programming applications for Windows when it was introduced, the fact that this can be accomplished with minimal effort and time is something of a small miracle. It used to take a few days just to construct the basic framework for an application (assuming that you didn't have a copy of a previous starting application saved as a pseudo-template). Now, depending on the speed of your computer, that same task takes only seconds. In fact, if you have never done any programming before, you can get a Windows Forms application up and running with little guidance from anyone else.

However, just because an application runs, that does not make it a good application. There are other things to consider when making that determination. The first factor is whether the application performs the function for which it was intended. The next consideration is how much effort it takes to maintain the application. Other aspects must also be considered, such as whether the code is readable, and so on. Without a basic understanding of how things are done in a Windows Forms application, it is impossible to create a well-formed application for which all the previous questions can be answered yes. In the following sections, you will gain a good understanding of the basics of Windows Forms programming.

Introducing the `Main` Method

Every Windows Forms application created in C# must contain a static method called `Main`. This method serves as the starting point for every application and serves as a pseudo-control point for this application. Because the `Main` method serves as the entry point, if you omit it, your application cannot run and the compiler will return an error that looks something like the following message:

```
Program
'F:\Visual C#.NET Unleashed\Chapter 23\Code Examples\HelloWorld\obj\Debug\
HelloWorld.exe'
 does not have an entry point defined.
```

The `Main` method is a static method that can return either an `int` or `void` type and can be declared with or without parameters. Without any parameters, the `Main` method takes one of the following forms:

```
static int Main()
```

```
static void Main()
```

If you want to allow your program to receive command-line arguments, simply use one of the following forms of the `Main` method:

```
static int Main(string[] args)
```

```
static void Main(string[] args)
```

To run a Windows Forms application, you must make a call to the `Application.Run` method. `Application.Run` takes the following forms, which are excerpted from Visual Studio .NET's help file:

```
// Begins running a standard application message loop on
// the current thread, without a form.
```

15

Windows Forms Basics

```
public static void Run();
// Begins running a standard application message loop on
// the current thread, with an ApplicationContext
public static void Run(ApplicationContext);
// Begins running a standard application message loop on
// the current thread, and makes the specified form visible
public static void Run(Form);
```

In C#, the Main method can be placed in any object that you choose, but there can be only one occurrence of this method per application. If you have multiple Main methods in an application, you will receive a compiler error similar to the following:

```
F:\Visual C#.NET Unleashed\Chapter 23\Code Examples\HelloWorld\Form1.cs(70):
Program 'F:\Visual C#.NET Unleashed\Chapter 23\Code Examples\HelloWorld\obj\Debug\
HelloWorld.exe' has more than one entry point defined: 'HelloWorld.Form1.Main()'
```

The following code snippet shows what a simple Main method for a Windows Forms application could look like:

```
[STAThread]
static void Main()
{
  Application.Run(new Form1());
}
```

Understanding the Forms Designer

In a way, the Forms Designer is similar to the Resource Editor that was used in the early days of Windows application development, or if you come from Visual C++, the not-so-distant past. The Forms Designer is essentially a graphical display/interface of the GUI code that is constructed within the code file. You can drag and drop components and controls from the toolbox to the form (the easy way) or create all the necessary code inside the code file so that the information will appear in the Forms Designer. Figure 15.1 shows an example of a Button control that has been dragged and dropped on the form.

Creating the Button control took only a few seconds to do and was not difficult to do by any stretch of the imagination. The following code snippet shows all the code that the Windows Forms Designer created in order for this Button to appear in the correct location on the form and with the appropriate properties:

```
#region Windows Form Designer generated code
/// <summary>
/// Required method for Designer support - do not modify
/// the contents of this method with the code editor.
```

```
///   </summary>
private void InitializeComponent()
{
    this.button1 = new System.Windows.Forms.Button();
    this.SuspendLayout();
    //
    // button1
    //
    this.button1.Location = new System.Drawing.Point(120, 96);
    this.button1.Name = "button1";
    this.button1.TabIndex = 0;
    this.button1.Text = "button1";
    //
    // Form1
    //
    this.AutoScaleBaseSize = new System.Drawing.Size(5, 13);
    this.ClientSize = new System.Drawing.Size(360, 266);
    this.Controls.Add(this.button1);
    this.Name = "Form1";
    this.Text = "Form1";
    this.ResumeLayout(false);
}
#endregion
```

15

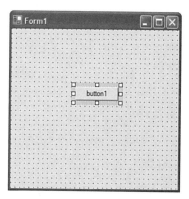

FIGURE 15.1   Design view of
a newly created
button on a
Windows Form.

In this snippet, you can see that the text of the button is set to button1. If you change the text in the code file to This is your button! and then switch to the Design View window, you will see the change reflected on the button (as shown in Figure 15.2).

Windows Forms Basics

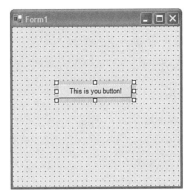

FIGURE 15.2   Design view of a button with the `Text` property changed from the Code View window.

If you use the Properties toolbar of the Design View window to change the `Text` property of the `Button` control to `Changed Again!` and go back to the Code View window, you will see that change reflected in the code:

```
//
// button1
//
this.button1.Location = new System.Drawing.Point(120, 96);
this.button1.Name = "button1";
this.button1.TabIndex = 0;
this.button1.Text = "Changed Again!";
```

Hello World

Now that a basic understanding of a Windows Forms application and the Windows Forms Designer have been established, it is time to create your first Windows Forms application. In the following sections, you will learn to create, compile and run a simple Hello World application.

Creating an Application Using the Windows Application Wizard

The first step in creating this simple application is invoking the Windows Application Wizard from the Visual Studio .NET New Project dialog as shown in Figures 15.3 and 15.4.

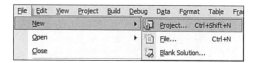

FIGURE 15.3 Select the File, New, Project menu item to invoke the Visual Studio .NET New Project dialog window.

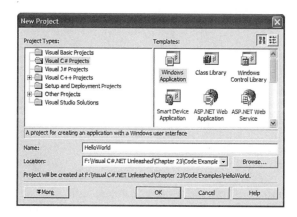

FIGURE 15.4 Selecting the Windows Application Wizard.

When the New Project dialog window appears, select the Windows Application Wizard shown in Figure 15.4 and type in the name and location of the project that you want to create. After you've entered all the required information, click the OK button and watch Visual Studio .NET create your application, as shown in Figure 15.5.

You will notice that the Solution Explorer contains three files. One file (App.ico) is the application icon. This file contains the icon image that will be used in your application. Another file (AssemblyInfo.cs) contains all information about the assembly, such as signing and general assembly and version information. The final file (Form1.cs) contains the Web Form that is the basis of our application. By default, it is a blank form that has the name Form1.

Hello World

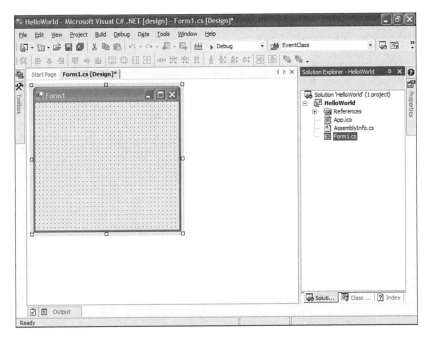

FIGURE 15.5   Visual Studio .NET showing the newly created Windows
Forms application.

Now that the basic application has been created, examine the Solution Explorer.

If you want to change any of the basic information of this project, including the
name of the icon file to be associated with it, you can invoke the application property pages by right-clicking on the project file in the Solution Explorer and selecting
the Properties menu item. From these pages, you can change properties in Tables
15.1 and 15.2.

TABLE 15.1

Common Properties

Property Page	Description
General	This page contains information such as the type of application, assembly name, and default namespace.
Designer Defaults	This page is used in Web Forms development.
References Path	This page lists the directories used for the assemblies that were added with the Add Reference command. Note that this is not stored with the project, but is stored in the *project name*.user file.
Build Events	This page specifies events that should take place before and after a build. You can also specify whether or not a post-build event should always take place, or only upon a successful build or when the build updates the project output. Note that this is not available to web applications.

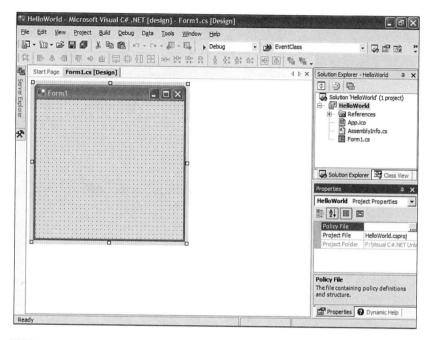

FIGURE 15.6   The Solution Explorer displaying the newly created Windows Forms application.

TABLE 15.2

Configuration Properties

Property Page	Description
Build	This page contains properties for setting code generation, errors and warnings, and outputs.
Debugging	This page specifies debugging specific information such as debuggers, start actions, and start options.
Advanced	This page contains settings for general configuration properties, such as whether the compiler should perform an incremental build, base address, file alignment, and whether to use the mscorlib assembly.

Setting the Properties

Now that all the files that will be used in the project have been identified, the form must be loaded in the Design View window. To do that, simply right-click on the file in the Solution Explorer, and select the View Designer menu option.

Hello World

TIP

Instead of right-clicking on the file and selecting the View Designer menu option to view the form in Design mode, you can simply double-click on the file and the Design View window will appear.

Next, drag and drop a `Label` control from the Windows Forms tab in the toolbox to the form. After the `Label` control has been placed on the form (as shown in Figure 15.7), change the control's `Text` property to `Welcome to Windows Forms Development!`.

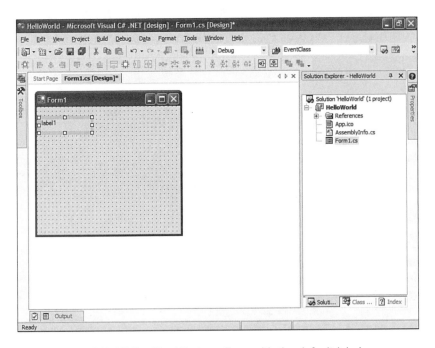

FIGURE 15.7   The Windows Form with the default label.

While you are in the Properties window, change the font size from its default value to a larger font size of 24. You will notice that the label now extends past the end of the form. That's okay; resize the form by clicking the mouse cursor on the lower-right side of the form and dragging to the right until the entire `Label` control can be seen (see Figure 15.8).

Compiling and Running the Application

After you have completed the visual design of the Hello World application, you must compile the application before it can be run. The compilation of a program can be accomplished in a few different ways: You can choose to compile the application from the keystroke Ctrl+Shift+B (assuming that you are using the default keystroke mapping); you can select the Build, Build *<Project Name>* menu option; or you can click the Build Solution toolbar button (by default, this button does not appear on the toolbar). Each of these techniques accomplishes the same thing, but seems faster than the other. Compile the program. Figure 15.9 shows the output of the compiler when it has successfully completed its task.

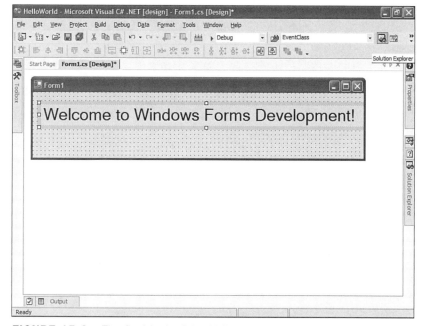

FIGURE 15.8   The final look of the Hello World application.

You have a few different options to run the application: You can press the F5 key; you can select the Debug, Start option from the main menu; or you can click the Start button on the toolbar. Using the F5 key seems faster than using the other options.

TIP
Instead of performing two different steps—compiling and then building the application—you can just click the Start button. If the application must be rebuilt, Visual Studio .NET will automatically perform this process. If the application does not require a rebuild, Visual Studio .NET simply starts it.

After the application has been started, you can see your welcome message, as shown in Figure 15.10.

Hello World

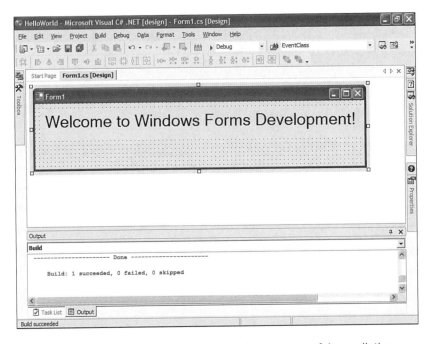

FIGURE 15.9   Output of the compiler after a successful compilation.

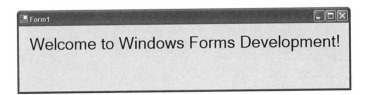

FIGURE 15.10   The Hello World application in action.

Responding to a Button Click

The welcome message is a great start, but it is not very useful. In fact, displaying the message did not require any coding, so the example was perhaps too simple. In Chapter 10, "Events and Delegates," you learned what an event was and why it is used. By default, a Button control has several events ready for your use (see Figure 15.11).

To add an event handler to any of the provided events, simply double-click the space next to the event name. The Forms Designer will automatically add the event handler, with a default name, in the Code View window and place your cursor inside the event handler method. All you have to do is add the code that you want to handle the event. To better illustrate this, add a `Button` control to the Hello World application form, as shown in Figure 15.12.

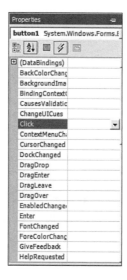

FIGURE 15.11   Default events of the `Button` control in the Properties window.

FIGURE 15.12   Design view of the Hello World application after the addition of a `Button` control.

After the button has been added, add an event handler to the `Button.Click` event. When that has been accomplished, the Forms Designer should place your cursor in a method that resembles the following code snippet:

```
private void button1_Click(object sender, System.EventArgs e)
{

}
```

Hello World

When that has been achieved, add the following line of code to this event handler:

```
MessageBox.Show("Button Clicked!");
```

The event handler should now look something like this:

```
private void button1_Click(object sender, System.EventArgs e)
{
  MessageBox.Show("Button Clicked!");
}
```

When the application is run, you will see the same welcome message with the addition of one Button control (see Figure 15.13).

FIGURE 15.13   The new Hello World application in action.

If you click the button, you will see a MessageBox appear with the message Button Clicked!.

Listing 15.1 contains all the code necessary to create the Hello World application.

LISTING 15.1

Form1.cs

```
using System;
using System.Drawing;
using System.Collections;
using System.ComponentModel;
using System.Windows.Forms;
using System.Data;

namespace HelloWorld
{
  /// <summary>
  /// Summary description for Form1.
  /// </summary>
  public class Form1 : System.Windows.Forms.Form
  {
```

LISTING 15.1
Continued

```csharp
private System.Windows.Forms.Label label1;
private System.Windows.Forms.Button button1;
/// <summary>
/// Required designer variable.
/// </summary>
private System.ComponentModel.Container components = null;

public Form1()
{
    //
    // Required for Windows Form Designer support
    //
    InitializeComponent();

    //
    // TODO: Add any constructor code after InitializeComponent call
    //
}

/// <summary>
/// Clean up any resources being used.
/// </summary>
protected override void Dispose( bool disposing )
{
    if( disposing )
    {
            if (components != null)
            {
                    components.Dispose();
            }
    }
    base.Dispose( disposing );
}

#region Windows Form Designer generated code
/// <summary>
/// Required method for Designer support - do not modify
/// the contents of this method with the code editor.
/// </summary>
private void InitializeComponent()
{
  this.label1 = new System.Windows.Forms.Label();
```

15

Hello World

LISTING 15.1
Continued

```csharp
this.button1 = new System.Windows.Forms.Button();
this.SuspendLayout();
//
// label1
//
this.label1.Font =
  new System.Drawing.Font("Microsoft Sans Serif", 24F,
    System.Drawing.FontStyle.Regular,
    System.Drawing.GraphicsUnit.Point, ((System.Byte)(0)));
this.label1.Location = new System.Drawing.Point(16, 24);
this.label1.Name = "label1";
this.label1.Size = new System.Drawing.Size(656, 40);
this.label1.TabIndex = 0;
this.label1.Text = "Welcome to Windows Forms Development!";
//
// button1
//
this.button1.Location = new System.Drawing.Point(296, 80);
this.button1.Name = "button1";
this.button1.TabIndex = 1;
this.button1.Text = "Click Me!";
this.button1.Click += new System.EventHandler(this.button1_Click);
//
// Form1
//
this.AutoScaleBaseSize = new System.Drawing.Size(5, 13);
this.ClientSize = new System.Drawing.Size(656, 126);
this.Controls.Add(this.button1);
this.Controls.Add(this.label1);
this.Name = "Form1";
this.Text = "Form1";
this.ResumeLayout(false);
}
#endregion

/// <summary>
/// The main entry point for the application.
/// </summary>
[STAThread]
static void Main()
{
```

LISTING 15.1
Continued

```
    Application.Run(new Form1());
  }

  private void button1_Click(object sender, System.EventArgs e)
  {
    MessageBox.Show("Button Clicked!");
  }
 }
}
```

15

Summary

In the previous sections, you learned the basics of Windows Forms programming and the Windows Forms Designer. Next, you learned how to construct and run a simple Hello World application. Finally, you learned to modify the application and add event handlers to the `Button.Click` event.

Further Reading

For more information on Windows Forms programming, the largest and most comprehensive reference available on a bookshelf right now is Charles Petzold's book from Microsoft Press, *Programming Windows with C# (Core Reference)*, ISBN 0735613702. Anything that you need more detail on, you will probably find in that book.

IN BRIEF

This chapter will give you an introduction to the user interface controls available to you in the .NET Framework for Windows forms. The first section will familiarize you with the standard controls provided in the .NET Framework. Finally, you will learn the basics of creating and using user controls.

WHAT YOU NEED

RECOMMENDED SOFTWARE	.NET Framework C# .NET environment
RECOMMENDED HARDWARE	.NET-enabled desktop client
SKILLS REQUIRED	C# coding

WINDOWS FORMS USER INTERFACE CONTROLS AT A GLANCE

Standard Windows Forms User Interface Controls	330		
Performing Actions with Controls	330	Maintaining Lists with Controls	337
Storing and Changing Values with Controls	334		

User Controls	347
Summary	349
Further Reading	349

Standard Windows Forms User Interface Controls

As does just about any other language that is capable of creating application for Windows, the .NET Framework provides a few standard controls for use in your applications. These controls enable you to perform actions, store values, maintain lists of information, and contain other controls. For most programmers, these controls are expected and often taken for granted. In the next few sections, you will learn the basics of some of the standard controls provided in the .NET Framework.

Performing Actions with Controls

The first set of controls are ones whose main function is to provide a means of signaling that an event or some sort of action should occur. These controls include the `Button` and `Toolbar`.

The `Button` Control

The `Button` control is a familiar one that looks just like what its name implies. Its sole purpose is to signal that an event or action should occur. The `Button` control, as shown in Figure 16.1, is useful when you want to place the burden of starting an event on the user of the application.

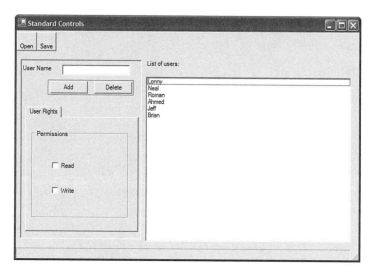

FIGURE 16.1   A Button control on a Windows Form.

The action of the `Button` can generally be triggered by clicking the `Button` with your mouse, by pressing the Enter button on your keyboard, or by pressing the spacebar while the focus is on the `Button`. If you set the `CancelButton` or `AcceptButton` property on the form to a particular `Button`, you can cause that `Button` to respond to the pressing of the Escape and Enter keys even when the `Button` does not have focus. In addition, when a window is used as a dialog by using the `ShowDialog` method, you can use the `DialogResult` property to set the return value of the `ShowDialog` method. The following code snippet shows how to create a `Button` control on a form:

```
private void CreateButton()
{
  // create the button
  Button myButton = new Button();
  // Set the button's caption
  myButton.Text = "Click Me!";
  // add the button to the control container
  Controls.Add(MyButton);
}
```

The `Toolbar` Control
The `ToolBar` control is used to contain and display `ToolBarButton` ▮1▮ controls. It can display any `ToolBarButton` that can be shown as a toggle-style

Standard Windows Forms User Interface Controls

button, a drop-down style button, or a standard button. The following code snippet shows how to create a `ToolBar` control along with two `ToolBarButtons`:

```
private void CreateToolBar()
{
  // create the button
  myToolBar = new ToolBar();

  // create the two ToolBarButtons
  ToolBarButton openButton = new ToolBarButton();
  ToolBarButton saveButton = new ToolBarButton();

  // add the two buttons to the ToolBar
  myToolBar.Buttons.Add(openButton);
  myToolBar.Buttons.Add(saveButton);

  // add the toolbar to the control container
  Controls.Add(myToolBar);
}
```

The `ToolBar`, as shown in Figure 16.2, receives the click event from the `ToolBarButtons` it contains.

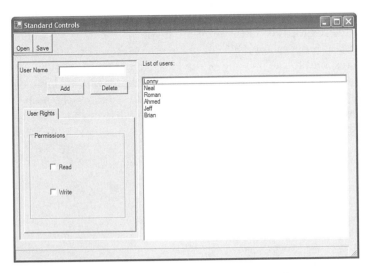

FIGURE 16.2   A `ToolBar` control on a Windows Form.

It's the responsibility of the `ToolBar` to figure out which button was responsible for the click. To receive the click notification, the `ToolBar` must have an event handler.

The following code snippet demonstrates how to add an event handler to the
ToolBar:

```
private void AddEventHandler()
{
  myToolBar.ButtonClick += new ToolBarButtonClickEventHandler(myToolbarButtonClick);
}
```

The next code fragment demonstrates how to determine which ToolBarButton was
pressed.

```
private void myToolbarButtonClick(Object sender, ToolBarButtonClickEventArgs e)
 {
   // Evaluate the Button property to determine which button was clicked.
   switch(myToolBar.Buttons.IndexOf(e.Button))
   {
      case 0:
         openFileDialog1.ShowDialog();
         // Insert code to open the file.
         break;
      case 1:
         saveFileDialog1.ShowDialog();
         // Insert code to save the file.
         break;
   }
 }
```

TIP

As you build and design your application, you will often change the location of different user interface
elements. To insulate yourself from breaking your code due to the position and layout of elements,
you can use a stronger method of identifying the source of an event. In the case of a button click on
a toolbar, you can query the name of the button that was pushed. You can also use the Tag property
to add arbitrary data to virtually any control. Numerical or name-based identification of controls is far
more reliable than relying on indexes or relative positions.

In addition to hosting the ToolBarButton controls, the ToolBar also has a few
methods and events that enable you to control the way that it is drawn. If you set
the Appearance property to Flat, the ToolBar will appear with a flat style and
when the mouse passes over any of its contained buttons, the ToolBarButton will
raise up to show that it is the target of any mouse input at that point. If you set the
Style property to ToolBarButtonStyle.Separator, a spacer will appear
between buttons.

Storing and Changing Values with Controls

The next set of controls is used to store and or change values. These controls include the `Label`, `TextBox`, and `StatusBar`. Although there are other controls in this category, the three just named will give you a general understanding of what this set of controls is used for and how to utilize them.

The `Label` Control

The `Label` control, as shown in Figure 16.3, is one of the easiest controls to understand. It simply displays a label on a form.

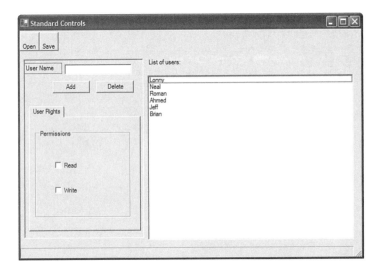

FIGURE 16.3   A `Label` control on a Windows Form.

Although the `Label` control participates in the tab order of a form or control, it does not receive focus.

TIP

To make a `Label` transparent, set `Label.BackColor` to `Transparent`. However, to ensure that the control is drawn properly, make sure to use only the coordinate system of the current device.

The following code snippet shows how to create a `Label`, set its text to `User Name`, and place it on a form:

```
private void CreateLabel()
{
  myLabel = new Label();
```

```
    myLabel.Text = "User Name";
    Controls.Add(myLabel);
}
```

The `TextBox` Control

Another useful control is the `TextBox`, shown in Figure 16.4. A `TextBox` provides the basis for most text input on Windows Forms and is by far the most common input control.

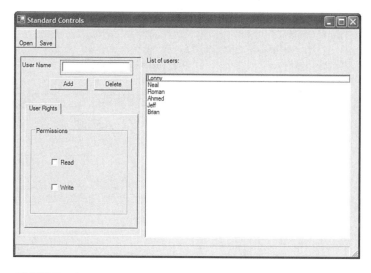

FIGURE 16.4   A `TextBox` control on a Windows Form.

When a `TextBox` control is used, the user can set focus to the control and type in some textual information. Although the user can type essentially anything he chooses, you can add an event handler to process the information as the user types it and to validate it against your business rules.

Unlike the standard Windows `TextBox`, the control provided in the .NET Framework enables you to use multiline editing, as well as password masking, simply by setting a property on the `TextBox`. The following code snippet demonstrates how to create a multiline `TextBox` that accepts the Return (or Enter) key as just another character:

```
private void CreateTextBox()
{
    // Create the TextBox control.
    TextBox myTextBox = new TextBox();

    // Allow for multiline capability.
```

Standard Windows Forms User Interface Controls

```
myTextBox.Multiline = true;
// Allow the use of the Return key.
myTextBox.AcceptsReturn = true;
// Set WordWrap to True.
myTextBox.WordWrap = true;

// Add the TextBox to the forms Controls container.
Controls.Add(myTextBox);
}
```

The StatusBar Control

Another common control is the StatusBar, shown in Figure 16.5. Just about every Windows application contains at least one of these controls.

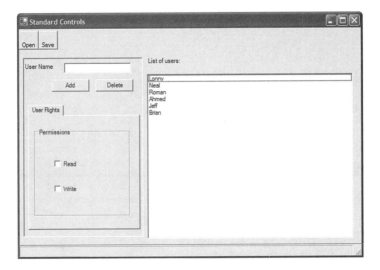

FIGURE 16.5   A StatusBar control on a Windows Form.

This control can contain one or many StatusBar panels. These panels are typically used to display information about the current object on a form or the application itself. As with all controls, you can customize the panels to display anything you prefer, such as a clock, progress bars, or images.

The following code snippet demonstrates how to create a status bar and display the default panel that is created along with the StatusBar:

```
private void CreateStatusBar()
{
  // Create the StatusBar control.
```

```
myStatusBar = new StatusBar();

// Display the Panels that are created in the StatusBar.
  myStatusBar.ShowPanels = true;

  // Add the StatusBar to the forms Controls container.
  Controls.Add(myStatusBar);
}
```

Maintaining Lists with Controls

The next set of controls is used to display lists of information. These controls are useful when multiple objects need to be displayed. Among these controls are the `ListBox`, `ListView`, and `TreeView`. The next few sections will give you a basic understanding of each control and an idea of how and when to use them.

The `ListBox` Control

The `ListBox` control, shown in Figure 16.6, is a relatively simple list control that enables you to display multiple items in list form. To reduce the amount of scrolling that a user must perform, the `ListBox` control enables you to display these items in a multicolumn format.

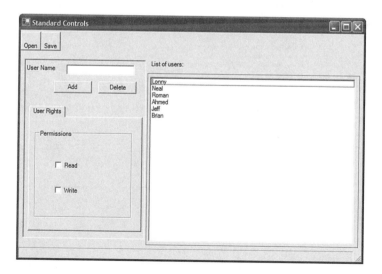

FIGURE 16.6   A `ListBox` control on a Windows Form.

The `ListBox` control also allows the user to select any item, or multiple items, by clicking them with the mouse. The following code snippet demonstrates how to create a `ListBox` control and add some items to the control to be displayed:

Standard Windows Forms User Interface Controls

```
private void CreateListBox()
{
  // Create the ListBox control.
  myListBox = new ListBox();

  string displayText;

  for(int i=0; i<5; i++)
  {
    displayText = "This is the first item " + i.ToString();
    myListBox.Items.Add(displayText);
  }

  // Add the ListBox to the forms Controls container.
  Controls.Add(displayText);
}
```

The ListView Control

The ListView control, shown in Figure 16.7, enables you to display items in its list in multiple ways.

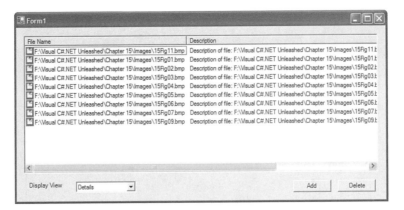

FIGURE 16.7   A ListView control on a Windows Form.

By setting the ListView.View property to one of the values in Table 16.1, you can change the appearance of the list. The following list of property values is taken from the MSDN Library documentation for the ListView.View property.

TABLE 16.1

`ListView.View` Property Values

Property Name	Description
Details	Each item appears on a separate line with further information about each item arranged in columns. The leftmost column contains a small icon and label, and subsequent columns contain subitems as specified by the application. A column displays a header which can display a caption for the column. The user can resize each column at runtime.
LargeIcon	Each item appears as a full-sized icon with a label below it.
List	Each item appears as a small icon with a label to its right. Items are arranged in columns with no column headers.
SmallIcon	Each item appears as a small icon with a label to its right.

Listing 16.1 contains the source code for the `ListView` example. It demonstrates how to add and delete items from the `ListView` control **2** as well as how to change the way these items are displayed.

LISTING 16.1

The `ListView` Example

```
using System;
using System.Drawing;
using System.Collections;
using System.ComponentModel;
using System.Windows.Forms;
using System.Data;

namespace ListViewExample
{
    /// <summary>
    /// Summary description for Form1.
    /// </summary>
    public class Form1 : System.Windows.Forms.Form
    {
        private System.Windows.Forms.ListView listView1;
        private System.Windows.Forms.Button addButton;
        private System.Windows.Forms.Button deleteButton;
        private System.Windows.Forms.ImageList imageList1;
        private System.Windows.Forms.OpenFileDialog openFileDialog1;
        private System.Windows.Forms.ComboBox viewCombo;
        private System.Windows.Forms.Label label1;
        private System.ComponentModel.IContainer components;

        public Form1()
        {
```

16

Standard Windows Forms User Interface Controls

LISTING 16.1
Continued

```
    //
    // Required for Windows Form Designer support
    //
    InitializeComponent();
```

```
    listView1.Columns.Add("File Name",     -2, HorizontalAlignment.Left);
    listView1.Columns.Add("Description",   -2, HorizontalAlignment.Left);

    viewCombo.SelectedIndex = 0;

    viewCombo_SelectedIndexChanged(viewCombo, null);
  }
```

```
  /// <summary>
  /// Clean up any resources being used.
  /// </summary>
  protected override void Dispose( bool disposing )
  {
    if( disposing )
      {
      if (components != null)
      {
        components.Dispose();
      }
      }
      base.Dispose( disposing );
  }
```

```
// windows forms designer code intentionally left out for clarity of sample.
```

```
  /// <summary>
  /// The main entry point for the application.
  /// </summary>
  [STAThread]
  static void Main()
  {
    Application.Run(new Form1());
  }
```

```
  private void AddItem(string fileName, string description)
  {
    string[] itemList = new string[2];
    itemList[0] = fileName;
```

Standard Windows Forms User Interface Controls

LISTING 16.1
Continued

```csharp
    itemList[1] = description;

    ListViewItem item = new ListViewItem(itemList, 0);
    listView1.Items.Add(item);
}

private void addButton_Click(object sender, System.EventArgs e)
{
  if(openFileDialog1.ShowDialog() == DialogResult.OK)
  {
    for(int i=0; i<openFileDialog1.FileNames.GetUpperBound(0); i++)
    {
      AddItem(openFileDialog1.FileNames[i],
        "Description of file: " + openFileDialog1.FileNames[i]);
    }
  }
}


private void deleteButton_Click(object sender, System.EventArgs e)
{
  if(MessageBox.Show("The selected items will be deleted",
    "Warning", MessageBoxButtons.OKCancel) == DialogResult.OK)
  {
    for(int i=listView1.SelectedItems.Count-1; i>=0; i--)
    {
      listView1.Items.Remove(listView1.SelectedItems[i]);
    }
  }
}


private void viewCombo_SelectedIndexChanged(object sender, System.EventArgs e)
{
  switch(viewCombo.SelectedIndex)
  {
    case 0:
      listView1.View = View.Details;
      break;
    case 1:
      listView1.View = View.LargeIcon;
      break;
    case 2:
      listView1.View = View.List;
      break;
```

Standard Windows Forms User Interface Controls

LISTING 16.1
Continued

```
        case 3:
            listView1.View = View.SmallIcon;
            break;
        }
    }
}
}
```

The `TreeView` Control

The `TreeView` control, shown in Figure 16.8, is a popular control for displaying hierarchical representations of data.

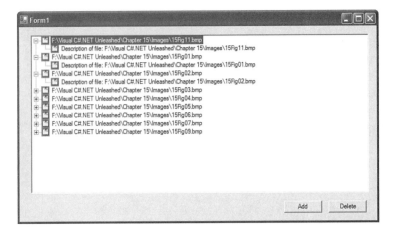

FIGURE 16.8   A `TreeView` control on a Windows Form.

The `TreeView` control is capable of displaying items, called *tree nodes*, in a fashion that resembles a tree of data. Each tree node added to the tree can contain its own collection of nodes, called *child nodes*, and so on. For example, if you were to add a root tree node called `Galaxies`, it could contain child nodes that were specific galaxies. Each galaxy could contain solar systems, each solar system could contain planets, each planet could contain moons, bodies of water, and so forth. You can see how you could get lost at any point of a tree.

Although items displayed in a `TreeView` are fairly easy to visualize conceptually, it is another thing to try to programmatically load and parse the data contained in this view. For this reason, the `TreeView.FullPath` property enables you to view the entire hierarchy from the root node to the current tree node. The code in Listing 16.2 is an example of using a `TreeView` control.

LISTING 16.2
The `TreeView` Sample Program

```csharp
using System;
using System.Drawing;
using System.Collections;
using System.ComponentModel;
using System.Windows.Forms;
using System.Data;

namespace TreeViewExample
{
  /// <summary>
  /// Summary description for Form1.
  /// </summary>
  public class Form1 : System.Windows.Forms.Form
  {
    private System.Windows.Forms.Button deleteButton;
    private System.Windows.Forms.Button addButton;
    private System.Windows.Forms.TreeView treeView1;
    private System.Windows.Forms.ImageList imageList1;
    private System.Windows.Forms.OpenFileDialog openFileDialog1;
    private System.ComponentModel.IContainer components;

    public Form1()
    {
      //
      // Required for Windows Form Designer support
      //
      InitializeComponent();

      //
      // TODO: Add any constructor code after InitializeComponent call
      //
    }

    /// <summary>
    /// Clean up any resources being used.
    /// </summary>
    protected override void Dispose( bool disposing )
    {
      if( disposing )
      {
        if (components != null)
        {
```

Standard Windows Forms User Interface Controls

LISTING 16.2
Continued

```csharp
            components.Dispose();
        }
    }
    base.Dispose( disposing );
}

    #region Windows Form Designer generated code
//Windows Forms designer code intentionally left out for clarity.
    #endregion

    /// <summary>
    /// The main entry point for the application.
    /// </summary>
    [STAThread]
    static void Main()
    {
      Application.Run(new Form1());
    }

    private void AddItem(string fileName, string description)
    {
      TreeNode item = new TreeNode(fileName, 0, 0);
      TreeNode subItem = new TreeNode(description, -1, -1);
      item.Nodes.Add(subItem);

      treeView1.Nodes.Add(item);
    }

    private void addButton_Click(object sender, System.EventArgs e)
    {
      if(openFileDialog1.ShowDialog() == DialogResult.OK)
      {
        for(int i=0; i<openFileDialog1.FileNames.GetUpperBound(0); i++)
        {
          AddItem(openFileDialog1.FileNames[i],
            "Description of file: " + openFileDialog1.FileNames[i]);
        }
      }
    }
```

LISTING 16.2
Continued

```
private void deleteButton_Click(object sender, System.EventArgs e)
{

    if(MessageBox.Show("The selected items will be deleted",
        "Warning", MessageBoxButtons.OKCancel) == DialogResult.OK)
    {
      treeView1.Nodes.Remove(treeView1.SelectedNode);
    }
  }
 }
}
```

Nesting Child Controls Within Controls

Similar to the list controls, controls that can contain other controls are often used to group items. The GroupBox, Panel, and TabControl are some of this type of control. In the next few sections, you will gain a basic understanding of these controls and how they are used.

The GroupBox Control

The GroupBox control, shown in Figure 16.9, is used to logically group other controls.

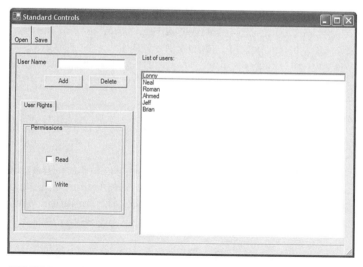

FIGURE 16.9   A GroupBox control on a Windows Form.

Standard Windows Forms User Interface Controls

This control is often used to display a set of radio buttons or check boxes in a group. The GroupBox control can display a border around the items along with or without a caption.

The Panel Control

Similar to the GroupBox control, the Panel control in Figure 16.10 is used to group a collection of other controls.

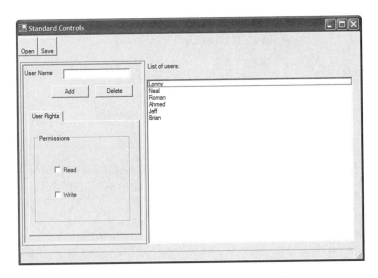

FIGURE 16.10   A Panel control on a Windows Form.

By default, the Panel control is displayed without a border. You can modify the Panel.BorderStyle property to add a Fixed3D, FixedSingle, or no style to the border. As with all other container type controls, setting the Enabled property to true or false will in turn set the Enabled property of all the contained controls to the same value.

The TabControl Control

The TabControl control, shown in Figure 16.11, is a control that can have one or more TabPages.

Unlike the other grouping controls, the TabControl control is used to separate groups of data onto separate sheets (TabPages). By displaying only the data that the user needs to view or modify, the TabControl eases the confusion that a user might experience by seeing too much information at the same time.

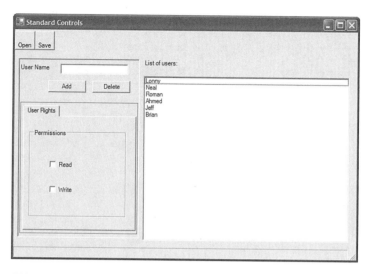

FIGURE 16.11   A `TabControl` control on a Windows Form.

User Controls

Similar to the grouping controls, a user control enables you to group a set of controls. Unlike the grouping controls, a user control allows the group of controls to act as one control. You can create your own properties and events on this control that will affect the way in which the grouped items behave. To better illustrate this point, consider the `OpenDialog` control. This control has many subcontrols, such as the `ListView`, `TextBox`, and `Label`, and OK and Cancel buttons. When you use the `OpenDialog` control, you don't write event handlers for all of these controls—they already exist. Similarly, a user control enables you to visually create your own controls by designing the control exactly as you would a form. You can then use the control by dragging and dropping it from the toolbox to a desired form. Listing 16.3 contains the source code for a simple `Logon` user control.

LISTING 16.3
Logon User Control

```
using System;
using System.Collections;
using System.ComponentModel;
using System.Drawing;
using System.Data;
using System.Windows.Forms;

namespace UserControlExample
{
```

User Controls

LISTING 16.3
Continued

```csharp
      /// <summary>
      /// Summary description for UserControl1.
      /// </summary>
  public class LogonUserControl : System.Windows.Forms.UserControl
  {
    private System.Windows.Forms.Button okButton;
    private System.Windows.Forms.Button cancelButton;
    private System.Windows.Forms.Label label1;
    private System.Windows.Forms.Label label2;
    private System.Windows.Forms.TextBox userName;
    private System.Windows.Forms.TextBox password;
    /// <summary>
    /// Required designer variable.
    /// </summary>
    private System.ComponentModel.Container components = null;

    public LogonUserControl()
    {
      // This call is required by the Windows.Forms Form Designer.
      InitializeComponent();

      // TODO: Add any initialization after the InitComponent call
    }

    /// <summary>
    /// Clean up any resources being used.
    /// </summary>
    protected override void Dispose( bool disposing )
    {
      if( disposing )
      {
        if( components != null )
          components.Dispose();
      }
      base.Dispose( disposing );
    }

    #region Component Designer generated code
// Windows Forms designer code intentionally left out for clarity.
    #endregion
  }
}
```

Summary

In this chapter, you learned how to use some of the standard controls that are provided in the .NET Framework. You learned about the four basic categories of controls: action, value, list, and container controls. Although not an exhaustive list of all the controls that fit into these categories, the controls examined in this chapter gave you an understanding of the four basic categories of controls and when to use each type. At the end of the chapter, you learned how to customize and create reusable user controls.

Further Reading

Programming Windows with C#, Core Reference by Charles Petzold. ISBN: 0735613702.

16

17 Creating Visually Compelling Windows Forms Applications

IN BRIEF

So far in the section of this book dealing with Windows Forms, you've seen a basic introduction to WinForms programming followed by an introduction to creating reusable controls and using attributes on those controls to make them easier to use.

This chapter will introduce some advanced user interface topics that you might not be familiar with. Continuing the discussion of reusable interface elements, this chapter will illustrate *visual inheritance*, a technology that allows one form to inherit the user interface of another.

That discussion is followed by an overview of creating dynamic context menus. After that is a discussion of creating custom-drawn elements, complete with samples of custom list boxes and menu items. The chapter finishes with a discussion of custom-shaped forms and form transparency.

WHAT YOU NEED

REQUIRED SOFTWARE	.NET Framework SDK v1.1 Visual Studio .NET 2003 with C# installed
RECOMMENDED HARDWARE	PC that meets .NET SDK minimum requirements
SKILLS REQUIRED	C# and .NET familiarity Familiarity with Windows Forms

CREATING VISUALLY COMPELLING WINDOWS FORMS APPLICATIONS AT A GLANCE

Visual Inheritance	**351**		
Using Inherited Forms	351	Visual Inheritance Best Practices	358
WinForms Visual Inheritance in Action	352		
Creating and Using Dynamic Context Menus	**359**		
Introduction to Contextual, Adaptive User Interfaces	360	A Sample Dynamic Context Menu in Action	360
Drawing Custom List Elements	**363**		
Using the DrawMode Property	**363**		
Creating a Custom ListBox	365	Creating Custom Menu Items	365
Shaped Forms	**368**		
Introduction to Shaped Forms	368	Creating a Sample Shaped Form	368

CREATING VISUALLY COMPELLING WINDOWS FORMS APPLICATIONS AT A GLANCE

Summary   370

Further Reading   370

Visual Inheritance

Visual inheritance is a concept that most people seem to be familiar with. However, when programmers are asked whether they're using visual inheritance, most say that they don't take advantage of it. The next section will show you what visual inheritance is, and how to take advantage of it quickly and easily within your applications. By the time you're done with this section, you will have become a convert and will use visual inheritance in all your Windows Forms applications in the future.

Using Inherited Forms

When you create a class that inherits from another class, the newly created class inherits those members and methods that the child class is allowed to inherit. The same is true for an inherited form. When you look at it from the lowest level, forms are just classes. A form that inherits from another form is still just one class inheriting from another class. The trick to remember is that a form renders its GUI through inheritable members, properties, and methods. By virtue of this inheritance, child forms inherit their GUI look and feel from their parents.

Just as with standard child classes, child forms are free to reuse any behavior or property of a parent. In addition, they can choose to override and provide their own implementation for any property or method where it is applicable.

You have already seen how to create reusable controls and you have seen their benefits. With a reusable control, you have a self-contained piece of functionality and user interface that you can reuse across multiple forms. With an inherited form, you create some piece of the user interface and functionality that will be provided free of charge to all child forms inheriting from the same parent. This gives you the ability to rapidly create a consistent look and feel throughout your Windows Forms application as well as giving you the ability to easily change that look and feel.

To truly see the power of visual inheritance, consider a scenario in which not using it could be disastrous. As an example, assume that you have created a large Windows Forms application that has at least 50 forms in it. On each of those forms, you have placed the company logo and an area within the logo that you can click to bring up the company's home page. Now assume that your boss has just told you to replace

17

all 50 of those forms with the new company logo, and that the link should no longer open the company website; it should instead open a Word document that will be installed with the application.

If you haven't used visual inheritance to create the application, you will be stuck making the change manually to all 50 forms. In addition, you will have to retest every one of the forms because the code is duplicated on each and a mass-change operation like this is highly prone to errors and typos.

However, if you had used visual inheritance, you could have simply made the change to the topmost ancestor in the hierarchy of inherited forms. All the child forms would be aware of the change automatically, and you would not have to rewrite a single line of code in any of them.

WinForms Visual Inheritance in Action

This section will show you an example of creating a system that uses visual inheritance. This example illustrates a sample company that wants to create a few standard forms that will be used to create a consistent look and feel for all of their applications.

To build this sample yourself, first create a library that contains a hierarchy of inherited forms. The sample will be finished by creating an application that takes advantage of the forms that use visual inheritance.

Open Visual Studio .NET 2003 and create a new solution called `VisualInheritance`. In that solution, add a new Windows Application called `FormsLibrary`. `FormsLibrary` will become a class library eventually. It was started as a Windows Application because doing so enables a developer to right-click the project and choose Add Windows Form, which can't be done with a standard class library.

Start coding with the form at the top of the hierarchy of company forms, `CompanyDefault`. Add a new Windows Form to the `FormsLibrary` project and call it `CompanyDefault`. To that form, add a panel that docks on top. You can decorate this any way you like, but at some point, add a label to the top panel and call it `lblApplicationName`. Next, add a new property to the form like the following:

```
protected string ApplicationName
{
  get
  {
    return lblApplicationName.Text;
```

```
    }
    set
    {
        lblApplicationName.Text = value;
    }
}
```

This property will be used by child forms that want to set the application name. This gives the child forms the capability to change the display of something that was created by the parent form. Although the code could have exposed the label itself as protected, doing so violates some of the guidelines of encapsulation that are always good to follow and also gives a cleaner, more maintainable interface. The protected keyword was used so that only forms that inherit from this form, but not unrelated forms, can set this property.

Now right-click the FormsLibrary project and choose Add Inherited Form. Do not add a regular form; make sure that you choose Inherited. From there, navigate down to the user interface node and choose Inherited Form. Call the form CompanyOKCancel and when Visual Studio .NET asks you for the parent form, make sure that you choose CompanyDefault.

When the form first appears, you will see that it looks just like the CompanyDefault form. The difference between this form and the parent form is that the inherited user interface elements are locked in position and are read-only. This is an important distinction. What you see in the designer is a partial render. The user interface elements inherited from the parent are not actually part of your design surface; they are drawn in place so that you can see what your form will look like at runtime to help you position new controls.

As its name might suggest, you are going to add an OK button and a Cancel button to this form. To do so, create another panel and set the Dock property to the bottom of the form. I set the background to white to make it stand out against the content area of the form. To keep your code in sync with the example, name the OK button btnOK and the Cancel button btnCancel. Figure 17.1 shows the CompanyOKCancel form from inside the Visual Studio .NET designer.

Before moving on to writing the code that will inherit from these two forms, some event handling must be added. The OK and Cancel buttons are no good to the user if forms that inherit from CompanyOKCancel cannot make use of them. To allow child forms to use these buttons and still maintain proper encapsulation, some events must be created for the child form to consume and respond to. Listing 17.1 shows the complete code-behind for the CompanyOKCancel form.

Visual Inheritance

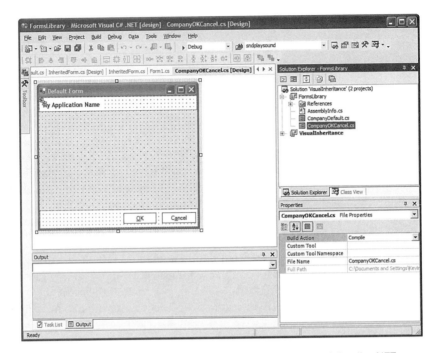

FIGURE 17.1   The `CompanyOKCancel` form in the Visual Studio .NET designer.

LISTING 17.1

The `CompanyOKCancel` Inherited Form

```
using System;
using System.Collections;
using System.ComponentModel;
using System.Drawing;
using System.Windows.Forms;

namespace SAMS.Evolution.CSharpUnleashed.VisualInheritance.Library
{
  public class CompanyOKCancel :
    SAMS.Evolution.CSharpUnleashed.VisualInheritance.Library.CompanyDefault
  {
    private System.Windows.Forms.Panel panel2;
    private System.Windows.Forms.Button btnCancel;
    private System.Windows.Forms.Button btnOK;

    private System.ComponentModel.IContainer components = null;
```

LISTING 17.1
Continued

```
    protected delegate void ButtonClickDelegate(object sender, System.EventArgs e);

    protected event ButtonClickDelegate OKClicked;

    protected event ButtonClickDelegate CancelClicked;
public CompanyOKCancel()
{
  // This call is required by the Windows Form Designer.
  InitializeComponent();
}

/// <summary>
/// Clean up any resources being used.
/// </summary>

protected override void Dispose( bool disposing )
{
  if( disposing )
  {
    if (components != null)
    {
     components.Dispose();
    }
}

base.Dispose( disposing );

}

  // *** Designer Generated Code Hidden from Listing
  private void btnOK_Click(object sender, System.EventArgs e)
  {
   if (OKClicked != null)
   {
     OKClicked(sender, e);
   }
  }

  private void btnCancel_Click(object sender, System.EventArgs e)
  {
```

17

Visual Inheritance

LISTING 17.1
Continued

```
    if (CancelClicked != null)
    {
        CancelClicked(sender, e);
    }
}
}
}
```

The important parts of this listing are the delegates and the events. The delegates dictate the type of the event, and the events are exposed as `protected` members. This allows child forms that inherit from this form to consume these events, but no other forms can do so.

As you can see with the event handlers for the `btnOK` and `btnCancel Click` events, if a child form has subscribed to listen to the appropriate events, it will be notified. This method of deferring events to a child from the parent is an excellent way of maintaining encapsulation and good object-oriented design while still maintaining flexibility and functionality.

Continue this example by creating some forms that inherit from the forms in the base library. The first step is to change the `FormsLibrary` Windows application to a class library. You can do that by changing the output type to Class Library in the Project Properties dialog.

Next, add a Windows application to the solution called `Visual Inheritance`. Add a reference from the new Windows application to the class library project that we just finished building. Add a new inherited form called `InheritedForm`, and choose `CompanyDefault` as the parent form. Then add another inherited form called `InheritedOKCancel` and choose `CompanyOKCancel` as the parent form.

To add some event handlers for the `CompanyOKCancel` form's events to the `InheritedOKCancel` form, set the code for the `InheritedOKCancel` form to the code shown in Listing 17.2.

LISTING 17.2
The `InheritedOKCancel` Form Code-Behind

```
using System;
using System.Collections;
using System.ComponentModel;
using System.Drawing;
using System.Windows.Forms;


namespace SAMS.Evolution.CSharpUnleashed.VisualInheritance
{
```

LISTING 17.2
Continued

```
public class InheritedOKCancel :
   SAMS.Evolution.CSharpUnleashed.VisualInheritance.Library.CompanyOKCancel
   {
   private System.Windows.Forms.Label label1;
   private System.ComponentModel.IContainer components = null;

public InheritedOKCancel()
{
// This call is required by the Windows Form Designer.

     InitializeComponent();

     this.CancelClicked += new ButtonClickDelegate(InheritedOKCancel_
     CancelClicked);
     this.OKClicked += new ButtonClickDelegate(InheritedOKCancel_OKClicked);
}



/// <summary>
/// Clean up any resources being used.
/// </summary>
     protected override void Dispose( bool disposing )
{
if( disposing )
 {
   if (components != null)
 {

components.Dispose();

}
}
  base.Dispose( disposing );
}



// Windows forms designer code hidden for listing

  private void InheritedOKCancel_CancelClicked(object sender, EventArgs e)
  {
     MessageBox.Show(this, "You clicked Cancel.");
```

17

LISTING 17.2
Continued

```
  }

  private void InheritedOKCancel_OKClicked(object sender, EventArgs e)
  {
    MessageBox.Show(this, "You clicked OK.");
  }
}
}
```

The code in Listing 17.2 sets up the event handlers in the child form to respond to events fired from controls in the parent form. This particular fact is extremely important to remember because it will help you create powerful hierarchies of reusable form templates for your applications in the future.

Now that you have created your inherited forms, create a few test controls on the main form. Create two buttons on the main form. The first button will launch the first form you created, and the second button will launch the second form.

Figure 17.2 shows the first form after it has been launched. Figure 17.3 shows the second form after it has been launched. Click the OK button on the InheritedOKCancel form to test the event-handling setup.

FIGURE 17.2   The InheritedForm Windows Form.

Visual Inheritance Best Practices

As you saw in the previous code sample, a separate library was created that contained the forms from which the code would inherit. This is a design pattern that I highly recommend you adopt. When creating a hierarchy of reusable forms, you want to be able to use those forms across multiple projects to provide your developers with a consistent look and feel, and a minimum set of functionality. If your forms are in a separate library that is designed to stand on its own, but that can be easily integrated by child forms, you will find that the whole experience of creating a Windows Forms application might become easier and less frustrating.

FIGURE 17.3   The `Inherited`
`OKCancel` Windows
Form.

Another design pattern that you should follow is that of maintaining encapsulation. As you saw, the code ensured that properties, methods, and events to be used by child forms were set as `protected`, and they didn't allow the controls used by parent forms to be accessed directly by child controls. Forcing this kind of encapsulation also forces you to think more closely about the interaction model between the hierarchy of forms.

Inherited forms and visual inheritance can be extremely powerful tools, and if you spend a little extra design time up front, the rewards will more than pay for the time spent.

Creating and Using Dynamic Context Menus

This next section is all about dynamic context menus. You might think that context menus are a small little piece of Windows Forms, and they're easy to do—so why bother dedicating a whole section to them in a chapter on advanced graphical user interfaces?

As you will see in the next section, the reason is that contextual functionality is often overlooked by many application developers. This section will show you how to create dynamic context menus and where they are appropriate.

Introduction to Contextual, Adaptive User Interfaces

Contextual functionality isn't just about making sure that you can right-click a control. It is also about providing relevant functionality that is related to whatever the user is working on.

If a user is editing a contact, and that contact can appear in 10 different other areas of that application, the application should provide some kind of contextual menu either through a ContextMenu (right-click menu) or through some other kind of dynamically changing menu that directs the user to those other areas. If your application also stores things such as email addresses, phone numbers, and personal information on a contact, but you don't have room to display all that information on the screen at once, a contextual menu or navigational system of some kind should be provided to get the user to those related areas.

The bottom line is that within the context of whatever action the user is performing, he should be able to perform any other tasks that are relevant to that action without requiring a significant amount of effort on his part. This is usually accomplished with contextual menus that appear when you right-click something that you are working on.

A Sample Dynamic Context Menu in Action

The next code sample is more an illustration of a design pattern than it is coding. The code is fairly simple, but the pattern it uses to provide dynamic contextual functionality is something that every Windows Forms application can benefit from.

To create this sample, follow the following steps:

1. Create a new Windows Forms application called DynamicContext.

2. Drop a ListView control onto the form and call it lvUsers.

3. Add the following columns to the ListView and place it in Report mode: Name, Address, Email.

4. Next, drop a ContextMenu onto the form and call it cmUserContext.

5. Add the following items to it: Assign Work, View Details, Send Email.

6. Associate the contextual menu with the list view by setting the list view's ContextMenu property to cmUserContext.

You should be ready to write some code for the dynamic context menu. Rig up an event handler (click the lightning-bolt icon in the Properties window and double-click the empty space next to the event name) for the Popup event. The code for the Popup event is shown in Listing 17.3.

LISTING 17.3
The Pop-up Context Menu Event Handler

```
private void cmUserContext_Popup(object sender, System.EventArgs e)
{
  if (lvUsers.SelectedItems.Count == 0)
    Disable_AllItems();
  else
  {
    Reset_DefaultItems();
    // evaluate which items to show based on the currently selected user
    cmiAssignWork.Enabled = (bool)lvUsers.SelectedItems[0].Tag;
    if (lvUsers.SelectedItems[0].SubItems[2].Text == "")
      cmiSendEmail.Enabled = false;
  }
}
private void Reset_DefaultItems()
{
  foreach (MenuItem mni in cmUserContext.MenuItems)
  {
    mni.Enabled = true;
  }
}

private void Disable_AllItems()
{
  foreach (MenuItem mni in cmUserContext.MenuItems)
  {
    mni.Enabled = false;
  }
}
```

There are a couple of $I~pop-up context menu event handler>things going on in this pop-up handler. If there is no selected item, there can be no user context, so all the context menu's menu items need to be disabled. If there is a user context, the menu items are first restored to their default position. Our sample has them all enabled, but the default position for your application could be anything; it could even be determined by a database query.

Finally, the code examines the selected ListViewItem. If the Tag property evaluates to true, the Assign Work menu item is enabled. The Send Email menu item is enabled only if the current user's email address isn't blank.

Before running the application, set up the following code (shown in Listing 17.4) for the form's constructor to populate some dummy values into the ListView.

Creating and Using Dynamic Context Menus

LISTING 17.4
Populating the `ListView` with Sample Values

```csharp
public Form1()
{
  //
  // Required for Windows Form Designer support
  //
  InitializeComponent();

  //
  // TODO: Add any constructor code after InitializeComponent call
  //
  SetupFakeUsers();
}
private void SetupFakeUsers()
{
  ListViewItem lvi = null;
  lvUsers.Items.Clear();

  lvi = new ListViewItem();
  lvi.Text = "Joe User";
  lvi.SubItems.Add( "1 Joe St");
  lvi.SubItems.Add("joe@joe.com");
  lvi.Tag = true;
  lvUsers.Items.Add( lvi );
  lvi = new ListViewItem();
  lvi.Text = "John Doe";
  lvi.SubItems.Add("???? Somewhere St");
  lvi.SubItems.Add("anonymous@somewhere.com");
  lvi.Tag = false;
  lvUsers.Items.Add( lvi );
  lvi = new ListViewItem();
  lvi.Text= "Jane Doe";
  lvi.SubItems.Add("1 Jane St");
  lvi.SubItems.Add("");
  lvi.Tag = true;
  lvUsers.Items.Add( lvi );
}
```

Run the application and right-click in various places on the `ListView` control. You should notice that this kind of dynamic control gives the user a feeling of freedom. Rather than having to fumble through toolbar icons he might not recognize, the user can right-click anything he likes and intuitively know that he will be presented only with relevant options. After the user knows that your application supports context menus, he will immediately begin trying to right-click in other areas as he finds your application easier to use and navigate.

Drawing Custom List Elements

Custom element drawing is another way in which you can give an ordinary, plain-looking Windows Forms application a little extra flare to make it stand out from its competitors. The concept involves overriding the way that certain controls draw their items and replacing that logic with your own code. This enables you to create list boxes that have decorated appearances and much more. The next section will show you the technology behind creating these custom elements and present a few sample custom elements created from a ListBox and a MenuItem.

Using the DrawMode Property

The DrawMode property is implemented by many Windows Forms controls. It dictates the method by which the control is rendered on the surface of a form or within another container control. Three different drawing modes are available:

▶ DrawMode.Normal—This mode is the default. When a control is set to this drawing mode, it will render itself according to the properties of the control using its default display. Every element in this control is drawn by the operating system, and each element within the control is a uniform size.

▶ DrawMode.OwnerDrawFixed—This mode will override the default drawing behavior, allowing manual drawing of each element. Each element will, however, be assumed to be the same size.

▶ DrawMode.OwnerDrawVariable—This mode allows for the manual drawing of each element. Each of those elements can be a different size.

Elements refer to items within a control such as a ListBox , a ComboBox, a ListView, and so on. When you indicate that you will be manually drawing the items within a control, you need to provide your own implementation for two events: DrawItem and MeasureItem. The next section will illustrate the use of custom drawing methods to create advanced controls.

Creating a Custom ListBox

The first custom-drawn items we will experiment with are the items of a ListBox. If you have seen any of the Longhorn demonstrations, you've seen how the Longhorn ListBox can automatically size each individual item and can contain anything, including graphics. Its default behavior has a nice gradient in the background.

Using the `DrawMode` Property

Until Longhorn comes out, developers have to code behavior like this by hand. Fortunately, with a little GDI+ magic, it isn't all that difficult to do as long as you remember the two important methods: `DrawItem` and `MeasureItem`.

To get started, create a new Windows Forms application called `CustomElements`. Don't bother deleting Form1; it's just a testbed anyway. Drop a `ListBox` onto the main form and set its `DrawMode` property to `DrawMode.OwnerDrawVariable`. Now switch over to the events list (the lightning-bolt Icon in the Properties window) and double-click the blank spaces next to `DrawItem` and `MeasureItem` to create some new event handlers.

The `MeasureItem` event handler is designed to provide the programmer with the ability to tell the Windows Forms system the dimensions of the custom item being drawing. It wouldn't matter if we were using `OwnerDrawFixed`, the custom item would be confined to the standard item space provided by the control.

The `DrawItem` event handler is called when Windows wants the code to perform the actual graphical output of the control. This is where we draw each item within the control. The method comes with a `DrawItemEventArgs` parameter that contains some valuable information, such as the bounding rectangle in which the item is being rendered. The code in Listing 17.5 shows these two event handlers for the `ListBox` that was added to the form.

LISTING 17.5
The `DrawItem` and `MeasureItem` Event Handlers for a `ListBox`

```
private void lbCustomDraw_MeasureItem(object sender,
  System.Windows.Forms.MeasureItemEventArgs e)
{
  string displayText = (string)lbCustomDraw.Items[ e.Index ];
  SizeF size = e.Graphics.MeasureString( displayText, this.Font );
  size.Height += 10;
  e.ItemHeight = (int)size.Height;
}

private void lbCustomDraw_DrawItem(object sender,
  System.Windows.Forms.DrawItemEventArgs e)
{
  // used to keep the background drawing consistent in case our code
  // doesn't completely cover the background
  e.DrawBackground();
  Rectangle r = new Rectangle(0,0, lbCustomDraw.Width, 100);
  bool selected= ((e.State & DrawItemState.Selected) == DrawItemState.Selected);
  LinearGradientBrush lgb = null;
  if (!selected)
    lgb = new LinearGradientBrush( r, Color.Red,
```

LISTING 17.5
Continued

```
        Color.Yellow, LinearGradientMode.Horizontal);
    else
      lgb = new LinearGradientBrush( r, Color.Cyan,
        Color.White, LinearGradientMode.Horizontal);

    e.Graphics.FillRectangle( lgb, e.Bounds );
    e.Graphics.DrawRectangle(SystemPens.WindowText, e.Bounds);

    Rectangle r2 = e.Bounds;
    string displayText = (string)lbCustomDraw.Items[ e.Index ];
    SizeF size = e.Graphics.MeasureString( displayText, this.Font );
    r2.Y = (int)(r2.Height / 2) - (int)(size.Height/2) + e.Bounds.Y;
    r2.X = 2;
    e.Graphics.DrawString( displayText , this.Font, Brushes.Black, r2 );
    e.DrawFocusRectangle();
}
```

17

The first method, MeasureItem, sets the item's height to 10 pixels more than the height required to draw the string contained in that item. You might also notice that I'm referring to lbCustomDraw directly. This is actually something to avoid, particularly if you are planning to create reusable controls out of the new display logic. You should instead refer to sender as a ListBox if you know ahead of time that the custom code is applicable for ListBox controls.

The second method, DrawItem, actually performs the rendering of the item. First, we call DrawBackGround so that we can be sure that the control has taken care of all transparency and overlay issues for us. Second, we create a LinearGradientBrush. This brush will fade from red to yellow if the ListBox item is not selected, and it will face from cyan to white if the item is selected. Finally, we fill the gradient into the appropriate rectangle and use DrawString to place the appropriate text into the rendered area.

Don't worry if the gradient code seems strange. As long as you know what methods to implement for your custom controls, you can always use a good GDI+ reference to aid you in drawing what you need.

Creating Custom Menu Items

The next thing to do is create some custom menu items. The good thing about this example is that if you know how to put a gradient behind an item, you know how to do virtually anything to it, including putting an image or an icon in front of it. Rather than showing you how to add icons to your menus, the code will illustrate how to add a graphical flare to them with more gradients.

Using the `DrawMode` Property

Add about 10 menu items to the form in a `MainMenu` control. It doesn't matter how many; just make sure that you add a few top-level menus and a few regular menu items. Don't use the ampersand (&) in menu item names because the custom rendering code in this sample won't handle it.

After you have added your new menu items, set the `OwnerDraw` property on *all* of them to `true`, and then make sure that the `DrawItem` and `MeasureItem` event handlers for all of those menu items point to the same two methods. Now set the code for your measure and draw methods to the code shown in Listing 17.6.

LISTING 17.6
The `DrawItem` and `MeasureItem` Event Handlers for Custom `MenuItems`

```
private void mniTEst_DrawItem(object sender, System.Windows.Forms.DrawItemEventArgs
e)
{
  e.DrawBackground();
  string displayText=  (string)(sender as MenuItem).Text;
  SizeF size = e.Graphics.MeasureString( displayText, SystemInformation.MenuFont );


  LinearGradientBrush lgb = null;
  bool selected=  ((e.State & DrawItemState.Selected) == DrawItemState.Selected );
  if (selected)
    lgb = new LinearGradientBrush( e.Bounds,
        Color.LightCoral, Color.AntiqueWhite, LinearGradientMode.Horizontal);
  else
   lgb = new LinearGradientBrush( e.Bounds,
        Color.LightBlue, Color.AntiqueWhite, LinearGradientMode.Horizontal);

  e.Graphics.FillRectangle( lgb, e.Bounds );

  Rectangle r2 = e.Bounds;
  r2.Y = (int)(e.Bounds.Height / 2) - (int)(size.Height/2) + e.Bounds.Y;
  r2.X = e.Bounds.X + 1;
  e.Graphics.DrawString( displayText, this.Font, Brushes.Black, r2 );
}

private void mniTEst_MeasureItem(object sender,
  System.Windows.Forms.MeasureItemEventArgs e)
{
  string displayText = (string)(sender as MenuItem).Text;
  SizeF size = e.Graphics.MeasureString( displayText, this.Font );
  size.Width = 50;
  size.Height += 4;
  if ( (sender as MenuItem).Text == "-")
```

17

LISTING 17.6
Continued

```
   e.ItemHeight = 3;
 else
   e.ItemHeight = 22;
   e.ItemWidth = (int)size.Width + 30;
}
```

The event handlers for these menu items are virtually identical to those for the list box. Pay close attention to the way the e.Bounds property is used, and how the Windows Forms GUI system informs your application of where it needs to render specific items.

You will probably be unable to make out the colors in Figure 17.4, but it should illustrate just how much of a radical difference you can make in the visual quality of your application just by taking a little extra effort to make some OwnerDraw controls.

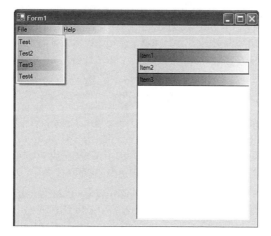

FIGURE 17.4   The OwnerDraw sample application, with colorful list boxes and menu items.

Nothing shown in this chapter has been dramatic or earth-shattering. On the contrary, this code is fairly simple. The next time your design calls for some visual effect that doesn't come standard with the .NET controls, take a look at OwnerDraw controls instead of backing away in fear of GDI+. There is no reason why every application developer shouldn't have a library of reusable controls that go beyond the capabilities provided by the .NET controls. The controls that come with Visual Studio .NET should be considered starter controls.

Shaped Forms

The next section of this chapter deals with the concept of shaped forms. A shaped form is a kind of `OwnerDraw` control that enables you to provide an advanced (and attractive) interface that doesn't conform to the standard Windows rectangle form factor.

Introduction to Shaped Forms

A shaped form is essentially just a Windows Form that doesn't appear to be rectangular. There are actually two ways in which you can create a shaped form using Windows Forms: an easy way and a hard way. I will cover the easy way here and let you do some experimenting to play with the hard way. The hard way involves using the `GraphicsPath` class to physically change the clipping region of your form at runtime by overriding some of your forms events (essentially making it an `OwnerDraw`).

The easy way gives you the most creativity and gets you up and running as soon as possible. It is, however, not quite as powerful or flexible as the hard way, so you will have to decide for yourself which method you need. Most people's needs can be met with the method shown next.

Creating a Sample Shaped Form

Building shaped forms relies on the ability for a Windows Form to set its `TransparencyKey`. This property basically tells .NET that anytime the color indicated by the `TransparencyKey` shows up on the form, it should be treated as transparent, and whatever is underneath the window in that position will show through.

Many people create odd-shaped forms by opening up their favorite paint program and drawing the surface of the form. The area outside the form that they don't want to show up is painted a different (usually an extremely bright and unusual) color. Then the transparency key of the form is set to the color of the outside area of the image. With that in place, all they do is set the background image of the form to the image with the bright color, and the form appears to be a custom shape.

There are some minor details to concern yourself with, but that process is basically all you have to do. To get started, create a new Windows Forms application called `ShapedForms`. To set up the background, set the background image of the form to an image you have created. Create the shape that you want your form to be, fill in the surrounding area with a bright color, and remember that color.

The background image of your form will tile and repeat by default, so you need to shrink your form so that it reveals only one of your images and you don't see the extra tiles. Now set the `TransparencyKey` property of the form to the same color as the one you used to fill the "hidden" area of your shaped form. I can't draw with a mouse, so I borrowed a news container panel from my friends at WarCry.com and filled in the transparent area with white.

TIP

Before you run the application, make sure to set the `FormBorderStyle` to None. If you don't set the `FormBorderStyle` to None, Windows will wrap your shaped form in a big square box equipped with a title bar and any other controls you have specified, shattering the illusion of a form shape. Remember that shaped forms like the ones in this chapter rely on transparency and borderless forms.

If you run the application now, you will see your nice, fancy shaped form. However, there are two problems: You can't close the form and you can't move the form because you don't have a title bar. To close the form, you can add a simple button to the form that closes it, or you can add another clickable image to do that if you want to make the Close button fit in with the style of your form.

To make the form move, you need to trap the `MouseDown` and `MouseMove` events so that you can allow the form to move when the user holds down the left mouse button anywhere on the form. MSDN comes to the rescue with the code in Listing 17.7 that illustrates these two event handlers.

LISTING 17.7

The `MouseDown` and `MouseMove` Event Handlers

```
private void button1_Click(object sender, System.EventArgs e)
{
  this.Close();
}


private void Form1_MouseDown(object sender, System.Windows.Forms.MouseEventArgs e)
{
  mouse_Offset = new Point(-e.X, -e.Y);
}


private void Form1_MouseMove(object sender, System.Windows.Forms.MouseEventArgs e)
{
  if (e.Button == MouseButtons.Left)
  {
    Point mousePos = Control.MousePosition;
    mousePos.Offset(mouse_Offset.X, mouse_Offset.Y);
    Location = mousePos;
  }
}
```

17

This code tracks the position of the mouse when it was clicked. Whenever the mouse moves, the location of the form is then moved to the location of the mouse, offset so that the form doesn't jerk the top-left corner of the form to the mouse location.

When it's all done and set to go, you might end up with a form that looks something like the one shown in Figure 17.5. I've moved the form into position over a window so that you can see the transparency effect and how the form appears to be rounded in multiple places.

FIGURE 17.5   The shaped form with the transparency effect in action.

Summary

This chapter has given you a glimpse at some of the real power you can unleash within a Windows Forms application if you follow some good design guidelines and are not afraid to dig into the WinForms object hierarchy a little. You've seen how you can customize the behavior of context menus to be incredibly dynamic and increase the richness of the user experience. You also saw how you can create graphically rich controls with only a little bit of effort through the `DrawItem` and `MeasureItem` events. Finally, we looked at how to create forms with nonrectangular custom shapes by using images and transparency layers. Now that you are a firm believer that Windows Forms programming is not boring and stuffy, you can do some pretty amazing things with Windows Forms if you spend a little extra effort up front.

Further Reading

Programming Windows with C# by Charles Petzold, Microsoft Press.
ISBN: 0735613702.

18 Consuming Web Services

IN BRIEF

Many of the samples available for consuming web services consist mainly of a simple application that makes a synchronous call to a Hello World web service, and that's the end of the sample. In the real world, however, a programmer needs to be aware of quite a few things in order to provide high-quality web service consumption. One such concern is how to obtain the proper and current definition of the web service and how to integrate that definition into the application. Another concern might be how to deal with asynchronous access to avoid creating an unfriendly user experience, as well as issues such as network detection, reliability, and keeping the application functional when the web service is unavailable or offline.

This chapter will show you how to deal with all of these things and more. Follow along with the code samples, and by the time you reach the end of the chapter you should feel extremely confident in your skills to not only consume a web service, but to consume it properly and with sufficient error handling, reliability, and ease of use.

WHAT YOU NEED

REQUIRED SOFTWARE	.NET Framework SDK v1.1 Visual Studio .NET 2003 with C# installed IIS version 5+
RECOMMENDED HARDWARE SKILLS REQUIRED	PC that meets .NET SDK minimum requirements C# and .NET familiarity Familiarity with ASP.NET

CONSUMING WEB SERVICES AT A GLANCE

Adding Web References	**373**		
Adding References in Visual Studio .NET	373	Using WSDL.EXE	377
Supporting Dynamic URLs	**378**		
Storing URLs in `app.config`	379	Dynamic URLs via UDDI Consumption	382
Storing URLs in Isolated Storage	379		
Consuming Web Services Asynchronously	**383**		
Multithreaded Service Consumption Sample	384		
Web Service Client Reliability	**385**		
Testing for Network Connection	386	Supporting Offline Actions	387
Handling Web Service Errors	387		
Summary	**388**		
Further Reading	**388**		

Adding Web References

Whether you are creating a Web Application or a Windows Forms application, you will need to provide some method by which your code accesses a web service. Thankfully, with .NET, you don't have to write your own SOAP headers and send your own manually created HTTP messages. The .NET Framework enables you to communicate with a web service via a proxy class that is generated on your behalf. You can generate this code proxy in one of two ways: via Web References in Visual Studio .NET or via a command-line tool called WSDL.EXE. This next section will show you how to create this proxy class using both methods.

Adding References in Visual Studio .NET

The easier of the two methods of creating a proxy for a web service is to use Visual Studio .NET's built-in features. To make use of a web service from within Visual Studio .NET, first create a new Windows Forms application.

When you have a new application, right-click the References folder and choose Add Web Reference. You will then be prompted with the search dialog box shown in Figure 18.1. This dialog enables you to supply the URL for a web service that you want to consume. When you are satisfied that you are looking at the correct service, clicking the Add Reference button will create a proxy class for you.

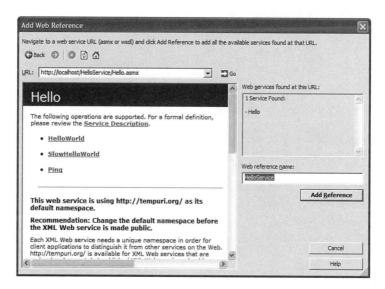

FIGURE 18.1   Visual Studio .NET 2003's Add Web Reference dialog.

To see that you have had a special class created for you, go to the solution explorer and choose Show All Files. At this point, the Web References folder will appear, with

Adding Web References

the `HelloService` web service node. Beneath that you will see three more files: `Hello.disco`, `Hello.wsdl`, and a node called `Reference.map`. These names were all generated automatically. When you create a web reference, you can choose the name of that web reference from the dialog box. This name becomes a namespace qualifier for the proxy class that has been created for you.

To continue exploring the new reference, expand the `Reference.map` node and you will see a file called `Reference.cs`. This sample is a deliberately simple web service (the ubiquitous Hello World service) so that you can see the generated proxy class without wading through 30 pages of code. Listing 18.1 shows this auto-generated proxy class. As you can see, it contains both synchronous ■1 and asynchronous ■2 method invocations for the three methods of the web service: `Ping`, `HelloWorld`, and `SlowHelloWorld`.

LISTING 18.1

The Visual Studio .NET Auto-Generated Web Service Client Proxy

```
//------------------------------------------------------------------------------
// <autogenerated>
//     This code was generated by a tool.
//     Runtime Version: 1.1.4322.573
//
//     Changes to this file may cause incorrect behavior and will be lost if
//     the code is regenerated.
// </autogenerated>
//------------------------------------------------------------------------------

//
// This source code was auto-generated by Microsoft.VSDesigner, Version
1.1.4322.573.
//
namespace HelloConsumer.HelloService {
using System.Diagnostics;
using System.Xml.Serialization;
using System;
using System.Web.Services.Protocols;
using System.ComponentModel;
using System.Web.Services;


/// <remarks/>
[System.Diagnostics.DebuggerStepThroughAttribute()]
[System.ComponentModel.DesignerCategoryAttribute("code")]
[System.Web.Services.WebServiceBindingAttribute(
  Name="HelloSoap", Namespace="http://tempuri.org/")]
```

LISTING 18.1
Continued

```
public class Hello : System.Web.Services.Protocols.SoapHttpClientProtocol {

/// <remarks/>
public Hello() {
this.Url = "http://localhost/HelloService/Hello.asmx";
}


/// <remarks/>
[System.Web.Services.Protocols.SoapDocumentMethodAttribute(           1
  "http://tempuri.org/Ping",
   RequestNamespace="http://tempuri.org/",
   ResponseNamespace="http://tempuri.org/",
   Use=System.Web.Services.Description.SoapBindingUse.Literal,
   ParameterStyle=System.Web.Services.Protocols.SoapParameterStyle.Wrapped)]
public bool Ping() {
  object[] results = this.Invoke("Ping", new object[0]);
  return ((bool)(results[0]));
}

/// <remarks/>                                                         2
public System.IAsyncResult BeginPing(System.AsyncCallback callback, object async-
State) {
  return this.BeginInvoke("Ping", new object[0], callback, asyncState);
}


/// <remarks/>
public bool EndPing(System.IAsyncResult asyncResult) {
  object[] results = this.EndInvoke(asyncResult);
  return ((bool)(results[0]));
}


/// <remarks/>
[System.Web.Services.Protocols.SoapDocumentMethodAttribute(
  "http://tempuri.org/HelloWorld",
  RequestNamespace="http://tempuri.org/",
  ResponseNamespace="http://tempuri.org/",
  Use=System.Web.Services.Description.SoapBindingUse.Literal,
  ParameterStyle=System.Web.Services.Protocols.SoapParameterStyle.Wrapped)]
public string HelloWorld() {
  object[] results = this.Invoke("HelloWorld", new object[0]);
  return ((string)(results[0]));
}
```

18

Adding Web References

LISTING 18.1
Continued

```csharp
/// <remarks/>
public System.IAsyncResult
  BeginHelloWorld(System.AsyncCallback callback, object asyncState) {
    return this.BeginInvoke("HelloWorld", new object[0], callback, asyncState);
}


/// <remarks/>
public string EndHelloWorld(System.IAsyncResult asyncResult) {
    object[] results = this.EndInvoke(asyncResult);
    return ((string)(results[0]));
}


/// <remarks/>
[System.Web.Services.Protocols.SoapDocumentMethodAttribute(
  "http://tempuri.org/SlowHelloWorld",
  RequestNamespace="http://tempuri.org/",
  ResponseNamespace="http://tempuri.org/",
  Use=System.Web.Services.Description.SoapBindingUse.Literal,
  ParameterStyle=System.Web.Services.Protocols.SoapParameterStyle.Wrapped)]
public string SlowHelloWorld() {
    object[] results = this.Invoke("SlowHelloWorld", new object[0]);
    return ((string)(results[0]));
}


/// <remarks/>
public System.IAsyncResult BeginSlowHelloWorld(
  System.AsyncCallback callback, object asyncState) {
    return this.BeginInvoke("SlowHelloWorld", new object[0], callback, asyncState);
}


/// <remarks/>
public string EndSlowHelloWorld(System.IAsyncResult asyncResult) {
    object[] results = this.EndInvoke(asyncResult);
    return ((string)(results[0]));
}
}
}
```

This chapter is not about how to create complex or advanced web services. It is about the various ways in which you can intelligently consume any service to provide a valuable user experience. As such, the server-side examples that are dealt with throughout this chapter are far more simplistic than real-world services in order to focus on the client-side consumption.

With this web reference in place, drop a simple button onto the main form and change the text to `Hello World`. Double-click it to generate the following event handler:

```
private void btnHelloWorld_Click(object sender, System.EventArgs e)
{
  HelloService.Hello helloProxy = new HelloService.Hello();
  MessageBox.Show(this,
    "Web Service returned " + helloProxy.HelloWorld(),
    "HelloService.Hello Proxy");
}
```

As you can see, you create the web service proxy just as you do any other managed class. The name you supplied in the Web Reference dialog becomes the namespace name, and the name of the service (in this case, the name is Hello) becomes the class name. To use a standard synchronous method invocation, just call the method and handle the results. You'll see more about asynchronous invocation later in this chapter. Figure 18.2 shows the message box created by this simple invocation.

FIGURE 18.2   MessageBox demonstrating a simple web service invocation.

This section has shown you how to use the built-in Visual Studio .NET 2003 tool to generate a proxy from a web service. Next you'll see how to use the WSDL command-line tool.

Using WSDL.EXE

You might occasionally run into a situation in which you have some special needs surrounding your client proxy. You might need to generate the class outside of Visual Studio .NET, or you might want to generate the class into a precompiled assembly and then simply reference that assembly from within Visual Studio .NET. For whatever reason, if you need manual control over proxy generation, WSDL is the tool to get it done.

As with all .NET command-line tools, running them at the command prompt gives you the basic syntax for operation. In this case, we want to use `WSDL.EXE` to grab the WSDL (Web Services Definition Language; the discussion of WSDL syntax is beyond the scope of this chapter) from the web service and generate a client proxy. With the sample "Hello World" service in place, the following command was issued to create the proxy:

```
wsdl /language:CS /namespace:HelloServiceWSDL /o:HelloServiceWSDL.cs
http://localhost/HelloService/Hello.asmx?wsdl
```

This command tells the WSDL tool to generate a client proxy using the namespace `HelloServiceWSDL` with an output file of `HelloServiceWSDL.cs`, using the WSDL contract defined at the URL `http://localhost/HelloService/Hello.asmx?wsdl`. By appending `?wsdl` to the end of a .NET web service URL, you get the raw WSDL contract for the service instead of the friendly greeting page that you get without that parameter.

The important thing to note about this class is that you can get more flexibility and more power by obtaining the reference manually, but it is easier to use from within Visual Studio .NET 2003. Which method you use is up to you, but you can be sure that the code generated for each proxy will be syntactically identical.

The Internet would be one really boring place if the only thing we ever did with web services was say "Hello World." The truth is that web services are far more complex than that. They take longer to return results, the results are more complicated, and the way in which client applications make use of them is almost always more complex. The rest of this chapter will show you best practices, tips, techniques, and code for consuming web services for professional-grade applications.

Supporting Dynamic URLs

One of the ways in which a great deal of sample code falls short of demonstrating how web services are consumed in professional applications is that the samples typically show a hard-coded service URL. Even if the web service being consumed is never scheduled to change its URL, it is possible that domain names could change, the file name of the service could change, and even more likely, the server will change depending on whether you are consuming a test service or a production service. Another possibility is that different vendors provide services that conform to the same contract. Assume, for the sake of example, that three different vendors provide a news publication service. You are building an application that can consume news from any service that conforms to the appropriate WSDL contract. The only way to accomplish that is through the use of dynamic URLs. In other words, real-world applications don't hard-code web service URLs; they enable users to enter them through the GUI, configuration files, database tables, and so on.

Storing URLs in `app.config`

One of the ways in which your application can support dynamic URLs is by providing the URL in the application's configuration file. In the case of a WinForms application, that is the `app.config` file. (Remember that an `app.config` file is automatically renamed and copied to the deployment directory when the application is built in Visual Studio .NET.)

To see how the storage of a URL works in the `app.config` file, highlight the web reference in the solution explorer with the Properties window open. You will see a property called `URL Behavior`. This is set to `Static` by default. Change it to dynamic, and you will see that a change has been made to your `app.config` file. The following few lines show the new addition to the file:

```
<?xml version="1.0" encoding="utf-8"?>
<configuration>
  <appSettings>
    <add key="HelloConsumer.HelloService.Hello"
      value="http://localhost/HelloService/Hello.asmx"/>
  </appSettings>
</configuration>
```

Instead of using the URL that you supplied when you first discovered the web service, your application is now dynamically loading the URL from the `app.config` at runtime, using that value as the default. If you're not convinced, go ahead and change the URL in this file to something nonexistent and then run the application to see the results. As you might expect, the application throws an exception when it tries to communicate with the bogus URL you supplied in the `app.config` file.

Storing URLs in Isolated Storage

Another option for storing the URL is a very powerful, but often ignored, method of storing configuration and user options data. Although information can be stored in the `app.config` file, that file is read-only and can be easily located and edited. In addition, that file only has one scope: the application. If you want to allow different users to access different URLs, you would need to come up with a very complex and custom scheme for storing information in the `app.config` file that might confuse users.

Enter isolated storage. Isolated storage is a concept that allows for scoped, isolated, secure, quota-limited storage of arbitrary files. The beauty of the system is that not only can you easily differentiate between files stored for different users as well as applicationwide data files, but the physical location of those files is completely irrelevant to your application. It doesn't make any difference to you where the isolated storage files are being stored. All you have to do is use the API methods and you get all that functionality for free.

Supporting Dynamic URLs

The following code demonstrates how you could store a URL in an XML document. This technique can be adapted to use with any kind of file you like as long as it can be represented as a stream.

The concept of isolated storage is beyond the scope of this chapter. Simply put, it is a sandbox for files separated by AppDomain, user, machine, or all of these. In the case of this sample, it is merely a tool to further show ways to enhance your web service consumers. The basic idea is that stores can be specific to your application, or they can be specific to your application and each user within your application. Within a store, you can create, update, and delete files. This store is configurable and managed by a computer administrator, and that administrator can do things such as specify a maximum disk size for each store, and so forth. Think of a store as a virtual folder and the files within that store as virtual files. You don't have to concern yourself with the physical implementation of isolated storage, just its stream-based API.

TIP

Isolated storage is not the only system within the .NET Framework that relies on streams. In fact, everywhere in the Framework where you would think a stream might be an option as a parameter, it *is*. The more comfortable you are with a streams-based programming model, the shorter your road to .NET mastery.

18

This example adds a text box and two buttons to the main form. The first button is for retrieving the URL from isolated storage, and the second button is for setting the URL in isolated storage. The code in Listing 18.2 shows the event handlers for both buttons, including all the isolated storage code.

LISTING 18.2

The Isolated Storage Retrieval and Update Code for an XML Document

```
private void btnGetURL_Click(object sender, System.EventArgs e)
{
  IsolatedStorageFile isoStore = IsolatedStorageFile.GetStore(
  IsolatedStorageScope.Assembly | IsolatedStorageScope.User, null, null );
  string[] fileNames = isoStore.GetFileNames( "WebServiceConfig.xml" );
  if (fileNames.Length == 0)
  {
    // file wasn't found, create it.
    IsolatedStorageFileStream isoFS =
      new IsolatedStorageFileStream( "WebServiceConfig.xml",
    FileMode.Create, isoStore );
    XmlDocument doc = new XmlDocument();
    string defaultXml =
      @"<configuration><serviceUrl>" +
      "http://localhost/HelloService/Hello.asmx</serviceUrl></configuration>";
```

LISTING 18.2
Continued

```
    doc.LoadXml(defaultXml);
    doc.Save( isoFS );
    isoFS.Close();
    tempURL = @"http://localhost/HelloService/Hello.asmx";
  }
  else
  {
    // load from existing file
    IsolatedStorageFileStream isoFS =
      new IsolatedStorageFileStream( "WebServiceConfig.xml",
      FileMode.Open, isoStore );
    XmlDocument doc = new XmlDocument();
    doc.Load( isoFS );
    isoFS.Close();
    XmlNode node = doc.SelectSingleNode("//serviceUrl");
    tempURL = node.InnerText;
  }
  MessageBox.Show(this, "URL loaded from options data: " + tempURL , "Options Data" 1
}

private void btnSetURL_Click(object sender, System.EventArgs e)
{
  IsolatedStorageFile isoStore = IsolatedStorageFile.GetStore(
  IsolatedStorageScope.Assembly | IsolatedStorageScope.User, null, null );
  string[] fileNames = isoStore.GetFileNames( "WebServiceConfig.xml" );
  tempURL = textBox1.Text;
  if (fileNames.Length ==0 )
  {
    //file doesn't exist, create it.
    IsolatedStorageFileStream isoFS =
      new IsolatedStorageFileStream( "WebServiceConfig.xml",
      FileMode.Create, isoStore );
    XmlDocument doc = new XmlDocument();
    string defaultXml =
      @"<configuration><serviceUrl></serviceUrl></configuration>";
    doc.LoadXml(defaultXml);
    doc.SelectSingleNode("//serviceUrl").InnerText = tempURL;
    doc.Save( isoFS );
    isoFS.Close();
  }
  else
  {
```

18

Supporting Dynamic URLs

LISTING 18.2
Continued

```
  IsolatedStorageFileStream isoFS =
    new IsolatedStorageFileStream( "WebServiceConfig.xml",
    FileMode.Open, isoStore );
  XmlDocument doc = new XmlDocument();
  doc.Load( isoFS );
  XmlNode node = doc.SelectSingleNode("//serviceUrl");
  node.InnerText = tempURL;
  isoFS.Close();
  isoFS = new IsolatedStorageFileStream( "WebServiceConfig.xml",
  FileMode.Create, isoStore );
  doc.Save( isoFS );
  isoFS.Close();
}
MessageBox.Show(this, "URL written to Isolated Storage.");
}
}
```

Running the preceding sample and clicking the button to retrieve the URL from isolated storage produces the dialog shown in Figure 18.3.

FIGURE 18.3   Retrieving the dynamic web service URL from isolated storage.

As you can see, this method obviously requires more code than the app.config method. However, you should be able to see the power in using isolated storage to store files that belong to specific users of your application or files that belong to everyone who uses your application. As mentioned earlier, the files you can place in isolated storage are completely arbitrary. You can easily store the XML serialization of a DataSet in isolated storage, giving you full data-binding functionality. When you are ready to save the changes, all you have to do is open an output stream as in the preceding code and save the changes to the DataSet.

Dynamic URLs via UDDI Consumption

Another way to get access to dynamically changing URLs is to make use of UDDI as a client. *UDDI* stands for *Universal Description, Discovery, and Integration*. It is a web service that is used to discover services available on local networks within an enterprise as well as services available publicly on the Internet.

UDDI has a far lower adoption rate than a lot of people expected. I have found that the most practical use of UDDI is by consuming it as a client within an intranet to obtain the true and current URL of an Intranet web service, such as a time-tracking, defect-tracking, or work-item-tracking service tool.

You can make use of public UDDI servers such as https://uddi.microsoft.com or you can make use of internal corporate UDDI servers such as those that can be hosted within Windows Server 2003.

Each entry in a UDDI directory can contain multiple URLs for a given service. You can use this entry in a UDDI directory like a phone book. Each time you want to invoke a web service you precede that call with a UDDI request. This request gives you the current URL of the web service. If the URL has changed, you can update your application and react accordingly.

The use of UDDI as a predecessor call allows the publishers of a web service to instantly change the location of a web service without negatively affecting any of the clients so long as the clients are using the UDDI entry. In addition, UDDI can be used to provide redundancy. If the UDDI entry returns a list of URLs, your application can try each of those URLs until one of the web service applications responds. If one of them fails, your application can then move to the next URL in the list to provide failover functionality.

Although your application might not need the degree of sophistication offered by using dynamic URLs and UDDI, there is no doubt that your application can benefit from providing at least some form of allowing the user to change the URL of the web service. This change can be done through GUI and private settings storage via isolated storage, or it can be done through the app.config file. Regardless of which method you choose, providing this dynamic, agile functionality will certainly enhance the end-user experience for your WinForms application.

Consuming Web Services Asynchronously

Not every web service returns results instantly, and those results often comprise extremely large amounts of data. Due to the latency of construction of SOAP envelopes and message overhead, web services lend themselves more toward a messaging infrastructure rather than an RPC (Remote Procedure Call) infrastructure. Because of that, the most efficient way to use web services is to make fewer calls with more data per call, rather than making frequent, small-data calls. As a result, some method calls to web services can take a significant amount of time to execute.

For example, you might be using a web service to perform some kind of search through a vast amount of records. The search itself could take a significant amount of time, as could the delivery of the results to the client depending on the number of rows in the result set. Now think about how upset the users of your application would be if your application were completely unresponsive for the entire time it took to locate and return all of those rows.

Fortunately there is an answer. If you make a request of the web service in a background thread while the main UI thread is still active and listening for input messages from the user, it will be able to respond and the user experience will not be harmed by long-running web service requests.

Multithreaded Service Consumption Sample

The following code will show you how to use a background thread to invoke a web service and obtain results. After the results have been obtained, the Invoke method is used to forward the request to display the results to the main thread.

There is a detail that you have to be aware of when doing multithreaded WinForms applications. When you are doing something in a background thread, any attempt to affect the UI at all will fail. In other words, you cannot do things such as open new forms or change properties of controls. You won't throw an exception, but it will appear as though nothing happened. For your background thread to affect the user interface, you have to use Invoke to cause a method to be executed on the main (GUI) thread. Listing 18.3 shows the code that invokes a method on the web service that waits for 30 seconds to simulate a CPU-intensive process. This code uses asynchronous multithreading to accomplish this without halting the foreground UI and it displays a dialog that tells the user that an action is taking place.

LISTING 18.3

The Asynchronous Execution of the `SlowHello` Web Service Method

```
private void btnSlowHello_Click(object sender, System.EventArgs e)
{
  HelloService.Hello helloProxy = new HelloService.Hello();
  progress.Show();
  helloProxy.BeginSlowHelloWorld(
    new AsyncCallback(FinishSlowHelloWorld), null );
}


private void FinishSlowHelloWorld( IAsyncResult ar )
{
  HelloService.Hello helloProxy = new HelloService.Hello();
  try
  {
    string helloWorld = helloProxy.EndHelloWorld( ar );
    this.Invoke( new DialogMethod( DisplayHelloWorldResult ),
      new object[] { helloWorld } );
  }
```

18

LISTING 18.3
Continued

```
catch (Exception ex)
{
  this.Invoke( new DialogMethod( DisplayError ),
    new object[] { ex.ToString() } );
}
}

private void DisplayHelloWorldResult( string message )
{
  progress.Close();
  MessageBox.Show(this, message, "SlowHelloWorld");
}
private void DisplayError( string message )
{
  if (progress.Visible)
    progress.Close();
  MessageBox.Show(this, message, "SlowHelloWorld Failure");
}
```

The asynchronous execution of the web service method centers around the fact that when the proxy was created for us by Visual Studio .NET, it created two methods: BeginSlowHelloWorld and EndSlowHelloWorld. The begin method takes as an argument a delegate to a callback function that will be called when the execution of the web service method has completed. When this delegate is called, it can then call EndSlowHelloWorld to obtain the actual results of the method. From there, the Invoke method is used on the Windows Form to push the execution of the DisplayHelloWorldResult method onto the main UI thread to allow the MessageBox to show up. Although the supposedly arduous background task is taking place, the application can leave open a dialog indicating that there is work taking place. If you want to be more subtle, you can simply display a message in a status bar or even change an icon to animate, indicating that web service communication is taking place.

Web Service Client Reliability

Making an application that consumes a web service perform in such a way that provides a rich user experience involves many things. One of those things, as you've seen, is the ability to deal with making requests of the web service in the background so as not to inconvenience a user or interrupt other work she might be performing at the same time.

Another thing that must be done for rich web service consumption is to provide some sense of reliability to your application. If your application hangs every time there are network problems or the web service throws an exception, your users won't find your application very compelling. They might also think your application is too limited to use if the application doesn't queue up work when it is offline. A lot of applications these days are being required to work on laptops, tablets, PDAs, and so forth. These environments are often referred to as *occasionally connected* or *loosely tethered* environments. Such environments sometimes have network access and sometimes they don't. Your application will need to be able to work offline in order to provide a rich experience in an occasionally connected environment.

Testing for Network Connection

If your application is to be able to work offline or handle unexpected circumstances, it will need to be able to determine whether it is indeed offline. Your application should be able to easily determine whether the web service is available.

There are a couple of approaches you can take here. One approach would be to use all kinds of highly complex code to detect whether a current network connection is available and whether that connection is available to the Internet, and so on. When you start to think about it, the amount of information that your code would have to sift through and keep track of to detect network connectivity at a hardware and driver level would be ridiculous.

A simpler method, typically called the Ping, requires very little code and allows for maximum flexibility because it has no dependency on how the user is connecting to your web service; it could be through a firewall, VPN, dial-up, or home DSL.

To ping a web service, set a very short timeout period on the proxy client class and then invoke a method on the web service that you know takes a very short amount of time to complete. If the method does not return in a timely fashion or an error is encountered, you can safely assume that your application has a bad network connection and you should be operating in offline mode. Here's a sample ping method:

```
private bool Ping()
{
  HelloService.Hello helloProxy = new HelloService.Hello();
  try
  {
    helloProxy.Timeout = 10000; // 10k milliseconds or 10 seconds.
    return helloProxy.Ping();
  }
  catch (Exception ex)
  {
    // an error occurred, do something with information
  }
  return false;
}
```

Using this type of method to detect network connection is probably the safest bet. Any attempt to use hardware or driver-level code to detect network connection will give you only the information that the user is on *a* network, not necessarily the right network. In addition, that method doesn't specifically test the connectivity between your application and the web service.

Handling Web Service Errors

Errors that occur during web service calls are handled in much the same way as standard errors. If an exception occurs during server-side execution, that exception will be serialized and then stored in the SOAP header as a SOAP fault. That SOAP fault will then be deserialized by the .NET Framework web services infrastructure and turned again into managed .NET exceptions. This mechanism allows it to appear as though when an exception is thrown on a web service server, it is caught by the client application.

The issue is that the serialization is just that: pure serialization. If you are throwing custom exceptions that have custom behavior, you cannot expect that behavior to carry over to the client that ends up catching the exception. For this reason, if your web service does throw exceptions of any kind, it should do so in a well-published, consistent, well-documented manner so that the client can tell what went wrong and why and be able to give the end user some important information about the source of the error.

Supporting Offline Actions

Offline access is something that you have to decide on; there isn't one piece of code that will enable your application to work in offline mode. What your application requires to work while untethered is dictated by the design and architecture of your application.

However, there are some things that you can do that will certainly help. The first is that you could possibly use the network detection ping code to determine whether your application is offline. If the application is not able to connect to the web service, you will need some method of storing the user actions that would ordinarily have been web service calls. You could use isolated storage (as shown earlier) to store an XML document or a `DataSet` that contains a history of user actions committed while offline. When the application detects (or is told) that it is connected again, you can then take the queued list of actions (essentially deserializing it) and push those actions out to the web service. This functionality enables personnel such as remote salespeople to do business offline. As soon as they are connected, the business they did offline can synch up, much like your PDA synchronizes with your desktop applications.

Summary

This chapter has been all about consuming web services from within Windows Forms application. Not only did you see the very basics of adding web references to your projects via Visual Studio .NET 2003 and the WSDL.EXE command-line tool, but we also went through various ways to keep your end-user experience rich, reliable, stable, fast, responsive, and agile. You saw how to do this by using multithreaded, asynchronous access to the web service, using dynamic URLs, trapping exceptions, consuming UDDI, and supported untethered offline access.

Further Reading

Microsoft NET XML Web Services by Robert Tabor, Sams Publishing. ISBN: 0672320886.

Programming Windows with C# by Charles Petzold, Microsoft Press. ISBN: 0735613702.

www.windowsforms.net—The official Microsoft Windows Forms community website.

18

19 Smart Clients

This chapter explains the smart client application.

In this chapter, you will first learn about some of the advantages and disadvantages of using a smart client.

Next, you will learn how to create an application that serves as a very thin loader client. On startup, it loads all the necessary assemblies to use the application.

Finally, you will learn how to load assemblies from a URL and how to connect your smart client to a web service.

WHAT YOU NEED

RECOMMENDED SOFTWARE	.NET Framework C# .NET environment
RECOMMENDED HARDWARE	.NET-enabled desktop client
SKILLS REQUIRED	C# coding

SMART CLIENTS AT A GLANCE

Smart Clients	**390**		
Understanding the Smart Client	391	Deciding Whether to Process on the Server Side or Client Side for Efficiency	400
Deploying Smart Client Updates from a Centralized Server	392	Make Use of Online and Offline Functionality	400
Make Use of Web Services for Smart Client Back-End Support	396		
Summary	**401**		
Further Reading	**401**		

Smart Clients

At the start of the client/server evolution, there were mainframes and dumb terminals. The terminals were *dumb* in that all they did was enable the user to input data and submit that data to the mainframe for processing. For a while, that was enough.

Then came the advent of the PC (personal computer) and the model shifted a bit. The shift occurred because it became apparent that if they could network a bunch of personal computers together and have the software run on the client as a "fat" client, the processing load could be distributed, saving expensive time on the mainframe. (In the past, processor cycles on the mainframe used to be billable.) This enabled the user to have a much more pleasurable experience in that the software had a rich GUI (graphical user interface).

After the PC and fat client came the browser-based model. Among other things, this model allowed for a single point distribution and automatic updates of the software. This model also took away the rich client and made the PCs into pseudo dumb terminals. The term *dumb terminal* was also used in the first sentence of this section. Yes, computing had come full circle in its evolution and was back to the mainframe and dumb terminal. The difference was that the extremely expensive piece of equipment from IBM was done away with and replaced with PC server and client machines.

Anytime you start with something, move to something else, and then return to the starting point, you wonder why you changed in the first place. Even more so, you wonder why you came back to the thing that you determined was inadequate enough to move from in the first place. In the following sections, you will learn why the next evolution takes the best parts of the rich client model and the browser-based model and combines them into one model: the smart client.

Understanding the Smart Client

To understand a smart client, as shown in Figure 19.1, it is helpful to define the term. A *smart client* is an application that leverages the best features of rich-client and web-client applications. As defined by Microsoft (msdn.microsoft.com/smartclient/understanding/definition/), a smart client is characterized by the following attributes:

▶ High fidelity user experience—The smart client leverages the latest graphics technology to bring a high fidelity experience to the user. In addition, it is personalized for each user based upon the context of the presentation.

▶ Intelligent connection—The smart client is capable of working in online or offline mode. It takes advantage of local data caching and processing. In addition, the smart client is a distributed application, taking advantage of web services.

▶ Information-centric—In the smart client, data access is loosely coupled, and easy to retrieve, cache, and post.

▶ Designed for operations—Smart clients make use of local CPU processing intelligently, and are secure, centrally deployable, and versionable.

By looking at the earlier definition, you might think that it's quite a list of things for an application to perform. However, decisional really means that when you make a decision about what type of application to build—a rich client or web application—it is not an all-or-nothing decision. A smart client application makes intelligent use of the best features of both programming paradigms. Here is a list of the most

Smart Clients

commonly included features to aid you when making a decision about what features to leverage in a smart client:

▶ Deploy the application and updates from a centralized server.

▶ Use web services to provide richer functionality.

▶ Use local processing power of the device when it is advantageous.

▶ Make use of online and offline functionality. This ensures that the user is always capable of being productive even when a connection to the server is not possible.

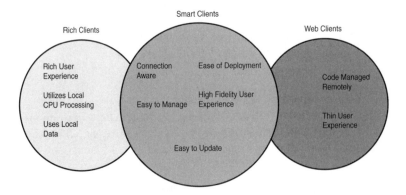

FIGURE 19.1   The smart client.

In the following sections, you will learn how to create a smart client application using each of the four bullet points just described.

Deploying Smart Client Updates from a Centralized Server

One of the first things you ask a client who is having difficulty with an application (other than "Is the power on?") is "What version do you have?" This is a necessary question to determine whether the client has the most recent version of your software. If not, you are wasting your time because the client's problem might have already been fixed in the latest version of the application.

To avoid this problem, you can deploy your application to a centralized server and tell everyone to check for updates there. This enables you to sidestep the issues that arise when a co-worker passes out the three-year-old copy of your software that she saved on a CD in her filing cabinet. However, this solves only part of the trouble. Just because someone knows that there is an update to the software doesn't mean that she will actually update the program. That kind of person understands only one thing: a forced update. But how do you know that this employee is running an older version of software in the first place? How do you force him to install the update? The answer is a self-updating application. There are many methods to achieve this goal, and the next few sections describe how to do so using .NET.

Web Server Deployment

Deploying your applications from a web server is easy and can offer quite a few advantages. Some of those advantages are as follows:

- ▶ Ensures that the client is always using the latest version—This avoids any problems with employees who don't want to upgrade. They no longer have an option.

- ▶ Assemblies are downloaded when needed or referenced—This means that the assembly will be downloaded only when it is referenced by the client, and then only when the local copy is out of date.

- ▶ Local copies of the assemblies are used when they're up to date—Therefore the network is not overburdened by unnecessary downloads of the same assembly.

There are three basic ways to deploy your application from a web server: using a URL-based executable, using the `Assembly.LoadFrom` method, and creating a custom self-updating application. These methods are discussed individually in the sections that follow this one.

Deploying a Smart Client with a URL-Based Executable

Using a URL-based executable is very easy. Essentially all you have to do is create a virtual directory on a web server and place all of your assemblies inside it. You can then deploy your application via a web link such as http://companysite/myapplication.exe. When a user launches your application, .NET automatically searches the specified location for every referenced assembly unless instructed not to do so.

Using the `Assembly.LoadFrom` Method

Using the `System.Reflection` method `Assembly.LoadFrom` **1** is useful in two situations. The first is when you need to load an assembly that is physically located in a location that is not in .NET's assembly resolution path. The second situation is when you create a stub application whose sole purpose is to load the real functionality of the application. That stub application typically contains very little code; it simply loads and kicks off the main method for the application. Listing 19.1 shows a typical stub application. These types of stubs are often referred to as *loaders* or *front-end loaders*.

LISTING 19.1
Stub Application Using the `Application.LoadFrom` Method

```
using System;
using System.Reflection;

namespace SAMS.VisualCSharpDotNetUnleashed.Chapter19
```

19

LISTING 19.1
Continued

```
{
    /// <summary>
    /// Summary description for Form1.
    /// </summary>
    public class StubApplicationClass
    {
        public static void Main()
        {
            Assembly.LoadFrom(
                "http://localhost/SampleApplication/SampleApplicationLibrary.dll");

            // Create a object for the Class
            Type typeContent = assemblyContent.GetType(sClassName);
            try
            {
                // Find the main method and start the execution.
                typeContent.InvokeMember ("Main", BindingFlags.Public |
BindingFlags.InvokeMethod |
                                        BindingFlags.Static, null, null, null);
            }
            catch(Exception e)
            {
                // Code omitted for brevity
            }
        }
    }
}
```

19

Creating a Custom Self-Updating Application

Creating a custom application for self-updating can be the best solution for your needs, but can also prove to be a challenge. The first thing you need to do when creating a custom solution is decide on three important things: Where do you check for updates, when do you check for updates, and how do you check for updates? The answers to these three questions will have a great influence on how you choose to implement the custom solution.

Determining the Location to Check for Updates   Deciding where to check for updates should be a fairly simple question to answer. Your code needs to determine if it should check a location on the network or check anywhere on an intranet or the Internet. If you want to check a location on the network, you can use simple file operations as a method for checking for necessary updates. However, if your answer was an intranet or the Internet, you will have to go with something such as an HTTP protocol or web services. For more information about file operations, see Chapter 7, "File and Stream I/O and Object Persistence." For more information about web services, see Chapter 32, "Introduction to Web Services," and Chapter 33, "Using WSE 2.0."

Determining When to Check for Updates   Although the question of when to check for updates seems like a simple question, it is doubtful that you want to make that assumption for the client. For example, in the case of virus-checking software, you might want to check for updates every five minutes, every hour, or every day. For other applications, it might be that you want to check for updates daily, weekly, or every time the application starts. Some people don't want an application to make a decision for them. For them, the task of checking for updates is a manual process. They want to tell the application when it is convenient to check for updates.

Determining How to Check for Updates   The task of actually checking for updates can be solved in a number of ways. In the first approach, you could check the server and directly compare the versions of assemblies with the ones that the application is currently using.

Alternatively, you could use a manifest approach. In this technique, you place a manifest of the assemblies, along with the current version numbers and download locations, on the server. From there the software can download the manifest and check the assemblies that reside on the local machine to see whether they are up to date. This has an advantage over the direct method in that if an additional assembly is required in the update, it can be included in the update as well. For example: If your application starts with two assemblies and checks for updates on the server, it might find that one of the assemblies is out of date and download the update. However, because the application doesn't know about the third assembly, it can't check the version and therefore doesn't download the newly required file.

As a third option, you could use a web service. This approach enables you to use a web service to receive a manifest. From there, the same rules apply here that were in effect for the manifest download. This gives you an advantage over both of the previously described methods in that you can tailor the manifest to each user. In other words, if you have two classes of users and an update is available for one class, you could send the new manifest to that class. When users from the other class log in, they would not receive an updated manifest and would therefore not get the update. This can be useful in the case of a beta program. For example, if you want to revoke a user's ability to test the software, you could refuse to send an updated manifest and therefore inhibit that user's ability to participate in the program.

After you've figured out that files need to be updated, you need to decide how to best accomplish this. When you decide to update an application, two things must happen: The download of the updated files must commence and the application cannot be left in an unusable state if the download fails. Downloading the updated files presents a few challenges: The server from which you are downloading could go

Smart Clients

down; your Internet connectivity could be interrupted; the power could go out; or the user could terminate the process. If any of these things happen, it is considered unacceptable to leave the application in any state other than usable. For that reason, the download must take place in such a way that it does not interfere with the application until the update process has actually started.

For the purposes of this discussion, the update process is considered to start after all files have been downloaded and verified to be okay. To accomplish this, you could design your download component to run as a separate service similar to the Windows XP update service (BITS). In this paradigm, you would first download the manifest and then download each assembly one at a time. After downloading an assembly, you would check off that item as complete. If at any time a failure occurs, such as the server going down, power outage, or user terminating the service, you could resume at the point after the last successful download when the service is restarted.

After the chore of downloading all the necessary files comes the necessity of actually updating the system to the new version. With this task comes another set of opportunities. First, if you are running the application (it is assumed that you are or you wouldn't have found the updated files), how do you update files that are in use? If you terminate the application so that the files are no longer in use, you terminate the process that was updating these files. If you don't, you can't update anyway.

There are two possible solutions. In the first approach, you spawn a separate process that updates the application and then terminate the existing application. However, with this approach, you would need to know how to update the application if it needed to be updated. The second approach is to create a stub application that does nothing more than launch the real application. By doing this, you can download the new files and place them in an alternative location (such as a sub folder). This enables you to build a new version of the application while still keeping the old one (just in case something breaks). Then all you would have to do is update the stub application to point to the new executable.

Make Use of Web Services for Smart Client Back-End Support

Another key point in the smart client is its capability to work in a distributed environment. This allows the smart client to offload some of the processing to a server. One way to accomplish this is through the use of web services. Web services are a way of distributing an application using platform-neutral protocols. With Visual Studio .NET, you can write an application that consumes a web service with just a few lines of code. Listing 19.2 shows the source code for a console application that connects to Amazon.com through its published web service API. To create an application that consumes Amazon.com's Keyword Search method in the Amazon Web Services (AWS) Kit version 3.0, follow these steps:

1. Start Visual Studio .NET and create a console application in a new solution.

2. Right-click on the project and select the Add Web Reference menu item, as shown in Figure 19.2.

FIGURE 19.2   Select the Add Web Reference menu item.

3. In the Add Web Reference dialog, shown in Figure 19.3, enter the address **http://soap.amazon.com/schemas3/AmazonWebServices.wsdl** in the URL text box and press the Enter key.

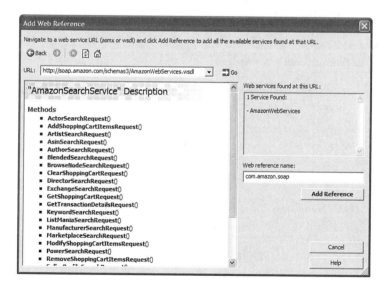

FIGURE 19.3   Connect to Amazon.com and add a web reference.

4. When the web service is located, you will see a list of all available methods in this web service, as you saw Figure 19.3. Click the Add Reference button to add the web reference.

Smart Clients

The web reference is now added to the solution and you can access the functionality just as you would any other class, Figure 19.4.

FIGURE 19.4   The web reference to Amazon.com is complete.

As shown in Listing 19.2 **2** , you create an instance of the `AmazonSearchService` class in the same way you create an instance of any other class. After the instance has been created, you can call the method `KeywordSearch`. This enables you to search Amazon.com for anything that matches the keywords that were entered earlier in the application.

LISTING 19.2
Connecting to Amazon.com's Web Service

```
using System;
using WebServiceConsumer.com.amazon.soap;

namespace SAMS.VisualCSharpDotNetUnleashed.Chapter19
{
  /// <summary>
  /// Summary description for WebServiceConsumer.
  /// </summary>
  class WebServiceConsumer
  {
    /// <summary>
    /// The main entry point for the application.
    /// </summary>
    [STAThread]
    static void Main(string[] args)
    {
      AmazonSearchService amazonSearch  = new AmazonSearchService();
      KeywordRequest       keywordReq    = new KeywordRequest();
```

LISTING 19.2
Continued

```
    keywordReq.devtag               = "DJYVGQ3AW0XX8";
    keywordReq.mode                 = "books";
    keywordReq.type                 = "heavy";
    keywordReq.sort                 = "+pmrank";

    ProductInfo productInfo         = null;
    try
    {
      System.Console.Write("Enter the keywords and press enter: ");
      keywordReq.keyword = System.Console.ReadLine();

      productInfo = amazonSearch.KeywordSearchRequest(keywordReq);
    }
    catch (Exception ex)
    {
      System.Console.WriteLine(ex.Message);
    }

    if (productInfo != null)
    {
      System.Console.WriteLine("{0} items were returned in your search.",
  productInfo.Details.Length);
      for(int i=0; i<productInfo.Details.Length; i++)
      {
        System.Console.WriteLine("{0}", productInfo.Details[i].ProductName);
      }
    }

    System.Console.WriteLine("** Press the Return Key to Continue. **");
    System.Console.ReadLine();
  }
 }
}
```

19

Web services give you the power to distribute your application. They also give you the freedom to easily publish an API to your system for external users to use. This opens up your application to a whole new world of users and developers. For more information on web services, please see Chapters 32 and 33.

Deciding Whether to Process on the Server Side or Client Side for Efficiency

In a normal web application, all the work is performed on the server. The advantage of doing this is that it enables you to create one monster server (or farm of servers) that has enough horsepower to accomplish all of your tasks. The problem with this is that all the work is done on the server. Doing all the processing on the server can be both an advantage and a disadvantage, depending on the situation. Being able to choose when and where such work is performed gives your application quite a bit of flexibility.

For example, suppose that you had to do some special processing on a string. You would have to get the text, send it to the server, and wait for the server to return with the modified text. This is a simple task that could have been done instantly (at least from the user's perspective) and now the user has to wait for the response from the server. From the perspective of responsiveness, performing simple tasks locally allows the user to have a more pleasurable experience. Performing tasks locally also enables you to take advantage of local APIs and applications. As an example, try to use a GDI+ library on the server and have it render locally. Sorry, it can't be done.

TIP

Although web-based applications can use client-side scripting and ActiveX controls to perform some tasks locally, they come with limitations. For example, scripted applications cannot read or write from a user's local disks. In addition, client scripts cannot interact with locally installed applications such as Microsoft Word or Excel. Additionally, users have the ability to disable client-side script as a security precaution, effectively breaking your application.

Make Use of Online and Offline Functionality

Smart clients have another advantage: They have the capability to work offline. Have you ever tried to do that with a web application? Unless you install the web server and all of its functionality locally, it will be difficult to work offline.

For many professions, it is a requirement that the system be able to work offline. For example, imagine that you are a nurse who works for a homecare agency. Your job is to go out and visit patients in their homes. When you arrive at the patient's home, do you ask if you can borrow the telephone line before you access the patient's records? How about if you plugged your cell phone into the computer and tried to connect to the Internet from inside a home when there is no signal on the cell phone? The only way to reliably accomplish these tasks is to have an application that can connect to the server, download the information, and then store it locally. This enables you to start the application at a later time and access the information without being connected to the server.

Summary

In this chapter, you got an introduction to the concept of a smart client application. You first learned the definition of a smart client and the advantages that the smart client approach has over traditional and web application development. You then learned that there were four commonly used features of a smart client. At the end of the chapter, you learned the reasons for implementing those features and how to use them.

Further Reading

Enterprise J2ME: Developing Mobile Java Applications, Chapter 3, by Michael Juntao Yuan, Prentice Hall PTC. ISBN: 0131405306.

Programming Windows with C#, Core Reference by Charles Petzold, Microsoft Press. ISBN: 0735613702.

19

20 Deploying Windows Applications

IN BRIEF

An often overlooked factor in software development is that the successful deployment of an application is just as important as the completion of the application itself. This chapter deals with the issue of deploying Windows Forms applications. The first section discusses the basics surrounding the installation of .NET applications. The next section shows you how to deploy an application using the Web. Finally, you learn how to install services and create a sample Microsoft Installer (MSI) installation project.

WHAT YOU NEED

RECOMMENDED SOFTWARE	.NET Framework
	C#.NET environment
RECOMMENDED HARDWARE	.NET-enabled desktop client
SKILLS REQUIRED	C# coding

DEPLOYING WINDOWS APPLICATIONS AT A GLANCE

Installing .NET Applications	402		
Understanding Assembly Deployment	403	Private Installations	409
Placing Assemblies in the Global Assembly Cache	404		

Web Installations	410		
Deploying from a URL	410	Deploying Smart Client Applications	412

MSI/Project Installations	415
Creating an Installation Project	415
Summary	421
Further Reading	421

Installing .NET Applications

Most everyone understands that it will take a fair amount of time to develop a useful software application. However, it might take some convincing that it will also take a fair amount of time to develop an installation program for that application. After all, an installation program is just that: a software program. The only difference is that its sole purpose is to install your application. Unfortunately, not enough emphasis is placed upon developing the installation program and all too often it is rushed and lacks the necessary functionality. Fortunately, when it comes to the installation of .NET applications, there are many different solutions ranging from traditional installation programs and private deployments to Web deployment.

Understanding Assembly Deployment

Assemblies are the basic unit of deployment for any .NET application. It can be the main application (.exe) or a separate library file (.dll). When an application references an assembly, the Common Language Runtime must be able to locate and load the file in order for the application to function properly.

Locating the Correct Assembly to Load

Although you can override this behavior in the configuration file, by default the Common Language Runtime attempts to load and bind to an assembly with the exact version number as was built with the application. The Common Language Runtime determines the correct assembly by performing the following steps:

1. The Common Language Runtime determines the correct version of the assembly by checking the following configuration files (in the order specified here):

   ▶ Application configuration file—The Common Language Runtime checks the application configuration file for any information that might override the version information stored in the calling assembly's manifest.

   ▶ Publisher policy file—Next, the Common Language Runtime checks the publisher policy file, if one exists. The publisher policy file is used by component makers to override all applications to direct the use of an assembly to the newer version. This is useful when a publisher provides hot fixes of service packs.

   ▶ Machine configuration file—Finally, the Common Language Runtime checks the machine configuration file. This file is used to set local (machine-specific) policies. Any setting in this file overrides configurations set in the application or publisher configuration files.

2. The Common Language Runtime checks to see whether the desired assembly name has been previously bound. If so, it uses the previously loaded assembly.

3. Next, the Common Language Runtime checks the global assembly cache (GAC). In order for an assembly to be placed in the GAC, it must have a strong name.

4. Finally, the Common Language Runtime probes for the desired assembly. This is done by performing the following steps:

   ▶ The directory specified by the codebase element specified in the configuration file is checked for the assembly.

   ▶ If no codebase element is found in the configuration file, the Common Language Runtime probes for the desired assembly using the following criteria: application base, culture, name, and private bin path.

20

Installing .NET Applications

Placing Assemblies in the Global Assembly Cache

The global assembly cache (GAC) is used as a central repository to store shared assemblies for use by varying .NET applications. The GAC allows for multiple versions of the same assembly to be stored and used by a requesting .NET assembly. To add an assembly to the GAC, a utility named gacutil.exe is provided. Use the -i parameter **1** to add an assembly to the GAC and the -r parameter **2** to remove one. Listing 20.1 displays all the attributes that the gacutil.exe accepts. To display this list on your computer, simply type **gacutil.exe** at the command prompt.

LISTING 20.1
Output of the gacutil.exe Default Execution

```
Microsoft (R) .NET Global Assembly Cache Utility.  Version 1.1.4322.573
Copyright (C) Microsoft Corporation 1998-2002. All rights reserved.


Usage: Gacutil <command> [ <options> ]
Commands:
```

1
```
/i <assembly_path> [ /r <...> ] [ /f ]
    Installs an assembly to the global assembly cache.
  /il <assembly_path_list_file> [ /r <...> ] [ /f ]
    Installs one or more assemblies to the global assembly cache.
```

2
```
/u <assembly_display_name> [ /r <...> ]
    Uninstalls an assembly from the global assembly cache.
```

20

```
  /ul <assembly_display_name_list_file> [ /r <...> ]
    Uninstalls one or more assemblies from the global assembly cache.


/ungen <assembly_name>
    Uninstalls a native image installed via the NGEN utility.


/l [ <assembly_name> ]
    List the global assembly cache filtered by <assembly_name>


/lr [ <assembly_name> ]
    List the global assembly cache with all traced references.


/cdl
    Deletes the contents of the download cache


/ldl
    Lists the contents of the download cache


/?
```

LISTING 20.1
Continued

```
    Displays a detailed help screen

Options:
  /r <reference_scheme> <reference_id> <description>
    Specifies a traced reference to install (/i, /il) or uninstall (/u, /ul).

  /f
    Forces reinstall of an assembly.

  /nologo
    Suppresses display of the logo banner

  /silent
    Suppresses display of all output
```

Because the GAC is a common place to store shared assemblies and to allow for side-by-side versioning, the GAC requires that all assemblies have a strong name. Therefore, to add an assembly to the GAC, you must first give it a strong name and sign the assembly.

TIP
Although the GAC enables you to store common assemblies for use by running applications, you must still keep a private copy of this assembly for the compilation of any assemblies that reference this assembly. The compiler will not find any assembly that is in the GAC at compile time.

20

Creating a Strongly Named Assembly

A strongly named assembly consists of its test name, version number, culture information, public key, and digital signature. A strongly named assembly grantees name uniqueness. This is done by using unique key pairs.

Generating Public and Private Key Pairs

To create a strongly named assembly, you must first generate a private and public key pair. The private key is used to create a digital signature. The private key should be kept, as its name implies, private. The public key is used as part of the strong name and is used by the Common Language Runtime to validate the digital signature of the assembly. You can use the strong name utility (sn.exe) to create a private/public key pair. The following sample illustrates how to create a random key pair and store it in a file called keypair.snk:

```
sn.exe -k keypair.snk
```

Installing .NET Applications

To view the public key stored in the `keypair.snk` file, use the following command:

```
sn.exe -tp keypair.snk
```

Listing 20.2 shows the contents of this file.

LISTING 20.2
Public Key Information Stored in the `keypair.snk` File

```
Public key is
07020000002400005253413200040000010001007b4a659111bf02da73fb30902e75b88d03b5f7
9f94b26563a57b102ea9e794a254b67d8a0a576abddd2eadebf6f61d24c172e7ab7f10cce5fa64
766e4b9ef9b5b8449e1dbd860a765f3bb2f7c64f82513a2c6dc44b26dfd15ec51995e22e35c8d4
882662cc4450aee73eb3708de79d1764dba8af90f31581328d675a22a5c0a1a35992d60f8205b2
3a3563a6624960d8eca999b3f7129648aeb622a3b316339fedb3474ab7271af2d769274cfc8091
417b204ec1afe93c4be8f8c96762b315d14909a17f8014184ab8454d1bc8a8da9f8acb1b04b5b6
6f3803bb8eba979c3f2492072aebda258522264a30467ce7f46a8905b0359d8519b5a11aadf8d2
120cc6d184fb1d42f86e915fd583b2ba393ee855f0d2423019db0756f672154c0b37f7c965eaa6
6c05659b37001bf4dcc81253cad9eacdde44585ef667f234a4a26e7af117d9936225486396382f
c335ba38fcc29dd548b0c2fe452bac6c1f34a3f05a15f52a528d56bec5952cdf2fef6507a40315
23e1b1df626bcc489042e27b5c5ad6cfb98702da24badd3afde117e014d6b8a29ba6073690113e
f61b2872516d5633a037d56e8cb2d9f8f7154f0ed4f65bc821a233ac8a503b09b453a3f59f7ec3
6150984e929e126617e705aa5a6deb13abc8f23cc6039800a2df06e64b56d1ccb3742b23e62b4b
ba16148f2cfbc8aeca8034a0cbffc01d929019a0803768cff828968575151b5933ecdb2b710817
6f8abcbe82c4de3a5f2a6face2837fc34dc96b60fe1e8960bc9f2ca77231c7cdf8c945670ae3b5
4f88b16d8871ba3d403853

Public key token is 7ba943661cd72246
```

Modifying the `AssemblyInfo.cs` File

The next step in creating a strong name for an assembly is specifying the version number, culture information and key pair information. To do this, you can modify the `System.Reflection.AssemblyCulture` and `System.Reflection.AssemblyVersion` attributes. If you are using Visual Studio .NET for your development, it automatically creates a file called `AssemblyInfo.cs` with these attributes already included. All you have to do is fill in the information. Listing 20.3 shows a default `AssemblyInfo.cs` file that was created for this sample project.

LISTING 20.3
Default `AssemblyInfo.cs` File

```
using System.Reflection;
using System.Runtime.CompilerServices;

//
```

LISTING 20.3
Continued

```
// General Information about an assembly is controlled through the following
// set of attributes. Change these attribute values to modify the information
// associated with an assembly.
//
[assembly: AssemblyTitle("")]
[assembly: AssemblyDescription("")]
[assembly: AssemblyConfiguration("")]
[assembly: AssemblyCompany("")]
[assembly: AssemblyProduct("")]
[assembly: AssemblyCopyright("")]
[assembly: AssemblyTrademark("")]
[assembly: AssemblyCulture("")]


//
// Version information for an assembly consists of the following four values:
//
//      Major Version
//      Minor Version
//      Build Number
//      Revision
//
// You can specify all the values or you can default the Revision and Build Numbers
// by using the '*' as shown below:
[assembly: AssemblyVersion("1.0.*")]                                              3

//
// In order to sign your assembly you must specify a key to use. Refer to the
// Microsoft .NET Framework documentation for more information on assembly signing.
//
// Use the attributes below to control which key is used for signing.
//
// Notes:
//    (*) If no key is specified, the assembly is not signed.
//    (*) KeyName refers to a key that has been installed in the Crypto Service
//        Provider (CSP) on your machine. KeyFile refers to a file which contains
//        a key.
//    (*) If the KeyFile and the KeyName values are both specified, the
//        following processing occurs:
//        (1) If the KeyName can be found in the CSP, that key is used.
//        (2) If the KeyName does not exist and the KeyFile does exist, the key
//            in the KeyFile is installed into the CSP and used.
//    (*) In order to create a KeyFile, you can use the sn.exe (Strong Name) utility.
```

20

Installing .NET Applications

LISTING 20.3
Continued

```
//       When specifying the KeyFile, the location of the KeyFile should be
//       relative to the project output directory which is
//       %Project Directory%\obj\<configuration>. For example, if your KeyFile is
//       located in the project directory, you would specify the AssemblyKeyFile
//       attribute as [assembly: AssemblyKeyFile("..\\..\\mykey.snk")]
//   (*) Delay Signing is an advanced option - see the Microsoft .NET Framework
//       documentation for more information on this.
//
```
4 `[assembly: AssemblyDelaySign(false)]`
```
[assembly: AssemblyKeyFile("")]
[assembly: AssemblyKeyName("")]
```

If you modify the `AssemblyVersion` **3** attribute to

```
[assembly: AssemblyVersion("1.1.2.3")]
```

you will set the version for this assembly to 1.1.2.3. By leaving the culture to its default, you are File saying that this assembly is suitable for all cultures.

The next step is to set the `AssemblyKeyFile` **4** attribute to the correct location. You will recall that in the previous section you created a key pair and stored it in the file `keypair.snk`. To tell the compiler to use this file, change the `AssemblyKeyFile` attribute as follows:

```
[assembly: AssemblyKeyFile("keypair.snk")]
```

Please note that the example this assumes that the `keypair.snk` file is in the search path for this project. If not, simply use a fully qualified path for the `keypair.snk` file. If you chose to store your keys in the Windows Cryptographic Service Provider (CSP) container, you should modify the `AssemblyKeyName` attribute instead.

With all the preceding changes made to a Visual Studio .NET project, when you next compile the project, the output will be a strongly named assembly.

Delayed Signing of an Assembly

For some organizations, usually larger ones, it is unacceptable to allow anyone access to the private key that is used to sign assemblies. In the previous example, this presents a problem when you need to sign the assembly. To overcome this challenge, .NET allows for the delayed signing of assemblies. This enables you to test your assembly and still have one person or group maintain ownership over the private key for the organization. In order for you to instruct the .NET compiler to delay the signing of an assembly, you must first change the `AssemblyDelaySign` attribute from false to true.

```
[assembly: AssemblyDelaySign(true)]
```

You must then specify, in the same manner as you did in the previous section, a file or CSP container that contains the public key. To extract the public key from the keypair.snk file to a separate file, you can use the strong name utility (sn.exe). The following command extracts the public key from the keypair.snk file and copies it to the publickey.snk file:

```
sn -p keypair.snk publickey.snk
```

Now that you have the public key stored in the publickey.snk file, modify the AssemblyKeyFile attribute to point to the publickey.snk file:

```
[assembly: AssemblyKeyFile("publickey.snk")]
```

Now, as before, simply compile the project. However, this time, the assembly does not have a strong name. It is simply ready to be signed by the person or group in your organization that has ownership of the private key. To sign the assembly now, simply use the -R argument with the strong name utility (sn.exe) as follows:

```
sn -R StrongNamedAssemblyExample.dll keypair.snk
```

This will create a strong name for this assembly.

Verify a Strongly Named Assembly

Sometimes just believing that a particular task was performed correctly is not enough. You or your QA department might want to verify this action. To verify that an assembly has a strong name, you can again use the strong name utility (sn.exe) along with the -v argument to accomplish the task. By typing the command

```
sn -v StrongNamedAssemblyExample.dll
```

you should receive an output similar to that in Listing 20.4.

LISTING 20.4
Verifying the Strong Name of an Assembly

```
sn -v strongnamedassemblyexample.dll

Microsoft (R) .NET Framework Strong Name Utility  Version 1.1.4322.573
Copyright (C) Microsoft Corporation 1998-2002. All rights reserved.

Assembly 'strongnamedassemblyexample.dll' is valid
```

Private Installations

If your application does not require that you share assemblies, you can choose to perform a private installation. A private installation is simply taking your files

20

(assemblies) from the distribution disk and placing them in a directory or directories on the designated machine. Because the .NET Framework does not require the registration of files, all you have to do is simply copy the files from one place and put them in another. Because it will automatically reproduce the correct directory structure, generally, you will use the XCopy command to perform this task.

Web Installations

With the gaining popularity of the Web, it is becoming increasing important, if not expected, to be able to download and run applications by simply going to a website. .NET provides several mechanisms for you to make this task easier. You can choose to deploy an application from a URL or your can create a smart client application that is capable of downloading itself.

Deploying from a URL

One of the coolest things with .NET is the attempts that the Framework makes to resolve the locations of an assembly it wants to bind. Because the Framework looks in so many locations, and one of them is the application base, you can simply set up an application for deployment from a URL by dropping all the required assemblies in a folder on the web server. To illustrate this point, take SimpleApplication.exe and the assembly that it references, SimpleApplicationLibrary.dll, and place them in a folder called SimpleExample off of the root of your web server.

20

TIP

Because the web server that you use to deploy your application simply serves as a distribution mechanism, you do not need to have the .NET Framework installed on that web server. In fact, the web server does not even have to be a Windows machine.

When the files are in this folder, you can open the Internet Explorer and, as shown in Figure 20.1, type the following URL:

http://localhost/SimpleExample/SimpleApplication.exe

When the application appears, click the button and a message should appear, as shown in Figure 20.2. The text for this message is not contained within the SimpleApplication.exe application, but is stored in the SimpleApplicationLibrary.dll assembly. This shows that the .NET Framework not only downloaded the requested file, but when needed, also downloaded the required assembly.

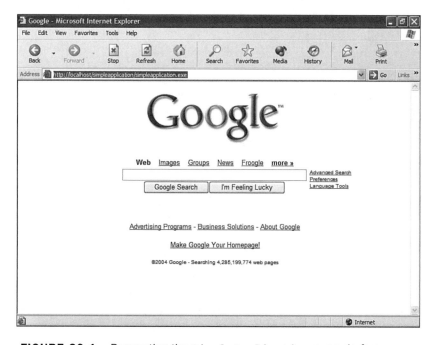

FIGURE 20.1 Requesting the SimpleApplication example from a URL.

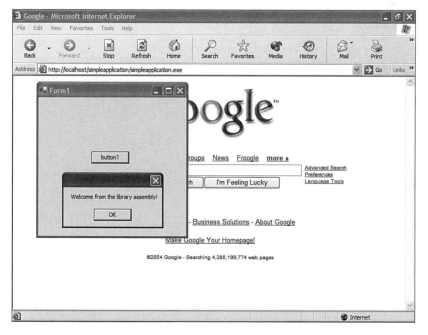

FIGURE 20.2 Requesting the SimpleApplication example from a URL.

Deploying Smart Client Applications

A *smart client* is an application that captures the best features of rich client and web client applications and adds to them. One of the features of a smart client is that it is centrally deployable and self-updating. That means when a smart client is deployed, the assemblies and required files should be deployed in one location and the client application should be capable of retrieving all the necessary files from that location. It also means that if any of the assemblies are updated, the smart client should be capable of detecting that a newer version is available and retrieve that version of the assembly.

Unlike the example in the previous section, when the application was started from a URL and it automatically loaded the referenced assembly from that location, a smart client application is generally stored on the user's machine. When the smart client application starts, it checks a predefined location for the required assemblies and if a newer version is available, it downloads this version to the client machine. In .NET, this is possible by using the `Assembly.LoadFrom` **5** method. By using this method, the .NET Framework will automatically check for, download, and use the latest version of the assembly. Listing 20.5 shows the source code for a pseudo smart client application. Although this application is capable of meeting the centrally deployable requirement of being a smart client, it does not meet all the requirements, so we will call it a *pseudo* smart client.

LISTING 20.5
Psuedo Smart Client Application

```
using System;
using System.Drawing;
using System.Collections;
using System.ComponentModel;
using System.Windows.Forms;
using System.Data;
using System.Reflection;

namespace PsuedoSmartClientExample
{
    /// <summary>
    /// Summary description for Form1.
    /// </summary>
    public class Form1 : System.Windows.Forms.Form
    {
        private System.Windows.Forms.Button button1;
        /// <summary>
```

LISTING 20.5
Continued

```csharp
    /// Required designer variable.
    /// </summary>
    private System.ComponentModel.Container components = null;

    public Form1()
    {
        //
        // Required for Windows Form Designer support
        //
        InitializeComponent();

        //
        // TODO: Add any constructor code after InitializeComponent call
        //
    }

    /// <summary>
    /// Clean up any resources being used.
    /// </summary>
    protected override void Dispose( bool disposing )
    {
        if( disposing )
        {
            if (components != null)
            {
                components.Dispose();
            }
        }
        base.Dispose( disposing );
    }

    #region Windows Form Designer generated code
    /// <summary>
    /// Required method for Designer support - do not modify
    /// the contents of this method with the code editor.
    /// </summary>
    private void InitializeComponent()
    {
        this.button1 = new System.Windows.Forms.Button();
```

20

Web Installations

LISTING 20.5
Continued

```
        this.SuspendLayout();
        //
        // button1
        //
        this.button1.Location = new System.Drawing.Point(104, 96);
        this.button1.Name = "button1";
        this.button1.TabIndex = 0;
        this.button1.Text = "button1";
        this.button1.Click += new System.EventHandler(this.button1_Click);
        //
        // Form1
        //
        this.AutoScaleBaseSize = new System.Drawing.Size(5, 13);
        this.ClientSize = new System.Drawing.Size(292, 266);
        this.Controls.Add(this.button1);
        this.Name = "Form1";
        this.Text = "Form1";
        this.ResumeLayout(false);

    }
    #endregion

    /// <summary>
    /// The main entry point for the application.
    /// </summary>
    [STAThread]
    static void Main()
    {
        Assembly.LoadFrom(
            "http://localhost/SimpleApplication/SimpleApplicationLibrary.dll");
        Application.Run(new Form1());
    }

    private void button1_Click(object sender, System.EventArgs e)
    {
        MessageBox.Show(SimpleApplicationLibrary.MessageContainer.MessageOne);
    }
  }
}
```

MSI/Project Installations

> **TIP**
>
> For any serious project or application, it is generally necessary to use professional installation software. This not only enables you to use someone else's resources to create and maintain the latest installation technology, but it also makes it possible for you to customize and perform tasks, such as adding shortcuts to the desktop, that you cannot do with an XCopy installation. Visual Studio .NET is just one provider of professional installation software. Other installation products include InstallShield and WISE InstallMaster. The next section will show you how to create a basic installation project using Visual Studio .NET.

Creating an Installation Project

The fist thing to do when creating a setup project is to invoke the Setup Project Wizard from the New Project dialog, as shown in Figure 20.3.

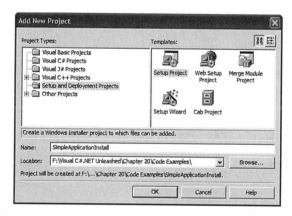

FIGURE 20.3   Select the Setup Project Wizard from the New Project dialog.

Just like any other project that you create, after you've invoked the Setup Project Wizard, Visual Studio .NET creates a setup project in your solution, as shown in Figure 20.4.

Now that the setup project has been created, you must now add the files that you want to distribute. To do this, invoke Add Project Output dialog (see Figure 20.5) by right-clicking the Application Folder item and selecting the Add, Project Output menu item.

Next, select Primary Output and press the Enter button. This will add the primary output (DLL or EXE) as well as other project dependencies to this folder, as shown in Figure 20.6.

MSI/Project Installations

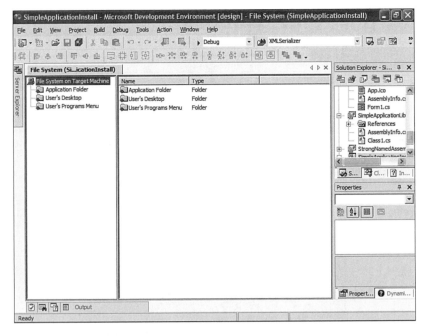

FIGURE 20.4   Visual Studio .NET creates a setup project in your active solution.

FIGURE 20.5   The Add Project Output dialog.

Now that the distributable files have been added to the project, you need to create a shortcut on the desktop for the application. To do this, right-click the desired location for the shortcut and select the Create New Shortcut menu item, as shown in Figure 20.7. For the purposes of this example, you should select the User's Desktop for the location of this shortcut.

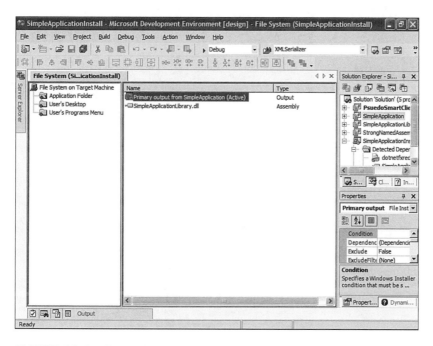

FIGURE 20.6   The SimpleApplication.exe and SimpleApplicationLibrary.dll assemblies are added to the application folder.

Next, select the folder in which the application is located (Application Folder) by double-clicking on the folder, as shown in Figure 20.8.

Now select the Primary Output from SimpleApplication item to create the shortcut, as shown in Figure 20.9.

MSI/Project Installations

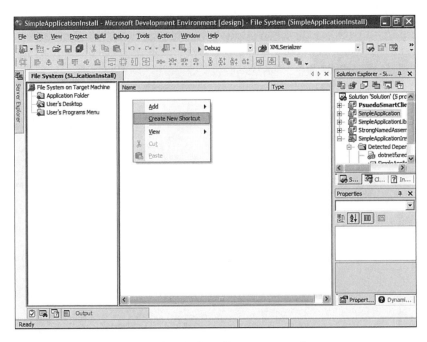

FIGURE 20.7   Select the Create New Shortcut menu item.

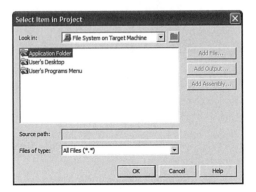

FIGURE 20.8   Select the location of the file in which to create the shortcut.

After you've selected the appropriate item, you are given the chance to rename the shortcut. Simply rename the shortcut to the desired name. Figure 20.10 shows the created shortcut.

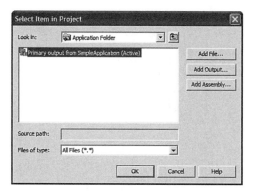

FIGURE 20.9   Select the desired file in which to create the shortcut.

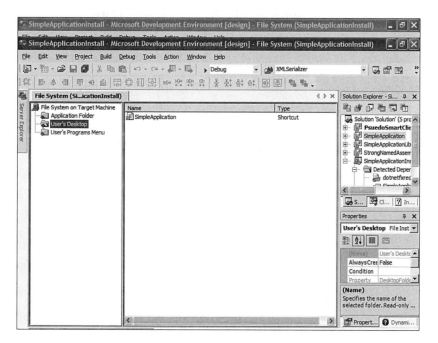

FIGURE 20.10   A shortcut to the `SimpleApplication.exe` file has been created.

Now that all the items are created and you are ready to compile the setup application, it might be helpful to look at the Solution Explorer, as shown in Figure 20.11. It shows all the assemblies that are included in the setup program.

MSI/Project Installations

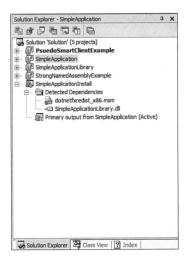

FIGURE 20.11 The dependencies of the `SimpleApplication` example.

Finally, compile the setup application. You should see a result similar to that in Figure 20.12.

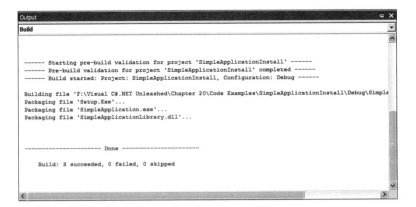

FIGURE 20.12 The setup program has been compiled and is ready to go.

Summary

In this chapter, you learned several techniques for deploying your application. First, you learned the basics of deploying applications, such as assemblies, GAC, and private deployments. Next, you learned about web deployments and smart clients. Finally, you learned how to create an installation program.

Further Reading

Programming Windows with C# (Core Reference) by Charles Petzold, Microsoft Press. ISBN: 0735613702.

20

Part IV

Web Applications

CHAPTER 21   Introduction to Web Forms and ASP.NET

CHAPTER 22   Web UI Controls

CHAPTER 23   State Management in ASP.NET

CHAPTER 24   Caching

CHAPTER 25   Advanced ASP.NET

CHAPTER 26   Deploying ASP.NET Applications

21 Introduction to Web Forms and ASP.NET

IN BRIEF

This chapter introduces you to the concept of creating world-class web applications using ASP.NET. The first section talks about the Web Forms Designer and how to visually design your web pages using Visual Studio .NET. Next, you will learn how to create your first ASP.NET application using the familiar Hello World example. Finally, you will explore adding some interactivity to your applications using the new concept of server-side ASP.NET event handling.

WHAT YOU NEED

RECOMMENDED SOFTWARE	.NET Framework
	C# .NET environment
RECOMMENDED HARDWARE	.NET-enabled desktop client with IIS
SKILLS REQUIRED	C# coding

INTRODUCTION TO WEB FORMS AND ASP.NET AT A GLANCE

Understanding the Web Forms Designer	424
Creating an ASP.NET "Hello World" Application	426
Basic Event Handling	433
Summary	438
Further Reading	438

Understanding the Web Forms Designer

Although an ASP.NET application can be created using the most basic of editors—Notepad, for example—it is often much easier to create a sample application using one of the wizards provided with Visual Studio .NET. When a wizard is invoked, Visual Studio .NET creates all the code, HTML, and C# code necessary to implement an empty framework behind an ASP.NET application. Even though this will be an application that compiles, it will not be very useful unless you add some sort of visual components or make the application do something in addition to appearing in the web browser.

To make the task of adding components to the Web Form easier, Visual Studio .NET provides the two different views of a form shown in Figure 21.1: the Design view and the HTML view.

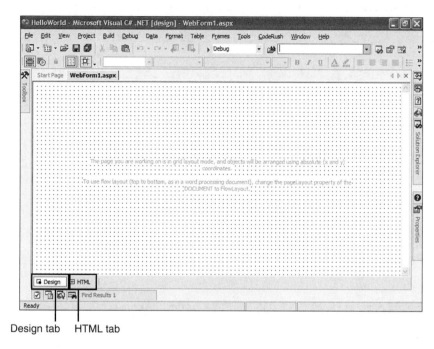

Design tab   HTML tab

FIGURE 21.1   Design view of the Web Forms Designer.

Adding components to the form can be done in a few different ways. The Design view enables you to add components to a form by simply dragging and dropping them from the toolbox to the form. Visual Studio .NET will then add all the necessary HTML code to the form. If you are an HTML expert and prefer to manually type the code, or if you want to see what the Designer generated, click the HTML tab and you will see the code that was generated, as shown in Figure 21.2.

Now that you have a basic understanding of the Web Forms Designer, it is time to create your first ASP.NET application. In the next section, you will learn how to create a Hello World application by using the ASP.NET Application Wizard.

21

Understanding the Web Forms Designer

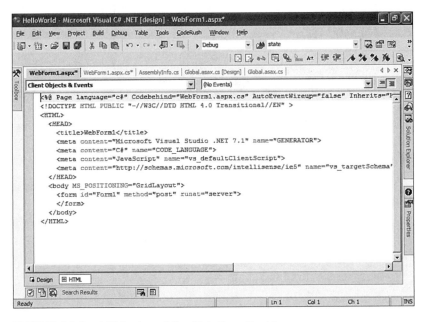

FIGURE 21.2   HTML view of the Web Form Designer.

Creating an ASP.NET "Hello World" Application

In this section, you will create your first ASP.NET application. This application is a simple but useful Hello World application. This application, upon execution, displays the message `Welcome from ASP.NET Web Forms!`, as shown in Figure 21.9. This application is simple in that you only have to drag and drop a Label component on the form and change the Text property; no coding is required. To create this application, first select New Project from the File, New, Project menu, as shown in Figure 21.3.

FIGURE 21.3   Select New Project from the File, New, Project menu.

Next, select the ASP.NET Web Application from the Visual C# Projects menu, as shown in Figure 21.4, and enter `http://localhost/HelloWorld` in the Location section of the dialog.

Creating an ASP.NET "Hello World" Application

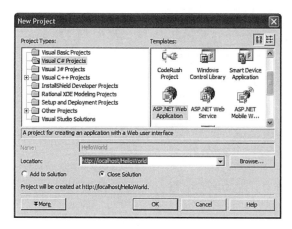

FIGURE 21.4   Select ASP.NET Web Application to create the Hello World application.

This will create a new C# ASP.NET application in a directory off of the Web Root folder. Visual Studio .NET will also create a virtual directory and point it to the specified location, as shown in Figure 21.5.

FIGURE 21.5   A look at Visual Studio .NET creating the Hello World application.

After the Hello World application has been created, you can see the application and all of its files in the Solution Explorer, as shown in Figure 21.6.

In the Solution Explorer, you can see that Visual Studio .NET not only created the project, but added four files as well. Three of these four files will always exist in every web application. These files are discussed in Table 21.1.

21

Creating an ASP.NET "Hello World" Application

FIGURE 21.6   The Solution Explorer with the new Hello World application displayed.

TABLE 21.1

Files Added as Part of the Default Web Application Template

File	Description
Web.config	This file contains all the configuration settings for the web application.
Global.asax	This file contains a class called Global that inherits from System.Web.HttpApplication. You can modify this file to wire up global event handlers, such as application start/end and session start/end, and any other event available from the System.Web.HttpApplication class.
AssemblyInfo.cs	This file contains all information about the assembly, such as general assembly information, version information, and information about signing the assembly.

The last file is the Web Form that was created for the application. By default, this form is given the name WebForm1. Now that you have an understanding of what Visual Studio .NET does when it creates a web application and what files are created along with the application, you can modify the form to display the welcome message. First, select the Web Forms tab from the toolbox and drag the Label component to the WebForm1 Design view, as shown in Figure 21.7. After you've dropped this component on the form, you will see a component that displays Label as its Text property, as shown in Figure 21.8.

Now change the message displayed by the Label component from Label to Welcome from ASP.NET Web Forms!. You do this by selecting the Label component and modifying the Text property in the Properties window, as shown in Figure 21.9.

Now that the application is finished and displays the correct message in the Design view, as shown in Figure 21.10, it is time to run the application and see whether the application does what you expect.

Creating an ASP.NET "Hello World" Application

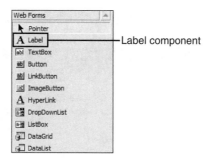

Label component

FIGURE 21.7 Drag and drop the label from the toolbox onto the Web Form.

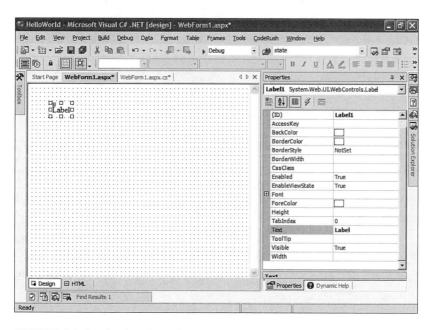

FIGURE 21.8 Design view after the Label control is dropped on the form.

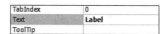

FIGURE 21.9 Modify the Text property to set the message.

Creating an ASP.NET "Hello World" Application

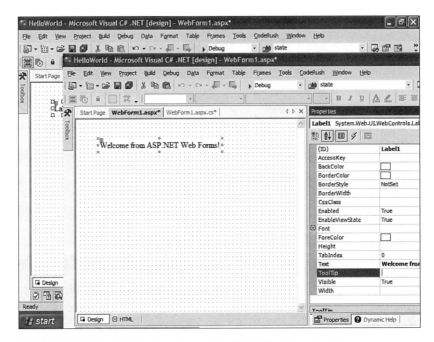

FIGURE 21.10   The Design view of the Hello World application.

To run the application, select the Debug, Start menu item or simply press the F5 key (assuming that you are using the Visual Studio Developer profile). When the program is running, you should be able to see the application in the browser and it should display the message `Welcome from ASP.NET Web Forms!`, as shown in Figure 21.11.

Listings 21.1 and 21.2 show the complete source code that it took to create the Hello World application. Listing 21.1 is the HTML code that displays the Web Form. The following line is the only line that was necessary to add in order to display the desired message **4**:

```
<asp:Label id="Label1" style="Z-INDEX: 101; LEFT: 48px;
 POSITION: absolute; TOP: 40px" runat="server">Welcome from ASP.NET Web
Forms!</asp:Label>
```

All other lines of code were generated by the ASP.NET Application Wizard.

Creating an ASP.NET "Hello World" Application

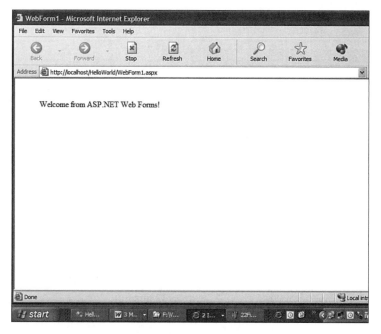

FIGURE 21.11 The Hello World application in action.

LISTING 21.1

WebForm1.aspx

```
<%@ Page language="c#" Codebehind="WebForm1.aspx.cs"
  AutoEventWireup="false" Inherits="HelloWorld.WebForm1" %>
<!DOCTYPE HTML PUBLIC "-//W3C//DTD HTML 4.0 Transitional//EN" >
<HTML>
  <HEAD>
    <title>WebForm1</title>
    <meta name="GENERATOR" Content="Microsoft Visual Studio .NET 7.1">
    <meta name="CODE_LANGUAGE" Content="C#">
    <meta name="vs_defaultClientScript" content="JavaScript">
    <meta name="vs_targetSchema" content="http://schemas.microsoft.com/
              intellisense/ie5">
  </HEAD>
  <body MS_POSITIONING="GridLayout">
    <form id="Form1" method="post" runat="server">
      <asp:Label id="Label1"                                              1
          style="Z-INDEX: 101; LEFT: 48px; POSITION: absolute; TOP: 40px"
          runat="server">Welcome from ASP.NET Web Forms!</asp:Label>
    </form>
  </body>
</HTML>
```

21

Creating an ASP.NET "Hello World" Application

LISTING 21.2

`WebForm1.aspx.cs`

```csharp
using System;
using System.Collections;
using System.ComponentModel;
using System.Data;
using System.Drawing;
using System.Web;
using System.Web.SessionState;
using System.Web.UI;
using System.Web.UI.WebControls;
using System.Web.UI.HtmlControls;

namespace HelloWorld
{
  /// <summary>
  /// Summary description for WebForm1.
  /// </summary>
  public class WebForm1 : System.Web.UI.Page
  {
    protected System.Web.UI.WebControls.Label Label1;

    private void Page_Load(object sender, System.EventArgs e)
    {
        // Put user code to initialize the page here
    }

    #region Web Form Designer generated code
    override protected void OnInit(EventArgs e)
    {
        //
        // CODEGEN: This call is required by the ASP.NET Web Form Designer.
        //
        InitializeComponent();
        base.OnInit(e);
    }

    /// <summary>
    /// Required method for Designer support - do not modify
    /// the contents of this method with the code editor.
    /// </summary>
    private void InitializeComponent()
    {
      this.Load += new System.EventHandler(this.Page_Load);
    }
```

LISTING 21.2
Continued

```
    #endregion
  }
}
```

Basic Event Handling

Displaying a Web Form is a relatively simple task, but if all it did was display static text, there would be no need for ASP.NET. To make an application more usable, it needs to respond to events and perform certain actions based upon these events. The following example builds on the Hello World application. You will modify the original form to add a Button control, as shown in Figure 21.12.

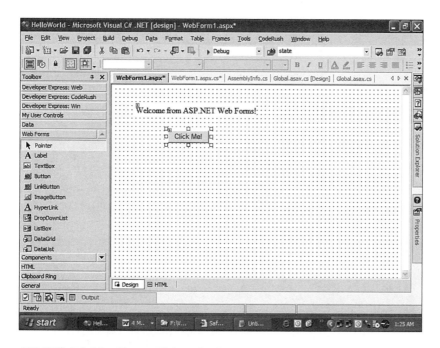

FIGURE 21.12   Drag and drop the Button control onto the Web Form.

After this control has been added to the form, modify the Text property of the button to be "Click Me!", as shown in Figure 21.13.

Next, select the Button control and add the Click event handler in the Events section of the Properties window, as shown in Figure 21.14. To add the event handler,

Basic Event Handling

simply double-click on the event and an event handler with a default name will be added.

FIGURE 21.13   The button caption is changed to Click Me!.

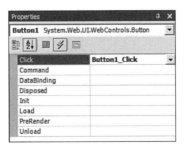

FIGURE 21.14   An event handler is associated with the Button Click event.

TIP

You can add a default event handler to a control simply by double-clicking the control itself. For buttons, the default event handler is the Click event.

After the event handler has been added to the Button control, add the following line of code to the event handler:

```
Label1.Text = "This label was changed by the Click event handler!";
```

This code will change the welcome message that was originally displayed when the button was clicked. Now that the modifications are complete, run the application. You will notice that the application looks the same as it did in the first example, with the exception of the addition of the button, as shown in Figure 21.15.

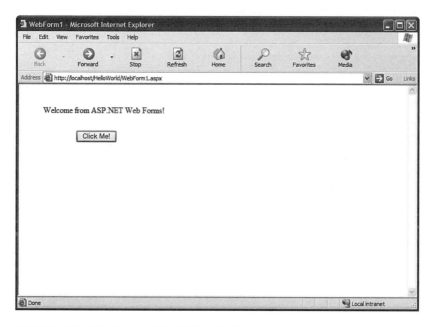

FIGURE 21.15   The modified Hello World application.

When the application appears, click the Click Me! button. You will notice that the displayed message changes to "This label was changed by the Click event handler!", as shown in Figure 21.16.

In this section, you learned the importance of event handlers and how to employ them. You can now take any web application and add the necessary event handlers to make the application useful. Listings 21.3 and 21.4 list all the code necessary to run this modified application.

21

Basic Event Handling

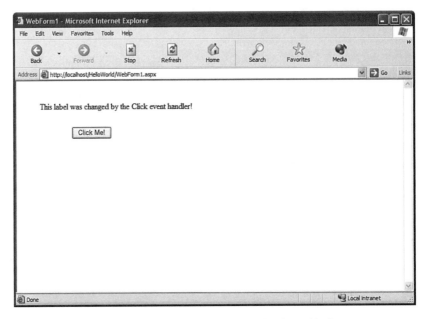

FIGURE 21.16   The modified Hello World application with the new
message created in the Click event handler.

LISTING 21.3

WebForm1.aspx

```
<%@ Page language="c#" Codebehind="WebForm1.aspx.cs"
AutoEventWireup="false" Inherits="HelloWorld.WebForm1" %>
<!DOCTYPE HTML PUBLIC "-//W3C//DTD HTML 4.0 Transitional//EN" >
<HTML>
  <HEAD>
    <title>WebForm1</title>
    <meta name="GENERATOR" Content="Microsoft Visual Studio .NET 7.1">
    <meta name="CODE_LANGUAGE" Content="C#">
    <meta name="vs_defaultClientScript" content="JavaScript">
    <meta name="vs_targetSchema" content="http://schemas.microsoft.com/
            intellisense/ie5">
  </HEAD>
  <body MS_POSITIONING="GridLayout">
    <form id="Form1" method="post" runat="server">
      <asp:Label id="Label1"
      style="Z-INDEX: 101; LEFT: 48px; POSITION: absolute; TOP: 40px"
       runat="server">Welcome from ASP.NET Web Forms!</asp:Label>
      <asp:Button id="Button1"
        style="Z-INDEX: 102; LEFT: 112px; POSITION: absolute; TOP: 88px"
```

LISTING 21.3
Continued

```
        runat="server"
        Text="Click Me!"></asp:Button>
    </form>
  </body>
</HTML>
```

LISTING 21.4
WebForm1.aspx.cs

```csharp
using System;
using System.Collections;
using System.ComponentModel;
using System.Data;
using System.Drawing;
using System.Web;
using System.Web.SessionState;
using System.Web.UI;
using System.Web.UI.WebControls;
using System.Web.UI.HtmlControls;

namespace HelloWorld
{
  /// <summary>
  /// Summary description for WebForm1.
  /// </summary>
  public class WebForm1 : System.Web.UI.Page
  {
    protected System.Web.UI.WebControls.Button Button1;
    protected System.Web.UI.WebControls.Label Label1;

    private void Page_Load(object sender, System.EventArgs e)
    {
        // Put user code to initialize the page here
    }

    #region Web Form Designer generated code
    override protected void OnInit(EventArgs e)
    {
        //
        // CODEGEN: This call is required by the ASP.NET Web Form Designer.
        //
        InitializeComponent();
```

Basic Event Handling

LISTING 21.4
Continued

```
        base.OnInit(e);
    }

    /// <summary>
    /// Required method for Designer support - do not modify
    /// the contents of this method with the code editor.
    /// </summary>
    private void InitializeComponent()
    {
      this.Button1.Click += new System.EventHandler(this.Button1_Click);
      this.Load += new System.EventHandler(this.Page_Load);
    }
    #endregion

    private void Button1_Click(object sender, System.EventArgs e)
    {
      Label1.Text = "This label was changed by the Click event handler!";
    }
  }
}
```

Summary

This chapter provided you with a brief introduction to Microsoft's new .NET-based web development platform: ASP.NET. In the previous sections, you received an introduction to ASP.NET and a basic understanding of how to create a Web Forms application. This introduction gave you the foundation that you need for the upcoming chapters in which you will learn all you need to know about ASP.NET to create robust web applications for everything from the smallest application need to large, enterprise-class scalable web applications.

Further Reading

Programming ASP.NET, Second Edition by Jesse Liberty and Dan Hurwitz, O'Reilly. ISBN: 0596004877.

Programming Microsoft ASP.NET by Dino Esposito. ISBN: 0735619034.

ASP.NET Unleashed, Second Edition by Stephen Walther, Sams Publishing. ISBN: 067232542X.

The .NET Framework enables you to create web applications with pages and controls using the technology of ASP.NET. ASP.NET provides many built-in, predefined UI controls that are either wrappers for standard HTML elements or implementations of some standard functionality that is often used when accessing websites.

For example, you could represent an input text box as simple static HTML text, but you are allowed to use the predefined server HTML ASP.NET control `System.Web.UI.HtmlControls.HtmlInputText` or the web server control `System.Web.UI.WebControls.TextBox`. Web controls are very similar to HTML controls, but they implement more advanced functionality and enable you to create more complex UI.

Basically, ASP.NET gives you all the web controls that are necessary for creating web applications. However, developers often need to create their own web controls for advanced functionality or to create a more complex and advanced UI. For this purpose, ASP.NET provides the ability to create your own web controls that contain custom logic, code, or user interface elements.

This chapter will explain what HTML and web controls are, the differences between server and user controls, how to use web controls, and how to create and use your own control.

WHAT YOU NEED

RECOMMENDED REQUIRED SOFTWARE	.NET Framework v1.1 Visual Studio .NET 2003 (C#) IIS version 5.0 or greater Windows XP Professional, Windows 2000 Professional, or Windows Server 2003
RECOMMENDED HARDWARE	.NET-enabled coding familarity desktop client
SKILLS REQUIRED	C# coding familarity

WEB UI CONTROLS AT A GLANCE

Server Controls	440
User Controls	444
Summary	455
Further Reading	455

Server Controls

If you have already worked with HTML, you should be familiar with controls such as the text box, buttons, check boxes, radio buttons, and so forth. Each of them is represented on a web page as a visual control. These HTML controls are processed completely on the client side of a web application. So, only the browser can work with and represent them. But you could make these controls available to the server side of an application by adding one attribute: `runat`. You set the value of this attribute to server. In this case, on the server side of the application, you could have access to these controls through variables. So, you could access all public properties and methods of these variables. After you've finished using these controls, they generate HTML code that is included in the content of the HTML page generated by the server.

Notice that each HTML element has a corresponding control on the server side. The following example shows how to transform a client-side control to server side:

```
Client-side: <div class="text" id="topicBody"> </div>
Server-side: <div class="text" runat="server" id="topicBody"> </div>
```

Transformation has been achieved in a very easy way: by adding the parameter runat="server".

In the preceding example, the server creates a variable of the type HtmlGenericControl. When the client requests a page, ASP.NET generates the necessary HTML code for representing this control as div. As soon as you change a control to be managed on the server side, you can use all its public properties and methods to manage it. For example, you can change text that should be represented inside this element by using property InnerText:

```
MyDiv.InnerText = "Some Text";
```

NOTE

Notice that all HTML server controls are located in the namespace System.Web.UI.HtmlControls.

The following list contains all HTML controls that are available for use in .NET:

▶ HtmlAnchor—Represents a hyperlink (<a> HTML element).

▶ HtmlButton—Represents the <input type="button"> HTML element. This control has many possibilities related to the behavior and view of the button. It is not supported by several browsers.

▶ HtmlForm—Defines an HTML form with all properties of it. Values of other controls are located inside it, and are sent to the server side after a submit action.

▶ HtmlGenericControl—Defines the base model of any HTML object (properties, methods, events, and so on). Each HtmlGenericControl control can be transformed to any HTML control.

▶ HtmlImage—Defines an HTML control that contains an image. It corresponds to the <img> HTML element.

22

Server Controls

▶ `HtmlInputButton`—Performs an action. This button is supported by all browsers. It corresponds to the `<input type="submit">` HTML control. After you click this button, all data inside the form will be posted to the server.

▶ `HtmlInputCheckBox`—Creates a flag that supports two states: on and off. Also this element contains a caption property. `HtmlInputCheckBox` corresponds to the `<input type="checkbox">` HTML element.

▶ `HtmlInputFile`—Enables users to upload files to the server. The form where this control is located should be configured to support this feature. Corresponds to the `<input type="file">` HTML element.

▶ `HtmlInputHidden`—Represents a hidden text box that contains all auxiliary information about the form (some persistent data that should be always available in the form, but should not be visible to or edited by the user). Represents the `<input type="hidden">` HTML control.

▶ `HtmlInputImage`—Very similar to a button control, but enables you to view a picture. Corresponds to the `<input type="image">` HTML element.

▶ `HtmlInputRadioButton`—Represents a set of radio buttons. This control is normally employed for user selection as one of the available choices. Corresponds with `<input type="radio">`.

▶ `HtmlInputText`—Represents a text box that is initialized to a value that is set during development process. This control allows the user to edit text and post it to the server. Corresponds to `<input type="text">` HTML element. Also, this control could be used as a password text box that corresponds to the `<input type="password">` HTML element.

▶ `HtmlSelect`—Represents a list of items with markers (bullets, circles, squares, and so forth). Corresponds to the `<select>` HTML element.

▶ `HtmlTable`—Corresponds to the `<table>` HTML element and allows user to read and write a table's properties (add rows, add cell, change look and feel, and so on).

▶ `HtmlTableCell`—Creates one cell inside some table. Corresponds to the `<td>` HTML element.

▶ `HtmlTableRow`—Creates one row inside some table. Corresponds to the `<tr>` HTML element.

▶ `HtmlTextArea`—Represents area with text (something like a memo). This control is used to read and write large pieces of text. Corresponds to the `<textarea>` HTML element.

There is another type of control that can be used by server-side code: web server controls. Web server controls are very similar to HTML server controls. They are created on the server side and enable you to design complex interfaces with an advanced look and feel. It is obligatory to set the attribute `runat="server"` in the declaration of a web server control. If you do not set this attribute, the web server control will not be shown on the browser, nor will it be accessible to server-side code.

Web server controls do not always corresponded to an HTML element. They could contain complex HTML constructs with complex business logic. Also they could contain other HTML and nested web server controls (this approach is very often used in the development practice).

Let's discuss how to declare web server controls in web pages or other controls. The following example demonstrates how to declare text box web server control:

```
<asp:TextBox
  CssClass="control" ID="searchRequestTextBox"
  name="searchRequestTextBox" MaxLength="30" Width="100%"
  Runat="server"></asp:TextBox>
```

On the page, this element represents a text box that is called `searchRequestTextBox` that has a max length equal to 30 characters, and a width equal to 100%. The CSS class of this control is set to "`control`".

Work with web server controls on the server side is very similar to work with HTML server controls. They are created at the server side and are available for developers through variables (instances of web server controls' classes). As mentioned earlier, these variables enable you to use all public properties and methods that are declared inside.

NOTE

Notice that each web server control has been rendered into ordinary HTML code before it was transferred to the browser. So, if you take a look at the HTML passed to the browser, you will not find anything unusual. You will see just simple HTML code. The purpose behind this is to give you extensive ability to choose what is rendered to the client by manipulating server-side objects.

The following list contains the most commonly used web server controls that are provided by ASP.NET:

22

▶ `Button`—Is used for performing some action. It's very similar to the `HtmlButton` HTML server control.

▶ `Calendar`—Represents graphical calendar and encapsulates its logic. You are allowed to select some date by using this control.

▶ `CheckBox`—Represents a flag, which could be checked or unchecked. The state of the check box is always sent to the server.

▶ `CheckBoxList`—Defines a group of check boxes and enables you to group check boxes with similar meaning.

Server Controls

- ▶ `DataGrid`—Represents some information (retrieved from a database or other data storage) that is formatted as a table with columns and cells. Allows the user to sort and edit data.

- ▶ `DataList`—Very similar to the `Repeater` control, but has more advanced possibilities for formatting and locating data. Also this control supports several modes of editing behavior.

- ▶ `DropDownList`—Enables user to select one item from a drop-down list or to type a custom item (like a text box).

- ▶ `HyperLink`—Creates a hyperlink.

- ▶ `Image`—Show image by the predefined path.

- ▶ `ImageButton`—Very similar to the `Button` web server control, but contains an image instead of text.

- ▶ `Label`—Contains read-only text (only for viewing).

- ▶ `LinkButton`—Similar to the `Button` control, but has a view like a hyperlink.

- ▶ `ListBox`—Creates a list of items. It enables you to select several items simultaneously.

- ▶ `Panel`—Creates part of a form that is a container for others controls.

- ▶ `RadioButton`—Represents a set of radio buttons. This control is normally used to select one of the available choices.

- ▶ `RadioButtonList`—Creates a group of radio buttons. Only one of elements can be selected inside one group.

- ▶ `Repeater`—Shows information that is retrieved from some data storage (such as a database). It uses other server controls, and repeats them for each record in the dataset.

- ▶ `Table`—Creates a table and enables the user to read and write the table's properties (add rows, add cell, change look and feel, and so on).

- ▶ `TableCell`—Creates one cell inside some table.

- ▶ `TableRow`—Creates one row inside some table.

- ▶ `TextBox`—Represents a text box that is initialized with a value that is set during development process. Allows the user to edit text and post it to the server.

22

User Controls

An ASP.NET user control is a group of one or more server controls or static HTML elements that encapsulate some functionality. The power of a user control comes from ASP.NET treating the user control as a standalone object. The user control is presented as a separate class in the code-behind so that other classes in your application can interact with it indirectly by using its public methods and properties. For developers, this approach has greatly simplified the process of creating web applications. The main idea is to give developers the possibility of using a control as a simple class. In terms of how ASP.NET handles user controls, you can think of them as mini-pages. Each user control has its own sequence of events that take it through the process of rendering output.

One of the ways in which you can create custom controls is to inherit your own control from an existing ASP.NET control just to extend its functionality. For example, assume that you want to have some additional functionality related to the representation and behavior of HTML input text box. You could create your own class, extend it from `System.Web.UI.WebControls.TextBox`, and implement your own additional functionality.

Another way to create custom controls is by aggregating existing controls and/or simple HTML elements inside your own. For example, you might want to create some kind of questionnaire that could be used in several applications or several different places within the same application. The best way is to implement your own web control that will contain several existing controls (check boxes, combo boxes, images, text boxes, and so on) and encapsulate all logic related to the questionnaire.

After you've created your own control, you could use it in different parts of your application, in different applications, insert it in different places during the design process, or use it dynamically as well as in predefined ASP.NET controls. So, you could customize your functionality and GUI, and make your application unique.

NOTE

Developers often ask what the difference is between user and server controls. User and server controls are very similar, but there is one essential difference.

A server control is compiled in a DLL file and cannot be edited on an interactive design surface. However, you can manipulate it by using its public methods and properties at runtime. It is possible to build a custom server control (sometimes called a *custom* control or a *composite* control).

In contrast, a user control consists of previously built server controls. It has an interface that can be completely edited and changed using the ASP.NET visual design surface. It can be manipulated at design time and runtime via properties that you are responsible for creating.

Although third-party vendors will build a multitude of controls for every possible function of ASP.NET, they will exist in the form of compiled server controls, as mentioned earlier.

22

Now that you have a good foundation, you can get to the coding of a custom control. This control will encapsulate some kind of help system. It will contain an area with some information and a search text box (see Figure 22.1).

Server Controls

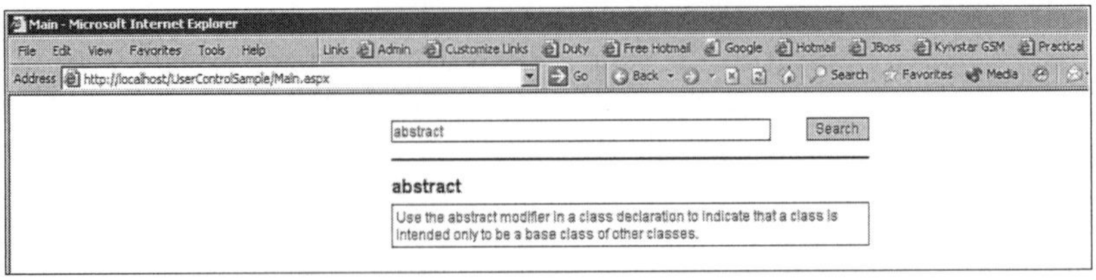

FIGURE 22.1   Sample interface using a custom control.

NOTE

Note that this chapter will not explain how to set up the environment for working with a web application in .NET. All examples in this chapter assume that you are already familiar with IIS (how it works, and how it could be set up and configured) and the process of creating a web application. If you are uncertain in those areas, you should read additional articles related to setting up web applications in .NET.

Listings 22.1–22.4 present the HTML and source code of a web page and the custom user control that the web page uses.

LISTING 22.1
HTML Code of the Web Page

```
<%@ Page language="c#" Codebehind="Main.aspx.cs"
   AutoEventWireup="false" Inherits="UserControlSample.Main" %>
<%@ Register TagPrefix="UserControl" TagName="Help" Src="help.ascx"%>
<!DOCTYPE HTML PUBLIC "-//W3C//DTD HTML 4.0 Transitional//EN" >
<html>
  <head>
    <title>Main</title>
    <meta name="GENERATOR" Content="Microsoft Visual Studio .NET 7.1">
    <meta name="CODE_LANGUAGE" Content="C#">
    <meta name=vs_defaultClientScript content="JavaScript">
    <meta name=vs_targetSchema
 content="http://schemas.microsoft.com/intellisense/ie5">
  </head>
  <body MS_POSITIONING="GridLayout">
    <form id="Main" method="post" runat="server">
            <div align="center">
                <table width="40%">
                    <tr>
                        <td>
                            <UserControl:Help runat="server"
ID="HelpControl"></UserControl:Help>
```

22

LISTING 22.1
Continued

```
                            </td>
                        </tr>
                    </table>
                </div>
        </form>
    </body>
</html>
```

LISTING 22.2
The Source Code (Code Behind) of the Sample Web Page

```
using System;
using System.Collections;
using System.ComponentModel;
using System.Data;
using System.Drawing;
using System.Web;
using System.Web.SessionState;using System.Web.UI;using System.Web.UI.WebControls;
using System.Web.UI.HtmlControls;
namespace UserControlSample {
        public class Main : System.Web.UI.Page {
                protected         UserControlSample.Help HelpControl;

                private void Page_Load(object sender, System.EventArgs e) {
                        HelpControl.SearchRequest =
HttpContext.Current.Request.Form.Get("HelpControl:searchRequestTextBox");
                        HelpControl.HelpInformation = HelpInformation();
                }

                #region Web Form Designer generated code
                override protected void OnInit(EventArgs e) {
                        InitializeComponent();
                        base.OnInit(e);
                }

                private void InitializeComponent() {
                        this.Load += new System.EventHandler(this.Page_Load);
                }
                #endregion

                private IDictionary HelpInformation () {
                        IDictionary helpInformation = new Hashtable();
```

Server Controls

LISTING 22.2
Continued

```
                helpInformation.Add("abstract", "Use the abstract modifier
in a class declaration to indicate that a class is intended only to be a base class
of other classes.");
                helpInformation.Add("base", "The base keyword is used to
access members of the base class from within a derived class.");
                helpInformation.Add("break", "The break statement terminates
the closest enclosing loop or conditional statement in which it appears. Control is
passed to the statement that follows the terminated statement, if any.");
                helpInformation.Add("delegate", "A delegate declaration
defines a reference type that can be used to encapsulate a method with a specific
signature. A delegate instance encapsulates a static or an instance method. Dele-
gates are roughly similar to function pointers in C++; however, delegates are type-
safe and secure.");
                helpInformation.Add("readonly", "The readonly keyword is a
modifier that you can use on fields. When a field declaration includes a readonly
modifier, assignments to the fields introduced by the declaration can only occur as
part of the declaration or in a constructor in the same class.");
                return helpInformation;
            }
        }
}
```

LISTING 22.3
HTML Code of Custom User Control

```
<%@ Control Language="c#" AutoEventWireup="false" Codebehind="Help.ascx.cs"
Inherits="UserControlSample.Help" TargetSchema="http://schemas.microsoft.com/
intellisense/ie5"%>
<style type="text/css">
        .control {
                BORDER-RIGHT: #000000 1px solid;
                BORDER-TOP: #000000 1px solid;
                BORDER-LEFT: #000000 1px solid;
                BORDER-BOTTOM: #000000 1px solid;
                FONT-SIZE: 12;
                FONT-FAMILY: Verdana, Arial;
        }
        .text {
                BORDER-RIGHT: #000000 1px solid;
                BORDER-TOP: #000000 1px solid;
                BORDER-LEFT: #000000 1px solid;
```

22

LISTING 22.3
Continued

```
                        BORDER-BOTTOM: #000000 1px solid;
                        FONT-SIZE: 12;
                        PADDING: 3 3 3 3;
                        FONT-FAMILY: Verdana, Arial;
        }
</style>

<table cellpadding="2" cellspacing="2" border="0" width="100%">
        <tr>
                <td width="80%" align="left">
                        <asp:TextBox CssClass="control" ID="searchRequestTextBox"
name="searchRequestTextBox" MaxLength="30" Width="100%"
Runat="server"></asp:TextBox>
                </td>
                <td align="right">
                        <input class="control" type="submit" value="Search"/>
                </td>
        </tr>
        <tr>
                <td width="100%" colspan="2">
                        <hr class="control">
                </td>
        </tr>
        <tr>
                <td width="100%" colspan="2"><b><span runat="server" id="topic-
Name"> </span></b></td>
        </tr>
        <tr>
                <td width="100%" colspan="2">
                        <div class="text" runat="server" id="topicBody"> </div>
                </td>
        </tr>
</table>
```

22

> **NOTE**
>
> Notice the lack of `<BODY>` tags. A user control does not need these tags because it will be placed on another page (or another user control) and rendered inline. The hosting page will be responsible for these common tags. The user control will, therefore, inherit all the host tags (including styles), unless they are specified otherwise.

Server Controls

LISTING 22.4
Source Code of Custom User Control

```
using System;
using System.Data;
using System.Drawing;
using System.Collections;
using System.Web;
using System.Web.UI.WebControls;
using System.Web.UI.HtmlControls;
namespace UserControlSample {
        public class Help : System.Web.UI.UserControl {
                protected HtmlGenericControl topicBody;
                protected HtmlGenericControl topicName;

                private void Page_Load(object sender, System.EventArgs e) {
                    if (this._helpInformation != null) {
                            if (_searchRequest != "" && _searchRequest != null) {
                                    IEnumerator enumerator =
_helpInformation.Keys.GetEnumerator();
                                    string searchResult = null;
                                    while (enumerator.MoveNext()) {
                                            if
(enumerator.Current.ToString().IndexOf(_searchRequest) != -1) {
searchResult = enumerator.Current.ToString();
                                                    break;
                                            }
                                    }
                                    if (searchResult != null) {
                                            topicName.InnerText = searchResult;
                                            topicBody.InnerText =
                                            _helpInformation[searchResult].
                                            ToString();
                                    } else {
                                            topicName.InnerText = "";
                                            topicBody.InnerText = ERROR_MESSAGE;
                                    }
                            }
                            else {
                                    topicName.InnerText = "";
                                    topicBody.InnerText = EMPTY_MESSAGE;
                            }
                    } else {
                            topicName.InnerText = "";
                            topicBody.InnerText = ERROR_MESSAGE;
                    }
```

22

LISTING 22.4
Continued

```csharp
        }

        #region Web Form Designer generated code
        override protected void OnInit(EventArgs e) {
                InitializeComponent();
                base.OnInit(e);
        }

        private void InitializeComponent() {
                this.Load += new System.EventHandler(this.Page_Load);
        }
        #endregion

        public IDictionary HelpInformation {
                set {
                        if (value != null) {
                                this._helpInformation = value;
                        } else {
                                this._helpInformation = new Hashtable();
                        }
                }
        }

        public string SearchRequest {
                set {
                        this._searchRequest = value;
                }
        }

        private IDictionary _helpInformation;
        private string _searchRequest;
        private const string ERROR_MESSAGE = "No topics were found by your
                                              request.";
        private const string EMPTY_MESSAGE = "No request was entered.";
    }
}
```

This control contains an information area that displays the name of some topic and description for it. Also, the control contains a Search button and a text box in which you could enter your search request. The control is built by way of aggregation of existing ASP.NET server controls. So, let's discuss the process of control creation and implementation.

Server Controls

To create a user control, you need to add a user-control file to a project.

1. First, create a new C# ASP.NET Web application.

2. Right-click on the project in the Project Explorer, click Add\Add New Item, and select a Web User Control item (see Figures 22.2 and 22.3). This adds a file with the extension .ascx to the project. This is the file that the user control will use to expose its interface. An ASCX file cannot be viewed directly in the browser. It must be placed within a container (such as another Web form) to be viewed.

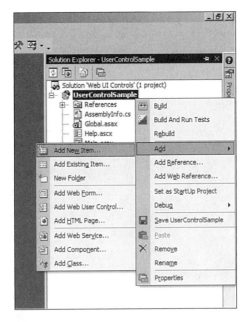

FIGURE 22.2   Selecting a Web User Control item.

The web project contains the web page Main.aspx. Let's include the control inside it. In the HTML code of the Main.aspx web form, you could find the following line:

```
<%@ Register TagPrefix="UserControl" TagName="Help" Src="help.ascx"%>
```

The @ Register directive registers the control on the page. After the control has been registered on the page, you can freely add many instances of the controls to the page. The TagPrefix attribute specifies the prefix to use for the control(s). It is sort of like a namespace in which several controls might share a single prefix value. This is why all ASP.NET server controls specify the <asp: prefix. The only difference is that the ASP.NET server control directive is implied and not explicitly declared.

`TagName` specifies the name of the control. Together, the tags create an instance of the control specified at the location of the `Src` attribute. You must also include the `runat="server"` name/value pair to manipulate the user control programmatically. Otherwise, only the raw HTML is sent back to the browser.

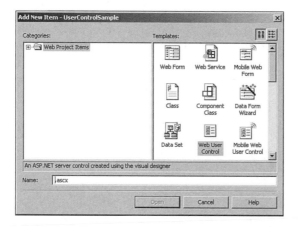

FIGURE 22.3   The Add New Item dialog box.

Next, open the user-control file in HTML mode and put into it other HTML and Web controls.

```
<asp:TextBox CssClass="control"
  ID="searchRequestTextBox" name="searchRequestTextBox" MaxLength="30" Width="100%"
  Runat="server"></asp:TextBox>
<input class="control" type="submit" value="Search"/>
<span runat="server" id="topicName"> </span>
<div class="text" runat="server" id="topicBody"> </div>
```

This inserts in our custom control one predefined Web control (`TextBox` server control) and three HTML controls (one of them is also a server-side control).

22

NOTE

The Search button HTML control is not registered as a server control (without `runat="server"`). It's because we do not need to manage this control on the server side (to be more precise, we do not need to use its public properties and methods in the code behind).

The `searchRequestTextBox` control is marked as `runat="server"`, but is not used in the code behind because `searchRequestTextBox` is a web control (not an HTML control). All web controls should be marked with the `runat="server"` tag to be visible in the browser. If you don't mark a web control with that tag, it will not be shown on the browser and you will not be allowed to access to it in the code-behind.

Server Controls

Now that the HTML view of the control has been defined, you could start defining the code-behind of the control. The code in the code-behind works exactly the same as a web form. HTML will be rendered and sent to the browser exactly as if the user control's resulting HTML were simply pasted into the hosting page's markup. The sample code declares two public properties of the control (SearchRequest and HelpInformation). These properties will be used in the page or other web control where our control will be included. All logic of the control is concentrated on the Page_Load function. This code searches in keys of the help information dictionary for the first key that includes the requested string.

The last step is to use the control in a web page or other control. How to register a user control in a web page has already been discussed. So, let's discuss how to use it in the code-behind of the page. In the code behind, the control is presented as a protected variable of type UserControlSample.Help. You could access all public properties and methods of this variable. The code initializes the Help control with the dictionary with some information and a search request that is retrieved from an HTTP request.

You also could insert several Help controls on the same page and initialize them with different data (see Figures 22.4 and 22.5).

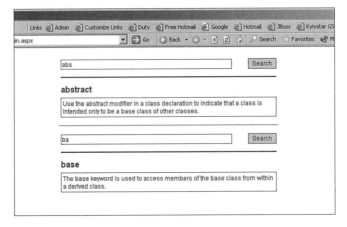

FIGURE 22.4   The code-behind of the control.

22

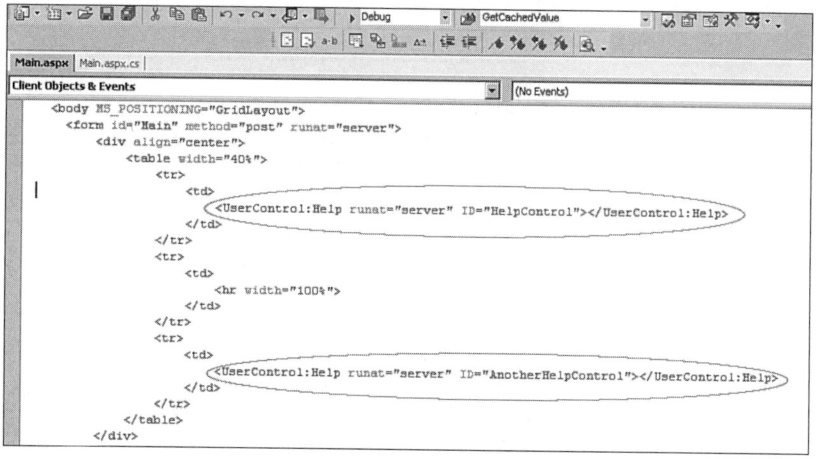

FIGURE 22.5 Example of different `Help` controls.

Summary

This chapter discussed what server and user controls are, and showed how to create a user control step by step. Also, you reviewed the most used predefined HTML and web server controls in ASP.NET.

Further Reading

Programming ASP.NET, Second Edition by Jesse Liberty and Dan Hurwitz, O'Reilly. ISBN: 0596004877.

ASP.NET Unleashed, Second Edition by Stephen Walther, Sams Publishing. ISBN: 067232542X.

22

23 State Management in ASP.NET

IN BRIEF

This chapter explains and demonstrates the different techniques that are available to maintain state within an ASP.NET application. The first section talks about the different ways to maintain state by using client-side techniques. The final section explores the different methods of maintaining state by using server-side techniques.

WHAT YOU NEED

RECOMMENDED SOFTWARE	.NET Framework C# .NET environment
RECOMMENDED HARDWARE	.NET-enabled desktop client with IIS
SKILLS REQUIRED	C# coding

STATE MANAGEMENT AT A GLANCE

Client-Side State Management   **456**

Understanding View State	456	Understanding Query Strings	471
Using Hidden Form Fields	463	Passing Server Control Values	
Explaining Cookies	467	Between Forms	474

Server-Side State Management   **479**

Explaining Application State	480	Understanding Session State	481

Summary   **482**

Further Reading   **483**

Client-Side State Management

When it comes to state management, there are two basic choices to make: Should you maintain the state by using server-side techniques or should you maintain the state on the client? In the following sections, you will learn how to maintain state using some client-side techniques such as `ViewState`, hidden form fields, cookies, and query strings.

Understanding View State

A very simple way of managing the view state of an ASP.NET server control is through the use of the `Control.ViewState` property.

> **TIP**
>
> The `Control.ViewState` property returns a `System.Web.UI.StateBag` object. A `StateBag` object is the primary storage method employed by HTML and server controls. It stores this information as name/value pairs and implements a dictionary to do so. Therefore you can perform operations, such as adding and removing of objects, on the `StateBag` object in the same manner as you would on the `Dictionary` object itself. The `ViewState` property is persisted by the ASP.NET Framework as strings, and is passed to the client by using a hidden form variable.

To store a value in the `ViewState` property, simply access the `StateBag` as you would a `Dictionary` object:

```
someControl.ViewState["Value Name"] = someValue;
```

A value can be written to the `ViewState` anytime after a page has been initialized from persistent settings, but you should avoid writing to it while the control is rendering. Reading from the `ViewState` is simply the opposite of writing to it:

```
someValue = someControl.ViewState["Value Name"];
```

You can read from the `ViewState` at any time. If you want your data to be displayed on a form, you should read it from the `ViewState` in the `Form.OnPreRender` event. The `ViewStateExample` project in Listings 23.1 and 23.2 illustrates how to store and retrieve values from the `ViewState` property.

LISTING 23.1

ViewStateExampleForm.aspx

```
<%@ Page language="c#"
  Codebehind="ViewStateExampleForm.aspx.cs"
  AutoEventWireup="false" Inherits="ViewStateExample.WebForm1" %>
<!DOCTYPE HTML PUBLIC "-//W3C//DTD HTML 4.0 Transitional//EN" >
<HTML>
  <HEAD>
    <title>WebForm1</title>
    <meta content="Microsoft Visual Studio .NET 7.1" name="GENERATOR">
    <meta content="C#" name="CODE_LANGUAGE">
    <meta content="JavaScript" name="vs_defaultClientScript">
    <meta content="http://schemas.microsoft.com/intellisense/ie5"
     name="vs_targetSchema">
  </HEAD>
  <body MS_POSITIONING="GridLayout">
    <form id="Form1" method="post" runat="server">
      <asp:textbox id="userName"
```

23

Client-Side State Management

LISTING 23.1
Continued

```
        style="Z-INDEX: 101; LEFT: 73px; POSITION: absolute; TOP: 115px"
runat="server">
    </asp:textbox>
    <asp:label id="userLabel"
      style="Z-INDEX: 102; LEFT: 73px; POSITION: absolute; TOP: 82px"
      runat="server">User Name</asp:label>
    <asp:label
      id="userGreeting"
      style="Z-INDEX: 103; LEFT: 73px; POSITION: absolute; TOP: 39px"
      runat="server">
    Please enter your user name below and press the submit button.</asp:label>
    <asp:button id="submitButton"
      style="Z-INDEX: 104; LEFT: 73px; POSITION: absolute; TOP: 166px"
      runat="server" Text="Submit"></asp:button></form>
  </body>
</HTML>
```

LISTING 23.2
ViewStateExampleForm.aspx.cs

```
using System;
using System.Collections;
using System.ComponentModel;
using System.Data;
using System.Drawing;
using System.Web;
using System.Web.SessionState;
using System.Web.UI;
using System.Web.UI.WebControls;
using System.Web.UI.HtmlControls;

namespace ViewStateExample
{
  /// <summary>
  /// Summary description for WebForm1.
  /// </summary>
  public class WebForm1 : System.Web.UI.Page
  {
    protected System.Web.UI.WebControls.TextBox userName;
    protected System.Web.UI.WebControls.Label userLabel;
    protected System.Web.UI.WebControls.Button submitButton;
    protected System.Web.UI.WebControls.Label userGreeting;
```

LISTING 23.2
Continued

```csharp
private void Page_Load(object sender, System.EventArgs e)
{
}


#region Web Form Designer generated code
override protected void OnInit(EventArgs e)
{
  //
  // CODEGEN: This call is required by the ASP.NET Web Form Designer.
  //
  InitializeComponent();
  base.OnInit(e);
}

/// <summary>
/// Required method for Designer support - do not modify
/// the contents of this method with the code editor.
/// </summary>
private void InitializeComponent()
{
  this.submitButton.Click += new System.EventHandler(this.Submit_Click);
  this.Load += new System.EventHandler(this.Page_Load);
  this.PreRender += new System.EventHandler(this.WebForm1_PreRender);
}
#endregion

private void WebForm1_PreRender(object sender, System.EventArgs e)
{
  string userResponse = (string) this.ViewState["User Name"];
  if((null != userResponse) && !userResponse.Equals(string.Empty))
  {
    submitButton.Visible = false;
    userLabel.Visible    = false;
    userName.Visible     = false;
    userGreeting.Text    = "Thank you " + userResponse + " for entering your
                            name.";
  }
}

private void Submit_Click(object sender, System.EventArgs e)
{
```

23

Client-Side State Management

LISTING 23.2
Continued

```
    this.ViewState["User Name"] = userName.Text;
  }
 }
}
```

This example uses two label controls and one edit control 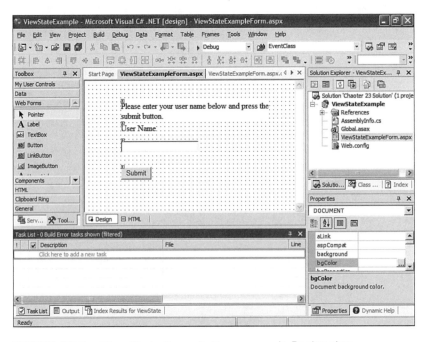. Figure 23.1 shows that the first label control is a greeting that invites the user to enter his username.

FIGURE 23.1 `ViewStateExampleForm.aspx` in Design view.

When the user enters his username (see Figure 23.2) and submits the form, the application stores the value entered by the user in the `ViewState` with a named value of `User Name`. When the form is posted back to the user, the application reads the `User Name` value from `ViewState` and populates the greeting label with a personalized thank you to the user for entering his information. This is demonstrated in Figure 23.3.

23

Client-Side State Management

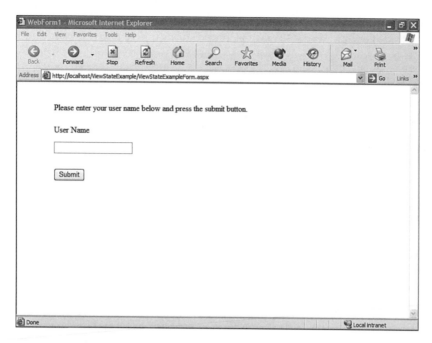

FIGURE 23.2   This is the initial screen before entering a username.

FIGURE 23.3   The same screen after the post back occurs.

Client-Side State Management

Customizing the `ViewState`

Because the `ViewState` serializer is optimized for primitive types, it is sometimes desirable to customize the way `ViewState` persists property data. However, if you customize the way that the `ViewState` stores these values, you must also customize the way the `ViewState` retrieves the values. The ASP.NET Framework offers two methods to customize this behavior: `Control.SaveViewState` and `Control.LoadViewState`. To customize the way in which `ViewState` is saved, simply override the `SaveViewState` method and save the data as described in the following code snippet:

```
protected override object SaveViewState()
{
  // Save State as an array of objects.  This could also be a class or anything
else.
  object baseState = base.SaveViewState();
  string password  = EncryptPassword(passwordText);
  object[] viewStates = new object[2];
  viewStates[0] = baseState;
  viewStates[1] = password;

  return viewStates;
}
```

Reading the data back is done in a similar way. Simply override the `LoadViewState` method and read back the data. This is demonstrated by the following code fragment:

```
protected override void LoadViewState(object savedState)
{
  if(null != savedState)
  {
    // Since the data was saved as an array of objects, we must read it back the
same way.
    base.LoadViewState(savedState[0]);
    // Some error checking should be placed here, but is omitted for brevity.
    string password = (string) savedState[1];
    passwordText = DecryptPassword(password);
    ... // Do something here with the passwordText that was decrypted.
  }
}
```

23

Using Hidden Form Fields

Using hidden form fields is another easy way to implement client-side state management. ASP.NET enables you to use standard HTML hidden fields to store a single variable in its `value` property. When a form is submitted to the server, the hidden field is available to you in just the same way as all other fields on that page.

TIP

In order for the variable stored in the hidden field to be available to you, the form must be sent to the server using the submit method. Using a page redirect or the HTTP get command will not enable you to use the variable.

Although the use of hidden fields is an easy way to manage state, it presents something of a security concern. The variable stored in these fields is available to any user who chooses to view the source of the page. Therefore, if you have any data that is privacy-sensitive or if you just don't want anyone to see its value, you should not use this technique to manage your form's state. By modifying the `ViewStateExample` program listed in the previous section, you will get a better understanding of what it will take to use a hidden variable. First, drop an `HtmlInputHidden` control on the form and change the `ID` to `userInputState`. The design view of the form after this control has been added. Next, switch to the HTML view, as shown in Listing 23.3, and make the new control a server control by adding the `runat="server"` attribute to the control. This is demonstrated in the following code snippet:

```
<INPUT style="Z-INDEX: 105; LEFT: 72px; POSITION: absolute; TOP: 248px"
type="hidden" name="userNameState"
runat="server" id="userNameState">
```

TIP

When you add an HTML control to a form and you need to access the variable in the code-behind page, you must manually add the declaration to the class and make the control a server-side control. You also must use as the variable name the same name that is listed in the `ID` attribute of the control. If you don't, ASP.NET will not link the control and the variable declaration together and you will receive an `Object reference not set to an instance of an object` exception when you try to access the variable.

23

Next, change the submit event to set the value of the hidden variable to the value of the text control:

```
userNameState.Value = userName.Text;
```

Client-Side State Management

Finally, change the `OnPreRender` event to read the value from the hidden field and populate the text control with this value:

```
string userResponse = (string) userNameState.Value;
```

If you now run the application, you will see that the sample program runs the same way it did when you ran the `ViewStateExample` program. The one difference occurs when you view the HTML source of the running page. If you select the menu items View, and then Source from the Internet Explorer menu, the source for the page will appear. You will notice that the value of the hidden variable appears in this listing. This is demonstrated in Listing 23.5. If you don't mind that this variable is visible to anyone who cares to view it, this side effect will not mean much. However, if this is a concern to you, do not use this method.

LISTING 23.3

HiddenVariableExample.aspx

```
<%@ Page language="c#"
    Codebehind="HiddenVariableExample.aspx.cs" AutoEventWireup="false"
    Inherits="HiddenVariableStateExample.WebForm1" %>
<!DOCTYPE HTML PUBLIC "-//W3C//DTD HTML 4.0 Transitional//EN" >
<HTML>
  <HEAD>
    <title>WebForm1</title>
    <meta content="Microsoft Visual Studio .NET 7.1" name="GENERATOR">
    <meta content="C#" name="CODE_LANGUAGE">
    <meta content="JavaScript" name="vs_defaultClientScript">
    <meta content="http://schemas.microsoft.com/intellisense/ie5"
name="vs_targetSchema">
  </HEAD>
  <body MS_POSITIONING="GridLayout">
    <form id="Form1" method="post" runat="server">
      <asp:textbox id="userName"
       style="Z-INDEX: 101; LEFT: 73px; POSITION: absolute; TOP: 115px"
       runat="server"></asp:textbox>
      <asp:label id="userLabel"
       style="Z-INDEX: 102; LEFT: 73px; POSITION: absolute; TOP: 82px"
       runat="server">User Name</asp:label>
      <asp:label id="userGreeting"
        style="Z-INDEX: 103; LEFT: 73px; POSITION: absolute; TOP: 39px"
        runat="server">Please enter your user name below and press the submit
                    button.
      </asp:label>
      <asp:button id="submitButton"
```

LISTING 23.3
Continued

```
        style="Z-INDEX: 104; LEFT: 73px; POSITION: absolute; TOP: 166px"
        runat="server" Text="Submit"></asp:button>
    <INPUT style="Z-INDEX: 105; LEFT: 72px; POSITION: absolute; TOP: 248px"
        type="hidden" name="userNameState" runat="server" id="userNameState">
    </form>
  </body>
</HTML>
```

LISTING 23.4

HiddenVariableExample.aspx.cs

```
using System;
using System.Collections;
using System.ComponentModel;
using System.Data;
using System.Drawing;
using System.Web;
using System.Web.SessionState;
using System.Web.UI;
using System.Web.UI.WebControls;
using System.Web.UI.HtmlControls;

namespace HiddenVariableStateExample
{
  // <summary>
  // Summary description for WebForm1.
  // </summary>
  public class WebForm1 : System.Web.UI.Page
  {
    protected System.Web.UI.HtmlControls.HtmlInputHidden userNameState;
    protected System.Web.UI.WebControls.TextBox userName;
    protected System.Web.UI.WebControls.Label userLabel;
    protected System.Web.UI.WebControls.Label userGreeting;
    protected System.Web.UI.WebControls.Button submitButton;

    private void Page_Load(object sender, System.EventArgs e)
    {
      // Put user code to initialize the page here
    }

    #region Web Form Designer generated code
```

23

Client-Side State Management

LISTING 23.4
Continued

```csharp
override protected void OnInit(EventArgs e)
{
  //
  // CODEGEN: This call is required by the ASP.NET Web Form Designer.
  //
  InitializeComponent();
  base.OnInit(e);
}


/// <summary>
/// Required method for Designer support - do not modify
/// the contents of this method with the code editor.
/// </summary>
private void InitializeComponent()
{
  this.submitButton.Click += new System.EventHandler(this.submitButton_Click);
  this.Load += new System.EventHandler(this.Page_Load);
  this.PreRender += new System.EventHandler(this.WebForm1_PreRender);
}
#endregion

private void submitButton_Click(object sender, System.EventArgs e)
{
  userNameState.Value = userName.Text;
}

private void WebForm1_PreRender(object sender, System.EventArgs e)
{
  string userResponse = (string) userNameState.Value;
  if((null != userResponse) && !userResponse.Equals(string.Empty))
  {
    submitButton.Visible  = false;
    userLabel.Visible     = false;
    userName.Visible      = false;
    userGreeting.Text     = "Thank you " + userResponse + " for entering your
                            name.";
  }
}
}
}
```

23

LISTING 23.5
Source View

```
<!DOCTYPE HTML PUBLIC "-//W3C//DTD HTML 4.0 Transitional//EN" >
<HTML>
  <HEAD>
    <title>WebForm1</title>
    <meta content="Microsoft Visual Studio .NET 7.1"
name="GENERATOR">
    <meta content="C#" name="CODE_LANGUAGE">
    <meta content="JavaScript" name="vs_defaultClientScript">
    <meta content="http://schemas.microsoft.com/intellisense/ie5"
    name="vs_targetSchema">
  </HEAD>
  <body MS_POSITIONING="GridLayout">
    <form name="Form1" method="post" action="HiddenVariableExample.aspx" id="Form1">
    <input type="hidden" name="__VIEWSTATE"
value="dDwzNDY2NjIxNTU7dDw7bDxpPDE+Oz47bDx0PDtsPGk8MT47aTwzPjtpPDU+O2k8Nz47PjtsPHQ8
DxwPGw8VGV4dDtWaXNpYmxlOz47bDxMb25ueTtvPGY+Oz4+Oz47dDxwPHA8bDxWaXNpYmxlOz47bDxvP
GY+Oz4+Oz47dDxwPHA8bDxUZXh0Oz47bDxUaGFuayB5b3UgTG9ubmkgZm9yIGVudGVyaW5nIHlvdX-
IgbmFtZS47Pjs7Pjt0PHA8cDxsPFZpc2libGU7Pjts PG88Zj47Pjs7Pjs+Pjs+3ixLXN1-
HEiVE3uZwiE/gsLivikQ=" />
        <span id="userGreeting" style="Z-INDEX: 103; LEFT: 73px; POSITION: absolute;
TOP: 39px">Thank you Lonny for entering your name.</span>
        <input name="userNameState" id="userNameState" type="hidden" style="Z-INDEX:
105; LEFT: 72px; POSITION: absolute; TOP: 248px" value="Hidden Variable Value Is
Shown Here" />
    </form>
  </body>
</HTML>
```

Explaining Cookies

Although a cookie is nothing more then a text file that can store user actions, values, and preferences, it is both a popular and convenient way of storing state information on the client side. Some of the benefits of using cookies are that they are lightweight, they have a configurable expiration, and they don't require any server resources. Unfortunately, along with these benefits come some pretty serious disadvantages. Among the disadvantages of cookies are that they can be easily manipulated by malicious users, they can be disabled by the user, and they are limited in size.

Although some newer browsers support a maximum cookie size of 8192 bytes, most older browsers support a maximum size of only 4192 bytes. If your goal is to simply store some user preferences or some identifying information for the user, this should not be a problem. However, if your goal is to store information that is of a sensitive

23

Client-Side State Management

nature, you might want to think about a different way of managing state. The values that you store in a cookie can be viewed by a user by simply loading the cookie file in Windows Notepad. In addition, a user could modify this information and potentially expose a security flaw in your application.

Cookies are generally used to store user preferences, and possibly an identity key that allows the system to automatically identify the user. In addition, cookies generally have an expiration date. This can be set by using the `HttpCookie.Expires` property. When the cookie expires, the system deletes it.

The example in Listings 23.6 and 23.7 takes the code example introduced in the `ViewState` section and modifies it slightly to store information in a cookie. This example contains one page that, upon initialization or postback, checks for the existence of a cookie. If the cookie exists, the system loads the "user" value and displays a message to the user welcoming her back to the website. If a cookie does not exist, the system prompts the user to enter her username. After the user has entered her username and submitted the form, the system rechecks for the existence of the cookie. If the cookie exists, the system welcomes the user.

LISTING 23.6
`CookieExample.aspx` Design View

```
<%@ Page language="c#" Codebehind="CookieExample.aspx.cs"
  AutoEventWireup="false" Inherits="CookieExample.WebForm1" %>
<!DOCTYPE HTML PUBLIC "-//W3C//DTD HTML 4.0 Transitional//EN" >
<HTML>
  <HEAD>
    <title>WebForm1</title>
    <meta content="Microsoft Visual Studio .NET 7.1" name="GENERATOR">
    <meta content="C#" name="CODE_LANGUAGE">
    <meta content="JavaScript" name="vs_defaultClientScript">
    <meta content="http://schemas.microsoft.com/intellisense/ie5"
name="vs_targetSchema">
  </HEAD>
  <body MS_POSITIONING="GridLayout">
    <form id="Form1" method="post" runat="server">
      <asp:textbox id="userName"
        style="Z-INDEX: 101; LEFT: 73px; POSITION: absolute; TOP: 115px"
        runat="server"></asp:textbox>
      <asp:label id="userLabel"
        style="Z-INDEX: 102; LEFT: 73px; POSITION: absolute; TOP: 82px"
        runat="server">User Name</asp:label>
      <asp:label id="userGreeting"
        style="Z-INDEX: 103; LEFT: 73px; POSITION: absolute; TOP: 39px"
        runat="server">Please enter your user name below and press the submit button.
      </asp:label>
```

23

LISTING 23.6
Continued

```
      <asp:button id="submitButton"
        style="Z-INDEX: 104; LEFT: 73px; POSITION: absolute; TOP: 166px"
        runat="server" Text="Submit"></asp:button>
    </form>
  </body>
</HTML>
```

LISTING 23.7
`CookieExample.aspx.cs` Source View

```csharp
using System;
using System.Collections;
using System.ComponentModel;
using System.Data;
using System.Drawing;
using System.Web;
using System.Web.SessionState;
using System.Web.UI;
using System.Web.UI.WebControls;
using System.Web.UI.HtmlControls;

namespace CookieExample
{
  /// <summary>
  /// Summary description for CookieExample.
  /// </summary>
  public class WebForm1 : System.Web.UI.Page
  {
    protected System.Web.UI.WebControls.Label userGreeting;
    protected System.Web.UI.WebControls.Button submitButton;
    protected System.Web.UI.WebControls.TextBox userName;
    protected System.Web.UI.WebControls.Label userLabel;

    private void Page_Load(object sender, System.EventArgs e)
    {
      // Put user code to initialize the page here
    }

    #region Web Form Designer generated code
    override protected void OnInit(EventArgs e)
    {
      //
```

23

Client-Side State Management

LISTING 23.7
Continued

```
    // CODEGEN: This call is required by the ASP.NET Web Form Designer.
    //
    InitializeComponent();
    base.OnInit(e);
}
/// <summary>
/// Required method for Designer support - do not modify
/// the contents of this method with the code editor.
/// </summary>
private void InitializeComponent()
{
  this.submitButton.Click += new System.EventHandler(this.submitButton_Click);
  this.Load += new System.EventHandler(this.Page_Load);
  this.PreRender += new System.EventHandler(this.WebForm1_PreRender);
}
#endregion

private void submitButton_Click(object sender, System.EventArgs e)
{
  HttpCookie userCookie = new HttpCookie("User Name");
  DateTime now          = DateTime.Now;

  userCookie.Value      = userName.Text;
  userCookie.Expires    = now.AddHours(5);

  Response.Cookies.Add(userCookie);
}

private void WebForm1_PreRender(object sender, System.EventArgs e)
{
  HttpCookie userCookie = Request.Cookies.Get("User Name");

  if(null != userCookie)
  {
    string userResponse = (string) userCookie.Value;

    if((null != userResponse) && !userResponse.Equals(string.Empty))
    {
      submitButton.Visible  = false;
      userLabel.Visible     = false;
      userName.Visible      = false;
      userGreeting.Text     =
```

LISTING 23.7

Continued

```
"Thank you " + userResponse + " for entering your name.";
        }
      }
    }
  }
}
```

TIP

The contents of a cookie are easily viewed and manipulated by a user. The contents of the cookie that was created by the `CookieExample` program are listed here:

User Name<CR>Lonny Kruger<CR>localhost/<CR>1024

<CR>1478352000<CR>29641125<CR>1876798432<CR>29641083<CR>*

As you can see, the username entered in the file is Lonny Kruger. If you change this name to something else and run the program again, you will see a welcome message that welcomes the user with the modified name.

Understanding Query Strings

Query strings are by far the easiest form of state management to understand. Using query strings to manage state has the following advantages: There are no server resources used, this approach is easy to implement, and just about all browsers support this method of state management. There are, however a few minor disadvantages. Some of these disadvantages are that most browsers support a maximum of only 255 characters in a query string and, like cookies, query strings are easily manipulated.

To use the query string method, simply append a question mark (?) to the URL, followed by the name and value pair that you want to pass to the next form. If you need to pass multiple values, simply separate the multiple name/value pairs by using an ampersand (&) character.

Passing a single value:

```
http://localhost/QueryStringExample/QueryStringExample.aspx?userName=Lonny
```

Passing multiple values:

```
http://localhost/QueryStringExample/QueryStringExample.aspx?firstName=
Lonny&lastName=Kruger
```

The following example, Listing 23.8, again modifies the original `ViewState` example and accomplishes the same task by using query strings.

23

Client-Side State Management

LISTING 23.8

QueryStringExample.aspx HTML View

```
<%@ Page language="c#" Codebehind="QueryStringExample.aspx.cs"
  AutoEventWireup="false" Inherits="QueryStringExample.WebForm1" %>
<!DOCTYPE HTML PUBLIC "-//W3C//DTD HTML 4.0 Transitional//EN" >
<HTML>
  <HEAD>
    <title>WebForm1</title>
    <meta content="Microsoft Visual Studio .NET 7.1" name="GENERATOR">
    <meta content="C#" name="CODE_LANGUAGE">
    <meta content="JavaScript" name="vs_defaultClientScript">
    <meta content="http://schemas.microsoft.com/intellisense/ie5"
name="vs_targetSchema">
  </HEAD>
  <body MS_POSITIONING="GridLayout">
    <form id="Form1" method="post" runat="server">
      <asp:textbox id="userName"
        style="Z-INDEX: 101; LEFT: 73px; POSITION: absolute; TOP: 115px"
        runat="server"></asp:textbox>
      <asp:label
        id="userLabel" style="Z-INDEX: 102; LEFT: 73px; POSITION: absolute; TOP:
82px"
        runat="server">User Name</asp:label>
      <asp:label
        id="userGreeting" style="Z-INDEX: 103; LEFT: 73px; POSITION: absolute; TOP:
39px"
        runat="server">Please enter your user name below and press the submit
button.</asp:label>
      <asp:button id="submitButton"
        style="Z-INDEX: 104; LEFT: 73px; POSITION: absolute; TOP: 166px"
        runat="server" Text="Submit"></asp:button>
      <INPUT
        style="Z-INDEX: 105; LEFT: 72px; POSITION: absolute; TOP: 248px"
        type="hidden" name="userNameState"
        runat="server" id="userNameState">
    </form>
  </body>
</HTML>
```

LISTING 23.9

QueryStringExample.aspx.cs Source View

```
using System;
using System.Collections;
```

LISTING 23.9
Continued

```csharp
using System.ComponentModel;
using System.Data;
using System.Drawing;
using System.Web;
using System.Web.SessionState;
using System.Web.UI;
using System.Web.UI.WebControls;
using System.Web.UI.HtmlControls;

namespace QueryStringExample
{
  /// <summary>
  /// Summary description for WebForm1.
  /// </summary>
  public class WebForm1 : System.Web.UI.Page
  {
    protected System.Web.UI.HtmlControls.HtmlInputHidden userNameState;
    protected System.Web.UI.WebControls.TextBox userName;
    protected System.Web.UI.WebControls.Label userLabel;
    protected System.Web.UI.WebControls.Label userGreeting;
    protected System.Web.UI.WebControls.Button submitButton;

    private void Page_Load(object sender, System.EventArgs e)
    {
        // Put user code to initialize the page here
    }

    #region Web Form Designer generated code
    override protected void OnInit(EventArgs e)
    {
        //
        // CODEGEN: This call is required by the ASP.NET Web Form Designer.
        //
        InitializeComponent();
        base.OnInit(e);
    }

    /// <summary>
    /// Required method for Designer support - do not modify
    /// the contents of this method with the code editor.
    /// </summary>
    private void InitializeComponent()
```

23

Client-Side State Management

LISTING 23.9
Continued

```
    {
      this.submitButton.Click += new System.EventHandler(this.submitButton_Click);
      this.Load += new System.EventHandler(this.Page_Load);
      this.PreRender += new System.EventHandler(this.WebForm1_PreRender);
    }
    #endregion

    private void submitButton_Click(object sender, System.EventArgs e)
    {
      Response.Redirect(
        "http://localhost/QueryStringExample/QueryStringExample.aspx?userName=" +
        userName.Text);
      //userNameState.Value = userName.Text;
    }

    private void WebForm1_PreRender(object sender, System.EventArgs e)
    {
      string userResponse = (string) Request.QueryString["userName"];
      if((null != userResponse) && !userResponse.Equals(string.Empty))
      {
        submitButton.Visible  = false;
        userLabel.Visible     = false;
        userName.Visible      = false;
        userGreeting.Text     = "Thank you " + userResponse + " for entering your
                                  name.";

      }
    }
  }
}
```

Passing Server Control Values Between Forms

One reason for using state management is to pass data between forms. ASP.NET offers a few different ways to accomplish this feat: ViewState, query strings, and SessionState. Although these are good ways of accomplishing the task, there is a better way of achieving the same result.

Instances of Web Forms exist for only a short period of time. They usually exist only long enough to perform page processing. As such, it is difficult to pass data between the pages. Fortunately, ASP.NET enables you to transfer control to another form. When you transfer control from one Web Form to another, you gain access to the

Web Form that transferred control and, as such, you also gain access to the properties exposed by this form.

The example in Listings 23.10–23.13 demonstrates how to transfer control from one form to another. This sample program again slightly modifies the example introduced in the `ViewState` section earlier in the chapter.

LISTING 23.10

`FirstForm.aspx` HTML View

```
<%@ Page language="c#"
  Codebehind="FirstForm.aspx.cs"
  AutoEventWireup="false" Inherits="PassingServerControlValuesExample.FirstForm" %>
<!DOCTYPE HTML PUBLIC "-//W3C//DTD HTML 4.0 Transitional//EN" >
<HTML>
  <HEAD>
    <title>WebForm1</title>
    <meta content="Microsoft Visual Studio .NET 7.1" name="GENERATOR">
    <meta content="C#" name="CODE_LANGUAGE">
    <meta content="JavaScript" name="vs_defaultClientScript">
    <meta content="http://schemas.microsoft.com/intellisense/ie5"
name="vs_targetSchema">
  </HEAD>
  <body MS_POSITIONING="GridLayout">
    <form id="Form1" method="post" runat="server">
      <asp:textbox
        id="userName" style="Z-INDEX: 101; LEFT: 73px; POSITION: absolute; TOP:
115px"
        runat="server"></asp:textbox>
      <asp:label
        id="userLabel" style="Z-INDEX: 102; LEFT: 73px; POSITION: absolute; TOP:
82px"
        runat="server">User Name</asp:label>
      <asp:label id="userGreeting"
        style="Z-INDEX: 103; LEFT: 73px; POSITION: absolute; TOP: 39px"
        runat="server">
        Please enter your user name below and press the submit button.</asp:label>
      <asp:button
        id="submitButton" style="Z-INDEX: 104; LEFT: 73px; POSITION: absolute; TOP:
166px"
        runat="server" Text="Submit"></asp:button>
    </form>
  </body>
</HTML>
```

23

Client-Side State Management

LISTING 23.11
`FirstForm.aspx.cs` **Code View**

```csharp
using System;
using System.Collections;
using System.ComponentModel;
using System.Data;
using System.Drawing;
using System.Web;
using System.Web.SessionState;
using System.Web.UI;
using System.Web.UI.WebControls;
using System.Web.UI.HtmlControls;

namespace PassingServerControlValuesExample
{
  /// <summary>
  /// Summary description for WebForm1.
  /// </summary>
  public class FirstForm : System.Web.UI.Page
  {
    protected System.Web.UI.WebControls.TextBox userName;
    protected System.Web.UI.WebControls.Label userLabel;
    protected System.Web.UI.WebControls.Label userGreeting;
    protected System.Web.UI.WebControls.Button submitButton;

    private void Page_Load(object sender, System.EventArgs e)
    {
        // Put user code to initialize the page here
    }

    #region Web Form Designer generated code
    override protected void OnInit(EventArgs e)
    {
        //
        // CODEGEN: This call is required by the ASP.NET Web Form Designer.
        //
        InitializeComponent();
        base.OnInit(e);
    }

    /// <summary>
    /// Required method for Designer support - do not modify
    /// the contents of this method with the code editor.
    /// </summary>
```

LISTING 23.11
Continued

```
private void InitializeComponent()
{
  this.submitButton.Click += new System.EventHandler(this.submitButton_Click);
  this.Load += new System.EventHandler(this.Page_Load);

}
#endregion

private void submitButton_Click(object sender, System.EventArgs e)
{
  Server.Transfer("SecondForm.aspx");
}

public string UserName
{
  get
  {
    return userName.Text;
  }
}
}
}
```

> **TIP**
>
> Although `Server.Transfer` might seem to solve a lot of your problems, it can be used only in a single-server situation.

LISTING 23.12
SecondForm.aspx HTML View

```
<%@ Page language="c#"
    Codebehind="SecondForm.aspx.cs" AutoEventWireup="false"
    Inherits="PassingServerControlValuesExample.SecondForm" %>
<!DOCTYPE HTML PUBLIC "-//W3C//DTD HTML 4.0 Transitional//EN" >
<HTML>
  <HEAD>
    <title>SecondFom</title>
    <meta name="GENERATOR" Content="Microsoft Visual Studio .NET 7.1">
    <meta name="CODE_LANGUAGE" Content="C#">
    <meta name="vs_defaultClientScript" content="JavaScript">
    <meta name="vs_targetSchema"
```

23

Client-Side State Management

LISTING 23.12
Continued

```
        content="http://schemas.microsoft.com/intellisense/ie5">
  </HEAD>
  <body MS_POSITIONING="GridLayout">
    <form id="Form1" method="post" runat="server">
      <asp:label id="userGreeting"
        style="Z-INDEX: 103; LEFT: 80px; POSITION: absolute; TOP: 40px"
        runat="server">
        Please enter your user name below and press the submit button.</asp:label>
    </form>
  </body>
</HTML>
```

LISTING 23.13
SecondForm.aspx.cs Code View

```csharp
using System;
using System.Collections;
using System.ComponentModel;
using System.Data;
using System.Drawing;
using System.Web;
using System.Web.SessionState;
using System.Web.UI;
using System.Web.UI.WebControls;
using System.Web.UI.HtmlControls;

namespace PassingServerControlValuesExample
{
  /// <summary>
  /// Summary description for SecondForm.
  /// </summary>
  public class SecondForm : System.Web.UI.Page
  {
    protected System.Web.UI.WebControls.Label userGreeting;
    public FirstForm firstForm;

    private void Page_Load(object sender, System.EventArgs e)
    {
      if(!IsPostBack)
      {
        firstForm = (FirstForm) Context.Handler;
        userGreeting.Text      =
```

LISTING 23.13
Continued

```
            "Thank you " + firstForm.UserName + " for entering your name.";
    }
}


    #region Web Form Designer generated code
    override protected void OnInit(EventArgs e)
    {
        //
        // CODEGEN: This call is required by the ASP.NET Web Form Designer.
        //
        InitializeComponent();
        base.OnInit(e);
    }
    /// <summary>
    /// Required method for Designer support - do not modify
    /// the contents of this method with the code editor.
    /// </summary>
    private void InitializeComponent()
    {
        this.Load += new System.EventHandler(this.Page_Load);
    }
    #endregion
    }
}
```

Server-Side State Management

Client side state management techniques enable you to store information on the client side in a lightweight fashion and are a relatively quick and easy way to do so. The problem with this approach is that for applications requiring a higher degree of security around their information, client-side state management might not be the right answer. Because server-side state management allows information to be stored on the server, there is less likelihood of this information being tampered with and it therefore poses less of a security risk.

When looking at the previous statement, you might ask yourself, "If server-side state management offers increased security, why wouldn't I use it all the time?" The answer is scalability. Although increased security is certainly a benefit, storing all the information comes at a price. Imagine a large system with approximately one million users. If every user stored the same amount of information that can be stored in a cookie (4096 bytes), the server would have to manage approximately 4 terabytes of

23

information just for some simple user preferences. Not only is this a lot of information to store, but it can affect performance and scalability.

In the following sections, you will learn how to maintain state using the following server-side techniques: application state, session state, and using a database to store state.

Explaining Application State

Before you learn how to use the application state technique, it is important for you to understand the concept of an application in ASP.NET. An *application*, in ASP.NET, is all the contents (forms, code, handlers, files, and so on) that fall under a virtual directory. This includes all the subdirectories of that directory as well.

Storing Data

Storing data using the `HttpApplicationState` object is a relatively easy task. An instance of the `HttpApplicationState` class is created the first time the server receives a request for anything within the application scope and is not destroyed until the application process is terminated. The instance of the class that is created is exposed via the `Application` object. To use this class, simply reference the `Application` object as you would a hash table:

```
Application["User Name"] = username.Text;
```

Retrieving values is equally simple:

```
userName.Text = (string) Application["User Name"];
```

Because the class returned is an object, you must cast it to the appropriate type.

TIP

Even though using `HttpApplicationState` class is similar to using a global variable, it is important to note that it is global to only the application process. It does not persist across web farms or web gardens. In other words, if you have an application that spans multiple processes or is run on several different machines, it is possible for each instance of the application to have different values for each name/value pairs.

23

Synchronizing Application State

Because an `Application` begins with the first request to an ASP.NET application and ends when the process terminates, it is possible to have multiple browsers and users trying to access the same variable at the same time. This could cause problems, so it is necessary to provide some sort of synchronization between the requests.

To assist with the synchronization, HttpApplicationState provides two methods: Lock and UnLock. Before writing to the state object, you should lock the object. As soon as you are done writing, you should unlock the object. The following code fragment demonstrates how to properly access an application state value. Note that the lock and unlock calls are wrapped in a resource protection block. This allows the Application object to continue to be accessed by other threads in the event of an unexpected exception while setting the value.

```
Application.Lock();
try
{
  Application["Global Counter"] = (int) Application["Global Counter"] + 1;
}
finally
{
  Application.UnLock();
}
```

Understanding Session State

Session state is very similar to application state. It allows the system to store information on the server for retrieval at a later time. Unlike the application state, session state is valid only during the current browser session. If the browser session terminates or a new session starts, the session state is either destroyed or a new one is created.

Configuring sessionState

Including being disabled, sessionState can be configured in one of four different modes: Off, InProc, StateServer, and SQLServer. This enables you to specify which method of storage to use when using sessionState.

sessionState **Mode** Off

When the mode is set to Off, sessionState is disabled. To turn off sessionState, simply change the mode in the configuration file to "Off".

```
<configuration>
   <system.web>
      <sessionState mode="Off" />
   </system.web>
</configuration>
```

23

sessionState **Mode** InProc

When the mode is set to InProc, the session information is stored locally. When using this mode, use the cookieless attribute to specify whether cookies should be used to store state information. The following example configures sessionState to be in the InProc mode, not to use cookies, and to have a timeout of 20 minutes:

Server-Side State Management

```
<configuration>
   <system.web>
      <sessionState mode="InProc" cookieless="true" timeout="20" />
   </system.web>
</configuration>
```

sessionState **Mode** StateServer

When the mode is set to StateServer, the session information is stored on a remote host. When using the StateServer mode, the attributes stateConnectionString and stateNetworkTimeout must be used. The following configuration section demonstrates how to configure the server for StateServer mode:

```
<configuration>
   <system.web>
      <sessionState
       mode="StateServer"
       stateConnectionString="tcpip=127.0.0.1:999"
       stateNetworkTimeout="10" />
   </system.web>
</configuration>
```

SQLServer

Placing the sessionState mode to SQLServer allows the system to store the information in a SQL Server database. When using SQLServer mode, the sqlConnectionString attribute must be used. The following configuration section demonstrates how to configure the system to use SQLServer mode:

```
<configuration>
   <system.web>
      <sessionState mode="SQLServer"
         sqlConnectionString="data source=localhost;Initial Catalog=testdb" />
   </system.web>
</configuration>
```

Summary

In the previous sections, you learned the different methods of storing state information in ASP.NET. Although all the methods are relatively simple and basically perform the same functions, all the methods mentioned accomplish the tasks in different manners. Each approach offers different advantages and disadvantages. When deciding which method to use, you should carefully balance the ease of use and speed with the need for scalability, durability, and security.

Further Reading

Programming Windows with C#, by Charles Petzold, Microsoft Press. ISBN: 0735613702.

ASP.NET Unleashed, Second Edition, by Stephen Walther, Sams Publishing. ISBN: 067232542X.

24 Caching

This chapter introduces you to the world of data caching in ASP.NET. You will learn the different techniques of caching data in ASP.NET and when you should use each of the different means of caching. Next, you will learn about the `OutputCache` directive and how to use it. Finally, you will learn about the `HttpCachePolicy` and `Cache` objects.

WHAT YOU NEED

RECOMMENDED SOFTWARE	.NET Framework Visual Studio .NET IIS
RECOMMENDED HARDWARE	.NET-enabled desktop client
SKILLS REQUIRED	C# coding

CACHING AT A GLANCE

Caching	484		
Introduction to ASP.NET Caching	485	Using `HttpCachePolicy`	489
`OutputCache` Directive	486	Using the `Cache` Object	491

Summary	496

Further Reading	496

Caching

Developers often need to temporarily put data (temporary data) in a storage medium (for example, a database or some location in memory) for quick access. The storage of this temporary data is called a *cache*.

A cache provides a number of possibilities. For example, imagine that you're working with a database in which data will be changed very rarely. When a user requests data, you will retrieve the same data each time from the database. Each time, the server will process the same operation to the retrieve the data and the performance of the application will be decreased. The best solution in such a situation is to store retrieved data in storage (at least for a short period of time). After storing the data, you can read it directly from the cache. In the cache, you could store database data as well as whole HTML pages—it depends on the logic of the application being implemented. Experience in web application development will teach you that developers often store data retrieved from a database in static variables (static hash tables, arrays, and so on), but do not often store HTML pages on the server side with help of ASP.NET's cache toolkit. But ASP.NET's mechanism of caching is very powerful and helpful (especially in small web applications).

All cached data is stored in memory so that it can be retrieved and processed significantly faster than if it were stored on magnetic media such as a hard disk. If a developer uses the cache correctly, he can greatly increase the performance of his application.

ASP.NET presents simple and very powerful possibilities of working with data caching. It enables you to cache whole HTML pages (or just parts of them) and other data in the global object `HttpCache`.

Introduction to ASP.NET Caching

The code in Listing 24.1 is a simple example that shows how to use a cache in ASP.NET.

LISTING 24.1

Caching HTML Pages by Using the `OutputCache` Directive

```
<%@ Page language="c#"
    Codebehind="Main.aspx.cs"
    AutoEventWireup="false" Inherits="OutputCacheSample.Main" %>
<%@ OutputCache Duration="60" VaryByParam="none"%>
<!DOCTYPE HTML PUBLIC "-//W3C//DTD HTML 4.0 Transitional//EN" >
<html>
        <head>
                <title>OutputCache using Sample</title>
                <meta name="GENERATOR" Content="Microsoft Visual Studio .NET 7.1">
                <meta name="CODE_LANGUAGE" Content="C#">
                <meta name=vs_defaultClientScript content="JavaScript">
                <meta name=vs_
    targetSchema content="http://schemas.microsoft.com/intellisense/ie5">
        </head>
        <body MS_POSITIONING="GridLayout">
                <table cellpadding="0" cellspacing="0" border="0">
                        <tr>
                                <td>
                                        Page's invocation time:
                                </td>
                                <td>
                                        <%=DateTime.Now.ToString("F")%>
                                </td>
                        </tr>
                </table>
        </body>
</html>
```

24

Caching

This example simply outputs the server's time on a web page. When the page first appears, it is cached because of the `OutputCache` directive in the second line of Listing 24.1. The page will be stored in the cache for 60 seconds. If a user requests this page, his browser will show the cached page with the old time. After the cache has been cleared, the user can view the updated page.

We have two ways to cache HTML pages:

- Using the `OutputCache` directive
- Using the `HttpCachePolicy` class

`OutputCache` and `HttpCachePolicy` are very similar, but using `OutputCache` is more user friendly. The following section discusses how to use the `OutputCache` directive in detail.

`OutputCache` **Directive**

Listing 24.1 showed how to use the `OutputCache` directive to quickly retrieve HTML pages from the cache. That example is very simple because it uses just one attribute from the available set of predefined parameters of the `OutputCache` directive. It uses the parameter `Duration`, which declares the time (in seconds) that pages should be stored in the cache. The example also declares that the page will have just one cached version, independent of the set of parameters of this one.

The `OutputCache` directive has the following attributes:

```
<%@ OutputCache Duration="value"

  Location="value" VaryByParam="value" VaryByHeader="value" VaryByCustom="value" %>
```

The following list describes each attribute in more detail:

- `Duration`—Sets the period of time (in seconds) during which pages should be saved in the cache (in Listing 24.1. it is set to 60 seconds). If a user requests a cached page before 60 seconds have expired, the page will not be processed at the server side, but will be read from the cache. This attribute is mandatory. If it's omitted, ASP.NET will throw an exception.

- `Location`—Indicates the location where cached pages should be stored. With help of this attribute, we can indicate whether a page should be cached in the server's RAM or in the client's browser. Location can be set to the following values:

  - `Any`—The page will be cached anywhere: on the server, on the client's browser, and so on. This value is the default.

  - `Client`—The page will be cached just on the client side (if it supports caching).

▶ `Downstream`—The page will be cached on the sending server.

▶ `None`—Caching is disabled.

▶ `Server`—The page will be cached on the server that processes the user's request.

To use the `Location` attribute in `OutputCache`, you should change the second line in Listing 24.1 to the following:

```
<%@ OutputCache Duration="60" VaryByParam="none" Location="Server"%>
```

In this case, the page will be cached for 60 seconds only on the server side.

TIP

Note that different values of the `Location` attribute will cause different behavior by the application. You should use it very carefully, taking into account the settings of the server and client browsers.

▶ `VaryByParam`—Enables you to have several instances of one page in the cache. A page could be cached in different ways, depending on the set of parameters that are passed over the query string (`GET` parameters) and the form's parameters (`POST` parameters). Caching could also depend on HTTP headers. If this attribute is set to `none`, the page will be cached only once (without taking into account parameters that are passed over the `GET` and `POST` mechanisms). But web pages are often built dynamically with different sets of parameters, so in that case you should use the `VaryByParam` attribute to define pages that should be cached (for example, you could cache a page by the value of some `GET` parameter).

Imagine that you need to create a forum. The probability of anyone changing already-posted messages in the forum is very small, so you could cache those messages. For example, the name of the page that shows the text of some message is `message.aspx` and it contains the `MID` (message ID) parameter in the `request` string. For caching each message in the forum, you should use the following format of the `OutputCache` directive:

```
<%@ OutputCache Duration="60" VaryByParam="MID" Location="server"%>
```

In this case, the server will cache the `message.aspx` page and take into account the value of the `MID` parameter. The `message.aspx` page will have several cached copies on the server side (the number of copies is equal to the number of messages that have been reviewed by different users during the previous 60 seconds). If several users want to review the same message in the forum, the page with that message will be generated just one time (meaning that there will be just one request in the database, too). Other users will see a

24

Caching

cached copy of `message.aspx` with a particular value of the `MID` parameter. This approach will result in greatly improved performance by the application.

You can also set several parameters for filtering cached pages inside `VaryByParam` attribute by using a semicolon. For example:

```
<%@ OutputCache Duration="60" VaryByParam="FID;MID" Location="server"%>
```

In this case, messages will be put in the cache by forum ID (`FID`) and message ID (`MID`). You can also use an asterisk in the `VaryByParam` attribute's value. In such a case, the page will be cached according to values of all parameters that are passed to it.

▶ `VaryByHeader`—With the help of this attribute, we can manage HTML page caching according to the values of the HTTP headers. This attribute could be set in one of following values: `Accept`, `Accept-Charset`, `Accept-Encoding`, `Accept-Language`, `Authorization`, `Content-Encoding`, `Expect`, `From`, `Host`, `If-Match`, `If-Modified-Since`, `If-None-Match`, `If-Range`, `If-Unmodified-Since`, `Max-Forwards`, `Proxy-Authorization`, `Range`, `Referer`, `TE`, and `User-Agent`.

You can use a semicolon to define several values of HTTP headers in the `VaryByHeader` attribute.

```
<%@ OutputCache Duration="60" VaryByHeader=" If-None-Match; Range "
VaryByParam="none"%>
```

The preceding example declares that the page caching depends on the values of `If-None-Match` and `Range` HTTP headers. It means that every new combination of these headers will cause a new copy of the page to be written in the cache.

▶ `VaryByCustom`—Use of this attribute enables you to manage page caching according to parameters, which are defined by the developer. The default value of this attribute is `Browser`. If you use this attribute with the `Browse` value, the page will be cached according to the client's browser type and the elder numbers of its version identifier.

```
<%@ OutputCache Duration="60" VaryByCustom="Browse" VaryByParm="none"%>
```

As mentioned earlier, developers can create custom values for the `VaryByCustom` attribute. Developers can do so by redefining the `HttpApplication.GetVaryByCustomString` method. That method could be redefined in the `global.asax` file.

24

Using HttpCachePolicy

As mentioned earlier, ASP.NET provides two ways to cache HTML pages. The first approach—the OutputCache directive—was discussed earlier. So, the following section covers the second approach: the HttpCachePolicy class.

To be more precise, the OutputCache directive is just an intuitive interface of the HttpCachePolicy class. But OutputCache gives more limited possibilities than HttpCachePolicy. For example, you aren't allowed to set an absolute expiration time for storing an object in the cache with the help of OutputCache, but HttpCachePolicy allows you to do so. You could retrieve access to that object via the Response.Cache object represented in ASP.NET.

Listing 24.2 is an example that shows the simplest way of using HttpCachePolicy. (The ASPX representation of this example is the same as in Listing 24.1, but without the use of the OutputCache directive.)

LISTING 24.2
Caching HTML Pages by Using the HttpCachePolicy Class

```
using System;
using System.Collections;
using System.ComponentModel;
using System.Data;
using System.Drawing;
using System.Web;
using System.Web.SessionState;
using System.Web.UI;
using System.Web.UI.WebControls;
using System.Web.UI.HtmlControls;

namespace HttpCachePolicySample
{
  public class Main : System.Web.UI.Page
  {
    private void Page_Load(object sender, System.EventArgs e)
    {
      Response.Cache.SetCacheability(HttpCacheability.Server);
      Response.Cache.SetExpires(DateTime.Now.AddSeconds(60));
    }

    #region Web Form Designer generated code
    override protected void OnInit(EventArgs e)
    {
      InitializeComponent();
      base.OnInit(e);
    }
```

24

Caching

LISTING 24.2
Continued

```
private void InitializeComponent()
{
    this.Load += new System.EventHandler(this.Page_Load);
}
#endregion
}
}
```

This example caches the page by using two methods of the HttpCachePolicy class: SetExpires and SetCacheability. In this case, the page will be cached on the server side for 60 seconds. You could also use the HttpCacheability.Public enumeration member for caching page anywhere (doing so is the same as using the Any value for the OutputCache.Location attribute).

TIP

Note that this article doesn't describe all the members and methods of the HttpCachePolicy class in detail. You can find all necessary information about them on any website related to ASP.NET technology and on Microsoft's MSDN site. In this chapter, we review only the most demonstrative methods of the class.

The SetExpires method helps to set an absolute expiration time for a page in the cache. The example in Listing 24.2 shows how to use SetExpires in tandem with the DateTime class. You are also allowed to use it in the following way:

```
Response.Cache.SetExpires(DateTime.Now.AddSeconds(60));
Response.Cache.SetExpires(DateTime.Parse("04:00"));
```

In this case, the page will be deleted from the cache at 4 o'clock local time.

Both methods that have been discussed enable you to set an absolute expiration time. But there is one more ASP.NET method that enables you to set the caching type to a sliding mode:

```
Response.Cache.SetSlidingExpiration( true );
```

When you use absolute caching, the page is stored in the cache until a particular amount of time expires, without taking into account the quantity of requests that have been performed to this page. When you use a sliding expiration, the page will be deleted from cache only when the page has not been requested by any user for a

24

certain length of time (in the sample case, it's 60 seconds). If a user requests the page during that length of time, the page will again be stored in the cache for an interval equal to the previous one.

Using the `Cache` Object

There is another class in ASP.NET that enables you to cache data. This class is called `Cache`, and you get access to it via the `Cache` property of the current context of the web application (for example, `Context.Cache`).

This object enables you to both store data and to retrieve stored data. It also supports the following:

- ▶ Memory management—It automatically removes an object from the cache to prevent memory overflow.

- ▶ Deleting object after some event—An object could be put in the cache with some rules that dictate when it will be removed automatically.

- ▶ Callback—`Cache` supports the ability to notify your code when an item is removed from the cache.

Listing 24.3 shows how to use the `Cache` object. This example puts some data into the cache and shows that data in the browser. It also checks the source from which the data has been retrieved.

LISTING 24.3
Using the `Cache` Object (Code-Behind)

```
using System;
using System.Collections;
using System.ComponentModel;
using System.Data;
using System.Drawing;
using System.Web;
using System.Web.SessionState;
using System.Web.UI;
using System.Web.UI.WebControls;
using System.Web.UI.HtmlControls;

namespace CacheSample
{
  public class Main : System.Web.UI.Page
  {
    protected HtmlTableCell DataCell;
    protected HtmlTableCell SourceCell;
```

Caching

LISTING 24.3
Continued

```csharp
private void Page_Load(object sender, System.EventArgs e)
{
  String data = "Some data that should be cached.";
  String source = "";
  if (Cache[SOME_DATA_KEY] != null)
  {
    data = Cache[SOME_DATA_KEY].ToString();
    source = "Cache";
  }
  else
  {
    Cache[SOME_DATA_KEY] = data;
    source = "Not Cache";
  }

  DataCell.InnerText = data;
  SourceCell.InnerText = source;
}

private const string SOME_DATA_KEY = "SOME_DATA_KEY";
#region Web Form Designer generated code
override protected void OnInit(EventArgs e)
{
  InitializeComponent();
  base.OnInit(e);
}

private void InitializeComponent()
{
  this.Load += new System.EventHandler(this.Page_Load);
}
#endregion
}
}
```

Listing 24.4 shows the HTML version of this example.

LISTING 24.4
Using Cache Object (HTML Representation)

```
<%@ Page language="c#" Codebehind="Main.aspx.cs"
  AutoEventWireup="false" Inherits="CacheSample.Main" %>
<!DOCTYPE HTML PUBLIC "-//W3C//DTD HTML 4.0 Transitional//EN" >
```

24

LISTING 24.4
Continued

```html
<html>
  <head>
    <title>Cache using Sample</title>
    <meta name="GENERATOR" Content="Microsoft Visual Studio .NET 7.1">
    <meta name="CODE_LANGUAGE" Content="C#">
    <meta name=vs_defaultClientScript content="JavaScript">
    <meta name=vs_targetSchema
content="http://schemas.microsoft.com/intellisense/ie5">
  </head>
  <body MS_POSITIONING="GridLayout">
    <table width="100%" cellpadding="0" cellspasing="0" border="0">
      <tr>
        <td width="20%">Data: </td>
        <td runat="server" id="DataCell"></td>
      </tr>
      <tr>
        <td>Source: </td>
        <td runat="server" id="SourceCell"></td>
      </tr>
    </table>
  </body>
</html>
```

After the first request to the page shown in Listings 24.3 and 24.4, you will see that the source of the data is Not Cache. All other requests (until the page is deleted from the cache) will return that data retrieved from the cache.

TIP

Note that it is mandatory to check whether an object is located in the cache; otherwise, ASP.NET will throw the exception NullReferenceException when you attempt to reference an item in the cache that does not exist.

The preceding example used an implicit approach to putting objects in the cache. You also could use the following method invocation:

```
Cache.Insert("SOME_DATA_KEY", data);
```

The Insert method also has three additional overloads that are discussed in the upcoming sections. Assume that you've read data from a file and put it in the cache. There is some chance that file could be changed, so data in the cache also should be

Caching

updated or deleted. The `Cache` object enables you to trace all changes in a file with data by using an additional parameter (in `Cache.Insert` method) with type `System.Web.Caching.CacheDependency`. To use this feature, you create an instance of the `CacheDependency` class and pass it to the `Cache.Insert` method:

```
System.Web.Caching.CacheDependency dependency = new
  System.Web.Caching.Dependency(Server.MapPath(someFileName));
Cache.Insert(SOME_DATA_KEY, data, dependency);
```

Before returning an object, `Cache` traces changes in the file that the object depends on. If the file has changed, the object is removed from `Cache`; otherwise, it is returned to `Cache`'s user.

The `System.Web.Caching.CacheDependency` class has overloads for the constructor, which enables you to trace the changes in the following:

- ▶ In a file
- ▶ In a folder
- ▶ In a set of files
- ▶ In a set of folders
- ▶ In other objects in `Cache`

TIP

Unfortunately, due to the transient nature of instances of Page classes, there is no built-in way in ASP.NET to create a dependency that removes an item from the cache in response to changes in a DataSet.

Another feature is that `Cache` enables you to set absolute and sliding expiration times for objects that should be inserted in it. (The differences between absolute and sliding time were discussed earlier in this chapter.)

```
Cache.Insert("SOME_DATA_KEY", data, null, DateTime.Now.AddMinutes(5),
  System.Web.Caching.Cache.NoSlidingExpiration);
Cache.Insert("SOME_DATA_KEY", data, null,
  System.Web.Caching.Cache.NoAbsoluteExpiration, TimeSpan.FromMinutes(2));
```

The first line shows how to use absolute object expiration time. The second line presents a sliding expiration time.

24

TIP

Notice that the `System.Web.Caching.Cache.NoSlidingExpiration` **constant is of type** `System.TimeSpan`, **and** `System.Web.Caching.Cache.NoAbsoluteExpiration` **is of type** `System.DateTime`.

As was mentioned earlier, `Cache` can manage memory and automatically remove objects from memory if an overflow occurs. An algorithm for this mechanism is encapsulated in the `Cache` object, and you cannot review or change it, but you're allowed to exert some influence on the process. You can do this with the help of the priority parameter in the `Cache.Insert` method. This one is of type `System.Web.Caching.CacheItemPriority`.

An object of lower priority will be deleted from the cache faster than objects with higher priority. You can also prohibit deletion of an object from the cache.

To set an object's priority in the cache, you use the enumeration `System.Web.Caching.CacheItemPriority`, which has the following values: `Low`, `BelowNormal`, `Default`, `Normal`, `AboveNormal`, `High`, and `NotRemovable`. An object of `CacheItemPriority.NotRemovable` priority will not be deleted during cache clearing.

The last parameter of the `Cache.Insert` method to be discussed is the `onRemoveCallback` parameter of type `System.Web.Caching.CacheItemRemovedCallback`. This parameter takes as its value a delegate that will be invoked during the deletion of a particular object from the cache. This allows your code to notify you about the deletion of an object from the cache.

```
Cache.Insert("SOME_DATA_KEY", data, null, DateTime.Now.AddMinutes(5),
   System.Web.Caching.Cache.NoSlidingExpiration,
   System.Web.Caching.CacheItemPriority.Low,
   new System.Web.Caching.CacheItemRemovedCallback(SomeDelegate));
...
...
...


private void SomeDelegate(string key, object val,
   System.Web.Caching.CacheItemRemovedReason reason)
{
   ...
}
```

> **TIP**
>
> You could remove an object from the cache manually by using the Cache.Remove method, which requires just one parameter: `key` (the name of object).

```
Cache.Remove("SOME_DATA_KEY");
```

The final capability of the Cache object discussed in this chapter is that Cache implements the IEnumerable interface. That is why you can very simply and quickly gain access to all objects located in the Cache object.

```
foreach(DictionaryEntry cacheEntry in Cache)
{
        //access to key - cacheEntry.Key.ToString();
        //access to value - Cache[cacheEntry.Key.ToString()].ToString();
}
```

Summary

This chapter discussed the ASP.NET toolkit that enables developers to store pages in a cache. You also reviewed how to manage the behavior of the cache.

Use of a cache could greatly increase the performance of your application, but you should use it very carefully because you could get surprising results: incorrect data representation (retrieving an incorrect version of the page from the cache) or memory overflow on the server side.

Further Reading

Programming Data-Driven Web Applications with ASP.NET, Chapter 16, by Donny Mack and Doug Seven, Sams Publishing. ISBN: 0672321068.

ASP.NET Unleashed, Second Edition, Chapter 17, by Stephan Walther, Sams Publishing. ISBN: 067232542X.

Special Edition Using Microsoft ASP.NET, Chapter 21, by Richard Leinecker, Que Publishing. ISBN: 0789725606.

24

IN BRIEF

This chapter is designed to provide you with valuable techniques and solutions to real-world problems faced by people creating production ASP.NET applications.

When building enterprise-scale ASP.NET websites, you very rarely find that a showstopper problem involves a programmer not knowing how a specific method of a control works or how to display something a certain way. More frequently the problems occur in trying to build applications that work in web farms, or applications that take into account user location, language, and culture.

This chapter will show you how to build ASP.NET applications that work properly within a web farm context, as well as how to build applications that take into account geographic location, user language, and cultural identity. Wrapping up this chapter will be a discussion of two advanced techniques for enhancing and empowering ASP.NET applications: HttpModules and HttpHandlers.

WHAT YOU NEED

REQUIRED SOFTWARE	.NET Framework SDK v1.1
	Visual Studio .NET 2003 with C# installed
	IIS 5.0 or greater
	Windows XP Pro, Windows 2000, or Windows Server 2003
RECOMMENDED HARDWARE	PC that meets .NET SDK minimum requirements
SKILLS REQUIRED	C# and .NET familiarity
	Familiarity with ASP.NET and IIS

ADVANCED ASP.NET AT A GLANCE

Creating ASP.NET Applications in a Web Farm — 499

ViewState in a Web Farm — 499
Session State Maintenance in a Web Farm — 501
Application State in a Web Farm — 503

Web Farm Configuration and Deployment — 504
Web Farm Best Practices, Recommendations, and Caveats — 505

Localization and Globalization in ASP.NET — 506

Using Localized Resources — 506
Displaying Localized Content — 507

"Out of the Box" Localization Functionality — 511

Creating Custom HttpModules — 513

Understanding the ASP.NET Application Events — 513

Creating a Custom HttpModule — 513

ADVANCED ASP.NET AT A GLANCE

Creating Custom HttpHandlers	**516**
Building a Synchronous HttpHandler	516
Summary	**518**
Further Reading	**519**

Creating ASP.NET Applications in a Web Farm

The following section of this chapter deals with the issue of creating websites that function in a web farm. A *web farm* is essentially a cluster of web servers, all running the same web application. That cluster allows increased user volume, load, and capacity on a website by providing additional hardware, memory, and processing power to sustain and scale the website.

In addition to providing increased scalability by allowing your application to support more concurrent users and higher volume, the use of a farm also can provide increased availability. What do you do if your main web server has a hard drive crash? What is your plan for surviving hardware failure, or server crashes due to other software problems? If you have only one server, you can be guaranteed that you won't survive any of those circumstances without your website being completely unavailable.

Some hardware devices (and some software as well) that create web farms also support the notion of *failover*. The concept is that when one of the servers in a farm becomes too slow, unresponsive, or completely crashes, other servers in the farm can temporarily handle the troubled server's load until it can be repaired or replaced. This provides a continuously available online presence, even when a server is down. In addition to giving you the ability to recover from hardware problems, a farm like this enables you to install new versions of your website one machine at a time, gradually transferring users from the old version to the new version as you upgrade each server. This type of upgrade can take place without any downtime experienced by any of your users.

Unfortunately, creating websites that not only take advantage of this scalability but function properly within such an environment is anything but trivial. There are quite a few things that a developer needs to do and be aware of to create applications that function in a web farm. The following section will prepare you for creating farm-friendly web applications in ASP.NET.

ViewState in a Web Farm

ViewState is a feature provided by ASP.NET that allows a web page to maintain state between requests. Because HTTP is a stateless protocol, developers often had to come

Creating ASP.NET Applications in a Web Farm

up with their own methods for maintaining state between pages to support items such as dynamic controls and wizards, and to support progressive activities such as shopping carts and wish lists. The code to create those features by hand is fairly extensive. ViewState makes dealing with those situations much easier, but at a price: ViewState is very large and adds quite a bit of weight to pages because of the encryption used.

The encryption is where some of the problems show up with ViewState and web farms. The scenario that gives many of us painful headaches is when the user receives a page from one server that has encrypted ViewState. The user then performs some action on that same page, sending the ViewState back, but the page ends up on a different server at the back-end. ViewState is often validated based on encryption. A MAC (message authentication code) is used to tell ASP.NET whether the ViewState has been tampered with. This is a very handy thing because it protects you from potential attacks involving modified ViewState contents. The downside is that the MAC is machine-specific. In other words, the MAC generated by one server will not be the same as the MAC generated by another server, even if they are in the same farm.

In the `web.config` file, you can set `<enableViewStateMAC>` to false to turn it off if you aren't worried about security and you want your ViewState to work properly within the farm.

If you do need the security of tamper-proof ViewState (this also applies to session keys), you can provide a `<machineKey>` tag in the `web.config` file. This key sets up a validation key and a decryption key that is used for generating the MAC that becomes the tool for verifying the validity of state variables. If every server in your farm has the same validation and decryption key, they all know how to read and interpret ViewState generated by any other server in the farm.

When specifying the validation key and encryption key, Microsoft recommends that keys be no smaller than 20 bytes (40 hexadecimal characters) and no greater than 64 bytes (128 hexadecimal characters).

The following is an example of an entry in a `web.config` file that, when set on each application server within a farm, will allow ViewState and session state keys to be handled by any server in the farm:

```
<machinekey
   validationkey=".. random sequence of 128 hex characters ..."
   decryptionkey=".. another random sequence of 128 hex characters ..."
   validation="SHA1" />
```

With code like this in place in your application's `web.config` file, you can rest easy that you're well on your way to being able to run within a farm. This is just the first step, however. There are still quite a few more things that you need to keep in mind in order to build a farm-friendly application.

Session State Maintenance in a Web Farm

If you have worked with ASP.NET for any length of time, you are probably already familiar with the concept of session state. A user's session begins when his browser makes the first request to the website. This session then continues until the server has not received any communication from the client within a certain timeout period. In this way, the stateless limitation of HTTP can be overcome and provide a rich and interactive experience for users. Session state is used to store everything from information on the current user to things such as shopping carts, wizard state, search results, cached data, and pretty much anything else that a developer felt should be easily accessible and divided on a per-session basis.

In its default configuration, ASP.NET session state is a large set of name-value pairs. Every time a piece of code accesses a session state variable, it does so by name. One level of abstraction that is deliberately abstracted from this model is that the session state dictionary is actually a nested dictionary. The top-level dictionary contains a mapping of unique session identifiers to a dictionary containing all the state variables.

Each time a page that has session state enabled is loaded, it retrieves from memory all the name/value pairs that are appropriate for the current session identifier.

Because this session state variable dictionary is stored at the `AppDomain` scope, it doesn't work within a web farm. Each process would be maintaining its own session state. Used in this default form, users could lose all of their session information if they were transferred from one server to another.

A way around this is to use an *out-of-process* session state provider. This essentially means that you can configure ASP.NET to use a *shared* session state provider. In this configuration, when pages are loaded, the session state variables are retrieved from the shared provider. During the page's execution, those values can be changed. Finally, when the page is done executing, changes to the current session are saved to the out-of-process session state provider.

TIP

There is one caveat, however, when writing ASP.NET code that utilizes background threads and out-of-process session state servers. When a *background* thread makes changes to the (out-of-process) session state, the foreground thread will not automatically be made aware of that change. Take care when creating multithreaded ASP.NET applications that use out-of-process session state.

Although you can create your own if you are feeling ambitious, two out-of-process session state servers ship with ASP.NET: the SQL Server session state provider and the ASP.NET State Server. Both are discussed in the following sections.

Session State Maintenance with SQL Server

SQL Server session state is, obviously enough, a session state provider that uses SQL Server as the persistence medium. The first time your ASP.NET page loads, a call is

25

Creating ASP.NET Applications in a Web Farm

made to SQL Server to obtain the list of name-value pairs that are applicable to the current session ID. The session ID is retrieved from either a cookie or the URL of the current page, depending on how the site is configured.

Throughout the execution of the page, changes made to the session state are stored in a temporary, in-memory session state dictionary. When the page finishes its execution, the changes made to session state are sent to SQL Server to be saved.

As you might have guessed, this method of using SQL Server for a session state manager isn't as fast or as efficient as using the in-process provider that is the ASP.NET default. It does have its benefits, however. It is far more reliable than the default session state provider, and it can be used as a shared provider for multiple web servers in a farm. In fact, you can even use the same SQL Server instance to provide session state management services for multiple web farms if you play with configurations a little.

To set up a SQL Server instance to be used as a session state provider, you first need to run a script that will configure all the appropriate data structures. You actually have two choices of scripts to run: `InstallSqlState.sql` and `InstallPersistSqlState.sql`. These are both SQL text files that you can execute from within SQL Query Analyzer or by running a SQL command-line tool. The first script will configure SQL Server to act as a host for session state management, with the information being stored in the `tempdb` database. As you might know, SQL Server empties the contents of that database on startup.

If you want the information contained in a user's session to survive a reboot of the SQL Server machine, you can use the second script, `InstallPersistSqlState.sql`. The second script creates a persistent database called `ASPState` that will maintain user session data even after the server has been rebooted. In addition to creating the data structures, it creates a job that periodically empties out the database of expired session state data. For this feature to work properly, the SQL Agent service must be running on the state management server. As with all session state providers, the interface for accessing session state variables is the same without regard for provider or provider location.

TIP

Even though the interface looks the same, you cannot assume that it will work the same. For example, all out-of-process session state servers work via *serialization*; they do not pass object references like the in-process provider. This means that any object instance you store in the session must not only be serializable, but it must also be stable. Here *stable* means that if you serialize an object and then reconstruct its graph by deserializing it, the object should have the same state. To avoid potential problems with serialization, always make your session objects serializable, and always make sure that you don't make use of private fields or one-way (only a get or set accessor provided, not both) properties.

To configure your web application to use SQL Server session state, set your `<sessionState>` tag in `web.config` to (note that the `mode` attribute is actually case-sensitive):

```
<sessionState mode="SQLServer"
    sqlConnectionString=
      "server=( server); user id=(user); password=(password); initial catalog=ASP-
State;"
    cookieless="false"
    timeout="60" />
```

The `sqlConnectionString` attribute follows all the original rules for creating a SQL Server connection. You can either specify the user credentials in the connection string (generally considered a security risk), or you can indicate integrated security, and so forth.

Session State Maintenance with the ASP.NET State Service

If you don't work for a SQL Server shop, you don't want or need the additional over-head of maintaining a separate SQL Server machine for state maintenance, or you just have something against servers made from three-letter acronyms, there is a more lightweight alternative in the ASP.NET State Service. The ASP.NET State Service is a Windows service that you can activate to handle requests from an ASP.NET applica-tion for state management. It is installed by default in the `(system)\Microsoft.NET\Framework\(version)` directory as the filename `aspnet_state.exe`.

To configure State Server in the `web.config` file, use the following `<sessionState>` tag format (again, the `mode` attribute is case sensitive):

```
<sessionState mode="StateServer"
  stateConnectionString="tcpip=(host):(port)"
  cookieless="false"
  timeout="60" />
```

The advantages of State Server are that it is already installed on every machine with ASP.NET, it has a smaller memory and processor footprint than SQL Server, and you don't have to worry about licensing issues and database load. However, although you can configure SQL Server to maintain a persistent state database that survives reboots, the ASP.NET State Service loses all of its state information when it is shut off for any reason.

Application State in a Web Farm

Whereas session state refers to information that is specific to a particular session on a website, *application state* refers to information that persists throughout the lifetime of an application (the time between reboots or restarts of IIS).

Creating ASP.NET Applications in a Web Farm

25

Each ASP.NET application runs in its own process. Within that process is an area that is available to be used for maintaining state. In fact, the AppDomain object has a dictionary built into it that enables you to get and set name/value pair data via the GetData and SetData methods. Although this might seem handy, it can be troublesome in a web farm.

You can't share application state between applications without writing your own custom code. You'll see some alternatives and options for sharing application state in the best practices and recommendations section later in the chapter. If you must use application state, you will have to come up with your own scheme for sharing or synchronizing application data—be it with a database or some other method.

Web Farm Configuration and Deployment

As you have seen so far, one of the most important issues when dealing with web farms and ASP.NET is in the configuration of the website. You've seen that multiple modifications have to be made to the web.config file to allow ViewState and session state keys to be properly interpreted. Changes must also be made to configuration sections for setting up out-of-process session state management.

There are a few more elements that need to be taken care of in order to properly configure and deploy a web farm. The first and foremost item is the actual creation of a farm. The creation of server sharing, farming, and clustering is outside the scope of this book. It should suffice to know that there are devices that enable you to set up one IP address that forwards to any number of other IPs in the farm, based on a variety of factors such as load and availability. Users come into your site using the external, single IP address, and are then sent seamlessly to one of the machines within the farm. You always need to remember that in a true farm, you have no control over which machine your code is currently executing within and you need to set up your design and architecture with that fact in mind.

IIS Configuration in a Web Farm

After your application has been designed, coded, and configured to run properly within the context of a web farm, and the farm has been created and is running properly, there is one last step: You need to make sure that IIS is configured properly.

If you are using out-of-process session state management in your web farm, and IIS is configured incorrectly, you can actually see data inconsistencies or session state simply not being maintained. The reason for this is that the out-of-process session state is keyed to the application path within the IIS metabase. Each web application in IIS is given a path, such as \LM\W3SVC\1 or \LM\W3SVC\2. If this path doesn't match for every single server in your web farm, those servers will not be able to share session state within that farm. There are two tools that you can use to obtain the application path from the IIS metabase: AdsUtil (a script written in VBScript; available with the NT option pack) and MetaEdit, a tool that you can get from the NT option pack and Windows 2000 CDs.

Before you give the word that your farm-friendly application is live, in production, and ready to go, check your metabase and make sure that every application in your web server has the same application path.

Web Farm Best Practices, Recommendations, and Caveats

As was mentioned earlier in the chapter, ViewState can add a considerable amount of overhead to a page. It can take a relatively long period of time to decrypt and verify the ViewState form variable. In addition, depending on how much information is stored in ViewState, it can actually increase the download time of a web page. On many projects, pages store a complete `DataGrid` control in the ViewState. For large results, the ViewState form variable can actually consume several hundred kilobytes of space, sometimes reaching over 1MB in size. On a LAN, you might not complain too much about that, but over a slow or weak internet connection, users will certainly notice that page taking too long to load and render.

It is recommend that you disable ViewState unless you are sure that you absolutely need the features it provides. In fact, you should probably disable ViewState throughout your entire web site as a rule, and turn it on only when you have discovered that no other alternative will work. Programmers often store data in ViewState to avoid requerying that same data on subsequent loads of the page. Get out your stopwatch and measure it. Which takes longer? Processing the download and upload of ViewState, or querying the database on the back-end? Before you quickly turn to ViewState as a catch-all to make things easier, examine your options regarding your database and server-side caching to see whether you can avoid using it.

If you are using out-of-process session state, you need to be aware of a crucial fact: Out-of-process session state performs two tasks that are both considered performance issues. The first task is that it makes a network connection to a server somewhere. Although it might be a fast connection, any off-machine connection will always be slower than an in-process data operation. The second task, all out-of-process state management, is accomplished via serialization. The more complex an object is, the larger its serialized representation and the longer it takes to serialize and deserialize on the network stream. In particular, `DataSets` (prior to .NET 2.0) serialize into extremely large XML representations that can potentially cause severe delays in state management. Also keep in mind that connections are made to the session state provider at both the beginning and at the end of page rendering, so any large object that you have in session state can potentially slow down the pipeline twice per page view.

It has been mentioned before, but it's worth mentioning again: Any object that is stored in out-of-process session state has to be serializable. You must be able to restore the state from a serialized graph for that object to work properly with session state. Keep the data you store in the session small and simple. Sticking to base .NET Framework types will make things a lot easier (and faster).

25

Application state is an area that can easily be abused. Because the state data stored in the `AppDomain` object is globally scoped throughout the `AppDomain`, any large data there is a burden on the garbage collector. Large data will stay in memory for an extremely long time, even if you don't use it. Keep your use of this dictionary (many consider it a crutch to be avoided) to a minimum. If you have to use it, store primitive types or small classes that are easily (and quickly) serialized (no `DataSets`).

If you truly need shared application state, resist the urge to do something cool and fancy and rig up some kind of Remoting system. Something like that will probably generate a lot of development work and a maintenance headache, when you probably could have used a table in your application's database for application state information. Granted, there are situations in which Remoting or using web services to synchronize application data within a farm is necessary, but those situations are rare and usually not practical.

TIP

Many developers easily fall into the habit of assuming that their desktop is the same as the deployment environment. With a few extra configuration steps, and keeping a few tips in mind, you can seamlessly take your single-server application and make it work smoothly within a 2-server, 20-server, or 200-server web farm.

Localization and Globalization in ASP.NET

Sitting at our desks and developing web applications, it's very easy for most of us to assume that the only language that will be used for the application is English. The truth is less short-sighted than that, however.

Even if your application server is hosted in an English-speaking country, that doesn't necessarily mean that all the users of your website will be native speakers of English. Language isn't the only cultural concern that developers need to consider at design time. Cultural locales dictate other things, such as the way that currency and date/time values are displayed. If you display 05-10-2003 to someone from the United States and 05-10-2003 to someone from England, they will more than likely disagree on the dates. The reader from the United States will think the date refers to May 10, 2003, whereas the reader from England will think that the date is referring to the October 5 of the same year. Ignoring issues like this can be disastrous. It is best to determine what level of support for globalization your application needs when you are designing it, because it is far more difficult to add support for this kind of architecture after your application has been released. The next section of this chapter will take you through various scenarios and solutions for creating globally aware ASP.NET applications.

Using Localized Resources

When most people think about globalization, they think about language first. A *resource* is any data that is available to an application, such as text, images, XML files, and so on. As you saw in

25

Chapter 12, "Assemblies and AppDomains," the .NET Framework uses a hub-and-spoke model for locating and using resources. If you have resources in your application for Spanish (neutral) and English (USA), and the user of your application has her cultural information set to Spanish (Mexico), the hub-and-spoke model will allow the .NET Framework to locate the Spanish language resources and use those before using the default language resources.

Displaying Localized Content

In Chapter 12, you saw how to use a `ResourceManager` to get access to resources embedded within your assembly, whether they were custom embedded resources or contained within an assembly resource file, such as a string table.

Instead, this chapter discusses the architectural impact of designing an ASP.NET application for displaying localized content. There are several things you need to concern yourself with when dealing with localized content in a web page:

- ▶ Displaying images
- ▶ Displaying text
- ▶ Displaying and querying data

It is very common for the cultural information to be stored in the URL; for example, `http://somesite.com/content/en-us/article1.html`. Duplicating your content for each location you support is definitely not something you want to do if you can avoid it. It creates a maintenance nightmare for both you and your translators. Your goal in creating a multicultural site is to support multiple cultures with a single code base. The concept of satellite assemblies enables you to do this easily if you put some thought into the design up front.

Displaying Localized Images

As with virtually everything in the .NET Framework, there are many different ways to accomplish any task. Displaying images with globalization in mind is no different.

One option, a brute-force style method, would be to create a different images directory for each supported culture and just retrieve images from the appropriate directory. Although this approach might seem appealing in that you don't have to write very much additional code, it would be a maintenance problem. In addition to being hard to maintain (every time you change an image, you have to change it in each culture's directory), you are duplicating quite a bit of data unnecessarily. Think about a typical content site. That site's graphics will usually contain dozens of images used to frame, highlight, box, and render content. These graphics are probably the same regardless of culture. Only images that have different significance in different cultures or that must be sized differently need to be changed with different cultures.

The preferred method is to use an assembly resource file. For each image, create a string that has the image's URL as a value. Because of the way .NET locates resources

Localization and Globalization in ASP.NET

and its resource default fallback logic, you need supply only overriding resource names for images that vary by culture, such as a flag or other culturally significant icons.

Displaying Localized Text

Displaying globalized text should follow the same rules as images. Instead of duplicating your content in multiple places throughout your site, you should retrieve your text from resources. However, keep in mind that resources involve a decent amount of overhead. You should use assembly resource files to store things such as prompts, button labels, menu items, and so on. Don't use .resx files for things such as very large text items like articles, essays, and so forth. For large text or binary resources, you should use a system more suited to the storage and retrieval of large amounts of data, such as an RDMBS like MS SQL Server, Oracle, mySQL, and others.

A picture is worth a thousand words, so a screenshot is probably worth pretty close to that. Figure 25.1 shows the output of a website that uses a resource file to store the URLs of globalized images, as well as another resource file to store the captions for each image.

FIGURE 25.1   Screenshot of a simple application using localized image and text resources.

To create this application, create a new solution called `CultureResource`. To that solution, add a class library called `CultureData` and a website called `CultureResource`. One of the best things about the .NET Framework resource handling is that satellite assemblies make it possible for you to add additional resources to an existing application without having to recompile anything.

> **TIP**
>
> A common misconception when dealing with resource localization is that the programmer is the one who will be compiling the resources into the assembly. In reality, more often than not, an outsourcing firm will be given the task of translation, and the XML file for building resources. Because of this, make sure that all your resource files are in an assembly that has *no other code contained within*. This makes it very easy to ship off to a third party for translation or for additional language resources.

Add four resource files to `CultureData`: `Strings`, `Strings.en-ca`, `Images`, and `Images.en-ca`. Add a string called `FlagCaption` to both `Strings` (the default culture) and `Strings.en-ca` (English/Canada). These captions match what you saw in Figure 25.1. To the `Images` file, add a string called `flag`, with the image URL `Images/usa.jpg`. The `Images.en-ca` file got a `flag` string with the value `Images/canada.jpg`.

Finally, write the code shown in Listing 25.1 to utilize the new resources.

LISTING 25.1
The Code for a Web Form Utilizing the New Resources

```
private void Page_Load(object sender, System.EventArgs e)
{
  // when using a ResourceManager, _ALWAYS_ remember the full namespace name
  // oh, and never use a hardcoded path like this :)
  Assembly cultureData = Assembly.LoadFrom(
  Server.MapPath("~/bin/CultureData.dll"));
  ResourceManager images = new ResourceManager("CultureData.Images",
    cultureData, null );
  ResourceManager strings = new ResourceManager("CultureData.Strings",
    cultureData, null );

  Response.Write( strings.GetString("FlagCaption") + "<BR>");
  Response.Write(
    string.Format("<img src=\"{0}\"/><br>",
    images.GetString("flag")));

  CultureInfo ci= new CultureInfo("en-ca");
  System.Threading.Thread.CurrentThread.CurrentCulture = ci;
  System.Threading.Thread.CurrentThread.CurrentUICulture = ci;
```

LISTING 25.1
Continued

```
Response.Write( strings.GetString("FlagCaption") + "<BR>");
Response.Write(
    string.Format("<img src=\"{0}\"/><br>",
    images.GetString("flag")));


}
```

The first step is to load the assembly. Because the assembly has no actual code in it, you can't use a shortcut and use the `Assembly` property of a `Type`; the assembly must be loaded manually. After the code has a reference to the resource assembly, two `ResourceManagers` are created: one for the images and one for the text captions. The rest of the code is pretty straightforward. It displays the default resource (the flag of the United States, in this case) and then changes the thread to indicate Canada (English) and displays that localized resource (the Canadian flag).

Using this model and architecture for localization, your application's support for multiple cultures will be robust and scalable, and provide a wide range of features for the consumers of your application.

Displaying and Querying Localized Data

So far you have seen code dealing with displaying information to the user in multiple languages and culture formats. You've seen some good ways to deal with localizing images as well as text. A more difficult task exists in providing localization services for large amounts of data and for data that exists in a database.

It is fortunate that you can provide the same kind of default fallback functionality that you get with resources against database structures like tables or stored procedures. You can provide a default stored procedure, and override it only for the cultures in which it makes sense to do so. Taking the previous model of storing URLs and text in resource files, you can also store the names of stored procedures and database tables in those resource files. For example, assume that you have a stored procedure called `sp_GetLocalTaxInfo`. This stored procedure works perfectly fine for 80% of your users, but the other 20% are from a country where the data in that stored procedure is incorrect. If you store the name of that stored procedure in a resource file as a string named "LocalTaxInfo", you can then override that string in a localized resource for cultures that might need to call `sp_GetAlternateLocalTaxInfo`.

You might be thinking that all of this sounds like a lot of work. The truth is that it is a lot of work. However, if you put in more effort up front, the rewards later on during the product's life cycle will be more than worth it. Assume you produce an application that follows the models and examples discussed earlier, and your architecture supports all facets of globalization. Now assume that your boss tells you that you need to get your application ready to support French and Spanish and you have only a short time period in which to do it.

If you followed the earlier advice, you could simply hand your .resx files and image directories to a translation company and have both the Spanish and French versions of your site completed simultaneously and still maintain only one single code base. Now picture the other alternative: You coded your site with no resources, everything defaulted to English, and no preparation done for globalization. It should be obvious where the payoff is in early investment in globalization.

"Out of the Box" Localization Functionality

In addition to you providing your own functionality as far as obtaining language strings, image references, and data references from resource files, ASP.NET (and the .NET Framework) provides quite a bit of localized functionality for you by default. This next section shows you a few of the elements for localizing your application that you get for free from ASP.NET.

Localized Dates

As you probably know, different cultures write dates in different formats. A United Kingdom date starts with the day, and a United States date starts with the month when displayed in short format. When you display the date in long format, .NET displays the name of the month in either abbreviated or full form. What happens if the viewer of that date is not from an English-speaking country? Fortunately, when you output date and time formats using .NET built-in methods, those formats *automatically* take into consideration the thread's current culture (not the current user interface culture).

Localized Currency Details

Currency is another thing that many developers take for granted. Too many developers will automatically just output a dollar ($) sign in front of a currency variable and think they're done. Each culture not only writes its currency in different ways (some use commas instead of decimal points), but they all have different names and symbols for their currency. By using the .NET built-in formatters for currency, you can be sure that the values you are displaying will be displayed in the appropriate way for the culture viewing the value.

To show how much built-in functionality .NET provides, add a few lines of code to the earlier resource sample. First, drop a placeholder control onto the Web Form, and then add the following lines of code to the end of the Page_Load event handler:

```
ci= new CultureInfo("hi-in");
System.Threading.Thread.CurrentThread.CurrentCulture = ci;
System.Threading.Thread.CurrentThread.CurrentUICulture = ci;
System.Web.UI.WebControls.Calendar cal = new System.Web.UI.WebControls.Calendar();
PlaceHolder1.Controls.Add(cal);
```

25

```
Response.Write(DateTime.Now.ToLongDateString() + " " +
   DateTime.Now.ToLongTimeString());
Response.Write("<br>");
Response.Write( string.Format("{0:C}", 12.75) );
```

This code is pretty simple. Essentially all that's being done is setting the current thread's UI Culture and Culture to Hindi (India), and then using stock functions to display a date, a calendar, and some currency. Figure 25.2 shows the new output of the `Default.aspx` page.

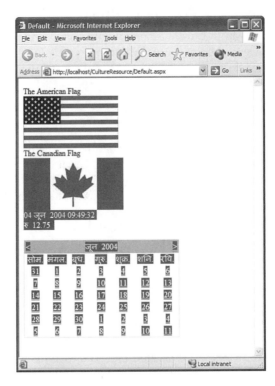

FIGURE 25.2   The new output of the `Default.aspx` page, showing localized dates, calendars, and currency.

Localization and Time Zones

Another somewhat egocentric thing that many do as developers is store and display time without regard to time zone. If your website stores content and the time and date that the content appeared is important—how does someone know that the content was added at 9 a.m. in their time zone, or 9 a.m. in the time zone of the host server?

One more thing that you can do to ensure that your users have the richest possible localized experience is to store all relevant times and dates in the GMT central time zone, and then simply convert the times when rendered to the time zone of the viewing user. You can do this by storing the user's home time zone in his profile in your database, in a cookie, or using some other means.

Creating Custom HttpModules

An *HttpModule* is a reusable piece of code that you can plug into the execution chain of an ASP.NET application. You can think of it as a piggyback mechanism whereby any application that receives a specific module can take advantage of the behavior of that module. An added benefit of HttpModules is that they can be reused among multiple applications because you need only to modify `web.config` to install them.

Understanding the ASP.NET Application Events

When an HttpModule has been installed, its `Init` method is invoked when the application begins. Within this method, any initialization code is run, and event handlers are attached to various application events. The following is a list of some of the more commonly utilized application events within an HttpModule:

- `AcquireRequestState`—This event is fired when an application acquires the state associated with a particular request, such as session state.

- `AuthenticateRequest`—This event is fired after a security module has determined the identity of the current request's user.

- `AuthorizeRequest`—This event is fired after a security module has determined the authorization for the current user.

- `BeginRequest`—This is the first event in the HTTP pipeline chain of events that starts when a request comes in for a page.

- `EndRequest`—This is the last event in the HTTP pipeline chain of events that takes place after a page has been rendered.

There are many more events, and you can find documentation on them all in the MSDN library installed with Visual Studio .NET at the following URL: `ms-help://MS.VSCC.2003/MS.MSDNQTR.2003FEB.1033/cpref/html/frlrfSystemWebHttpApplicationEventsTopic.htm`. The URL might be different if you have a newer version of the MSDN library installed.

Creating a Custom HttpModule

Now that you know what events you can trap using an HttpModule, take a look at some code for a custom HttpModule that can be used on a localized website.

Creating Custom HttpModules

Create a new solution called CustomModule. In that solution, start with a website called CustomModule and a class library called SampleHttpModule. Create a Default.aspx and drop a calendar on the page. Switch to the Page_Load event handler for that page and add the following line of code:

```
Response.Write("The price of that item is " +
    string.Format("{0:C}", 21.89) );
```

When you run this web page, you get a standard calendar, and you see that the price for an item is $21.89. What if your users could all specify their own local culture, regardless of the culture of the server? To do something like that, create an HttpModule. Add a class to the SampleHttpModule project called SampleModule. The code for that class is shown in Listing 25.2.

LISTING 25.2

The SampleModule HttpModule Implementation

```csharp
using System;
using System.Web;
using System.Collections;
using System.Globalization;

namespace SampleHttpModule
{
  /// <summary>
  /// Summary description for SampleModule.
  /// </summary>
  public class SampleModule : IHttpModule
  {
    public void Init( HttpApplication application )
    {
      application.AcquireRequestState
        +=new EventHandler(application_AcquireRequestState);
    }

    public void Dispose()
    {
      // take care of anything that needs discarding here
    }

    private void application_AcquireRequestState(object sender, EventArgs e)
    {
      CultureInfo ci = new CultureInfo("es-es");
      System.Threading.Thread.CurrentThread.CurrentCulture = ci;
      System.Threading.Thread.CurrentThread.CurrentUICulture = ci;
```

LISTING 25.2
Continued

```
    }
  }
}
```

During the `Init` method, we rig up an event handler for the
`AcquireRequestState` event. That handler sets the culture information for the
current culture and user interface culture. Here it has been hand-coded to Spanish
(Spain), but you could easily do something like read that information from the
browser's identification information from a cookie or from some user preference data
in your own database. `es-es` is used here just to make the demonstration easier.

The last step before trying this module is to set it up in `web.config` with the
following tag:

```
<httpModules>
    <add type="SampleHttpModule.SampleModule, SampleHttpModule"
      name="SampleHttpModule" />
</httpModules>
```

After building the solution and running the web page, you can probably guess that
both the calendar and currency will change to support the new culture. As indicated
by Figure 25.3, the currency information for Spain is, in fact, euros. Thanks to the
.NET Framework, we don't have to remember details like that.

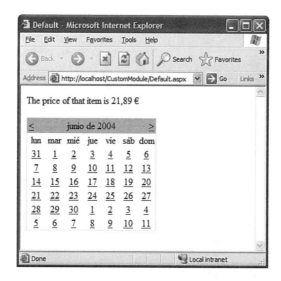

FIGURE 25.3   The new web page with its
culture set by an HttpModule.

Creating Custom HttpHandlers

An *HttpHandler* is a class that has a single method that is invoked to handle a request. Rather than attaching itself to application events, an HttpHandler registers itself to listen for requests that match a specific path or wildcard expression. For example, you can create an HttpHandler that will respond to requests for all files ending in the .myHandler extension.

Another really good use for HttpHandlers is to create a handler that deals with .html files. Rather than have a single product.aspx page, you can have a virtual .html page for every product ID in your catalog. This allows a page to be bookmarked (and possibly spidered by search engines) and still be every bit as dynamic as a regular ASP.NET page.

Building a Synchronous HttpHandler

If you still have the HttpModule solution, you can add HttpHandler code to it. Add a new class to the SampleHttpModule project and call it HtmlHandler. Listing 25.3 shows the contents of that class.

LISTING 25.3
The HtmlHandler Class

```
using System;
using System.Web;
using System.Collections;


namespace SampleHttpModule
{
  /// <summary>
  /// Summary description for HtmlHandler.
  /// </summary>
  public class HtmlHandler : IHttpHandler
  {
    public HtmlHandler()
    {
      //
      // TODO: Add constructor logic here
      //
    }
    #region IHttpHandler Members

    public void ProcessRequest(HttpContext context)
```

LISTING 25.3
Continued

```
    {
      string prodId = context.Request.FilePath.Substring(
      context.Request.FilePath.IndexOf("/custommodule/")+18,
      context.Request.FilePath.Length-23-
        context.Request.FilePath.IndexOf("/custommodule/"));
      HttpResponse Response = context.Response;

      Response.Write("<html>");
      Response.Write("<body>");
      Response.Write("The following is the detail for product ID " + prodId +
"<Br>");
      Response.Write("This product costs: " +
      string.Format("{0:C}<br>", 49.99));
      Response.Write("</body>");
      Response.Write("</html>");

    }

    public bool IsReusable
    {
    get
    {
      // TODO:  Add HtmlHandler.IsReusable getter implementation
      return false;
    }
  }

  #endregion
  }
}
```

The `ProcessRequest` method takes an instance of the `HttpContext` class and
provides processing for it. In this case, I create a simple HTML document that
contains product details. Instead of passing something like "`productId=222`", I can
browse to "`prod222.aspx`" and it will have the same effect. To rig up this handler,
add the following lines to your `web.config`:

```
<httpHandlers>
  <add verb="*" path="prod*.aspx"
    type="SampleHttpModule.HtmlHandler, SampleHttpModule" />
</httpHandlers>
```

Creating Custom HttpHandlers

> **TIP**
>
> If the handler you are creating is not for an extension that is already managed by .NET, you will need to go into the IIS management console and change the configuration of the application's virtual directory. Add a file extension mapping of your custom extension to the .NET ISAPI filter (aspnet_isapi.dll) and your custom HttpHandler should then work properly. To test it out before making a change to IIS, you can always set your path to use an existing extension, such as `.aspx`.

Rebuild the solution and then browse to
`http://localhost/custommodule/prod222.aspx`. Figure 25.4 shows that not only do we get a custom implementation of an `.aspx` page, but that the HttpModule we built previously is still active and controlling the format of our currency, even though the currency was displayed inside an HttpHandler.

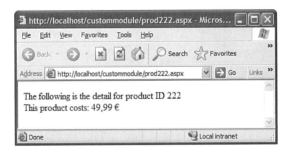

FIGURE 25.4   The custom `HtmlHandler` in action.

Summary

This chapter has introduced you to some advanced ASP.NET techniques. They aren't advanced because they're difficult; they're advanced because they usually escape the notice of most programmers. Thinking about globalization and localization is something that far too few of us do on a daily basis. The same is true for creating applications that not only function properly in a web farm, but that also thrive and excel in that environment. Finally, we took a look at two ways in which you can extend the HTTP processing pipeline from within ASP.NET: HttpHandlers and HttpModules. This chapter has given you some insight not only on various coding techniques, but on the architecture and design of advanced and powerful ASP.NET applications that are ready for today's demanding and global market.

Further Reading

ASP.NET Unleashed, 2nd Edition by Stephen Walther, Sams Publishing.
ISBN: 067232542X.

Professional ASP.NET 1.1, Wrox Press. ISBN: 0764558900.

www.asp.net

www.gotdotnet.com

msdn.microsoft.com/netframework

25

26 Deploying ASP.NET Applications

IN BRIEF

As you are probably painfully aware, there is a big difference between the effort involved in creating an application and the effort involved in deploying an application. For that reason alone, many IT departments have a configuration manager whose sole responsibility is the managing of builds, deployments, and installations.

This chapter will introduce some of the concepts and tasks involved in deploying an ASP.NET application. You will see how to perform these deployments manually with Visual Studio .NET tools and simply by copying files from one place to another. In addition, you'll see how to create a Setup project that can be used to install the application on other machines. Finally, you'll learn a little bit about deployment concerns when publishing your application to a hosted environment over which you have no control, such as Brinkster or another third-party hosting firm.

WHAT YOU NEED

REQUIRED SOFTWARE	.NET Framework SDK v1.1
	Visual Studio .NET 2003 with C# installed
	IIS 5.0 or greater
	Windows XP Pro, Windows 2000, or Windows Server 2003
RECOMMENDED HARDWARE	PC that meets .NET SDK minimum requirements
SKILLS REQUIRED	C# and .NET familiarity
	Familiarity with ASP.NET and IIS

DEPLOYING ASP.NET APPLICATIONS AT A GLANCE

Manually Deploying an ASP.NET Application	521		
Deploying via "Copy Project"	521	When to XCopy	522
XCopy Deployment	522		
Automated Deployment	**523**		
Creating a Setup Project	523	Deploying a Setup Project	529
Advanced ASP.NET Deployment	**529**		
Web Farm Considerations	530	Hosted Environment Considerations	532
Firewalls, DMZs, Routers, and Security Constraints	530		
Summary	**533**		
Further Reading	**533**		

Manually Deploying an ASP.NET Application

It seems almost like overkill to dedicate a chapter to ASP.NET deployment because it is such a breath of fresh air compared to previous deployment models for COM and legacy ASP. Before the chapter gets into building setup projects using Visual Studio .NET, it covers how to deploy your web application manually. Knowing where the files go, how you can get them there, and how to configure the target environment will make it easier for you to build setup applications later. The next section will show you how to deploy your ASP.NET applications manually using Visual Studio or using the command-line tool, XCopy. Finally, you'll see some of the problems with XCopy deployment and when you can and cannot make use of it.

Deploying via "Copy Project"

Within Visual Studio .NET is an option under the Project menu called *Copy Project*. This option is a double-edged sword, unfortunately. On one hand, it gives you nearly one-click deployment of your application (typically residing on your local PC) to another server somewhere in your network. On the other hand, the method used to publish that application will almost never be sufficient to get your production applications out the door. For copying simple applications to other servers that are unsecured for development use, it is an ideal tool. Figure 26.1 shows the dialog box that opens when you choose Project, Copy Project.

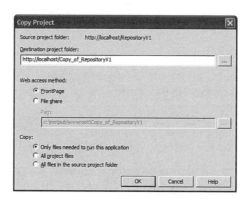

FIGURE 26.1   The Copy Project dialog box.

There are two publish methods: FrontPage and file share. If your production machine is even remotely secured against attack, you know that neither of these publishing methods will work, regardless of how much administrative access your account has on the remote server. FrontPage extensions are typically disabled when IIS security is locked down for a production machine. File sharing is almost always disabled on production web servers.

If you are lucky enough to be able to deploy to a machine this way, it is a handy way of duplicating web sites. There is even an option to exclude source code files from the deployment so that only those files necessary to run the application are copied.

The real issue with Copy Project is that you can't control how your dependencies are deployed or whether they are deployed at all. Referenced assemblies will show up in the bin directory on the website, but if you have any other complex dependencies, such as COM objects or requirements for the global assembly cache, the Copy Project tool won't help you deploy your application.

XCopy Deployment

XCopy deployment doesn't actually refer to deployment that you must do using the XCopy command-line utility. It actually refers to dependency-free deployment that can be accomplished simply by copying files from one location to another location. This means that you can XCopy deploy using FTP, drag-and-drop file copy, file sharing, or any other means of transferring files to the destination server.

To XCopy a web application from one location to another is a very simple command-line task. To do so, open any command prompt (you don't need the Visual Studio .NET command prompt) and type the following command:

```
xcopy c:\inetpub\wwwroot\devapplication z:\prodapplication
```

That's all you need to do. Specify the source directory and the destination directory and XCopy will copy the files and preserve the tree structure.

When to XCopy

A few guidelines and pieces of advice can be given with regard to when you should XCopy your projects to deploy them:

If it is physically possible to XCopy deploy your project, you should XCopy deploy your project.

Determining whether or not your application qualifies for XCopy deployment is something else entirely. Also, keep in mind that when this chapter discusses deploying, it is discussing deployment of the application as a functional unit. If some pieces of the application don't work after XCopy deployment, but some do, the application doesn't support XCopy deployment.

The following is a quick list of some of the most common things that can cause your application to be unable to take advantage of XCopy deployment:

▶ Your application makes use of COM objects.

▶ Your application makes use of components assumed to be in the global assembly cache.

- ▸ Your application is a Windows service.

- ▸ Your application is a COM+/Enterprise Services package that cannot be auto-registered.

- ▸ Your application makes use of event logs, performance counters, message queues, and other system resources that must be preconfigured before your application can run properly.

If your application is built to run without any dependencies on things such as COM objects, preconfigured OS services, and so on, you can probably XCopy deploy your application.

If your application requires any kind of configuration outside the setup of the `web.config` file, has COM/COM+ dependencies, or depends on things such as the GAC or even operating system resources such as event logs and the like, it will be unable to take advantage of XCopy deployment and you will have to create a setup application for deployment.

Automated Deployment

At one time or another, we've all sat through an InstallShield process or downloaded something from the Web that began installing itself, or installed something that was packaged using the Microsoft installer tool (packages with `.msi` file extensions).

When you can't deploy your applications simply by dragging the files from the development machine to the deployment machine, you need to use some extra tools to create deployment and installation packages to help distribute your applications.

The next section of the chapter deals with creating and deploying automated installations using the Visual Studio .NET 2003 Setup project type, built specifically for a web application. Although you can use this project type to create installation packages for Windows Forms, that aspect of the tool will not be discussed in this chapter.

Creating a Setup Project

This next section covers the creation of an MSI (Windows Installer) package that will install your website on a server. There are many different reasons why you would want to package your website in a self-installing executable.

The first and probably most common reason is that your server deployment environment is incredibly secure. The only way you can install applications on that server is to provide someone with access to your server (either IT or configuration management) with an easy-to-install installation package and instructions for how to answer the prompts.

Automated Deployment

A second scenario is that your application is a website that you sell "shrink-wrapped" to other clients. For example, you might produce a bug-tracking application that installs on the web servers in other IT departments. In that case, you would definitely want to provide an easy-to-use installation package that someone could run from a CD and have everything configured properly.

To discuss the creation of a complete setup project, the first thing to be done is to create the website to be deployed. The website will be simple so that you can focus on the deployment of that website and not the development of the site itself.

The first step is to create a new Web Application project. Call this project `Deployment`. Don't worry about changing any values or setting up anything else. Next, add a new class library to the solution called `DeploymentLibrary`. Add a reference from the `Deployment` project to the `DeploymentLibrary` project.

Now that you have a website set up and you've got a class library that it references to create a representation of some kind of dependency, create the setup project. Add a new Web Setup project to the solution and call it `DeploymentInstall`.

You will be presented with a new view that contains a folder called `Web Application Folder` and some properties for that folder in the properties window. This new view is shown in Figure 26.2.

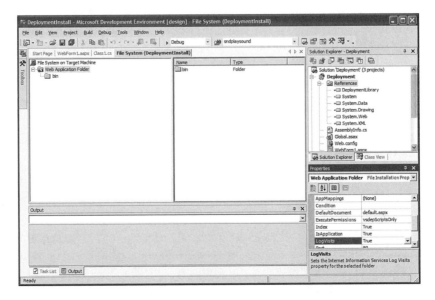

FIGURE 26.2   Empty web setup project.

There is a plethora of properties that you can set on the web application folder. This view, called the File System view, represents the file system as you would like it to be after the installation has completed. As such, the properties of the `Web`

`Application Folder` are those that you want to have set on your application when it is installed and configured in IIS. Table 26.1 is a short list of some of the more commonly used properties of the `Web Application Folder`.

TABLE 26.1

Properties Available for Configuration of the `Web Application Folder`

Property	Description
`AllowDirectoryBrowsing`	Controls whether the destination application directory will allow browsing
`AllowReadAccess`	Controls whether the destination application will allow Read access
`AllowScriptSourceAccess`	Allows script source access on the destination application directory
`DefaultDocument`	Indicates the filename of the website's default document (default is `default.aspx`)
`ExecutePermissions`	Sets the IIS Execute permissions property on the folder
`Index`	Boolean indicates whether the site's content will be indexed
`IsApplication`	Boolean indicates whether the site is an application (defaults to true)
`LogVisits`	Boolean indicates whether to log visits to the website after it has been installed
`Port`	Indicates the port number on which the application will run (default is 80)
`VirtualDirectory`	Indicates the name of the virtual directory in which the application will be installed

As you can see, you have quite a bit of control over the installation of your website using a setup project. To add the files that your website is going to install, right-click the `Web Application Folder` and choose Add, Project Output. You will be prompted for the kind of project output you want. Select Primary Output to add the website's `bin` directory. Do the same thing again, except choose Content Files this time. This will include all the `.aspx`, `.asmx`, and `.ascx` files from the website.

Highlight the Content Files from Deployment (Active) node and look at the properties window. You should see a host of configuration options that control how, when, and where you install that particular item.

This is just a small number of the things that a setup project can accomplish. Take a look at the View, Editor menu options. You'll see the following different kinds of views that you can examine within your setup project:

- ▶ File System (this is the default and initial view)
- ▶ Registry
- ▶ File Types

Automated Deployment

26

- ▶ User Interface
- ▶ Custom Actions
- ▶ Launch Conditions

Open the User Interface section. You will see a hierarchical view of dialogs and other pieces of the user interface, such as the progress dialog, and so on. Figure 26.3 shows what the default user interface of a setup application looks like.

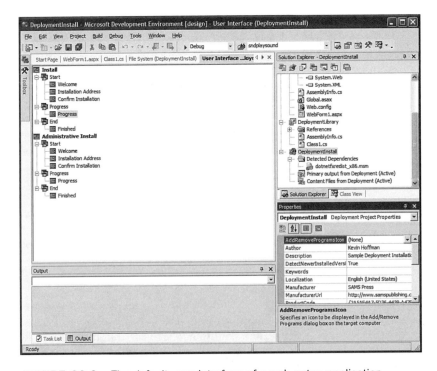

FIGURE 26.3   The default user interface of a web setup application.

There is too much that you can configure in a setup project to cover in one short chapter on ASP.NET deployment. To keep things short and to the point, this chapter discusses some of the more interesting ASP.NET installation features and lets you play with the remaining settings on your own. The setup project really is quite intuitive and very easy to use. When you start to find out everything the setup project can do, you'll be really surprised at how powerful it is.

To demonstrate some of these powerful features, we're going to password-protect the setup project so that only people who have the proper password can install the application. This isn't exactly practical, but it shows you just how easily you can customize your setup project.

First, get into the User Interface view and right-click the standard install's Start node. Choose Add Dialog and select Textboxes (A). Make sure that you move that dialog to the top so that it appears before the Address input dialog. Although you can't actually drag and drop buttons and things onto a design surface, you can control the behavior of the dialog via properties. Set the `BannerText` and `BodyText` properties to anything you like. Table 26.2 shows some of the properties for this dialog.

TABLE 26.2

Properties Available for a Custom Dialog

Property	Value
BannerText	Security Identification Required
BodyText	This sample website ... (and so on)
Edit1Label	Enter the Password:
Edit1Property	SUPERSECRET
Edit2Visible	False
Edit3Visible	False
Edit4Visible	False

The most important part of this dialog is the `Edit1Property` value SUPERSECRET. You can think of this as a variable. Whatever the user performing the install enters when prompted for Edit1 will be stored in a property called SUPERSECRET that will be accessible to other parts of the installation system for querying.

One of those parts is a launch condition. A *launch condition* is a prerequisite that must be met in order for the installation to actually begin. By default, ASP.NET setup projects require a minimum version of IIS and a minimum version of ASP.NET. You can require anything you like in order to prevent your application from being installed in an unsuitable environment.

For this security demo, you're going to create a launch condition that prevents the installation from occurring if the password isn't correct.

1. To do add a custom launch condition, change the editor view to the Launch Conditions window (View, Editor, Launch Conditions).

2. Right-click the `Launch Conditions` folder and add a new condition. ˆ

3. Call the condition `SuperSecretPassword` and set the `Condition` property to the following text:

   SUPERSECRET=password

4. Set the message property to "You entered the wrong Password. Installation cannot continue."

With that in place, you have a launch condition that prevents the installation from being launched if the user-entered property called SUPERSECRET is not equal to the value password.

Automated Deployment

Build the installation project so you can test it out. The actual MSI file will be in the project's `bin\debug` directory. Executing the setup project, you'll see the opening welcome screen, as illustrated in Figure 26.4.

FIGURE 26.4   The opening welcome screen of the Installation Wizard.

Clicking on the Next button, you are prompted for the password, as shown in Figure 26.5. Take a good look at this dialog, and remember that you had to set up only a couple of properties in order to get it to appear.

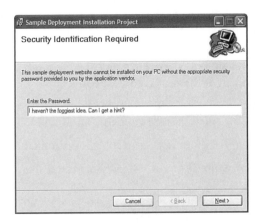

FIGURE 26.5   The custom password prompt dialog.

Note that we obviously didn't enter the correct password. The wizard will continue gathering information from the user, and then when it gets to the step where it validates all the launch conditions, the error message shown in Figure 26.6 appears just before the installation aborts.

FIGURE 26.6 The error message indicating an install abort due to invalid password.

You've now seen that with a few changes to some properties and just a small amount of effort, you can turn your stock, default installer into an incredibly powerful deployment tool. Unless you need the most state-of-the-art features for your deployment package, you shouldn't need to use any third-party deployment packaging tools because the one that you get for free in Visual Studio .NET 2003 is sufficient for the majority of most deployment needs.

Deploying a Setup Project

Fortunately, deploying a setup project is one of the easiest parts of the whole deployment process. To deploy your setup project, you simply transfer the MSI file to the destination machine, and then run it. If the destination machine is in a data center or a DMZ, or you can't get physical console access, installations are typically performed using Terminal Services.

If you have additional tasks to be performed as part of the installation, you can bundle executable files or assemblies with special installer classes embedded in them. With the Custom Actions section of the setup project, you can specify pieces of code that can take care of specialized configuration needed just for your project to run during different portions of the installation. You also don't have to worry about the global assembly cache. You can specify the global assembly cache as a target folder and your code will be registered there without a problem.

Advanced ASP.NET Deployment

So far, this chapter has discussed the various ways in which you can get the files that belong to your website onto a production server or some other deployment destination. The next section of the chapter focuses on more advanced and difficult concerns with deployment, such as deploying to web farms, deploying to secure environments, and deploying to limited environments such as public web hosts.

Web Farm Considerations

In Chapter 25, "Advanced ASP.NET," you saw how to design, architect, and code your web applications so that they can take advantage of the scalability, reliability, and availability that are provided by the use of web farms.

Before .NET, deploying applications to web farms could be unbelievably complex and very painful. Imagine trying to make sure that every GUID for every COM object on every server in a 10-server farm was the appropriate value, that every version matched, and that all the ASP files were synchronized.

It might not be that difficult now, but it's not an automatic thing, either. When deploying to a web farm, if you can't afford the downtime involved in bringing down the entire farm, you need to figure out a strategy for leaving the old version of the site up and running on other servers while you upgrade each box. This could pose a problem because if the new version of your application makes changes to the database, you obviously can't make changes to the same database—doing so would break the old application while upgrading the new one.

That is just one example of the many things that you must be concerned with when deploying an upgrade or an installation to a web farm when availability is critical. As mentioned in Chapter 25, configuration issues must be taken care of, such as various `Web.config` settings, and you also have to make sure that application IDs within the IIS metabase are synchronized or ASP.NET won't work properly within the context of a farm.

Other deployment issues center around dependencies such as files on disk. What if your application requires that various resource files be available for download by the users of the application? Do you deploy all of those files to another server that acts as a singleton file server and is not part of the farm? Or do you deploy the files redundantly to all the servers and make sure that you have some method for resolving the local pathnames? There is no one right answer because the solution varies depending on the problem. This chapter can't give you the solution to your web farm deployment issues, but it can give you a list of some of the issues that you will need to address when deploying to a farm.

TIP
Make sure that you know whether your application will be running on a farm before you've written a single line of code. The deployment environment of an application should be determined in the Analysis and Design phases of a project. Preparing early for a web farm with considerations for session state, application state, and hardware dependencies will save you a lot of trouble when it comes time to deploy.

Firewalls, DMZs, Routers, and Security Constraints

A fairly common joke among developers is that there is an inverse ratio between productivity and security. Most of that is a joke...most of it. It wouldn't be funny if there wasn't some truth behind it. When you deploy your application into a secure environment, a myriad of things must be considered and properly configured for your application to work.

In a typical secure environment, the production web application is in a *DMZ* (*demilitarized zone*; an IT term for the barrier zone between your secure network and the Internet). Connections to the secure network behind your firewall(s) where the databases live can be limited. Some networks actually limit the number of open connections, and others restrict the available ports. Either way, you'll need to work it out with your infrastructure folks to enable the appropriate ports for your data access calls (for example, SQL Server's default instance starts at port 1650, but you can configure it to listen on any port).

You have connections that go from your DMZ to your secure network, allowing your public-facing application to access secure data behind the corporate firewall. What if you need data from another source? What if your application actually is a web service consumer and you need to establish connections to other websites for some or all of your back-end data? If you don't tell the infrastructure and security people about that need, your application probably won't work. In most cases, applications on boxes in the DMZ are forbidden direct Internet access, and have to use virtual IP addresses that allow them access to a specific host on the Internet. Without that virtual IP in the DMZ allowing your application to communicate with the outside world, your web service and any other connection will fail.

Many people fail to see the importance of taking all of this into consideration, and those same people end up with chronic headaches and spend far too many weekends in the office putting out fires. When you build your applications, you need to make sure that you are *designing for deployment*. Don't simply build your application so that it compiles and don't be satisfied that your application works on your nice, clean development machine. You need to build your application with deployment in mind. Before you write a single line of code in your ASP.NET application, you should know the answer to every one of the following questions:

▶ Where will my application be deployed? To a data center, a third-party host, a server under my control, or a server from another department?

▶ How will my application be deployed? Does it qualify for XCopy deployment or will I have to create a web setup project?

▶ What external dependencies does my application have? What does it need to access from the operating system and from the client (via cookies, session, and so on). What does it need from the outside world? Does it consume web services outside my network? Does it make other proprietary network connections outside my network?

▶ How will my application communicate with the database? Can that communication type be supported in a secure production environment through firewalls and still work properly and efficiently?

Advanced ASP.NET Deployment

26

▶ How big is my application? What kind of disk storage will I need for the application? Will consumers of the application be using up a lot of bandwidth in doing so? If so, can I afford the cost of that bandwidth?

▶ How important is privacy to my application? Will I need SSL support from the operating system and from the networking infrastructure? Will I need the ability to encrypt and decrypt on the fly?

▶ How scalable must the application be? Will I need a farm? If so, how many servers do I need and what are my maintenance plans, deployment plans, and failover contingency plans?

VISUAL STUDIO .NET 2005

Visual Studio .NET 2005 will address much of what is being discussed here. In several different versions of this package that will be available, there is a design tool (formerly codenamed *Whitehorse*) that enables the developer to draw a conceptual structure diagram of an application, including all connectivity to both internal and external sources. IT personnel can then draw the physical layout of a data center, describing the machines, their connectivity, and their restrictions in great detail. Finally, the developer can then drag assets from the application layout diagram onto the data center diagram to illustrate the deployment plan. After the deployment plan has been created, the user of this tool can then simply click a button to validate. The validation process compares the needs of the application with the restrictions of the data center and the location of everything and will tell you, before you have written a single line of code, whether that deployment plan will work.

By the time this book comes out, the beta of Visual Studio Team System will more than likely already be available for download by MSDN subscribers and might even be a public beta. If you have access to it, you should definitely get a copy of it, and give a demonstration of that feature to your IT/infrastructure team. D*esigning for deployment* is an absolute life-saver for complex applications in secure environments.

Hosted Environment Considerations

A *hosted environment* is a third-party company, such as Brinkster, Mavweb, or any of thousands of others that provides hosting services for your application.

These hosting companies maintain their own Internet presence, their own data center, their own bandwidth, and their own servers. In exchange for a monthly fee, they allow you to rent space on their servers in which your application can run. Because of the incredible acceptance rate of the .NET Framework, it is actually becoming pretty difficult to find a hosting company that doesn't provide at least one option in which it hosts ASP.NET applications.

There are a number of benefits to these systems. The foremost benefit is cost savings. You don't have to own your own server or run your own data center or pay for your own bandwidth if you are using an external host. The hosting company takes care of everything. The hosting company might charge you extra for additional bandwidth, but you don't actually have to have a T1 or a T3 running through the back door of your house to host your application.

You need to be concerned with a number of things when you use an external host. These issues are related to the fact that not everything is under your control, and external hosts have restrictions and rules by which your applications must abide.

One of those restrictions is data access. Most hosting companies provide the capability for your application to read and write to the disk, so you can use XML and Access databases fairly easily. Others allow you to pay extra for SQL data access, but have disk space limitations.

You also should be aware of other limitations to third-party hosting, such as limited authentication methods. To provide hosting services to a large number of applications, some hosting companies disable the ability to set the authentication mode in the web.config file to keep people from tampering. Add to that the fact that most hosting sites limit things such as disk space, network access, operating system privileges, bandwidth, and more, and you will quickly realize that certain applications just can't be affordably hosted by third-party hosting companies.

If you plan to release a large commercial application, you probably are not going to want to make use of an external host. However, if your application is small or has limited needs, you can create an affordable presence on the web with all the speed, reliability, and productivity inherent in ASP.NET and the .NET Framework.

Summary

This chapter might have been a little light on the code, but that is actually a good thing. The main thing to take away from this chapter is that deployment should be something that you not only consider, but plan for well in advance of actually writing any code.

Designing for the purpose of deployment is something that should be part of every application's design process. Even though ASP.NET applications are much easier to deploy than their predecessors, the environments into which those applications are being deployed are becoming more and more complex with increasing restrictions and requirements. After reading this chapter, you not only have some idea of how you can deploy your applications, but also a more thorough understanding of all the issues surrounding deployment in general.

Further Reading

Deploying .NET Applications, by Microsoft Corporation, Microsoft Press. ISBN: 0735618461.

Part V

Data Access

CHAPTER 27   Using .NET Data Providers

CHAPTER 28   Creating a Custom ADO.NET Data Provider

CHAPTER 29   Typed DataSets and XSD

CHAPTER 30   Windows Forms Data Binding

CHAPTER 31   Web Forms Data Binding

27

Using .NET Data Providers

IN BRIEF

This chapter will show you how to use the various data providers that ship with the .NET Framework, as well as mention some alternative data providers that are available. A *data provider* is a collection of classes that provides programmatic access to some source of data. That data source could be a flat file on a disk, an MS Access database, an Excel spreadsheet, an Oracle server, SQL Server, or virtually any other data source on the market.

You will see how the SQL and OLEDB data providers work, as well as how to attach a DataSet to a data provider for automatic propagation of changes to the DataSet to the data source. By the end of this chapter, you will have a firm grasp on the concept of a data provider, how to use data providers, and how to use a data provider in combination with a DataSet for dynamic binding and updating.

WHAT YOU NEED

REQUIRED SOFTWARE	.NET Framework SDK v1.1 Visual Studio .NET 2003 with C# installed SQL 2000 Sample DB and/or MS Access sample DB
RECOMMENDED HARDWARE SKILLS REQUIRED	PC that meets .NET SDK minimum requirements C# and .NET familiarity

USING .NET DATA PROVIDERS AT A GLANCE

SQL Server Data Provider   **537**

Introduction to the SQL Server Data Provider	537	The SqlCommand Class — 540
Using the SqlConnection Class	537	The SqlDataReader Class — 542
Using Database Connection Strings with a SqlConnection	539	The SqlDataAdapter Class — 542

Working with the OLEDB Data Provider   **544**

Overview of the OLEDB Data Provider	545	Using the OleDbDataReader — 546
Using the OleDbConnection	545	Using the OleDbDataAdapter — 546
Using the OleDbCommand	545	

Additional Data Providers   **547**

The Oracle .NET Data Provider (ODP.NET)	547	The .NET ODBC Data Provider — 548
The Microsoft .NET Data Provider for Oracle	547	The mySQL .NET Data Provider — 548

USING .NET DATA PROVIDERS AT A GLANCE

`DataSet` **and** `DataAdapter`
Binding   **548**

    `DataSet` Review   548

    Associating a `DataSet` with a

    `DataAdapter`   549

Sample: Hooking Up a `DataSet` to a Live Data
Source   549

Summary   **552**

Further Reading   **552**

27

SQL Server Data Provider

This section will show you how to use the SQL Server Data Provider, including all the classes that are part of it.

Introduction to the SQL Server Data Provider

The SQL Server Data Provider is a set of classes that enable you to access data and metadata within an instance of SQL Server. All operations require an open connection to the database. After you have established a connection, you can perform various operations such as executing stored procedures and retrieving rows of data. The following is a description of each of the classes that make up the SQL Server Data Provider.

Using the `SqlConnection` Class

As with all data sources that require an active connection, the connection is the heart of the provider. You cannot get data from or send data to the database without an open, functioning connection. In the case of SQL Server, the connection is a network connection (can be sockets or named pipes) between the client application and the database server.

TIP

When working with connections, the most important thing to remember is that when the connection goes out of scope, *it will not be closed.* You must close or dispose of the connection manually when you are done with it; you cannot rely on the garbage collector to properly release the resources associated with the connection.

The basic flow for interacting with the database is as follows:

- Create an instance of `SqlConnection`
- Set the connection string and other properties (such as timeout, and so on)

SQL Server Data Provider

- ▶ Open the connection
- ▶ Perform the data operations
- ▶ Close the connection—this is extremely important!

Table 27.1 is a list of the properties available on the `SqlConnection` class.

TABLE 27.1

`SqlConnection` **Properties**

Property	Description
ConnectionString	The connection string used to connect to the SQL database
ConnectionTimeout	The maximum elapsed time that can occur while attempting to connect before throwing an exception
Database	The name of the database to which the connection has been attached
DataSource	The name of the SQL Server instance to which to connect
PacketSize	The size in bytes of the network packets used for transmission of data to and from SQL Server
ServerVersion	A string that indicates the version of the server to which the instance is connected
State	The current state of the connection (Open, Closed, Closing, and so on)
WorkstationId	The ID of the client as it will appear in the list of clients connected to SQL Server; useful for troubleshooting during development

Table 27.2 is a list of some of the more commonly used methods provided by the `SqlConnection` class. For a more complete reference, consult your MSDN documentation.

TABLE 27.2

`SqlConnection` **Methods**

Method	Description
BeginTransaction	Starts a new database transaction (not to be confused with DTS/COM+ transactions).
ChangeDatabase	Switches the active connection to the indicated database. All other connection properties remain the same.
Close	Closes the database connection and allows the resources to be freed.
CreateCommand	Creates a new `SqlCommand` instance that is pre-associated with this connection. `SqlCommand` will be discussed shortly.
Dispose	Disposes the current connection.
Open	Opens the database connection.

In addition to the properties and methods in the preceding tables, you can also consume the following events that are provided by the `SqlConnection` class:

- ▶ `Disposed`

- ▶ `InfoMessage`—This event is fired when SQL Server returns a warning or other informational message.

- ▶ `StateChange`— This event is fired whenever the connection state changes.

Using Database Connection Strings with a `SqlConnection`

Perhaps one of the most important properties of any database connection class is the connection string. The *connection string* tells the client API the server or file to connect to; it also provides information on security and the method of connection. The connection string for SQL Server is a semicolon-delimited list of key-value pairs. Each key and value are separated by an equal (=) sign, and extraneous whitespace is ignored. Table 27.3 is a list of some of the parameters that you can supply to the connection string property. Also note that you can supply the connection string in the `SqlConnection` class's constructor.

TABLE 27.3

Connection String Parameters

Parameter	Description
`Application Name`	The name of the client application. If this is not specified, ' .Net SqlClient Data Provider' will be used. This can be used to distinguish one application from another when examining usage on the SQL Server instance.
`Connect Timeout` or `Connection Timeout`	The maximum time in seconds that can elapse before the connection is established without throwing an exception.
`Current Language`	The current SQL Server language.
`Data Source` or `Server` or `Address` or `Addr` or `Network Address`	The machine name, alias, or network address of the SQL Server nstance. Note that if you are connecting to a nondefault instance name, you must specify the instance name preceded by a ibackslash; for example, `MyServer\TestInstance`.
`Encrypt`	Whether to use SSL encryption between the client and the server. Incurs a hefty performance cost and is rarely needed.
`Initial Catalog` or `Database`	The name of the database to which to connect.
`Integrated Security` or `Trusted Connection`	Whether to use Windows credentials (true, yes, or *sspi*) or to use credentials supplied in the connection string (false). The default is false.
`Network Library`	Specifies which communications method to use to connect to the database. Some of the valid options are as follows:

27

SQL Server Data Provider

TABLE 27.3

Continued

dbnmpntw—Named pipes dbmsrpcn—Multiprotocol dbmslpcn—Shared memory dbmsspxn—IPX/SPX dbmssocn—TCP/IP	If you are using a server on localhost and don't specify a library, shared memory will be used.
Password	Password of the user authenticating against the database.
User ID	User ID of the user authenticating against the database.
Workstation ID	The name of the PC connecting to the server.
Pooling	Whether SQL connections should be pooled for better performance in enterprise scenarios.
Min Pool Size	The minimum size of the connection pool.
Max Pool Size	The maximum size of the connection pool.
Enlist	When this value is true, the connection is automatically enlisted in the current thread's transaction (if applicable).
Connection Reset	Whether the connection state will be reset when retrieving it from the connection pool. The default is true.
Connection Lifetime	How long a pooled connection will remain in the pool. If set to 0 (the default), it will have the maximum allowable timeout period.

The SqlCommand Class

The SqlCommand class is responsible for actually performing the operations against the database, whether you are executing a stored procedure or issuing TSQL commands such as SELECT and UPDATE directly to the database. Rather than start you off with a boring table of properties and methods, take a look at how to use the SqlCommand class in Listing 27.1.

LISTING 27.1
A Sample Use of the SqlCommand Instance

```
using System;
using System.Data;
using System.Data.SqlClient;

namespace SqlClient
{
class Class1
{
  /// <summary>
  /// The main entry point for the application.
  /// </summary>
  [STAThread]
```

LISTING 27.1
Continued

```
static void Main(string[] args)
{
  SqlConnection conn = new SqlConnection(
    "Server=localhost; Initial Catalog=Northwind; User ID=sa; Password=password;");
  conn.Open();

  // get the history for customer ALFKI
  SqlCommand cmd = conn.CreateCommand();
  cmd.CommandText = "CustOrderHist";
  cmd.CommandType = CommandType.StoredProcedure;
  cmd.Parameters.Add( new SqlParameter("@CustomerID", SqlDbType.VarChar, 5 ) );
  cmd.Parameters[0].Value = "ALFKI";
  SqlDataReader dr = cmd.ExecuteReader();
  Console.WriteLine(
    "Order History for ALFKI\nItem\t\tTotal\n-----------------------------------");
  while (dr.Read())
  {
    Console.WriteLine("{0}\t\t{1}",
      dr.GetString(0), dr.GetInt32(1));
  }
  // never leave a connection or reader open!
  dr.Close();
  conn.Close();
  Console.ReadLine();
  }
 }
}
```

There are two different types of commands that you will be primarily concerned with when working with the SQL data provider: Text and StoredProcedure. Listing 27.1 executes one of the stored procedures that come with the Northwind sample database on SQL Server 2000. After creating an instance of the command, a parameter is set up and its value is set. It is worth pointing out that you can use parameters with Text commands just as easily as you can with StoredProcedure commands, so long as you format your text properly. After the command has been set up, all you need to do is execute it and the database will perform the requested operation. The preceding sample executes the CustOrderHist stored procedure. The code also introduces a SqlDataReader, which will be covered in an upcoming section.

Commands can have input parameters, output parameters, or parameters that go in both directions. After the command has executed, you can examine the value of the

Value property of a given parameter to see the output. Similarly, before the execution of a command, you can set the Value property of a parameter to supply input to the command.

A command can be executed using any of the following methods:

- ExecuteNonQuery—This method will execute a command and return only the number of rows affected. Output parameters will be populated.

- ExecuteScalar—This method will execute a command and return the first column of the first row in the resulting output.

- ExecuteReader—This method will execute a command and return the output in the form of a DataReader that runs against the result set returned from the command.

The SqlDataReader Class

The SqlDataReader class implements a forward-only, read-only cursor-style model for reading and traversing result sets returned from SQL Server. As you saw in the previous sample, you can get a SqlDataReader by calling ExecuteReader on a SqlCommand instance.

The SqlDataReader advances from one record to the next via the Boolean method, Read. If Read returns false, there is no more data left to read. Table 27.4 is a list of the properties exposed by the SqlDataReader.

TABLE 27.4

Properties Exposed by SqlDataReader

Property	Description
Depth	Indicates how deeply nested the current row is within multiple row sets.
FieldCount	Gets the number of columns in the current row.
HasRows	Indicates whether the reader contains rows.
IsClosed	Indicates whether the reader is currently closed.
Item	This is the indexer property in C#, exposed as Item for other languages. This gets the value of a column in its original data type format.
RecordsAffected	Indicates the number of records affected by the execution of the command that generated the reader.

The SqlDataAdapter Class

Data adapters are classes that provide the "glue" that attaches DataSets and DataTables to the data source. I like to think of them using an analogy of an electrical adapter. On the small side of the adapter is the DataSet. On the big side are for plugs for attaching to the database, a `Select` command, an `Insert` command, an `Update` command, and a `Delete` command. Figure 27.1 contains an illustration of this principle.

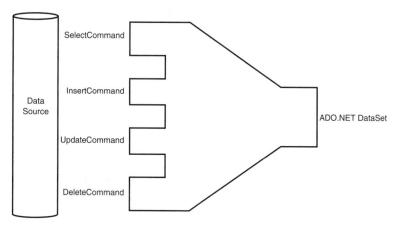

FIGURE 27.1 A data adapter is a plug between a DataSet and a data source.

The code in Listing 27.2 shows how to take an existing `SqlCommand` and use it to store data in a `DataSet`. To do this, we'll modify the code from Listing 27.1 slightly.

LISTING 27.2

Using a `SqlCommand` and a `SqlDataAdapter` to Populate a `DataSet`

```
using System;
using System.Data;
using System.Data.SqlClient;

namespace SqlClient
{
  class Class1
  {
    /// <summary>
    /// The main entry point for the application.
    /// </summary>
    [STAThread]
    static void Main(string[] args)
    {
      SqlConnection conn = new SqlConnection(
        "Server=localhost; Initial Catalog=Northwind; User ID=sa; Password=password;");
      conn.Open();

      // get the history for customer ALFKI
```

SQL Server Data Provider

LISTING 27.2
Continued

```
SqlCommand cmd = conn.CreateCommand();
cmd.CommandText = "CustOrderHist";
cmd.CommandType = CommandType.StoredProcedure;
cmd.Parameters.Add( new SqlParameter("@CustomerID", SqlDbType.VarChar, 5 ) );
cmd.Parameters[0].Value = "ALFKI";
DataSet ds = new DataSet();
SqlDataAdapter da = new SqlDataAdapter( cmd );
da.Fill(ds);
Console.WriteLine(
  "Order History for ALFKI\nItem\t\tTotal\n------------------------------------");
foreach (DataRow row in ds.Tables[0].Rows)
{
  Console.WriteLine("{0}\t\t{1}", row["ProductName"], row["Total"]);
}
// never leave a connection or reader open!
conn.Close();
Console.ReadLine();
  }
 }
}
```

In Listing 27.2, the code re-used the same command from the previous sample. Instead of using it to create a `SqlDataReader`, the command was passed as the constructor argument to the `SqlDataAdapter`. The `SqlDataAdapter` takes the `SelectCommand` as an argument. The `SelectCommand` is one of the four command instances that the `SqlDataAdapter` maintains. Whenever the adapter needs to query data from the data source, it does so using the `SqlCommand` instance in the `SelectCommand` property.

In this sample the code used the `Fill` method, which takes information returned from the `SelectCommand` and places it in a `DataSet` (or a single `DataTable`, depending on the arguments you supply for the method). You will see some of the other methods of the `DataReader` later in the chapter.

Working with the OLEDB Data Provider

This next section gives you a brief introduction to using the OLEDB data provider. One of the main goals of data providers is to provide a standardized, unified method of access to differing types of data. As a result, the way you use the OLEDB data provider is extremely similar to the way in which you use any other valid data provider for the .NET Framework. As a result, this section focuses mainly on the differences between the two providers, rather than how they are alike.

Overview of the OLEDB Data Provider

The OLEDB provider is a set of classes that provides a managed wrapper around an OLEDB data source. Unlike the SQL Server Data Provider, which only connects to a single type of server, the OLEDB provider can connect to any OLEDB data source. These data sources can include everything from Microsoft Access databases, to MS Office documents such as Excel, and even SQL Server using the OLEDB drivers. As a result, some functionality that is exposed by the provider might not be available depending on the type of data source being used, and some functionality may behave differently. For a complete list of what functionality is and is not available for a particular OLEDB data source, consult the manufacturer's documentation for its OLEDB driver.

Using the `OleDbConnection`

`OleDbConnection` provides a connection to a data source that is exposed through an OLE DB server. OLE (Object Linking and Embedding) is the pre-cursor to COM and OLEDB data sources are exposed through a standardized set of binary interfaces. Any server that implements these interfaces can expose its data to OLEDB, making a large number of varying and diverse types of data available to the same client API.

The connection string is the key property of the `OleDbConnection` class. Like the SQL connection string, it is divided into name-value pairs that are separated by semi-colons. The most important name-value pair is the keyword `Provider`. This defines the type of OLEDB data source to which the class instance will be connecting. The `Data Source` parameter defines the source of that data. For some providers, this indicates a filename, whereas other providers use this parameter to specify a server name or network address.

Using the `OleDbCommand`

The `OleDbCommand` class works in an almost identical fashion to that of the `SqlCommand` class, except that the underlying data source is an OLEDB provider instead of SQL Server. It enables you to execute stored procedures (if the underlying provider supports it) or execute SQL-syntax queries. Parameters can also be input or output, just as with the SQL command class.

The tricky part about the OLEDB command is that, even though the API is the same regardless of the underlying OLEDB provider, not all providers support stored procedures. So, if you attempt to execute a stored procedure using one of those OLEDB providers, you will get an exception.

27

Working with the OLEDB Data Provider

Using the `OleDbDataReader`

The `OleDbDataReader` is a class that provides a read-only, forward-only cursor model for traversing data that was returned as a result from an `OleDbCommand`. If you know how to use one provider's data reader, you should have no trouble using a data reader for a different provider. The `OleDbDataReader` list of exposed methods and properties doesn't differ from that of the SQL data reader.

Using the `OleDbDataAdapter`

The `OleDbDataAdapter` is, just like all other data adapters, designed to *adapt* data between the original data source and a `DataSet` or `DataTable`. Using the `Fill` and `Update` methods, you can establish a bi-directional, dynamic binding that was never possible using any of ADO.NET's ADO predecessors. You will see how to accomplish this later in the chapter. Take a look at the code in Listing 27.3 illustrating the use of the Microsoft Access OLEDB provider.

LISTING 27.3
A Sample Use of an OLEDB Provider to Query an Access Database

```csharp
using System;
using System.Data;
using System.Data.OleDb;

namespace OleDbClient
{
  class Class1
  {
    /// <summary>
    /// The main entry point for the application.
    /// </summary>
    [STAThread]
    static void Main(string[] args)
    {
      OleDbConnection conn = new OleDbConnection(
        @"Provider=Microsoft.JET.OLEDB.4.0;Data Source=..\..\testdatabase.mdb");
      conn.Open();

      OleDbCommand cmd = conn.CreateCommand();
      cmd.CommandText = "SELECT * FROM SampleTable ORDER BY Description";
      cmd.CommandType = CommandType.Text;

      // store in a DataSet
      DataSet ds = new DataSet();
      OleDbDataAdapter da = new OleDbDataAdapter( cmd );
      da.Fill(ds);
```

27

LISTING 27.3
Continued

```
    foreach (DataRow row in ds.Tables[0].Rows)
    {
      Console.WriteLine("{0}\t{1}", row["ID"], row["Description"]);
    }
    cmd.Dispose();
    conn.Close();
    Console.ReadLine();
  }
 }
}
```

27

Additional Data Providers

There are more data providers than just the two just covered. The beauty of the data provider system is that the interfaces required to implement a data provider are part of the .NET Framework itself. This means that any vendor that wants to create a managed wrapper around their own data source can do so quickly and easily using the established interfaces and guidelines for data access. As a result, many different providers have popped up and more are appearing every day.

The Oracle .NET Data Provider (ODP.NET)

Oracle has created its own managed provider that exposes all the Oracle client functionality that you might expect, as well as some extra bonuses such as the ability to use cursors as parameters to stored procedures and much more. The benefit of having a managed provider developed directly by the product vendor is that, in general, you get a richer API with more functionality and possibly better performance. In most cases, there hasn't been much visible difference in speed between Oracle's data provider and Microsoft's data provider for Oracle. Both of those managed providers make use of OCI (Oracle Call Interface), the low-level C-based API that allows for the fastest consumption of Oracle features. The main difference between the two providers is in the depth of their functionality.

The Microsoft .NET Data Provider for Oracle

With the release of version 1.1 of the .NET Framework, programmers are now able to reference `System.Data.OracleClient.dll`, Microsoft's own OCI client implemented as a managed provider for .NET. This provider gives you access to a host of features such as transactions, CLOBS, BLOBS, and many more. As mentioned earlier, it is up to you whether you choose Oracle's provider or Microsoft's provider. They are functionally quite similar, so it probably boils down to choosing the support you want: Oracle's or Microsoft's.

The .NET ODBC Data Provider

The ODBC data provider is a wrapper for the older database connectivity standard ODBC (Object Database Connectivity). The ODBC provider used to be an optional download, but it is now included with the 1.1 version of the .NET Framework. The only real guideline for using ODBC is that you should use it as a last resort. If there is any other way to get at your data, you should use that. If you can use OLEDB, SQL, Oracle, or even XML, you should use one of those methods in favor of the older, slower, and less reliable standard. Most companies no longer provide updated ODBC drivers, so you might be putting your code at risk by relying on ODBC. However, for backward compatibility and for getting at outdated sources of data, the ODBC provider is available if you need it. It implements all the appropriate provider interfaces so it should be very easy to pick up and use.

The mySQL .NET Data Provider

mySQL is a popular (free) database that is used on Unix and Windows systems alike. It is an extremely powerful, fast alternative to some of the bigger commercial databases, such as Microsoft SQL Server and Oracle.

Several different managed providers allow managed access to mySQL from the .NET Framework, including some commercial projects and a free provider found on SourceForge. A project on SourceForge.net, formerly referred to as ByteFX.Data, has been merged with the mySQL project and is now the official managed client provider for mySQL. You can find updates on this project on the mysql.com website. You can keep up to date on the latest news from the SourceForge.net site at sourceforge.net/projects/mysqlnet/.

DataSet and DataAdapter Binding

One of the most powerful features of ADO.NET and managed data providers is that any managed provider that implements a DataAdapter is fully, and automatically, compatible with the DataSet. In this next section, you will see how to configure a DataAdapter in such a way that you can push changes made in the DataSet to the original data source in a seamless, integrated, and almost invisible fashion.

DataSet Review

As you probably know by now, a DataSet is an in-memory representation of a table and column structure. Tables within a DataSet can be related to each other through relationships that establish parent/child relationships, and tables in a DataSet support the notion of primary and foreign keys. They are essentially a miniature, in-memory database. You have no doubt seen the DataSet used throughout this book and you will see it again. Rather than devote a single chapter to the DataSet, what we've done is simply use the DataSet whenever it was appropriate to accomplish a task—something that you will more than likely do for your own projects.

Associating a DataSet with a DataAdapter

As you have seen, the DataAdapter has the capability to store four different database commands: SelectCommand, UpdateCommand, DeleteCommand, and InsertCommand. On their own they are just simple commands that don't do anything more than a standard database command. However, when placed on the DataAdapter class, they can perform some very powerful tasks. When a DataAdapter has these four commands configured, it can examine a DataSet for recent changes and commit them to the database.

The DataAdapter essentially looks at all the rows in the DataSet. For each row that has been inserted, the InsertCommand will be invoked. For each row that has been updated, the UpdateCommand will be invoked. As you've probably guessed, for each row that has been deleted, the DeleteCommand will be invoked.

Sample: Hooking Up a DataSet to a Live Data Source

This next example illustrates how to create the four commands required by a DataAdapter and how to make changes on the DataSet that will be propagated to the original data source via the adapter. The code in Listing 27.4 shows the sample that illustrates this ability to link a DataSet with a DataAdapter.

LISTING 27.4

A Demonstration of Linking a DataSet and DataAdapter Using SQL Server and the Northwind Database

```
using System;
using System.Data;
using System.Data.SqlClient;

namespace DataAdapterBinding
{
class Class1
{
  [STAThread]
  static void Main(string[] args)
  {
    SqlConnection conn = new SqlConnection(
      "server=localhost; User ID=sa; Password=password; Initial Catalog=Northwind;");
```

DataSet **and** DataAdapter **Binding**

LISTING 27.4
Continued

```
conn.Open();

SqlCommand selectCommand = conn.CreateCommand();
selectCommand.CommandText =
  "SELECT CustomerID, CompanyName, ContactName, ContactTitle FROM Customers";
selectCommand.CommandType = CommandType.Text;

// update command
SqlCommand updateCommand = conn.CreateCommand();
updateCommand.CommandText =
  "UPDATE Customers SET CompanyName = @CompanyName, @ContactName = ContactName, " +
  "ContactTitle = @ContactTitle WHERE CustomerID = @CustomerID";
updateCommand.Parameters.Add(
  new SqlParameter("@CompanyName", SqlDbType.NVarChar,40, "CompanyName"));
updateCommand.Parameters.Add(
  new SqlParameter("@ContactName", SqlDbType.NVarChar, 30, "ContactName"));
updateCommand.Parameters.Add(
  new SqlParameter("@ContactTitle", SqlDbType.NVarChar, 30, "ContactTitle"));
updateCommand.Parameters.Add(
  new SqlParameter("@CustomerID", SqlDbType.NChar, 5, "CustomerID"));

// insert command
SqlCommand insertCommand = conn.CreateCommand();
insertCommand.CommandType = CommandType.Text;
insertCommand.CommandText =
  "INSERT INTO Customers(CustomerID,CompanyName, ContactName, " +
  "ContactTitle) VALUES(@CustomerID, @CompanyName, @ContactName, @ContactTitle)";
insertCommand.Parameters.Add(
  new SqlParameter("@CompanyName", SqlDbType.NVarChar,40, "CompanyName"));
insertCommand.Parameters.Add(
  new SqlParameter("@ContactName", SqlDbType.NVarChar, 30, "ContactName"));
insertCommand.Parameters.Add(
  new SqlParameter("@ContactTitle", SqlDbType.NVarChar, 30, "ContactTitle"));
insertCommand.Parameters.Add(
  new SqlParameter("@CustomerID", SqlDbType.NChar, 5, "CustomerID"));

// delete command
SqlCommand deleteCommand = conn.CreateCommand();
deleteCommand.CommandText = "DELETE Customers WHERE CustomerID = @CustomerID";
deleteCommand.Parameters.Add(
```

LISTING 27.4
Continued

```
new SqlParameter("@CustomerID", SqlDbType.NChar, 5, "CustomerID"));


SqlDataAdapter da = new SqlDataAdapter( selectCommand );
da.UpdateCommand = updateCommand;
da.InsertCommand = insertCommand;
da.DeleteCommand = deleteCommand;

DataSet ds = new DataSet();
da.Fill(ds);

// this will cause an update
ds.Tables[0].Rows[0]["CompanyName"] = "Modified";

// this will cause an insert
DataRow newrow = ds.Tables[0].NewRow();
newrow["CustomerID"] = "KEVCO";
newrow["CompanyName"] = "KevCorp Inc Limited";
newrow["ContactName"] = "Kevin Hoffman";
newrow["ContactTitle"] = "Owner";
ds.Tables[0].Rows.Add( newrow );


// this will cause a delete
ds.Tables[0].Rows[5].Delete();

// you must call this before trying to perform inserts and deletes
ds.AcceptChanges();

da.Update(ds);
conn.Close();
Console.WriteLine("DB changes committed.");
Console.ReadLine();
  }
 }
}
```

Just to make sure that the changes that we expect to see in the Customers table are actually there, open up Enterprise Manager and look at the table. If everything went well, the first row has been modified and a new row has been created, and one of the customers is missing. Figure 27.2 shows this screenshot from SQL Enterprise Manager.

DataSet and **DataAdapter** **Binding**

CustomerID	CompanyName	ContactName	ContactTitle	Address	City	Region	PostalCode	Country	Phone
ALFKI	Modified	Maria Anders	Sales Representati	Obere Str. 57	Berlin	<NULL>	12209	Germany	030-0074321
ANATR	Ana Trujillo Empare	Ana Trujillo	Owner	Avda. de la Constit	México D.F.	<NULL>	05021	Mexico	(5) 555-4729
ANTON	Antonio Moreno Ta	Antonio Moreno	Owner	Mataderos 2312	México D.F.	<NULL>	05023	Mexico	(5) 555-3932
AROUT	Around the Horn	Thomas Hardy	Sales Representati	120 Hanover Sq.	London	<NULL>	WA1 1DP	UK	(171) 555-778
BERGS	Berglunds snabbköp	Christina Berglund	Order Administrato	Berguvsvägen 8	Luleå	<NULL>	S-958 22	Sweden	0921-12 34 65
BLAUS	Blauer See Delikate	Hanna Moos	Sales Representati	Forsterstr. 57	Mannheim	<NULL>	68306	Germany	0621-08460
BLONP	Blondesddsl père e	Frédérique Citeaux	Marketing Manager	24, place Kléber	Strasbourg	<NULL>	67000	France	88.60. 15.31
BOLID	Bólido Comidas prep	Martín Sommer	Owner	C/ Araquil, 67	Madrid	<NULL>	28023	Spain	(91) 555 22 82
BONAP	Bon app'	Laurence Lebihan	Owner	12, rue des Bouche	Marseille	<NULL>	13008	France	91.24.45.40
BOTTM	Bottom-Dollar Mark	Elizabeth Lincoln	Accounting Manage	23 Tsawassen Blvd	Tsawassen	BC	T2F 8M4	Canada	(604) 555-472
BSBEV	B's Beverages	Victoria Ashworth	Sales Representati	Fauntleroy Circus	London	<NULL>	EC2 5NT	UK	(171) 555-121
CACTU	Cactus Comidas pa	Patricio Simpson	Sales Agent	Cerrito 333	Buenos Aires	<NULL>	1010	Argentina	(1) 135-5555
CENTC	Centro comercial M	Francisco Chang	Marketing Manager	Sierras de Granada	México D.F.	<NULL>	05022	Mexico	(5) 555-3392
CHOPS	Chop-suey Chinese	Yang Wang	Owner	Hauptstr. 29	Bern	<NULL>	3012	Switzerland	0452-076545
COMMI	Comércio Mineiro	Pedro Afonso	Sales Associate	Av. dos Lusíadas, 2	Sao Paulo	SP	05432-043	Brazil	(11) 555-7647
CONSH	Consolidated Holdir	Elizabeth Brown	Sales Representati	Berkeley Gardens 1	London	<NULL>	WX1 6LT	UK	(171) 555-228
DRACD	Drachenblut Delikat	Sven Ottlieb	Order Administrato	Walserweg 21	Aachen	<NULL>	52066	Germany	0241-039123
DUMON	Du monde entier	Janine Labrune	Owner	67, rue des Cinqua	Nantes	<NULL>	44000	France	40.67.88.88
EASTC	Eastern Connection	Ann Devon	Sales Agent	35 King George	London	<NULL>	WX3 6FW	UK	(171) 555-029
ERNSH	Ernst Handel	Roland Mendel	Sales Manager	Kirchgasse 6	Graz	<NULL>	8010	Austria	7675-3425
FAMIA	Familia Arquibaldo	Aria Cruz	Marketing Assistan	Rua Orós, 92	Sao Paulo	SP	05442-030	Brazil	(11) 555-9857
FISSA	FISSA Fabrica Inter	Diego Roel	Accounting Manage	C/ Moralzarzal, B6	Madrid	<NULL>	28034	Spain	(91) 555 94 44
FOLIG	Folies gourmandes	Martine Rancé	Assistant Sales Age	184, chaussée de T	Lille	<NULL>	59000	France	20.16.10.16
FOLKO	Folk och fä HB	Maria Larsson	Owner	Åkergatan 24	Bräcke	<NULL>	S-844 67	Sweden	0695-34 67 21
FRANK	Frankenversand	Peter Franken	Marketing Manager	Berliner Platz 43	München	<NULL>	80805	Germany	089-0877310
FRANR	France restauration	Carine Schmitt	Marketing Manager	54, rue Royale	Nantes	<NULL>	44000	France	40.32.21.21
FRANS	Franchi S.p.A.	Paolo Accorti	Sales Representati	Via Monte Bianco 3	Torino	<NULL>	10100	Italy	011-4988260
FURIB	Furia Bacalhau e Fr	Lino Rodriguez	Sales Manager	Jardim das rosas n.	Lisboa	<NULL>	1675	Portugal	(1) 354-2534
GALED	Galería del gastróni	Eduardo Saavedra	Marketing Manager	Rambla de Cataluñ	Barcelona	<NULL>	08022	Spain	(93) 203 4560
GODOS	Godos Cocina Típica	José Pedro Freyre	Sales Manager	C/ Romero, 33	Sevilla	<NULL>	41101	Spain	(95) 555 82 82
GOURL	Gourmet Lanchone	André Fonseca	Sales Associate	Av. Brasil, 442	Campinas	SP	04876-786	Brazil	(11) 555-9482
GREAL	Great Lakes Food N	Howard Snyder	Marketing Manager	2732 Baker Blvd.	Eugene	OR	97403	USA	(503) 555-755
GROSR	GROSELLA-Restaur	Manuel Pereira	Owner	5ª Ave. Los Palos G	Caracas	DF	1081	Venezuela	(2) 283-2951
HANAR	Hanari Carnes	Mario Pontes	Accounting Manage	Rua do Paço, 67	Rio de Janeiro	RJ	05454-876	Brazil	(21) 555-0091
HILAA	HILARION-Abastos	Carlos Hernández	Sales Representati	Carrera 22 con Ave	San Cristóbal	Táchira	5022	Venezuela	(5) 555-1340
HUNGC	Hungry Coyote Imp	Yoshi Latimer	Sales Representati	City Center Plaza 5	Elgin	OR	97827	USA	(503) 555-687
HUNGO	Hungry Owl All-Nigh	Patricia McKenna	Sales Associate	8 Johnstown Road	Cork	Co. Cork	<NULL>	Ireland	2967 542
ISLAT	Island Trading	Helen Bennett	Marketing Manager	Garden House Cres	Cowes	Isle of Wight	PO31 7PJ	UK	(198) 555-888
KEYCO	KeyCorp Inc Limited	Kevin Hoffman	Owner	<NULL>	<NULL>	<NULL>	<NULL>	<NULL>	<NULL>

FIGURE 27.2   Customers table after being modified by a DataSet/DataAdapter combination.

Summary

This chapter introduced you to some of the more commonly used managed data providers and how to communicate with the databases. Rather than show you a mountain of code specific to each type of database, the chapter showed you how similar the code is regardless of which database or provider you are accessing. Finally, you saw the power of dynamically connecting a DataSet to a DataAdapter to allow for the automatic propagation of changes made in the DataSet to the database. Having read this chapter, you should be more familiar with ADO.NET in general, as well as the means by which .NET applications access data and how you can use the DataSet as an incredibly powerful intermediary between your user interface (whether it is Windows or Web) and the underlying data source.

Further Reading

www.asp.net

www.gotdotnet.com

Programming Data-Driven Web Applications with ASP.NET by Donny Mack and Doug Seven ("ADO.NET Managed Providers" chapter), Sams Publishing. ISBN: 0672321068.

msdn.microsoft.com/netframework

ADO.NET Cookbook by Bill Hamilton, O'Reilly. ISBN: 0596004397.

27

IN BRIEF

As you saw in the previous chapter, using the ADO.NET data providers gives you a consistent user experience, whether you're connecting to some OLE DB data source, SQL, Oracle, or even an ODBC data source. The goal of the consistent data provider model is that programmers need to learn to use only one set of interfaces, regardless of which database they are accessing.

You've seen it from the consumer point of view, and this chapter will show you ADO.NET data providers from the perspective of the data provider. In this chapter, you will see a lot of code for creating your own custom data provider. In addition to the code for a custom provider, you will also see the details on all the interfaces required to implement a provider, as well as guidelines for when you should and should not implement your own custom provider.

WHAT YOU NEED

REQUIRED SOFTWARE	.NET Framework SDK v1.1
	VSVisual Studio .NET 2003 w/with C# Installedinstalled
RECOMMENDED HARDWARE	PC that meets .NET SDK minimum requirements
SKILLS REQUIRED	C# and .NET Familiarityfamiliarity
	Familiarity with web services (see Chapters 18 and 32)

CREATING A CUSTOM ADO.NET DATA PROVIDER AT A GLANCE

Custom Data Providers   555

When to Create a Data Provider   555

Steps for Implementing a Custom Data Provider   556

Sample Data Provider Scenario   556

Overview of the Remote Data Provider   557

Implementing `IDataParameter` and `IDataParameterCollection`   558

The `IDataParameter` Interface   558

The `IDataParameterCollection` Interface   559

The `RDPParameter` Class   559

The `RDPParameterCollection` Class   563

Implementing a Custom Connection   565

The `IDbConnection` Interface   566

The `RDPConnection` Class   566

Implementing a Custom Command   569

The `IDbCommand` Interface   569

The `RDPCommand` Class   570

Implementing a Custom DataReader   575

The `IDataReader` Interface   575

The `RDPDataReader` Class   576

CREATING A CUSTOM ADO.NET DATA PROVIDER AT A GLANCE

Implementing a Custom DataAdapter	582		
The IDbDataAdapter Interface	582	The RDPDataAdapter Class	582
Summary	587		

Custom Data Providers

A custom data provider, in the context of ADO.NET and the .NET Framework, is a suite of classes that provide programmatic access to some data source using a set of consistent interfaces. The data source can be anything you like. There are custom providers for flat-file databases that have no corresponding ODBC driver, providers for Reflection, and even a provider for MSMQ (Microsoft Message Queuing) data communication.

The point is that, whatever the data source, the interface and API to gain access to that data is consistent between your provider, Microsoft's providers, and any other implemented providers. The next section gives you guidelines to determine when you should create a custom provider, how you should create one, and why you should do so, using a hypothetical scenario as an example.

When to Create a Data Provider

There are plenty of reasons to create a data provider. The first and foremost reason is that your data cannot be accessed via one of the standard access methods:

- ▸ SQL Server (managed ADO.NET provider)
- ▸ OLE DB (managed ADO.NET provider)
- ▸ ODBC (managed ADO.NET provider)
- ▸ XML (standard .NET XML classes)

If your data cannot be accessed by any of the preceding means, you should definitely consider creating your own provider to give consumers of your data a familiar, fast, and consistent interface.

Another situation in which you might need to create your own data provider is when an ADO.NET provider can access your data, but its access isn't native. Creating your own managed provider might give programmers faster and more powerful functionality as well as access to more features of your particular data source.

28

Custom Data Providers

If your data source doesn't make use of things such as connections or transactions, and it is pure data, creating your own provider might be overkill. It might be more work than is necessary and you could be able to accomplish what you need by exposing your data as XML instead of through a custom provider.

Also, if your data source is a fully functional RDBMS that has all the features associated with common database servers such as SQL and Oracle, you might want to consider writing an OLE DB provider and using the .NET managed OLE DB provider to access it. If you think you can create faster access by writing your own provider and bypassing OLE DB, doing so might be your best bet.

Steps for Implementing a Custom Data Provider

Even though it might look like a lot of work, implementing a custom ADO.NET data provider is a very straightforward process. The .NET Framework provides a series of interfaces that you can implement. By creating a library that contains class implementations for those classes, you can create your own custom data provider. You can choose to implement as many or as few of the data provider interfaces as you like, provided you can still provide the appropriate functionality. The interfaces that can be implemented in a custom provider library are as follows:

- IDataParameter

- IDataParameterCollection

- IDbConnection

- IDbCommand

- IDbDataReader

- IDbDataAdapter

As the chapter steps through the process of building a custom provider, you will see each of these interfaces, their intended functionality, and a custom implementation of each interface. Before getting to the code, take a look at the sample scenario for which a data provider will be built.

Sample Data Provider Scenario

As mentioned earlier, you should not create a data provider if your data can be accessed via one of the standard data providers that ships with the .NET Framework or if your data can be exposed and accessed via XML.

The example discussed throughout this chapter creates a custom data provider to solve a unique problem. A fictitious company has decided that it needs to have its applications access data remotely. For some reason (IT security, firewalls, and so on), the ports normally used to transmit SQL data are not available to the client. Also, for various business reasons, the company has decided that the business logic must reside on the client side. Finally, the company must be able to write the client code in such a way that if the data were to become local (instead of remote behind a firewall), the application could be quickly modified to work in that way.

What the client programmers need is an ADO.NET provider that they can use generically via interfaces that will give them firewall-friendly access to a data tier on the other side. For this solution, you are going to create a data provider that works just like any other data provider, but instead of connecting to a database, it will connect to a web service that will blindly forward queries to a secure back-end.

The architecture shown in Figure 28.1 provides a good illustration of the network topology in which this provider will exist.

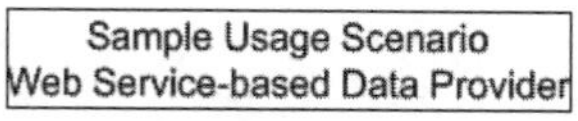

```
┌─────────────────────────────┐
│    Sample Usage Scenario     │
│Web Service-based Data Provider│
└─────────────────────────────┘
```

FIGURE 28.1   Architecture of the sample data provider.

Overview of the Remote Data Provider

The sample architecture you saw in Figure 28.1 provides a good high-level overview of what you're trying to accomplish. On a lower level, the main concept is changing the concept of a connection within the ADO.NET data provider paradigm from a database connection to a web service connection.

When commands are executed against this new custom provider, they will be serialized and then sent to the web service. The data will be returned from the web service, and the data provider clients can do whatever they want with the results, such as open a `DataReader` or fill a `DataSet`, and so forth. Not all the methods that are part of the provider have been implemented, so you will notice that things such as `Fill()` on a `DataSet` are not supported. After you've completed this chapter, it might be a useful exercise to modify this provider to give additional functionality and to support the `DataAdapter`'s `Fill` operation and so on.

The following code is a sample of the code that will be used to access the custom provider:

```
RDPConnection conn =
  new RDPConnection("http://localhost/DataService/DataHost.asmx");
conn.Open();
RDPCommand cmd = conn.CreateCommand();
cmd.CommandText = "SELECT * FROM Customers";
```

Custom Data Providers

```
cmd.CommandType = CommandType.Text;
RDPDataReader reader = cmd.ExecuteReader( CommandBehavior.Default );
while (reader.Read())
{
  Console.WriteLine("{0}\t{1}\t\t\t{2}",
    reader.GetString(0), reader.GetString(1), reader.GetString(2));
}
```

Because this particular provider simply forwards requests to a web service, the client application need not store things such as the SQL Server connection string, passwords, IP addresses for database servers, and so on. All it needs is the URL to the database back-end web service. Figure 28.2 shows the console output of the preceding program (you might recognize the data from the Northwind database).

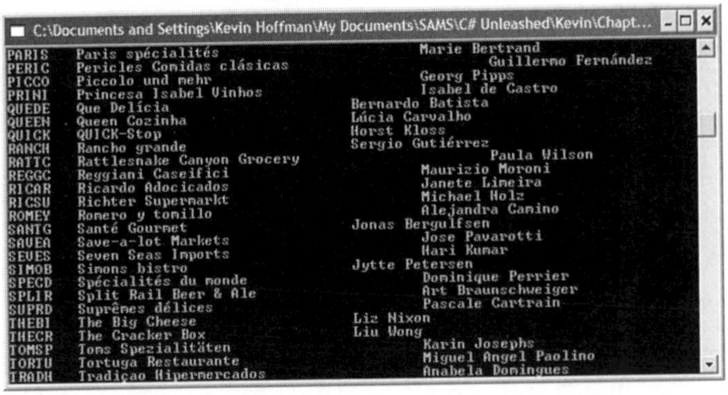

FIGURE 28.2   The sample remote data provider consumer application in action.

Implementing IDataParameter and IDataParameterCollection

The first items to deal with when creating the custom provider are parameters. Parameters are associated with commands and can be input parameters, output parameters, or both. Those parameters are associated with data commands via a customized collection of parameters.

The IDataParameter Interface

The IDataParameter interface is fairly simple. Table 28.1 lists the properties defined by the IDataParameter interface.

TABLE 28.1

`IDataParameter` **Properties**

Property	Description
DbType	Indicates the database type of the parameter. The value is an element of the `DbType` enumeration.
Direction	Indicates whether the parameter is input, output, or both.
IsNullable	Indicates whether the parameter can contain null values.
ParameterName	Indicates the name of the parameter.
SourceColumn	When using a `DataSet` mapping, this property indicates the source column that is mapped to the value of this parameter. Used for row updates and so forth.
SourceVersion	Indicates the `DataRowVersion` when obtaining the value of the parameter.
Value	Contains the actual parameter value.

The `IDataParameterCollection` Interface

The `IDataParameterCollection` isn't much more than a marker interface. It is used to tell the custom provider that the collection of parameters supports a minimal set of collection functionality. Table 28.2 lists the properties and methods defined by the `IDataParameterCollection` interface.

TABLE 28.2

`IDataParameterCollection` **Properties and Methods**

Property or Method	Description
Item	This is the indexer property for the class (appears as the `Item` property in VB .NET).
Contains()	Indicates whether the collection contains the given parameter.
IndexOf()	Returns the index of the supplied parameter.
RemoveAt()	Removes the parameter from the collection at the given index.

The `RDPParameter` Class

Now that you've seen the basic interfaces that will be implemented, take a look at the code. The code in Listing 28.1 shows the `RDPParameter` class. If you really feel like typing this all in (as opposed to copying it from the book's media), create a new C# Class library called `RemoteDataProvider` and add the `RDPParameter` class as shown here.

Implementing `IDataParameter` and `IDataParameterCollection`

LISTING 28.1
The Remote Data Provider Parameter Class

```
using System;
using System.Data;

namespace SAMS.CSharpUnleashed.RemoteDataProvider
{
public class RDPParameter : IDataParameter
{
  private DbType dbType;
  private ParameterDirection direction = ParameterDirection.Input;

  private string paramName;
  private string sourceColumn;
  private object paramValue;
  private DataRowVersion sourceRowVersion = DataRowVersion.Current;

  public RDPParameter()
  {
  }

  public RDPParameter( string parameterName, DbType type)
  {
    paramName = parameterName;
    dbType = type;
  }

  public RDPParameter( string parameterName, object value )
  {
    paramName = parameterName;
    paramValue = value;
  }

  public RDPParameter( string parameterName, DbType type, string sourceColumn )
  {
    paramName = parameterName;
    dbType = type;
    this.sourceColumn = sourceColumn;
  }
  #region IDataParameter Members

  public System.Data.ParameterDirection Direction
  {
```

Implementing `IDataParameter` and `IDataParameterCollection`

LISTING 28.1
Continued

```
    get
    {
      return direction;
    }
    set
    {
      direction = value;
    }
  }

  public System.Data.DbType DbType
  {
    get
    {
      return dbType;
    }
    set
    {
      dbType = value;
    }
  }

  public object Value
  {
    get
    {
      return paramValue;
    }
    set
    {
      paramValue = value;
    }
  }

  public bool IsNullable
  {
    get
    {
      return false;
    }
```

Implementing `IDataParameter` and `IDataParameterCollection`

LISTING 28.1
Continued

```
  }

  public System.Data.DataRowVersion SourceVersion
  {
    get
    {
      return sourceRowVersion;
    }
    set
    {
      sourceRowVersion = value;
    }
  }

  public string ParameterName
  {
    get
    {
      return paramName;
    }
    set
    {
      paramName = value;
    }
  }

  public string SourceColumn
  {
    get
    {
      return sourceColumn;
    }
    set
    {
      sourceColumn = value;
    }
  }

  #endregion
  }
}
```

Implementing `IDataParameter` and `IDataParameterCollection`

You might have noticed that this class isn't doing anything special or unusual. The code just provides a stock implementation of the appropriate interfaces for most of the interfaces discussed in this chapter. There are two reasons for creating the custom implementation: to show you a sample implementation, and so that if you want to customize any of this later, you can simply take the provided implementation and add to it without much effort.

The `RDPParameterCollection` Class

The `RDPParameterCollection` class shown in Listing 28.2 is just as simple as the `RDPParameter` class, if not simpler. It provides a simple `ArrayList` implementation to store the list of `RDPParameter` instances to be used for an `RDPCommand`.

LISTING 28.2
The Remote Data Provider Parameter Collection Class

```
using System;
using System.Data;
using System.Collections;


namespace SAMS.CSharpUnleashed.RemoteDataProvider
{
  public class RDPParameterCollection : ArrayList, IDataParameterCollection
  {
    public RDPParameterCollection() : base()
    {}

    #region IDataParameterCollection Members

    public object this[string parameterName]
    {
      get
      {
        return this[IndexOf(parameterName)];
      }
      set
      {
        this[IndexOf(parameterName)] = value;
      }
    }

    public void RemoveAt(string parameterName)
    {
```

Implementing `IDataParameter` and `IDataParameterCollection`

LISTING 28.2
Continued

```csharp
      RemoveAt(IndexOf(parameterName));
    }

    public bool Contains(string parameterName)
    {
      return ( -1 != IndexOf(parameterName) );
    }

    public int IndexOf(string parameterName)
    {
      int idx = 0;
      foreach (RDPParameter param in this)
      {
        if ( parameterName == param.ParameterName)
          return idx;
        idx ++;
      }
      return -1;
    }

    #endregion

    public override bool IsReadOnly
    {
      get
      {
        return false;
      }
    }

    public override int Add(object value)
    {
      return Add((RDPParameter)value);
    }

    public int Add( RDPParameter value)
    {
      if (value.ParameterName != null)
        return base.Add(value);
      else
```

LISTING 28.2
Continued

```
      throw new ArgumentException("RDP Parameter must have a name");
  }

  public int Add( string parameterName, DbType dbType )
  {
    return Add ( new RDPParameter( parameterName, dbType ) );
  }

  public int Add( string parameterName, object value )
  {
    return Add( new RDPParameter( parameterName, value) );
  }

  public int Add( string parameterName, DbType type, string sourceColumn )
  {
    return Add( new RDPParameter( parameterName, type, sourceColumn ) );
  }


  }
}
```

As you can see, it's a pretty simple class. All it's really doing is providing an implementation of the interface and some strongly typed implementations of the collection methods to make things easy for other programmers to use.

Implementing a Custom Connection

A *connection* is an abstraction of a physical link between the data provider and the source of the data itself. In most cases, that means a network connection between the client application code and the database server code (such as a TCP/IP connection on port 1560 for SQL Server, and the like).

In the case of this sample remote data provider, the connection is an implied or logical connection rather than a physical connection. As you know, HTTP is a stateless protocol. When you request information from a web server, the connection is opened at the time of the request, not ahead of time as with database connections.

For this reason, the connection being implemented is just a storage place for the connection string, and a state machine that indicates whether the connection is open or closed (although it has no real impact).

The `IDbConnection` Interface

The `IDbConnection` interface defines the properties and methods given in Table 28.3.

TABLE 28.3

Properties and Methods of the `IDbConnection` Interface

Property or Method	Description
`ConnectionString`	The connection string used to connect to the database (or web service, in the case of this example).
`ConnectionTimeout`	The timeout period for establishing a connection.
`Database`	The name of the database to which the connection is attached. This property is irrelevant for the sample provider in this chapter, so it will always be the empty string.
`State`	The state of the connection (for example, `Open`, `Closed`, `Closing`, and so on).
`BeginTransaction()`	Begins a new transaction on the connection.
`ChangeDatabase()`	Forces the connection to point to a different database within the same context. This method won't be supported by the RDP.
`Close()`	Closes the connection to the database.
`CreateCommand()`	Creates a new command object that is pre-associated with this connection.
`Open()`	Opens the connection.

The `RDPConnection` Class

The code in Listing 28.3 illustrates the `RDPConnection` class. Note that no physical or networking connections are made. All that's done is store a connection string that will be used by the `RDPCommand` object to issue web service method invocations.

LISTING 28.3
The Remote Data Provider Connection

```
using System;
using System.Data;

namespace SAMS.CSharpUnleashed.RemoteDataProvider
{
  public class RDPConnection : IDbConnection
  {
    private ConnectionState state;
    private string connectionString;
```

LISTING 28.3
Continued

```csharp
public RDPConnection()
{
  state = ConnectionState.Closed;
  connectionString = "";
}

public RDPConnection( string connString )
{
  state = ConnectionState.Closed;
  connectionString = connString;
}

#region IDbConnection Members

public void ChangeDatabase(string databaseName)
{
  throw new NotSupportedException("RDP does not dynamic change of Database.");
}

public IDbTransaction BeginTransaction(System.Data.IsolationLevel il)
{
  throw new NotSupportedException("Transactions not supported in RDP.");
}

IDbTransaction System.Data.IDbConnection.BeginTransaction()
{
  throw new NotSupportedException("Transactions not supported in RDP.");
}

public System.Data.ConnectionState State
{
  get
  {
    return state;
  }
}

public string ConnectionString
{
  get
  {
```

Implementing a Custom Connection

LISTING 28.3
Continued

```
      return connectionString;
  }
  set
  {
     connectionString = value;
  }
}

IDbCommand IDbConnection.CreateCommand()
{
  RDPCommand cmd = new RDPCommand();
  cmd.Connection = this;
  return (IDbCommand)cmd;
}

public RDPCommand CreateCommand()
{
  RDPCommand cmd = new RDPCommand();
  cmd.Connection = this;
  return cmd;
}

public void Open()
{
  state = ConnectionState.Open;
}

public void Close()
{
  state = ConnectionState.Closed;
}

public string Database
{
  get
  {
     return "";
  }
}

public int ConnectionTimeout
```

LISTING 28.3
Continued

```
  {
    get
    {
      return 0;
    }
  }

  #endregion

  #region IDisposable Members

  public void Dispose()
  {
    this.Dispose(true);
    System.GC.SuppressFinalize(this);
  }

  private void Dispose( bool disposing )
  {
    if (state == ConnectionState.Open)
      Close();
  }

  #endregion
  }
}
```

Implementing a Custom Command

When you think about implementing a custom data provider, you should usually start your thinking at the command level. The command is the workhorse of the entire provider. When a `DataAdapter` fills a `DataSet`, it uses a command to generate a `DataReader` that is then used to populate the `DataSet`. The command utilizes the existing connection to perform the actual data operation, including sending parameters, obtaining results, and populating output parameters.

The `IDbCommand` Interface

The `IDbCommand` interface defines the properties and methods listed in Table 28.4.

Implementing a Custom Command

TABLE 28.4

Properties and Methods of the IDbCommand Interface

Property or Method	Description
CommandText	The text of the command. In most implementations, this is the name of a stored procedure or a SQL statement such as SELECT, DELETE, and so on.
CommandTimeout	The elapsed time that can occur before the completion of the command before an exception will be thrown.
CommandType	Indicates whether the command is a stored procedure or plain text, and so on.
Connection	Indicates the connection currently associated with this command.
Parameters	Indicates an IDataParameterCollection of parameters. In the sample case presented in this chapter, this property contains an RDPDataParameterCollection.
Transaction	Indicates the current transaction.
UpdatedRowSource	Indicates how commands are applied to the DataRow when a DataAdapter performs an update.
Cancel()	This method tries to cancel the currently executing command, if possible.
CreateParameter	Creates a new parameter.
ExecuteNonQuery	Executes the current command and returns the number of rows affected.
ExecuteReader	Executes the current command, returning a DataReader on the results.
ExecuteScalar	Executes the current command, returning the first column of the first row in the result set.
Prepare	Creates a compiled version of the command (if applicable).

The RDPCommand Class

Listing 28.4 shows the implementation of IDbCommand, the RDPCommand class.

LISTING 28.4
The Remote Data Provider Command Class

```
using System;
using System.Data;

namespace SAMS.CSharpUnleashed.RemoteDataProvider
{
  public class RDPCommand : IDbCommand
  {
    private RDPConnection connection = null;
    private string cmdText;
    private RDPParameterCollection parameters = null;
```

LISTING 28.4
Continued

```csharp
  private UpdateRowSource urs;

  public RDPCommand()
  {
    cmdText = "";
  }

  public RDPCommand(string commandText)
  {
    cmdText = commandText;
  }

  public RDPCommand( string commandText, RDPConnection connection )
  {
    cmdText = commandText;
    this.connection = connection;
  }

  #region IDbCommand Members

  public void Cancel()
  {
    throw new NotSupportedException("Cancel method not supported by the RDP.");
  }

  public void Prepare()
  {
    throw new NotSupportedException("Prepare method not supported by the RDP.");
  }

  public System.Data.CommandType CommandType
  {
    get
    {
      return CommandType.Text;
    }
    set
    {
      if (value != CommandType.Text)
        throw new
        NotSupportedException("Only text commands are supported by the RDP
Provider.");
```

Implementing a Custom Command

LISTING 28.4
Continued

```
  }
}

private RDPDataReader GetReader()
{
  DataSet ds;
  int rowsAffected;
  RemoteDataHost.DataHost dhProxy = new RemoteDataHost.DataHost();
  dhProxy.Url = connection.ConnectionString;
  ds = dhProxy.ExecuteDataSet( cmdText, out rowsAffected );
  RDPDataReader reader = new RDPDataReader( ds.Tables[0] , connection );
  return reader;
}

public RDPDataReader ExecuteReader(System.Data.CommandBehavior behavior)
{
  return GetReader();
}

IDataReader
System.Data.IDbCommand.ExecuteReader( System.Data.CommandBehavior behavior)
{
  return (IDataReader)GetReader();
}

IDataReader System.Data.IDbCommand.ExecuteReader()
{
  return (IDataReader)GetReader();
}

public object ExecuteScalar()
{
  DataSet ds;
  int rowsAffected;
  RemoteDataHost.DataHost dhProxy = new RemoteDataHost.DataHost();
  dhProxy.Url = connection.ConnectionString;
  ds = dhProxy.ExecuteDataSet( cmdText, out rowsAffected );
  return ds.Tables[0].Rows[0][0];
}
```

LISTING 28.4
Continued

```
public int ExecuteNonQuery()
{
    DataSet ds;
    int rowsAffected;
    RemoteDataHost.DataHost dhProxy = new RemoteDataHost.DataHost();
    dhProxy.Url = connection.ConnectionString;
    ds = dhProxy.ExecuteDataSet( cmdText, out rowsAffected );
    return rowsAffected;
}

public int CommandTimeout
{
    get
    {
        return 0;
    }
    set
    {
    }
}

public IDbDataParameter CreateParameter()
{
    return (IDbDataParameter)(new RDPParameter());
}

public IDbConnection Connection
{
    get
    {
        return connection;
    }
    set
    {
        connection = (RDPConnection)value;
    }
}

public System.Data.UpdateRowSource UpdatedRowSource
{
```

Implementing a Custom Command

LISTING 28.4
Continued

```
      get
      {
        return urs;
      }
      set
      {
        urs = value;
      }
    }

    public string CommandText
    {
      get
      {
         return cmdText;
      }
      set
      {
        cmdText = value;
      }
    }

    public IDataParameterCollection Parameters
    {
      get
      {
        return parameters;
      }
    }

    public IDbTransaction Transaction
    {
      get
      {
        throw new NotSupportedException("Transactions not supported by RDP.");
      }
      set
      {
        throw new NotSupportedException("Transactions not supported by RDP.");
      }
    }
```

LISTING 28.4
Continued

```
    #endregion

    #region IDisposable Members

    public void Dispose()
    {
      this.Dispose(true);
      System.GC.SuppressFinalize(this);
    }

    private void Dispose(bool disposing)
    {
      // get rid of any resources that need to be disposed
    }

    #endregion
  }
}
```

Implementing a Custom `DataReader`

As you know, a `DataReader` is a class that provides a fast, forward-only method for traversing data returned from a command execution. In the case of SQL Server, this reader is live and connected to the server. In most cases, a `DataReader` is faster than filling a `DataSet` because it is a forward-only cursor.

The sample case simulates external data from the web service. That data is actually simulated using a `DataTable`. For that reason, the `RDPDataReader` isn't any faster than a `DataSet`. As mentioned earlier, this is only a sample implementation. In the real world, you would have some kind of proprietary data format for interfacing with the web service. In addition, you might be able to limit the number of rows returned on the first access, so that with subsequent calls to the `DataReader.Read` method, you could actually hit the web service for additional data in the background. If you feel really motivated, you can try adding that functionality to this provider.

The `IDataReader` Interface

The `IDataReader` interface defines the properties and methods described in Table 28.5.

Implementing a Custom DataReader

TABLE 28.5

Properties and Methods of the IDataReader Interface

Property or Method	Description
Depth	Indicates the nesting depth for the current row
IsClosed	Indicates whether the DataReader is closed
RecordsAffected	Where applicable, returns the number of rows affected by the SQL statement that created the reader
Close()	Closes the reader
GetSchemaTable()	Returns a DataTable that describes the schema of the information on which the reader is operating
NextResult()	Advances the reader to the next set of records when operating on SQL result batches
Read()	Moves the reader to the next record

The RDPDataReader Class

The code in Listing 28.5 shows the custom version of the DataReader developed for the example in this chapter.

LISTING 28.5
The Remote Data Provider DataReader Class

```
using System;
using System.Data;

namespace SAMS.CSharpUnleashed.RemoteDataProvider
{
  public class RDPDataReader : IDataReader
  {
    private bool open = true;
    private DataTable resultSet;
    private int currentPosition = 0;
    private RDPConnection connection;


    internal RDPDataReader( DataTable tbl )
    {
      resultSet = tbl;
    }


    internal RDPDataReader( DataTable tbl, RDPConnection connection )
    {
      this.connection = connection;
```

LISTING 28.5
Continued

```
    resultSet = tbl;
}

#region IDataReader Members

public int RecordsAffected
{
  get
  {
    return -1;
  }
}

public bool IsClosed
{
  get
  {
    return !open;
  }
}

public bool NextResult()
{
  // TODO:  Add RDPDataReader.NextResult implementation
  return false;
}

public void Close()
{
  open = false;
}

public bool Read()
{
  if (++currentPosition >= resultSet.Rows.Count)
    return false;
  else
    return true;
}

public int Depth
{
```

Implementing a Custom DataReader

LISTING 28.5
Continued

```csharp
    get
    {
      return 0;
    }
  }

  public DataTable GetSchemaTable()
  {
   throw new NotSupportedException();
  }

  #endregion

  #region IDisposable Members

  public void Dispose()
  {

  }

  #endregion

  #region IDataRecord Members

  public int GetInt32(int i)
  {
    return (int)resultSet.Rows[currentPosition][i];
  }

  public object this[string name]
  {
    get
    {
      return resultSet.Rows[currentPosition][name];
    }
  }

  object System.Data.IDataRecord.this[int i]
  {
   get
   {
     return resultSet.Rows[currentPosition][i];
```

LISTING 28.5
Continued

```
  }
}

public object GetValue(int i)
{
  return resultSet.Rows[currentPosition][i];
}

public bool IsDBNull(int i)
{
  return ( (resultSet.Rows[currentPosition][i] == DBNull.Value) ||
    (resultSet.Rows[currentPosition][i] == null ) );
}

public long
  GetBytes(int i, long fieldOffset, byte[] buffer, int bufferoffset, int length)
{
  throw new NotSupportedException();
}

public byte GetByte(int i)
{
  return (byte)resultSet.Rows[currentPosition][i];
}

public Type GetFieldType(int i)
{
    return resultSet.Rows[currentPosition][i].GetType();
}

public decimal GetDecimal(int i)
{
  return (decimal)resultSet.Rows[currentPosition][i];
}

public int GetValues(object[] values)
{
  throw new NotSupportedException();
}

public string GetName(int i)
{
```

28

Implementing a Custom DataReader

LISTING 28.5
Continued

```csharp
      return resultSet.Columns[i].ColumnName;
   }

   public int FieldCount
   {
     get
     {
      return resultSet.Columns.Count;
     }
   }

   public long GetInt64(int i)
   {
      return (long)resultSet.Rows[currentPosition][i];
   }

   public double GetDouble(int i)
   {
       return (double)resultSet.Rows[currentPosition][i];
   }

   public bool GetBoolean(int i)
   {
      return (bool)resultSet.Rows[currentPosition][i];
   }

   public Guid GetGuid(int i)
   {
      return (Guid)resultSet.Rows[currentPosition][i];
   }

   public DateTime GetDateTime(int i)
   {
      return (DateTime)resultSet.Rows[currentPosition][i];
   }

   public int GetOrdinal(string name)
   {
      return resultSet.Columns.IndexOf(name);
   }
```

LISTING 28.5
Continued

```csharp
public string GetDataTypeName(int i)
{
  return resultSet.Rows[currentPosition][i].GetType().ToString();
}

public float GetFloat(int i)
{
  return (float)resultSet.Rows[currentPosition][i];
}

public IDataReader GetData(int i)
{
  throw new NotSupportedException();
}

public long
  GetChars(int i, long fieldoffset, char[] buffer, int bufferoffset, int length)
{
  throw new NotSupportedException();
}

public string GetString(int i)
{
  return (string)resultSet.Rows[currentPosition][i];
}

public char GetChar(int i)
{
  return (char)resultSet.Rows[currentPosition][i];
}

public short GetInt16(int i)
{
  return (short)resultSet.Rows[currentPosition][i];
}

  #endregion
  }
}
```

28

Implementing a Custom DataAdapter

As you saw in the previous chapter, the DataAdapter is essentially a plug that takes data from commands and plugs it into DataSets and DataTables. The DataAdapter implementation in this example takes a shortcut and inherits from an abstract base class called DbDataAdapter.

The IDbDataAdapter Interface

The IDbDataAdapter interface defines the properties listed in Table 28.6.

TABLE 28.6

Properties of the IDbDataAdapter Interface

Property	Description
SelectCommand	Contains the IDbCommand instance that is called to query data from the database
InsertCommand	An IDbCommand instance that is called to create new rows in the data source
UpdateCommand	An IDbCommand instance that is used to perform updates on rows
DeleteCommand	An IDbCommand instance that is used to delete existing rows from the data source

The RDPDataAdapter Class

Listing 28.6 illustrates a custom DataAdapter class. Make note of where IDbDataAdapter interface methods are implemented, and where properties and methods from the parent abstract class, DbDataAdapter, are overridden.

LISTING 28.6

The Remote Data Provider Data Adapter Class

```
using System;
using System.Data;
using System.Data.Common;

namespace SAMS.CSharpUnleashed.RemoteDataProvider
{
  public class RDPDataAdapter : DbDataAdapter, IDbDataAdapter
  {
    private RDPCommand selectCommand;
    private RDPCommand insertCommand;
    private RDPCommand deleteCommand;
    private RDPCommand updateCommand;
```

LISTING 28.6
Continued

```
static private readonly object EventRowUpdated = new object();
static private readonly object EventRowUpdating = new object();

public RDPDataAdapter()
{ }

#region Properties
public RDPCommand SelectCommand
{
  get
  {
    return selectCommand;
  }
  set
  {
    selectCommand = value;
  }
}

IDbCommand IDbDataAdapter.SelectCommand
{
  get
  {
    return selectCommand;
  }
  set
  {
    selectCommand = (RDPCommand)value;
  }
}

public RDPCommand InsertCommand
{
  get
  {
    return insertCommand;
  }
  set
  {
    insertCommand = value;
  }
}
```

28

Implementing a Custom DataAdapter

LISTING 28.6
Continued

```csharp
IDbCommand IDbDataAdapter.InsertCommand
{
  get
  {
    return insertCommand;
  }
  set
  {
    insertCommand = (RDPCommand)value;
  }
}

public RDPCommand UpdateCommand
{
  get
  {
    return updateCommand;
  }
  set
  {
    updateCommand = value;
  }
}

IDbCommand IDbDataAdapter.UpdateCommand
{
  get
  {
    return updateCommand;
  }
  set
  {
    updateCommand = (RDPCommand)value;
  }
}

public RDPCommand DeleteCommand
{
  get
  {
    return deleteCommand;
  }
```

LISTING 28.6
Continued

```
    set
    {
      deleteCommand = value;
    }
  }

  IDbCommand IDbDataAdapter.DeleteCommand
  {
    get
    {
      return deleteCommand;
    }
    set
    {
      deleteCommand = (RDPCommand)value;
    }
  }
  #endregion


  override protected RowUpdatedEventArgs CreateRowUpdatedEvent(DataRow dataRow,
    IDbCommand command, StatementType statementType, DataTableMapping
    tableMapping)
  {
    return new RDPRowUpdatedEventArgs(dataRow, command, statementType,
    tableMapping);
  }

  override protected RowUpdatingEventArgs CreateRowUpdatingEvent(DataRow dataRow,
    IDbCommand command, StatementType statementType, DataTableMapping
    tableMapping)
  {
    return new RDPRowUpdatingEventArgs(dataRow, command, statementType,
    tableMapping);
  }

  override protected void OnRowUpdating(RowUpdatingEventArgs value)
  {
    RDPRowUpdatingEventHandler handler =
      (RDPRowUpdatingEventHandler) Events[EventRowUpdating];
    if ((null != handler) && (value is RDPRowUpdatingEventArgs))
    {
```

28

Implementing a Custom DataAdapter

LISTING 28.6
Continued

```
        handler(this, (RDPRowUpdatingEventArgs) value);
    }
}

override protected void OnRowUpdated(RowUpdatedEventArgs value)
{
  RDPRowUpdatedEventHandler handler =
    (RDPRowUpdatedEventHandler) Events[EventRowUpdated];
  if ((null != handler) && (value is RDPRowUpdatedEventArgs))
  {
    handler(this, (RDPRowUpdatedEventArgs) value);
  }
}

public event RDPRowUpdatingEventHandler RowUpdating
{
  add { Events.AddHandler(EventRowUpdating, value); }
  remove { Events.RemoveHandler(EventRowUpdating, value); }
}

public event RDPRowUpdatedEventHandler RowUpdated
{
  add { Events.AddHandler(EventRowUpdated, value); }
  remove { Events.RemoveHandler(EventRowUpdated, value); }
}
}

public delegate
  void RDPRowUpdatingEventHandler(object sender, RDPRowUpdatingEventArgs e);
public delegate
  void RDPRowUpdatedEventHandler(object sender, RDPRowUpdatedEventArgs e);

public class RDPRowUpdatingEventArgs : RowUpdatingEventArgs
{
  public RDPRowUpdatingEventArgs(DataRow row, IDbCommand command,
    StatementType statementType, DataTableMapping tableMapping)
  : base(row, command, statementType, tableMapping)
  {
  }

  // Hide the inherited implementation of the command property.
  new public RDPCommand Command
```

28

LISTING 28.6
Continued

```
    {
      get   { return (RDPCommand)base.Command; }
      set   { base.Command = value; }
    }
  }

  public class RDPRowUpdatedEventArgs : RowUpdatedEventArgs
  {
    public RDPRowUpdatedEventArgs(DataRow row, IDbCommand command,
      StatementType statementType, DataTableMapping tableMapping)
      : base(row, command, statementType, tableMapping)
    {
    }

    // Hide the inherited implementation of the command property.
    new public RDPCommand Command
    {
      get   { return (RDPCommand)base.Command; }
    }
  }
}
```

As you've seen in the preceding listings, the framework for creating your own data provider is already in place and written for you within ADO.NET. With a little imagination and a connection-style data source, you can create some extremely flexible and compelling code with your own custom data providers.

Summary

In the previous chapter, you saw how to access various forms of data using a standardized model outlined for you by the ADO.NET data providers for SQL, Oracle, OLE DB, and so on. This chapter showed the reasons why you might create your own provider, and gave you information on how to create a provider and the interfaces that are required for data providers. Finally, you saw the code for a sample, custom data provider that gets its data from a web service connection instead of from a standard data source. After finishing this chapter, you should have a good idea of when and when not to create custom data providers. And if you decide you need to create a data provider, you should now have the information and the tools necessary to do so.

29

Typed DataSets and XSD

IN BRIEF

This chapter will show you how to extend the power of the DataSet with XML-driven schemas written in an XML dialect called *XML Schema Definition (XSD)*. These schemas can define the structure of any data, including things such as keys, relationships, constraints, and much more. Because it is a human-readable dialect, XSD also gives you the ability to annotate schemas and in doing so, to provide documentation about them.

This chapter will show you how to work with XSD, how to integrate XSD into your DataSets, and how to create a strongly typed wrapper around a DataSet based on an XSD schema.

WHAT YOU NEED

REQUIRED SOFTWARE	.NET Framework SDK v1.1 Visual Studio .NET 2003 with C# installed
RECOMMENDED HARDWARE	PC that meets .NET SDK minimum requirements
SKILLS REQUIRED	C# and .NET familiarity Familiarity with security concepts helpful

TYPED DATASETS AND XSD AT A GLANCE

XML Schema Definition	**589**		
Introduction to XSD	589	Annotating XML Schemas	593
Primitive Data Types in XSD	591	XML Schema Facets	594
Derived Data Types	591	Programming XML Schemas—	
Complex Data Types	592	The Xml Schema Class	595
Grouping Elements	593		

Structuring DataSets with Schema	**599**		
Defining Tables and Columns Using XML Schema	599	Defining DataSet Keys and Constraints with XML Schema	600

Typed DataSets	**603**		
Creating Typed DataSets in Visual Studio .NET	606	Using Typed DataSets	607
Building Typed DataSets Using XSD.EXE	607	Annotating Typed DataSets	609

Summary	**611**

Further Reading	**611**

XML Schema Definition

Before looking at the code involved in working with XSD, you need to spend some time learning about XSD itself. This section of the chapter will show you the basics of XSD, and the basic syntax for defining the elements, attributes, and data types that exist within structured XML documents.

Introduction to XSD

As mentioned earlier, XSD itself is written in XML. You can think of it as a standardized XML format for describing other XML documents. When defining an XML schema, you always start with the `<schema>` element. Before getting into the details of the syntax and structure of an XSD document, look at a few samples of XSD documents to get a frame of reference for the rest of this section. Listing 29.1 shows a sample XSD file.

LISTING 29.1

A Sample XSD File

```
<?xml version="1.0" encoding="IBM437"?>
<xs:schema xmlns:xs="http://www.w3.org/2001/XMLSchema"> <xs:annotation>
  <xs:documentation xml:lang="en">
    This is an example schema that dictates the format of an XML
    document that contains information on books and their authors.
  </xs:documentation>
 </xs:annotation>

  <xs:complexType name="AuthorType">
    <xs:sequence>
      <xs:element name="Name" type="xs:string" />
      <xs:element name="Age" type="xs:positiveInteger" />
    </xs:sequence>
  </xs:complexType>
  <xs:complexType name="ChapterType">
    <xs:sequence>
      <xs:element name="Title" type="xs:string" />
      <xs:element name="Pages" type="xs:positiveInteger" />
    </xs:sequence>
  </xs:complexType>
  <xs:complexType name="ChaptersType">
    <xs:sequence>
      <xs:element minOccurs="0" maxOccurs="unbounded" name="Chapter"
      type="ChapterType" />
    </xs:sequence>
```

29

LISTING 29.1

Continued

```xml
  </xs:complexType>
  <xs:complexType name="LibraryType">
    <xs:sequence>
      <xs:element name="Book" type="BookType" />
    </xs:sequence>
  </xs:complexType>
  <xs:complexType name="BookType">
    <xs:sequence>
      <xs:element name="Author" type="AuthorType" />
      <xs:element name="Chapters" type="ChaptersType" />
    </xs:sequence>
    <xs:attribute name="title" type="xs:string" />
    <xs:attribute name="publisher" type="xs:string" />
  </xs:complexType>

  <xs:element name="Library" type="LibraryType" />

</xs:schema>
```

Each piece of this schema will be discussed as you progress through this section of the chapter, but you need to see a working XSD file before moving on to the details to give you some context. An XML file that conforms to the preceding XSD might appear as follows:

```xml
<Library>
  <Book title="My Summer Vacation" publisher="Small Shop Press">
    <Author>
      <Name>Kevin Hoffman</Name>
      <Age>2</Age>
    </Author>
    <Chapters>
      <Chapter>
        <Title>Introduction</Title>
        <Pages>12</Pages>
      </Chapter>
      <Chapter>
        <Title>Chapter Two</Title>
        <Pages>42</Pages>
      </Chapter>
    </Chapters>
  </Book>
</Library>
```

Primitive Data Types in XSD

As you saw in the XSD document in Listing 29.1, you are defining the position, location, name, and data type of elements and attributes within a document. When you define elements and attributes, you also define the data type. Data types can be simple primitive types, such as integers or strings, or they can be complex types or user-defined types. Table 29.1 shows a list of the most commonly used primitive types. For a complete list of all types, you should consult a book or reference guide dedicated to XML schemas. When indicating a data type in an XSD document, prefix the name of the data type with the `xs:` XML schema namespace prefix.

TABLE 29.1

Commonly Used XSD Primitive Types

Type	Description
`xs:anyUri`	Represents a uniform resource locator, as defined by RFC 2396.
`xs:Bool`	Indicates a Boolean. Values are written as `true` or `false`.
`xs:dateTime`	Represents a fixed timestamp including both date and time.
`xs:decimal`	Represents floating-point numbers of varying precision.
`xs:double`	Indicates a double-precision floating-point number (64-bit).
`xs:duration`	Indicates a length of time. The pattern for storing lengths of time is PnYnMnDTnHnMnS, where *n* is numeric values and the capital letters are fixed pieces of the pattern. For example, `P1Y2M3DT1H3M1S` is equivalent to the duration 1 year, 2 months, 3 days, 1 hour, 3 minutes, and 1 second.
`xs:date`	Indicates a date. This value cannot contain timestamps, only valid dates.
`xs:float`	A floating-point number in single precision (32-bit).
`xs:string`	Indicates a variable-length character string.
`xs:time`	Contains a timestamp with no date portion.
`xs:hexBinary`	Indicates a string of binary data encoded in hexadecimal notation.
`xs:base64Binary`	Indicates encoded binary data in base-64.

29

Derived Data Types

Also available to you is a set of more specialized data types that are part of the XSD language definition. If you are building an XSD, you might save yourself a lot of time and effort if you take a look at the list of derived types to see whether the XSD language definition hasn't already taken care of a particular data scenario for which you are preparing. If it makes things clearer, you can think of derived types as XML data types that inherit from the primitive XML data types listed in Table 29.1, and restrict, constrain, or limit those types in some way. Table 29.2 lists some of the more common derived data types.

TABLE 29.2

Common Derived Data Types in XSD

Type	Description
languagexs:Language	Contains a string that represents a standard language identifier. Language identifiers are enumerated in RFC 1766.
xs:Name	Indicates a valid XML token name. Starts with a letter, underscore, or colon. Derived from the token type.
tokenxs:Token	Derived from normalizedString.
xs:normalizedString	Indicates a white-space normalized string (all duplicate whitespace is reduced to a single whitespace character, trailing and leading whitespace is trimmed).
xs:integer	A whole number that can be preceded by a + or –; derived from decimal.
xs:nonPositiveInteger	Any integer that is either 0 or negative. Can be preceded by a negative (–) sign.
xs:positiveInteger	An integer that is greater than 0.
xs:unsignedLong	An unsigned long. Means that the space normally used for storing the values below zero is used for positive numbers, allowing a maximum value of 18,446,744,073,709,551,615.
xs:unsignedInt	As with long, only with integer values. Maximum value is 4,294,967,295.
xs:unsignedShort	Unsigned 16-bit value, maximum 65535.
xs:unsignedByte	Unsigned 8-bit value, maximum 255.

Remember that in any place that you need to define the data type of an element or attribute, you can use any of the data types in Table 29.2 without having to include extra files because they are part of the XSD language specification.

Complex Data Types

Primitive data types and derived data types belong to a single category of data types called *simple types*. A simple type is just that; it contains a type definition for a simple structure, such as an element or attribute.

A complex type defines the set of attributes and child content of an element. The reason it is called *complex* is that because the element doesn't have a simple data type, it can contain as its children other elements that are either simple or complex. You saw several complex types in the sample in Listing 29.1. The complex type is indicated in an XSD document as <complexType>. For example:

```
<xs:complexType name="AuthorType">
    <xs:sequence>
        <xs:element name="Name" type="xs:string"/>
        <xs:element name="Age" type="xs:positiveInteger" />
```

```
    </xs:sequence>
  </xs:complexType>
```

It should be fairly evident from the preceding sample that the complex type called `AuthorType` defines a sequence of child elements. These elements are called `Name` and `Age`   **1** . Any time an `<xs:element>` is used in a schema with the type of `AuthorType`, it is assumed that, in the instance document, the element will always contain both a `Name` and `Age` child element. The term *instance document* always refers to the XML document containing the data that conforms to the structure defined by the XSD document. The XSD document is often referred to as the *schema document*.

Grouping Elements

In the previous section, you saw how to define a complex type. A complex type is a nesting of other complex or simple types. The use of complex types enables you to control very intricate structures, but also enables you to keep your schema document clear and easy to read.

You can define the grouping structure of the child elements of a complex type by using one of four group control attributes: `<group>`, `<all>`, `<sequence>`, and `<choice>`.

- ▸ group—This element defines a grouping of elements to be contained as a complex type. You can define the properties of a grouping, such as the min and max occurrence values, as well as the name. You place the simple or complex type definitions that you want to appear as children beneath the group element.

- ▸ choice—This element indicates that one and only one of the elements defined as a child can appear in the instance document.

- ▸ all—This element indicates that all child elements beneath this element can appear in the containing element in any order. This doesn't require that all elements appear in the containing element, however.

- ▸ sequence—This element indicates that all child elements beneath this element must appear in the order listed in the schema document. If the document order in the instance document does not match the order defined in the schema document, document validation will fail.

Annotating XML Schemas

Even if you know every attribute and element defined by the XSD language definition, reading someone else's XSD file can often be a daunting task. You might not be able to infer the intent of the schema author from the schema itself. In such a case,

XML Schema Definition

the schema author can provide annotation, which enables him to include documentation in the schema document to complement external documentation such as MS Word or PDF documents.

An annotation element (`<xs:annotation>`) occurs as a child element of the element it is documenting. For example, the following section of XSD provides an annotation for a complex type:

```
<xs:complexType name="MyComplexType" >
  <xs:annotation>
    <xs:documentation>
      The MyComplexType allows you to do something. It is a very
      valuable element, etc, etc, etc.
    </xs:documentation>
  </xs:annotation>
</xs:complexType>
```

Even if your code is the only code using the schema and humans might never see it, you can still use annotation to record information about the application for which the schema was created. The `<xs:appinfo>` element (a child of `<xs:annotation>`) can be used to store application-specific information that can be read programmatically from the schema file.

> **TIP**
> There are tools to make creating and annotating schemas much easier, such as XML Spy, a tool capable of producing graphical, hierarchical XML rendering as well as creating Microsoft Word documents containing schema annotations.

XML Schema Facets

Any simple type (either primitive or derived, as shown in the earlier tables) can have a *facet*. According to Webster's Dictionary, a *facet* is a definable aspect that makes up a subject or an object. In the case of XSD, facets are definable aspects of data types that further refine the definition of that data type.

Just like annotations, a facet describes or constrains the element in which it is defined (its parent element). Facets are described in XSD using elements. For example:

```
<xs:simpleType name="AgeOfWoman">
  <xs:restriction base="xs:integer">
    <xs:maxExclusive value="29" />
  </xs:restriction>
</xs:simpleType>
```

The preceding facet restricts all elements defined as the type AgeOfWoman in such a way that the data can never reflect an age that exceeds 29 years.

Programming XML Schemas—The XmlSchema Class

The XmlSchema class is one that is provided with the .NET Framework to give you an object-oriented view of the structure and construction of an XML schema definition file. The code in Listing 29.2 illustrates how to create the XSD file shown earlier in the chapter in Listing 29.1. The code might seem overly complex, but when you compare the output file and the code, you'll see the relationship between each class and each element in the XSD file, and the code will become clear and useful.

LISTING 29.2
The Code to Create the XSD File in Listing 29.1

```
using System;
using System.Xml;
using System.Xml.Schema;

namespace XmlSchemaBuilder
{
  class Class1
  {
    /// <summary>
    /// The main entry point for the application.
    /// </summary>
    [STAThread]
    static void Main(string[] args)
    {
      XmlNamespaceManager nsMan = new XmlNamespaceManager( new NameTable() );
      nsMan.AddNamespace("xs", "http://www.w3.org/2001/XMLSchema");
      XmlSchema schema = new XmlSchema();

      XmlSchemaComplexType ctAuthorType = new XmlSchemaComplexType();
      ctAuthorType.Name = "AuthorType";
      XmlSchemaSequence seqAuthor = new XmlSchemaSequence();
      XmlSchemaElement elemName = new XmlSchemaElement();
      elemName.Name = "Name";
      elemName.SchemaTypeName = new XmlQualifiedName("string",
        @"http://www.w3.org/2001/XMLSchema");
      seqAuthor.Items.Add( elemName );
      XmlSchemaElement elemAge = new XmlSchemaElement();
      elemAge.Name = "Age";
      elemAge.SchemaTypeName = new XmlQualifiedName("positiveInteger",
```

29

LISTING 29.2
Continued

29

```
        @"http://www.w3.org/2001/XMLSchema");
seqAuthor.Items.Add( elemAge );
ctAuthorType.Particle = seqAuthor;
schema.Items.Add( ctAuthorType );

XmlSchemaComplexType ctChaptersNested = new XmlSchemaComplexType();
ctChaptersNested.Name = "ChapterType";
schema.Items.Add( ctChaptersNested );
  XmlSchemaSequence seqChapter = new XmlSchemaSequence();
  XmlSchemaElement elemTitle = new XmlSchemaElement();
  elemTitle.Name = "Title";
  elemTitle.SchemaTypeName = new XmlQualifiedName("string",
    @"http://www.w3.org/2001/XMLSchema");
  seqChapter.Items.Add( elemTitle );

  XmlSchemaElement elemPages = new XmlSchemaElement();
  elemPages.Name = "Pages";
  elemPages.SchemaTypeName = new XmlQualifiedName("positiveInteger",
    @"http://www.w3.org/2001/XMLSchema");
  seqChapter.Items.Add( elemPages );
  ctChaptersNested.Particle = seqChapter;

XmlSchemaComplexType ctChapters = new XmlSchemaComplexType();
ctChapters.Name = "ChaptersType";
XmlSchemaSequence seqChapters = new XmlSchemaSequence();

XmlSchemaElement elemChapter = new XmlSchemaElement();
elemChapter.Name = "Chapter";
elemChapter.SchemaTypeName = new XmlQualifiedName("ChapterType");
elemChapter.MinOccursString = "0";
elemChapter.MaxOccursString = "unbounded";
seqChapters.Items.Add( elemChapter );

ctChapters.Particle = seqChapters;
schema.Items.Add( ctChapters );

XmlSchemaComplexType ctLibrary = new XmlSchemaComplexType();
ctLibrary.Name = "LibraryType";
XmlSchemaSequence seqLibrary = new XmlSchemaSequence();
ctLibrary.Particle = seqLibrary;
XmlSchemaElement elemBook = new XmlSchemaElement();
elemBook.Name = "Book";
```

LISTING 29.2
Continued

```
    elemBook.SchemaTypeName = new XmlQualifiedName("BookType");
    seqLibrary.Items.Add( elemBook );
    schema.Items.Add( ctLibrary );


    XmlSchemaComplexType ctBook = new XmlSchemaComplexType();
    ctBook.Name = "BookType";
    XmlSchemaSequence seqBook = new XmlSchemaSequence();
    ctBook.Particle = seqBook;


    XmlSchemaElement elemAuthor = new XmlSchemaElement();
    elemAuthor.Name = "Author";
    elemAuthor.SchemaTypeName = new XmlQualifiedName("AuthorType");
    seqBook.Items.Add( elemAuthor );
    XmlSchemaElement elemChapters = new XmlSchemaElement();
    elemChapters.Name = "Chapters";
    elemChapters.SchemaTypeName = new XmlQualifiedName("ChaptersType");
    seqBook.Items.Add( elemChapters );


    XmlSchemaAttribute attribTitle = new XmlSchemaAttribute();
    attribTitle.Name = "title";
    attribTitle.SchemaTypeName = new XmlQualifiedName("string",
      @"http://www.w3.org/2001/XMLSchema");
    ctBook.Attributes.Add( attribTitle );
    XmlSchemaAttribute attribPublisher = new XmlSchemaAttribute();
    attribPublisher.Name = "publisher";
    attribPublisher.SchemaTypeName = new XmlQualifiedName("string",
      @"http://www.w3.org/2001/XMLSchema");
    ctBook.Attributes.Add( attribPublisher );
    schema.Items.Add( ctBook );
    XmlSchemaElement elemLibrary = new XmlSchemaElement();
    elemLibrary.Name = "Library";
    elemLibrary.SchemaTypeName = new XmlQualifiedName("LibraryType");
    schema.Items.Add( elemLibrary );


    schema.Compile( new ValidationEventHandler( ValidationCallback ));    2

    schema.Write( Console.Out, nsMan );
}


public static void ValidationCallback(object sender, ValidationEventArgs e )
{
  Console.WriteLine(e.Message);
```

29

XML Schema Definition

LISTING 29.2
Continued

```
    }
   }
}
```

Figure 29.1 shows the console output of the preceding code.

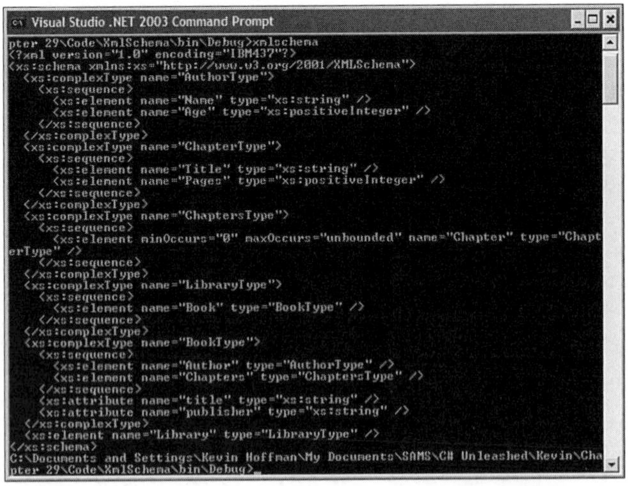

FIGURE 29.1   Console output of the XSD builder console application.

There's a lot of code to take in from the preceding sample, but if you take a little time to read it, it should make perfect sense. There is a class in the System.Xml.Schema namespace for every single type of structure that you can place in an XSD document. If you know what you want your XSD to look like, you know what classes you want to instantiate and insert into the document.

The XmlSchema class forces you to think about everything the way an XSD parser would think about it. For example, even though you can create elements in an XSD that don't appear to have a namespace qualification, everything you do with the XmlSchema class has to be namespace qualified. The output document will remove redundant or unnecessary declarations, which is something XSD authors do without thinking about what they're doing.

Another handy feature of the XmlSchema class is that you can specify a callback method **2**. This method will be invoked whenever there is a schema validation failure. Instead of throwing an exception and stopping the validation process, it actually makes a callback for *every* validation issue so that you can decide for yourself which validation problems are worth halting program execution.

Structuring DataSets with Schema

As mentioned in the introduction, this chapter isn't just about XML schemas and XSD documents. This chapter is about how XSD documents relate to DataSets and the additional power and features you can enable when combining XML schemas with the power and flexibility of DataSets.

Defining Tables and Columns Using XML Schema

The first thing we need to do is figure out how to create XSD documents that will describe the data structure of a DataSet. When you describe XML data, you can very easily describe semi-structured, hierarchical data that might or might not have a consistent format. However, with a DataSet, you are talking about a consistent format of tables, rows, columns, relationships, keys and constraints.

The first thing you'll see are tables and columns. To create a DataSet, the first element you need in your XSD is a DataSet. As you'll see, there are some Microsoft-supplied extensions to XSD that control the behavior of XSD-structured DataSets. The following piece of XSD is the bare definition of an empty DataSet:

```
<xs:schema id="MyDataSetSchema"
           xmlns=""
           xmlns:xs="http://www.w3.org/2001/XMLSchema"
           xmlns:msdata="urn:schemas-microsoft-com:xml-msdata">
   <xs:element name="MyDataSet" msdata:IsDataSet="true">
   </xs:element>
 </xs:schema>
```

It should look somewhat familiar. You'll notice that there is a new namespace declaration: `msdata`. The `DataSet` class knows about the various tags that are part of that namespace and knows how to modify DataSets according to the `msdata` instructions in the XSD document.

When a DataSet is obtaining its structure from an XSD document, only the top-level complex types are used to generate tables. Items below that are used to generate the columns within those tables. Simple types such as integers and strings cannot generate tables.

TIP

Just because an XSD is valid doesn't mean that it will generate a valid DataSet structure. DataSets are inherently relational data, and require a structure that can be interpreted as a list of tables, with columns that are constrained or related to each other in some way. If that structure cannot be extrapolated, the XSD will not be able to generate a valid DataSet.

29

Structuring DataSets with Schema

Given this information, the following XSD should represent a DataSet that has two tables (Book and Author), each with two columns:

```xml
<xs:schema id="MyDataSetSchema"
           xmlns=""
           xmlns:xs="http://www.w3.org/2001/XMLSchema"
           xmlns:msdata="urn:schemas-microsoft-com:xml-msdata">
  <xs:element name="MyDataSet" msdata:IsDataSet="true">
   <xs:complexType>
     <xs:choice maxOccurs="unbounded">
       <xs:element name="Book" >
         <xs:complexType >
           <xs:sequence>
             <xs:element name="Title" type="xs:string"
                         minOccurs="0" />
             <xs:element name="ISBN" type="xs:string"
                         minOccurs="0" />
           </xs:sequence>
         </xs:complexType>
       </xs:element>

       <xs:element name="Author" >
         <xs:complexType>
           <xs:sequence>
             <xs:attribute name="Name" type="xs:string" />
             <xs:attribute name="Age" type="xs:positiveInteger" />
           </xs:sequence>
         </xs:complexType>
       </xs:element>
     </xs:choice>
   </xs:complexType>
  </xs:element>
</xs:schema>
```

Defining DataSet Keys and Constraints with XML Schema

Now that you've seen the basics of defining DataSet structure with XSD documents that can create tables and columns, let's move on to something slightly more advanced.

Tables and columns are great, but most relational databases and relational data containers have the capability to set keys and constraints. A key is an indicator of uniqueness. The key is the list of columns whose unique value distinguishes one row from the next in any given table.

A *constraint* is a restriction on a column within the table. When you define a key on a table, there is automatically an implied unique constraint. You can have a unique constraint on a nonunique column, but you can also have other kinds of constraints on other columns.

Key Constraints

The following XSD will create a key on a given column in a table (element within a top-level complex type):

```
<xs:key  msdata:PrimaryKey="true"
            msdata:ConstraintName="KeyConstraintISBN"
            name="KeyISBN" >
   <xs:selector xpath=".//Books" />
   <xs:field xpath="ISBN" />
   </xs:key>
```

This key element creates a key on the ISBN column within the Books table. The reason that the `<xs:selector>` and `<xs:field>` elements use XPath notation is that you can have elements that are columns, and you can also have attributes that function as columns as well, and they can be defined anywhere in the document. To allow for this kind of flexibility, the key element uses XPath to locate the elements for which the key is applicable. The msdata attributes control the way the DataSet key is created such as whether the key is a primary key, the name of the key and the constraint, and so forth. KeyConstraintISBN creates a unique constraint on the column, and the other msdata attribute sets that key as a primary key.

Unique Constraints

Unique constraints work very much like key constraints. You define one against an attribute or element that will be interpreted as a column within the XSD as follows:

```
<xs:unique msdata:ConstraintName="UniqueAuthorName"
    name="UniqueConstraintAuthorName" >
   <xs:selector xpath=".//Books" />
   <xs:field xpath="Author" />
</xs:unique>
```

Relationships

You can't call it relational data unless you can relate one set of data with another. That's where relationships come in. XSD doesn't call them relationships, it calls them *references*. There are, however, some msdata tags that you can apply to a reference that will create a proper DataSet relationship between rows in tables.

29

Structuring DataSets with Schema

Keyref Constraints

As you might expect, a *keyref* is an element that refers to a key. These references from one key to another create relationships between tables. Probably the most well-known (and overused) example of a parent-child relationship between tables is the Order and OrderDetail tables. The Order table contains header or summary information, and the OrderDetail table contains individual line items. Rather than continuing that tradition, I'll continue with the books and author data I've been using so far.

Consider the following schema:

```xml
<xs:schema id="MyDataSet" xmlns=""
           xmlns:xs="http://www.w3.org/2001/XMLSchema"
           xmlns:msdata="urn:schemas-microsoft-com:xml-msdata">


  <xs:element name="MyDataSet" msdata:IsDataSet="true">
   <xs:complexType>
     <xs:choice maxOccurs="unbounded">
        <xs:element name="Book">
          <xs:complexType>
            <xs:sequence>
              <xs:element name="ISBN" type="xs:string" />
              <xs:element name="Title" type="xs:string" />
              <xs:element name="Author" type="xs:string" />
            </xs:sequence>
          </xs:complexType>
        </xs:element>
        <xs:element name="Author">
          <xs:complexType>
            <xs:sequence>
              <xs:element name="Name" type="xs:string" />
              <xs:element name="Age" type="xs:integer" />
            </xs:sequence>
          </xs:complexType>
        </xs:element>
     </xs:choice>
   </xs:complexType>

  <xs:key name="AuthorKey"  >
    <xs:selector xpath=".//Author" />
    <xs:field xpath="Name" />
  </xs:key>
```

```
<xs:keyref name="AuthorBooksKeyRef" refer="AuthorKey">
  <xs:selector xpath=".//Book" />
  <xs:field xpath="Author" />
</xs:keyref>
</xs:element>
</xs:schema>
```

Most of the schema above you should be able to recognize. It creates a DataSet with two tables: Author **3** and Book **4**. In addition, there is a key called AuthorKey on the Name field in the Author table. Keys are vitally important to relationships between tables because you cannot create a relationship without a keyref, and you cannot create a keyref without a key.

When the code sets the keyref, it is creating a relationship between two tables. In the preceding case, the keyref refers to the AuthorKey, indicating that the AuthorKey is the parent. The child is indicated by the <xs:selector> and <xs:field> elements.

A DataSet whose structure was created with the preceding XSD will have a parent-child relationship between the Author table and the Book table, as well as a nonprimary, unique key on the Author table. By virtue of the relationship, a foreign key will be created on the Book table.

Typed DataSets

Typed DataSets solve a very specific problem. Before you look at typed DataSets themselves, look at an example of the problem they solve. Examine the schema in Listing 29.3. It is a nested version of the schema that was generated earlier. DataSets are very finicky about the format of the schemas they can read, so the preceding schema has been modified to work with a DataSet.

LISTING 29.3
Nested Schema Example

```
<?xml version="1.0" standalone="yes"?>
<xs:schema id="Library"
    xmlns=""
    xmlns:xs="http://www.w3.org/2001/XMLSchema"
    xmlns:msdata="urn:schemas-microsoft-com:xml-msdata">
  <xs:element name="Library" msdata:IsDataSet="true">
    <xs:complexType>
      <xs:choice maxOccurs="unbounded">
```

29

Typed DataSets

LISTING 29.3
Continued

```
5        <xs:element name="Book">
          <xs:complexType>
            <xs:attribute name="author" type="xs:string" />
            <xs:attribute name="isbn" type="xs:string" use="required" />
            <xs:attribute name="title" type="xs:string" />
            <xs:attribute name="publishdate" type="xs:string" />
            <xs:attribute name="publisher" type="xs:string" />
          </xs:complexType>
        </xs:element>
        <xs:element name="Author">
          <xs:complexType>
            <xs:sequence>
              <xs:element name="ID" type="xs:string" minOccurs="0" />
              <xs:element name="Name" type="xs:string" minOccurs="0" />
              <xs:element name="Age" type="xs:string" minOccurs="0" />
            </xs:sequence>
          </xs:complexType>
        </xs:element>
6        <xs:element name="Chapter">
          <xs:complexType>
            <xs:sequence>
              <xs:element name="ISBN" type="xs:string" minOccurs="0" />
              <xs:element name="Title" type="xs:string" minOccurs="0" />
              <xs:element name="Pages" type="xs:string" minOccurs="0" />
            </xs:sequence>
          </xs:complexType>
        </xs:element>
        </xs:choice>
      </xs:complexType>
      <xs:unique name="PK_BookISBN" msdata:PrimaryKey="true">
        <xs:selector xpath=".//Book" />
        <xs:field xpath="@isbn" />
      </xs:unique>
7        <xs:keyref name="BookChapters" refer="PK_BookISBN">
          <xs:selector xpath=".//Chapter" />
          <xs:field xpath="ISBN" />
        </xs:keyref>
      </xs:element>
    </xs:schema>
```

This schema still describes the basic data model you saw before. This new schema
describes two tables: Book **5** and Chapter **6**. Each book can have multiple

chapters, so there is a relationship defined between the Book table and the Chapters table **7**.

Here is some code that reads the schema and then displays some basic information about the DataSet to the console. It also displays the books and their associated chapters:

```csharp
using System;
using System.Data;

namespace DataSetSchema
{
  class Class1
  {
    /// <summary>
    /// The main entry point for the application.
    /// </summary>
    [STAThread]
    static void Main(string[] args)
    {
      DataSet ds = new DataSet();
      ds.ReadXmlSchema(@"MoreBooks.XSD");

      foreach (DataTable table in ds.Tables)
      {
        Console.WriteLine("Table: {0}\n--------------------", table.TableName);
        foreach (DataColumn column in table.Columns)
        {
          Console.Write("{0} ({1})\t", column.ColumnName,
column.DataType.ToString());
        }
        Console.WriteLine("\n");
      }

      foreach (DataRelation rel in ds.Relations)
      {
        Console.WriteLine( "Relation: {0}, Nested: {1}",
          rel.RelationName, rel.Nested.ToString() );
      }

      ds.ReadXml("Morebooks.xml");
      Console.WriteLine("{0} Authors Found.", ds.Tables["Author"].Rows.Count);

      foreach (DataRow book in ds.Tables["Book"].Rows)
      {
```

Typed DataSets

```
    Console.WriteLine("Book {0}", book["title"]);
    foreach (DataRow chapter in book.GetChildRows("BookChapters"))
    {
      Console.WriteLine("\tChapter: {0}", chapter["Title"]);
    }
  }
  Console.ReadLine();
  }
 }
}
```

The output from running the preceding program is shown in Figure 29.2.

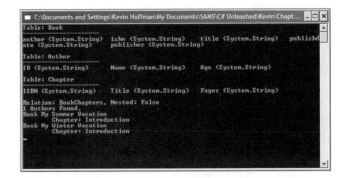

FIGURE 29.2   Constructing a DataSet from an XSD file.

This shows you that you can create a DataSet structure from an XSD file at runtime. The problem is that this is very inefficient. As you probably noticed, the code is treating each row and column generically, and is doing a lot of type casting and the code doesn't look all that elegant. What's more, we know the structure of our DataSet at compile time, so why should the code wait until runtime to set the structure of the DataSet? It would be great if we could blend the XSD-supplied structure with the DataSet at compile time to create strongly typed wrappers around all the tables and columns. The great thing is that we can.

Creating Typed DataSets in Visual Studio .NET

A typed DataSet is a class that inherits from the DataSet class. It enables you to access data members generically, such as:

```
typedDataSet.Tables["MyTable"].Rows[0]["MyColumn"];
```

This access method is what you should be very familiar with as the standard way of getting at data within a DataSet. However, because a typed DataSet creates strongly typed members that are wrappers for the generic access methods, you can actually write code that looks like this:

```
typedDataSet.MyTable[0].MyColumn;
```

Obviously, this is much easier to read. Even more useful than the ease of reading and maintenance is the fact that each member will already be cast to the appropriate type.

To create a typed DataSet in Visual Studio .NET, right-click any existing project, select Add, and then select Add New Item. When prompted for the type of item to add, select DataSet.

Visual Studio .NET will create a new .xsd file and provide you with an interactive design surface and an XML view of the schema. In addition, a new class will be added to your project, but it won't be visible unless you have the Show All Files option turned on. The chapter doesn't cover the design surface because it focuses on XSD. Enter the XSD from Listing 29.3 in the XML view of the DataSet. You'll see some code for using a typed DataSet shortly. The next section is about using the XSD.EXE command-line tool for generating a typed DataSet.

29

Building Typed DataSets Using XSD.EXE

The XSD tool is a utility that comes with the .NET Framework SDK to enable you to create XML schemas from existing .NET classes. It also gives you the ability to create typed DataSets from XSD files.

Issue the following command line in the same directory as the Morebooks.XSD file:

```
xsd /dataset /namespace:SAMS.SampleDataSet /language:CS Morebooks.xsd
```

This command creates a new typed DataSet class called SAMS.SampleDataSet.Library. This chapter will spare you the waste of paper and eyestrain from reading the typed DataSet code. In general, it basically creates members that match each of the columns and tables in the XSD schema for the generated class. The code is extremely lengthy. There are reasons why this class is normally hidden from you by Visual Studio .NET, the biggest of which is the sheer volume of the code in the file. To see this code in Visual Studio .NET, make sure that Show All Files is turned on in this project, and you will be able to see the .CS file below the .XSD schema.

Using Typed DataSets

Thankfully, using a typed DataSet is far easier than reading the code that is used to create one. All you have to do is instantiate it as you would any other

Typed DataSets

DataSet. Instead of using generic DataSet members, you can use the members of the class that were automatically generated by the XSD tool or by Visual Studio .NET.

Listing 29.4 shows the code that instantiates a new library typed DataSet, and uses strongly typed members and methods to display the data and navigating relationships.

LISTING 29.4
Code to Manipulate a Typed DataSet

```
using System;

namespace UsingTypedDataSets
{
  class Class1
  {
    /// <summary>
    /// The main entry point for the application.
    /// </summary>
    [STAThread]
    static void Main(string[] args)
    {
      Library library = new Library();
      library.ReadXml(@"..\..\..\morebooks.xml");

      foreach (Library.BookRow book in library.Book)
      {
        Console.WriteLine("Book : {0}, Written by {1}",
          book.title, book.author );
        foreach (Library.ChapterRow chapter in book.GetChapterRows())
        {
          Console.WriteLine("\tChapter : {0}, Pages {1}",
            chapter.Title, chapter.Pages);
        }
      }

      Console.ReadLine();
    }
  }
}
```

Annotating Typed DataSets

After looking at the code in Listing 29.4, you should be convinced that using a typed DataSet (if you know the structure of your DataSet at compile/design-time) is beneficial for multiple reasons.

There is a little bit more that can be done. You probably noticed that all the nested classes that represent the strongly typed rows end with the `Row` postfix. In addition, the name of each column is exactly as it appears in the XML schema, so the `title` and `author` attributes also become lowercased column names.

Microsoft provides an additional set of instructions that you can supply in a DataSet's XML schema to allow for annotation. The following list contains the annotations that you can supply to control the definition of the typed DataSet at generation time:

- ▸ `typedName`—The name of this item as it will appear in the DataSet. This annotation is used to override a name so that it doesn't have to match the name in the XML schema.

- ▸ `typedPlural`—Sets the name of a collection of typed objects in the DataSet.

- ▸ `typedParent`—Sets the name of the parent item.

- ▸ `typedChildren`—Gets the name of the method that returns child objects of a given typed row.

- ▸ `nullValue`—If the data row is null, this specifies what value should be stored in the DataSet in place of `DBNull`.

Being able to annotate an XML schema for DataSet generation requires the addition of the following namespace declaration to the file:

```
xmlns:codegen="urn:schemas-microsoft-com:xml-msprop"
```

Now look at Listing 29.5, the newly annotated XML schema. The highlighted portions indicate the new annotations ■8■.

LISTING 29.5
The Annotated Typed DataSet

```
<?xml version="1.0" standalone="yes"?>
<xs:schema id="LibraryAnnotated" xmlns=""
xmlns:xs="http://www.w3.org/2001/XMLSchema"
     xmlns:msdata="urn:schemas-microsoft-com:xml-msdata"
     xmlns:codegen="urn:schemas-microsoft-com:xml-msprop">
  <xs:element name="LibraryAnnotated" msdata:IsDataSet="true">
    <xs:complexType>
```

29

Typed DataSets

LISTING 29.5
Continued

```xml
            <xs:choice maxOccurs="unbounded">
              <xs:element name="Book" codegen:typedName="Book"
codegen:typedPlural="Books">
                <xs:complexType>
                  <xs:attribute name="author" type="xs:string"
codegen:typedName="Author"/>
                  <xs:attribute name="isbn"
                       type="xs:string" use="required" codegen:typedName="ISBN"/>
                  <xs:attribute name="title" type="xs:string" codegen:typedName="Title"/>
                  <xs:attribute
                       name="publishdate" type="xs:string" codegen:typedName="Publish-
Date"/>
                  <xs:attribute
                       name="publisher" type="xs:string" codegen:typedName="Publisher"/>
                </xs:complexType>
              </xs:element>
              <xs:element name="Author" codegen:typedName="Author">
                <xs:complexType>
                  <xs:sequence>
                    <xs:element name="ID" type="xs:string" minOccurs="0" />
                    <xs:element name="Name" type="xs:string" minOccurs="0" />
                    <xs:element name="Age" type="xs:string" minOccurs="0" />
                  </xs:sequence>
                </xs:complexType>
              </xs:element>
              <xs:element name="Chapter"
                  codegen:typedName="Chapter" codegen:typedPlural="Chapters">
                <xs:complexType>
                  <xs:sequence>
                    <xs:element name="ISBN" type="xs:string" minOccurs="0" />
                    <xs:element name="Title" type="xs:string" minOccurs="0" />
                    <xs:element name="Pages" type="xs:string" minOccurs="0" />
                  </xs:sequence>
                </xs:complexType>
              </xs:element>
            </xs:choice>
          </xs:complexType>
          <xs:unique name="PK_BookISBN" msdata:PrimaryKey="true">
            <xs:selector xpath=".//Book" />
            <xs:field xpath="@isbn" />
          </xs:unique>
          <xs:keyref name="BookChapters" refer="PK_BookISBN" codegen:typedParent="Book"
                  codegen:typedChildren="GetChapters">
```

LISTING 29.5
Continued

```
        <xs:selector xpath=".//Chapter" />
        <xs:field xpath="ISBN" />
    </xs:keyref>
  </xs:element>
</xs:schema>
```

With the new annotations, you are now able to rewrite the previous code as follows:

```
LibraryAnnotated libraryA = new LibraryAnnotated();
libraryA.ReadXml(@"..\..\..\morebooks_annotated.xml");

foreach (LibraryAnnotated.Book book in libraryA.Books)
{
  Console.WriteLine("Book: {0}, Written by {1}", book.Title, book.Author );
  foreach (LibraryAnnotated.Chapter chapter in book.GetChapters())
  {
    Console.WriteLine("\tChapter: {0}, Pages {1}", chapter.Title, chapter.Pages);
  }
}
```

29

Summary

This chapter started with an introduction to the XML Schema Definition (XSD) language. You saw how to read schemas, how to create schemas using text editors, and how to create schemas programmatically using the XmlSchema class.

With the introduction to XSD out of the way, you saw how to use XSD to generate structure within a DataSet. Finally, you saw how to create typed DataSets that not only enforce structure, but do so at compile time, giving you IntelliSense support and compile-time type checking, as well as the ability to use annotations to make the DataSets even easier to use.

With this new knowledge, you should begin to consider using typed DataSets for your next applicable project rather than resorting to the quick and easy fix of using a generic DataSet. If you know the structure of your data at design-time, you should definitely think about taking advantage of typed DataSets.

Further Reading

Microsoft ADO.NET (Core Reference), Microsoft Press. ISBN: 0735614237.

ADO.NET In a Nutshell by Matthew MacDonald and Bill Hamilton, O'Reilly. ISBN: 0596003617.

30 Windows Forms Data Binding

IN BRIEF

In this section of the book, you have been learning about and experimenting with ADO.NET. You have seen how the `DataSet` works, including how relationships can be established between multiple tables within a single `DataSet` and how you can create strongly typed `DataSets` from XML schema information. If you've been reading the chapters in order, you have also seen how to combine a `DataSet` and a data adapter to a linked system that automatically pushes changes made to the `DataSet` back to the original data source through either stored procedures or SQL statements such as `INSERT`, `UPDATE`, and so on.

All of this is incredibly useful information, but it doesn't do anyone any good if the user never sees all of this powerful data access. If the user interface doesn't take advantage of all the various features of ADO.NET, the user won't have benefited at all. This chapter shows you how to create compelling, data-driven user interfaces with ADO.NET using Windows Forms technology.

WHAT YOU NEED

REQUIRED SOFTWARE	.NET Framework SDK v1.1 Visual Studio .NET 2003 with C# installed
RECOMMENDED HARDWARE	PC that meets .NET SDK minimum requirements
SKILLS REQUIRED	C# and .NET familiarity

WINDOWS FORMS DATA BINDING AT A GLANCE

Data Binding Overview	**613**			
Introduction to Windows Forms Data Binding	613	Complex Data Binding	616	
Simple Data Binding	613	One-Way and Two-Way Data Binding	616	
Data Binding Mechanics	**616**			
The `BindingContext` Class	617	The `PropertyManager` Class	620	
The `CurrencyManager` Class	617			
Data Binding Samples	**621**			
Simple Binding	621	`DataGrid` Binding	622	
Binding to a `ComboBox`	622			
Advanced Binding Samples	**625**			
Header/Detail Forms	625	Cascading Header/Detail	628	
Summary	**632**			

Data Binding Overview

Data binding is the act of attaching a source of data to a user interface control. As you will see, data binding can be done in a read-only mode or in a bi-directional mode in which data can flow from the source to the control and data can flow from the control (via the user) to the data source. The next section will introduce you to some of the basic concepts of WinForms data binding and show you the various ways in which data binding can be done on a Windows Form. If you have any preconceived notions about data binding based on your COM, Visual Basic 6, or MFC experience, you should leave those behind.

Introduction to Windows Forms Data Binding

Windows Forms data binding provides an extremely powerful, easy-to-use method for linking data between a data source and a GUI control. The controls that are typically bound are `DataGrids`, `ComboBoxes`, `TextBoxes`, and many more. They can be bound to all kinds of data, including objects that implement the `IList` interface, arrays, `ArrayLists`, `DataSets`, `DataTables`, and much more. As you will see later in this chapter, you can even bind different properties of controls (such as size, position, color, and so on) to different data sources.

Simple Data Binding

Simple data binding refers to a situation in which a single value within the data source is bound to a single property on the interface control. For example, you can bind a value in the data source to the `Text` property of a `TextBox`. In other cases, you might want to bind some of the numeric properties of a control to data source values, such as the size, position, or any other aspect of the control that can be managed with a single property.

The ability to bind the value of a property to a single value within a data source is accomplished through the `DataBindings` collection. Every control that can be bound has a `DataBindings` collection. When you add a binding to this collection, you specify the property on the control to which you will be binding. Then you specify the object that provides the binding value and the property name on that object that will supply the value. Listing 30.1 shows how to use the `DataBindings` collection to create two different controls that have their `Text` properties dynamically bound to the `TextProperty` property on the `SimpleBindingClass` class instance.

To create the sample shown in Listing 30.1, just create a new Windows Forms application called `SimpleBinding` and change the main form class to be called `frmMain.cs`.

Data Binding Overview

LISTING 30.1
The Main Form of a Simple Data Binding Demonstration Application

```csharp
using System;
using System.Drawing;
using System.Collections;
using System.ComponentModel;
using System.Windows.Forms;
using System.Data;

namespace SimpleBinding
{

  public class frmMain : System.Windows.Forms.Form
  {
    private System.Windows.Forms.Label lblSimpleBinding;
    private System.Windows.Forms.TextBox txtSimpleBinding;
    /// <summary>
    /// Required designer variable.
    /// </summary>
    private System.ComponentModel.Container components = null;
    private System.Windows.Forms.Button btnExamine;
    private SimpleBindingClass simpleBind = new SimpleBindingClass();

    public frmMain()
    {

      InitializeComponent();

      simpleBind.TextProperty = "Hello World";
      lblSimpleBinding.DataBindings.Add("Text", simpleBind, "TextProperty");
      txtSimpleBinding.DataBindings.Add("Text", simpleBind, "TextProperty");
    }

    /// <summary>
    /// Clean up any resources being used.
    /// </summary>
    protected override void Dispose( bool disposing )
    {
      if( disposing )
      {
        if (components != null)
        {
```

1

LISTING 30.1
Continued

```
            components.Dispose();
        }
    }
    base.Dispose( disposing );
}

// Windows Forms designer code cut for ease of reading

/// <summary>
/// The main entry point for the application.
/// </summary>
[STAThread]
static void Main()
{
    Application.Run(new frmMain());
}

private void btnExamine_Click(object sender, System.EventArgs e)
{
    MessageBox.Show(simpleBind.TextProperty);
}
}
}
```

The most important lines of code are the following lines taken from the form's
constructor ▮1▮:

```
simpleBind.TextProperty = "Hello World";
lblSimpleBinding.DataBindings.Add("Text", simpleBind, "TextProperty");
txtSimpleBinding.DataBindings.Add("Text", simpleBind, "TextProperty");
```

The preceding code binds both UI controls' Text property to the simpleBind
class's TextProperty property. One important thing to note is that the mechanism
performing the binding will not update the source of the data (in this case, the
simpleBind class instance) until you tab out of the text box. In other words, the
code will not waste time trying to update bindings every time a character changes in
the TextBox control.

Figure 30.1 shows the preceding application in action, after having changed the text
box value and allowing the text box to lose focus.

Data Binding Overview

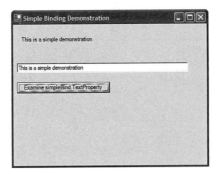

FIGURE 30.1   The simple data binding sample application.

Complex Data Binding

Complex data binding involves binding a user interface control to a list of data instead of a single, scalar value. This list can be virtually any list of data, including an array, an `ArrayList`, `Hashtables`, and so forth—virtually anything that implements the `IList` interface. You will see more about binding to complex data structures later in this chapter.

One-Way and Two-Way Data Binding

As mentioned earlier, Windows Forms allow both one and two-way data binding. When you want to accomplish one-way data binding, you bind the user interface controls to some object that does not propagate changes back to the original data source. This enables you to feed the user interface the data that you want, as well as to explicitly control what data does and does not make it back into the database, text file, XML source, or whatever your data source might be. Two-way data binding refers to associating the user interface control with an object that propagates its changes back to the data source (such as the dynamically bound `DataSet`/`DataAdapter` combination demonstrated in Chapter 27, "Using .NET Data Providers").

Data Binding Mechanics

So far all you've seen code for has been some very simple data binding. Before getting into more involved data binding code, you should know how the guts of the data binding system works. Three classes are present within Windows Forms data binding, whether you notice them or not. The main class responsible for all binding is `BindingContext`. This class can give you an instance of the `CurrencyManager` or the `PropertyManager`, depending on whether you are using simple binding (as in the example you saw earlier) or complex binding to a list-type data source.

The `BindingContext` Class

Every control on a form can have a single `BindingContext` instance associated with it. Each `BindingContext` class is the designated manager for a collection of `BindingManagerBase` objects (such as a `CurrencyManager` or a `PropertyManager`). The most common use of the `BindingContext` class is to obtain a Windows Form's current `BindingContext` to gain access to the binding managers for all the controls on that form.

If subsections of your form require independent data binding code, you can create a `BindingContext` for a container control such as a `GroupBox` or a `Panel` to provide a separate set of binding code for the grouped control.

The `BindingContext` class contains the expected methods for managing a collection, so you can add, remove, and clear the collection of `BindingManagerBase` classes. The most commonly used method is the indexer method, which enables you to access an individual `BindingManagerBase` class based on a data source object and the name of the binding (this is often the name of a table, `DataRelation`, or property). The indexer is two-dimensional. The first dimension is the data source for which you are trying to obtain a `BindingManagerBase` class. The second dimension is the name of the data member. As mentioned previously, this data member can be the name of a `DataTable` or the name of a property.

To illustrate how to obtain a `BindingContext` and use it to get a `BindingManagerBase` class, the following two lines are added to the beginning of the `btnExamine_Click` event handler from Listing 30.1:

```
BindingManagerBase bmLabel = BindingContext[ lblSimpleBinding, "Text" ];
MessageBox.Show(bmLabel.GetType().ToString());
```

When you run the new application, you'll see that the `BindingManagerBase` class for the `lblSimpleBinding` control is a `RelatedPropertyManager` class. Property managers will be discussed shortly.

The `CurrencyManager` Class

The `CurrencyManager` class is used to maintain the current position within the bound list for a given control. Obviously, you can't have the same position for each bound control, so each control bound to a list-type data source will have its own `CurrencyManager` that you can access via the `BindingContext` class. Table 30.1 provides a list of the public properties exposed by the `CurrencyManager` class.

30

Data Binding Mechanics

TABLE 30.1

Public Properties Exposed by the `CurrencyManager` **Class**

Property	Description
`Bindings`	Contains the collection of bindings maintained by the `CurrencyManager`.
`Count`	Indicates the number of rows in the underlying data source.
`Current`	The current object. In a `CurrencyManager`, this is one element within the list-type data source.
`List`	Gets the list to which the `CurrencyManager` is bound.
`Position`	Indicates the current position within the list.

Additional control over your data binding code can be exerted through the various events that are published by the `BindingManagerBase` class and its descendants. Table 30.2 lists the events to which you can subscribe on the `CurrencyManager` class.

TABLE 30.2

Events of the `CurrencyManager` **Class**

Event	Description
`CurrentChanged`	This event is fired when the bound value changes.
`ItemChanged`	This event is fired when the current item changes.
`MetaDataChanged`	This event is fired when the metadata associated with the list changes.
`PositionChanged`	This event is fired when the current position changes. This should not be confused with events that indicate the bound data is changing.

Listing 30.2 illustrates a sample Windows Forms application that makes use of the currency manager. Although you could accomplish what this application does in other ways, it is extremely valuable and important for you to learn to work with the `CurrencyManager` if you will be writing any kind of complex, data-driven Windows Forms applications in the future.

LISTING 30.2

A Sample Application That Illustrates the Use of the `CurrencyManager` **Class and Complex Data Binding**

```
using System;
using System.Drawing;
using System.Collections;
using System.ComponentModel;
using System.Windows.Forms;
using System.Data;


namespace CurrencyManager
```

30

LISTING 30.2
Continued

```
{
  public class frmCurrencyManager : System.Windows.Forms.Form
  {
    private System.Windows.Forms.ListBox listBox1;
    private System.Windows.Forms.Label label1;
    private System.Windows.Forms.Label lblCurrentValue;
    private System.Windows.Forms.Label label2;
    private System.Windows.Forms.Label lblPosition;
    private ArrayList al;

    /// <summary>
    /// Required designer variable.
    /// </summary>
    private System.ComponentModel.Container components = null;

    public frmCurrencyManager()
    {
      InitializeComponent();

      al = new ArrayList();
      al.Add( "Monday" );
      al.Add( "Tuesday" );
      al.Add( "Wednesday" );
      al.Add( "Thursday" );
      al.Add( "Friday" );
      al.Add( "Saturday" );
      al.Add( "Sunday" );

      listBox1.DataSource = al;

      System.Windows.Forms.CurrencyManager cm =
        (System.Windows.Forms.CurrencyManager)BindingContext[ al ];
      cm.CurrentChanged += new EventHandler(cm_CurrentChanged);
      cm_CurrentChanged(this, null);
    }

    /// <summary>
    /// Clean up any resources being used.
    /// </summary>
    protected override void Dispose( bool disposing )
    {
      if( disposing )
      {
```

30

Data Binding Mechanics

LISTING 30.2
Continued

```
    if (components != null)
    {
      components.Dispose();
    }
  }
  base.Dispose( disposing );
}

// Windows Forms designer code edited out for clarity.

[STAThread]
static void Main()
{
  Application.Run(new frmCurrencyManager());
}

private void cm_CurrentChanged(object sender, EventArgs e)
{
  System.Windows.Forms.CurrencyManager cm =
    (System.Windows.Forms.CurrencyManager)BindingContext[ al ];
  lblCurrentValue.Text = cm.Current.ToString();
  lblPosition.Text = cm.Position.ToString();
  }
 }
}
```

Here a standard list box is bound to an `ArrayList` that represents the days of the week. At the end of the form's constructor, a reference to the `CurrencyManager` is obtained (note that you don't have to keep that reference in scope for all of this code to work because the form itself has the original references) and then an event handler for the `CurrentChanged` event is rigged up.

When this event is fired, the code updates a display that shows the current value and the current position of the binding context. Figure 30.2 shows how this application looks when running.

The `PropertyManager` Class

The `PropertyManager` class is used when dealing with simple binding. When you create a simple binding via `Bindings.Add`, the resulting `BindingManagerBase` class is a `PropertyManager`. The properties in Table 30.3 apply to the `PropertyManager` class.

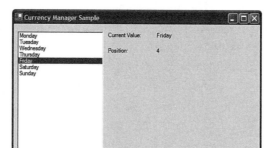

FIGURE 30.2 The CurrencyManager sample illustrating the use of a CurrencyManager class in binding.

TABLE 30.3

Properties of the PropertyManager Class

Property	Description
Bindings	Contains the collection of bindings managed by this class.
Count	Gets the number of rows being managed by the class. For property managers, this is always 1.
Current	Gets the object to which the data-bound property has been associated.
Position	Gets the current position within the list-based data source. In a property manager, this is always 0.

30

Data Binding Samples

The next section will show you some samples of data binding. Some of these samples will be review (such as the simple binding and ComboBox binding), but the DataGrid sample will be entirely new. Before going on to discuss more advanced data binding topics, you should see the DataGrid binding in action and understand how it works in conjunction with the currency manager and the BindingContext.

Simple Binding

As you saw earlier, simple binding involves the association of a single value on a data source with a single property value on a control. This is accomplished by adding a new binding instance to the DataBindings collection, as shown here:

```
lblDescription.DataBindings.Add("Text", objDataSource, "Description");
```

Data Binding Samples

All the code that you saw earlier dealing with the `PropertyManager` (obtained through the `BindingContext` class) applies to simple binding concepts. One of the most common uses for simple binding is to automatically store and retrieve control properties such as size, location, colors, and so forth in an effort to remember user preferences.

Binding to a `ComboBox`

Earlier in the chapter, you saw an example of binding to a `ListBox` control. Binding to a `ComboBox` control is no different. All you do is set the `DataSource` property of the control, as well as the `DisplayMember` and `ValueMember` properties, if applicable. After that has been done, you can use the control properties and the members of the `CurrencyManager` class to create a rich, data-bound user experience.

`DataGrid` Binding

This brings up the topic of binding to a `DataGrid`. The `DataGrid` is at once one of the most powerful WinForms controls and the most frustrating. It can save you a lot of time if it is used properly, but it can cause you an endless amount of frustration if it isn't used properly.

The `DataGrid` sample you are going to see doesn't allow inline editing within the grid. Although it is useful to know how this works, there are very few actual user interfaces where this is actually a desired behavior. More often than not, the `DataGrid` is used to display columnar data and to allow the user to browse. After the user has found the record he wants to work with, he double-clicks it to open an additional editor that might also display data related to that record. You'll see how to use a `CurrencyManager` to take care of that.

Listing 30.3 shows a sample form that has on it a single `DataGrid`, two buttons, and a context menu associated with the grid. The first button simply retrieves data from the Northwind sample database in SQL 2000 (you can change your code to get it from the Access database if you don't have a copy of SQL installed). The second button and the context menu simulate what the code might look like if you were to launch a user editor dialog based on the current position of the cursor within the `DataGrid`. The most refreshing thing to notice is that this code doesn't do any hit testing, nor does it look at any two-dimensional array of cells; all it does is look at the `BindingContext`, which is always the simplest way to get at the current row of any data source.

LISTING 30.3

An Illustration of `DataGrid` Binding and Interaction with a `CurrencyManager`

```
using System;
using System.Drawing;
using System.Collections;
```

LISTING 30.3
Continued

```csharp
using System.ComponentModel;
using System.Windows.Forms;
using System.Data;
using System.Data.SqlClient;

namespace DataGridBinding
{

public class Form1 : System.Windows.Forms.Form
{
  private System.Windows.Forms.DataGrid dataGrid1;
  private System.Windows.Forms.Button button1;
  private System.Windows.Forms.Button btnEdit;
  private System.Windows.Forms.ContextMenu cmGrid;
  private System.Windows.Forms.MenuItem cmiEditUser;

  private System.ComponentModel.Container components = null;

  public Form1()
  {
    InitializeComponent();

  }

  protected override void Dispose( bool disposing )
  {
    if( disposing )
    {
      if (components != null)
      {
        components.Dispose();
      }
    }
    base.Dispose( disposing );
  }

  // Windows Forms designer code cut out for clarity

  [STAThread]
  static void Main()
  {
    Application.Run(new Form1());
```

Data Binding Samples

LISTING 30.3
Continued

```
    }

    private void button1_Click(object sender, System.EventArgs e)
    {
      SqlConnection conn =
        new SqlConnection(
        "server=localhost; User ID=sa; Password=password; Initial Catalog=Northwind;");
      conn.Open();
      SqlDataAdapter da = new SqlDataAdapter("SELECT * FROM Customers", conn);
      DataSet dsCustomers = new DataSet();
      da.Fill(dsCustomers,"Customers");
      dataGrid1.DataSource = dsCustomers.Tables["Customers"];
    }


    private void btnEdit_Click(object sender, System.EventArgs e)
    {
      CurrencyManager cm = (CurrencyManager)BindingContext[ dataGrid1.DataSource ];
      DataRowView drv = (DataRowView)cm.Current;
      System.Diagnostics.Debug.WriteLine(
        "About to edit customer " + drv["CustomerID"].ToString());

      // launch user editor with drv as parameter
    }

    private void cmiEditUser_Click(object sender, System.EventArgs e)
    {
      CurrencyManager cm = (CurrencyManager)BindingContext[ dataGrid1.DataSource ];
      DataRowView drv = (DataRowView)cm.Current;
      System.Diagnostics.Debug.WriteLine(
        "About to edit customer " + drv["CustomerID"].ToString());

      // launch user editor with drv as parameter
    }


    }
}
```

When you play around with this sample, you'll begin to see how powerful it really is. Although it might not be flashy or complicated, it does illustrate a very powerful principle. When using a DataGrid that can be extremely complicated visually, especially when displaying entire hierarchies of data, all you need to remember is that you can always rely on the `BindingContext` and the `CurrencyManager`. These classes will always be there, and they will always give you the right information quickly and easily. When many developers are first learning Windows Forms, they often learn nothing of the `BindingContext` class or of the `CurrencyManager` class. As a result, many think that Windows Forms data binding is complex and difficult. After developers obtain a firm grasp on the big picture of how everything works and how all the data binding facets are interrelated, Windows Forms data binding is actually very pleasant, quick, and powerful.

After you have played with a technology to the point where the information no longer intimidates you, you can begin to create some incredible solutions, especially with powerful tools such as Windows Forms data binding. Tinker with the samples you have seen in this chapter until you feel that you have mastered the samples. The following advanced binding samples will be much easier to follow at that point.

Advanced Binding Samples

The next section will take you through the process of creating some complex header/detail forms using Windows Forms data binding, parent/child relationships within `DataSets`, and (of course) the `BindingContext` and `CurrencyManager` classes.

30

Header/Detail Forms

A header/detail form is a scenario in which a grid is bound to a data source. In addition, there is a grid bound to some child relationship. For example, if you are looking at a grid of customers and you select a customer row, you would expect the child grid (containing that customer's orders) to automatically refresh to display just the orders for that customer. This is an example of a header/detail form, where the header is the grid bound to the parent rows and the detail grid is bound to the child rows of each row to which the header grid is bound.

To create the sample in Listing 30.4, two grids, called `dgCustomers` and `dgOrders`, respectively, are dropped onto a form. Then a Get Data button is added to fetch information from the database to populate the grids. The tricky part here is that data is fetched from two different queries into the same table, and then a parent-child relationship is created between those tables. This relationship is what enables the header/detail grid binding.

LISTING 30.4
A Form That Demonstrates Header/Detail Grid Binding

```
using System;
using System.Drawing;
using System.Collections;
```

Advanced Binding Samples

LISTING 30.4
Continued

```
using System.ComponentModel;
using System.Windows.Forms;
using System.Data;
using System.Data.SqlClient;

namespace AdvGridBinding
{
  public class Form1 : System.Windows.Forms.Form
  {
    private System.Windows.Forms.Button btnGetData;
    private System.Windows.Forms.DataGrid dgCustomers;
    private System.Windows.Forms.DataGrid dgOrders;
    private System.ComponentModel.Container components = null;

    public Form1()
    {
      InitializeComponent();
    }

    /// <summary>
    /// Clean up any resources being used.
    /// </summary>
    protected override void Dispose( bool disposing )
    {
     if( disposing )
     {
        if (components != null)
        {
          components.Dispose();
        }
     }
      base.Dispose( disposing );
    }

    // Windows Forms designer code cut out for clarity

    /// <summary>
    /// The main entry point for the application.
    /// </summary>
    [STAThread]
    static void Main()
    {
```

LISTING 30.4
Continued

```csharp
      Application.Run(new Form1());
  }

  private void btnGetData_Click(object sender, System.EventArgs e)
  {
    SqlConnection conn = new SqlConnection(
      "server=localhost; User ID=sa; Password=password; Initial Catalog=Northwind;");
    conn.Open();
    DataSet ds = new DataSet();
    SqlDataAdapter custDA = new SqlDataAdapter("SELECT * FROM Customers", conn);
    SqlDataAdapter ordersDA = new SqlDataAdapter("SELECT * FROM Orders", conn);
    custDA.Fill(ds, "Customers");
    ordersDA.Fill(ds, "Orders");

    DataRelation dr = new DataRelation("CustOrders",
      ds.Tables["Customers"].Columns["CustomerID"],
      ds.Tables["Orders"].Columns["CustomerID"]);
    ds.Relations.Add( dr );

    dgCustomers.DataSource = ds;
    dgCustomers.DataMember = "Customers";

    dgOrders.DataSource = ds;
    dgOrders.DataMember = "Customers.CustOrders";

    BindingContext[ dgCustomers.DataSource, "Customers" ].CurrentChanged +=
      new EventHandler(Form1_CurrentChanged);

  }

  private void Form1_CurrentChanged(object sender, EventArgs e)
  {
    CurrencyManager cm =
     (CurrencyManager) BindingContext[ dgCustomers.DataSource,
        "Customers" ];
    DataRowView drv = (DataRowView)cm.Current;
    dgOrders.CaptionText = string.Format("{0}'s Order History",
    drv["ContactName"]);
  }
 }
}
```

30

Advanced Binding Samples

When retrieving the data, you can see that the code uses two DataAdapters so that the results of two different SQL queries can be placed into the same DataSet by specifying unique table names as destinations. If you don't specify a destination table name, the SqlDataAdapter will name the first table Table, the second Table1, and so on.

For the parent/child relationship to work properly, both grids must be bound to the same data source and differ by only the name of the data member. For example, if you bound the dgCustomers grid to the Customers table with no data member instead of to the DataSet using Customers as a data member, the child grid would never be updated with currency changes.

Finally, just to show you some more uses for the BindingContext and CurrencyManager, the detail grid's CaptionText is changed to indicate the name of the customer who owns the list of orders in the grid. This shows how, with just a small amount of effort, you can add little touches to your applications that will increase the usability of your application and the depth of its user experience.

Cascading Header/Detail

Cascading header/detail forms refers to the situation in which each row in a detail grid is also the parent row to another grid. This cascading effect of parents that are details that are parents is often daunting and overwhelming for programmers to implement. It was especially difficult before .NET was available when most people turned to third-party grid controls to accomplish this task.

The code in Listing 30.5 is a modified version of the previous sample. The difference is that a third grid has been added to the form. This grid displays the list of items that belong to a specific order (which in turn belongs to a specific customer). To keep things interesting, inner join is performed to obtain the product name of each item in the order. This should add to your impression of how powerful and flexible Windows Forms data binding can be.

LISTING 30.5

A Modified Advanced Grid Binding Form That Illustrates a Cascade or Waterfall of Parent/Detail Records

```
using System;
using System.Drawing;
using System.Collections;
using System.ComponentModel;
using System.Windows.Forms;
using System.Data;
using System.Data.SqlClient;
```

LISTING 30.5
Continued

```
namespace AdvGridBinding
{
  public class Form1 : System.Windows.Forms.Form
  {
    private System.Windows.Forms.Button btnGetData;
    private System.Windows.Forms.DataGrid dgCustomers;
    private System.Windows.Forms.DataGrid dgOrders;
    private System.Windows.Forms.DataGrid dgOrderDetails;

    private System.ComponentModel.Container components = null;

    public Form1()
    {

      InitializeComponent();

    }

    /// <summary>
    /// Clean up any resources being used.
    /// </summary>
    protected override void Dispose( bool disposing )
    {
      if( disposing )
      {
        if (components != null)
        {
          components.Dispose();
        }
      }
      base.Dispose( disposing );
    }

// Windows Forms designer code excluded for clarity

    /// <summary>
    /// The main entry point for the application.
    /// </summary>
    [STAThread]
```

30

Advanced Binding Samples

LISTING 30.5
Continued

```
static void Main()
{
  Application.Run(new Form1());
}

private void btnGetData_Click(object sender, System.EventArgs e)
{
  SqlConnection conn = new SqlConnection(
    "server=localhost; User ID=sa; Password=password; Initial Catalog=Northwind;");
  conn.Open();
  DataSet ds = new DataSet();
  SqlDataAdapter custDA = new SqlDataAdapter("SELECT * FROM Customers", conn);
  SqlDataAdapter ordersDA = new SqlDataAdapter("SELECT * FROM Orders", conn);
  SqlDataAdapter orderitemsDA = new SqlDataAdapter(
    "SELECT p.ProductName, od.ProductId, od.UnitPrice, od.Quantity, " +
    "od.Discount, od.OrderID " +
    "FROM [Order Details] od INNER JOIN Products p ON " +
    "od.ProductId = p.ProductID", conn);
  custDA.Fill(ds, "Customers");
  ordersDA.Fill(ds, "Orders");
  orderitemsDA.Fill(ds,"OrderItems");

  DataRelation dr =
    new DataRelation("CustOrders", ds.Tables["Customers"].Columns["CustomerID"],
    ds.Tables["Orders"].Columns["CustomerID"]);
  ds.Relations.Add( dr );
  dr = new DataRelation("OrderDetails", ds.Tables["Orders"].Columns["OrderID"],
    ds.Tables["OrderItems"].Columns["OrderID"]);
  ds.Relations.Add( dr );

  dgCustomers.DataSource = ds;
  dgCustomers.DataMember = "Customers";

  dgOrders.DataSource = ds;
  dgOrders.DataMember = "Customers.CustOrders";

  dgOrderDetails.DataSource = ds;
```

30

LISTING 30.5
Continued

```
    dgOrderDetails.DataMember = "Customers.CustOrders.OrderDetails";

    BindingContext[ dgCustomers.DataSource, "Customers" ].CurrentChanged +=
      new EventHandler(Form1_CurrentChanged);
    BindingContext[ dgOrders.DataSource, "Customers.CustOrders"].CurrentChanged +=
      new EventHandler(CustOrders_CurrentChanged);
    conn.Close();
  }

  private void Form1_CurrentChanged(object sender, EventArgs e)
  {
    string custName;
    CurrencyManager cm = (CurrencyManager) BindingContext[ dgCustomers.DataSource,
      "Customers" ];
    DataRowView drv = (DataRowView)cm.Current;
    custName = drv["ContactName"].ToString();
    dgOrders.CaptionText = string.Format("{0}'s Order History",
      custName);
  }

  private void CustOrders_CurrentChanged(object sender, EventArgs e)
  {
    CurrencyManager cm = (CurrencyManager)BindingContext[ dgOrders.DataSource,
      "Customers.CustOrders"];
    DataRowView drv = (DataRowView)cm.Current;
    DataRow customer = drv.Row.GetParentRow("CustOrders");
    dgOrderDetails.CaptionText = string.Format("{0}'s Order on {1} ({2})",
      customer["ContactName"], ((DateTime)drv["OrderDate"]).ToShortDateString(),
      drv["OrderID"]);
  }
 }
}
```

One of the more subtle things taking place in the new event handler for the second grid is that because the `DataSet` has built-in relationships, the `DataRowView` instance can be used to get at the underlying row, which can then obtain a reference to its parent via the `GetParentRow` method. When you compile and run the preceding Windows Forms application, you will be presented with the form shown in Figure 30.3.

Advanced Binding Samples

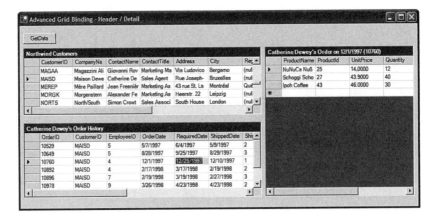

FIGURE 30.3   A cascading header/detail data binding application.

Summary

Some reactions of developers when discussing WinForms data binding are that it is too complicated, too difficult to use, and not as flexible as ASP.NET data binding. The truth is that ASP.NET and Windows Forms data binding serve two different purposes, and therefore act, function, and look very different.

This chapter showed you that Windows Forms data binding is indeed extremely powerful and very flexible. After reading this chapter, you won't believe any of the rumors that WinForms data binding is difficult or too complex.

You saw how you can do everything from simple binding of one property on a control to a field in a data source to cascading a long series of parent/child relationships in related `DataGrid` objects. You saw the mechanics of WinForms data binding and the importance of learning how to use the `BindingContext`, `CurrencyManager`, and `PropertyManager` classes.

After reading this chapter and doing the samples included, you should not only feel comfortable using Windows Forms data binding, but also realize that it has far more power and flexibility than many people realize.

31 Web Forms Data Binding

IN BRIEF

This section of the book is focused entirely on ADO.NET and dealing with data in various forms. Data binding is a very broad topic, especially when you are talking about data binding within the .NET Framework.

Both Windows Forms and Web Forms (ASP.NET) have completely unique implementations of data binding. Rather than this being a hindrance to developers, it is actually very helpful. The reason for the difference is that web applications have different data binding needs than Windows applications, and the data binding mechanisms supplied for each application type are optimized for that.

ASP.NET data binding is a lengthy subject that we can't provide complete coverage for in a chapter of this size in a book this size. However, this chapter aims to provide a good summary of the code and design involved in binding your data to ASP.NET controls.

WHAT YOU NEED

REQUIRED SOFTWARE	.NET Framework SDK v1.1Visual Studio .NET 2003 with C# installed IIS version 5+ Windows XP, 2000 Pro+, 2003
RECOMMENDED HARDWARE	PC that meets .NET SDK minimum requirements
SKILLS REQUIRED	C# and .NET familiarity ADO.NET familiarity

WEB FORMS DATA BINDING AT A GLANCE

Data Binding Overview	**635**		
Introduction to Web Forms Data Binding	635	Simple Data Binding	636
		Complex Data Binding	638
`<%# %>` Binding Syntax	635	The `DataBind()` Methods	638
Data Binding Mechanics	**639**		
`Container.DataItem`	639	The `ItemDataBound` Event	640
`DataBinder.Eva`	639		
Data Binding Samples	**641**		
Simple Binding	641	`DataList` Binding	645
`Repeater` Binding	641	`DataGrid` Binding	647
Advanced Binding Samples	**647**		
Header and Detail Forms	652	Cascading Header and Detail	652
Summary	**657**		
Further Reading	**658**		

Data Binding Overview

The next section will give you a good idea of how ASP.NET data binding works and how your code can take advantage of the various binding mechanisms available. You will see examples of simple binding, complex binding, and the methods available in controls and page classes that facilitate data binding.

Introduction to Web Forms Data Binding

Web Forms data binding is much different from the dynamic, bi-directional update model that you saw in Chapter 30, "Windows Forms Data Binding." The ASP.NET model is specifically designed with the notion that the vast majority of all data-related tasks involve retrieving data and rendering it in some fashion, whether it is simple output or an extremely complex grid. As a result, ASP.NET data binding is *read-only*. When you bind a control in ASP.NET, it does not have the capability to dynamically modify the original data source.

There are several reasons for that. The first and foremost reason is that for most data modifications to take place, a round-trip must occur and the client browser must re-request the page. On a re-request, the interface control has no way of knowing whether the data source it was originally bound to will exist after the round trip, or if the data will remain the same. This is why most data-bound controls allow their bound data to be stored in `ViewState` to appear again after a round trip to the server.

There are several aspects to ASP.NET data binding. The first is binding the data to a control, and the second is rendering the bound data. You can render the bound data in any number of ways. The next few sections show you some of the ways in which data can be rendered for a data-bound control.

<%# %> Binding Syntax

Those of you familiar with classic ASP applications might think that the `<%# %>` syntax looks very familiar. It is similar in purpose, but you need to make sure that you don't confuse the two because doing so could cause your application to function improperly.

Whereas in ASP (and ASP.NET), the `<%= %>` syntax causes whatever is inside the brackets to be evaluated at render time, the `<%# %>` brackets unique to ASP.NET are evaluated only during binding. As you will see later in this section, the page and each bindable control on the page have a `DataBind()` method. The expressions contained within the data binding brackets (`<%# %>`) are evaluated only when the control's `DataBind` method is invoked. You will see how to use this syntax shortly.

31

Simple Data Binding

Simple data binding refers to the situation in which you bind a single value to a property of a control. In addition to binding to the property of a control, you can also
simply insert directly into the document the result of a binding operation. Simple
data binding is accomplished via the bind evaluation brackets (<%# %>).

Listing 31.1 shows the ASP.NET page that illustrates some very simple data-binding
techniques. Listing 31.2 shows the code-behind C# code that provides the background data and method calls that are invoked by the controls.

LISTING 31.1
An ASP.NET Page That Makes Use of Simple Binding

```
<%@ Page language="c#"
    Codebehind="SimpleBinding.aspx.cs"
    AutoEventWireup="false" Inherits="WebFormsBinding.SimpleBinding" %>

<!DOCTYPE HTML PUBLIC "-//W3C//DTD HTML 4.0 Transitional//EN" >
<HTML>
<HEAD>
<title>SimpleBinding</title>
 <meta name="GENERATOR" Content="Microsoft Visual Studio .NET 7.1">
 <meta name="CODE_LANGUAGE" Content="C#">
 <meta name="vs_defaultClientScript" content="JavaScript">
 <meta name="vs_targetSchema"
content="http://schemas.microsoft.com/intellisense/ie5">
</HEAD>
<body>
  <form id="Form1" method="post" runat="server">
  <asp:TextBox ID="txtSample" Runat=server Text="<%# myFunction()
%>"></asp:TextBox><br>
  <asp:Panel ID="pnlSample" Height="<%# height %>"
            Width="<%# width %>"
            BorderColor="<%# Color %>"
    Runat=server BorderStyle=Solid>
      <%# GetPanelText() %>
  </asp:Panel>
</form>
</body>
</HTML>
```

31

LISTING 31.2

The Code-Behind for the ASP.NET Page in Listing 31.1

```csharp
using System;
using System.Collections;
using System.ComponentModel;
using System.Data;
using System.Drawing;
using System.Web;
using System.Web.SessionState;
using System.Web.UI;
using System.Web.UI.WebControls;
using System.Web.UI.HtmlControls;

namespace WebFormsBinding
{
  public class SimpleBinding : System.Web.UI.Page
  {
    public int width = 30;
    public int height= 30;
    public Color Color = Color.Red;

    private void Page_Load(object sender, System.EventArgs e)
    {
      // if you take this code out, none of the bound controls will be bound
      // and no <%# %> expressions will be evaluated
      DataBind();
    }

    public string myFunction()
    {
      return "This came from a bound function call";
    }

    public string GetPanelText()
    {
      return "This is inside a panel";
    }

    #region Web Form Designer generated code
    override protected void OnInit(EventArgs e)
    {

      InitializeComponent();
      base.OnInit(e);
```

31

LISTING 31.2
Continued

```
    }

    /// <summary>
    /// Required method for Designer support - do not modify
    /// the contents of this method with the code editor.
    /// </summary>
    private void InitializeComponent()
    {
      this.Load += new System.EventHandler(this.Page_Load);
    }
    #endregion
  }
}
```

A couple of different things are going on in this sample. The value of the text box is bound (remember this is read-only) to the result of the function myFunction. A panel's various properties are controlled by being bound to some public fields on the page class, such as the height, width, and color. In addition, the text that appears inside the panel is dictated by the GetPanelText() method. It can't be stressed enough that data binding in ASP.NET is a one-time deal. When the page loads, you choose when the DataBind() method is called and for which controls. That method then supplies data *to* controls based on the code you've written. The controls may maintain their own state between page views, but the data in the control is never automatically written back to the original source—that is something you will have to write manually.

Complex Data Binding

Simple data binding deals with simple scalar values, such as strings and integers. Complex data binding deals with list-type data. In fact, any data type that implements the IEnumerable interface can be bound as a list-type to any of the server controls that support multiple rows of data, such as the DataGrid, DataList, and Repeater. You will see these controls demonstrated shortly.

The DataBind() Methods

As you saw in the first sample on simple data binding, there is a method that you can invoke on the page class that will perform data binding for every control on the page in a cascading fashion. If there are containers of other controls on the page when the DataBind() method is called, those controls will be data-bound at the time. Each bindable control in the entire library of ASP.NET server controls has a DataBind() method.

Unlike WinForms, where you simply set the data source and everything magically appears, ASP.NET requires you to invoke the `DataBind()` method for any data binding to occur.

Data Binding Mechanics

The next section will dig a little deeper and cover some of the nuts and bolts of the data binding system for ASP.NET, including some of the most commonly called methods and properties, such as `Container.DataItem`, `DataBinder.Eval`, and the `ItemDataBound` event.

Container.DataItem

`Container.DataItem` is a property on a class that is made available to ASP.NET controls at runtime. The `Container` class instance's `DataItem` property indicates the item to which the current control's container has been bound. This property is used within templates to provide additional user interface functionality. *Templates* are formatting models that are instantiated for each row bound. When creating an item template, you can use `Container.DataItem` to refer to the piece of data to which the current item has been bound. You will see more of the `ItemTemplate` and other templates when you see some sample binding with `Repeaters`, `DataLists`, and `DataGrids`.

31

DataBinder.Eval

The `DataBinder` class is a noninheritable class that is used for one purpose: data binding shortcuts. It has a single method, `Eval`, that is used to evaluate data binding expressions at runtime and return type-safe results.

The reason for using this syntax instead of using the standard data binding expression syntax is because the `Eval` method uses Reflection to map the binding expression to a data-bound object. It performs type casting and type conversion so that the developer does not have to worry about it at design time. This method is what makes it possible for Visual Studio .NET 2003 to enable the developer to write data binding expressions in a design tool against an object that will not be instantiated until runtime.

The `Eval` method can take up to three arguments. The first two arguments are required. The first parameter is the data source object on which the evaluation should be performed. This is very often a dynamically bound object supplied by ASP.NET that you can refer to with the `Container.DataItem` syntax. The second parameter is the name of the member on the data source to evaluate. The third (and optional) parameter is a format string that dictates the format into which to convert the output.

For example:

```
<%# DataBinder.Eval( Container.DataItem, "RetailPrice", "{0:c}" %>
```

This outputs the value of the `RetailPrice` member on whatever object is currently bound in the localized currency format.

The only caveat here is that this method uses Reflection. If you know at design time everything you need to know to perform your binding, you can get away without using the `DataBinder.Eval` method and bypass the performance penalty you would incur by using Reflection.

The `ItemDataBound` Event

When you think of binding, you might think of it taking place in one big event. For example, you bind a `DataGrid` to a table that has 400 rows in it. To the naked eye, it looks like the grid was simply bound to the entire set of data and that's all that took place.

In reality, each row is individually bound to the data, and rendered using a template that dictates how that row is to be displayed and rendered to the client browser. When a row (or any element in an `IEnumerable` list) is taken from the data source and bound to the various templates, an event is triggered. This event is `OnItemDataBound`, and every bindable ASP.NET control implements it.

Everyone who has ever tried to use data binding knows that binding on its own is almost never enough. You might need custom formatting in some conditions; you might want to insert line breaks or an `<hr>` tag at certain points; you might want to enclose a specific record in a border if it is the currently selected record, and so on. Whatever the reason, if you want control over the process that takes place when an element is bound to a control, you can take advantage of the `OnItemDataBound` event. Each control that implements `OnItemDataBound` supplies its own special type of arguments to the event. Table 31.1 shows the class that implements the event and the name of the event argument class that is supplied with it. You can look the event argument class up in MSDN for a detailed list of all the properties.

TABLE 31.1

Control Classes and the Event Arguments Passed for Item Data Binding

Control Class	Event Argument Class Passed
Repeater	RepeaterItemEventArgs
DataGrid	DataGridItemEventArgs
DataList	DataListItemEventArgs

31

Data Binding Samples

This next section shows you some samples that involve basic ASP.NET Web Forms data binding. You will see how to bind data to simple properties, how to list type controls such as the `Repeater` and `DataList`, and finally you will see an example of using the ASP.NET `DataGrid` control in a data-bound situation.

Simple Binding

You have already seen plenty of examples of simple binding in this chapter. Whenever you use the `<%# %>` syntax to evaluate some expression in the ASP.NET page at bind time, you are using simple binding. A section is included here just as a refresher to remind you that you can accomplish some pretty amazing things using just simple data binding. You should always try to look for the simplest solution to any problem, and simple binding is often overlooked in favor of more complex binding.

`Repeater` Binding

The `Repeater` is a simple control that enables you to define output that will be repeated for each element in the bound list. You can define templates for the header, default items, alternating items (every even numbered element), separators between each element, and even the footer. The `Repeater` is an incredibly flexible control that can be used to display virtually anything that is described by list data. It is also the most basic control and contains the least amount of built-in functionality.

Listing 31.3 shows a `Repeater` control defined by an ASP.NET page, followed by the code-behind class in Listing 31.4. This chapter doesn't spend too much time on templates and template programming because that topic is better covered by chapters on developing GUI controls.

31

LISTING 31.3
An ASP.NET Page Demonstrating the Use of a Data-Bound `Repeater`

```
<%@ Page language="c#"
    Codebehind="RepeaterDemo.aspx.cs"
    AutoEventWireup="false"
    Inherits="WebFormsBinding.RepeaterDemo" %>
<!DOCTYPE HTML PUBLIC "-//W3C//DTD HTML 4.0 Transitional//EN" >
<HTML>
<HEAD>
  <title>RepeaterDemo</title>
    <meta name="GENERATOR" Content="Microsoft Visual Studio .NET 7.1">
    <meta name="CODE_LANGUAGE" Content="C#">
    <meta name="vs_defaultClientScript" content="JavaScript">
```

Data Binding Samples

LISTING 31.3
Continued

```
        <meta name="vs_targetSchema"
            content="http://schemas.microsoft.com/intellisense/ie5">
</HEAD>

<body MS_POSITIONING="GridLayout">

<form id="Form1" method="post" runat="server">
  <asp:Repeater ID="rptCustomer" Runat="server">
    <HeaderTemplate>
     <table width="100%" border="0" cellspacing="1" cellpadding="1">
     <tr>
      <th>
       Contact Name</th>
      <th>
       Company Name</th>
      <th>
       Contact Title</th>
     </tr>
    </HeaderTemplate>
    <FooterTemplate>
     </table>
    </FooterTemplate>
    <ItemTemplate>
     <tr>
       <td><%# DataBinder.Eval(Container.DataItem, "ContactName") %></td>
       <td><%# DataBinder.Eval(Container.DataItem, "CompanyName") %></td>
       <td><%# DataBinder.Eval(Container.DataItem, "ContactTitle") %></td>
     </tr>
    </ItemTemplate>
    <SeparatorTemplate>
     <tr>
       <td colspan="3"><hr>
       </td>
     </tr>
    </SeparatorTemplate>
    <AlternatingItemTemplate>
     <tr bgcolor="#c8c8c8">
       <td><%# DataBinder.Eval(Container.DataItem, "ContactName") %></td>
       <td><%# DataBinder.Eval(Container.DataItem, "CompanyName") %></td>
       <td><%# DataBinder.Eval(Container.DataItem, "ContactTitle") %></td>
     </tr>
    </AlternatingItemTemplate>
```

LISTING 31.3
Continued

```
</asp:Repeater>
</form>
</body>
</HTML>
```

LISTING 31.4
The Code-Behind for the ASP.NET Page in Listing 31.3

```csharp
using System;
using System.Collections;
using System.ComponentModel;
using System.Data;
using System.Data.SqlClient;
using System.Drawing;
using System.Web;
using System.Web.SessionState;
using System.Web.UI;
using System.Web.UI.WebControls;
using System.Web.UI.HtmlControls;

namespace WebFormsBinding
{
  public class RepeaterDemo : System.Web.UI.Page
  {
    protected System.Web.UI.WebControls.Repeater rptCustomer;

    private void Page_Load(object sender, System.EventArgs e)
    {
      SqlConnection conn = new SqlConnection(
        "server=localhost; user id=sa; password=password; Initial Catalog=Northwind;");
      conn.Open();
      SqlDataAdapter da=  new SqlDataAdapter("SELECT * FROM Customers", conn);
      DataSet ds = new DataSet();
      da.Fill(ds,"Customers");

      rptCustomer.DataSource = ds;
      DataBind();
    }

    #region Web Form Designer generated code
    override protected void OnInit(EventArgs e)
```

31

Data Binding Samples

LISTING 31.4
Continued

```
  {
    InitializeComponent();
    base.OnInit(e);
  }

  private void InitializeComponent()
  {
    this.Load += new System.EventHandler(this.Page_Load);

  }
  #endregion
  }
}
```

Figure 31.1 shows what the output of this page looks like. As you would expect, it is a simple repetition of customers from the Northwind database, separated by `<hr>` tags and distinguished with a differing background color for alternating items.

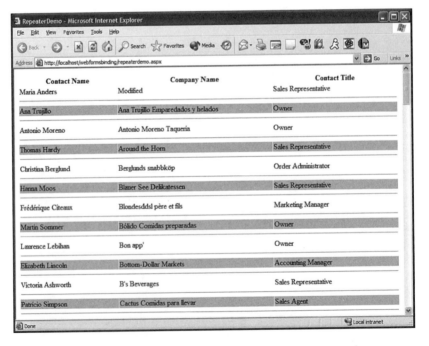

FIGURE 31.1   A `Repeater` control with an `ItemTemplate` and an `AlternatingItemTemplate`.

DataList **Binding**

The DataList is derived from the Repeater, but it adds quite a bit of functionality. Not only can you repeat items, but the DataList also enables you to *flow* items in a given direction. You can choose to have the items appear in sequence horizontally or vertically, and move to the next region of display space after presenting a certain number of items. In this way, you can simulate a display such as a newspaper column layout, and you also can create attractive photo thumbnail displays, product overview displays, and more. The RepeatDirection property controls the direction in which the DataList flows, and the RepeatColumns property indicates the number of items to display before switching (or breaking) to the next repeat of items. If you are flowing vertically, the next repeat of items is a column. If you are flowing horizontally, the next repeat of items will be in a new row.

Listing 31.5 shows that you can create a very attractive flow of data, and you can define visual styles for the items, alternating items, headers, and footers. Styles like that cannot be defined by the Repeater, and this is one area in which the DataList shows off its power. In Listing 31.5, you will see the ASP.NET markup that creates a powerful DataList control. The binding code is not shown because it is virtually identical to the binding code in Listing 31.4.

LISTING 31.5
An ASP.NET Page Demonstrating a Data-Bound DataList Control

```
<%@ Page language="c#" Codebehind="DataListDemo.aspx.cs"
    AutoEventWireup="false" Inherits="WebFormsBinding.DataListDemo" %>
<!DOCTYPE HTML PUBLIC "-//W3C//DTD HTML 4.0 Transitional//EN" >
<HTML>
<HEAD>
  <title>DataListDemo</title>
  <meta name="GENERATOR" Content="Microsoft Visual Studio .NET 7.1">
  <meta name="CODE_LANGUAGE" Content="C#">
  <meta name="vs_defaultClientScript" content="JavaScript">
  <meta name="vs_targetSchema"
content="http://schemas.microsoft.com/intellisense/ie5">
</HEAD>
<body>

<form id="Form1" method="post" runat="server">

  <asp:DataList ID="dlCustomers" Runat="server"
    RepeatColumns="3" RepeatDirection="Horizontal"
    AlternatingItemStyle-BackColor="#c8c8c8" ItemStyle-Height=150>
  <ItemTemplate>
```

31

Data Binding Samples

LISTING 31.5

Continued

```
    1   <table width="100%" border="1"
          bordercolor="#000000" cellspacing="0" cellpadding="0" height=150>
        <tr>
          <td valign="top">
            <table width="100%" border="0" cellspacing="2" cellpadding="2">
              <tr>
                <td colspan="2" align=center>
                  <b><%# DataBinder.Eval(Container.DataItem, "ContactName")%></b>
                </td>
              </tr>
              <tr>
                <td width="50%" >
                  <%# DataBinder.Eval(Container.DataItem, "CompanyName")%>
                </td>
                <td width="50%" >
                  <%# DataBinder.Eval(Container.DataItem, "ContactTitle")%>
                </td>
              </tr>
              <tr>
                <td colspan="2">
                  <%# DataBinder.Eval(Container.DataItem, "Address") %>
                  <br>
                  <%# DataBinder.Eval(Container.DataItem, "City") %>,
                  <%# DataBinder.Eval(Container.DataItem, "PostalCode") %>
                </td>
              </tr>
            </table>
          </td>
        </tr>
      </table>
    </ItemTemplate>

    <HeaderTemplate>
    </HeaderTemplate>
    <FooterTemplate>
    </FooterTemplate>
  </asp:DataList>
  </form>
  </body>
  </HTML>
```

From the preceding code, you should be able to see that each item is a self-contained table with its own border and a nested table to create a surrounding margin **1**. Within the table, the contact name is centered above the contact information, such as the address and postal code. The effect looks very much like a business card. Figure 31.2 shows the (much more attractive) output produced by the `DataList`.

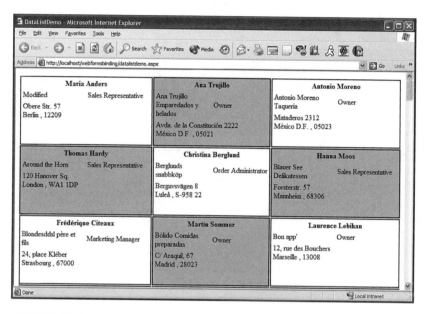

FIGURE 31.2   A `DataList` control bound to data with an `ItemTemplate`.

`DataGrid` **Binding**

The `DataGrid` is a complex and powerful control. It contains all the capability to visually style items that the `DataList` has and much more. It is designed to present data as a list of rows, with each row containing one or more columns. This output looks just like a worksheet in Excel. Not too much time will be spent on the basics of `DataGrid` binding because the advanced samples will cover many of the details of how to manipulate a `DataGrid`.

Advanced Binding Samples

This section will show you some of the more complex data binding types that can be accomplished with ASP.NET. Remember that when the user clicks something on the page, a postback is created, and your controls can either be rebuilt from the database or rebuilt from `ViewState`. The performance impact of the samples shown here will not be discussed. You should be able to look at the samples and see where the performance issues might be for a production system (such as caching the data instead of retrieving it each time).

Header and Detail Forms

One of the most common data binding tasks, as you might have seen in the previous WinForms chapter, is displaying data that exists in a parent-child relationship. This next sample will show you how to create two DataGrids. The first DataGrid contains the parent data (in this case, Customers), and the second DataGrid contains the child data (in this case, Orders). Listings 31.6 and 31.7 show the creation of these linked DataGrids. An explanation of how it works follows the code.

LISTING 31.6

An ASP.NET Page Demonstrating Two DataGrids Linked by a Parent-Child Relationship

```
<%@ Page language="c#" Codebehind="HeaderDetail.aspx.cs"
    AutoEventWireup="false" Inherits="WebFormsBinding.HeaderDetail" %>
<!DOCTYPE HTML PUBLIC "-//W3C//DTD HTML 4.0 Transitional//EN" >
<HTML>
<HEAD>
<title>HeaderDetail</title>
  <meta name="GENERATOR" Content="Microsoft Visual Studio .NET 7.1">
  <meta name="CODE_LANGUAGE" Content="C#">
  <meta name="vs_defaultClientScript" content="JavaScript">
  <meta name="vs_targetSchema"
content="http://schemas.microsoft.com/intellisense/ie5">
</HEAD>
<body>

<form id="Form1" method="post" runat="server">
<table width="100%" border="0" cellspacing="2" cellpadding="2">
<tr>
<td valign="top">
  <asp:DataGrid id="dgCustomers" runat="server"
    BorderColor="#999999" BorderStyle="None" BorderWidth="1px"
    BackColor="White" CellPadding="3" GridLines="Vertical"
    AutoGenerateColumns="False">
    <SelectedItemStyle
      Font-Bold="True" ForeColor="White"
      BackColor="#008A8C"></SelectedItemStyle>
    <AlternatingItemStyle BackColor="#DCDCDC"></AlternatingItemStyle>
    <ItemStyle ForeColor="Black" BackColor="#EEEEEE"></ItemStyle>
    <HeaderStyle Font-Bold="True" ForeColor="White" BackColor="#000084">
```

LISTING 31.6
Continued

```
</HeaderStyle>
    <FooterStyle ForeColor="Black" BackColor="#CCCCCC"></FooterStyle>
    <Columns>
      <asp:ButtonColumn Text="Select" HeaderText="Select"
        CommandName="cmdSelectCustomer"></asp:ButtonColumn>
      <asp:BoundColumn HeaderText="Customer" DataField="ContactName"></asp:BoundColumn>
      <asp:BoundColumn HeaderText="Company" DataField="CompanyName"></asp:BoundColumn>
    </Columns>
    <PagerStyle HorizontalAlign="Center"
      ForeColor="Black" BackColor="#999999" Mode="NumericPages"></PagerStyle>
  </asp:DataGrid>
</td>
<td valign="top" align="left">
  <asp:DataGrid ID="dgOrders" Runat="server" BorderColor="#999999"
    BorderStyle="None" BorderWidth="1px"
    BackColor="White" CellPadding="3" GridLines="Vertical"
AutoGenerateColumns="False">
  <SelectedItemStyle Font-Bold="True"
    ForeColor="White" BackColor="#008A8C"></SelectedItemStyle>
  <AlternatingItemStyle BackColor="Gainsboro"></AlternatingItemStyle>
  <ItemStyle ForeColor="Black" BackColor="#EEEEEE"></ItemStyle>
  <HeaderStyle Font-Bold="True" ForeColor="White" BackColor="#000084"></HeaderStyle>
  <FooterStyle ForeColor="Black" BackColor="#CCCCCC"></FooterStyle>
  <PagerStyle HorizontalAlign="Center"
    ForeColor="Black" BackColor="#999999" Mode="NumericPages"></PagerStyle>
  <Columns>
    <asp:TemplateColumn HeaderText="Order ID">
      <ItemTemplate>
      <%# ((System.Data.DataRow)Container.DataItem)["OrderID"] %>
      </ItemTemplate>
    </asp:TemplateColumn>
    <asp:TemplateColumn HeaderText="Employee">
    <ItemTemplate>
      <%# ((System.Data.DataRow)Container.DataItem)["EmployeeName"] %>
    </ItemTemplate>
  </asp:TemplateColumn>
</Columns>
</asp:DataGrid>
</td>
</tr>
```

31

Advanced Binding Samples

LISTING 31.6
Continued

```
</table>
</form>
</body>
</HTML>
```

The preceding ASP.NET code sets up two DataGrids. You can't see the parent-child relationship or the dynamic data binding without looking at the code-behind. The code-behind class is given in Listing 31.7.

LISTING 31.7
The Code-Behind for the HeaderDetail.aspx Page

```
using System;
using System.Collections;
using System.ComponentModel;
using System.Data;
using System.Data.SqlClient;
using System.Drawing;
using System.Web;
using System.Web.SessionState;
using System.Web.UI;
using System.Web.UI.WebControls;
using System.Web.UI.HtmlControls;

namespace WebFormsBinding
{
  /// <summary>
  /// Summary description for HeaderDetail.
  /// </summary>
  public class HeaderDetail : System.Web.UI.Page
  {
    protected System.Web.UI.WebControls.DataGrid dgOrders;
    protected System.Web.UI.WebControls.DataGrid dgCustomers;

    private void Page_Load(object sender, System.EventArgs e)
    {
      LoadData();
      DataBind();
    }

    private void LoadData()
    {
```

31

LISTING 31.7
Continued

```
      SqlConnection conn = new SqlConnection(
        "server=localhost; user id=sa; password=password; Initial Catalog=Northwind");
      conn.Open();
      SqlDataAdapter custDa =
        new SqlDataAdapter("SELECT * FROM Customers", conn);
      SqlDataAdapter orderDa = new SqlDataAdapter(
        "SELECT o.CustomerID, o.OrderID, EmployeeName = e.FirstName "+
        "' ' + e.LastName FROM Orders o " +
        "INNER JOIN Employees e ON o.EmployeeID = e.EmployeeID", conn);
    DataSet ds=  new DataSet();
    custDa.Fill(ds,"Customers");
    orderDa.Fill(ds, "Orders");

    DataRelation dr = new DataRelation("CustOrders",
    ds.Tables["Customers"].Columns["CustomerID"],
    ds.Tables["Orders"].Columns["CustomerID"]);
    ds.Relations.Add( dr );

  dgCustomers.DataSource = ds;
  dgCustomers.DataMember = "Customers";
}

#region Web Form Designer generated code
override protected void OnInit(EventArgs e)
{
//
// CODEGEN: This call is required by the ASP.NET Web Form Designer.
//
InitializeComponent();
base.OnInit(e);
}

/// <summary>
/// Required method for Designer support - do not modify
/// the contents of this method with the code editor.
/// </summary>
  private void InitializeComponent()
  {
    this.dgCustomers.ItemCommand +=
      new System.Web.UI.WebControls.DataGridCommandEventHandler(
        this.dgCustomers_ItemCommand);
```

31

Advanced Binding Samples

LISTING 31.7
Continued

```
      this.Load += new System.EventHandler(this.Page_Load);


   }
#endregion

private void dgCustomers_ItemCommand(object source,
   System.Web.UI.WebControls.DataGridCommandEventArgs e)
{
   if (e.CommandName == "cmdSelectCustomer")
   {
      dgCustomers.SelectedIndex = e.Item.ItemIndex;
      DataRow cust = ((DataSet)dgCustomers.DataSource).Tables["Customers"].Rows[
      dgCustomers.SelectedIndex];
      Response.Write("You selected " + cust["ContactName"].ToString());
      DataRow[] custOrders = cust.GetChildRows("CustOrders");

      dgOrders.DataSource = custOrders;
      DataBind();
   }
}


}
}
```

One of the things you might notice is that every time the page loads, it populates the
DataSet and creates the data relations. In a real-world scenario, you wouldn't make
database round-trips that often. You could use caching mechanisms or make more
complicated use of ViewState to avoid the round-trip. However, to keep the
example clear and easy to follow, the DataSet is created every time. The key to how
the sample works is that when the user clicks the select button on the form, the code
changes the currently selected row (highlighting it in the output), and binds the
child DataGrid to the array of child rows of the currently selected row. Figure 31.3
shows the page rendered by the preceding code.

Cascading Header and Detail

An even more complex problem occurs when your child rows are themselves parents
of yet deeper child rows. I apologize for using the Northwind database so much, but
it is one database that most people with either SQL Server or MS Access on their
machines already have. In the case of Northwind, the child rows of Orders are
Order Items.

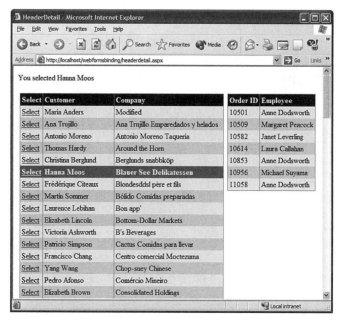

FIGURE 31.3   A parent-child data relationship illustrated
with two linked `DataGrid`s.

Rather than show you three `DataGrid`s, this section will modify the sample so that
it uses three list boxes. You'll notice that rather than grabbing all the rows at once
and doing the rebinding on events, the code actually queries for the child data
rather than using a child relationship. The reason for this is a state management
issue. You need to be able to ensure that certain bits of information are available at
the right times. To do this, the database is queried when additional child rows are
needed. You could query the session state, application state, or a cache if you wanted
to speed up the example. Listings 31.8 and 31.9 contain the code required to create
three linked `ListBox` controls.

LISTING 31.8
Three Simple `ListBox` Controls That Will Be Linked via Parent-Child Relationships

```
<%@ Page language="c#" Codebehind="CascadeDetail.aspx.cs"
    AutoEventWireup="false" Inherits="WebFormsBinding.CascadeDetail" %>
<!DOCTYPE HTML PUBLIC "-//W3C//DTD HTML 4.0 Transitional//EN" >
<HTML>
<HEAD>
<title>CascadeDetail</title>
  <meta name="GENERATOR" Content="Microsoft Visual Studio .NET 7.1">
  <meta name="CODE_LANGUAGE" Content="C#">
  <meta name="vs_defaultClientScript" content="JavaScript">
```

Advanced Binding Samples

LISTING 31.8
Continued

```
  <meta name="vs_targetSchema"
content="http://schemas.microsoft.com/intellisense/ie5">
</HEAD>
<body>
  <form id="Form1" method="post" runat="server">
  <table width="100%" border="0" cellspacing="1" cellpadding="1">
    <tr>
      <td width="33%" valign="top">
        <asp:ListBox ID="lstCustomers" Runat="server"
         Width="100%" AutoPostBack="True"></asp:ListBox>
      </td>
      <td width="34%" valign="top">
        <asp:ListBox ID="lstOrders" Runat="server"
          Width="100%" AutoPostBack="True"></asp:ListBox>
      </td>
      <td width="33%" valign="top">
        <asp:ListBox ID="lstOrderDetails" Runat="server" Width="100%"></asp:ListBox>
      </td>
    </tr>
  </table>
</form>
</body>
</HTML>
```

31

LISTING 31.9
The Code-Behind Class That Makes the Three `ListBox` Binding Possible

```
using System;
using System.Collections;
using System.ComponentModel;
using System.Data;
using System.Data.SqlClient;
using System.Drawing;
using System.Web;
using System.Web.SessionState;
using System.Web.UI;
using System.Web.UI.WebControls;
using System.Web.UI.HtmlControls;

namespace WebFormsBinding
{
```

LISTING 31.9
Continued

```
public class CascadeDetail : System.Web.UI.Page
{
  protected System.Web.UI.WebControls.ListBox lstCustomers;
  protected System.Web.UI.WebControls.ListBox lstOrders;
  protected System.Web.UI.WebControls.ListBox lstOrderDetails;

  private void Page_Load(object sender, System.EventArgs e)
  {
    if (!Page.IsPostBack)
    {
      SqlConnection conn = new SqlConnection(
        "server=localhost; user id=sa; password=password; initial catalog=northwind;");
      conn.Open();

      DataSet ds = new DataSet();
      SqlDataAdapter custDA = new SqlDataAdapter("SELECT * FROM Customers", conn );

      custDA.Fill(ds, "Customers");

      lstCustomers.DataSource = ds;
      lstCustomers.DataMember = "Customers";
      lstCustomers.DataTextField = "ContactName";
      lstCustomers.DataValueField = "CustomerID";
    }

    DataBind();
  }

  #region Web Form Designer generated code
  override protected void OnInit(EventArgs e)
  {
    //
    // CODEGEN: This call is required by the ASP.NET Web Form Designer.
    //
    InitializeComponent();
    base.OnInit(e);
  }

  /// <summary>
  /// Required method for Designer support - do not modify
```

31

Advanced Binding Samples

LISTING 31.9
Continued

```csharp
/// the contents of this method with the code editor.
/// </summary>
private void InitializeComponent()
{
  this.lstCustomers.SelectedIndexChanged +=
    new System.EventHandler(this.lstCustomers_SelectedIndexChanged);
  this.lstOrders.SelectedIndexChanged +=
    new System.EventHandler(this.lstOrders_SelectedIndexChanged);
  this.Load += new System.EventHandler(this.Page_Load);


}
#endregion

private void lstCustomers_SelectedIndexChanged(object sender, System.EventArgs e)
{
  string custID = lstCustomers.SelectedValue;
  SqlConnection conn = new SqlConnection(
    "server=localhost; user id=sa; password=password; initial catalog=
northwind;");
  conn.Open();
  SqlDataAdapter ordersDA =
    new SqlDataAdapter(
      "SELECT * FROM Orders WHERE CustomerID='" + custID+"'", conn );
  DataSet ds = new DataSet();
  ordersDA.Fill(ds, "Orders");
  lstOrders.DataSource = ds;
  lstOrders.DataMember = "Orders";
  lstOrders.DataValueField = "OrderID";
  lstOrders.DataTextField = "OrderDate";
  lstOrders.SelectedIndex =0;
  lstOrderDetails.Items.Clear();
  DataBind();
}

private void lstOrders_SelectedIndexChanged(object sender, System.EventArgs e)
{
  string orderID = lstOrders.SelectedValue;
  SqlConnection conn = new SqlConnection(
    "server=localhost; user id=sa; password=password; initial catalog=
northwind;");
  conn.Open();
```

LISTING 31.9
Continued

```
        SqlDataAdapter detailDA =
            new SqlDataAdapter("SELECT od.*, p.ProductName FROM [Order Details] od " +
                " INNER JOIN Products p on od.ProductID = p.ProductID WHERE OrderID=" +
orderID, conn);
        DataSet ds = new DataSet();
        detailDA.Fill(ds, "OrderDetails");
        lstOrderDetails.DataSource = ds;
        lstOrderDetails.DataMember = "OrderDetails";
        lstOrderDetails.DataValueField = "ProductID";
        lstOrderDetails.DataTextField = "ProductName";
        lstOrderDetails.SelectedIndex = 0;
        DataBind();
    }
  }
}
```

Basically what happens here is when the user clicks on a customer, the code retrieves the orders for that customer and places them in the second list box. The customer list remains intact because it is being copied from page view to page view via the ViewState mechanism. When you, the user, clicks on an order, the list of order details and items is retrieved from the database and bound to the third and final list box. Using this model, you can cascade parent/child relationships to any depth you like and are still able to retrieve the ID values of all the parents, even if the DataSet that originally generated the parents is not available.

31

Summary

This chapter took you on a brief tour through some of the highlights of data binding with Web Forms. It is by no means a complete reference; an entire book could be written to discuss data access with ASP.NET. However, you now have a clearer idea of what is involved in binding to controls using ASP.NET and you can determine what additional information you need, if any.

This chapter showed you the basic binding syntax for simple binding, as well as how to bind to simple list controls like the DataList and Repeater. Then you moved on to see a simple DataGrid binding, and wrapped up the chapter with discussions of parent-child binding with DataGrids and ListBox controls.

Further Reading

www.asp.net

www.gotdotnet.com

Building Web Solutions with ASP.NET and ADO.NET by Microsoft Press.
ISBN: 0735615780.

31

Part VI

Web Services

CHAPTER 32   Introduction to Web Services

CHAPTER 33   Introduction to WSE 2.0

32 Introduction to Web Services

IN BRIEF

If you have been reading this book from the beginning to the end (no small feat!), you undoubtedly have seen quite a few references to web services. Chapter 18, "Consuming Web Services," contains a detailed explanation of how to consume web services and create web services clients using Windows Forms and C#.

In this chapter, you will learn how to build some basic web services and get valuable information about how web services work. In addition, there will be some information at the end of the chapter on consuming web services in case you didn't read Chapter 18 or if you want a quick review.

WHAT YOU NEED

REQUIRED SOFTWARE	.NET Framework SDK v1.1 Visual Studio .NET 2003 with C# installed Windows XP/2000 Pro or Windows Server 2003 IIS version 5+
RECOMMENDED HARDWARE	PC that meets .NET SDK minimum requirements
SKILLS REQUIRED	C# and .NET familiarity

INTRODUCTION TO WEB SERVICES AT A GLANCE

Introduction to Web Services	663		
Defining Web Services	663	Overview of WSDL	665
Overview of SOAP	663		

Building Web Services	665		
Hello World	665	Maintaining State with a Web Service	673
Complex Serialization	669	Contract-First Programming with	
Using Transactions with a Web Service	673	Web Services	674

Review of Web Service Consumption	674		
Creating a Client Proxy for a Web Service	674	Making Synchronous Calls	674
		Making Asynchronous Calls	675

Summary	676

Further Reading	676

Introduction to Web Services

The next section will provide you with an introduction to web services and an overview of how they work and what they are. You will learn about wire formats such as SOAP, XML dialects such as WSDL, and how they all come together to enable the loose coupling, highly portable framework of web services.

Defining Web Services

Put simply, a *web service* is a service that is provided by a piece of software running on the Web. More specifically, it is a service that responds to requests on a specific TCP/IP port that are formatted in a specific way. The responses to these requests are also formatted in a specific fashion. Any network client that knows the format of sending and receiving messages can communicate with a web service.

Two of the main building blocks of web services are SOAP and WSDL. SOAP and WSDL are both discussed briefly later in the chapter. Entire books on the subject of web services will contain more specifics on both SOAP and WSDL; this book provides only a brief introduction of each topic and a discussion of how to create web services using Visual Studio .NET 2003.

Overview of SOAP

When a message is sent to a web service, it is sent via SOAP (Simple Object Access Protocol). SOAP is a *wire format*, which means some language or dialect that formats data transmitted on the wire. There are other wire formats, but SOAP is the format that is used to carry web service payloads from one endpoint to another.

In non-.NET applications, applications communicate with each other via RPCs (Remote Procedure Calls). The RPC mechanism is a standard that allows for one application to invoke a method hosted by another application and to obtain the results. There is a specific binary format for passing parameters on RPC calls and obtaining results. RPCs are almost always blocked by routers due to security problems.

Other binary standards for remote communication between applications (such as DCOM [Distributed Component Object Model or Distributed COM]) cannot be routed. As a result, RPC and DCOM fail when it comes to providing the capability for an application to communicate across routers or wide networks like the Internet.

SOAP provides an XML-based dialect for describing remote method invocations and message transmission between applications. If you encode a request to invoke a method at one end of a network connection and send it to a remote application, you can then receive the result of that method execution as another SOAP message sent back. This is the fundamental basis for web services.

Introduction to Web Services

A common misconception is that SOAP is a communication protocol, like HTTP. In fact, SOAP is only a wire format—a specification for encoding messages that will be transmitted via network. When a client communicates with a web service via SOAP, the client is actually sending SOAP messages (called *envelopes*) within the body of an HTTP request. If you have played with Remoting much, you know that you can use SOAP to encode messages sent on non-HTTP TCP ports. It is important to realize the distinction between communication protocol and wire format because it will help you understand the more complex topics later.

Everything relevant to web services communications that utilize SOAP (some web services communication can be done with pure HTTP) takes place within the SOAP envelope. The idea of messages (rather than Remote Procedure Calls) is more and more becoming the preferred way of viewing web services.

The following is a sample of what an empty SOAP envelope might look like. Remember that SOAP is a specific dialect of XML, so all SOAP must be well-formed XML and SOAP elements must be included within the appropriate namespace for proper validation:

```
<?xml version="1.0"?>
<soap:Envelope
    xmlns:soap="http://www.w3.org/2001/12/soap-envelope"
    soap:encodingStyle="http://www.w3.org/2001/12/soap-encoding">

    <soap:Header>
      <!-- Header information, can be any well-formed
           XML including user credentials, etc -->
    </soap:Header>

    <soap:Body>
      <!-- The actual body of the SOAP envelope  -->
      <!-- contains the serialized method invocation or results -->

      <soap:Fault>
        <!-- If an error occurred, it will be serialized here -->
      </soap:Fault>
    </soap:Body>
</soap:Envelope>
```

You don't have to spend too much time learning the SOAP format. Visual Studio .NET 2003 and the .NET Framework abstract most of the work for you so that you can view web service execution as either RPC-like calls or transmissions of messages. If you want more detail on SOAP itself, you can consult the actual W3C specification at www.w3.org/2000/xp/Group. The XML Protocol Working Group site contains links to all the information you need on the SOAP specification and status of standardization of the latest version.

Overview of WSDL

For a client to know what methods are exposed by a particular service, the parameters of those methods, and how to interact with the service, the client must be able to obtain information about the service. That information is stored in a specific format called *WSDL* (*Web Services Description Language*).

This format describes the interface to the web service, including information about whether the service is communicating using a message-style format or using a more RPC-like method. For more information about WSDL, its format, and other details, you can check out the W3C site at www.w3.org/TR/wsdl.

Building Web Services

This next section will show you how to create your own web services and give you information on dealing with irregular and complex data types, state maintenance, and more. More advanced web service topics will be covered in later chapters.

Hello World

The first sample of a web service that you'll see is the default web service that you create within Visual Studio .NET 2003. To follow along, create a new Web Service project in Visual Studio .NET 2003 and call it `WSChapter32`. Delete the `Service1.asmx` file and add a new web service to the project called `HelloService.asmx`. The code for `HelloService` is contained in Listing 32.1.

LISTING 32.1
The Code-Behind for the Simple Hello World Web Service

```csharp
using System;
using System.Collections;
using System.ComponentModel;
using System.Data;
using System.Diagnostics;
using System.Web;
using System.Web.Services;

namespace WSChapter32
{
  /// <summary>
  /// Summary description for HelloService.
  /// </summary>
  [WebService(Namespace="http://www.samspublishing.com/csharpunleashed/chapter32")]
  public class HelloService : System.Web.Services.WebService
  {
```

32

Building Web Services

LISTING 32.1
Continued

```
public HelloService()
{
   //CODEGEN: This call is required by the ASP.NET Web Services Designer
   InitializeComponent();
}

// Component designer code cut out for clarify

// WEB SERVICE EXAMPLE
// The HelloWorld() example service returns the string Hello World
// To build, uncomment the following lines then save and build the project
// To test this web service, press F5

[WebMethod(Description="This method will return 'Hello World'")]
public string HelloWorld()
{
  return "Hello World";
}
   }
}
```

To see what this actually produces, without writing a web service client, Visual Studio .NET gives you the ability to see the service from a web page. If your web server is your local machine, you should now be able to pull up `http://localhost/WSChapter32/Hello.asmx`. The page you see should look a lot like the page in Figure 32.1.

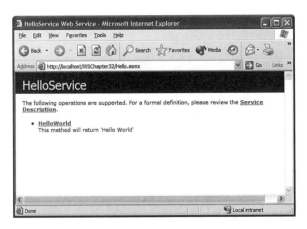

FIGURE 32.1   The `Hello.asmx` page rendered by Internet Explorer.

Figure 32.1 shows that the web service has only one method: `HelloWorld`. As per a code attribute in the code, this page indicates that the `HelloWorld` method will return the string 'Hello World'.

Clicking the link to the `HelloWorld` method, you see that the page actually shows you sample SOAP envelopes that can be used for communicating with the service. Those are shown here:

```
<?xml version="1.0" encoding="utf-8"?>
<soap:Envelope
  xmlns:xsi="http://www.w3.org/2001/XMLSchema-instance"
  xmlns:xsd="http://www.w3.org/2001/XMLSchema"
  xmlns:soap="http://schemas.xmlsoap.org/soap/envelope/">
  <soap:Body>
    <HelloWorld xmlns="http://www.samspublishing.com/csharpunleashed/chapter32" />
  </soap:Body>
</soap:Envelope>
```

The SOAP envelope will contain a response from the `HelloWorld` method:

```
<?xml version="1.0" encoding="utf-8"?>
<soap:Envelope
  xmlns:xsi="http://www.w3.org/2001/XMLSchema-instance"
  xmlns:xsd="http://www.w3.org/2001/XMLSchema"
  xmlns:soap="http://schemas.xmlsoap.org/soap/envelope/">
  <soap:Body>
    <HelloWorldResponse xmlns="http://www.samspublishing.com/csharpunleashed/
chapter32">
      <HelloWorldResult>string</HelloWorldResult>
    </HelloWorldResponse>
  </soap:Body>
</soap:Envelope>
```

If you click the sample Invoke button on the page, you will actually see the SOAP that is returned to the client:

```
<?xml version="1.0" encoding="utf-8" ?>
  <string xmlns="http://www.samspublishing.com/csharpunleashed/chapter32">Hello
World</string>
```

This is all great, but as you know, being able to return the string 'Hello World' to a client isn't exactly the most amazing thing. Take a look at what `HelloService.asmx` might look like if it accepts some simple input parameters. The code for the new `HelloService` is shown in Listing 32.2.

32

Building Web Services

LISTING 32.2
The `HelloService` Class with a New Method That Takes Parameters

```csharp
using System;
using System.Collections;
using System.ComponentModel;
using System.Data;
using System.Diagnostics;
using System.Web;
using System.Web.Services;

namespace WSChapter32
{
  /// <summary>
  /// Summary description for Service1.
  /// </summary>
  [WebService(Namespace="http://www.samspublishing.com/csharpunleashed/chapter32")]
  public class HelloService : System.Web.Services.WebService
  {
    public HelloService()
    {
      //CODEGEN: This call is required by the ASP.NET Web Services Designer
      InitializeComponent();
    }

// component designer commented out for clarity

    // WEB SERVICE EXAMPLE
    // The HelloWorld() example service returns the string Hello World
    // To build, uncomment the following lines then save and build the project
    // To test this web service, press F5

    [WebMethod(Description="This method will return 'Hello World'")]
    public string HelloWorld()
    {
      return "Hello World";
    }

    [WebMethod(Description="This method processes some parameters")]
    public string HelloWithParameters( DateTime inTime, int daysToAdd, string
userName )
    {
      return string.Format("Hello, {0}. Your method indicated {1}",
        userName, inTime.AddDays(daysToAdd).ToLongDateString());
    }
  }
}
```

The new method takes a couple of parameters, performs some processing on them, and returns a string. This is where you can start to see the real power of web services. Obviously the power of a web service isn't in its capability to simply return a static string; it's in the capability to perform some processing and return the result of that processing in a standardized, portable, XML-based format that can be read by any client with a network connection and an XML parser. The output of this method, when supplied with a name and October 10th, 2004 as a starting date with 10 additional days as a parameter, is as follows:

```
<?xml version="1.0" encoding="utf-8" ?>
  <string
    xmlns="http://www.samspublishing.com/csharpunleashed/chapter32">
    Hello, Kevin. Your method indicated Wednesday, October 20, 2004</string>
```

Complex Serialization

The preceding method and its parameters are fairly simple. You can imagine hundreds of uses for web services that use only simple arguments and simple return types. In addition to the simple types such as strings, integers, and dates, other types can also be utilized by a web service.

Any data type that is passed to or from a web service must be a type that you can represent with an XSD (XML Schema Definition Language) schema. Therefore, you automatically know that all the primitive types, such as integer, string, and date, are supported because they are supported by XSD. But what about things such as ArrayLists, simple arrays, or even very complex objects such as DataSets?

A complex data type can be used with a .NET web service if the data type can be serialized and if its data structure can be represented in XSD.

Listing 32.3 shows the new web service class, complete with a method that returns an ArrayList, one that returns an array of strings, and one that returns a DataSet. You will see that the web service will return very different responses based on these complex, serializable data types.

LISTING 32.3
The New HelloService Class That Returns Complex Data to The Client

```
using System;
using System.Collections;
using System.ComponentModel;
using System.Data;
using System.Diagnostics;
using System.Web;
using System.Web.Services;
```

Building Web Services

LISTING 32.3
Continued

```
namespace WSChapter32
{
  /// <summary>
  /// Summary description for Service1.
  /// </summary>
  [WebService(Namespace="http://www.samspublishing.com/csharpunleashed/chapter32")]
  public class HelloService : System.Web.Services.WebService
  {
    public HelloService()
    {
      //CODEGEN: This call is required by the ASP.NET Web Services Designer
      InitializeComponent();
    }

// Component Designer code commented out for clarity

    // WEB SERVICE EXAMPLE
    // The HelloWorld() example service returns the string Hello World
    // To build, uncomment the following lines then save and build the project
    // To test this web service, press F5

    [WebMethod(Description="This method will return 'Hello World'")]
    public string HelloWorld()
    {
      return "Hello World";
    }

    [WebMethod(Description="This method processes some parameters")]
    public string HelloWithParameters( DateTime inTime, int daysToAdd, string
userName )
    {
      return string.Format("Hello, {0}. Your method indicated {1}",
        userName, inTime.AddDays(daysToAdd).ToLongDateString());
    }

    [WebMethod(Description="This method returns an ArrayList of strings")]
    public ArrayList GetArrayList( int count )
    {
      ArrayList al = new ArrayList();
```

32

LISTING 32.3
Continued

```
      for (int x=0; x < count-1; x++)
      {
        al.Add( x.ToString());
      }

      return al;
    }

    [WebMethod(Description="Get String Array")]
    public string[] GetStrings( int count )
    {
      ArrayList al = GetArrayList(count);
      string[] results = (string[])al.ToArray(typeof(string));
      return results;
    }

    [WebMethod(Description="Returns a DataSet")]
    public DataSet GetDataSet( string dsName )
    {
      DataSet ds = new DataSet();
      ds.DataSetName = dsName;
      return ds;
    }
  }
}
```

32

When you test the `GetArrayList` method, you will get the following results (the results will vary slightly based on your input):

```xml
<?xml version="1.0" encoding="utf-8" ?>
 <ArrayOfAnyType xmlns:xsi="http://www.w3.org/2001/XMLSchema-instance"
    xmlns:xsd="http://www.w3.org/2001/XMLSchema"
    xmlns="http://www.samspublishing.com/csharpunleashed/chapter32">
  <anyType xsi:type="xsd:string">0</anyType>
  <anyType xsi:type="xsd:string">1</anyType>
  <anyType xsi:type="xsd:string">2</anyType>
  <anyType xsi:type="xsd:string">3</anyType>
  <anyType xsi:type="xsd:string">4</anyType>
  <anyType xsi:type="xsd:string">5</anyType>
  <anyType xsi:type="xsd:string">6</anyType>
  <anyType xsi:type="xsd:string">7</anyType>
```

Building Web Services

```
 <anyType xsi:type="xsd:string">8</anyType>
 <anyType xsi:type="xsd:string">9</anyType>
 <anyType xsi:type="xsd:string">10</anyType>
</ArrayOfAnyType>
```

As you can see, an XML document that conforms to the XSD schema is being sent to the client. If you run the test method against the GetStrings method (also using 10 as the count), you will get the following (much simpler) result:

```
<?xml version="1.0" encoding="utf-8" ?>
 <ArrayOfString
    xmlns:xsi="http://www.w3.org/2001/XMLSchema-instance"
    xmlns:xsd="http://www.w3.org/2001/XMLSchema"
    xmlns="http://www.samspublishing.com/csharpunleashed/chapter32">
  <string>0</string>
  <string>1</string>
  <string>2</string>
  <string>3</string>
  <string>4</string>
  <string>5</string>
  <string>6</string>
  <string>7</string>
  <string>8</string>
  <string>9</string>
 </ArrayOfString>
```

32

Finally, if you run the test method against the GetDataSet method, you will get output that looks similar to the following:

```
<?xml version="1.0" encoding="utf-8" ?>
 <DataSet xmlns="http://www.samspublishing.com/csharpunleashed/chapter32">
 <xs:schema id="MyDataSet"
    xmlns="" xmlns:xs="http://www.w3.org/2001/XMLSchema"
    xmlns:msdata="urn:schemas-microsoft-com:xml-msdata">
 <xs:element name="MyDataSet" msdata:IsDataSet="true">
 <xs:complexType>
  <xs:choice minOccurs="0" maxOccurs="unbounded" />
 </xs:complexType>
 </xs:element>
 </xs:schema>
<diffgr:diffgram
    xmlns:msdata="urn:schemas-microsoft-com:xml-msdata"
    xmlns:diffgr="urn:schemas-microsoft-com:xml-diffgram-v1" />
</DataSet>
```

As you can see, the `DataSet` comes across serialized into XML. There is no additional wrapper around the `DataSet` as there is with simple results. In addition, the schema for the `DataSet` is included along with a `DiffGram` that, if this `DataSet` had any data, would indicate all the data within the `DataSet`.

Keep in mind that the more complex your parameters and output types are, the less likely it will be that non-.NET clients will be able to create or interpret the information.

Using Transactions with a Web Service

One of the extra options available with .NET web services is the capability for a web service method to be the initiator of a distributed COM+ (see Chapter 40, "COM+ Enterprise Services"). Without going into too much detail, a *distributed transaction* is one in which actions taken by multiple software components in different locations can contribute to the commitment or rollback of a single unit of work or transaction.

You can use the `TransactionOption` enumeration as an argument to the `WebMethod` attribute to control the capability of your method to control a COM+ transaction. The options you can set are as follows:

- `Required, RequiresNew`—The method being invoked will create a new COM+ transaction.

- `NotSupported, Supported, Disabled`—The method being invoked will not participate in a COM+ transaction.

You will see much more about COM+ transactions and what they are in Chapter 41. You might want to use a distributed transaction if your web service makes several calls to remote systems, and if any of those calls fail, the desired behavior would be for all the actions to be rolled back.

Maintaining State with a Web Service

A common topic with web services is the issue of managing state. With standard ASP.NET web applications, it's pretty easy to assume that if a specific user hasn't requested a page from the server within a period of time, the user's session has expired. Can you be so certain about calls to a web service? What constitutes a session within a web service?

When defining a web service in .NET, session state can be enabled if it is needed through the `WebService` code attribute. The real problem with maintaining session state is that the client is required to be able to accept cookies, and some web service clients refuse cookies.

32

Contract-First Programming with Web Services

If you've been following along with the code samples, what you have been doing up until this point is code-first web service programming. In other words, you have been creating a class and using ASP.NET to generate the WSDL contract that clients consume.

A popular trend among web service programmers is to write the contract first and then build the code around the contract. This is done to maximize the ability to communicate between disparate systems. If you define the contract exactly the way you like it, you know that the communication between the client and server should be possible and interpreted properly. On the other hand, if you write the server code first and have ASP.NET generate the WSDL, there is a chance that the client might not be able to parse or interpret the WSDL (such as a Java client trying to deal with custom SOAP headers, and so on).

Review of Web Service Consumption

This next section will provide you with a quick review of consuming web services. In the samples that follow, the code consumes the service created earlier using both synchronous and asynchronous method calls. Much of this information can be seen in the section of this book that discusses Windows Forms and how to consume web services from a Windows Forms application.

Creating a Client Proxy for a Web Service

The first step toward consuming a web service is the creation of a client proxy. You can either let Visual Studio .NET 2003 create the proxy for you by adding a web reference or you can use the `WSDL.EXE` command-line tool to create the proxy class.

Whether you use Visual Studio or the command-line to create the proxy, the proxy will be identical. It will contain method definitions for both synchronous and asynchronous calls. When you invoke the methods on the proxy, they will be forwarded over the network in the appropriate wire format to the web service.

See Chapter 41 or another reference on web services for details on using `WSDL.EXE` to create client proxies. The next two samples will both be written using Visual Studio .NET 2003 and web references.

Making Synchronous Calls

Making synchronous calls is the easiest way to communicate with web services. The code in Listing 32.4 shows a very simple synchronous execution in response to a button press. It is made possible by creating a new Windows Forms application, adding a web reference to the web service created earlier (`HelloService`), and placing some input controls and some buttons on a form.

LISTING 32.4
The Code Supporting Synchronous Web Service Calls

```
private void button1_Click(object sender, System.EventArgs e)
{
  HelloService.HelloService proxy = new HelloService.HelloService();
  MessageBox.Show(this, proxy.HelloWithParameters(
    dtStartTime.Value, Int32.Parse(txtDaycount.Text), txtUserName.Text));
}
```

Making Asynchronous Calls

Making asynchronous calls is a little trickier because the processing of the call to the web service takes place on a background thread. The result of this is that you can make calls to long-running web service tasks without blocking the user interface so that the user doesn't think the application is hung or broken.

The code from Listing 32.5 shows the methods necessary to asynchronously invoke the web service and display the results. The `Invoke` method is used so that the foreground thread is asked to perform the operation. As was just mentioned, asynchronous web service processing is done on the background thread. Some tasks (such as opening new forms) don't happen unless they're performed by the foreground thread.

LISTING 32.5
Methods Supporting Asynchronous Execution of a Web Service Call

```
private void button2_Click(object sender, System.EventArgs e)
{
  statusBar1.Panels[0].Text = "Invoking HelloWithParameters Asynchronously....";
  HelloService.HelloService proxy = new HelloService.HelloService();
  proxy.BeginHelloWithParameters(
    dtStartTime.Value,
    Int32.Parse(txtDaycount.Text), txtUserName.Text,
    new AsyncCallback(FinishHelloWithParameters), null);
}


private void FinishHelloWithParameters(IAsyncResult ar )
{
  HelloService.HelloService proxy = new HelloService.HelloService();
  string result = proxy.EndHelloWithParameters( ar );
  statusBar1.Panels[0].Text = "Asynchronous Invocation Completed.";
  this.Invoke( new ShowMessageDelegate(ShowMessage), new object[] { result } );
}
```

32

Review of Web Service Consumption

LISTING 32.5
Continued

```
private void ShowMessage( string message )
{
  MessageBox.Show(this, message );
}
```

When a user clicks the button to invoke the code asynchronously, the BeginHelloWithParameters method is called with a new asynchronous callback delegate. When the method on the server finishes its work and returns, the callback delegate is invoked by the framework and the method can then extract the results. As mentioned earlier, the Invoke method is used to forward the request to display a message box to the foreground thread of the user interface.

Summary

This chapter has given you a brief introduction to the world of web services. Web services are a way in which functionality can be exposed over the Internet or corporate intranets by using standard HTTP protocols that can be consumed by clients on varying platforms so long as they conform to industry standards.

This chapter showed you how to create web services and how to consume them, as well as gave you information on the plumbing that makes web services work properly: SOAP and WSDL. The next few chapters go into more detail regarding web services and best practices when working with them.

Further Reading

www.asp.net

www.gotdotnet.com

msdn.microsoft.com/netframework

msdn.microsoft.com/webservices

.NET Web Services Architecture and Implementation by Keith Ballinger, Addison-Wesley. ISBN: 0321113594.

33 Introduction to WSE 2.0

IN BRIEF

The previous chapter provided an introduction to the basic concepts dealing with web services. You saw that a web service is essentially a method of transmitting messages over the Internet using an agreed-upon message format. Web Services Description Language (WSDL) defines the interface to the web service, whereas Simple Object Access Protocol (SOAP) defines the format of messages to be used in communicating between the service and the client.

This chapter will introduce you to additional web service standards, such as WS-Security, and other standards, such as DIME for attaching files to XML messages, and much more. Web Service Enhancements (WSE) 2.0 is a powerful set of tools and APIs that take the basic web service functionality to a whole new level. This chapter will show you just a few of the many different features available within WSE.

WHAT YOU NEED

REQUIRED SOFTWARE	.NET Framework SDK v1.1 Visual Studio .NET 2003 with C# installed Windows XP/2000 Pro or Windows Server 2003 IIS version 5+ WSE 2.0 Service Pack 1
RECOMMENDED HARDWARE	PC that meets .NET SDK minimum requirements
SKILLS REQUIRED	C# and .NET familiarity

INTRODUCTION TO WSE 2.0 AT A GLANCE

Introduction to WSE 2.0	679		
Overview of GXA	679	Evolution of WSE	679
TCP Messaging	**679**		
SOAP over TCP	680	The `SoapService` Class	683
`SoapSender` and `SoapReceiver`	680	The `SoapClient` Class	686
Security	**687**		
Introduction to WSE Security	687	X.509 Certificates	689
`UsernameTokens`	688	Signing Messages	690
Messaging with Attachments Using WSE 2.0	**690**		
Introduction to DIME	690	Transferring files via WSE	691
Summary	**691**		
Further Reading	**691**		

Introduction to WSE 2.0

WSE (Web Services Enhancements) v2.0 is a product from Microsoft that extends and enhances the web services offering provided by the .NET Framework version 1.1. WSE is a class library that provides utilities for writing code that works with some of the new web service industry standards such as WS-Security, WS-Attachments, WS-Addressing, WS-Policy, WS-SecurityPolicy, and WS-Trust. The next section will give you some insight as to the industry movements that spurred the development of WSE and how it came about.

Overview of GXA

With the advent of various implementations of web services by Microsoft, Sun, IBM, and others, it became apparent that simply being able to send simple messages and remotely invoke methods would not satisfy all the needs that companies had to use web services safely, reliably, and securely.

Over the past eight years, Microsoft has worked with multiple partners in the computing industry to create what we now know as XML Web Services. GXA, the Global XML Web Services Architecture, spawned the industry standards that support the business needs for doing business using web services. GXA defined the standards for secure, reliable messaging between end points using web services and much, much more.

Evolution of WSE

WSE originally showed up as a 1.0 Technical Preview that developers could download from MSDN. It provided a basic implementation of some of the additional standards that extend web services such as WS-Security and WS-Addressing, and so forth. Since the original 1.0 Technical Preview came out, WSE has evolved. And with the 2.0 Release Candidate (the current version as of the writing of this book), WSE has become an incredibly powerful set of tools for both web services programming and XML messaging without the aid of Internet Information Server.

33

TCP Messaging

WSE provides so many different features that it would be impossible to provide adequate coverage of them in a single chapter. Instead, this chapter will cover some of the more interesting features of WSE.

NOTE

If you want more information about the aspects of WSE that this chapter doesn't cover, you can always read up on WSE using MSDN at the Web Services Developer Center: msdn.microsoft.com/webservices/building/wse/default.aspx.

If you have been reading this book in order, you've already read the chapter introducing you to the basic concepts of web services. Although web services and the ability to send SOAP messages over HTTP might be empowering to quite a few applications, it doesn't do any good to those applications that aren't running on machines with an IIS web server. The next section will show you how some of the classes provided by WSE 2.0 can facilitate SOAP messaging over TCP where neither endpoint needs to have IIS installed.

SOAP over TCP

Web services operate by sending SOAP messages between the client and the server over HTTP. This is great if what you are doing is writing an application that is designed to sit on a web server running IIS. However, what if you want to create a situation that lends itself more to a peer-to-peer architecture? How do you send messages between two different applications that are able to communicate via TCP/IP, but aren't necessarily on machines that have web servers?

Without using WSE, there are a few options. You can use Remoting, but Remoting is a very RPC-like model, and becomes overly complex if all you are trying to do is exchange messages rather than remotely invoke methods. You could also write your own socket code. If you have a lot of experience with socket code, this might be a good alternative. However, in most situations, you don't have time to write your own low-level socket communication library.

Thankfully, WSE now provides the ability to send and receive SOAP messages on several levels. You can write code designed to read and write raw SOAP messages over TCP, or you can write code that works at a slightly higher level using the concepts of a service and a client. The four classes that make this possible are `SoapSender`, `SoapReceiver`, `SoapService`, and `SoapClient`.

One of the really important and powerful features of WSE 2.0 is that you can use the SOAP classes to send and receive SOAP messages on any of three different protocols: in-process (for communicating between two running applications on the same machine), TCP, and HTTP.

SoapSender **and** SoapReceiver

`SoapSender` and `SoapReceiver` are two classes that facilitate SOAP message transmission over any of the supported network protocols, such as HTTP, TCP, or the in-process memory protocol. Before you can start using these classes to their utmost, you need to make sure that you have switched to the mindset of messaging rather than remote procedure calls (RPCs). Because the messages are created and sent on the fly, the network connection between endpoints could actually go down between transmissions. As long as there is a network connection available at the time of message transmission, the message will be sent properly.

Another twist in thinking about message transmission is that either endpoint can be a sender or a receiver. The traditional concepts of client and server do not apply when dealing purely with senders and receivers.

To illustrate how `SoapSender` and `SoapReceiver` work, examine two sample applications. The first application is a Windows Forms application that listens on the `soap.tcp` protocol for SOAP messages. The second is a Console application that allows the user to send messages to the Windows Forms application. Although the applications themselves are fairly simple, powerful networking applications can be created with some of the features of WSE 2.0.

The first step to creating an application that can receive messages is to create a class that derives from `SoapReceiver`. Listing 33.1 shows the `MessageReceiver` class, part of the `SoapMessageReceiver` WinForms application.

LISTING 33.1

The `MessageReceiver` Class Derives from `SoapReceiver`

```
using System;
using Microsoft.Web.Services2.Messaging;
using Microsoft.Web.Services2;

namespace SoapMessageReceiver
{
  /// <summary>
  /// Summary description for MessageReceiver.
  /// </summary>
  public class MessageReceiver : SoapReceiver
  {
    public delegate void MessageReceivedDelegate(string message);
    public event MessageReceivedDelegate MessageReceived;

    protected override void Receive(SoapEnvelope envelope)
    {
      System.Diagnostics.Debug.WriteLine("Received a Message.");
      string message = envelope.SelectSingleNode("//msg").InnerText;
      System.Diagnostics.Debug.WriteLine("Message Received: " + message);
      if (MessageReceived != null)
        MessageReceived(message);
    }
  }
}
```

33

TCP Messaging

For the .NET Framework to know which class to call when a message is sent to a specific URI, that class instance must be registered. The following lines from the main form take care of registering the `SoapReceiver`:

```
Uri receiverUri = new Uri("soap.tcp://localhost/messages");
rcv = new MessageReceiver();
rcv.MessageReceived +=
  new SoapMessageReceiver.MessageReceiver.MessageReceivedDelegate(rcv_
MessageReceived);
SoapReceivers.Add(receiverUri, rcv);
```

The `SoapReceiver` class has one method, `Receive`, that takes a `SoapEnvelope` argument. The class shown previously extracts the information from the custom message that is created (an XML node called `msg`) and then fires another event, allowing the main GUI thread to respond to the new information. The main form simply handles the event and displays the information in a text box.

Next in the application construction process is the creation of code that sends the SOAP envelope to the receiver. For this sample, the code is in a Console application that creates a custom SOAP envelope and sends it to the listener. Listing 33.2 shows the code from the Console application that creates the custom SOAP envelope and sends it on the `soap.tcp` protocol ▇1▇ .

LISTING 33.2
SOAP Message Sender

```
using System;
using Microsoft.Web.Services2;
using Microsoft.Web.Services2.Messaging;

namespace SoapMessageSender
{
  /// <summary>
  /// Summary description for Class1.
  /// </summary>
  class Class1
  {
    /// <summary>
    /// The main entry point for the application.
    /// </summary>
    [STAThread]
    static void Main(string[] args)
    {
      Uri destUri = new Uri("soap.tcp://localhost/messages");
      string msg = "-";
      while (msg.Length > 0)
```

LISTING 33.2
Continued

```
      {
         Console.Write("Enter message to send (blank to quit): ");
         msg = Console.ReadLine();
         if (msg != string.Empty) {
            SoapEnvelope env = CreateTextMessage( msg );                    1
            env.Context.Addressing.Action =
               new Microsoft.Web.Services2.Addressing.Action("urn:messages:send");
            SoapSender sender = new SoapSender( destUri );
            sender.Send( env );
         }
      }
   }

   static SoapEnvelope CreateTextMessage(string msg)
   {
      SoapEnvelope e = new SoapEnvelope();
      e.CreateBody();
      e.Body.InnerXml = "<msg>" + msg + "</msg>";
      return e;
   }
  }
}
```

To test this application, first run the Windows Forms listener application. Because the `SoapReceiver` has been registered with the `SoapReceivers` collection, it will have its `Receive` method invoked and the transmitted SOAP envelope passed.

With the Windows Forms application running, launch the Console application and start typing in messages. You should notice that the text area in the Windows Forms application has been receiving the messages, as shown in Figure 33.1.

The `SoapService` Class

Using the `SoapSender` and `SoapReceiver` classes, you can implement some incredibly powerful network messaging for your applications. But implementing the SOAP envelope yourself, including all the logic to build and parse the SOAP body, can become tedious and introduce additional potential points of failure in your application.

A higher level set of messaging classes is available to reduce the complexity and make it even easier to use SOAP over TCP or HTTP in a pure messaging environment: `SoapService` and `SoapClient`. When dealing with `SoapSender` and `SoapReceiver`, you have to write all the code that differentiates between the

33

TCP Messaging

actions you want performed. For example, if you have three different methods you want to invoke from a client, you have to code the convention used to distinguish which method you want to invoke, and the service must be coded so that it recognizes that convention. Thankfully, Microsoft has provided the `SoapService` and `SoapClient` classes that automatically have support for determining which methods to invoke remotely.

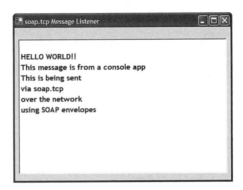

FIGURE 33.1   A Windows Forms application listening for `soap.tcp` messages.

The first step to implementing TCP/SOAP messaging using a `SoapService` is to create a class that derives from `SoapService`. Instead of overriding the default `Receive` method, individual methods can be created so long as they are marked with the `SoapMethod` attribute. Listing 33.3 shows a class that inherits from `SoapService`. Like the previous class, this one exposes a method that allows a WinForms GUI to listen for incoming messages.

33

LISTING 33.3

The `MessageService` Class Inherits from `SoapService`

```
using System;
using Microsoft.Web.Services2;
using Microsoft.Web.Services2.Messaging;
using Microsoft.Web.Services2.Addressing;

namespace SoapServiceWin
{
  /// <summary>
  /// Summary description for MessageService.
  /// </summary>
  public class MessageService : SoapService
  {
```

LISTING 33.3
Continued

```
public delegate void MessageReceivedDelegate(string message);
public event MessageReceivedDelegate OnMessageReceived;

[SoapMethod("ReceiveMessage")]
public SoapEnvelope ReceiveMessage(SoapEnvelope env)
{
  System.Diagnostics.Debug.WriteLine("Received message");
  string message = "test";
  try
  {
    message = env.Body.InnerText;
  }
  catch (Exception ex)
  {
    message = "Failed to find body: " + ex.ToString();
  }

  if (OnMessageReceived != null)
    OnMessageReceived(message);

  return new SoapEnvelope();

  }
 }
}
```

In the preceding code, there is a single method marked with the `SoapMethod` attribute. The string argument to that attribute must match the name of the method that a `SoapClient` invokes in order for a client and service to communicate. If results need to be sent back to the client, those results can be enclosed in a SOAP envelope. The preceding `ReceiveMessage` method takes a message contained in the raw SOAP body and passed it to the Windows Forms GUI via events. The code to register the `SoapService` looks virtually identical to the code to register a `SoapReceiver` and is located in the main form's constructor:

```
ms = new MessageService();
ms.OnMessageReceived +=
  new SoapServiceWin.MessageService.MessageReceivedDelegate(
    ms_OnMessageReceived);
Uri localUri = new Uri("soap.tcp://localhost/MessageService");
EndpointReference epr = new EndpointReference(localUri);
SoapReceivers.Add(epr, ms);
```

33

The `SoapClient` Class

To communicate with a `SoapService`, you need a `SoapClient`. The `SoapClient`, which inherits from `SoapSender`, abstracts the busywork of identifying the name of the method to execute on the remote server. Listing 33.4 shows a class that derives from `SoapClient` that can send requests to execute the `ReceiveMessage` remotely via the `soap.tcp` WSE protocol.

LISTING 33.4
The `MessagingSoapClient` Class Derives from `SoapClient`

```
using System;
using Microsoft.Web.Services2;
using Microsoft.Web.Services2.Messaging;
using Microsoft.Web.Services2.Addressing;

namespace SoapClientApp
{
  /// <summary>
  /// Summary description for SoapClient.
  /// </summary>
  public class MessagingSoapClient : SoapClient
  {
    public MessagingSoapClient(
      EndpointReference destination ) : base(destination) { }

    [SoapMethod("ReceiveMessage")]
    public void SendReceiveMessage(SoapEnvelope env)
    {
      base.SendRequestResponse("ReceiveMessage", env );
    }
  }
}
```

There are two different ways that you can send a message to a `SoapService`: `SendRequestResponse` and `SendOneWay`. The first method, used in the preceding code, expects that the service will supply a populated SOAP envelope as a response. The second method is a fire-and-forget style method: issue the call and it will be asynchronously invoked without expecting a value in return. The following code prompts a user at the console for a message to send to the Windows Forms service host:

```
Uri destination = new Uri("soap.tcp://localhost/MessageService");
EndpointReference epr = new EndpointReference( destination );
```

```
MessagingSoapClient msc = new MessagingSoapClient( epr );

Console.Write("Type message to send below:");
string message = Console.ReadLine();
SoapEnvelope env = new SoapEnvelope();
env.SetBodyObject(message);
msc.SendReceiveMessage( env );
```

With the Windows Forms application running and actively listening for those messages, the server application looks as shown in Figure 33.2.

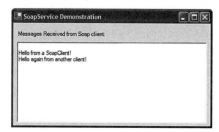

FIGURE 33.2   The GUI host for the `MessageService` class.

Security

One of the other features that WSE provides is the ability to extend the security of a web service by providing APIs and tools that deal with use name identity transmission, X.509 certificates, and digital signatures. The next section will show you how to write a web service that can not only accept a username and password combination embedded in the SOAP envelope, but can also validate the authenticity of the message itself using digital certificates.

Introduction to WSE Security

WSE security is built around adding various elements to the SOAP header. An element called a `UsernameToken` can be added to the header that identifies the username and password of the message sender. Additional elements include security verification elements for signatures and more.

Previous versions of WSE were more difficult to work with. To get certain things working, programmers had to manually add entries to the `web.config` file and add references and more. With WSE 2.0, the Visual Studio .NET 2003 integration is fairly complete. You can now right-click the web project and select WSE Settings 2.0.

33

Security

Doing so pulls up a multipage tabbed dialog of various policy settings, security settings, and options for WSE-based applications.

UsernameTokenS

A *UsernameToken* is a special element defined by the WS-Security standard. It can pass credentials from the client to a service. These credentials can either be a simple username, a username and a clear text password, or even a username and an encrypted username hash digest.

The WSE security subsystem automatically detects the presence of UsernameTokens in every message sent to a WSE-enabled web service. By default, the identity contained in the UsernameToken is compared against an Active Directory or the NT domain user list.

If you want to implement your own user identity system (most systems are based on a relational database that contains a list of usernames and encrypted passwords), WSE provides a pluggable architecture that allows for this.

To validate your own tokens, you can create a class that derives from UsernameTokenManager. Then override a method called AuthenticateToken **2** . Listing 33.5 shows such a sample class.

LISTING 33.5

A Custom UsernameToken Processing Class; Always Returns a Valid Result

```
using System;
using System.Security.Permissions;
using System.Security;
using Microsoft.Web.Services2.Security;
using Microsoft.Web.Services2.Security.Tokens;
using Microsoft.Web.Services2;

namespace Chap33WSE
{
  /// <summary>
  /// Summary description for CustomUsernameTokenManager.
  /// </summary>
  [SecurityPermission(SecurityAction.Demand,
    Flags= SecurityPermissionFlag.UnmanagedCode)]
  public class CustomUsernameTokenManager : UsernameTokenManager
  {
    public CustomUsernameTokenManager()
    {

    }
```

LISTING 33.5
Continued

```
    protected override string AuthenticateToken(UsernameToken token)      2
    {
        if (token == null)
            throw new ArgumentNullException();

        // the user will be considered valid if a string is returned.
        // if an empty string is returned, the user is not valid.
        // typically the username/password hash are compared against
        // a database

        byte[] userName =
            System.Text.Encoding.UTF8.GetBytes(token.Username);

        return System.Text.Encoding.UTF8.GetString( userName );
    }
    }
}
```

In order to register a custom token manager with WSE, you have to open up the WSE Settings 2.0 dialog and go to the Security tab. This tab will prompt you for the fully qualified type name of your class, followed by a comma, and then the name of the assembly in which the class can be found. The next prompt is for the namespace of the security token, and finally the name of the token. There are links for examples that will show you how to set up each of these items.

The following simple lines of code show how you can create an instance of a WSE proxy client and add a UsernameToken to it to pass credentials from client to server:

```
RemoteService.ServiceWse proxy = new RemoteService.ServiceWse();
UsernameToken ut = new UsernameToken("user", "pass", PasswordOption.SendHashed);
proxy.RequestSoapContext.Security.Tokens.Add( ut );
proxy.InvokeMethod();
```

X.509 Certificates

X.509 digital certificates are used in encryption. The way they work with WSE is that one half of the certificate's key is used to encrypt the data being sent to the server, and the other half is used to verify or decrypt the data on the other end of the communications.

33

Signing Messages

A message signature is essentially a hash of the message. The hash is completely unique to that message. In other words, when a message is signed by a client, the server can then verify the hash of the message against the signature and will be able to verify that the message sent by the client was indeed sent by the client. This prevents malicious attackers from intercepting and modifying messages en route to the server. There are multiple ways to sign a message, including using X.509 tokens and `UsernameTokens`. To sign a message using a `UsernameToken`, you can create a signature from a `UsernameToken`, and add that signature to the WSE context for the web service proxy client as shown here:

```
UsernameToken ut = new UsernameToken("Kevin", "password", PasswordOption.Send-
Hashed);
MyService.Service proxy = new MyService.Service();
Proxy.RequestSoapContext.Security.Tokens.Add( ut );
MessageSignature sig = new MessageSignature( ut );
Proxy.RequestSoapContext.Security.Elements.Add( sig );
```

Everything hinges on the WSE context's Security object. This object controls the serialization of all the tokens and security elements including signatures into the various industry-standard SOAP headers.

Messaging with Attachments Using WSE 2.0

You might have noticed a common theme in dealing with some of the extras that come with WSE with regard to web service communication. Many of the additional industry standards, such as WS-Attachments, WS-Security, and so on, can be accessed via methods and properties of the WSE `RequestSoapContext` and `ResponseSoapContext` properties.

The same is true of attachments. To attach a file to a message being sent to a web service (or any other WSE-based SOAP endpoint, such as the TCP samples from earlier in the chapter), all you need to do is simply add the file to the `Attachments` collection by creating a `DimeAttachment`.

Introduction to DIME

DIME (Direct Internet Message Encapsulation) is a standard for sending attachments between hosts on the Internet. Without spending too much time getting into the low-level details of DIME, there is some basic information that might prove useful: DIME breaks up a file being attached to a message into multiple records for efficient transmission over the Internet.

Transferring Files via WSE

To send a message from one WSE endpoint to another, you can create an instance of the `DimeAttachment` class and add it to the `Attachments` collection of the appropriate `SoapContext` class. The following few lines of code shows how easy it is to add a simple image file as an attachment by passing a stream to an image to the `DimeAttachment` constructor:

```
DimeAttachment da = new DimeAttachment(
  "image/gif", TypeFormatEnum.MediaType, gifStream );
da.id = "myfile.gif";
wseProxy.RequestSoapContext.Attachments.Add( da );
```

Summary

WSE is an extremely in-depth topic that covers far too much territory for a single chapter to do it justice. Instead of trying to cover all the aspects of WSE 2.0, this chapter covered some of the more exciting topics to whet your appetite to find out more about WSE 2.0. You can use what you've seen in this chapter and the information in other areas of this book to make WSE 2.0 do some incredible things for your application.

Further Reading

msdn.microsoft.com/webservices—Microsoft's Web Services Development Center

Web Services Enhancements: Understanding the WSE for .NET Enterprise Applications by Bill Evjen, Wiley. ISBN: 0764537369.

33

Part VII

Secure Applications

CHAPTER 34   Code Access Security

CHAPTER 35   Securing Sensitive Data

CHAPTER 36   Securing ASP.NET Web Applications

CHAPTER 37   Licensing and Intellectual Property

34 Code Access Security

IN BRIEF

Code access security (CAS) is one of those necessary technologies that is always there, but never noticed. We write code, compile it, run it, and know that the code works. If the code works properly, we don't often stop and think about the fact that code access security is being used in the background to ensure that managed code is never allowed to do more than it is allowed to do within the current enterprise, network, or computer.

Code access security defines a set of permissions that can be associated with managed code, as well as various ways of creating and querying those associations. It is the plumbing that prevents code downloaded from the Internet from making network requests to any location other than the host from which it was downloaded, and much, much more.

This chapter will introduce you to the key concepts surrounding CAS and give you the information you need so that you will be aware of the limitations imposed on your code by security, and how to write your code so that it takes security into account. You'll see the permissions and permission sets within which your code executes, and you'll see samples of how to create code that is security-aware and code that protects itself from being executed by unauthorized clients.

WHAT YOU NEED

REQUIRED SOFTWARE	.NET Framework SDK v1.1 Visual Studio .NET 2003 with C# installed
RECOMMENDED HARDWARE	PC that meets .NET SDK minimum requirements
SKILLS REQUIRED	C# and .NET familiarity

CODE ACCESS SECURITY AT A GLANCE

Introduction to CAS   695

Using Code Access Security Permissions	696	Identity Permissions	697
Code Access Permissions	696	Role-Based Security Permissions	698

CAS Administration   698

Modifying CAS Policy	698	Adjust Zone Security	701
Policy Administration Tools	699	Evaluate Assembly	701
Increasing Assembly Trust Levels	700	Creating a Deployment Package	703

Writing CAS-Aware Code   704

Using Imperative Security Syntax	704	Blocking Unwanted Clients	706
Using Declarative Security Syntax	705		

Summary   708

Further Reading   709

Introduction to CAS

Code Access Security is a mechanism that is built into the .NET Framework to limit access to resources for managed code. A *resource* can be anything that might need to be secured, such as a file on disk, a CD-ROM drive, a TCP/IP connection, a database connection, or any number of things.

CAS defines standard permissions and permission sets that apply to all activities and all code run within the .NET Framework. When code is written with CAS in mind, code can request permissions from the system based on the activities that it needs to perform. It can also list the permissions that it would like to have but are not required for proper operation. Administrators can configure a security policy that dictates which sets of code (called *code groups*) have which permissions.

This chapter covers permissions and code groups and requesting permissions later. For now, it might be helpful if you knew how the .NET Framework authorized code. The code authorization process determines the permissions granted to a piece of code that is running.

To do this, the .NET Framework iterates through all the methods in the call stack and compares the permissions that have been granted to each item on the call stack with the permissions being demanded by those items. Obviously, if an item is demanding more permission than it has been granted, a security exception will occur and the item will be unable to complete its process.

If a semi-trusted (or untrusted) assembly makes a call to a fully trusted assembly without some additional precaution, the untrusted assembly could take advantage of the second assembly's security clearance and potentially cause severe damage to the system. To counteract this, .NET assigns permissions to individual callers on the call stack. Each caller has its own set of permissions. When the highly trusted code requests a permission, the stack is walked backward and the aggregate of permissions is examined. If one of the previous callers has been denied that permission, the execution will fail even if the most recent caller has been granted that permission. Figure 34.1 supplies a visual overview of this process.

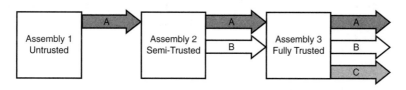

FIGURE 34.1   Illustration of call-stack based permission resolution.

From the figure, you can see that there are three different assemblies, each with a different trust level (set of permissions). When Assembly 1 initiates Action A, whenever subsequently executed code demands permissions, those permissions will be

34

resolved against the trust level of Assembly 1. Even if the request for permission occurs in Assembly 3 (a fully trusted assembly), the stack-walk that the .NET Framework performs will reveal that the call was initiated by a caller with little or no permissions granted and the call will more than likely fail. Action B is initiated by a semi-trusted assembly and will have more permissions than Action A, but less than Action C, because Action C is initiated by an assembly that has been fully trusted.

All of this complexity and depth in resolving permissions associated with code is designed to prevent your code from being abused by malicious code. The idea is that if someone writes malicious code that attempts to use an API that can destroy files, the malicious code will be unable to do so, even though that API has full permissions on the file system. This is possible because the stack of execution calls contains the permission information associated with the malicious code (hopefully untrusted) and can react accordingly.

Before discussing the permissions themselves, let's summarize the way that CAS works with assemblies. When an assembly is loaded, evidence such as the identity, public key, filename, version number, and zone (Internet, Intranet, so on) is combined with the configurable policy (you will see this policy later in the chapter) to produce a set of permissions that have been granted to the assembly. This set of permissions is then assigned to each caller on the stack to allow CAS to determine what callers from the assembly can and cannot do.

Using Code Access Security Permissions

By now you're probably wondering what a permission is. A *permission* is a discrete unit of ability. When code has a permission, it means that the code will be allowed to perform the task associated with the permission. In the list of permissions that you will see later, all the permissions refer to very specific actions to be taken by code when permission has been granted.

Code Access Permissions

Code access permissions are designed to protect resources and operations from unauthorized code and inappropriate, potentially harmful use. Each of the permissions in Table 34.1 grants the privilege to access a protected resource or to perform a particular secured task.

TABLE 34.1

Common Code Access Permissions

Permission Class	Privilege Granted
AspNetHostingPermission	The ability to access resources in ASP.NET-hosted environments
DirectoryServicesPermission	Access Directory services

TABLE 34.1

Continued

Permission Class	Privilege Granted
DnsPermission	Resolve hostnames via DNS
EnvironmentPermission	Access (read/write) environment variables
EventLogPermission	Read or write event log entries
FileDialogPermission	Open a file dialog
FileIOPermission	Read/write files on disk
IsolatedStorageFilePermission	Access isolated storage
MessageQueuePermission	Access MSMQ queues and messages
OdbcPermission	Access ODBC data sources
OleDbPermission	Access OLE DB data sources
OraclePermission	Access an Oracle database server
PerformanceCounterPermission	Access performance counters
PrintingPermission	Access printer resources
ReflectionPermission	Access the metadata of other objects via Reflection
RegistryPermission	Access the system registry
SecurityPermission	Assert permissions and bypass other security measures
ServiceControllerPermission	Start and stop currently installed services via the ServiceController class
SocketPermission	Initiate or receive network data via sockets
SqlClientPermission	Access a SQL server database
UIPermission	Manipulate the user interface
WebPermission	Initiate or accept connections on a Web address
DbDataPermission	Abstract permission class from which you can inherit to create your own database access permission
IsolatedStoragePermission	Abstract permission class from which you can inherit to create your own isolated storage permission
ResourcePermissionBase	Abstract permission class from which you can inherit to create your own system resource access permission

34

Identity Permissions

When protecting your code from unauthorized use, it is often necessary to require that only calling code with a certain identity be given execute access to your code. For this purpose, and many others, there are identity permissions. Identity permissions are designed to represent various pieces of identity-related evidence that is associated with an assembly. Table 34.2 is a list of the identity permissions in the .NET Framework.

TABLE 34.2

Common Identity Permissions

Permission Class	Privilege Granted
`PublisherIdentityPermission`	Indicates the software publisher's digital signature.
`SiteIdentityPermission`	The identity of the website where the code originated.
`StrongNameIdentityPermission`	Refers to the strong name of an assembly.
`URLIdentityPermission`	The URL where the code originated. This is not the same as `SiteIdentityPermission`, and can be from any protocol such as HTTP, FTP, HTTPS, and so on.
`ZoneIdentityPermission`	Refers to the zone from which the code originated. Can be any of the following: `Internet`, `Intranet`, `MyComputer`, `NoZone`, `Trusted`, `Untrusted`.

Role-Based Security Permissions

There is only one role-based security permission class within CAS: `PrincipalPermission`. This is an identity-style permission. Instead of checking for the identity of the calling code, it checks the identity of the current security context, allowing code to demand identity and role membership of the current security context.

CAS Administration

Administering code access security is a task that programmers and users both need to know how to accomplish. Programmers need to know how to administer CAS in order to set up their development and deployment environments. Users need to know how to administer code access security and security policies in order to grant rights to different applications on their computers or in their corporate networks.

Modifying CAS Policy

Policy is the set of permissions, permission sets, and code groups for your computer and your enterprise. The policy is essentially the set of rules by which all managed code executed on your machine must abide.

There are some guidelines as to when you should modify policy. The policies that are configured by default when the .NET Framework is installed on your PC are configured that way for a specific reason. If you modify that policy, you run the risk of opening holes in security that malicious applications can take advantage of or holes in security that will enable careless code to cause damage.

34

If there is an application installed on your PC that originated from an untrusted or partially trusted zone (such as the Internet or an intranet) that requires more than the default permissions, you will need to modify the default policy in order to trust that code.

Often publishers will create suites of applications. If you want your computer to automatically apply the same trust level to all applications created by the same publisher, you will need to modify the default security policy. Although there are several reasons for promoting applications to a more trusted level of security, there are also reasons for tightening the security policy. For example, you could modify the security policy in such a way that even applications that are part of the fully trusted zone cannot access certain resources unless you specify otherwise.

Policy Administration Tools

There are several tools that you can use to modify the security policy for your .NET Framework installation. There are both command-line utilities and MMC (Microsoft Management Console) snap-ins that enable you to administer various aspects of the .NET Framework configuration, including security policy. A command-line tool called CASPOL.EXE gives you manual (and fairly complex) access to the security policy configuration. The security policy for the .NET Framework is stored in .config files on the system.

The most commonly used tool (and easiest to use) is the .NET Configuration tool. You can find this tool by either launching Start, Run, **mscorcfg.msc**, or by opening your Administrative Tools folder and launching Microsoft .NET Framework 1.1 Configuration. When you launch this application, you will see various options in a tree view on the left side. The option of interest for this chapter is the Runtime Security Policy folder icon. Expand that tree and you will see that you can set policy for the enterprise, for the current machine, and for the current user.

TIP

Note that policies overwrite each other in descending scope. Therefore, if you allow code to have certain permissions at the enterprise level and you deny those same permissions on that machine, the code will be denied those permissions when executed on your computer. The same type of descending-order filtering applies to user-scope security policy.

34

When you click on the Runtime Security Policy folder icon, the main content panel will show you the following list of tasks:

▶ Increase Assembly Trust—This task launches a wizard that will enable you to increase the level of trust that belongs to a specific assembly. The wizard will let you browse for a specific filename.

CAS Administration

▶ Adjust Zone Security—This task launches a wizard that enables you to increase the permissions granted to code originating from the different zones such as Internet, Intranet, My Computer, and the rest.

▶ Evaluate Assembly—This is a handy new wizard that enables you to browse for an assembly. You will then receive a report showing you the permissions and security policy associated with that assembly.

▶ Create a Deployment Package—This is perhaps one of the most underutilized tools. It launches a wizard that creates a deployment package that actually bundles a collection of security policy settings that will be committed to a destination system when the package is installed. Because the output is an .msi file, it can be distributed throughout an enterprise via group policy, manual copies, or through the Systems Management Server update mechanism.

▶ Reset All Policy Levels—This task resets your entire security policy to the settings they were at the time of the original install (the default settings). Because this will destroy all changes that you have made to your security policy since installing .NET, make sure that this is really what you want to do before executing this task.

Increasing Assembly Trust Levels

Click on the Trust an Assembly hyperlink and you will see a wizard form appear. The first question you will be asked is whether the changes to the trust level apply to the current user or the current machine. This enables you to let certain applications run with additional security permissions while certain users are using the application, or to let those applications run with additional privilege for everyone using the current computer.

After you have browsed to the assembly (typically a DLL or EXE) that you want to trust and have clicked the Next button, you will see the screen shown in Figure 34.2.

This dialog prompts you for whether you want to trust the assembly or all assemblies created by the assembly publisher. This happens if the assembly you are trying to trust has a strong name. If the assembly doesn't have a strong name, you can't identify the publisher, so the wizard will never give you the option of trusting the publisher. The dialog illustrates a user having browsed to a sample class library called CASLibrary.

If you have a strongly named assembly (or want to create one for this example), choose to increase the trust for just that one assembly and set the trust level to Full Trust. Confirm the settings and you have completed the Increase Assembly Trust wizard.

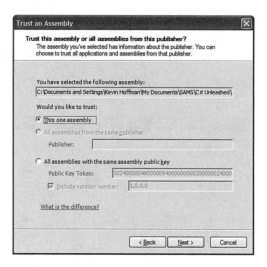

FIGURE 34.2   The Trust an Assembly
dialog, prompting for
assembly or publisher.

Adjust Zone Security

The Adjust Zone Security wizard prompts you to change the trust level that is associated with each zone. Unless you are really sure what you are doing, you probably don't want to mess with the settings in this area. The reason is that if you give too much trust to a zone without knowing the full consequences, you could be opening your computer to intrusion, malicious code, or poorly written code that can do damage to your system.

The dialog in Figure 34.3 shows the security adjustment screen for the various zones. If you have ever opened the security adjustment dialog from within Internet Explorer, this dialog should look familiar. In fact, it should look exactly the same—these settings are also used by Internet Explorer.

Evaluate Assembly

The Evaluate Assembly task enables you to examine the current security permissions of a specific assembly. When the security policy is displayed, it takes into account enterprise, machine, and user policy as well as explicitly granted security systems.

When you start this wizard, it asks whether you want to view permissions that have been explicitly granted to the assembly or view all the code groups that grant permissions to the assembly.

A *code group* is a logical organization of similar code defined by some criteria. When you earlier told the Trust wizard that you wanted to trust the assembly, it created a code group that consisted of that one assembly and only that assembly. It then

34

CAS Administration

granted that one code group full trust. The way CAS works is that permissions and policy only apply to code groups; they do not apply to individual files. As shown in Figure 34.4, one of the code groups currently granting permissions to the assembly is Wizard_0. Wizard_0 is the code group that was automatically generated by the wizard when you trusted the test assembly.

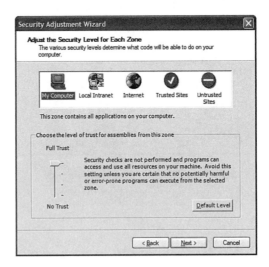

FIGURE 34.3 The Security Adjustment Wizard dialog for .NET security.

FIGURE 34.4 The results of evaluating the code groups contributing to my assembly's permissions.

You might be wondering how you can know that the code group `Wizard_0` is actually the one that was created by the wizard you ran earlier. To verify this fact, you can take a look at the list of code groups on your machine. Expand the Machine node under the Runtime Security Policy, and then expand the Code Groups node, and finally expand the All_Code parent group (code groups are arranged in hierarchies of inherited characteristics). At the bottom, you'll see `Wizard_0` (if you were following along, you might see other automatically generated code groups if you have been playing with security). Click it (you'll notice that its description indicates it was auto-generated by the .NET configuration tool) and then click Edit Code Group Properties. The screen shown in Figure 34.5 will appear.

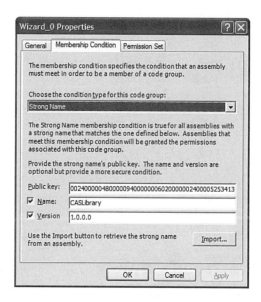

FIGURE 34.5   The Code Group Properties dialog, showing the Membership Condition tab.

By clicking the Membership Condition tab, you can see that the configuration tool set up a code group that indicates a strong name, including the public key, name, and version number of the assembly created earlier. Click the Permission Set to see that the code group has indeed been granted full trust.

Creating a Deployment Package

A deployment package is one of the most important tools for a programmer creating an application that will be deployed to servers or desktops that requires special treatment by security policy. You can't assume that all installations will have the same default policy. Many organizations disable the capability for managed code to make

34

use of the network, even if that code was installed directly on the computer. In such a case, your code must be specifically granted the permissions it needs in order to access the network.

To make sure that your code has the permissions it needs, you can create a code group for your code by specifying the public key and possibly the version number of your strongly named assemblies and grant it the appropriate permissions. Then when you create a deployment package, it will contain that code group and permission set. Any client installing that package will have its security policy modified in order to grant trust to your code.

Writing CAS-Aware Code

At this point, you should have a pretty good idea of what CAS is, how it works behind the scenes of all managed code, and what options you have for administering security policy. This next section will show you some of the various coding techniques that you can employ to not only make your applications aware of security, but to better interact with security policy and CAS.

There are two different ways in which your application can specify which permissions it needs or the permissions that are required of the caller in order to invoke it. You can use an imperative security syntax, which uses specific methods from the security namespace to interact with CAS. The other method you can employ is to use declarative security, specifying code attributes that will interact with the security system through Reflection.

Using Imperative Security Syntax

Imperative security involves creating an instance of the security permission you need before performing the task for which the permission is required. In addition to creating an instance of a single permission, you can create an instance of a permission set that allows you to demand specific sets of permissions from the .NET Framework.

For example, to create an instance of the `FileIOPermission` class and then issue a demand indicating that all callers on the stack prior to the demand must have at least the amount of privilege indicated in the constructor to the `FileIOPermission` class, use the following code:

```
FileIOPermission fileIo =
  new FileIOPermission(
    FileIOPermissionAccess.Write, @"C:\SEC\myfile.txt");
fileIo.Demand();
```

To see this in action, you can write a simple console application that performs this action. Before setting up security policy, write the code and see that it executes just fine. Then modify security policy using the earlier instructions to set the permission set of your application to Internet. The Internet zone does not (by default) have permission to access the local file system, so when you run the code under the Internet privilege, you will get a security error.

Another important thing to note is that the `Demand()` method protects the entire method in which it was invoked. In other words, if that demand fails, no code within the method will ever be called. When a `Demand()` is compiled, the MSIL is modified so that the permission is checked before the method is invoked. You can verify this by putting a `Debug.WriteLine` method call before you issue the `Demand()`. This output will show in the debug window only if the demand passes. If the demand fails, you will see that your code is never executed. This is an important point to remember about protecting entire methods from illegal execution.

Using Declarative Security Syntax

Declarative security works by using code attributes to protect methods and classes from being executed when the permissions of the caller or callers are not sufficient. This can mean demanding that the call stack have sufficient file I/O permission, or it can demand that somewhere on the call stack be the identity of an assembly with a particular public key, or version number, and so on.

To protect a method, you use an attribute like the one that follows. (For a list of the attributes, see the list of permissions. Each permission has its own attribute that can be used in your code.)

```
[FileIOPermission(SecurityAction.Demand,
    PathDiscovery="C:\\SEC\\myfile.txt")]
public void CreateAnotherFile()
{
  // perform file I/O
  System.Diagnostics.Debug.WriteLine(
    "Executing CreateAnotherFile");
}
```

As with the other test, if you deny your code the capability to access the file system, *none of the code in the method protected by the attribute will execute.* That is one of the really beneficial features of CAS. If, at design time, you know that your code is going to need several privileges, you can demand them up front. If you don't get the results you want, you can provide the user with a friendly error indicating the reason for failure. This enables you to prevent data loss, break of workflow, and even data corruption due to a security failure in the middle of the application.

34

Blocking Unwanted Clients

Consider the following scenario: You have created a Windows Forms application that you want to be distributed to all of your clients. This application performs several actions that you don't want to be performed by any application but your own. In most circumstances, any .NET programmer could find out all the methods exposed by your application and consume it. This would allow other programmers to use functionality that might corrupt data or circumvent measures that prevent users from using features of an application for which they haven't paid.

Using security demand features, you can write your code in such a way that certain methods in your application cannot be called by client code unless that client code was also written by you or your organization. You can tell that the code was written by you or your organization if the code has a strong name and the public key token is the same for the calling code as it is for your code.

This security demand involves the `StrongNameIdentityPermission` attribute class. If you protect a class, method, or other member with that attribute, you can control the identity of calling clients; thereby ensuring that only those you want to call your code can call your code.

The first thing you need to do to make this work is get the public key token that you want to require. Remember that the public key token is virtually synonymous with a manufacturer or publisher. If a company is consistent, it will use the same strong name for all of its software, enabling you to write security policy against that manufacturer.

So, if you want all the code in a particular utility library to be available only to your own applications, you will restrict access to that library to only that code with the right public key token.

To get the public key token, use a tool called `SECUTIL.EXE`. This tool is part of the Framework SDK. Here is a sample invocation:

```
secutil -hex -s CASLibrary.dll
```

This will display all the strong name information associated with the `CASLibrary.dll` assembly. The output is as follows (for my sample library; your output will vary with your own assemblies):

```
Microsoft (R) .NET Framework SecUtil 1.1.4322.573
Copyright (C) Microsoft Corporation 1998-2002. All rights reserved.


Public Key =
0x0024000004800000940000000602000000240000525341310004000001000100073F835D64CDBD4
348C6B9EB55C23BEB3B66880512E07602ED508AB038C5AE68AE2A72C0F3F403B08A637667DDBE6F5
DAF2ADC96EFB7BAF6096C220A2F272807B91885FEB436FFBF1455337FDB06F74A44213DBCFB5384B
146AFC0C078E0E336BC96BAE3791CB514FEF3DEBC7DB49E684F002261BEB84E7F6BAE35304F7706A
B4
Name =
CASLibrary
Version =
1.0.0.0
Success
```

The public key piece is what we are looking for as publisher identification. To test this security feature, create a new class called `PublisherProtected` in `CASLibrary.dll`. The code is shown in Listing 34.1(note that the preceding `0x` hex indicator contained in the original string output by `secutil` has been removed):

LISTING 34.1
Identity-Protected Method

```
using System;
using System.Security;
using System.Security.Permissions;

namespace CASLibrary
{
  /// <summary>
  /// Summary description for PublisherProtected.
  /// </summary>
  [StrongNameIdentityPermission(SecurityAction.Demand,

PublicKey="0024000004800000940000000602000000240000525341310004000001000100073F835D64
C" +

"DBD4348C6B9EB55C23BEB3B66880512E07602ED508AB038C5AE68AE2A72C0F3F403B08A637667DDBE6F
5" +

   "DAF2ADC96EFB7BAF6096C220A2F272807B91885FEB436FFBF1455337FDB06F74A44213DBCFB5384B"
+

"146AFC0C078E0E336BC96BAE3791CB514FEF3DEBC7DB49E684F002261BEB84E7F6BAE35304F7706AB4"
)]
```

34

LISTING 34.1
Continued

```
public class PublisherProtected
{
  public PublisherProtected()
  {

  }

  public string GetMessage()
  {
    return "This message is from a protected method.";
  }
}
}
```

Execute this code from an application that has been signed with the same strong-name key pair file to see that the application works properly and when you try to call GetMessage everything works as it should.

However, to ensure that unwanted consumers of your code cannot use it, create a new assembly that is signed with a different strong-name key pair file. When you try to execute this method, you will get a security exception.

As mentioned before, these attributes are evaluated before code within any protected method is executed. This means that if a protected class requires a public key identity from its callers, no property or method of that class can be accessed by any code that doesn't have the appropriate public key.

Summary

This chapter has presented you with a lot of information about code access security. You've seen the underlying structure of how permissions work, what permissions and permission sets are, and what CAS is. The discussion moved to learning how to administer and configure CAS as well as to create deployment packages to accommodate the needs of your own application. Finally, you saw a sample of CAS in action in the appearance of a class that can be used only by classes written by the same publisher with the same public key. At this point, you should have a thorough understanding of CAS—you will not take its existence for granted the next time you set out to create a new project.

Further Reading

msdn.microsoft.com/netframework

Essential .NET, Volume I: The Common Language Runtime by Don Box, Addison-Wesley. ISBN: 0201734117.

.NET Common Language Runtime Unleashed by Kevin Burton, Sams Publishing. ISBN: 0672321246.

34

35 Securing Sensitive Data

IN BRIEF

This chapter is about data protection. There are countless ways that you can protect your data, using everything from simple homemade techniques of data disguise to full-blown encryption algorithms.

This chapter will show you how to protect your data using the facilities available within the .NET Framework and within the operating system itself. You will see an explanation of the concepts behind secret key encryption, public key encryption, and the Windows Data Protection API (DPAPI). In addition to getting introductions to each of those topics, you will see samples of how to use each type of encryption technology within the .NET Framework so that at the end of the chapter you should be confident in your ability to secure any kind of data for any type of transmission or storage using C#.

WHAT YOU NEED

REQUIRED SOFTWARE	.NET Framework SDK v1.1 Visual Studio .NET 2003 with C# installed
RECOMMENDED HARDWARE	PC that meets .NET SDK minimum requirements
SKILLS REQUIRED	C# and .NET familiarity Familiarity with security concepts helpful

SECURING SENSITIVE DATA AT A GLANCE

Secret Key (Symmetric) Encryption   711

DESCryptoServiceProvider	711	TripleDESCrypto-ServiceProvider	713
RC2CryptoServiceProvider	712		
RijndaelManaged	713		

Using Hashes to Protect Data   716

MACTripleDES	716	MD5CryptoServiceProvider	719
SHA1Managed	718		

Public Key Encryption and Signatures   720

DSACryptoServiceProvider	721	RSACryptoServiceProvider	723

Windows Data Protection API   723

Using DPAPI	724	Protecting Data in .NET with DPAPI	732
Creating a DPAPI Wrapper	726		

Summary   733

Secret Key (Symmetric) Encryption

Secret key encryption, also called *symmetric encryption* because of its two-way nature, relies on something called a *shared secret* or *secret key*. Before discussing code, consider a hypothetical scenario:

Bob wants to send information to John, but Bob doesn't want anyone to be able to intercept the communication and be able to read the information being sent. To accomplish this, Bob comes up with a secret code that he uses to encrypt his message. Bob makes sure that John has this secret code through some means. When John receives the encrypted message, John can use that same secret key to decrypt the message that Bob sent.

There are two important aspects of this type of encryption:

▶ There is a secret shared between parties that allows for the secure transmission of data.

▶ The same key that is used to encrypt the data is used to decrypt the data (hence the term *symmetric* to describe this encryption type).

Secret key encryption works on single blocks of data at a time. Blocks are then chained together and operated on sequentially. If the secret key was used to encrypt each block without any modification, the same encrypted results would appear for the same block all the time. All someone would have to do is search for patterns in your blocks of encrypted data to get a head start on deciphering your key. To deal with this, an initialization vector (IV) is used. This is essentially a starter key that is used to encrypt the first block of data. Then data from each block is mixed with the data from the block, preventing duplicate blocks from producing the same encrypted output.

Thus, a common characteristic of all secret key encryption is the use of a secret key and an initialization vector key. The combination of these two keys is used to encrypt and decrypt information in a symmetric fashion. The next few sections will show you samples of some of the .NET cryptographic service providers that implement secret key encryption: `DESCryptoServiceProvider`, `RC2CryptoServiceProvider`, `RijndaelManaged`, and `TripleDESCryptoServiceProvider`.

DESCryptoServiceProvider

The `DESCryptoServiceProvider` is a managed class that inherits from `System.Security.SymmetricAlgorithm`. It provides an implementation of the DES (Data Encryption Standard) algorithm.

As with all symmetric algorithms, it requires a key and an IV to operate properly. These values are stored as byte arrays in the .NET Framework. For the examples in

35

Secret Key (Symmetric) Encryption

this chapter, some random keys have been generated on the fly to make them easier to read. For real-world scenarios, these keys would be kept secret somewhere inaccessible to most users.

The best way to encrypt data with a symmetric algorithm is to create a CryptoStream. A CryptoStream functions just like any other stream, but with one major difference: When nonencrypted data is written to the stream, it is encrypted by the stream itself. The following code creates an instance of the DESCryptoServiceProvider and sets up a CryptoStream:

```
// DES
DESCryptoServiceProvider des = new DESCryptoServiceProvider();
des.GenerateKey();
des.GenerateIV();
FileStream fsOut_DES = new FileStream("outputDES.txt", FileMode.Create,
FileAccess.Write);
CryptoStream desStream = new CryptoStream( fsOut_DES,
  des.CreateEncryptor( des.Key, des.IV ), CryptoStreamMode.Write);
```

In a real-world scenario, instead of calling GenerateKey and GenerateIV, you would assign the Key and IV properties to byte arrays that you created with your own keys.

Keep in mind that each of the algorithms has its own requirements for key size, so you will need to consult the documentation on each algorithm before creating your key and IV.

RC2CryptoServiceProvider

RC2CryptoServiceProvider is an implementation of the SymmetricAlgorithm abstract base class that provides access to the RC2 encryption algorithm. The following code shows how to set up a CryptoStream to an output file where the contents of the file will be RC2-encrypted:

```
// RC2
RC2CryptoServiceProvider rc2 = new RC2CryptoServiceProvider();
rc2.GenerateIV();
rc2.GenerateKey();
FileStream fsOut_RC2 = new FileStream("outputRC2.txt", FileMode.Create,
FileAccess.Write);
CryptoStream rc2Stream = new CryptoStream( fsOut_RC2,
  rc2.CreateEncryptor(), CryptoStreamMode.Write);
```

35

RijndaelManaged

The `RijndaelManaged` class is an implementation of the managed version of the `Rijndael` symmetric encryption algorithm. The following code illustrates creating a `CryptoStream` to an output file that will create a Rijndael-encrypted output:

```
// RijndaelManaged
RijndaelManaged rm = new RijndaelManaged();
rm.GenerateIV();
rm.GenerateKey();
FileStream fsOut_RM = new FileStream("outputRM.txt", FileMode.Create,
FileAccess.Write);
CryptoStream rmStream = new CryptoStream( fsOut_RM,
  rm.CreateEncryptor(), CryptoStreamMode.Write);
```

TripleDESCryptoServiceProvider

The TripleDES encryption algorithm is a symmetric encryption algorithm based on the data encryption standard. The following code illustrates how to set up an output `CryptoStream` that will create an encrypted text file based on TripleDES:

```
// TripleDES
TripleDESCryptoServiceProvider tripleDes = new TripleDESCryptoServiceProvider();
tripleDes.GenerateIV();
tripleDes.GenerateKey();
FileStream fsOut_3Des =
  new FileStream("output3DES.txt", FileMode.Create, FileAccess.Write);
CryptoStream tripleStream = new CryptoStream( fsOut_3Des,
  tripleDes.CreateEncryptor(), CryptoStreamMode.Write);
```

To put all of these encryption algorithms together into a simple program that will take an unencrypted text file and produce an encrypted version for each one of the symmetric algorithms, you can use the code shown in Listing 35.1.

LISTING 35.1
A Symmetric Encryption Demonstration

```
using System;
using System.IO;
using System.Text;
using System.Security.Cryptography;

namespace SecretKeyCrypto
{
  /// <summary>
```

35

Secret Key (Symmetric) Encryption

LISTING 35.1
Continued

```
/// Summary description for Class1.
/// </summary>
class Class1
{
  /// <summary>
  /// The main entry point for the application.
  /// </summary>
  [STAThread]
  static void Main(string[] args)
  {

    byte[] bin = new byte[100]; // 100 byte buffer

    FileStream fsIn = new FileStream("input.txt", FileMode.Open, FileAccess.Read);

    // buffer data
    long rdLen = 0;
    long totLen = fsIn.Length;
    int len;



    // DES
    DESCryptoServiceProvider des = new DESCryptoServiceProvider();
    des.GenerateKey();
    des.GenerateIV();
    FileStream fsOut_DES =
      new FileStream("outputDES.txt", FileMode.Create, FileAccess.Write);
    CryptoStream desStream = new CryptoStream( fsOut_DES,
      des.CreateEncryptor( des.Key, des.IV ), CryptoStreamMode.Write);

    // RC2
    RC2CryptoServiceProvider rc2 = new RC2CryptoServiceProvider();
    rc2.GenerateIV();
    rc2.GenerateKey();
    FileStream fsOut_RC2 =
      new FileStream("outputRC2.txt", FileMode.Create, FileAccess.Write);
    CryptoStream rc2Stream = new CryptoStream( fsOut_RC2,
      rc2.CreateEncryptor(), CryptoStreamMode.Write);

    // RijndaelManaged
```

35

LISTING 35.1
Continued

```
    RijndaelManaged rm = new RijndaelManaged();
    rm.GenerateIV();
    rm.GenerateKey();
    FileStream fsOut_RM =
      new FileStream("outputRM.txt", FileMode.Create, FileAccess.Write);
    CryptoStream rmStream = new CryptoStream( fsOut_RM,
      rm.CreateEncryptor(), CryptoStreamMode.Write);

    // TripleDES
    TripleDESCryptoServiceProvider tripleDes = new TripleDESCryptoServiceProvider();
    tripleDes.GenerateIV();
    tripleDes.GenerateKey();
    FileStream fsOut_3Des =
      new FileStream("output3DES.txt", FileMode.Create, FileAccess.Write);
    CryptoStream tripleStream = new CryptoStream( fsOut_3Des,
      tripleDes.CreateEncryptor(), CryptoStreamMode.Write);


    while ( rdLen < totLen )
    {
      len = fsIn.Read(bin, 0, 100);
      System.Diagnostics.Debug.WriteLine("Read " + len.ToString() + " bytes.");
      desStream.Write(bin, 0, len );
      rc2Stream.Write(bin, 0, len );
      rmStream.Write(bin, 0, len );
      tripleStream.Write(bin, 0, len );
      rdLen += len;
      Console.WriteLine("{0} Bytes Read.", rdLen );
    }

    desStream.Close();
    fsOut_DES.Close();
    fsIn.Close();
  }
 }
}
```

35

Creating a decryption stream is just as easy as creating an encryption stream. All you do is use the symmetric algorithm's CreateDecryptor method with the appropriate key and IV when creating a CryptoStream with the mode set to CryptoStreamMode.Read.

Using Hashes to Protect Data

Hashes are at the core of most real-world encryption algorithms and solutions. A *hash* is a one-way encryption algorithm that takes a variable-length string and uses a mathematical formula to reduce that string to a fixed-length hash. For a formula to qualify as a hashing algorithm, the formula must be able to guarantee that it is mathematically impossible for two different strings to ever produce the same hash value, no matter how similar they are. It also must be computationally impossible to write an algorithm that can determine the original message based on the digest (hash value). There are several different kinds of hashing algorithms. The MD (Message Digest) series of algorithms (MD2, MD4, MD5) all produce hashes of 128 bits. Both SHA and SHA-1 (Secure Hash Algorithm) produce digests that are 160 bits in size.

Hashes are used as verifiers. For example: A message is produced, and that same message is then hashed using a one-way algorithm. If the message is then hashed in some other location and compared to the original hash and the two hash values are not the same, you know the message has been tampered with. As you will see in an upcoming section, hashes combined with public key encryption form the basis for digital signatures.

MACTripleDES

The `MACTripleDES` class inherits from the `KeyedHashAlgorithm` class. It creates a one-way hash based on a key value. A *MAC* is a *message authentication code*; it is a signal from the receiver to the transmitter that the message being transmitted has not been tampered with.

The MAC scenario works like this: The client creates a hash of a message using some encryption algorithm. The client then sends both the message and the hash to the receiver. The receiver (who also knows the secret key) computes a hash from the message received. If the computed hash does not match the transmitted hash, the receiver knows that the message has been tampered with.

The code in Listing 35.2 shows how to hash a phrase (or password or any other arbitrary-length data) to a fixed-length hash code using the `MACTripleDES` algorithm.

35

LISTING 35.2
A Demonstration of the `MACTripleDES` Hash Algorithm

```
using System;
using System.Security.Cryptography;

namespace HashCrypto
{
    /// <summary>
```

LISTING 35.2
Continued

```
/// Summary description for Class1.
/// </summary>
class Class1
{
  /// <summary>
  /// The main entry point for the application.
  /// </summary>
  [STAThread]
  static void Main(string[] args)
  {
   string dataToHash = "The quick brown fox " +
     "ran over the lazy dog with a 50 horsepower " +
     "lawnmower. The carnage was horrible.";
    string key = "ABCDEFGHIJKLMNOPQRSTUVWX";

    byte[] dataToHash_Bytes =
      System.Text.Encoding.Unicode.GetBytes( dataToHash );
    byte[] key_Bytes =
      System.Text.Encoding.ASCII.GetBytes( key );

    MACTripleDES mac = new MACTripleDES( key_Bytes );

    byte[] result_Bytes = mac.ComputeHash( dataToHash_Bytes );

    Console.WriteLine("Phase has been hashed to {0} bytes length.",
      result_Bytes.Length );
    Console.WriteLine(
      System.Text.Encoding.ASCII.GetString( result_Bytes ));
    Console.ReadLine();

  }
 }
}
```

When you run this application, you will see that the hash code was reduced to 8 bytes (the size of the hash code is dependent on the size of the key). The MACTripleDES algorithm can use a key that is 8, 16, or 24 bytes and will *always* produce a hash that is 8 bytes, regardless of the size of the message being hashed. Note that MACTripleDES is a keyed hash algorithm. As such, it requires a secret key in order to create the hash code. Other algorithms, such as SHA1 (Secure Hash Algorithm), do not require a key to hash data.

35

Using Hashes to Protect Data

SHA1Managed

The SHA1Managed class provides a managed implementation of the SHA-1 secure hash algorithm. The SHA-1 hash algorithm is ideal for hashing large amounts of data, such as text and messages being sent over the wire or passwords. The reason is that even the smallest change in the source data can produce extremely variant changes in the hash output. As mentioned before, it is statistically impossible for any two different sources of data ever to produce a *collision* (a case where two different data sources produce the same hash). Because this algorithm doesn't require a key, it doesn't require very much effort to produce a hash, as shown in Listing 35.3.

LISTING 35.3

A Demonstration of the SHA-1 Managed Hash Algorithm Class

```
using System;
using System.Security.Cryptography;

namespace HashCrypto
{
  /// <summary>
  /// Summary description for Class1.
  /// </summary>
  class Class1
  {
    /// <summary>
    /// The main entry point for the application.
    /// </summary>
    [STAThread]
    static void Main(string[] args)
    {
     string dataToHash = "The quick brown fox " +
       "ran over the lazy dog with a 50 horsepower " +
       "lawnmower. The carnage was horrible.";

      byte[] dataToHash_Bytes =
        System.Text.Encoding.Unicode.GetBytes( dataToHash );

      // Produce a SHA1 hash of the original message.
      SHA1Managed sha1 = new SHA1Managed();
      byte[] sha1_Bytes = sha1.ComputeHash( dataToHash_Bytes);
      Console.WriteLine("SHA1 has produced a hash that is {0} bytes long.",
        sha1_Bytes.Length);
      Console.WriteLine( System.Text.Encoding.ASCII.GetString( sha1_Bytes ));

      Console.ReadLine();
```

35

LISTING 35.3
Continued

```
    }
  }
}
```

When you run this modified version of the previous sample, you will see that it produces an output hash that is 20 bytes long. This hash is a favorite for hashing passwords and similar information because the output is always 20 bytes (160 bits), which fits into a database column quite nicely. As mentioned earlier, the SHA1 hash algorithm always produces 160-bit hashes (160 bits equals 20 bytes).

MD5CryptoServiceProvider

The MD5 cryptographic service provider is another popular method for obtaining a one-way hash for verification of data. Because it also inherits from HashAlgorithm, and not KeyedHashAlgorithm, you do not need to provide it with a key to obtain hashed data. A slight modification to the preceding code can be made to produce an MD5-encryption-based hash of the original string, as shown in Listing 35.4.

LISTING 35.4
A Demonstration of the MD5 Cryptographic Service Provider

```csharp
using System;
using System.Security.Cryptography;

namespace HashCrypto
{
  /// <summary>
  /// Summary description for Class1.
  /// </summary>
  class Class1
  {
    /// <summary>
    /// The main entry point for the application.
    /// </summary>
    [STAThread]
    static void Main(string[] args)
    {
     string dataToHash = "The quick brown fox " +
       "ran over the lazy dog with a 50 horsepower " +
       "lawnmower. The carnage was horrible.";

      byte[] dataToHash_Bytes =
        System.Text.Encoding.Unicode.GetBytes( dataToHash );
```

35

Using Hashes to Protect Data

LISTING 35.4
Continued

```
    // Produce an MD5 hash of the original message.
    MD5CryptoServiceProvider md5 = new MD5CryptoServiceProvider();
    byte[] md5_Bytes = md5.ComputeHash( dataToHash_Bytes);
    Console.WriteLine("MD5 has produced a hash that is {0} bytes long.",
      md5_Bytes.Length);
    Console.WriteLine( System.Text.Encoding.ASCII.GetString( md5_Bytes ) );

    Console.ReadLine();

  }
 }
}
```

Running this application shows you that the MD5 algorithm will produce a hash that is 16 bytes long (128 bits).

Public Key Encryption and Signatures

Public key encryption involves the use of a key pair. That pair consists of a secure, private key, and a public key that can be made available to anyone. This type of encryption is called *asymmetric* because you don't use the same key to encrypt the data that you use to decrypt the data. Data that has been encrypted with the public key can be decrypted only by the private key, and data signed (encrypted) with the private key can be verified only by using the public key.

In a typical scenario, the public key is made available to anyone, and is used to encrypt data being sent to the owner of the private key. The other main difference between secret key (symmetric) and public key (asymmetric) encryption is that public key encryption is not designed to work with varying length blocks of data. You can't link together blocks of data in a public key encryption scenario.

So, if public key encryption only works with fixed-length sets of relatively small data, how do you secure a conversation over an open wire like the Internet? The answer involves using public key encryption to encrypt a shared secret.

A typical conversation might go like this: Bob and Joe already have key pairs defined. Bob and Joe also have each other's public keys because they know they want to talk to each other. Bob decides to start a conversation by encrypting a secret key using Joe's public key. He then sends the encrypted secret key to Joe, who then decrypts it using Joe's private key. Now both Bob and Joe know a secret key that can be used for symmetric encryption of large amounts of data, and they never transmitted that secret key unencrypted over the wire. Bob and Joe are then free to exchange large files, documents, images, or just chat, with full symmetric encrypted security.

DSACryptoServiceProvider

These examples will show you the basic technique for providing a validation, or digital signature, for a message transmission of some kind. The way it works is that a client uses a hash algorithm (one of the ones shown in Listings 35.2–35.4) to create a hash of the message. The hash of the message (called the *message digest*) is then encrypted using the sender's private key to create a personalized digital signature. When the receiver gets the message and the signature, the receiver decrypts the message digest using the sender's public key. The receiver then performs a hash on the message body. If the computed hash and the hash that was transmitted via public key encryption do not match, the receiver can assume that the message has been tampered with. Anyone can verify a *signature* (an array of bytes) because the only thing required to do so is the public key of the person who issued the signature.

The code in Listing 35.5 will show you how to verify a hash value using the DSACryptoProvider. The basic flow of code here is to create a hash. That hash is then used to create a signature. The signature can then be transmitted with the message. The receiving end creates a hash (in the sample case, just copies the previous hash) and then uses a signature deformatter to verify that the signature matches the hash.

LISTING 35.5

A Demonstration of the DSACryptoServiceProvider to Verify a Signature with a Key Pair

```
using System;
using System.Security.Cryptography;

namespace PublicKeyCrypto
{
  /// <summary>
  /// Summary description for Class1.
  /// </summary>
  class Class1
  {
    /// <summary>
    /// The main entry point for the application.
    /// </summary>
    [STAThread]
    static void Main(string[] args)
    {
      // create a hash that we will use to sign data.
      string dataToSign =
```

35

Public Key Encryption and Signatures

LISTING 35.5
Continued

```
                "The quick brown fox pulled a sub-machine gun on the lazy dog.";

        byte[] data_Bytes =
          System.Text.Encoding.ASCII.GetBytes( dataToSign );

        SHA1Managed sha1 = new SHA1Managed();
        byte[] hash_Bytes = sha1.ComputeHash( data_Bytes );

        // sign the hash
        DSACryptoServiceProvider dsa =
          new DSACryptoServiceProvider(); // creates a new key pair!
        DSASignatureFormatter sigFormatter = new DSASignatureFormatter(dsa);
        sigFormatter.SetHashAlgorithm("SHA1");
        byte[] signedHash = sigFormatter.CreateSignature( hash_Bytes );

        // for the sake of example, assume that the message and the signed hash have
        // been sent across a wire and stored in the remote_* variables.
        byte[] remote_SignedHash = signedHash;
        byte[] remote_HashedValue = hash_Bytes;

        // create a signature DEformatter, point it at the original DSA provider
        // to make sure the key pair is the same. In the 'real world', you would have
        // to see the provider with the right key
        // pair to make it able to decrypt the signature.
        DSASignatureDeformatter sigDeformatter = new DSASignatureDeformatter( dsa );
        sigDeformatter.SetHashAlgorithm( "SHA1" );

        if (sigDeformatter.VerifySignature( remote_HashedValue, remote_SignedHash ))
          Console.WriteLine("The signature used to sign the hash has been verified.");
        else
          Console.WriteLine("The signature used to sign the hash does not match the
                            hash.");
        Console.ReadLine();
      }
    }
  }
```

The only concern with this code is that it is easy to forget that you are actually working with a key pair. When you create a new instance of the DSA provider, it actually creates a public and private key pair for you that will be useable until the instance of the DSA provider is disposed of. Obviously, for production-quality code, you will need a permanent key pair for signing and verifying. Also keep in mind that the DSACryptoService provider is not an encryption provider; it is instead used for verifying signatures and hashes.

RSACryptoServiceProvider

The RSACryptoServiceProvider uses public and private key pairs to encrypt and decrypt data. The following section of code shows a quick and easy (again with an auto-generated key pair) method of encrypting data with a private key:

```
RSACryptoServiceProvider rsa=  new RSACryptoServiceProvider();
byte[] dataToEncrypt = System.Text.Encoding.Unicode.GetBytes( "Encrypt THIS!" );
byte[] encrypted_Bytes;
byte[] decrypted_Bytes;

// no OAEP padding, as that is an XP-only service.
encrypted_Bytes = rsa.Encrypt( dataToEncrypt, false );
Console.WriteLine("RSA-encrypted data is {0} bytes long.", encrypted_Bytes.Length);
decrypted_Bytes = rsa.Decrypt( encrypted_Bytes, false );
Console.WriteLine("RSA-decrypted string is {0}.",
System.Text.Encoding.Unicode.GetString( decrypted_Bytes ));
```

The code involved in creating encrypted strings is fairly simple with the RSA provider. It will always create encrypted data that is 128 bytes in length. As a result, you can't use RSA to encrypt long streams of data. Instead, it is used for encrypting keys and phrases.

Windows Data Protection API

Windows Data Protection API (DPAPI) appeared with the release of Windows 2000. It was obvious at the time that developers and users needed the ability to protect their data through the use of encryption. The DPAPI interface is extremely simple, and provides two functions for users: protect data and unprotect data.

Because of the way key-based encryption works, there needs to be some way to protect one user's data from another user. Because DPAPI is part of the operating system, and it requires a password in order to perform data protection operations, it only makes sense that it would use your Windows credential information.

This brings up another problem. There are cases where many different people use the same account to log in to a machine. In this case, data protection based on a user's credentials would be pretty meaningless—everyone who logged in as that user would be able to unprotect that user's data. To deal with this, DPAPI enables you to provide an additional secret that is used in combination with the user's password to allow an

35

application or a user to provide additional security on the data. The same additional secret used to protect the data is required to unprotect the data.

Another chapter could be written on the details on the DPAPI, but to keep it short, only one more additional detail will be mentioned before beginning a discussion of how to use DPAPI. As you now know, DPAPI data protection is based on user credentials. Through a fairly complicated process, encryption keys are rebuilt when users change their passwords and the data is reprotected so that when the user attempts to unprotect data, the correct password will be used. Older keys based on older user passwords are kept around in order to allow data to remain protected. As has already been said, it's a fairly complex process. Rather than burden you with all the details, you can be content in knowing that the operating system handles all the details associated with keeping DPAPI safe, backed up, reliable, and backwards compatible with user password changes.

The last point to be made before getting into the code is this: DPAPI provides only protection for your data; it does not provide a means to store protected data. You have to provide your own storage mechanism for protected and unprotected data. All of DPAPI's functions operate on in-memory data only.

Using DPAPI

The API for data protection is very simple. There are only two main things that you can do with it: protect data and unprotect data. The first method that you need to learn how to use is `CryptProtectData`. The DPAPI is not implemented in managed code, so you will need to use some P/Invoke conventions and marshalling to get the job done. Thankfully, the API is fairly simple and is pretty easy to wrap.

Here is the C++ prototype for the `CryptProtectData` function:

```
BOOL WINAPI CryptProtectData (
    DATA_BLOB                    *pDataIn,
    LPCWSTR                       szDataDescr,
    DATA_BLOB                    *pOptionalEntropy,
    PVOID                         pvReserved,
    CRYPTPROTECT_PROMPTSTRUCT    *pPromptStruct,
    DWORD                         dwFlags,
    DATA_BLOB                    *pDataOut)
```

There are two `struct`s in the preceding API call: DATA_BLOB, which contains the actual data to be protected, and the output return value of the function. The following is a description of the parameters of the method call:

▶ pDataIn—A pointer to a DATA_BLOB struct containing the plain text that is to be protected by encryption.

▶ szDataDescr—A string describing the data to be protected. This description is placed into the protected output blob. *Optional.*

35

▸ pOptionalEntropy—A pointer to an additional blob of data that will be used to add more randomness to the data, further separating it from data encrypted by the same Windows logon. *Optional*

▸ pvReserved—This will always be NULL.

▸ pPromptStruct—A pointer to a CRYPTPROTECT_PROMPTSTRUCT structure that is used to indicate where and when prompts occur, and the contents of those prompts. The CRYPTPROTECT_PROMPTSTRUCT is defined later.

▸ dwFlags—A list of possible flags for further configuration of data protection. Possible flags are as follows:

CRYPTPROTECT_LOCALMACHINE—Uses a machine key to encrypt.

CRYPTPROTECT_UI_FORBIDDEN—Cannot display UI during protection.

CRYPTPROTECT_AUDIT—Records an audit of protection.

CRYPTPROTECT_CRED_SYNC—Causes a re-encryption of master keys, more than likely after a password change.

CRYPTPROTECT_SYSTEM—Causes the call to fail.

▸ pDataOut—A pointer to a blob of data that contains the protected data.

Now the C++ prototype for CryptUnprotectData:

```
BOOL WINAPI CryptUnprotectData (
    DATA_BLOB                  *pDataIn,
    LPCWSTR                     *ppszDataDescr,
    DATA_BLOB                  *pOptionalEntropy,
    PVOID                        pvReserved,
    CRYPTPROTECT_PROMPTSTRUCT   *pPromptStruct,
    DWORD                        dwFlags,
    DATA_BLOB                  *pDataOut)
```

You can probably guess what these parameters mean given the previous parameter description. If you need even more detail than what is described here, you can always consult the Windows Platform SDK documentation; these functions are part of the Windows 2000, Windows XP, and Windows Server 2003 operating systems.

The following is the C++ prototype for the CRYPTPROTECT_PROMPTSTRUCT structure. This structure gives the operating system information that allows it to prompt the user to configure the data protection that will take place, including the security level and the additional entropy password.

```
typedef struct _CRYPTPROTECT_PROMPTSTRUCT {
    DWORD      cbSize;
    DWORD      dwPromptFlags;
```

35

Windows Data Protection API

```
    HWND      hwndApp;
    LPCWSTR   szPrompt;
} CRYPTPROTECT_PROMPTSTRUCT, *PCRYPTPROTECT_PROMTPSTRUCT;
```

The fields in this structure are as follows:

▶ cbSize—Contains the size of the structure in bytes

▶ dwPromptFlags—When used to encrypt data, any of the following flags may
   be passed:

   CRYPTPROTECT_PROMPT_ON_PROTECT—Prompts the user for information
           when the data is protected

   CRYPTPROTECT_PROMPT_ON_UNPROTECT—Prompts the user for information
           when the data is unprotected

   CRYPTPROTECT_STRONG—Uses strong security by default

▶ hwndApp—Handle to the parent window

▶ szPrompt—String containing the text for the security prompt

Creating a DPAPI Wrapper

To create a DPAPI wrapper class, you must create definitions for all the unmanaged
functions that you need to use. In addition, you'll have to define the data structures
that you will use to pass data back and forth between the API.

To do this, create a simple Console Application and add a class called
DPAPIWrapper to it. Inside the DPAPI namespace, outside the class wrapper, add the
following structs:

```
[StructLayout(LayoutKind.Sequential, CharSet=CharSet.Unicode)]
public struct DATA_BLOB
{
  public int cbData;
  public IntPtr pbData;
}


[StructLayout(LayoutKind.Sequential, CharSet=CharSet.Unicode)]
public struct CRYPTPROTECT_PROMPTSTRUCT
{
  public int cbSize;
  public int dwPromptFlags;
  public IntPtr hwndApp;
  public string szPrompt;
}
```

With these `structs` in hand, you can build a wrapper class that wraps around the functionality of the `CryptProtectData` and `CryptUnprotectData` functions available in `crypt32.dll`. You can also statically link to `crypt32.lib` if you are writing C++ or managed C++ code. Listing 35.6 shows the `DPAPIWrapper` class. The code in Listing 35.6 was inspired by an article you can find on MSDN entitled "How to Create a DPAPI Library" (msdn.microsoft.com/library/default.asp?url=/library/en-us/secmod/html/secmod21.asp). The code comes from the security patterns and practices recommendations. Because Microsoft recommends that you utilize DPAPI from .NET in this manner, code similar to the article is used in Listing 35.6.

LISTING 35.6
The `DPAPIWrapper` Class

```
using System;
using System.Runtime.InteropServices;

namespace DPAPI
{
  public enum EncryptionKeyType
  {
    User = 1,
    Machine
  }

  [StructLayout(LayoutKind.Sequential, CharSet=CharSet.Unicode)]
  public struct DATA_BLOB
  {
    public int cbData;
    public IntPtr pbData;
  }

  [StructLayout(LayoutKind.Sequential, CharSet=CharSet.Unicode)]
  public struct CRYPTPROTECT_PROMPTSTRUCT
  {
    public int cbSize;
    public int dwPromptFlags;
    public IntPtr hwndApp;
    public string szPrompt;
  }

  /// <summary>
  /// Summary description for DPAPIWrapper.
  /// </summary>
  public class DPAPIWrapper
  {
    private const int CRYPTPROTECT_UI_FORBIDDEN  = 0x1;
    private const int CRYPTPROTECT_LOCAL_MACHINE = 0x4;
```

35

Windows Data Protection API

LISTING 35.6
Continued

```csharp
[DllImport( "crypt32.dll",
  SetLastError=true,
  CharSet=System.Runtime.InteropServices.CharSet.Auto)]
private static extern bool CryptProtectData(
  ref DATA_BLOB pDataIn,
  string szDataDescr,
  ref DATA_BLOB pOptionalEntropy,
  IntPtr pvReserved,
  ref CRYPTPROTECT_PROMPTSTRUCT pPromptStruct,
  int dwFlags,
  ref DATA_BLOB pDataOut);


[DllImport( "crypt32.dll",
  SetLastError=true,
  CharSet=System.Runtime.InteropServices.CharSet.Auto)]
private static extern bool CryptUnprotectData(
  ref DATA_BLOB pDataIn,
  ref string ppszDataDescr,
  ref DATA_BLOB pOptionalEntropy,
  IntPtr pvReserved,
  ref CRYPTPROTECT_PROMPTSTRUCT pPromptStruct,
  int dwFlags,
  ref DATA_BLOB pDataOut);

private static CRYPTPROTECT_PROMPTSTRUCT CreateEmptyPromptStruct()
{
  CRYPTPROTECT_PROMPTSTRUCT cpps = new CRYPTPROTECT_PROMPTSTRUCT();

  cpps.cbSize = Marshal.SizeOf( typeof( CRYPTPROTECT_PROMPTSTRUCT) );
  cpps.dwPromptFlags = 0;
  cpps.hwndApp = IntPtr.Zero;
  cpps.szPrompt = null;

  return cpps;
}

private static DATA_BLOB InitBlobFromByteArray( byte[] data )
{
  DATA_BLOB blob = new DATA_BLOB();

  blob.pbData = Marshal.AllocHGlobal( data.Length );
  if (blob.pbData == IntPtr.Zero)
```

LISTING 35.6
Continued

```
      throw new Exception("Could not allocate BLOB buffer.");

  blob.cbData = data.Length;
  Marshal.Copy(data, 0, blob.pbData, data.Length);
  return blob;
}

public static string Protect(
  string dataToProtect,
  string entropy,
  string dataDescription )
{
  return Convert.ToBase64String(
    Protect(
      EncryptionKeyType.User,
      System.Text.Encoding.UTF8.GetBytes( dataToProtect ),
      System.Text.Encoding.UTF8.GetBytes( entropy ),
      dataDescription ) );
}

// Start overloads of Protect
public static byte[] Protect(
  EncryptionKeyType keyType,
  byte[] inputData,
  byte[] entropyData,
  string dataDescription )
{
  DATA_BLOB inputBlob = InitBlobFromByteArray( inputData );
  DATA_BLOB entropyBlob = InitBlobFromByteArray( entropyData );
  DATA_BLOB outputBlob = new DATA_BLOB();

  try
  {
    CRYPTPROTECT_PROMPTSTRUCT prompt = CreateEmptyPromptStruct();

    int dwFlags = CRYPTPROTECT_UI_FORBIDDEN;
    if (keyType == EncryptionKeyType.Machine)
      dwFlags |= CRYPTPROTECT_LOCAL_MACHINE;

    // Finally, invoke DPAPI
    bool result = CryptProtectData(
      ref inputBlob,
      dataDescription,
      ref entropyBlob,
```

35

Windows Data Protection API

LISTING 35.6
Continued

```csharp
                IntPtr.Zero,
                ref prompt,
                dwFlags,
                ref outputBlob );


        if (result == false)
        {
          throw new Exception("Failed to Protect Data.");
        }

        byte[] outputBytes = new byte[outputBlob.cbData];
        Marshal.Copy( outputBlob.pbData,
          outputBytes,
          0,
          outputBlob.cbData );

        return outputBytes;
      }
      catch (Exception ex)
      {
        throw new Exception("DPAPI Failure: " + ex.ToString());
      }
      finally
      {
        if ( inputBlob.pbData != IntPtr.Zero)
          Marshal.FreeHGlobal( inputBlob.pbData );
        if ( entropyBlob.pbData != IntPtr.Zero )
          Marshal.FreeHGlobal( entropyBlob.pbData );
        if ( outputBlob.pbData != IntPtr.Zero )
          Marshal.FreeHGlobal( outputBlob.pbData );
      }
    }

    public static string Unprotect(
      string protectedString,
      string entropyData,
      out string dataDescription )
    {
      return System.Text.Encoding.UTF8.GetString(
        Unprotect( Convert.FromBase64String( protectedString ),
        System.Text.Encoding.UTF8.GetBytes( entropyData ),
        out dataDescription ) );
    }
```

35

LISTING 35.6
Continued

```
public static byte[] Unprotect(
  byte[] protectedData,
  byte[] entropyData,
  out string dataDescription )
{
  DATA_BLOB unprotectedBlob = new DATA_BLOB();
  DATA_BLOB protectedBlob = InitBlobFromByteArray( protectedData );
  DATA_BLOB entropyBlob = InitBlobFromByteArray( entropyData );

  CRYPTPROTECT_PROMPTSTRUCT prompt = CreateEmptyPromptStruct();

  dataDescription = string.Empty;

  try
  {
    int dwFlags = CRYPTPROTECT_UI_FORBIDDEN;

    bool result = CryptUnprotectData(
    ref protectedBlob,
    ref dataDescription,
    ref entropyBlob,
    IntPtr.Zero,
    ref prompt,
    dwFlags,
    ref unprotectedBlob );

    if (!result)
      throw new Exception("CryptUnprotectData Failure.");

    byte[] unprotectedBytes = new byte[ unprotectedBlob.cbData ];
    Marshal.Copy(
      unprotectedBlob.pbData, unprotectedBytes,
      0, unprotectedBlob.cbData );

    return unprotectedBytes;
  }
  catch (Exception ex)
  {
    throw new Exception("Failed to decrypt via DPAPI: " + ex.ToString());
  }
  finally
  {
    if (unprotectedBlob.pbData != IntPtr.Zero)
      Marshal.FreeHGlobal( unprotectedBlob.pbData );
```

35

Windows Data Protection API

LISTING 35.6
Continued

```
    if (protectedBlob.pbData != IntPtr.Zero)
      Marshal.FreeHGlobal( protectedBlob.pbData );
    if (entropyBlob.pbData != IntPtr.Zero)
      Marshal.FreeHGlobal( entropyBlob.pbData );
  }
 }
 }
}
```

It might look like a lot of up-front work, but putting the effort up front gives you a very powerful, very reusable class that you can use in all of your applications that might need DPAPI support for data protection.

When dealing with the pbData field in the DATA_BLOB struct, it is important to remember that it is an allocated HGlobal. Without going too deep into the Win32 API or unmanaged C++, an HGlobal is a global handle that is allocated to an application by the operating system. When the application is done with that handle, it needs to make sure that it gets the operating system to release the handle; otherwise, there will be a slow leak in the application that could eventually cause a crash.

Protecting Data in .NET with DPAPI

Now that you have a reusable class that you can use to protect and unprotect data using DPAPI, look at the following few lines of code to see how incredibly easy it now is to use DPAPI in your application:

```
[STAThread]
static void Main(string[] args)
{
  string dataToProtect = "The quick brown fox got ran over by a reindeer.";
  string entropy = "Entropic Entropicality";

  string encryptedData =
    DPAPIWrapper.Protect( dataToProtect, entropy, "My Data" );

  Console.WriteLine("Successfully protected the string : {0}\nNow encrypted into :
{1}",
    dataToProtect, encryptedData );

  string dataDescription;
  string decryptedData =
    DPAPIWrapper.Unprotect( encryptedData, entropy, out dataDescription );
```

35

```
Console.WriteLine("Successfully unprotected the string : {0}\n" +
   "Now descripted into : {1}\nDescription : << {2} >>",
   encryptedData, decryptedData, dataDescription );

Console.ReadLine();
}
```

As you can see, it's pretty simple to make use of the new wrapper class. As you find
new needs for the wrapper class and new needs for DPAPI interaction, you can
simply add method overrides to support your required functionality. The output of
the DPAPI protection sample is shown in Figure 35.1.

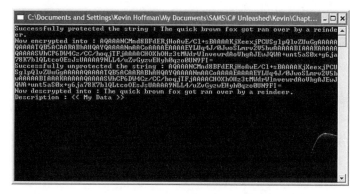

FIGURE 35.1   A console application using the newly created
DPAPI wrapper class.

Summary

This goal of this chapter was to show you how to protect your data and protect
communications between applications using security. You saw the symmetric
algorithms that use a secret key to encrypt and decrypt data. You saw asymmetric
algorithms that use public-private key pairs to produce complex, secure, encrypted
data. In addition, you looked at creating hashes and took a whirlwind tour of the
Windows Data Protection API (DPAPI).

After having read this chapter, you should be confident in your own ability to
protect your application's data and protect information sent to and from your application using various methods. You should also feel fairly comfortable with the different concepts that are critical to encryption, such as key pairs, hashes, symmetric and
asymmetric algorithms, and DPAPI.

35

36

Securing ASP.NET Web Applications

IN BRIEF

This chapter continues the topic of security and applies it to the protection and security of ASP.NET web applications. Whether you are building a small ASP.NET application for your corporate intranet or an e-commerce application that will accept tens of thousands of transactions per day, you will at some point be faced with the questions: How do I protect my website? Ensure the privacy of my users? Protect and secure the data for my website?

This chapter will get you thinking about those questions and provide some design patterns for solving those problems as well as walk you through some sample code that shows you some of the ways in which ASP.NET and the .NET Framework can provide varying levels of security and protection for your users, your data, and your server.

WHAT YOU NEED

REQUIRED SOFTWARE	.NET Framework SDK v1.1
	Visual Studio .NET 2003 with C# installed
	IIS version 5+
RECOMMENDED HARDWARE	PC that meets .NET SDK minimum requirements
SKILLS REQUIRED	C# and .NET familiarity
	Familiarity with ASP.NET

SECURING ASP.NET APPLICATIONS AT A GLANCE

User Security	734		
Authenticating Users	735	Implementing IIdentity and	
Authorizing Users with Roles	740	IPrincipal	740
Data Security in ASP.NET Applications	748		
Protecting Connection Strings and Web.config Data	748	Deciding When to Use SSL	751
Protecting User Passwords	748	Data Security with ViewState Encryption	751
Summary	752		
Further Reading	752		

User Security

Every aspect of security is extremely important to the success of your website. Without users, you don't have a website. You will lose your users if you can't guarantee that their passwords are secure, and that you can reliably authenticate and authorize users if your site requires it.

Authenticating Users

The process of authentication is the process by which a user's identity is confirmed. Through some means, your web site determines who the user is. ASP.NET provides several different methods for authenticating users and determining identity. They are as follows:

- ▶ Windows authentication
- ▶ Forms authentication
- ▶ Passport authentication

Windows Authentication

Windows authentication mode uses the current user's Windows identity to authenticate the user. This is an extremely secure way of authenticating users when you can guarantee that the users of your website will be on machines within a domain that has some relationship to the server's domain. This authentication mode is done in combination with IIS authentication. IIS authentication can be done using basic (clear text), digest (hashed identity information), or integrated Windows authentication.

Windows Authentication through ASP.NET is accomplished through an authentication provider called the Windows Authentication Provider. This provider requires the smallest amount of code to implement security.

Everywhere that a user's security context is required in the .NET Framework, two types of objects are used: principals and identities. A principal is a container for an identity. You use the principal to find out the identity of the principal and the list of roles to which that principal belongs.

An identity contains the actual identity of the user. The identity enables the programmer to determine the method by which the user was authenticated (for example, Windows, Passport, or Forms), whether the identity has been authenticated, and the name of that user's identity.

When Windows authentication is used, ASP.NET will automatically provide a `WindowsPrincipal` and a `WindowsIdentity` object to every page for the programmer to use. To set up Windows authentication, just set the `<authentication>` element in `Web.config` to the following:

```
<authentication mode="Windows" />
```

You can then set the `<authorization>` element to choose whether your site allows anonymous or authenticated users or both. The comments in the default `Web.config` file explain the syntax of the `<authorization>` element.

36

User Security

The following section of code shows you a couple of the common ways in which you can use the `WindowsIdentity` and `WindowsPrincipal` objects that are part of the ASP.NET security model when you are using Windows authentication:

```
private void Page_Load(object sender, System.EventArgs e)
{
  // Put user code to initialize the page here
  WindowsPrincipal wp = (WindowsPrincipal)User;
  Response.Write("Welcome, " + wp.Identity.Name + "<br>");
  Response.Write("Authentication Mode: " +
    wp.Identity.AuthenticationType.ToString() + "<BR>");
  Response.Write("Is user authenticated? : " +
    wp.Identity.IsAuthenticated.ToString() + "<BR>");
  Response.Write("Is in Administrators Role? : " +
    wp.IsInRole( WindowsBuiltInRole.Administrator ) );
}
```

The preceding code prints out the user's name, whether the user is authenticated, and how authentication was performed. The `IsInRole` method is part of the `IPrincipal` interface. The `WindowsPrincipal` class provides an override that enables you to check whether a `WindowsPrincipal` belongs to one of the built-in Windows groups. If you supply a string, the `WindowsPrincipal` will check for group membership within the named NT group. The output from the preceding code is shown in Figure 36.1.

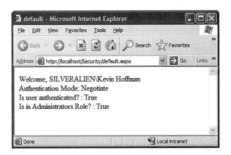

FIGURE 36.1 Output of some data using Windows authentication.

As you can see, using Windows authentication is pretty easy. With only a quick change to the `Web.config` file, you automatically gain access to the entire Windows security model and can make use of that functionality within your web application.

Forms Authentication

With Windows authentication, there is no need to log in. The login is already handled by Windows. If Windows knows who you are, the web application automatically knows who you are. This is not true with Forms authentication.

Windows authentication is great for intranet websites and private websites that you might find on the Internet, but it isn't a very good way of providing authentication for public websites.

For that, you need a more versatile way of providing authentication. For this, ASP.NET provides the Forms Authentication Provider. When a request is made for a protected page by an unauthenticated user, the user is redirected to a login page that performs the login and user authentication. After that user has been authenticated, she can access protected pages and the website can then identify her. The default mode is to use a cookie that provides a secure method of authenticating a request.

To change the website from the previous example to work with Forms authentication, make a change to the Web.config file. Change the <authentication> element to the following:

```
<authentication mode="Forms">
  <forms loginUrl="login.aspx" name=".SECURITYAUTH" />
</authentication>
```

The <forms> tag takes two attributes: loginUrl and name. The loginUrl specifies the URL of the login page to which an unauthenticated user will be redirected when he attempts to access a secured page. The name attribute is actually the suffix used for the authentication cookie that will be written to the client. If you have more than one secure website on the same server using Forms authentication, you will need to make sure that those suffixes are unique across the applications.

With the <forms> tag in place in Web.config, you need to create a login.aspx page to handle verification of the user's identity. To do that, add a new Web Form called login.aspx to whatever web project you're working on.

Add a TextBox for the user ID called txtLogin, a TextBox for the password called txtPassword (set the TextMode property to Password), a CheckBox called chkPersistCookie, and finally a button called btnLogin. If the user checks the box in the Persist Cookie check box, the authentication cookie will be persistent and the website will remember that user even after his session has ended.

Double-click the btnLogin button to wire up the following Click event handler:

```
private void btnSubmit_Click(object sender, System.EventArgs e)
{
  if (  (txtLogin.Text == "kevin") && (txtPassword.Text == "password" ))
  {
    FormsAuthentication.RedirectFromLoginPage( txtLogin.Text,
```

36

User Security

```
    chkPersistCookie.Checked );
  }
}
```

This method uses the FormsAuthentication class's static method RedirectFromLoginPage. This method not only writes out the authentication cookie, identifying the user by the first parameter, but it also redirects the user to the page he was trying to access before he was redirected to the login page.

Obviously you will not want to perform your real authentication like this. Hard-coded usernames and passwords were used in the example just to demonstrate authentication. Typically you would be using a database to perform secure password authentication. In fact, you'll see a way to ensure password security and privacy later in this chapter.

This redirection gets rid of the problem that many sites used to have with bookmarks on secured pages. If someone were to bookmark a page that required a login and the site didn't have this redirection logic, the bookmark would be useless because after logging in, the user would be directed to some home page. With ASP.NET and Forms authentication, the website knows what protected page the user initially requested and can return her to that page after she has been authenticated.

The FormsAuthentication class contains many other utilities and tools for dealing with forms-based security. Some of them are listed in Table 36.1.

TABLE 36.1

Static Methods of the FormsAuthentication Class

Method	Description
Authenticate	This method attempts to validate supplied credentials against credentials stored in the Web.config file in the <credentials> element. This is definitely not a recommended best practice for anything but the simplest of websites.
GetRedirectUrl	Obtains the URL that the user originally requested before being sent to a login page.
HashPasswordForStoringInConfigFile	This method takes a password and an identifier for the hash type and returns a hashed password suitable for storing as plain text.
RedirectFromLoginPage	This method sends the user back to the page he requested as well as writes his authentication cookie.
RenewTicketIfOld	This gives the programmer the ability to conditionally extend the expiration period on an authentication ticket.

36

TABLE 36.1

Continued

Method	Description
SetAuthCookie	This method sets the authentication cookie just as the RedirectFromLoginPage method does, except this method does not redirect.
SignOut	This method signs the user out by removing his authentication ticket.

After removing the WindowsPrincipal-specific code from default.aspx, I then tried to open that page in a browser. As expected, I was redirected to my quick-and-dirty login page. After logging in with my hard-coded username and password, I am presented with a default.aspx page, as shown in Figure 36.2.

FIGURE 36.2   The default.aspx page under the protection of Forms authentication.

The point to take away from this section of the chapter isn't that Forms authentication is the best authentication system in the world. It isn't; it is a starting point and you have to do a lot of the heavy lifting yourself to get it to work the way you need.

However, Forms authentication is the most commonly used form of website authentication on the Internet for ASP.NET websites. The reason for this is that it is the most available. Both Windows and Passport authentication have restrictions that make them less frequently used on public websites than standard Forms authentication. Forms authentication is extensible and configurable and with a little work, you can get it to work with just about any security needs you might have.

Passport Authentication

Passport authentication is an implementation of single sign-on technology. In other words, you have a single authentication ticket (a passport, if you will) that you own

36

and that you present to each site that you access. If the site you are accessing is aware of the Passport authentication scheme, that site can authenticate you on the spot without you having to go through the painstaking process of signing up as a new user including typing in your name, address, email, contact information, and so on.

There are several benefits and limitations to using the Passport Authentication Provider. The major benefit is, of course, the use of single sign-on technology and the ease of use for the end user as well as the ability to use something called a *Kids Passport* for compliance with the COPPA (Children's Online Privacy Protection Act). The problem is that this technology isn't easy to use nor is it free.

For your site to be able to recognize and authenticate valid Passport identities, you need to download and install the Passport SDK after reading the license agreement and documentation found at www.passport.com/business. Another downfall of this system is that your ability to authenticate users is at the mercy of some other party. Although that other party is Microsoft, that fact doesn't make it immune from downtime. I have had many days where my Passport simply wouldn't work anywhere because the central Passport authentication server was not responding or was having some other trouble.

Unfortunately, many of the sites that could benefit from Passport simply can't afford it. The current pricing at the time this book was being written is a periodic compliance testing fee of $1,500 and an annual per-company fee of $10,000.

Authorizing Users with Roles

As you saw earlier, the `IPrincipal` interface implements a method called `IsInRole`. Up to the implementer to define, this method determines whether the user is part of a named group or role. *Roles* are abstractions that relate different types of users together. For example, you can have roles that are for administrators, data base personnel, developers, and end users.

As you saw, the implementation of the `WindowsPrincipal` class determines membership within a Windows group. Other implementations of principal use that method for determining membership within their own custom groups. In the next section, you will see how to create your own implementation of `IIdentity` and `IPrincipal` and use your custom implementations to not only add your own functionality, but also to provide your own role-based security system that integrates seamlessly with ASP.NET security.

Implementing `IIdentity` and `IPrincipal`

Even though the default implementations of `IPrincipal` and `IIdentity` should be sufficient for most applications, there may be times when you want to create your own implementation and use it on top of the existing ASP.NET security functionality.

36

For example, if you want to be able to get an enumeration of all the roles to which a user belongs, you can't get that functionality with the default `IPrincipal` implementation. Or if you want to use your own data source for the list of roles assigned to each user for Forms authentication, you will want to create your own principal. You can implement your own custom `IPrincipal` without implementing a new `IIdentity`, but the example shown next uses custom implementations of both interfaces and shows you how to integrate those into ASP.NET.

This example will show you how to create your own `IIdentity` and `IPrincipal` implementations and integrate them into ASP.NET with very minimal effort. To start off, create a new Web Application and follow the same steps as you did in the previous sample to set it up for Forms authentication. This includes creating a `login.aspx` page and setting up the `Web.config` file to deny anonymous users and set up the authentication ticket. The following code simply authenticates whomever attempts to login. The goal of this exercise isn't to show secure authentication, but to show you how to enhance the existing user identity system.

```
private void btnLogin_Click(object sender, System.EventArgs e)
{
  // ordinarily you would call business tier to authenticate user
  // instead we're just going to authenticate them.

  FormsAuthentication.RedirectFromLoginPage(
    txtLogin.Text, chkRememberLogin.Checked );
}
```

This code will automatically accept whatever username is typed into the login form and create an authentication ticket for that user.

The next thing to do is create identity and principal objects. Listing 36.1 and Listing 36.2 show both of these classes.

LISTING 36.1
The `CustomIdentity` Class

```
using System;
using System.Security;
using System.Security.Principal;

namespace CustomSecurity.Classes
{
  /// <summary>
  /// Summary description for CustomIdentity.
  /// </summary>
  public class CustomIdentity : IIdentity
  {
```

36

User Security

LISTING 36.1
Continued

```csharp
      private string name = null;

      public CustomIdentity( string name)
      {
        this.name = name;
      }

      #region IIdentity Members

      public bool IsAuthenticated
      {
        get
        {
          // TODO:   Add CustomIdentity.IsAuthenticated getter implementation
          return !(name == null);
        }
      }

      public string Name
      {
        get
        {
          return name;
        }
      }

      public string AuthenticationType
      {
        get
        {
          // TODO:   Add CustomIdentity.AuthenticationType getter implementation
          return "Custom";
        }
      }

      #endregion
  }
}
```

The CustomIdentity class is a fairly simple class. All it needs to store is the authentication type and the name of the identity. The CustomPrincipal object shown in

Listing 36.2 is a little more complex because that is where all of the custom role-based security code goes.

LISTING 36.2
The `CustomPrincipal` Class

```
using System;
using System.Xml;
using System.Collections;
using System.Collections.Specialized;
using System.Security;
using System.Security.Principal;

namespace CustomSecurity.Classes
{
  /// <summary>
  /// Summary description for CustomPrincipal.
  /// </summary>
  public class CustomPrincipal : IPrincipal
  {
    private StringCollection sc = new StringCollection();
    private IIdentity identity;

    public CustomPrincipal( IIdentity identity )
    {
      this.identity = identity;
      LoadRolesFromDataSource();
    }

    private void LoadRolesFromDataSource()
    {
      // this is where we obtain the list of roles that belong
      // to the custom identity.
      XmlDocument doc = new XmlDocument();
      doc.Load( System.Web.HttpContext.Current.Server.MapPath("~/users.xml"));

      XmlNode user = doc.SelectSingleNode("//user[@id=\"" + identity.Name + "\"]");
      foreach (XmlNode node in user.SelectNodes("role") )
      {
        sc.Add( node.Attributes.GetNamedItem("name").Value );
      }
    }

    #region IPrincipal Members
```

36

LISTING 36.2
Continued

```
public IIdentity Identity
{
  get
  {
    return identity;
  }
}

public bool IsInRole(string role)
{
  return sc.Contains(role);
}

public bool IsInAllRoles(string roleList)
{
  bool inAll = true;
  string[] roles = roleList.Split('|');
  foreach (string role in roles)
  {
    if (!sc.Contains(role))
      inAll = false;
  }
  return inAll;
}

    #endregion
  }
}
```

When the CustomPrincipal is created via the constructor, it takes the CustomIdentity that is passed to it and uses that to retrieve the role membership for the user. If you wanted to do so, you could implement lazy-loading and request the role list only when the IsInRole or IsInAllRoles methods are called.

The LoadRolesFromDataSource method could have loaded the role list from a database, from a different kind of XML file, or even from Active Directory. The beauty of it is that even though the back-end store is something you can choose yourself, the CustomPrincipal class still integrates into ASP.NET security by virtue of implementing the IPrincipal interface. Here is a look at the users.xml file used for the sample:

```xml
<?xml version="1.0" encoding="utf-8" ?>
<users>
  <user id="kevin">
    <role name="Administrators"></role>
    <role name="Programmers"></role>
  </user>
  <user id="guest">
    <role name="Users"></role>
  </user>
</users>
```

For this example, the users.xml file was simply added to the project as content. Obviously it isn't secure to put user data in the root directory of an application. Again, the goal of this exercise is to show you how to add your own code to the security infrastructure. Ensuring data security is discussed in the next section.

Now you need to integrate the CustomPrincipal and CustomIdentity with the application. These should be available to any page in the application during any event handler, postback or otherwise. For this to happen, you need to insert code into the Application_AuthenticateRequest event handler. You could write an HttpModule that handles that event as you have seen in previous chapters. For the purposes of this example, just make the changes in global.asax. Listing 36.3 shows the new global.asax.cs file after modifications.

LISTING 36.3

The Application_AuthenticateRequest Event Handler in Global.asax.cs

```csharp
/// <summary>
/// This method is called to authenticate a given request. This is where we
/// should construct our custom principal and identity objects.
/// </summary>
/// <param name="sender"></param>
/// <param name="e"></param>
protected void Application_AuthenticateRequest(Object sender, EventArgs e)
{
  string authTicketId = FormsAuthentication.FormsCookieName;
  HttpCookie cookie = Context.Request.Cookies[ authTicketId ];

  if (cookie == null) return;

  FormsAuthenticationTicket ticket = null;
  try
  {
    ticket = FormsAuthentication.Decrypt( cookie.Value );
```

36

User Security

LISTING 36.3
Continued

```
    }
    catch
    {
      // insert code to log error
    }
    if (ticket == null) return;

    Classes.CustomIdentity ci = new Classes.CustomIdentity( ticket.Name );
    Classes.CustomPrincipal cp = new Classes.CustomPrincipal( ci );
    Context.User = cp;
}
```

This code first grabs a reference to an authentication cookie, if one exists. If it does, the code decrypts the contents of the cookie to create a new authentication ticket. From that ticket, you can obtain the user's name. The user's name is used to construct the identity and the principal. With the newly created principal, you can set that to the value of Context.User, essentially overriding the ASP.NET principal with your own. You won't break existing functionality because the principal class implements the IPrincipal interface and its identity implements the IIdentity interface.

The only thing left to do in this example is to write some code in the default.aspx page that makes use of the new principal, both as a generic IPrincipal and as a CustomPrincipal. That code is shown in Listing 36.4.

LISTING 36.4
The default.aspx Page Making Use of CustomPrincipal

```
private void Page_Load(object sender, System.EventArgs e)
{
  // Put user code to initialize the page here
  if (User.Identity.IsAuthenticated)
  {
    Response.Write("You are authenticated.<br>");
    Response.Write("Your name is : <b>" + User.Identity.Name + "</b><br>");
    Response.Write("You are in the Users Role? : " +
       User.IsInRole("Users").ToString() + "<BR>");
    Response.Write("You are in the Administrators Role? : " +
       User.IsInRole("Administrators").ToString() + "<BR>");
    Classes.CustomPrincipal cp = (Classes.CustomPrincipal)User;
    Response.Write("You are in both Administrators and Programmers : " +
       cp.IsInAllRoles("Administrators|Programmers").ToString() + "<BR>");
```

LISTING 36.4
Continued

```
    Response.Write("You are in Administrators, Programmers, and Users? : " +
        cp.IsInAllRoles("Administrators|Programmers|Users") + "<BR>");
    }
    else
        Response.Write("You are not an authenticated user.");
}
```

Build the application to make sure that everything is okay. Now try to open `default.aspx` in your browser. As expected, you should be redirected to the login page. For the first test, the login is `kevin`. The password is irrelevant because the code will authenticate you no matter who you are. After logging in as `kevin`, you will be presented with the output shown in Figure 36.3.

FIGURE 36.3   The `default.aspx` output, with an administrative user.

Now close the browser and log back in to the website, but this time as the user `guest`. You will notice that you have fewer privileges because you belong to fewer roles. Keep in mind that all the assignment of roles is being done by your code, and that list can be coming from an XML file, an Access database, a SQL Server instance, or even a web service. Figure 36.4 shows the output of `default.aspx` after logging in as a guest.

This section has shown you how to create custom implementations of `IPrincipal` and `IIdentity` so that you can extend the ASP.NET authentication mechanism to provide your own functionality or provide more advanced versions of existing functionality. The next section will show you how to secure the sensitive data pertaining to your website and your users to continue the discussion of ASP.NET security.

36

Data Security in ASP.NET Applications

FIGURE 36.4   The default.aspx output, with a guest user.

Data Security in ASP.NET Applications

You've seen how to add code to the existing security framework to add enhanced role-based security and other features. All of that won't do you much good if your website can't protect your data and your users' data. The next section discusses various things you can do to secure the data on which your site operates as well as the data that belongs to your users, such as sensitive information like credit card data and passwords.

Protecting Connection Strings and Web.config Data

Everything that resides in your Web.config file is human-readable text. That means that if anyone were to ever gain possession of your Web.config file, he would be able to read all the sensitive information contained therein.

In theory, the information contained in your Web.config file should do an attacker no good. For example, if he gains access to your database connection string, he should be physically unable to connect to your database, right? Wrong. Even if the database is in a secure zone, it is still possible to hijack the web server and make it do things that ordinary users cannot do, such as connect to a database.

A common dilemma is how to keep information in the Web.config file where it is most useful to the application, but make that information unreadable to anyone but the application.

There are two options. The first option is the most obvious: don't actually store your sensitive information in the Web.config file. Some security experts recommend not only encrypting the connection string, but also storing that encrypted connection string in the Registry rather than in the Web.config file. The second option is to encrypt the string data that you are storing in Web.config and then have your application perform the decryption once at run-time and cache the decrypted value.

36

The code for encrypting and decrypting a string was covered in depth in Chapter 35, "Securing Sensitive Data."

Protecting User Passwords

User passwords are some of the most important pieces of data that you can house within your website. Anyone who gains access to someone else's password gains access to all the information about that user within the website. With a stolen password, people can buy items on someone else's credit card and commit everything from fraud to identity theft.

For this reason, every website that maintains user passwords needs to be able to assure the users of that website that the passwords are secure and stored in such a way that they cannot be compromised.

The best way to do this is to store the user passwords in such a way that you are not actually storing the password. Instead, you are storing a hash of the password. The hash is the result of a mathematical encryption calculation that reduces (or *hashes*) a password or any other string into a fixed-length representation. The same string will always reduce to the same hash and it is mathematically impossible for two different strings to produce different hashes.

Although you can use the standard .NET encryption library for producing the hashes of user passwords, there is a far easier method. The `FormsAuthentication` utility class provides a method called `HashPasswordForStoringInConfigFile`. Even though the method name is pretty lengthy, it's actually pretty easy to use. The following is a demonstration of the syntax:

```
string pwdHash =
  FormsAuthentication.HashPasswordForStoringInConfigFile(
    password, "SHA1");
```

The SHA1 algorithm produces a 160-bit digest (20 ASCII characters), whereas the MD5 algorithm produces a digest that is 128 bits (16 ASCII characters).

The idea here is to accept a password from a user in some secure manner (such as via SSL) and then create a hash of that password to store in your database. When the user supplies a password to log in, that password is hashed and then compared to the value stored in the database. In this way, the comparison can be done without sending a nonencrypted password over any wire. A sample `ValidateUser` method is shown here:

```
public bool ValidateUser( string userName, string password )
{
    string userHash =
    FormsAuthentication.HashPasswordForStoringInConfigFile(
      password, "SHA1" );
    string storedHash = // get from database
```

Data Security in ASP.NET Applications

```
    return (userHash == storedHash);
}
```

All you need to do is store hashed passwords in your user database and you can be sure that no one will ever be able to hack your passwords off the wire or get into your user database, right? Wrong.

Remember the nature of hashes: When you hash a string, it will always return the same hash. That means two identical strings return identical hashes. This fact is an invitation for a hacker. A hacker can easily use the same hashing mechanism to hash a large dictionary and then start comparing hashes against hashes obtained from your website. Even easier is if the hacker finds two users with the same password. Both have the same hash and that will be the first step toward compromising your user data. Remember that a hacker doesn't need to break into *your* website to get a list of hashed passwords. Any site using the same hashing technique that is vulnerable could easily supply a hacker with a reference database he needs to hack yours.

The solution to this is to "salt" your hash. Although that sounds appetizing, it actually refers to adding an additional bit of information to the user's password *before* it is hashed. This way you can guarantee two things:

- ▶ No two users will ever have the same passwords.

- ▶ No password will ever match any entry from any language dictionary.

The way to implement this is to first come up with the unique salt for the user's password hash. Then concatenate the salt onto the user's password and hash the password. When storing the password in your database, store the salt value along with it so that you can properly hash that user's password with the attempt to authenticate against your website.

There are two very good ways of coming up with unique salts. The first is to create a new GUID when you create a new user, and use that GUID as the user's hash salt. The second is to use the RNGCryptoProvider (*RNG* in this case stands for *random number generator*) to come up with a "more random" random number sequence than the operating system can normally provide.

Many developers prefer to use random number sequences because everyone knows how long GUIDs are and they are easily recognizable as GUIDs. A random number sequence can be any length and you can easily disguise it as some value that might or might not be related to passwords.

The following code snippet performs user validation when a salt has been stored in the database alongside the user's hashed password:

```
public bool ValidateUser(string userName, string password)
{
    string storedHash = // get from database
    string salt = // get from database
```

```
string pwdHash = FormsAuthentication.HashPasswordForStoringInConfigFile(
  salt + password, "SHA1" );

return (pwdHash == storedHash);
}
```

The thing to remember is that just because something is encrypted when it is trans-mitted over the wire (via SSL or something else), that doesn't mean that it is completely secure. If your database is compromised, you want to make it as hard as possible for someone to figure out the passwords. Also, you want to make sure that the password hashes from your website are never the same as the hashes from another website. There are many .NET websites appearing, and many people are making security mistakes with those websites. After reading the information in this chapter, you won't make those same mistakes.

Deciding When to Use SSL

SSL is an encryption algorithm that protects data being sent over the wire via the HTTPS protocol. When someone pulls up a URL for a website via SSL, the contents of that entire page are encrypted. Everything sent on that port comes across encrypted, including all text, all images, all scripts, everything.

For this reason, SSL often incurs a performance overhead both on the server and on the client. With broadband clients, the speed difference isn't quite as visible as it is with dial-up, but it is still a good idea to use SSL only when you absolutely have to.

The following is a quick checklist of reasons why you should use SSL. There are obvi-ously more and every case is different, but these guidelines may help:

▶ You require that the information communicated between client and server must be secure for confidentiality reasons, such as transmission of medical or financial data.

▶ It is a login page and requires the user to enter her password.

▶ It is a checkout or shopping cart page and requires the user to enter credit card information.

Data Security with ViewState Encryption

When ASP.NET creates the hidden form field for the page's ViewState contents, it can be instructed to store the contents in an encrypted form to prevent people from tampering with your site by examining the contents of ViewState.

By setting the `validationKey` attribute on the `<machineKey>` element to `3Des`, you can provide a symmetric encryption algorithm by which all ViewState for all sites on that server are validated.

36

Summary

As you saw in the discussion of web farm scenarios in Chapter 25, "Advanced ASP.NET," if you want a farm to work properly, you must specify the same validation key for each server. This is to allow one server to decrypt the ViewState generated by another server.

Summary

Next to your application performing quickly and looking good, one of the most important things that your application can do is be secure.

Not only do you need to defend your website against hackers, which is something that you do as an application developer and the IT folks do at a network level, but you need to defend your users against other malicious attackers and intruders. User passwords need to be secure, and connection strings to the database need to be secure.

In addition, you need to be able to authenticate your own users and identify the roles to which they belong so that you can determine what functionality to provide for them.

After going through this chapter, you should now have a good idea of what it takes to authenticate users, provide custom role-based security implementations, and use encryption and hashing techniques to protect your data and the sensitive information belonging to your users.

Further Reading

Applied Cryptography: Protocols, Algorithms, and Source Code in C, Second Edition by Bruce Schneier, Wiley. ISBN: 0471117099.

www.asp.net

www.gotdotnet.com

msdn.microsoft.com/netframework

37 Licensing and Intellectual Property

IN BRIEF

When you are learning a new technology, such as .NET, there are many different approaches to absorbing the new material. You might seek out training and instruction from people who have more experience, you (obviously) read books, and you might check the Internet for newsgroups, communities, and samples. All of this gives you a wealth of knowledge and information to teach you how to write your code and create your applications.

But what do you do if you need to protect your applications and your investment in their development? We often spend so much time trying to figure out how to code our applications that we forget that we are indeed trying to make money. How do you make sure that only people who have paid for your applications or your controls can make use of them? How do you protect your application from prying eyes and curious hackers?

This chapter will show you how to create licensing schemes for your controls and how to protect your application's sensitive code.

WHAT YOU NEED

REQUIRED SOFTWARE	.NET Framework SDK v1.1 Visual Studio .NET 2003 with C# installed
RECOMMENDED HARDWARE	PC that meets .NET SDK minimum requirements
SKILLS REQUIRED	C# and .NET familiarity

LICENSING AND INTELLECTUAL PROPERTY AT A GLANCE

Licensing Overview	755		
Licensing Defined	755	Types of Licensing and Verification	756
When to License and Protect	755		
Implementing Custom Licensing	**757**		
Introduction to the License Provider and License Manager	757	Building Licensed Controls	764
Creating a License	759	Licensed Web Controls Versus Windows Forms Controls	768
Creating a License Provider	760		
Licensing Implementation Strategies	**768**		
Deciding on a Licensing Deployment Method	768	Deciding on a License Purchase Method	768
Deciding on a Licensing Verification Method	768	Deciding on a Licensing Method	769

LICENSING AND INTELLECTUAL PROPERTY AT A GLANCE

Protecting Your Intellectual Property 769

    Protecting Intellectual Property by
Hiding Your Licensing Algorithm 769

    Protecting Intellectual Property
Through Obfuscation 770

Protecting Intellectual Property with
Alternative Back-Ends 770

Summary 771

Further Reading 771

37

Licensing Overview

This section provides an overview of the concept of licensing as it applies to software purchasing and pricing. It discusses some common types of licensing as well as some guidelines on when to use licensing mechanisms and when they aren't appropriate.

Licensing Defined

Licensing is the means by which valid users of your software distinguish themselves from users who do not have permission (license) to use your software. Whether you are writing GUI controls, an API of classes, or a fully functional application, you need some way to identify those who have the right to use your software and those who don't. A section coming up shortly provides a list of the various ways of identifying a user's right to use the application.

When to License and Protect

When you see licensing mentioned in the context of the .NET Framework, it is almost always referring to the licensing of controls and classes, and not to application purchase plans. If you have created a control that requires some kind of action on the part of the user before he can use it, licensing is definitely something you should consider. However, if you have created an application that will require a CD key in order to install, that technology is covered elsewhere. For that type of scenario, you might want to see whether encryption technologies would be useful.

As far as protection is concerned, all .NET developers should be aware of the fact that every managed application can be disassembled into its corresponding MSIL (Microsoft Intermediate Language). If some aspect of the logic and code in your application is too sensitive to allow curious users of your application to see, you should consider protecting your intellectual property. You'll learn how to accomplish that near the end of this chapter.

37

Types of Licensing and Verification

There are countless ways in which you can license your applications, classes, and controls. As new delivery mechanisms are created and Internet access becomes more ubiquitous, more licensing schemes are being created every day. The following list describes just a few of the software licensing schemes that can be facilitated by the .NET Framework:

▶ Free—This type of software is pretty obvious. There is no need for code-enforced licensing because the assumption is that anyone is allowed to use the software. Also under this umbrella is the case in which users must accept a license agreement to use the software, but are not required to pay a fee.

▶ One-time fee—To use your control, class, or application, the user pays you a one-time fee. This is either by buying a shrink-wrapped package from the store or purchasing it through your website, and so on. The user is then granted a license that does not expire to use your application.

▶ Per CPU—Many enterprise software packages charge on a per-CPU basis. A license is granted to the user and there is usually some runtime check to make sure that the number of CPUs on the machine is less than or equal to the number of licensed CPUs.

▶ Per seat—This is another fairly common enterprise licensing scheme. Each time the application is installed in a physical location such as a user's hard drive, it consumes a seat. Licenses are granted on a per-seat or per-installation basis. This is often enforced via an Internet activation mechanism for each seat; the activation found in many Microsoft products, such as Windows XP and MS Office, is an example of this type of licensing.

▶ Per action—This is sometimes referred to as *per hit* licensing. Each time you perform some action within an application or control, a check is made to see whether your license allows the action. This can be accomplished with a control that allows you to perform an action 150 times before requiring you to buy the full version or purchase more uses.

▶ Subscription—The subscription model is a fairly simple to understand model in which the user pays to use the application, classes, or controls for a certain period of time. When the time period runs out, the user is either charged for another period or the ability to use the product is revoked.

Fortunately for product developers, the .NET Framework's built-in licensing scheme enables you to implement all the preceding models and many others. The number of licensing models available to you is limited only by your ability to design and come up with new models.

Implementing Custom Licensing

The flexibility of the .NET Framework licensing support enables you to build in any kind of licensing that you want, so long as your code supports the notion of being able to return a Boolean that indicates whether or not a control is licensed.

The licensing system actually works in two different modes: at design time when you are working in the Visual Studio .NET IDE, and at runtime when the application is active. The .NET Framework designers were aware of the fact that the need for validating licenses is different at design time than it is at runtime and built consideration for that into the code. For example, you might have an ASP.NET control that validates licenses at runtime via a web service call. You don't want to be making web service calls every time you look at the control in a designer, so a more static design-time system can be used to validate the control within the IDE.

Introduction to the License Provider and License Manager

The core of .NET's licensing scheme centers around the `LicenseManager` class. Even if you have never written a line of code that deals with licensing, you can be sure that your code is being run through the `LicenseManager` class. Each time a class is instantiated in the .NET Framework, the `LicenseManager` is invoked to make sure that the class has a valid license. By default, classes don't implement licensing and so are considered always valid.

To mark a class (which can be a standard class, a Web Forms control, or a Windows Forms control) as one that requires some kind of licensing, you mark it with the `LicenseProvider` attribute. The `LicenseProviderAttribute` custom attribute class indicates the custom license provider class that will be responsible for determining whether the class is licensed at runtime and/or design time.

The `LicenseProvider` class is a class from which you inherit to create your own licensing scheme. It provides a method that is used by the license manager to determine validity of the license for the class `GetLicense`. `GetLicense` obtains an instance of the `License` class.

When you create your own license provider, you will probably also be creating your own license class. For example, if you are implementing a license scheme in which the users purchase licenses on a per-CPU basis, your license class must contain a property that indicates the number of CPUs for which it has been licensed. The only trick to this is that all licenses are derived from *keys*, which are strings that can contain anything, including encrypted data. Therefore, if you need to store the number of CPUs for which a particular license was purchased, you have to come up with a way of storing that in the string. Don't worry about coming up with complex algorithms. As you'll see in the samples that follow, the string can be as secure as you like. Also, because you have control over the verification process at both design time and runtime, you can use a more secure runtime validation and a less secure

Implementing Custom Licensing

design-time validation to make development easier and more convenient for your customers.

The basic process for licensing is as follows. At design time, when the class is instantiated for display in the IDE, the license is queried. The license provider can do anything it wants in order to obtain a license, whether that be looking at a file on disk, querying a web service, or some other means of verification. In the case of the `LicFileLicenseProvider` (the only one that ships with the .NET Framework), the license obtained from the `.lic` file, if valid, is embedded into the assembly when it is compiled. At runtime, the key for the license is extracted from the assembly (if there is a license embedded) and checked for validity. For ASP.NET applications, the runtime license is stored in a binary file on disk that will be loaded when needed.

If you use Visual Studio .NET, the license key embedding is taken care of automatically for you at build time. If you are creating your assemblies manually, you will need to use the `LC.EXE` tool. This command-line tool reads a text file that contains a list of licensed classes used for a particular application and creates a binary `.licenses` file. This file can then be embedded into an assembly using the Assembly Linker tool (`AL.EXE`).

The next few sections will take you through the process of creating a licensed control, including describing the usage scenario and showing you the code required to use the control in an application.

The fictitious scenario is this: The Acme Stocks company provides live, real-time stock quotes to its customers. In addition, the company has created a Windows Forms control called `StockLabel`. This control dynamically displays the price of a stock on a Windows Form (presumably by obtaining that price from the Acme Stocks web service). To use this control, you need to purchase it from the Acme Stocks company.

Because stock price information is very sensitive, especially real-time data such as that provided by Acme Stocks, the vendor needs to make sure that only the appropriate people can use the control. To accomplish this, the company has implemented .NET licensing for its control.

At design time, the control displays some fixed information about a bogus stock that doesn't exist. This gives the developer the ability to lay out the control but the design-time environment doesn't need to be connected to the Internet. At runtime, however, the control makes use of the web service to obtain the stock quote. It also makes use of a web service to validate that the form containing the control has been authorized for use. When a developer purchases this control (or subscribes, pays in advance for 30 days, and so on), she provides Acme Stocks with the GUID (*globally unique identifier*) that belongs to the type that will contain the control. In this chapter's example, the type is a form, but it could be a panel or any other container.

At runtime, this GUID is detected by the stock quote control and sent to the validation web service. If the validation web service indicates that the GUID is still valid, the control allows itself to be executed. Otherwise, the request for a license fails and the application is unable to continue until the control has been properly licensed or removed from the form. The examples that follow will show you how to implement this model.

Creating a License

Creating a license is fairly simple. The first step is to create a class that inherits from the System.ComponentModel.License class and provide the appropriate overrides. If you want to maintain additional information about the license, such as number of processors allowed and so on, you could make that data properties of the license and extract it from whatever key you use. Listing 37.1 shows the very simple AcmeStockLicense.

LISTING 37.1

The Acme Stock Company's License Class Implementation

```
using System;
using System.ComponentModel;
using System.Collections;
using System.Collections.Specialized;
using System.IO;
using System.Diagnostics;

namespace StockLibrary
{
  /// <summary>
  /// Summary description for AcmeStockLicense.
  /// </summary>
  public class AcmeStockLicense : License
  {
    private string licenseKey = string.Empty;

    public AcmeStockLicense(string key)
    {
      licenseKey = key;
    }

    public override void Dispose()
    {
      // nothing needs disposing of
    }
```

Implementing Custom Licensing

LISTING 37.1
Continued

```
public override string LicenseKey
{
  get
  {
    return licenseKey;
  }
}


  }
}
```

As you can see, there is nothing all that exciting about this class. It is a simple property container for the license key that implements the right overrides from the
abstract license class. If complex logic on the license itself were needed for encrypted
license keys, it could be added to this class.

Creating a License Provider

As mentioned earlier, the LicenseProvider class is just a vehicle for the Common
Language Runtime's LicenseManager class to obtain a license for a given class.
Each time a class is initialized and the Validate method is invoked, the Common
Language Runtime looks to see whether it has a license provider defined. If so, that
license provider has its GetLicense method invoked. If an exception occurs or the
license returned is null, the control (or class) is considered unlicensed. If the license
is returned, the Common Language Runtime assumes that everything is okay.

To create a LicenseProvider class, create a class that inherits from
LicenseProvider and overrides the appropriate methods. In the case of the Acme
Stocks fictitious sample, the license provider being built needs to use a web service to
validate the container type's GUID.

This introduces an element of instability in the control. For example, if there is no
network connection, the control will fail to authorize itself and obtain a license. One
way to mitigate this involves creating a method of license caching that isn't illustrated in this chapter. However, by using other techniques described in this book, you
can extend this provider to contain license caching.

But for this sample control, the instability isn't of any concern. The control won't
display its data unless it can contact the stock quote web service, so having to rely on
the validation web service isn't a problem. Listing 37.2 shows the custom
LicenseProvider, AcmeStockLicenseProvider, and its use of the validation
web service to secure a license on behalf of the client.

LISTING 37.2
The Acme Stock Company License Provider Implementation

```csharp
using System;
using System.ComponentModel;
using System.Collections;
using System.Collections.Specialized;
using System.IO;
using System.Diagnostics;


namespace StockLibrary
{
  /// <summary>
  /// Summary description for AcmeStockLicenseProvider.
  /// </summary>
  public class AcmeStockLicenseProvider : LicenseProvider
  {
    public AcmeStockLicenseProvider()
    {

    }

    public override License
      GetLicense(LicenseContext context,
        Type type, object instance,
        bool allowExceptions)
    {
      AcmeStockLicense license = null;
      if (context.UsageMode == LicenseUsageMode.Designtime)
      {
        // always provide a 'fake' license for developers during design-time
        license = new AcmeStockLicense("");
      }
      else
      {
        // obtain the GUID attribute of the containing type
        string guid = type.GUID.ToString();
        // Invoke the web service
        AcmeValidator.Validator validator = new AcmeValidator.Validator();
        string licenseKey = validator.ValidateTypeGuid( guid );

        if (licenseKey != string.Empty)
        {
          license = new AcmeStockLicense(guid);
```

Implementing Custom Licensing

LISTING 37.2

Continued

```
        }
      }
      return license;
  }


  }
}
```

From this code, you can see that if the control is instantiated by the Visual Studio .NET 2003 IDE, it will create a default blank license and allow itself to function. A real control like this would also detect whether it is in design mode and would not display the live stock quotes.

If a control is instantiated at runtime, the preceding license provider attempts to contact the validation web service and supply the container type's GUID. The container type sets its GUID with the `System.Runtime.InteropServices.GuidAttribute` attribute that is typically used for COM InterOp but serves just as useful a purpose here. The validation web service will then compare the supplied GUID with the Acme Stock company's list of valid customers and their allocated GUIDs for container types. If the GUID matches in the database, it will return a license key for that GUID, granting the client permission to use the control at runtime. Again, for a more efficient use of networking and license code, the runtime license could be cached offline for a period of time to avoid overloading the validation service and slowing down the WinForms application.

Listing 37.3 shows a small web service written to validate controls. Instead of going to the trouble of creating a database of customer GUIDs, the code simply fakes it and returns the GUID back as a license key. To make a control fail validation, just return the empty string instead of the GUID.

LISTING 37.3

The Sample Validation Web Service Used by the License Provider to Authenticate Client Controls

```
using System;
using System.Collections;
using System.ComponentModel;
using System.Data;
using System.Diagnostics;
using System.Web;
using System.Web.Services;

namespace AcmeStockControlValidator
{
```

37

LISTING 37.3

Continued

```
/// <summary>
/// Summary description for Validator.
/// </summary>
public class Validator : System.Web.Services.WebService
{
   public Validator()
   {
    //CODEGEN: This call is required by the ASP.NET Web Services Designer
    InitializeComponent();
   }

   #region Component Designer generated code

   //Required by the Web Services Designer
   private IContainer components = null;

   /// <summary>
   /// Required method for Designer support - do not modify
   /// the contents of this method with the code editor.
   /// </summary>
   private void InitializeComponent()
   {
   }

   /// <summary>
   /// Clean up any resources being used.
   /// </summary>
   protected override void Dispose( bool disposing )
   {
     if(disposing && components != null)
     {
       components.Dispose();
     }
     base.Dispose(disposing);
   }

   #endregion


  [WebMethod]
  public string ValidateTypeGuid(string guid)
  {
```

37

LISTING 37.3
Continued

```
        // check the guid against the database of registered clients
        // if the guid is there, return their unique license key

        // for the sample, I will just return the guid back.
        return guid;
    }
  }
}
```

The service is very simple. It takes the GUID supplied by the client control, skips what would ordinarily be some database activity, and then returns a valid license key for that client. As mentioned earlier, to test what happens when the license is not valid, just return the empty string.

Building Licensed Controls

Now that you have a license, a license provider, and a well-defined scheme for obtaining and validating licenses, you can actually write your custom control. Adding licensing to a custom control is simple after you have done the hard work of creating the license provider and the license. It becomes even easier when you consider that multiple controls can use the same license provider. Companies often use the same license provider for every licensed class they produce. All the company has to do is add a little bit of code to each control, and they automatically become managed by the same licensing scheme as all other controls that the company produces.

To protect your control with your licensing scheme, you need to do two things:

- ▶ Decorate your control class with a `LicenseProviderAttribute` attribute class.

- ▶ Use either the `IsValid` or the `Validate` method of the `LicenseManager` control to enforce license validation on your class. You can also use the `IsLicensed` method to determine whether a license was found (regardless of whether that license is valid).

This chapter's example uses the `Validate` method. This method will throw a security exception if no license is found. If a license (any license) is found, no exception will be thrown and the code will be allowed to continue. Because it is known that the code will not return any license unless the license is valid, this works well. Listing 37.4 shows a sample user control that is protected by the `AcmeStockLicenseProvider`.

LISTING 37.4
A License-Protected Label Control

```
using System;
using System.Collections;
using System.ComponentModel;
using System.Drawing;
using System.Data;
using System.Windows.Forms;

namespace StockLibrary
{
  /// <summary>
  /// Summary description for StockLabel.
  /// </summary>
  [Description("Provides live stock quote information")]
  [LicenseProvider( typeof(AcmeStockLicenseProvider) )]
  public class StockLabel : System.Windows.Forms.UserControl
  {
    private System.Windows.Forms.Label label1;
    private System.Windows.Forms.Label label2;
    /// <summary>
    /// Required designer variable.
    /// </summary>
    private System.ComponentModel.Container components = null;

    public StockLabel()
    {
      // This call is required by the Windows.Forms Form Designer.
      InitializeComponent();

      try
      {
        LicenseManager.Validate(typeof( StockLabel), this.Container);
      }
      catch
      {
        MessageBox.Show(
          "Could not obtain a valid runtime license for the StockLabel control. " +
          "Please contact Acme Stocks to obtain a valid license for this control.",
          "Invalid License", MessageBoxButtons.OK, MessageBoxIcon.Error);
        this.Enabled = false;
        this.Visible = false;
      }

    }
```

1

Implementing Custom Licensing

LISTING 37.4
Continued

```csharp
/// <summary>
/// Clean up any resources being used.
/// </summary>
protected override void Dispose( bool disposing )
{
  if( disposing )
  {
    if(components != null)
    {
      components.Dispose();
    }
  }
  base.Dispose( disposing );
}

#region Component Designer generated code
/// <summary>
/// Required method for Designer support - do not modify
/// the contents of this method with the code editor.
/// </summary>
private void InitializeComponent()
{
  this.label1 = new System.Windows.Forms.Label();
  this.label2 = new System.Windows.Forms.Label();
  this.SuspendLayout();
  //
  // label1
  //
  this.label1.Location = new System.Drawing.Point(8, 16);
  this.label1.Name = "label1";
  this.label1.TabIndex = 0;
  this.label1.Text = "Live Stock Price:";
  //
  // label2
  //
  this.label2.ForeColor = System.Drawing.Color.IndianRed;
  this.label2.Location = new System.Drawing.Point(112, 16);
  this.label2.Name = "label2";
  this.label2.TabIndex = 1;
  this.label2.Text = "$31.50";
```

LISTING 37.4
Continued

```
    //
    // StockLabel
    //
    this.Controls.Add(this.label2);
    this.Controls.Add(this.label1);
    this.Name = "StockLabel";
    this.Size = new System.Drawing.Size(224, 64);
    this.ResumeLayout(false);
    }
    #endregion
  }
}
```

This class is protected by the AcmeStockLicenseProvider, as indicated by the LicenseProviderAttribute  custom attribute class. In addition, in the constructor of the class is a call to LicenseManager.Validate. This call will attempt to obtain a license based on the type of the form. As you know, this means it will try to reach the web service at runtime and obtain a valid license key based on the form's GUID.

Now that the example has a library that contains a license, a license provider, and a license-protected control, a Windows Forms application can be created to use this control. To do this, follow the usual procedure for adding a control to the toolbar (open a new tab group, right-click it, select Add New Items, and then browse to the DLL that contains the control).

You should notice that the control renders just fine in design mode. If you wrote the web service the way it appears in the earlier listing, the application should also render just fine. If you modify the web service so that it just returns the empty string, you will see the dialog box shown in Figure 37.1 when you run your application. In addition, the StockLabel control will become disabled and invisible. In a real-world situation, you might want to remove the control from the form to prevent a programmer from re-enabling the control after the license check failed.

FIGURE 37.1   A dialog that appears indicating that the license check for the StockLabel control failed.

37

Licensed Web Controls Versus Windows Forms Controls

When coming up with your licensing scheme and design, it is worth your time to take a look at what kind of control you are building. The environments in which these controls exist dictate what licensing methods might and might not be practical.

For example, if you are developing a Windows Forms control that requires licensing, you might not want to cause that runtime licensing check to make use of a network connection because most Windows applications should be able to run in an offline mode. If you are developing an ASP.NET application, the nature of the application enables you to assume that it will be connected to some kind of network.

Licensing Implementation Strategies

With the .NET Framework, arguably the hardest part of building license-protected controls and classes is determining how to license your control. The method you choose to implement for licensing could influence the usability of the control and its ease of use for developers and consumers. This section briefly discusses some of the issues that come up when designing a licensing scheme.

Deciding on a Licensing Deployment Method

How are developers going to gain access to your controls? If you are going to be sending out CDs and special installation media, your licensing scheme might differ from controls that you make publicly available on the Internet. Making sure that you have decided how you will be delivering your controls to developers before you come up with a licensing scheme could prove beneficial.

Deciding on a Licensing Verification Method

The verification method refers to how you plan to verify that the user of your control has the right to use your control. Several schemes have been mentioned throughout this chapter. If you can figure out how to code it, you can use it as a verification method. Common verification methods include special user-entered registration keys (stored in the registry or other locations), web services, files on disk, hardware serial numbers, and much more. With the proliferation of smart card readers with personal computers, even more verification methods could become popular, including the biometric verification (fingerprint scanning) that you can now find on many popular PDAs.

Deciding on a License Purchase Method

How are you planning to sell your application? Will it be shrink-wrapped and put on store shelves, mailed to the customer, or purchased and downloaded in an electronic-only environment? All of these issues affect your ability to differentiate between legitimate users of your application and those without license. Regardless of the method of purchase, you have to assume that some of the users who purchased your application legally will distribute your application to users who did not purchase it. This is why some licensing schemes require additional information that only the legitimate owner of the software can provide, such as an original serial number on a CD or some other unique piece of identifying information that would not transfer with a copy of the software.

Deciding on a Licensing Method

Finally, after deciding how your control will be distributed and purchased, and how the rightful owners of your software will be identified, you can choose an appropriate licensing scheme. *Licensing scheme* refers to the list mentioned earlier in the chapter, such as per seat, per CPU, subscription, one-time purchase, and so on. If you know all the other things about the licensing implementation of your application, the licensing scheme that you choose should be a fairly simple decision.

Protecting Your Intellectual Property

So far this chapter has been about how you can sell and license your application, make sure that the developers building with your controls have purchased them, and that the licenses are valid when the control runs.

Another aspect related to licensing and verifying the authenticity of the users of your application is the concept of protecting your intellectual property. Every .NET programmer knows that any managed code can be disassembled and examined. All managed code is expressed as MSIL. Therefore, any plain text information stored in your application is as visible as if it had been left in plain sight, as are most of your business logic, data access logic, and any other tasks that your code performs. The following sections provide a few ideas and concepts for coding your applications in such a way that you can protect your intellectual property.

Protecting Intellectual Property by Hiding Your Licensing Algorithm

As already mentioned, your code is basically an open book. If you are using an algorithm to determine whether the user is licensed to use your application and that algorithm is in a library sitting on the user's hard drive, all he needs to do is disassemble your code and spend some time reading MSIL to figure out how to get free access to your application.

One way around this is to store the license validation algorithm somewhere else and access it via the network through web services, remoting, or some other approach. Another possibility is to scatter the pieces of your licensing algorithm in such a way that once obfuscated (which is discussed next), it would be extremely difficult to

37

figure out what your code does to determine the authenticity of licenses and license keys.

Protecting Intellectual Property Through Obfuscation

As mentioned earlier, your code is basically an open book. The names of all the variables and methods, as well as the values of all constants, are visible to anyone with a disassembler. Anyone who has the .NET Framework has access to a disassembler (ILDASM.EXE). There is something that you can do to defend your code from prying eyes: obfuscation.

Obfuscation refers to performing a series of operations that disguises the true meaning, purpose, and logic of your application's code. This is done by changing your variable and method names to a series of unintelligible alphanumeric characters. After obfuscation, reverse-engineering MSIL code that might ordinarily be easily reversible quickly becomes a colossal task that would take so long that most people would be discouraged from attempting it.

Don't let this fool you: Anyone who wants to reverse-engineer your code badly enough will either do it or find the resources to get it done. As a result, you need to write your code defensively. If you really do have a trade secret embedded in your code, don't put it in the same place, scatter it around, and make sure that the obfuscated MSIL doesn't make it obvious what your code is doing. Visual Studio .NET 2003 comes with a program called Dotfuscator, which obfuscates .NET code. Several other commercial and free products are available as well.

TIP

Keep in mind that obfuscators work only on code you write. They cannot mangle the symbol names of code already in the .NET Framework or of assemblies that your application references. As a result, it will still be obvious when your code attempts to use a class from the System.Security.Cryptography **namespace.**

Protecting Intellectual Property with Alternative Back-Ends

As I mentioned, everyone with the determination and resources will be able to reverse-engineer any code that they have on their hard drive. There are products that can generate C# from MSIL code even if it has been obfuscated. In such a format, it would take only minutes for an intruder to search for what he needs to find out all the information he wants.

The only way to protect your trade secrets and intellectual property from every single prying eye is to simply not give them out. Don't distribute your trade secrets. With the proliferation of broadband access, assuming that your user base has some form of network or dial-up access to the Internet is no longer a sure bet. If some operation must be performed and you can't risk someone discovering and distributing the algorithm behind that operation, don't distribute the algorithm.

You can expose some or all of your business back-end as a web service. If your code must perform an operation that might reveal too much about the application, such as decrypting sensitive data or comparing encrypted hashes, you can delegate the work to a web service and know that your trade secrets are safely inside your corporate firewall. Even if the client application is reverse-engineered, the real work is done behind the veil of the web service, so the reverse-engineered application will not reveal any sensitive or private information.

Summary

This chapter has been about licensing and intellectual property. Far too often, people spend so much time worrying about the code and the functionality of their application that they ignore the financial aspects of selling software. You won't make money if people can figure out how to use your software for free.

You need the ability to tell the difference between users of your product who have full legal right to use your product and those who do not. This can be done through various licensing schemes and different classes within the .NET Framework that enable class-level license control.

A combination of approaches such as obfuscation, licensing, and delegated back-ends supported by web services can provide an application that is very resilient to attacks and nearly impossible to pirate. This chapter has given you some insight into the concept of software licensing and you can produce a better, more sellable and secure product as a result.

Further Reading

Applied Cryptography: Protocols, Algorithms, and Source Code in C, Second Edition by Bruce Schneier, Wiley. ISBN: 0471117099.

www.asp.net

www.gotdotnet.com

msdn.microsoft.com/netframework

Part VIII

Enterprise and Connected Applications

CHAPTER 38   Interface Programming

CHAPTER 39   Remoting

CHAPTER 40   COM+ Enterprise Services

CHAPTER 41   Enterprise Templates

38 Interface Programming

This chapter explains the ins and outs of interface programming. In this chapter, you will learn about the differences between abstract classes and interfaces. After reading this chapter, you will be familiar with the concepts surrounding programming with interfaces and related topics such as interface inheritance.

WHAT YOU NEED

RECOMMENDED SOFTWARE	.NET Framework
	C# .NET environment
RECOMMENDED HARDWARE	.NET-enabled desktop client
SKILLS REQUIRED	C# coding

INTERFACE PROGRAMMING AT A GLANCE

Interface Programming	774		
Understanding the Interface	774	Mapping the Interface	786
Declaring the Interface Implicitly	778	Inheriting the Interface	789
Declaring the Interface Explicitly	784		
Summary	**790**		
Further Reading	**790**		

Interface Programming

Allowing classes to have intimate knowledge of each other goes against the basic principle of object-oriented programming. That principle states that you should try to decouple classes from one another as much as possible. If you don't, you run the risk of creating spaghetti code. To understand what is meant by *spaghetti code*, imagine a bowl of spaghetti where every noodle represents a different object. As you can see, each class (or noodle) touches quite a few other classes. Therefore, if you change one class, you must revisit, redo, and/or recompile every other class that it touches. That might not be a problem for a small project, but for large projects that need to be maintained, that would be a big problem. One way to reduce the coupling of classes is to use interfaces. In the following sections, you will learn why you should use interfaces and how to implement them.

Understanding the Interface

An interface is essentially a contract. It is a contract to implement the methods and properties that are declared in the contract. In other words, if a class implements an interface, it is agreeing that it will implement *all* the properties and methods. If the class does not, it has broken the contract and the compiler will complain and will refuse to compile the project as shown in Figure 38.1.

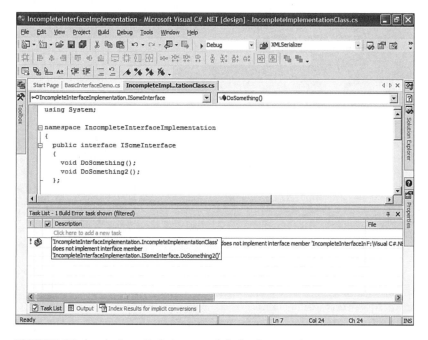

FIGURE 38.1   A class that does not fully implement the
ISomeInterface interface.

TIP

An interface is a contract. It can be a member of a namespace or class and can contain any of the
following: methods, properties, indexers, and events. Although an interface is very similar to an
abstract base class that contains only abstract methods (for the C++ people, it is similar to a pure
virtual method), there are some very important distinctions. In C#, a class can inherit from only one
base class, but it can implement multiple interfaces. An interface can inherit from one or more interfaces and can be implemented or realized by either classes or structs.

Figure 38.2 shows a class model of an application that uses interfaces.

In this diagram, you can see two distinct base classes: Animal and Person. You can
also see that these two base classes realize the ISpeak interface. Because both
species are capable of emitting sounds (speaking), they share a common trait. Other
than that, the two species (at least for the purposes of this demo) are completely
different. Because both base classes implement the ISpeak interface, you can
simply reference both classes by the ISpeak interface and cause the concrete implementations of the interfaces to speak. This will be demonstrated later in this chapter
(see Listing 38.2).

Interface Programming

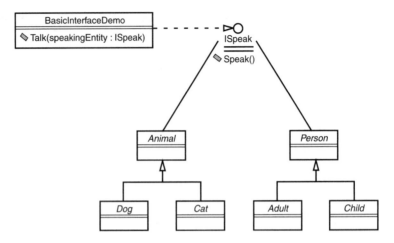

FIGURE 38.2   A class diagram of a sample program that uses inter-faces.

Declaring the Interface

An interface is declared in a similar fashion as a C# class. As shown in the MSDN help, an interface is declared in the following manner.

```
[attributes] [modifiers] interface identifier [:base-list]
{interface-body}[;]
```

- ▶ attributes—The attributes section is optional and can contain any additional declarative information. For more information on using or declaring attributes please refer to Chapter 11, "Reflection and Code Attributes."

- ▶ modifiers—The modifiers section is optional. The available modifiers are new, public, protected, internal, internal protected, and private.

- ▶ interface—The interface keyword is used to tell the compiler that this is an interface declaration.

- ▶ identifier—This is the place to put the name of the interface.

- ▶ :base-list—The base-list is an optional section that can contain a list of one or more interfaces from which to inherit. Each base interface is separated by a comma.

- ▶ {interface-body}—This section contains the methods, properties, indexers, and events associated with the interface.

Practical Declaration of Interfaces

When declaring an interface, the first thing to do is specify any attributes to be associated with the interface. In the following example, this is demonstrated by the attribute `SomeAttribute`. Next, you declare the visibility or access modifier, followed by the keyword `interface` and then the interface name. In the example, the interface is declared as a public interface with a name of `ISomeInterface`. Then you specify which (if any) interfaces to inherit from. This example shows that the interface inherits from two base interfaces: `BaseInterface1` and `BaseInterface2`. Finally, you specify the methods, properties, indexers, and events associated with this interface.

```
[SomeAttribute()]
public interface ISomeInterface : BaseInterface1, BaseInterface2
{
  // methods
  // properties
  // indexers
  // events
}
```

It is customary to begin the interface name with an uppercase I. This is demonstrated in the previous code snippet.

Declaring Methods

When declaring the methods of an interface, you do not specify an access modifier. That is because when they are implemented, all the methods must be public. This is demonstrated in the following code snippet:

```
public interface ISomeInterface
{
  void SomeMethod();
}
```

Declaring Properties

Just as with a method, when declaring a property for an interface, do not specify the access modifier. However, you must specify which property accessors must be present. By specifying the accessors, you are indicating whether the interface will be read only, read-write, or write only. For example, the following code snippet specifies that the property `SomeProperty` will have both a get and set accessor and will therefore be a read-write property:

```
public interface ISomeInterface
{
  int SomeProperty
  {
    get; set;
  }
}
```

Interface Programming

Declaring Indexers

An indexer is declared in the same way as a property. The exception is that instead of giving it a name, you must use the name `this` followed by the formal index parameter list. The following code snippet demonstrates how to declare an indexer in an interface:

```
public interface ISomeInterface
{
  string this[int index]
  {
    get; set;
  }
}
```

Declaring Events

For most of the `interface` declaration, there have been slight differences. Fortunately, some things don't change. Given the following `delegate`:

```
public delegate void CallbackDelegate(object sender, object event);
```

an event is declared, in a `class` in the following manner:

```
event CallbackDelegate OnCallback;
```

In an interface, an event is declared in the exact same way. For more information on events and delegates, please refer to Chapter 10, "Events and Delegates."

Declaring the Interface Implicitly

To realize an interface from a `class` or `struct`, you must first implement all the methods, properties, indexers, and events. To do this, you can choose to implicitly implement the interface members. According to the definition at www.dictionary.com, the word *implicit* means "implied or understood though not directly expressed." Essentially, that means that all we have to do is implement the members of the interface in a class without doing anything special (actually, you must declare the methods, properties, indexers, and events as public). Listing 38.1 demonstrates how to implement a method of an interface implicitly.

LISTING 38.1
Implementing an Interface Implicitly

```
using System;

namespace ImplicitInterfaceExample
{
  public interface ISpeak
```

LISTING 38.1
Continued

```csharp
{
  void Speak();
}

public abstract class Animal : ISpeak
{
  #region ISpeak Members

  public abstract void Speak();

  #endregion
}

public abstract class Person : ISpeak
{
  #region ISpeak Members

  public abstract void Speak();

  #endregion
}

public class Dog : Animal
{
  #region ISpeak Members

  public override void Speak()
  {
    System.Console.WriteLine("Woof!");
  }

  #endregion
}

public class Cat : Animal
{
  #region ISpeak Members

  public override void Speak()
  {
    System.Console.WriteLine("Meow!");
  }
```

38

Interface Programming

LISTING 38.1
Continued

```csharp
    #endregion
  }

  public class Adult : Person
  {
    #region ISpeak Members

    public override void Speak()
    {
      System.Console.WriteLine("Hello!");
    }

    #endregion
  }

  public class Child : Person
  {
    #region ISpeak Members

    public override void Speak()
    {
      System.Console.WriteLine("<<High Pitched>> Hi!");
    }

    #endregion
  }

  class ImplicitInterfaceExample
  {
    public static void Talk(ISpeak speakingEntity)
    {
      speakingEntity.Speak();
    }

    [STAThread]
    static void Main(string[] args)
    {
      Talk(new Adult());
      Talk(new Child());
      Talk(new Dog());
      Talk(new Cat());

      System.Console.ReadLine();
```

LISTING 38.1
Continued

```
    }
  }
}
```

In this example, the `Dog`, `Cat`, `Adult`, and `Child` classes realize the `ISpeak` interface. Because of this, they are contractually obligated to implement the `Speak` method that was specified by the contract (interface). Figure 38.3 shows the output of the program.

FIGURE 38.3   Output of the `ImplicitInterfaceImplementation` program.

Overriding a Previous Implementation

In the previous example, you learned how to implicitly implement a method from an interface. However, what happens if you implement an interface from a base class and then in one subclass, you decide that you need to change the implementation?

Your first thought might be to redeclare the method in the subclass with the `new` keyword. After all, that is how you would do it without using interfaces. This is almost correct. In addition to redeclaring the method in the subclass, you must also explicitly declare that the subclass implements the interface. For example, in Listing 38.2, you redeclare the method in the subclass without explicitly implementing the interface on the subclass. Figure 38.4 shows the result. This is not what was expected.

LISTING 38.2
Incorrectly Redeclaring the Interface Method

```
using System;
namespace OverridingImplicitInterfaceImplementations
{
```

Interface Programming

```
public interface ISpeak
{
  void Speak();
}

public class Child : ISpeak
{
  #region ISpeak Members

  public void Speak()
  {
    System.Console.WriteLine("<<High Pitched>> Hi!");
  }

  #endregion
}

public class Adolescent : Child
{
  #region ISpeak Members

  public new void Speak()
  {
    System.Console.WriteLine("Yo!");
  }

  #endregion
}

class ImplicitInterfaceExample
{
  public static void Talk(ISpeak speakingEntity)
  {
    speakingEntity.Speak();
  }

  [STAThread]
  static void Main(string[] args)
  {
    Talk(new Child());
    Talk(new Adolescent());

    System.Console.ReadLine();
  }
}
```

FIGURE 38.4   Output of Listing 38.2.

If you were to explicitly implement the ISpeak interface in the subclass
Adolescent as demonstrated in the following code snippet, you would get the
desired results. The output of the modified code is shown in Figure 38.5.

```
public class Adolescent : Child, ISpeak
{
  #region ISpeak Members

  public new void Speak()
  {
    System.Console.WriteLine("Yo!");
  }

  #endregion
}
```

FIGURE 38.5   Output of Listing 38.2 with the modified
                 section.

38

Declaring the Interface Explicitly

In Listing 38.1, you saw how to implicitly implement an interface. This works fine for interfaces that do not conflict with each other, but what happens when you have two interfaces that specify the same method name and signature and should have different implementations? The answer is that you can't. You can't, that is, unless you explicitly implement the interfaces. To explicitly implement the interfaces, you simply omit the access modifier and then prepend the interface name to the method. For example, the following code snippet demonstrates how to explicitly implement the method DoSomething in the ISomeInterface interface:

```
class SomeClass : ISomeInterface
{
  void ISomeInterface.DoSomething()
  {
    ...
  }
}
```

TIP

When explicitly implementing an interface method, you must omit the access modifier. If you do not, the compiler will complain and your code will not run. Consequently, by omitting the access modifier, you will no longer be able to access that method from the class. To access this method, you have to gain access to an instance of the interface that was explicitly declared. In other words, you will have to cast the class to the desired interface and then you will be able to use the desired method.

Consider the following example. In real life, there are animals that walk erect and those that walk on all fours. If you were to create two interfaces, IWalkUpright and IWalkOnAllFours, and then declare a method in those interfaces called Walk, you would be able to apply IWalkUpright to humans and IWalkOnAllFours to other animals such as dogs. However, what happens when you try to model a bear? A bear can walk on all fours, but it can also (with enough motivation) walk upright. Therefore the bear would implement the IWalkUpright and IWalkOnAllFours interfaces. The problem is that both interfaces have the same method (Walk) declared inside of them and the implementation of Walk should be different for both of them as well. Listing 38.3 shows how explicitly declaring the interface methods solves this problem **1**.

LISTING 38.3
Two Interfaces with the Same Method and Signature

```
using System;

namespace TwoInterfacesSameMethod
```

LISTING 38.3

Continued

```
{
    public interface IWalkOnAllFours
    {
        void Walk();
    }
    public interface IWalkUpright
    {
        void Walk();
    }


    public class Bear : IWalkUpright, IWalkOnAllFours
    {
        #region IWalkUpright Members

        void IWalkUpright.Walk()
        {
            System.Console.WriteLine("Walking upright....");
        }

        #endregion

        #region IWalkOnAllFours Members

        void IWalkOnAllFours.Walk()
        {
            System.Console.WriteLine("Walking on all fours....");
        }

        #endregion
    }
```

```
class TwoInterfacesSameMethod
{
    public static void WalkUpright(IWalkUpright animal)
    {
        animal.Walk();
    }

    public static void WalkOnAllFours(IWalkOnAllFours animal)
    {
        animal.Walk();
    }
```

LISTING 38.3
Continued

```
[STAThread]
static void Main(string[] args)
{
  Bear bear = new Bear();
  WalkOnAllFours(bear);
  WalkUpright(bear);

  System.Console.ReadLine();
}
}
}
```

Mapping the Interface

Mapping the interface refers to the process of locating the interface that a method, property, indexer, or event belongs to. For simple classes that implement only one interface, this is relatively simple. For example, in the following code snippet, it is easy to tell that the Speak method in the class Dog is the implementation of the ISpeak interface:

```
public interface ISpeak
{
  void Speak();
}

public abstract class Dog : ISpeak
{
  #region ISpeak Members

  public void Speak()
  {
    ...
  }

  #endregion
}
```

Consider the example in Listing 38.4. In this listing, you have two classes and one interface. You also have class two inheriting from class1 and from the interface SomeInterface. Unless you know some basic interface mapping rules, it would be difficult to determine which methods would be called by looking at the code.

Fortunately, the basic rules are simple. First, explicit implementations take precedence. Next, the current class is searched for the implementation. If the implementation is not found there, the base classes are searched starting from left to right in the declaration.

LISTING 38.4
Mapping the Interface

```csharp
using System;

namespace MappingTheInterface
{
  interface ISomeInterface
  {
    void DoSomething();
  }

  class Class1 : ISomeInterface
  {
    #region ISomeInterface Members

    public void DoSomething()
    {
      System.Console.WriteLine("Doing something in Class 1.");
    }

    #endregion

  }

  class Class2 : Class1, ISomeInterface
  {
    #region ISomeInterface Members

    void ISomeInterface.DoSomething()
    {
      System.Console.WriteLine("Explicitly doing something.");
    }

    public new void DoSomething()
    {
      System.Console.WriteLine("Doing something in Class 2.");
    }

    #endregion
  }
```

Interface Programming

LISTING 38.4
Continued

```
class MappingTheInterface
{
  [STAThread]
  static void Main(string[] args)
  {
    Class2 c2 = new Class2();

    c2.DoSomething();
    ((ISomeInterface) c2).DoSomething();

    ((Class1) c2).DoSomething();

    System.Console.ReadLine();
  }
}
}
```

If you know the basic rules, you can see that the code in Listing 38.4 will produce a result in the following manner (shown in Figure 38.6). First, because the class c2 explicitly implements the ISomeInterface interface and because you are accessing the method via a class reference, the Doing something in Class 2 message is printed. Next, because Class2 has an explicit implementation of the DoSomething method and you are casting the Class2 reference to an ISomeInterface interface, the Explicitly doing something message is printed. Finally, because you cast the Class2 reference to Class1, the Class1 class is searched first and the Doing something in Class 1 message is printed. The output of this listing is shown in Figure 38.6.

FIGURE 38.6   Output of Listing 38.4.

Inheriting the Interface

As previously mentioned in this chapter, interfaces can inherit from one or more base interfaces. When an interface inherits from another interface, it also inherits the contract. Therefore, if a class realizes an interface that inherits from another interface, it must implement all of the methods, properties, indexers, and events from both interfaces. For example, Listing 38.5 demonstrates an interface that inherits from another and a class that inherits from that interface.

LISTING 38.5
Inheriting from Interfaces

```
using System;

namespace InterfaceInheritance
{
  public interface Interface1
  {
    void DoSomething1();
  }

  public interface Interface2 : Interface1
  {
    void DoSomething2();
  }

  class Class1 : Interface2
  {
    #region Interface2 Members

    public void DoSomething2()
    {
      System.Console.WriteLine("Doing something 2.");
    }

    #endregion

    #region Interface1 Members

    public void DoSomething1()
    {
      System.Console.WriteLine("Doing something 1.");
    }

    #endregion
  }
```

Interface Programming

LISTING 38.5
Continued

```
class InterfaceInheritance
{
  [STAThread]
  static void Main(string[] args)
  {
  }
}
}
```

Summary

In this chapter, you learned the basics of using interfaces. First, you learned how to declare an interface. Next, you learned how to implicitly implement an interface and when it was useful. Then you learned some of the shortcomings of implicitly implementing an interface and how explicitly implementing an interface can help. Finally, you learned how to use interface inheritance to create a hierarchy of interfaces.

Further Reading

Special Edition Using C#, Chapter 11, by NIIT, Que Publishing. ISBN: 0789725754.

C# Web Development with ASP.NET: Visual QuickStart Guide, Chapter 8, by Jose Mojica, Peachpit Press. ISBN: 0201882604.

39 Remoting

IN BRIEF

This chapter gives you an understanding of how .NET Remoting works and how you can realize its benefits. In this chapter, you will learn how .NET isolates applications using application domains and contexts. Next, you will learn how to create a hosting server, Remoting object, and client application. Finally, you will learn how to use Internet Information Services (IIS) to host your remote objects and replace the hosting server application.

WHAT YOU NEED

RECOMMENDED SOFTWARE	.NET Framework C# .NET environment
RECOMMENDED HARDWARE	.NET-enabled desktop client
SKILLS REQUIRED	C# coding

REMOTING AT A GLANCE

Remoting Architecture	792		
Introduction to Remoting	792	Life and Death of the Remote Object	797
Explaining Application Domains	793	Building the Remoting Server Application	803
Understanding the Context	795	Building the Remoting Server Application	803
Choosing a Channel	796	Building the Client	805

IIS and Remoting	806

Summary	807

Further Reading	807

Remoting Architecture

Distributed applications enable you to leverage the power of additional machines to serve as the workhorses of your application. In the following sections, you will learn how to create distributed applications using .NET Remoting.

Introduction to Remoting

.NET Remoting, as shown in Figure 39.1, is a technology that enables you to easily distribute application components across processes and computers. It allows you to seamlessly integrate these distributed components into your application. To better understand .NET Remoting, it is important to understand its architecture and terminology.

When you look at an unmanaged application and how the operating system handles it, you can see that the unmanaged application is separated from other applications by a boundary around its code. The isolated code is known as a *process*. Without the use of some sort of interprocess communication (IPC) method, it is not possible for one application (process) to communicate with another. This can sometimes be a pain, but it comes with some benefits. The benefit of not being able to communicate with another process is that if you can't communicate with it, it is unlikely that your application will break it. In other words, if an application does manage itself well (overwriting memory and so forth), you probably don't want it interfering with your application and will be glad that it can't.

With .NET comes the concept of running multiple applications within the same process. This is possible because .NET ensures two things: type safety and that applications can't access invalid memory locations. In the old model (unmanaged code), you had a process. With the new .NET model, you still have a process, but .NET adds two more logical subdivisions: application domain and context.

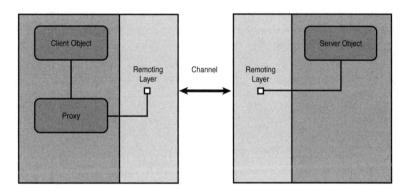

FIGURE 39.1   The .NET Remoting model.

Explaining Application Domains

At a basic level, operating systems host processes. In the unmanaged world, processes form a boundary around a single application. A process can be loaded and unloaded (terminated). However, with the loading and unloading of a process comes a lot of overhead. To overcome this, .NET takes a different approach. In .NET, applications and assemblies are hosted inside of an application domain (also known as an *AppDomain*). An AppDomain forms a boundary around your managed code, as shown in Figure 39.2.

A process can host one or more application domains. However, simply because a process can host more then one application domain does not eliminate the need for isolation. User code from one application domain cannot directly access code from another application domain, nor can data be shared directly.

Remoting Architecture

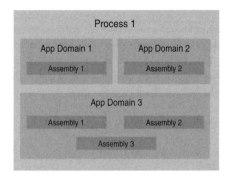

FIGURE 39.2   An application domain.

> **TIP**
>
> An AppDomain provides isolation, unloading, and security boundaries for the managed application. When the Common Language Runtime is first loaded into a process, it creates a default application domain to execute an application's code. From there, both the Common Language Runtime and user code can create additional AppDomains.
>
> Application domains are isolated from each other. In other words, information cannot be directly shared across AppDomains, nor can one AppDomain directly access another. The very fact that application domains are isolated from each other gives you the ability to unload an application domain. In fact, as it turns out, AppDomains are the smallest unit that can be unloaded from a process. Although you can load assemblies, you can not directly unload an assembly.

AppDomains and Domain-Neutral Assemblies

By default, the Common Language Runtime loads an assembly into an AppDomain that contains the code that references that assembly. This allows the code and assembly to be isolated. However, if an assembly is used by multiple domains in the same process, the code (not the data) can be shared among all the domains that reference that assembly. If an assembly can be used by all domains in the process, an assembly is said to be *domain neutral*. There are the options for loading domain-neutral assemblies:

- ▶ Don't load any assemblies as domain neutral

- ▶ Load all assemblies as domain neutral

- ▶ Load only strongly named assemblies as domain neutral

Each option gives you a different benefit and should be used in particular circumstances. Use the first option when there is only one application in the process. Use the second option if you have multiple domains, in the same process, which use the same code. Finally, use the third option when you are running multiple applications in the same process.

Global Exception Handler

When an unhandled exception is encountered, an application (managed or unmanaged) terminates. Because programs are written by programmers who are sometime forced to take shortcuts, this is often a little annoying (especially when you are trying to give a demo that you spent all night trying to produce and your manager presses a key that he knew he shouldn't touch). Fortunately, .NET enables you to associate a global exception handler with an application domain. A global exception handler enables you to trap and cover up any unforeseen code "opportunities." Listing 39.1 shows an example of a global exception handler.

LISTING 39.1
Global Exception Handler

```
// Project AppDomain/ExceptionHandler
using System;

namespace SAMS.VisualCSharpDotNetUnleashed.Chapter39
{
  class GEHApplication
  {
    static void GlobalExceptionHandler(Object sender,
      UnhandledExceptionEventArgs e)
    {
      Console.WriteLine(e.ExceptionObject.ToString());
    }

    public static void Main()
    {
      // Add a global exception handler to the current Application Domain
      AppDomain appDomain = AppDomain.CurrentDomain;
      appDomain.UnhandledException +=
        new  UnhandledExceptionEventHandler(GlobalExceptionHandler);

      // ***** From This point you should be protected! *****

      // throw an exception
      throw new Exception("It worked before you touched it!");
    }
  }
}
```

Understanding the Context

In .NET, a class can be configured to use different services such as synchronization, transactions, just-in-time (JIT) activation, and security. The way in which these services are configured for an object is called a *context*. Each time a class is

Remoting Architecture

instantiated, the runtime places it into a context. The runtime first searches for a compatible context. If a compatible context is not found, the runtime creates a new one. However, after an instantiated class has been placed into a context, it remains there for the rest of its life (which is over when the object is collected by the Garbage Collector).

A context resides in a application domain, as shown in Figure 39.3. An AppDomain can have one or more contexts. When an application domain is created, it creates a default context with a `Context.ContextID` of 0. Each subsequent `Context` that is created receives the next `ContextID`. It is important to note, however, that the `ContextID` is unique only within an application domain.

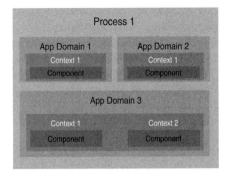

FIGURE 39.3   The context.

Choosing a Channel

A channel is a transport mechanism. It transports messages between Remoting boundaries such as application domains, process, and computers. Built into the .NET Framework are two channels: `HttpChannel` and `TcpChannel`. In addition, the .NET Framework enables you to create custom channels, although doing so is beyond the scope of this book.

The `HttpChannel` and `TcpChannel` channels are similar. However, they do have some differences. `TcpChannel` uses the binary formatter to serialize messages, whereas `HttpChannel` uses the SOAP-XML formatter. Now that you have a basic understanding of channels, it will be helpful for you to understand the common terms described in Table 39.1.

TABLE 39.1

Common Channel Terms

Term	Description
Object URI	This represents a well-known object that is registered on the server.
Channel URI	This string represents the connection information to the server. The Channel URI is specified in the form: `http://hostname:port`

TABLE 39.1

Continued

Server-Activated URL	This is a unique string that is used by the client to connect to the server object. It is in the format: *Channel-uri*/object-url For example: http://*hostname*:*port*/object-url
Client-Activated URL	This string is similar to the server-activated URL except that it does not have to be unique.

To choose between using an `HttpChannel` and a `TcpChannel`, it is useful to know some of the differences between the two. Table 39.2 describes some differences, benefits, and limitations.

TABLE 39.2

Choosing Between the Two Built-in Channels

Channel	Comments	Efficiency	Security
`HttpChannel`	This channel enables you to host objects on an HTTP server. This adds the ability to utilize some of the features that come with a web server, such as web farms and so on.	Because the `HttpChannel` uses HTTP as its transport, it has more overhead than the `TcpChannel`.	Because the `HttpChannel` is hosted by a web server (such as IIS), it can immediately take advantage of the Secure Sockets Layer (SSL).
`TcpChannel`	This channel enables you to host objects on a particular TCP port. Unfortunately, in today's world, it is very hard to get an IS department to expose a port to the Internet.	`TcpChannel` uses raw sockets to transmit the data and therefore has less overhead than the `HttpChannel`.	A TCP port is less secure then a web server. However, you can implement a custom security system using the class in the `System.Security` namespace.

Life and Death of the Remote Object

Every instance of a class has a beginning and an end to its life. The questions with remote objects involve when they are instantiated and when they are terminated. The answers depend upon the mode of the instantiation or, in the case of .NET Remoting, activation. .NET offers three ways of activating a remote object: single call, singleton, and client activated.

Single Call Remote Objects

With single call activation, the remote object is created with each call to it and is destroyed at the end of the call. Because the object is created and destroyed with each call, this object typically does not maintain state. Although it is possible to maintain state (you would have to maintain the state yourself), it would simply be

Remoting Architecture

too much overhead to make this practical. This type of activation is useful for stateless programming, such as web applications. Figure 39.4 shows the lifetime of the single call remote object.

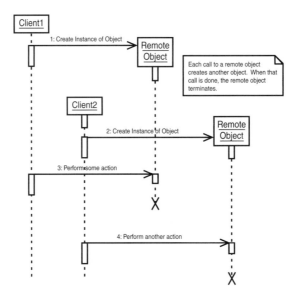

FIGURE 39.4   Single call remote object lifetime.

Singleton Remote Objects

Singleton activation is a little different from the other two methods. The remote object is activated upon the first call to the remote object, using the Singleton method. Subsequent calls to that remote object, regardless of which client is calling the remote object, use the same instance of the remote object. The remote object terminates only when its lifetime expires. As shown in Figure 39.5, each client uses the same instance of the remote object. This can make the chore of maintaining state fairly simple. However, because all clients share the same instance, you must take care to differentiate between the client calls.

Client-Activated Remote Objects

With client-activated remote objects, the server activates the object when the client requests its activation. This is different from the other two methods in that with the other methods, the server determines when the remote object is activated and when it is destroyed. As with the single call method, each client gets its own instance of the remote object. However, because the object is not terminated with each call, you have the option of easily maintaining state.

Terminating the remote object with the client-activated method is also a little different. In both the singleton and the single call methods, the server determines when to destroy the object. With the client-activated method, the object is either destroyed upon request or at the termination of its lease. The lease is actually a contract between the client and server. It specifies how long the remote object can live before it is marked for garbage collection. As it is in real life, when the lease is about to expire, the server contacts any of the object's sponsors and asks whether they would like to extend the lease. If not, the object is marked for garbage collection. In addition, you can set the lease to reset upon each call to the remote object. Figure 39.6 shows the activation process and lifetime of a remote object that is activated using the client activation method.

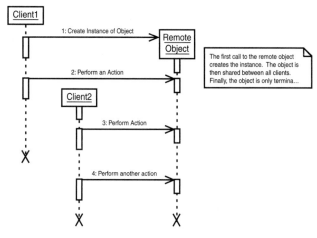

FIGURE 39.5   Singleton remote object lifetime.

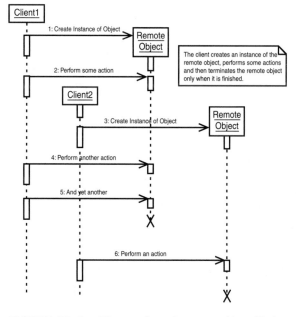

FIGURE 39.6   Client-activated remote object lifetime.

39

Registering the Remote Object

In the single call and singleton methods, you must register a remote object type before you can expose the object to other AppDomains. There are two ways to do this: by registering the types programmatically and by using a configuration file.

Registering Programmatically

The first step in exposing the Remoting object is to register the channel. As described earlier in this chapter, this can be accomplished by calling the `ChannelServices.RegisterChannel` method, as in Listing 39.2.

LISTING 39.2

Programmatically Registering the Single Call and Singleton Methods of Activation on the Server

```
// Project Remoting Sample
// This code listing does not contain the sources for
// the sample remote object.  It is only meant to show
// how to expose the object to other application domains.

using System;

namespace SAMS.VisualCSharpDotNetUnleashed.Chapter39
{
  class RemotingSample
  {
    public static void Main()
    {
      HttpChannel httpChannel = new HttpChannel(9000);
      ChannelServices.RegisterChannel(httpChannel);
      RemotingConfiguration.RegisterWellKnownServiceType(typeof(SampleService),
          "SAMSSampleService/SampleService.soap", WellKnownObjectMode.Singleton);
      Console.WriteLine("** Press enter to end the server process. **");
      Console.ReadLine();
    }
  }
}
```

To expose a client-activated object, replace the shaded area in Listing 39.2 **1** with the following code snippet:

```
RemotingConfiguration.RegisterActivatedServiceType(typeof(SampleService));
```

The code in Listing 39.3 illustrates programmatically registering single-call and singleton methods on the client.

LISTING 39.3

Programmatically Registering the Single Call and Singleton Method of Activation on the Client

```csharp
// Project Remoting Sample
// This code listing does not contain the sources for
// the sample remote object.  It is only meant to show
// how to expose the object to other application domains.

using System;

namespace SAMS.VisualCSharpDotNetUnleashed.Chapter39
{
  class RemotingSample
  {
    public static void Main()
    {
      HttpChannel httpChannel = new HttpChannel(8085);
      ChannelServices.RegisterChannel(httpChannel);

      RemotingConfiguration.RegisterWellKnownClientType(typeof(SampleService),
          "tcp://localhost:9000/SAMSSampleService/SampleService.soap",
          WellKnownObjectMode.Singleton);

      SampleService service = new SampleService();
      if(service == null)
      {
        Console.WriteLine("Service Not Found!");
      }
      else
      {
        Console.WriteLine("Calling Some Method on the server");
        Service.SomeMethod();
      }

      Console.WriteLine("** Press enter to end the client process. **");
      Console.ReadLine();
    }
  }
}
```

To expose a client-activated object, replace the appropriate area in Listing 39.3 with the following code snippet:

```csharp
RemotingConfiguration.RegisterActivatedClientType(
    GetType(SampleService), "tcp://localhost:9000");
```

Remoting Architecture

Registering with a Configuration File

Registering the remote object with a configuration file is fairly trivial. Simply make a call to the `RemotingConfiguration.Configure` method and pass in the configuration file and path. Listing 39.2 shows how to register a remote object using a config file. As with registering the remote object programmatically, there are slight differences between registering on the server and on the client. The following code snippet shows a sample configuration file for the server:

```
<configuration>
  <system.runtime.remoting>
    <application name="SampleServer">
      <service>
        <wellknown mode="SingleCall"
          type="SampleServer.SampleService, SampleService"
          objectUri="SampleServiceURI" />
      </service>
      <channels>
          <channel ref="tcp" port="9000" displayName="SampleService tcp channel" />
          <channel ref="http" port="9001" displayName="SampleService http channel" />
      </channels>
    </application>
  </system.runtime.remoting>
</configuration>
```

The following code snippet shows a sample configuration file for the client:

```
<configuration>
  <system.runtime.remoting>
    <application name="SampleServer">
      <service>
        <activated type="SampleServer.SampleService, SampleService"/>
      </service>
      <channels>
        <channel ref="tcp" port="9000" displayName="SampleService tcp channel" />
        <channel ref="http" port="9001" displayName="SampleService http channel" />
      </channels>
      <lifetime leaseTime="1000MS"
          sponsorshipTimeout="500MS" renewOnCallTime="100MS"
leaseManagerPollTime="10MS" />
    </application>
  </system.runtime.remoting>
</configuration>
```

LISTING 39.4
Registering a Remote Object Using a Config File

```
// Project Remoting Sample
// This code listing does not contain the sources for
// the sample remote object.  It is only meant to show
// how to expose the object to other application domains.

using System;

namespace SAMS.VisualCSharpDotNetUnleashed.Chapter39
{
  class RemotingSample
  {
    public static void Main()
    {
      HttpChannel httpChannel = new HttpChannel(9000);
      ChannelServices.RegisterChannel(httpChannel);

      RemotingConfiguration.Configure("SampleService.config");

      Console.WriteLine("** Press enter to end the server process. **");
      Console.ReadLine();
    }
  }
}
```

Building the Remoting Server Application

Building the server application consists of two things. In addition to the remote object that you want to host, you must also have a hosting application. As you will learn later in this chapter, you can use IIS to host your application, but for now, you will create a server host application. The only things required in this host application are to open a channel in which to host the remote object, register the type, and wait for a connection. Listing 39.5 shows the code necessary to create a host application that hosts and exposes the class SampleService.

LISTING 39.5
The Server Host Application

```
using System;
using System.Runtime.Remoting;
using System.Runtime.Remoting.Channels;
using System.Runtime.Remoting.Channels.Http;

namespace SAMS.VisualCSharpDotNetUnleashed.Chapter39
```

Remoting Architecture

LISTING 39.5
Continued

```
{
  class RemotingSample
  {
    public static void Main()
    {
      HttpChannel httpChannel = new HttpChannel(9000);
      ChannelServices.RegisterChannel(httpChannel);

      RemotingConfiguration.RegisterWellKnownServiceType(typeof(SampleService),
        "SAMSSampleService/SampleService", WellKnownObjectMode.SingleCall);

      Console.WriteLine("** Press enter to end the server process. **");
      Console.ReadLine();
    }
  }
}
```

Building the Common Files

As stated in the previous section, there are two parts to hosting a remote object. The first part is a host application and the second part is the remote object itself. Listing 39.6 shows the code necessary to produce a simple class that can act as the remote object. This class has one method: GetInformation. When called, this method returns the application domain in which the object is created.

LISTING 39.6
The Common File (Remote Object)

```
using System;

namespace SAMS.VisualCSharpDotNetUnleashed.Chapter39
{
  [Serializable]
  public class SampleService : System.MarshalByRefObject
  {
    public SampleService()
    {
    }

    public string GetInformation()
    {
      return "Thie application domain is: " +
System.AppDomain.CurrentDomain.ToString();
    }
```

LISTING 39.6
Continued

```
  }
}
```

Building the Client

The client application contains the most code. You must first open a channel. Remember that this is the client channel, not the channel on which the remote object is hosted, and therefore it must have a different port than the host. Next, you register the server type on the client. You can accomplish this by calling the `RemotingConfiguration.Configure` method or you can, as in Listing 39.6, programmatically register the type. After the type has been registered **2**, you can activate the remote object. You can use the `new` operator or you can use the `Activator.GetObject` or `Activator.CreateInstance` methods to accomplish the activation. Listing 39.7 demonstrates the use of the `new` operator. Finally, you can call the method on the remote object. When called, this method returns the application domain in which the object was created and is then output to the console. Listing 39.7 shows the code necessary to create the client application.

LISTING 39.7
The Client Console Application

```csharp
using System;
using System.Runtime.Remoting;
using System.Runtime.Remoting.Channels;
using System.Runtime.Remoting.Channels.Http;

namespace SAMS.VisualCSharpDotNetUnleashed.Chapter39
{
  class ClientSample
  {
    /// <summary>
    /// The main entry point for the application.
    /// </summary>
    [STAThread]
    static void Main(string[] args)
    {
      // Create the client channel on a different port then the remote object.
      HttpChannel httpChannel = new HttpChannel(8085);
      ChannelServices.RegisterChannel(httpChannel);

      // Get the remote object
      RemotingConfiguration.RegisterWellKnownClientType(typeof(SampleService),
        "http://localhost:9000/SAMSSampleService/SampleService.Soap");
```

2

Remoting Architecture

LISTING 39.7

Continued

```
    // Activate the remote object.
    SampleService service = new SampleService();
    if(service == null)
    {
      Console.WriteLine("Service Not Found!");
    }
    else
    {
      Console.WriteLine("Calling Some Method on the server");
      Console.WriteLine("");
      Console.WriteLine(service.GetInformation());
      Console.WriteLine("");
    }

    Console.WriteLine("** Press enter to end the client process. **");
    Console.ReadLine();
   }
  }
}
```

IIS and Remoting

As shown in the previous sections, the remote object must be hosted by some server application. Listing 39.5 showed the code necessary to build a bare-bones hosting application. That was fairly simple, but an application has already been written that can do this for you. Internet Information Services (IIS) is an application that comes with Windows and is quite capable of hosting the remote object for you with minor changes to the application. The first change is that you must tell IIS where your object is located and how to host the remote object. You accomplish this through the use of a virtual directory and web.config file. To better illustrate this, follow these steps:

1. Create a directory called SampleService in the Inetpub\wwwroot directory.

2. Under the SampleService directory, create a subdirectory named bin.

3. On your local machine, create a virtual directory called SAMSSampleService and point it to the SampleService directory you created in step 1. You can use all the defaults when creating the virtual directory.

4. Cut and paste the code in Listing 39.6 into a file named web.config and save that file in the SampleService directory.

5. Copy the Chapter41Common.dll file from the build directory to the SampleService\bin directory.

6. Modify the shaded code in Listing 39.5 by removing the port designation (`http://localhost:9000` should become `http://localhost`).

7. Build and run the client application.

After the application has been built and run, you should see the same results as you did by running the server and the client.

LISTING 39.8

Web.config

```
<configuration>
  <system.runtime.remoting>
    <application>
      <service>
        <wellknown mode="SingleCall"
         type="SAMS.VisualCSharpDotNetUnleashed.Chapter39.SampleService,
Chapter41Common"
          objectUri="SampleService.Soap" />
      </service>
    </application>
  </system.runtime.remoting>
</configuration>
```

Summary

In this chapter, you learned the basics of using .NET Remoting. First you got an understanding of the .NET Remoting architecture. Next you learned that .NET takes a different approach to isolating applications from one another through application domains and contexts. Next, you learned how to build a simple Remoting host server, Remoting object, and client application. Finally, you learned how to use IIS to host your Remoting objects.

Further Reading

Advanced .NET Remoting, by Ingo Rammer, Apress. ISBN: 1590590252. (Considered by many to be the definitive bible of .NET Remoting.)

.NET Common Language Runtime Unleashed, Chapter 13, by Kevin Burton, Sams Publishing. ISBN: 0672321246.

.NET Programming: A Practical Guide Using C#, Chapter 6, by Pradeep Tapadiya, Prentice Hall PTR. ISBN: 0130669458.

39

40 COM+ Enterprise Services

IN BRIEF

COM+ is a set of services that are provided to applications to facilitate enterprise-scale development. This chapter will provide you with an overview of how COM+ works and how it evolved. After a brief overview of COM+, you will spend the rest of the chapter developing serviced components. *Serviced components* are classes that are managed by COM+ services.

COM+ provides application developers with the ability to quickly and easily share property data and perform things such as two-phase commit transactions, just-in-time activation, object pooling, automatic object construction, and much more. After reading this chapter, you should have a good idea of what COM+ is, how it works, and how to write C# code that takes advantage of COM+.

WHAT YOU NEED

REQUIRED SOFTWARE	.NET Framework SDK v1.1 Visual Studio .NET 2003 with C# installed
RECOMMENDED HARDWARE	PC that meets .NET SDK minimum requirements
SKILLS REQUIRED	C# and .NET familiarity Familiarity with COM+

COM+ Enterprise Services at a Glance

Overview of COM+	809		
Transactions	809	Role-Based Security	811
JIT Activation in COM+	810	Queued Components	812
Object Pooling	810	Events	812
Construction Strings	811		

Building COM+ Components	813		
Transactions	813	Object Pooling	817
Construction Strings	815	Shared Properties	818
JIT Activation Sample	817		

Security in COM+	820		
Object and Security Contexts	820	Role-Based Security	821

Advanced COM+	823		
Events	823	Queued Components	826

Summary	827

Further Reading	827

Overview of COM+

This section will provide you with an overview of some of the services and features that COM+ provides for serviced components.

COM+ began its life as MTS (Microsoft Transaction Services). MTS was a system designed to facilitate distributed transactions across multiple software components. The advent of component-centric programming showed a need for the ability to extend the concept of a transaction outside a single database. Transactions needed to be able to deal with multiple components that performed data operations on multiple, possibly distant, data sources.

After the distributed transaction system was in place, other features began falling into place as well, turning MTS from a simple transaction coordinator into a full-fledged enterprise application hosting environment. MTS eventually grew into what is now COM+. COM+ can be managed through the Component Services section of your operating system's Administrative Tools section.

In COM+, you create an *application*, which is a container for COM+ components. Applications can exist in two different modes: Server mode and Library mode. An application in Server mode is hosted on the COM+ server by the COM+ process itself. When clients attach to a component in a Server mode application, they attach via Remoting and the components remain in the server host process's context. On the other hand, a Library mode application has the components instantiated within the thread context of the calling client. The difference between Server mode and Library mode applications is *where* the code is executed. COM+ Server mode applications execute all the code on the server in which they are configured, whereas COM+ Library mode applications execute on the client.

Transactions

A *transaction* can be thought of as a single, atomic unit of work. In a database, you begin a transaction and then perform several operations on multiple tables. If something goes wrong during one of those operations, you need to be able to restore the database to its state at the moment before the transaction began. If nothing goes wrong, you need to be able to commit the changes made during the transaction to make them permanent.

The same needs apply to a COM+ transaction. The only difference is that a COM+ transaction is a distributed transaction that can occur between multiple components. In a typical scenario, a component begins a transaction, creating a transaction root. Every method call on every component below that root can then be enlisted in the transaction, based on the configuration of the child components. If the component is involved in the transaction, it can then vote for whether the transaction is committed or is rolled back.

40

At the end of the execution of the method that started the transaction, if every involved component votes to commit the transaction, the transaction will be committed. If even one component votes against committing the transaction due to some application failure, the entire transaction will be rolled back. Every action performed by every involved component since the beginning of the transaction will be rolled back.

TIP

People often take it for granted that actions performed by their components will be rolled back. However, if the data source you are working with doesn't support the MS DTC transaction process, you will have to roll back those changes yourself. SQL Server, Access, and OLE DB can all be rolled back. But if you did something such as call a web service during a COM+ transaction, you'll have to call the web service again to undo the changes made when the transaction was rolled back.

40

JIT Activation in COM+

JIT is an acronym that stands for *just-in-time* activation. When a COM+ application is configured in Server mode with object pooling enabled (discussed shortly), the application can take advantage of JIT activation.

JIT is an advanced feature that allows for pooled objects to mitigate the sometimes high cost of instantiation. Certain applications require that when some components are first instantiated, they obtain resources and perform certain tasks that take a considerable amount of time. In a large, multiuser application in which objects are instantiated and disposed of constantly, that large initial overhead can bring an application to its knees and drastically reduce performance.

JIT allows for objects to be deactivated when not in use, even if clients are holding open references to them. This means that the resources the objects consume are temporarily given back to the system until they are needed again. When a deactivated reference to a JIT-managed object is invoked, the object is reactivated. These processes are called *deactivation* and *activation*. You can think of these as pseudo constructors and destructors. As a programmer, you can write code that will be executed upon activation and deactivation. If you know in advance that your application can take advantage of JIT, you can write your components to make the best use of the JIT system and activation.

Object Pooling

As mentioned in the previous section, components often have a high instantiation cost and high-volume systems that are constantly instantiating new objects can create a performance problem that can cripple an application.

Object pooling is one answer to this problem. When an object is first requested, it is instantiated and the full cost of instantiating the object is incurred. However, this is where the similarity between standard instantiation and pooling/JIT disappears. After it has been instantiated, the object is considered pooled. When the object becomes inactive for a set period of time, it will be returned to the pool. If the object is requested again, it will be fetched from a pool instead of instantiated from scratch. This defers a lot of the performance cost of instantiation and allows an application to handle higher volumes much more smoothly.

As a COM+ programmer, you can give your object event handlers that will handle the events of being placed into a pool (deactivated) or being retrieved from the pool for use by a client object (activated). As mentioned in the JIT section, you can perform the heavy lifting in the instantiation (construction) phase, and perform only minimal maintenance code in the activation and deactivation handlers. This will allow your COM+ application to function extremely well in a high volume environment that is constantly requesting new objects. Another thing you can do as the developer or administrator is to configure the size of the object pool for optimal performance.

Construction Strings

COM+ components (classes that derive from `ServicedComponent`) are instantiated by the COM+ system. Objects can also be constructed. This allows for an initial state to be given to the component by an administrator. Within the COM+ administration console, you can set the construction string for every component in the application. That string is then sent to the component by means of the `Construct` method. Every time a component is then constructed by the infrastructure, its `Construct` method is invoked, allowing variable initialization parameters to be passed as startup options.

Role-Based Security

Role-based security provides an easy-to-use system for administering users, groups, and permissions. The idea is that instead of giving specific privileges to specific users, privileges are granted to roles or groups. Users are then associated with those groups; the privileges of the users are obtained by looking at the privileges granted to the groups to which the user belongs.

In the case of COM+ Enterprise Services, security can be enabled at the protocol level. That means if a COM+ component is properly configured, it can be made aware of the security context under which it is running for any and all methods invoked. For example, if a user named `johndoe` in the domain `MYDOMAIN` uses an application that employs a COM+ application, the COM+ components within that application can be allowed to determine the identity of the user at runtime.

Not only can the components determine the identity of the user at runtime, they can determine the groups to which that user belongs. A special class called `ContextUtil`, which is made available to all `ServicedComponent` classes, can be used to detect whether security is enabled. If so, `ContextUtil` can determine whether the current user belongs to a given group with the method `IsCallerInRole`. If you have had experience with .NET security, you'll notice that this method looks a lot like the `IsInRole` method that is part of the `IPrincipal` interface. You will see how to write this security code later in the chapter in the "Building COM+ Components" section.

Queued Components

A queued component is actually a collection of several interconnected pieces of technology. Queued components provide an asynchronous method by which COM+ components can have their methods invoked. If the processing of a method is complicated and could take a long time, but the client code doesn't need to know the result right away, queued components can dramatically increase performance.

A queued component works by wiring up a Microsoft Message Queuing (MSMQ) queue to a COM+ component. Every time a method call is made to the component, the parameters for the invocation are serialized and stored in a message in the queue. At some later point (the actual time is determined by the CPU and resource load on the machine at the time), the queue is examined. Each message in the queue is deserialized and rebuilt into a method invocation. That method is then called on the COM+ component.

TIP

Because the method invocations are done out-of-sync with the client code, queued components cannot have any nonvoid methods. In other words, if you want to be able to queue method calls to a component, those methods calls need to take serializable parameters and cannot return any data.

As you will see later in the chapter, there is a special syntax to instantiating components that are associated with queues.

Events

Events are based on a publisher/subscriber model. When some event of importance takes place within a component, form, control, or class, that class can then fire the event. By firing an event, the class is actually notifying all the event subscribers that the important event took place, and it is providing additional information regarding the event. This model is referred to as *tightly coupled events*.

The event model supported and provided by COM+ is referred to as *loosely coupled events*. A loosely coupled event is actually a COM+ component. When an important event takes place in a COM+ application, the application can then publish that event. All subscribers of the event, which are also COM+ components, are then notified. It is considered loosely coupled because an event from one application can be subscribed to by another application and the applications will work. Subscriptions can be managed programmatically or through the COM+ administrative tools. Creating an event capable of participating in the COM+ event system requires the use of a custom attribute that you will see later.

Building COM+ Components

This next section will take you through the C# code that you can use to build the features described in the previous section. There are two key factors to building COM+ components in the .NET Framework: the `ServicedComponent` class from which all .NET COM+ components inherit, and various custom code attributes that give the COM+ environment detailed instructions on how to regulate the behavior of components and COM+ applications.

Transactions

As mentioned earlier, transactions indicate a single, cohesive unit of work. If something goes wrong during a transaction, the assumption must be that all work performed during that transaction will be rolled back or cancelled. If everything during the transaction goes properly, the assumption must be that all work performed during the transaction will be made permanent.

The easiest way to control transactions is through the use of code attributes. The following code attributes affect transaction processing behavior for COM+ components and methods:

- `AutoCompleteAttribute`—When this attribute decorates a method call, the COM+ system automatically assumes that if no exception occurs during the execution of the associated method, the transaction will complete and commit successfully.

- `TransactionAttribute`—This attribute defines information on how transaction processing should take place on a given method. Options include setting the isolation, timeout, and the value which is of type `TransactionOption` (`Disabled`, `NotSupported`, `Required`, `RequiresNew`, `Supported`).

The only time you should consider using COM+ transactions is if a single method encapsulates transactional calls to multiple, disparate sources; for example, if you need to encapsulate a call to an MSMQ, a SQL database, and an OLEDB data source in a single unit of work. For this, you would use a COM+ transaction. However, if everything you need to do takes place within a single data source such as SQL Server, you're better off using native T-SQL transactions. Distributed transactions have very high overhead.

The following code shows how you can manually control the commitment or rollback of a distributed COM+ transaction through the `ContextUtil` **1** class, as well

Building COM+ Components

as how to make the transaction automatically complete (if no exception occurs) via
the AutoComplete **2** attribute:

```csharp
using System;
using System.Data;
using System.Data.SqlClient;
using System.EnterpriseServices;

namespace ServicedApplication
{
  public class SampleClass : ServicedComponent
  {
    public SampleClass()
    {
    }

    public void ManualTransaction( string trxData )
    {
      // perform some work using trxData, using manual transactions
      SqlConnection conn = null;
      try
      {
        conn = new SqlConnection(" ... your connection string here ... ");
        conn.Open();
        SqlCommand cmd = conn.CreateCommand();
        cmd.CommandText = " .. some update .. ";
        cmd.CommandType = CommandType.Text;
        cmd.ExecuteNonQuery();
        conn.Close();
        ContextUtil.SetComplete();
      }
      catch (Exception ex)
      {
        ContextUtil.SetAbort();
      }
      finally
      {
        if ((conn != null) && (conn.State == ConnectionState.Open))
        {
          conn.Dispose();
        }
      }
    }

    [AutoComplete()]
    public void AutoTransaction( string trxData )
```

```
    {
      SqlConnection conn = null;
      try
      {
        conn = new SqlConnection(".. your connection string here ... ");
        conn.Open();
        SqlCommand cmd = conn.CreateCommand();
        cmd.CommandText = ".. your update here ..";
        cmd.ExecuteNonQuery();
        conn.Close();
      }
      catch (Exception ex)
      {
        // re-throw
        throw ex;
      }
      finally
      {
        if ( (conn != null) && (conn.State == ConnectionState.Open))
          conn.Dispose();
      }
    }
  }
}
```

As you can see, working with transactions from within a COM+ component isn't very difficult at all. If you inherit from `ServicedComponent`, reference `System.EnterpriseServices`, and know how to use the `ContextUtil` class, the `AutoComplete` attribute, and the `Transaction` attribute, you are ready to start creating COM+ components that participate in distributed transactions.

Construction Strings

The construction string is used to initialize a component during the construction phase. This is accomplished by the COM+ system calling the `Construct` method on the COM+ component. To implement this method, simply define it and provide an implementation for it on your class:

```
protected override void Construct(string s)
{
  connectionString = s;
}
```

This code is pretty simple; all it does is override a method called `Construct`. This method can be invoked by COM+ if the application is configured properly. The

Building COM+ Components

preceding sample, assumes that a database connection string will be provided by the construction method.

Another feature of .NET serviced components is that, upon initial execution, if the assembly contains the appropriate custom code attributes, the COM+ system can automatically register the assembly as a COM+ application. For example, the following code sets two attributes on a sample class library, ServicedApplication:

```
// Enterprise Services attributes
[assembly: ApplicationName("Chapter 43 Sample")]
[assembly: Description("Chapter 43 Serviced Component COM+ Sample")]
```

These attributes allow .NET and COM+ to create this application the first time a serviced component is invoked within this assembly.

Figure 40.1 shows what the COM+ (Component Services) administration console looks like after instantiating a serviced component in the sample class library.

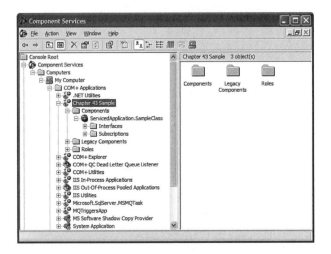

FIGURE 40.1   The Component Services administration console showing a recently auto-registered COM+ application.

Now right-click the registered application and choose the Properties option. When you click the Activation tab, you will see the place where you can define the construction string (in this case, a database connection string passed in by administrators). Figure 40.2 shows this tab.

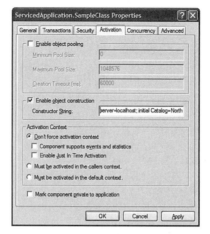

FIGURE 40.2   The Activation tab of the Properties dialog on the newly registered COM+ application.

JIT Activation Sample

As you saw in the overview at the beginning of the chapter, JIT refers to just-in-time activation. JIT is possible only when object pooling is enabled, so the next section will show a sample of both JIT and object pooling.

Object Pooling

Object pooling is a scenario in which a pool of pre-instantiated objects is maintained in memory in a server application managed by COM+. Object pooling is enabled and configured on a per-object basis. This means that you can have some components in your COM+ application be pooled and some others not be pooled. When pooling is enabled and the COM+ application is configured as a Library mode application, pooled objects are pooled within the AppDomain of the client. In Server-activation applications, the pool resides on the server in the AppDomain in which the application resides.

To configure object pooling, you can use the ObjectPooling attribute on a class. The following code shows you a sample of how to use this attribute:

```
[ObjectPooling(Enabled=true, MinPoolSize=1, MaxPoolSize=20, CreationTimeout=10000)]
public class MyPooledObject : ServicedComponent
{
    public override void Activate() { } // removed from pool
    public override void Deactivate() { } // returned to pool
    public override bool CanBePooled() { return true; }
}
```

The preceding component will be created in a pool. The first time that a request is made for the component, a pool with only one object will be created. At peak volume, when the most requests for the component are being made, 20 objects will belong to the pool. If a request for the component lasts more than 10 seconds without a response, the request will fail and the client will be unable to create an instance of the object.

Shared Properties

Shared properties and shared property groups are services provided by COM+ that allow objects to share state within a given server process. One of the requirements of many types of applications written for COM+ is that they not maintain state because doing so would diminish the returns provided by object pooling, activation, and JIT. However, sometimes information needs to be shared between objects. To do this, you can actually share resources, called *shared properties,* within a single COM+ application.

All of this work begins with the `SharedPropertyGroupManager` class. The Shared Property Manager (SPM) is designed to take the headache out of sharing data between objects in a server process in a multithreaded environment. It deals with access locks, name collision issues, multithreading synchronization issues, semaphores, and much more. All you have to do is create and access the properties—it's definitely a good trade-off.

The next sample uses two classes: `SPMGetter` **3** and `SPMSetter` **4** . Just as it appears, one class writes a value to a shared property and the other class reads a value from a shared property. To accomplish something like this without COM+, you would need to use complex memory-sharing APIs and implement your own thread synchronization and item-locking code. Fortunately, COM+'s SPM handles all that. Listings 40.1 and 40.2 show the two getter/setter classes that deal with the shared property. You can tell from the syntax that accessing shared properties is extremely simple.

LISTING 40.1

Class That Reads the Current Value of a Shared Property

```
using System;
using System.EnterpriseServices;

namespace ServicedApplication
{
  /// <summary>
  /// Summary description for SPMGetter.
  /// </summary>
 public class SPMGetter : ServicedComponent
  {
```

LISTING 40.1
Continued

```
    public string GetProperty()                                             3

    {
        SharedPropertyGroupManager spm = new SharedPropertyGroupManager();
        SharedPropertyGroup spg;
        PropertyLockMode plm = PropertyLockMode.Method;
        PropertyReleaseMode prm = PropertyReleaseMode.Process;
        bool groupExists;
        bool propExists;


        spg = spm.CreatePropertyGroup("SAMS",
            ref plm, ref prm, out groupExists );
        SharedProperty sp = spg.CreateProperty("TestProperty", out propExists );
        return (string)sp.Value;

    }

  }
}
```

LISTING 40.2
Class That Sets the Value of a COM+ Shared Property

```
using System;
using System.EnterpriseServices;

namespace ServicedApplication
{
  /// <summary>
  /// Summary description for SPMSetter.
  /// </summary>
  public class SPMSetter : ServicedComponent
  {
    public void SetProperty(string strValue)                                4

    {
        SharedPropertyGroupManager spm = new SharedPropertyGroupManager();
        SharedPropertyGroup spg;
        PropertyLockMode plm = PropertyLockMode.Method;
        PropertyReleaseMode prm = PropertyReleaseMode.Process;
        bool groupExists;
        bool propExists;


        spg = spm.CreatePropertyGroup("SAMS", ref plm, ref prm, out groupExists );
        SharedProperty sp = spg.CreateProperty("TestProperty", out propExists );
        sp.Value = strValue;

    }
```

40

Building COM+ Components

LISTING 40.2
Continued

```
  }
}
```

In the code so far, all that's been done is to create two classes: one that has a method that sets a value and one that has a method that reads a value. Finally, you can write some code that will test this theory and determine whether the code reads and writes the same value. That code is listed here:

```
Console.WriteLine("Setting shared property to the value 'Hello World'");
ServicedApplication.SPMSetter setter = new ServicedApplication.SPMSetter();
setter.SetProperty("Hello World");
ServicedApplication.SPMGetter getter = new ServicedApplication.SPMGetter();
Console.WriteLine("Value obtained from SPMGetter: " + getter.GetProperty());
```

As expected, this application produces the conventional hello world output. There is one caveat: This application won't work unless the COM+ components making use of the SPM are given an MTS object context. You'll learn more about contexts later in this chapter and in other COM+ reference manuals. The important thing to note here is that shared properties won't work without an MTS context. To provide a context for your components, the components must enforce sufficient security. On the Security tab of the application Properties dialog, make sure that the Perform Access Checks at the Component and Process Level radio button is checked.

Security in COM+

Security in COM+ is an extremely complex and involved topic. If you really want the full details, you should pick up a book devoted to COM+. The next section will provide you with an overview of how security works in a COM+ application, the security options available to you, and how you can program against that security model.

Object and Security Contexts

A security context identifies the principal (see other chapters in this book about IPrincipal and IIdentity) that is performing a given action. If a method is being invoked on a serviced component, COM+ can be configured to provide that component with an object context. That context gives the code the capability to query the identity of the calling client as well as the roles (discussed shortly) to which the user belongs. The object context allows a method on a ServicedComponent to obtain information about current transactions, whether security is enabled, and allows the code to vote for the commitment or rollback of the current transaction.

Table 40.1 is a quick list of some of the methods and properties available on the `ContextUtil` class, a class used for interfacing with the MTS (COM+) context object.

TABLE 40.1

Methods and Properties of the `ContextUtil` Class

Property / Method	Description
Properties	
ActivityId	Gets the GUID for the current activity
ApplicationId	Gets the GUID for the current COM+ application
ContextId	Gets the GUID for the current context
DeactivateOnReturn	Indicates to the COM+ system that the component will be deactivated when the current method finishes
IsInTransaction	Indicates whether the current method is participating in a transaction
IsSecurityEnabled	Indicates whether security is enabled at the component or process level
Transaction	Returns information about the current distributed transaction
TransactionId	Gets the GUID for the current transaction
Methods	
DisableCommit()	Disables transaction commits for the current method execution
EnableCommit()	Enables transaction commits for the current method execution
GetNamedProperty()	Gets a named property that belongs to the current object context; not to be confused with shared property groups
IsCallerInRole()	Indicates whether the client code's security context is within a certain COM+ role
SetAbort()	Votes to abort (roll back) the current transaction
SetComplete()	Votes to commit (complete) the current transaction

Role-Based Security

Role-based security refers to the concept of assigning roles or groups to specific users. What the user can and cannot do is dictated by the roles to which that user belongs.

Every COM+ application has a set of roles associated with it. These roles can then have user accounts or user groups placed in them. These accounts are part of an NT domain or part of an Active Directory. Therefore, you can create roles such as Finance, Shipping, Receiving, Billing, Administrators, and Users. Each of these groups could have different or overlapping members. Code within the COM+ application can then test whether the user belongs to a particular group before allowing the user to perform a given action.

Building COM+ Components

The code in Listing 40.3 shows a new class, `RoleSecurity`, that has methods whose use is restricted to specific roles within the application. The code is examined in more detail after the listing.

LISTING 40.3
A Class That Has Methods That Utilize Object and Security Contexts

```
using System;
using System.EnterpriseServices;

namespace ServicedApplication
{
  /// <summary>
  /// Summary description for RoleSecurity.
  /// </summary>
  [ComponentAccessControl(true),
   SecurityRole("App User", true),
   SecurityRole("App Administrator")]
  [Transaction(TransactionOption.Required)]
  [EventTrackingEnabled(true)]
  [JustInTimeActivation(true)]
  [Synchronization( SynchronizationOption.Required)]
  public class RoleSecurity : ServicedComponent
  {
     public string PerformAdministrativeAction()
     {
       if (!ContextUtil.IsSecurityEnabled)
         return "No Security Available";

       if (SecurityCallContext.CurrentCall.IsCallerInRole("App Administrator"))
       {
         return "Task Completed";
       }
       else
       {
         return "Task Failed";
       }
     }
     public string PerformStandardAction()
     {
       if (!ContextUtil.IsSecurityEnabled)
         return "No Security Available";

       if (SecurityCallContext.CurrentCall.IsCallerInRole("App Administrator") ||
           SecurityCallContext.CurrentCall.IsCallerInRole("App User"))
```

LISTING 40.3
Continued

```
    {
        return "Task Completed by " +
            SecurityCallContext.CurrentCall.DirectCaller.AccountName;
    }
    else
        return "Task Failed";
    }
}
}
```

The onslaught of attributes **5** at the top of the class defines the necessary COM+ configuration that is required for COM+ to provide the component with security and object contexts. The `SecurityRole` attribute is used so that when the assembly is self-registering with COM+, it will create those security roles. If a Boolean value of true is supplied for this attribute, it will automatically add the special group Everyone to the role.

The first method, `PerformAdministrativeAction` **6**, makes a call to `IsCallerInRole` to find out whether the calling client code's security context is in the administrative application user role. The second method **7** will let anyone execute it so long as they are a user or an administrator.

The console output from invoking both of these methods is as follows:

```
Administrative result: Task Failed
Standard result: Task Completed by SILVERALIEN\Kevin Hoffman
```

By default, the `Kevin Hoffman` account is not part of the administrators group, but because the special group Everyone is part of the standard users group, the second task was completed. To illustrate how to identify the calling client, the name of the user that requested the task is displayed.

Advanced COM+

This section will show you some of the more powerful features of COM+ and how to write code that utilizes those technologies, such as loosely coupled events and queued components.

Events

In the .NET Framework, you can write code that subscribes to events published by other classes. The classes that publish events can reside in other assemblies or within

40

the same assembly. One thing those classes can't do is publish events when the client applications aren't running.

With the COM+ loosely coupled event system, an event publisher (also a serviced component) can publish an event without knowing the list of subscribers. COM+ will handle transmitting the event to all subscribers, including activating dormant components that have registered as listeners for that event.

There are three requirements for creating a loosely coupled event system: The publisher and subscriber must both inherit from `ServicedComponent`, they must both implement the same interface, and there must be a subscription configured between the receiving (listening) component and the publishing component. The code in Listing 40.4 shows the event class, the event subscriber (often called the *sink*) class, and the shared interface between the two.

40

LISTING 40.4
The Event Class, Subscriber Class, and Shared Interface

```
using System;
using System.EnterpriseServices;
using System.Windows.Forms;

namespace ServicedApplication
{
  /// <summary>
  /// Summary description for LooselyCoupledEvent.
  /// </summary>
  [EventClass()]
  public class LooselyCoupledEvent : ServicedComponent, ILooselyCoupledEvent
  {
    public void EventMethod(string evtMessage) { }
  }


  public interface ILooselyCoupledEvent
  {
    void EventMethod( string evtMessage );
  }


  public class LooselyCoupledEventSubscriber : ServicedComponent,
ILooselyCoupledEvent
  {
    public void EventMethod(string evtMessage)
    {
      MessageBox.Show(evtMessage, "Event Subscriber");
    }
```

LISTING 40.4
Continued

```
  }
 }
}
```

One thing that might not be obvious at first is that you don't need to create an instance of the subscriber component for it to receive the event from the publisher. The following code in another serviced component actually publishes the event:

```
public void PublishEvent( string message )
{
  LooselyCoupledEvent lce = new LooselyCoupledEvent();
  lce.EventMethod( message );
}
```

All you need to do now is set up the subscription between the publisher and the subscriber and invoke the `PublishEvent` method from a client application and you will be able to see COM+ events in action.

To rig up the subscription, find the subscriber component, expand the node, and right-click the Subscriptions folder. When you add a new subscription, a wizard will appear, as shown in Figure 40.3.

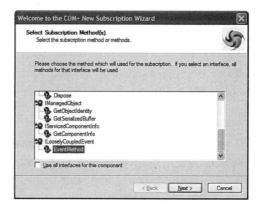

FIGURE 40.3   The COM+ New
Subscription Wizard.

When you add the following code to a client application, it will trigger an event publish, and you should see a message box appear:

```
ServicedApplication.SampleClass sc = new ServicedApplication.SampleClass();
sc.PublishEvent("Hello to all client events!");
```

When this code is executed after a subscription has been defined, the message shown in Figure 40.4 will appear.

FIGURE 40.4   The message that appears as a result of a COM+ event notification.

40

Queued Components

As mentioned earlier in the chapter, you can hook a COM+ component up to a message queue to provide deferred, asynchronous method execution. Instead of instantiating a component directly, you instantiate the component with a reference to its queue and the queued component will operate asynchronously with your method calls being serialized into messages in the queue.

With a few exceptions, every aspect of COM+ programming remains the same between queued components and regular (synchronous) components. The first exception is that methods of queued components cannot return values. The second is that clients need to use a specific syntax to bind to the queued component instead of creating an instance using the `new` keyword.

To instruct COM+ that queuing should be enabled, use the `ApplicationQueuing` attribute with the `Enabled` parameter set to true and the `QueueListenerEnabled` parameter set to true. This will set up a queue to service the component and immediately start listening on that queue. Use the `InterfaceQueuing` attribute to indicate the name of the interface that the particular class is implementing, allowing for proper message queue operation.

Finally, when you have created a queued component, you will need to create an instance of that component. Instead of using the `new` keyword, you need to use the `Marshal.BindToMoniker` method. For example, if you created a queued component that implements the interface `IAsyncComponent`, you might use the following code to create an instance of that component:

```
IAsyncComponent iac;
Iac = (IAsyncComponent) Marshal.BindToMoniker("queue:/new:MySampleClass.
AsyncComponent");
```

This will not only create an instance of a queued component, but will also obtain the resources necessary for writing serialized method calls to the associated queue.

Summary

This chapter started with a brief overview of some of the functionality provided by the COM+ system; such functionality allows for enterprise-scale applications and application services. The chapter then moved into a detailed discussion of how to write code that utilizes the different services provided by COM+. At this point, you should have a good understanding of what COM+ is, how it works, and how you can write code that utilizes its various services and features. For a more detailed look at COM+, you might want to consult a book or reference that is dedicated entirely to the subject of COM+.

Further Reading

Programming .NET Components, by Juval Lowy, O'Reilly. ISBN: 0596003471.

40

41 Enterprise Templates

IN BRIEF

This chapter explains the basics of enterprise templates. In this chapter, you will learn what enterprise templates are and why you should use them. Then you will learn how to create an enterprise template. Finally, you will learn how to control the usage of an enterprise template through the application of policy files.

WHAT YOU NEED

RECOMMENDED SOFTWARE	.NET Framework
	Visual Studio .NET Enterprise Edition
	C# .NET environment
	IIS
RECOMMENDED HARDWARE	.NET-enabled desktop client
SKILLS REQUIRED	JScript

ENTERPRISE TEMPLATES AT A GLANCE

Enterprise Templates	**828**		
Introducing the Enterprise Template	829	Subproject Wizards	831
Static and Dynamic Content	830	Custom Wizards	831
Static Prototypes	831		
Policy Files	**831**		
TDL Elements	832		
Teaching by Example	**834**		
Setting Up the Prerequisites	834	Making the Template	840
Laying Out the Template	835	Making the Template Available to Users	844
Creating the Template Structure	836		
Assigning a Policy to the Template	839	Testing the Template	845
Summary	**846**		
Further Reading	**847**		

Enterprise Templates

With the advent of .NET came a lot of power and flexibility. You can now develop an application in any language you like and can even easily develop different parts of the application in different languages. If you prefer C++, another developer prefers Visual Basic, and yet another developer prefers C#, it is possible for each of you to develop the assemblies you are responsible for in the language you prefer and put them to work seamlessly.

Although that ability is great for the developer, it is not necessarily the best business decision. For example, imagine that you work for a development shop that codes primarily Visual Basic and one of your developers decides to code his portion of the project in C#. Although in theory this is not a problem and everything should work, what happens if that person leaves the company? Does the company have another person that knows C# and can take over the maintenance of the project? For the business, this could be a major risk and liability. This is one of many things that using enterprise templates can help with. Not only can you restrict projects to certain languages and which components and classes can be used, you can actually enforce how the application will be structured as well.

Introducing the Enterprise Template

An enterprise template is a mechanism by which you can restrict developers from coding in ways that do not fall in line with the policies and directives of your business. In addition, an enterprise template is also a means by which you can automate the creation of basic or shell applications, assemblies, and components. To understand an enterprise template, it is important to understand its architecture.

Enterprise Template Architecture

An enterprise template consists of three main parts: prototype, policy file, and custom help, (see Table 41.1 for more information). It can contain two types of projects: an enterprise template project (.etp) and a language-specific project (for C#, .csproj).

TABLE 41.1

Enterprise Template Parts

Part	Description
Prototype	The prototype is the static content of the template. For example: In a Hello World program, the prototype would be the `helloworld.cs` file and any associated files that you choose to include.
Policy File	The policy file enables you to enforce the restrictions or policies of your company or development team.
Custom Help	Custom help enables you to add dynamic help or guidance to your template.

SOLUTIONS WITHIN SOLUTIONS

An interesting side effect of the enterprise template project is that it allows other enterprise template projects and language-specific projects to be contained within the project. In essence, this enables you to create solutions within solutions.

Even if you do not want to use any other feature available to enterprise templates, this is a significant benefit. By enabling you to contain multiple projects with an enterprise template, you are freed to break up your application logically. For example, many

Enterprise Templates

applications have a set of common libraries, common data libraries, and so on. Instead of creating a solution for each set of libraries, you can now create an enterprise template (.etp). The next time you need to work on those libraries while working on your project, all you have to do is add the enterprise template project to your solution.

Static and Dynamic Content

There are two types of content in the enterprise template. The first is static content. *Static* content is the material that remains the same for every instance of this template. For example, if you create a new console application by using the Visual Studio .NET Wizard, as in Listing 41.1, you will create an application created with a file called Class1.cs. With the exception of the namespace, it doesn't matter how many different times you create a project based on this template, the code file will always remain the same.

41

LISTING 41.1
`StaticAndDynamicContent` **Project**

```
using System;

namespace StaticAndDynamicContent
{
  /// <summary>
  /// Summary description for Class1.
  /// </summary>
  class Class1
  {
    /// <summary>
    /// The main entry point for the application.
    /// </summary>
    [STAThread]
    static void Main(string[] args)
    {
      //
      // TODO: Add code to start application here
      //
    }
  }
}
```

Dynamic content is the material that changes based upon user input. For example, when you create a new project, as in the new console project, you enter an application name. When the template generates the code for file Class1.cs, it generates a namespace that corresponds to the application name you entered. That is dynamic content.

Static Prototypes

Static prototypes are the easiest templates to understand and are a good example of static content. A *static prototype* is basically a shell application that can be used as the starting point for applications. Consider the following: Each time you create a Windows application, you have basically the same elements: a frame window with a menu, an About screen, and header comments for source control in each code file. In this situation, you could create a shell application that would contain these elements already laid out for you and save it as a static prototype template.

Unfortunately, there are two basic limitations with this approach. The first limitation is minor in that you cannot add dynamic content to the shell. Depending on the complexity of the requirements for your shell application, this might not be of much concern. The second limitation is a little more troubling in that this type of proto-type might not be compatible with future versions of enterprise templates.

Subproject Wizards

Using Microsoft JScript, subproject wizards enable you to write custom content into the enterprise template. In an example of dynamic content, subproject wizards not only enable you to change namespaces and class names, they also make it possible for you to customize the application content based on any criteria that you choose, such as user permissions, time of day, or a random sequence of events. Subproject wizards are a powerful feature that supplements static prototypes. In addition, they will easily port to the next version of enterprise templates.

Custom Wizards

Similar to static prototypes and subproject wizards, custom wizards enable you to create custom application content. However, unlike the other techniques, a custom wizard is not based on built-in wizards contained within the IDE, which makes it the most complex technique to create. To create a custom wizard, you must use native C++ and build in a GUI to gather the user inputs and requirements. For more infor-mation about custom wizards, see the MSDN documentation.

Policy Files

Policy files are XML files that enable you to enforce the restrictions or policies of your company or development team and are written in the Enterprise Template Definition Language (TDL). The policy files contain information and restrictions on every project that can be included in a solution.

TIP

Just like any programming language API, TDL has many options with specific parameters. In the old days, this was the reason for carrying a large book that contained the definitions and available parameters for the API. However, with the introduction of Intellisense and code completion, those books have become unnecessary. If you edit a TDL file with Visual Studio .NET, you will immediately see that you made the correct decision as Visual Studio .NET understands the TDL file and you can take advantage of code completion.

TDL Elements

Because it is always a good idea to learn the constructs and definitions of any language before you attempt to use it, each element and a brief description of its function are included in Table 41.2. Each element, known as a *node*, is written in uppercase and the structure and nesting of each node is enforced by the `TDLSchema.xsd` file. It is also worth noting that only nodes that are included in the `TDLSchema.xsd` file are allowed when creating policy files.

TABLE 41.2

TDL Elements as Indicated by MSDN Documentation

Element	Description
`<CATEGORIES>`	Defines a container for logically grouping similar elements defined in a different location of the policy file.
`<CATEGORY>`	Defines a reusable grouping of logically similar elements.
`<CATEGORYMEMBER>`	Defines a reference to a predefined policy file element.
`<CMDID>`	Defines the absolute position ID of a menu item in a menu hierarchy.
`<CONSTRAINTS>`	Defines a container for defining restrictions on IDE properties, menus, and toolbox items.
`<CONTEXT>`	Defines the content information displayed by the Dynamic Help Window when navigating between IDE elements.
`<CTXTATTRIBUTE>`	Defines a container for resolving contextual switching and initialization issues related to dynamic help within the Visual Studio .NET IDE.
`<DEFAULT>`	Defines a default value for automatically initializing a property.
`<DEFAULTACTION>`	Defines the default inclusion or exclusion setting to apply to a group of policy file elements.
`<DEFAULTSETTINGS>`	Defines global enterprise template policy file settings for each element.
`<DESCRIPTOR>`	Defines a unique ID for an IDE toolbox control.
`<ELEMENT>`	Defines a unique enterprise template building block.
`<ELEMENTS>`	Defines a collection of all building blocks available to an enterprise template.
`<ELEMENTSET>`	Defines a container for grouping building blocks.

TABLE 41.2

Continued

`<ENABLED>`	Defines an enabled or disabled state for a menu item or toolbox item.
`<EXCLUDE>`	Defines which template building blocks are not permitted to be referenced from within the context of another building block.
`<FEATURELINKS>`	Defines which set of menu or toolbox features may be associated to a specific template building block element.
`<FEATURES>`	Defines the collection of menu and toolbox items to be restricted via policy.
`<GUID>`	Defines a globally unique identifier for an IDE menu group.
`<ID>`	Defines a mechanism for referencing a node from other places in the policy file.
`<IDENTIFIER>`	Defines locating, identifying and configuration information about a specific policy file element.
`<IDENTIFIERDATA>`	Defines a name/value pair for processing references to elements.
`<IDENTIFIERS>`	Defines a collection of identifying nodes containing location, identification, and configuration information for specific elements.
`<INCLUDE>`	Defines the ID of an element to include in another place in the policy file.
`<MAXVALUE>`	Defines the maximum allowable value a property or element may contain.
`<MEMBERCONSTRAINT>`	Defines restrictions on a specific element based upon an ID.
`<MEMBERCONSTRAINTS>`	Defines a collection of restraints applying to specific menu, toolbox, or properties based upon an ID.
`<MENU>`	Defines a menu item for later reference in the policy file.
`<MENUCONSTRAINT>`	Defines the enabled or disabled restraint for a menu item.
`<MENUCONSTRAINTS>`	Defines a collection of context-based restricted menu items.
`<MENULINK>`	Defines a relationship where a menu item is disabled if the associated item is defined elsewhere in the policy file with an exclusion setting.
`<MENULINKS>`	Defines a collection of menu items to be disabled when the associated item has the exclusion property set.
`<MENUS>`	Defines a collection of menus to be included in the policy file.
`<MINVALUE>`	Defines a minimum allowable value for an element.
`<NAME>`	Defines a reference identifier for accessing the node containing the value.
`<ORDER>`	Defines the order in which include/exclude settings are evaluated within a policy file element.
`<POLICYMODE>`	Defines the mechanism for handling undefined or unrecognized items.
`<PROPERTYCONSTRAINT>`	Defines scope-restricted settings for properties displayed within the IDE properties browser window.
`<PROPERTYCONSTRAINTS>`	Defines a collection of scope-restricted settings for properties displayed within the IDE properties browser window.

41

TABLE 41.2

Continued

<PROTOTYPE>	Defines the location of a project, item, or enterprise template project from which a specific type of project can be created.
<PROTOTYPES>	Defines a collection of location information for finding and creating specific types of enterprise template projects.
<READONLY>	Defines if a property is allowed to be edited.
<TDL>	Defines the root node of a policy file, which contains all other policy file elements.
<TOOLBOXCONSTRAINT>	Defines if a specific toolbox item should be contextually enabled or disabled.
<TOOLBOXCONSTRAINTS>	Defines a collection of toolbox items that should be contextually enabled or disabled.
<TOOLBOXITEM>	Defines an item to display within the toolbox.
<TOOLBOXITEMS>	Defines a collection of items to display within the toolbox.
<TOOLBOXLINK>	Defines a relationship where a toolbox item is disabled if the associated item is defined elsewhere in the policy file with an exclusion setting.
<TOOLBOXLINKS>	Defines a collection of toolbox items to be disabled when the associated item has the exclusion property set.
<TYPE>	Defines a label identifying the type of the logical element.
<VALUE>	Defines the data portion of a name/value pair.

Teaching by Example

Some concepts are easy to understand simply by listening to a lecture or reading a book. Others require examples in order to fully comprehend them. Enterprise templates are a perfect example of the latter. Because much of an enterprise template is shell code, it is sometimes hard to explain. In the following sections, you will learn how to create a new enterprise template. The entire process can be broken up into several distinct parts.

Setting Up the Prerequisites

The first step in developing anything is to set up your environment. The same holds true with the development of an enterprise template. Before you start this example, make sure that you set up your system to display hidden files, folders, and file extensions in the Windows Explorer. Also, because this template will include a web service, ensure that IIS has been installed on your machine.

Laying Out the Template

The template that you will be developing is a standard *n*-tier application. As shown in Figure 41.1, it consists of a user interface layer (UIL), a business logic layer (BLL), and a data access layer (DAL).

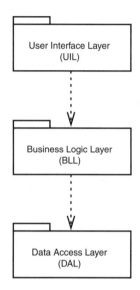

FIGURE 41.1   The enterprise template architecture is divided into three distinct layers.

In this template, the user interface layer will be a Windows Forms application. This layer enables you to display all the necessary information to the user. In addition, it makes it possible for you to collect information from the user. The next layer is the business logic layer. This layer is a set of web services that contain the logic necessary to perform the necessary operations of the system. The final layer is the data access layer. This layer contains the functionality needed to store and retrieve the database entities used in the application. Although these layers would normally contain the functionality needed to perform the functions of the system, this is only a template and therefore contains only a thin shell of functionality.

Naming the Parts of the Template

When laying out the template, it is useful to write down the names of each section. Later in the project, it will be necessary to refer to the correct names of each part of the template. If you choose not to write down the names, you run the risk of generating errors by using inconsistent names. For the purposes of this demonstration, the

Teaching by Example

name of this template will be `nTierTemplate.etp`. The three layers will use the name of the layer followed by `.etp`. For example, the data access layer will be `dal.etp`, the user interface layer will be `uil.etp`, and the business logic layer will be `bll.etp`.

Creating the Template Structure

The first thing to do in creating the template structure is to create the enterprise template. The following steps will create an empty enterprise template:

1. Start Visual Studio .NET.

2. Display the New Project dialog box by selecting File, New, Project menu item.

3. As shown in Figure 41.2, select the Enterprise Template Project by expanding the Other Projects folder in the Project Types pane.

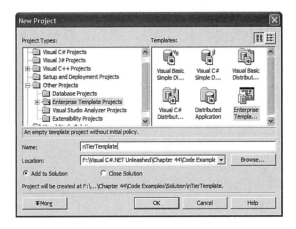

FIGURE 41.2   Create a new enterprise template project from the New Project dialog.

4. Type the name **nTierTemplate** in the Name section of the dialog.

5. Write down the location (path) of the template because you will need this information later in the section.

With this done, you will need to create the subproject templates. To do this, follow these steps:

1. Select the `nTierTemplate` node in the Solution Explorer.

2. As you did earlier, invoke the New Project dialog and select the Enterprise Template Project.

3. Change the name to **DAL** and create the project.

4. Repeat steps 1 through 3 two more times, changing **DAL** to **BLL** and **UIL**, respectively, to create the data access layer and user interface layer subprojects.

Figure 41.3 shows the completed template structure to this point.

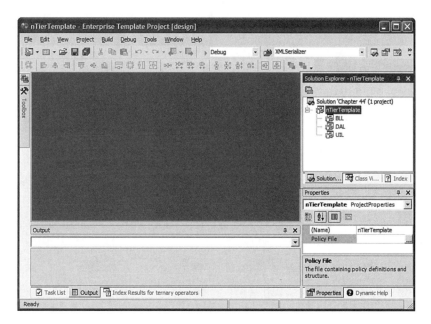

FIGURE 41.3   The empty structure of the `nTierTemplate` enterprise template.

Adding the Language Projects

Up to this point, the work you have done is similar to creating four separate solutions. The only difference is that these solutions are contained within a solution and are known as an enterprise template (although similar to a solution, enterprise template projects have additional features). The next step is to actually add some substance to the template by adding what are known as *language projects* to the template.

The following steps will create the DAL project:

1. Select the DAL node in the Solution Explorer.

2. Invoke the New Project dialog and select the Class Library project under the Visual C# Projects folder in the Project Types pane, as shown in Figure 41.4.

Teaching by Example

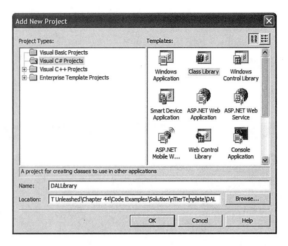

FIGURE 41.4   Create the DAL project.

3. Change the name of the project to **DALProject** and click OK.

After you've created the DAL project, you can create the UIL project template, as shown in the following steps:

1. Select the UIL node in the Solution Explorer.

2. Invoke the New Project dialog and select the Windows Application project under the Visual C# Projects folder in the Project Types pane, as in Figure 41.5.

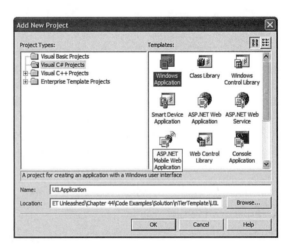

FIGURE 41.5   Create the UIL project.

3. Change the name of the project to **UILProject** and click OK.

Finally, you will want to create the BLL project. To do so, follow these steps:

1. Select the BLL node in the solution explorer.

2. Invoke the New Project dialog and select the ASP.NET Web Service project under the Visual C# Projects folder in the Project Types pane, as shown in Figure 41.6.

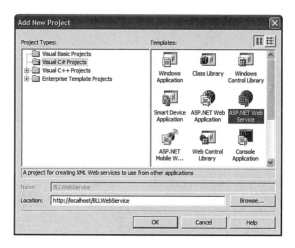

FIGURE 41.6   Create the BLL project.

3. Change the location of the project to **http://localhost/BLLWebService** and click OK.

The creation of the template structure is now complete and should resemble Figure 41.7. This structure will serve as the basis for all projects created with this template. As such, you can specify any additional settings that you want to be included with all of those projects. The settings could include compiler settings, such as warning levels, and other project defaults. You can also choose to add controls or other projects to these templates.

Assigning a Policy to the Template

Before you can use this structure as a template, you must assign a policy. Although you could create a policy from scratch, doing so is beyond the scope of this section. For the purposes of this demonstration, you will create a policy by cloning the default DAP.tdl file and modifying it as necessary.

Teaching by Example

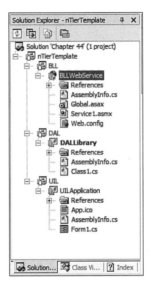

FIGURE 41.7   The completed
`nTierTemplate`
structure.

Follow these steps to configure the policy:

1. Copy the `DAP.tdl` file and rename the copy to `nTierTemplate.tdl`.

2. Select the `nTierTemplate` node in the Solution Explorer.

3. In the Properties window, enter the location and name of the policy file in the Policy File section, as shown in Figure 41.8.

4. Click Yes when prompted to reopen the project.

Making the Template

The previous sections created the basic structure from which to create the enterprise template. Unfortunately, those sections were the last of the automated processes (wizard based). This section will show you the manual steps that you must perform to finish the template and have it recognized by Visual Studio .NET.

Locate, Organize, and Clean Up

The following steps walk you through finalizing the process of creating and using an enterprise template. Before starting the following steps, save the projects, close the solution, and exit Visual Studio .NET.

FIGURE 41.8   Assign a policy to the `nTierTemplate` enterprise template.

1. Locate the `EnterpriseFrameworks` directory. By default, it should be located in a subdirectory of the `Microsoft Visual Studio .NET 2003` directory.

2. Copy the entire structure of the `nTierTemplate` project from its current location (you were instructed to write down this directory in a step earlier in this chapter) to the `EnterpriseFrameworks\Projects` directory.

3. Copy the web `BLLWebService` project (located in the web root directory) from its current location to the `EnterpriseFrameworks\Projects\nTierTemplate\BLL` directory.

Throwing Out the Trash

Applications such as those created by Visual Studio .NET require a few ancillary files and directories such as the solution file (`.sln`), `.suo` files, `.eto` files, and `bin` and `obj` directories. Although they serve a purpose in a regular application, they are not needed in an enterprise template and can therefore be deleted.

Modifying the Enterprise Template Project Files

This next section will show you how to make some minor modifications to all the associated enterprise template files (`.etp`).

1. Remove the Project ID.

2. Modify the Web project to prompt for a URL.

Teaching by Example

To remove the Project ID from the Enterprise Template Files, start by deleting the line

```
<GUIDPROJECTID>A GUID Will Be Here</GUIDPROJECTID>
```

from the following files: *nTierTemplate.etp*, *BLL\bll.etp*, *DAL\dal.etp*, and *UIL\uil.etp*.

The next thing you'll do in this sample is to modify the Web Project template to prompt for a URL. Listing 41.2 shows the contents of the business logic layer enterprise template project file. In order for the web project to prompt for the URL **1**, this file must be modified. The modified contents are shown in Listing 41.3.

LISTING 41.2

The `bll.etp` File Before Modifications

```xml
<?xml version="1.0"?>
<EFPROJECT>
    <GENERAL>
        <BANNER>Microsoft Visual Studio Application Template File</BANNER>
        <VERSION>1.00</VERSION>
        <Views>
            <ProjectExplorer>
                <File>http://localhost/BLLWebService/BLLWebService.csproj</File>
            </ProjectExplorer>
        </Views>
        <References>
            <Reference>
                <FILE>http://localhost/BLLWebService/BLLWebService.csproj</FILE>
            </Reference>
        </References>
    </GENERAL>
</EFPROJECT>
```

LISTING 41.3

The `bll.etp` File After Modifications

```xml
<EFPROJECT>
    <GENERAL>
        <BANNER>Microsoft Visual Studio Application Template File</BANNER>
        <VERSION>1.00</VERSION>
        <Views>
            <ProjectExplorer>
                <File>BLLWebService\BLLWebService.csproj</File>
            </ProjectExplorer>
        </Views>
        <References>
```

LISTING 41.3
Continued

```
        <Reference>
            <FILE>BLLWebService\BLLWebService.csproj</FILE>
            <REQUIRESURL>1</REQUIRESURL>                          1
        </Reference>
    </References>
    </GENERAL>
</EFPROJECT>
```

The next step is to add global entries to the Enterprise Template Project (.etp) and user properties to the language projects (.csproj) to allow the policy file (.tdl) to identify your project files as elements.

Add the following entry to the <GLOBALS> section in all four enterprise template projects:

```
<GLOBALENTRY>
  <NAME>TDLELEMENTTYPE</NAME>
  <VALUE>Insert Name Here</VALUE>
</GLOBALENTRY>
```

Make sure to replace *Insert Name Here* with the name of the template project. For example, after modifying the nTierTemplate.etp file, it should look like the following:

```
<GLOBALENTRY>
  <NAME>TDLELEMENTTYPE</NAME>
  <VALUE>nTierTemplate</VALUE>
</GLOBALENTRY>
```

Add the following entry after the <Files> section in all three of the language projects:

```
<UserProperties
  TDLFILE = "nTierTemplate.tdl"
  TDLELEMENTTYPE = "Insert Name Here"
/>
```

Make sure to replace the *Insert Name Here* to the name of the language project. For example, after modifying the DALLibrary.csproj, it should look like the following:

```
<UserProperties
  TDLFILE = "nTierTemplate.tdl"
  TDLELEMENTTYPE = "DALLibrary"
/>
```

Making the Template Available to Users

Now that you have a completed template and are ready to use it, how do you make sure that it is easily accessible to all users of the system? After all, if you spend all the time and effort necessary to plan and create a usable enterprise template, the last thing you want to hear is that "I didn't use it because I couldn't find it."

Creating a `.vsdir` File

To identify the appropriate files to display in the Add New Project dialog, Visual Studio .NET uses a `.vsdir` file. In this file, each line represents a different project or template. Within each line is a set of fields delimited by pipes (|), as described in Table 41.3.

41

TABLE 41.3

`.vsdir` File Fields

Field Name	Purpose
RelPathName	The path relative to the location of the `.vsdir` file to the template file.
{clsidpackage}	Optional GUID representing a product (Visual C#, and so on) that has a DLL containing localized resources.
LocalizedName	The name of the template. This name appears in the Add Item dialog box. This field is optional and can contain either a name or resource ID.
SortPriority	An integer representing the sort order and relative priority of the template in the dialog box.
Description	A description of the template. This description appears in the Add Item dialog box when the item is selected. This field can contain either a name or resource ID.
DLLPath or {clsidPackage}	Used to load an icon for the template from a DLL or EXE file. Either specifies a full path to the DLL or EXE, or a GUID of a product that has a DLL containing localized resources.
IconResourceId	Resource ID within the specified DLL. This field is optional and determines the icon to display. If no icon is defined, the shell substitutes the default icon for a file with the same extension as the item.
Flags	A group of flags that disable or enable the Name and Location fields on the Add Item dialog box. The flags can have the following values: Space (" "): enable filename 8192: disable filename
SuggestedBaseName	The default name for the template. This name will be displayed in the Name field in the dialog box.

To correctly expose your new template to users, you will need to create a `.vsdir` file that contains the appropriate information for your file and store it in the `EnterpriseFrameworks\ProxyProjects` directory. For the purposes of this discussion, create a new text file in Notepad, and copy and paste the following line into this file (space restrictions do not allow the code to be printed on a single line, but you should paste it into Notepad as one line):

```
..\Projects\nTierTemplate\nTierTemplate.etp|{AE77B8D0-6BDC-11d2-B354-0000F81F0C06}|
Visual C# n-Tier Project|1|This is the sample enterprise template created in chapter
41
of the Visual C#.NET Unleashed Book.|{AE77B8D0-6BDC-11d2-B354-0000F81F0C06}|
125|0|nTierProject
```

To complete the exposure of the template, save this file into the `EnterpriseFrameworks\ProxyProjects` directory.

Testing the Template

The final step in this example is to test the newly created template.

1. Start Visual Studio .NET.

2. Invoke the New Project dialog and select the newly created Visual C# n-Tier Project project, as shown in Figure 41.9.

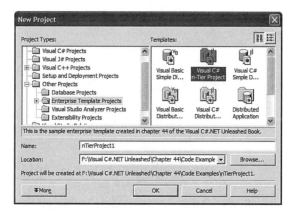

FIGURE 41.9   Select the template displayed in the New Project dialog.

3. Either leave the default or change the name and click OK.

4. Enter the path to store the Web Service BLL project, as in Figure 41.10.

As shown in Figure 41.11, when these steps have been completed, you should have an instance of the application that your template was designed to create.

Teaching by Example

FIGURE 41.10   Enter the path to create the BLL Web Service Project.

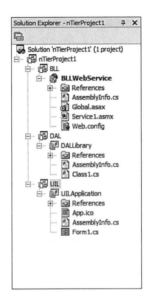

FIGURE 41.11   The solution created by the enterprise template.

Summary

This chapter provided an overview of enterprise templates and their uses. Because of the scope of enterprise templates, this was not meant to be an exhaustive description of all the available features and functions; it was meant only as an introduction and overview. In addition to the overview, you learned how to create a simple *n*-tier enterprise template and expose it to all the users of the system.

Further Reading

Developing Applications with Visual Studio .NET, Chapter 6, by Richard Grimes, Addison Wesley. ISBN: 0201708523.

41

Part IX

Debugging and Testing

CHAPTER 42   Debugging Your Applications

CHAPTER 43   Monitoring Your Applications

CHAPTER 44   Instrumenting Your Application

CHAPTER 45   The Future of C#

42

Debugging Your Applications

IN BRIEF

This chapter explains and demonstrates how to debug applications using the Visual Studio .NET environment. The first section talks about the Visual Studio .NET debugging environment and how to navigate the different windows that are available. Finally, you will explore how to use the Visual Studio .NET debugging environment to debug an application.

WHAT YOU NEED

RECOMMENDED SOFTWARE	.NET Framework C# .NET environment Visual Studio .NET
RECOMMENDED HARDWARE	.NET-enabled desktop client
SKILLS REQUIRED	C# coding

DEBUGGING YOUR APPLICATIONS AT A GLANCE

**The Visual Studio .NET
Debugging Environment**   **850**

Setting Up the Application for
Debugging   850

Understanding Syntax and Error
Messages   852

Understanding the Debugging
Tool Windows   854

Navigating the Application   858

Setting and Using Breakpoints   859

**Debugging with
Visual Studio .NET**   **861**

Debugging an Application   861

The Visual Studio .NET Debugging Environment

To most seasoned programmers, there is only one type of bug that ever exists in a program. This bug is the most aggravating thing that could ever happen. It is when the requirements that were given to you are wrong or the client simply changed his mind. All other bugs are simply "features of the application" that are misunderstood to everyone but the person who programmed the logic. In the following section, you will learn about the different tools that the Visual Studio .NET environment gives you to find these misunderstood features.

Setting Up the Application for Debugging

Before you can debug an application, it is important to understand the different configurations that Visual Studio .NET offers you for your application. Table 42.1 provides a list of the choices.

TABLE 42.1

Build Configurations

Configuration	Description
Release	This represents the Release build configuration. The code is optimized and debug information is removed.
Debug	This represents the Debug build configuration. The code is not optimized and debug information is generated.
All Configurations	Any changes made while this build configuration is selected will be made to all the configurations. This is used as an easy way to specify global settings.
Multiple Configurations	This option functions in basically the same way as the All Configurations option. However, when this option is available and selected, Visual Studio .NET enables you to select the configurations to which you want to apply the global settings.

In Visual Studio .NET, there are several ways to do just about everything and switching from Debug to Release mode is no exception. Figure 42.1 shows the quick way to change from Debug to Release mode. Just select the drop-down list and choose the configuration that you want to use.

42

FIGURE 42.1   You can choose the active build configuration you want very quickly with this option.

You can edit the build configurations, but you cannot change the active build configuration by right-clicking the project and selecting the Properties menu option. This will bring up the Project Properties dialog, as shown in Figure 42.2.

In addition to the methods just described, you can open the Configuration Manager dialog shown in Figure 42.3.

From here, you can select the active build configuration, create your own custom configurations, or edit an existing one, as shown in Figure 42.4.

Although you can debug an application without debug information (the Generate Debugging Information setting turned off), your debugging capabilities will be severely limited. To properly debug an application, it is necessary to generate the debugging information. This allows the debugger to insert the variable names and other helpful information.

The Visual Studio .NET Debugging Environment

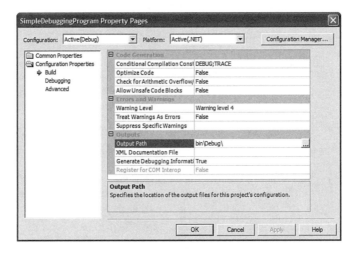

FIGURE 42.2   You can edit the different build configurations from the Project Properties dialog.

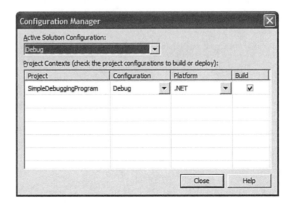

FIGURE 42.3   You can choose the build configuration you
want from the Configuration Manager.

Understanding Syntax and Error Messages

A *syntax error* is a bug, or error, that prevents the compiler from completing its job.
Visual Studio .NET looks at and checks for some syntax errors while you are typing.
When Visual Studio .NET encounters one of these syntax errors, it displays a squiggly line where the syntax error occurred, as shown in Figure 42.5, and adds the error
to the Task List, as in Figure 42.6.

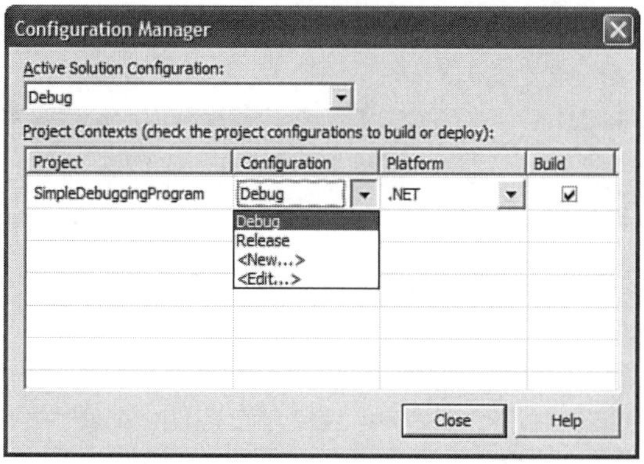

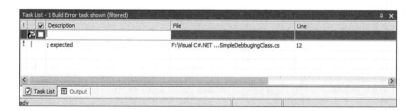

FIGURE 42.4   You can create your own custom
                 configurations using
                 Configuration Manager.

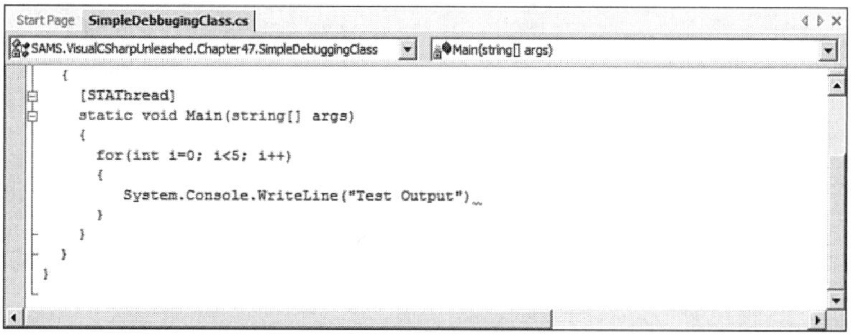

FIGURE 42.5   As indicated by the squiggly line, you can see where the
                 syntax error occurs in the code view.

FIGURE 42.6   You can view all encountered syntax errors in the Task
                 List.

When the compiler encounters a syntax error, it adds an error message to the Task
List, as in Figure 42.6, and the Output window, shown in Figure 42.7.

The Visual Studio .NET Debugging Environment

FIGURE 42.7   You can also see the syntax errors in the Output window.

When reviewing the Output window or Task List, if you want to quickly go to the line that generated the error, you can simply double-click on the error and Visual Studio .NET will place your cursor on the offending line of code, as shown in Figure 42.8.

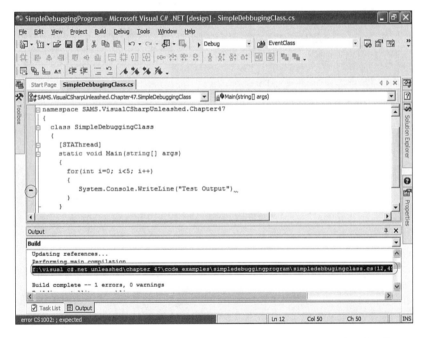

FIGURE 42.8   Double-clicking on the error brings you to the offending line of code.

Understanding the Debugging Tool Windows

As with everything in Visual Studio .NET, there are tool windows for just about everything that must be displayed. In addition to the code window, Visual Studio

.NET provides 12 tool windows just for debugging purposes. This section will list each of these windows and give a short description of each. Most of these windows will be used and explained later in this chapter.

Using the Autos Window

The Autos window displays all the variables for both the current and previous statements. In addition, it will display any return values for a method as well as values returned from methods that were called from that method. Figure 42.9 shows the Autos window.

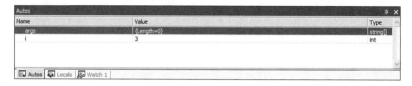

FIGURE 42.9   The Autos tool window.

Using the Locals Window

The Locals window displays local variables. This window is automatically populated when variables come in scope. The variables are removed when they go out of scope. Figure 42.10 shows the Locals window.

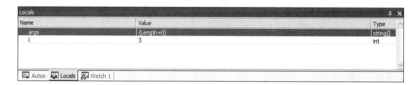

FIGURE 42.10   The Locals tool window.

Using the Watch Window

The Watch window displays variables that you specify. You can add variables to this window by simply dragging and dropping them into this window. You can also click on an empty space in the window grid and type the name of the variable that you want to add. Figure 42.11 shows a Watch window.

Using the This Window

The This window shows the object pointed to by the this pointer. Figure 42.12 shows the This window.

42

The Visual Studio .NET Debugging Environment

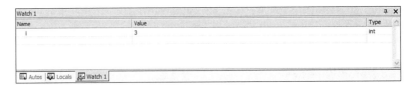

FIGURE 42.11   The Watch tool window.

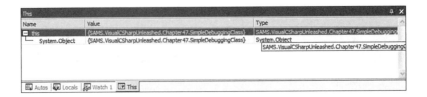

FIGURE 42.12   The This tool window.

Using the Call Stack Window

The Call Stack window displays the functions on the call stack. Figure 42.13 shows the Call Stack window.

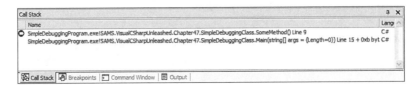

FIGURE 42.13   The Call Stack tool window.

Using the Threads Window

The Threads window displays information about the Threads that are being used by the application. Figure 42.14 shows the Threads window.

FIGURE 42.14   The Threads tool window.

Using the Breakpoints Window

The Breakpoints window displays information about all the breakpoints that are set for an application. Figure 42.15 shows the Breakpoints window.

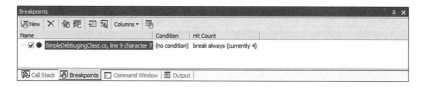

FIGURE 42.15   The Breakpoints tool window.

Using the Command Window

The Command window enables you to enter commands to take place for the currently running application. For example, if you are in a loop in the current program and the loop variable is i, you could enter the command i=0. This would set the i variable to 0. Figure 42.16 shows the Command window.

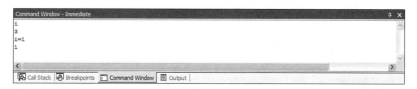

FIGURE 42.16   The Command tool window.

Using the Output Window

In addition to the Output window displaying any compiler errors, it can be used to display trace information or other types of debugging information. Figure 42.17 shows the Output window.

Using the Modules Window

The Modules window displays information about the modules that are used by your application. Figure 42.18 shows the Modules window.

Using the Memory Window

The Memory window displays information about memory used by your application. Figure 42.19 shows the Memory window.

Using the Registers Window

The Registers window displays the contents of each register. Figure 42.20 shows the Registers window.

42

The Visual Studio .NET Debugging Environment

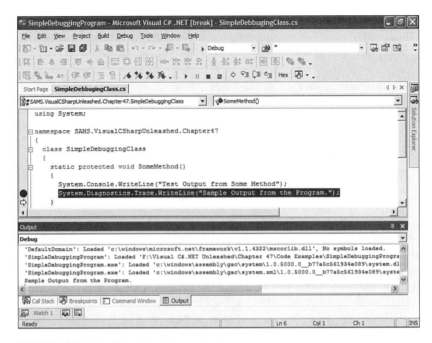

FIGURE 42.17   The Output tool window.

FIGURE 42.18   The Modules tool window.

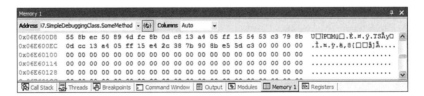

FIGURE 42.19   The Memory tool window.

Navigating the Application

The ability to navigate through an application while debugging is an essential part of the debugging process. Visual Studio .NET offers several commands for this very purpose. Table 42.2 displays the available commands and a brief description of each one.

FIGURE 42.20 The Registers tool window.

TABLE 42.2

Debug Navigation Commands

Command	Description
Step Into	Stepping into a function enables you to execute the next line of code. If the next line of code is a method call, the debugger stops executing when the first line of the method call is reached.
Step Over	Like the Step Into command, the Step Over command executes the next line of code. Unlike the Step Into command, if the next line of code is a method call, the Step Over command executes the method in its entirety.
Step Out	The Step Out command resumes execution until the method returns.
Start	The Start command starts the execution of a program and runs until a breakpoint is reached.
Stop	The Stop command stops the debugging of an application. Note: This command does not always terminate the application process.
Show Next Statement	The Show Next Statement command places the line with the yellow arrow (the current line of execution) in view.

Setting and Using Breakpoints

To debug an application, it is often necessary to stop the execution of that application at a certain point. TO do this, Visual Studio .NET offers breakpoints. When the debugger reaches a valid breakpoint, it stops the execution of that program until you resume the application. To set a breakpoint, click in the area to the left of the line of code at which you want to stop execution. Figure 42.21 shows a breakpoint that has been reached by a debugger.

If you display the Breakpoints window, you will now see the breakpoint that you just set listed in that window. You will also see that it does not have a condition associated with it and it has a hit count of Break Always (Currently 0). To set a condition for this breakpoint, right-click on the breakpoint and select the Properties menu option. This will bring up the Breakpoint Properties dialog shown in Figure 42.22.

The Visual Studio .NET Debugging Environment

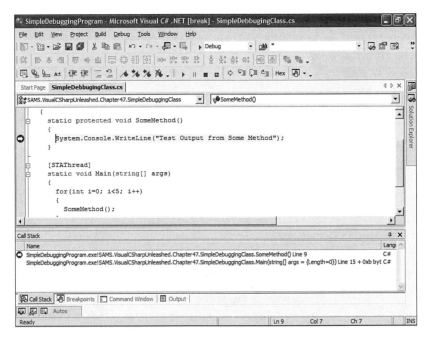

FIGURE 42.21   A valid breakpoint that has been reached by the debugger.

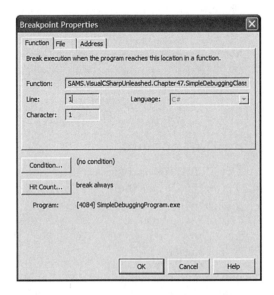

FIGURE 42.22   The Breakpoint Properties
dialog.

From the Breakpoint Properties dialog, you can click on either the Condition button to associate a condition, as in Figure 42.23, or the Hit Count button to associate a hit count condition with this breakpoint.

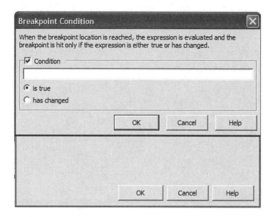

FIGURE 42.23   Associate a condition with a breakpoint through this dialog.

Debugging with Visual Studio .NET

In the next sections, you will learn how to debug the sample application. The sample application contains several syntax errors and a few "features" that the client did not expect. By stepping through and debugging a sample application, you will become familiar with the purpose of the debugger, and learn how to use it to be more productive by creating more stable, reliable, and efficient code.

Debugging an Application

When trying to fix syntax errors, it is not necessary to know what the application is attempting to accomplish. However, when attempting to debug an application, it is helpful, and in most cases a necessity, to know what the application is supposed to do. The following application, Listing 42.1, is a simple program that calculates the average scores in a class. It also prints out the smartest and least smartest person in the class (based upon grades).

LISTING 42.1
Sample Program with Syntax Errors

```
using System;
using System.Collections;
```

LISTING 42.1
Continued

```
namespace SAMS.VisualCSharpUnleashed.Chapter45
{
  class Student
  {
    private string  m_name;
    private double  m_grade;

    public Student(string name, double grade)
    {
      m_name  = name;
      m_grade = grade;
    }

    public double Grade
    {
      get { return m_grade; }
      set { m_grade = value; }
    }

    public string Name
    {
      get { return m_name; }
      set { m_name = value; }
    }
  }

  class SimpleDebuggingClass
  {
    private System.Collections.ArrayList m_list = new
System.Collections.ArrayList();

    protected void CreateStudentList()
    {
      m_list.Add(new Student("Lonny",   100.0));
      m_list.Add(new Student("Richard", 90.0));
      m_list.Add(new Student("Ahmed",   92.5));
      m_list.Add(new Student("Jeff",    75.0));
      m_list.Add(new Student("Neal",    46.8));
      m_list.Add(new Student("Roman",   70.0));
    }

    protected double CalculateAverageGrade()
```

42

LISTING 42.1
Continued

```csharp
{
  double totalScores = 0;

  for(int i=0; i<m_list.Count; i++)
  {
    totalScores += ((Student) m_list[i]).Grade;
  }

  return totalScores / m_list.Count;
}

protected Student GetSmartest()
{
  double highestScore = 0;
  Student result       = null;

  for(int i=0; i<m_list.Count; i++)
  {
    if(highestScore < ((Student) m_list[i]).Grade)
    {
      highestScore = ((Student) m_list[i]).Grade;
      result = (Student) m_list[i];
    }
  }

  return result;
}

protected Student GetLeastSmartest()
{
  double lowestScore  = 0;
  Student result       = null;

  for(int i=0; i<m_list.Count(); i++)
  {
    if(lowestScore > ((Student) m_list[i]).Grade)
    {
      lowestScore = ((Student) m_list[i]).Grade;
      result = (Student) m_list[i];
    }
  }
```

42

Debugging with Visual Studio .NET

LISTING 42.1
Continued

```
      return result;
   }

   [STAThread]
   static void Main(string[] args)
   {
     SimpleDebuggingClass sample = new SimpleDebuggingClass();
     sample.CreateStudentList();

     // Calculate and print the average grade in the class.
     double avgGrade = sample.CalculateAverageGrade()
     System.Console.WriteLine("Average grade in the class is: {0}", avgGrade);

     // Calculate the smartest and "least smartest" student in the class.
     Student smartest      = sample.GetSmartest();
     Student leastSmartest = sample.GetLeastSmartest();

     System.Console.WriteLine("The smartest person in the class is: {0}",
smartest.Name);
     System.Console.WriteLine("The least smartest person in the class is:
        {0}", leastSmartest.Name);

     System.Console.ReadLine();
   }
 }
}
```

When you compile this program you will see, as shown in Figure 42.24, that it generates two syntax errors.

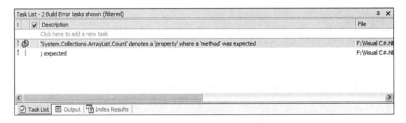

FIGURE 42.24   Two syntax errors generated from the sample program.

If you double-click on the first error, Visual Studio .NET will take you to the offending line of code, as in Figure 42.25. You will notice that this error states that `'System.Collections.ArrayList.Count'` denotes a `'property'` where a `'method'` was expected. This simply means that a method was made out of a property. Remove the `()` from the line:

```
for(int i=0; i<m_list.Count(); i++)
```

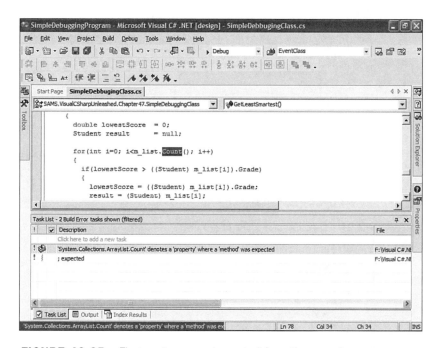

FIGURE 42.25 First syntax error generated from the sample program.

If you double-click on the second error, you will notice that this statement is just missing the semicolon (;) character, as in Figure 42.26. Simply add the semicolon to the end of this line and recompile.

The application should now compile. However, if you run the application, you will notice a more menacing problem. Running the application cause an exception to be thrown, as in Figure 42.27.

Fortunately, if you click the Break button in this message, the debugger places you at the offending line. If you put your cursor over the `leastSmartest` variable, you will notice that it is set to `null`, as shown in Figure 42.28.

Debugging with Visual Studio .NET

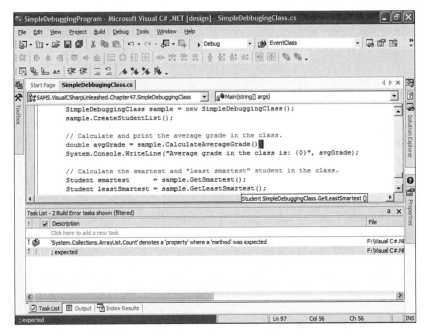

FIGURE 42.26　Second syntax error generated from the sample program.

FIGURE 42.27　Exception thrown from the application.

Now that you know that this is the problem causing the exception, you can start looking at the code where this variable is being set. However, because this is a simple application, there is no way to re-execute the code. When you restart the code, you will want to stop before the variable is set. This will enable you to inspect the process as it is happening. To cause the application to stop, set a breakpoint at the following line:

```
Student leastSmartest = sample.GetLeastSmartest();
```

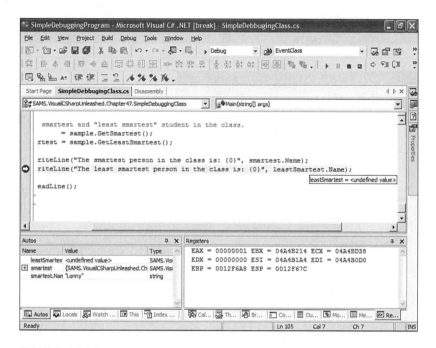

FIGURE 42.28 The offending line of code.

Now run the application. When the debugger reaches this line, it will stop. Next, step into the method call and make the Watch window visible. Add the following variables to the Watch window:

```
(Student) m_list[i]
lowestScore
```

Now step through the loop and inspect the variables, as in Figure 42.29.

Now that you can see the two variables in the Watch window, you will notice that the lowestScore is set to 0.0. Because this was set during initialization, no Student will have a lower grade then this. This means that the leastSmartest Student is always going to be set to null. Set the lowestScore to 100.0 in the initialization and rerun the application. The application now runs without problems. Listing 42.2 contains the corrected version of this application.

Debugging with Visual Studio .NET

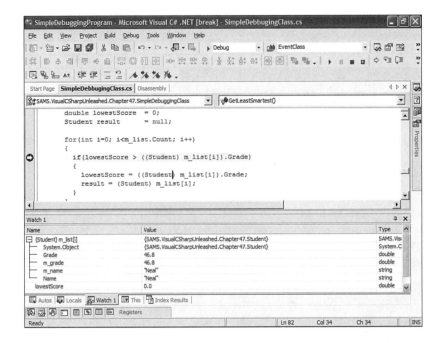

FIGURE 42.29 Inspecting the `GetLeastSmartest()` method.

LISTING 42.2
Corrected Sample Program

```csharp
using System;
using System.Collections;

namespace SAMS.VisualCSharpUnleashed.Chapter45
{
  class Student
  {
    private string  m_name;
    private double  m_grade;

    public Student(string name, double grade)
    {
      m_name  = name;
      m_grade = grade;
    }

    public double Grade
    {
```

LISTING 42.2
Continued

```csharp
      get { return m_grade; }
      set { m_grade = value; }
    }

    public string Name
    {
      get { return m_name; }
      set { m_name = value; }
    }
  }

  class SimpleDebuggingClass
  {
    private System.Collections.ArrayList m_list = new
System.Collections.ArrayList();

    protected void CreateStudentList()
    {
      m_list.Add(new Student("Lonny",    100.0));
      m_list.Add(new Student("Richard", 90.0));
      m_list.Add(new Student("Ahmed",    92.5));
      m_list.Add(new Student("Jeff",      75.0));
      m_list.Add(new Student("Neal",      46.8));
      m_list.Add(new Student("Roman",    70.0));
    }

    protected double CalculateAverageGrade()
    {
      double totalScores = 0;

      for(int i=0; i<m_list.Count; i++)
      {
        totalScores += ((Student) m_list[i]).Grade;
      }

      return totalScores / m_list.Count;
    }

    protected Student GetSmartest()
    {
      double highestScore = 0;
      Student result       = null;
```

42

Debugging with Visual Studio .NET

LISTING 42.2
Continued

```csharp
    for(int i=0; i<m_list.Count; i++)
    {
      if(highestScore < ((Student) m_list[i]).Grade)
      {
        highestScore = ((Student) m_list[i]).Grade;
        result = (Student) m_list[i];
      }
    }

    return result;
  }

  protected Student GetLeastSmartest()
  {
    double lowestScore = 100.0;
    Student result      = null;

    for(int i=0; i<m_list.Count; i++)
    {
      if(lowestScore > ((Student) m_list[i]).Grade)
      {
        lowestScore = ((Student) m_list[i]).Grade;
        result = (Student) m_list[i];
      }
    }

    return result;
  }

  [STAThread]
  static void Main(string[] args)
  {
    SimpleDebuggingClass sample = new SimpleDebuggingClass();
    sample.CreateStudentList();

    // Calculate and print the average grade in the class.
    double avgGrade = sample.CalculateAverageGrade();
    System.Console.WriteLine("Average grade in the class is: {0}", avgGrade);

    // Calculate the smartest and "least smartest" student in the class.
    Student smartest      = sample.GetSmartest();
    Student leastSmartest = sample.GetLeastSmartest();
```

LISTING 42.2
Continued

```
    System.Console.WriteLine("The smartest person in the class is: {0}",
      smartest.Name);
    System.Console.WriteLine("The least smartest person in the class is: {0}",
      leastSmartest.Name);

    System.Console.ReadLine();
  }
 }
}
```

43 Monitoring Your Applications

IN BRIEF

Very often developers need to review what actions are performed at runtime in some part of source code (this need is especially important in the case of complex applications). The simplest way to retrieve this information is by debugging an application step by step and using various features of the Visual Studio.NET IDE, such as watching, quick watching, command windows, local windows, and so on. But this approach provides developers only some information while debugging. Debugging enables you to track down finite pieces of information, single lines of trouble code, and so on.

Another important task is monitoring an application as it runs, and one approach is to write information in some storage (database, file, console, and so forth). In that case, the developer has a full overview of all actions (exceptions, warnings, critical situations, debugging information, and so on) that occurred during the application process execution. The common way of writing and storing auxiliary information during an application process execution is logging.

A logging facility lets an application write out information as it runs, and captures that information for later analysis. The information in the log can be very detailed or very sparse. Examining the log is a useful post-mortem tool, helping you pinpoint when and where a problem occurs for more detailed analysis. Logging facilities are especially handy when debuggers are not available or are too intrusive.

The simplest way to log information is by using `Console.WriteLine()` and `Console.Write()` statements. But this method is very crude and inflexible. The .NET Framework proposes its own mechanism of logging information: tracing, debugging statements and trace listeners.

WHAT YOU NEED

RECOMMENDED SOFTWARE	.NET Framework Visual Studio .NET
RECOMMENDED HARDWARE	.NET-enabled desktop client
SKILLS REQUIRED	C# coding

MONITORING YOUR APPLICATIONS AT A GLANCE

Debugging and Tracing Statements 872

Trace Listeners	876	Custom Trace Listeners	885
Trace Switches	882		

Debugging and Tracing Statements

Two important programming operations that help you debug and monitor applications are debugging and tracing. Debugging enables you to observe and correct programming errors. Tracing is a form of debugging that enables you to keep track of the health and sanitary conditions of our applications. Whereas debugging provides you with the ability to examine the state of data at any given line of code, tracing enables you to record information from events as they occur. Tracing is an extremely powerful feature and should not be ignored as a potential tool not only for debugging, but also for providing information on test systems during load tests, and much more.

The .NET Framework provides built-in support for various tracing mechanisms. In legacy languages and in COM, there are no facilities already written for you; traditionally, you had to write your own logging, tracing, and debugging code.

In .NET, a *trace listener* is an object that receive the trace output and redirects it to a location that is described in the listener's configuration. You could configure a trace listener to output information; for example, into a window in the IDE, a file, the event log, a SQL Server database, and so on.

A trace listener is just that: a listener. It listens for information from your application, and then sends that information to whatever persistence medium you've chosen. In a typical application, your code makes use of the Trace class and writes information. The listener hears the information arrive on the listener, and then forwards it to the persistence medium using configured rules. Using this process, you can trace any information, such as object instantiation, database operations, exceptions, user authentication, and much more.

All tracing-related interfaces, classes, structures, enumerations, and other languages' constructions are contained in the System.Diagnostics namespace. This namespace contains two classes, called Trace and Debug, which are used for writing errors and other application information to some persistence format. These classes are helpful during development (to output debug messages and so on) and after deployment (to output performance-related issues and so forth).

When you create a new project, you could define the DEBUG symbol to enable output with the Debug class and the TRACE symbol to enable output with the Trace class. If you create a project in Visual Studio .NET, its Debug version already has these symbols defined (see Figure 43.1).

43

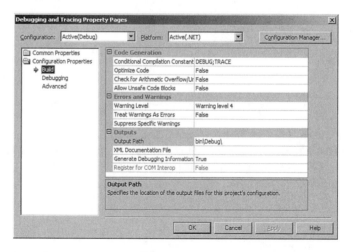

FIGURE 43.1 Debug symbols.

Debugging and Tracing Statements

There are several predefined trace listeners in the `System.Diagnostics` namespace. The default trace listener is `System.Diagnostics.DefaultTraceListener`. The `Write` and `WriteLine` methods of this class route the tracing information to the `OutputDebugString` and to the `Log` method of the attached debugger. Also, the .NET Framework contains a mechanism called *trace switches*. A trace switch is a variable that contains a value that helps you configure an application's debugging from an outside process. You could set values of trace switches outside of an application (in a configuration file), so you don't have to recompile each time the application's executable code changes this value. The only place you have to change the value is in the XML configuration file (`.config`). To be more precise, trace switches are simple objects that can be controlled externally through the application configuration files.

The code in Listing 43.1 uses the `Trace` and `Debug` classes to write log information.

LISTING 43.1
A Simple Example of Using the `Trace` and `Debug` Classes

```
using System;
using System.Diagnostics;
namespace DebuggingTracing {
        class DebuggingTracing {
                [STAThread]
                static void Main(string[] args) {
                        Trace.WriteLine("Some Trace information");
                        Debug.Indent();
                        Debug.WriteLine("Indented Debug information");
                        Trace.WriteLine("Indented Trace information");
                        Trace.Unindent();
                        Debug.WriteLine("Some Debug information");
                }
        }
}
```

This example uses the `WriteLine`, `Indent`, and `Unindent` methods of the `Debug` and `Trace` classes **1**. All log information will be written to the .NET Framework IDE's console. This is made possible by using the default trace listener: `System.Diagnostics.DefaultTraceListener`.

The following is a list of the common methods used in tracing:

▶ `WriteLine`—Enables you to write some information to the log and moves the cursor to the next line

▶ Unindent—Decreases current level of indention

▶ Indent—Increases current level of indention

You also could use the following methods of these classes for log writing:

▶ Write—Enables you to write some information to the log without moving the cursor to the next line.

▶ WriteIf—Very similar to the previous function, but uses condition. If condition is true, log information will be written into data storage. Otherwise, the information will be ignored.

▶ WriteLineIf—Enables you to write some information to the log and moves the cursor to the next line by using condition. The purpose of condition is the same as in the WriteIf function.

To test how Listing 43.1 works, you could start to debug your application by using the Debug/Step Over command (see Figure 43.2).

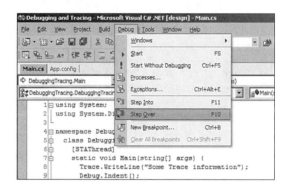

FIGURE 43.2 Stepping over code.

43

Listing 43.2 provides you with tracing information (see Figure 43.3).

LISTING 43.2
Trace of the Example in Listing 43.1

```
Some Trace information
    Indented Debug information
    Indented Trace information
Some Debug information
```

Debugging and Tracing Statements

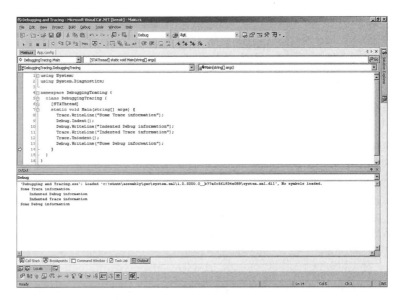

FIGURE 43.3   Trace information.

NOTE

There is a very important point in using `Trace` and `Debug` classes: If you change the compilation mode to Release, all the methods on the `Debug` class simply will be ignored. As mentioned earlier, the `Trace` class performs tracing only when the compilation symbol `TRACE` has been defined. Likewise, `Debug` calls are performed only when the `DEBUG` symbol has been defined. For information on which configurations support `Debug` and `Trace`, examine your project's configuration settings.

Trace Listeners

As mentioned earlier, trace listeners are objects that receive the trace information, store it, and then route it to its final target (file, event log, database, and so on). The final target of the tracing information is decided by the trace listener.

There are several predefined trace listeners in .NET:

- `DefaultTraceListener`

- `TextWriterTraceListener`

- `EventLogTraceListener`

All trace listeners are derived from the abstract `TraceListener` class. This class declares the methods that each trace listener should implement. If you want to inherit from this class, you must at least implement the `Write` and `WriteLine` methods.

Both the `Trace` and the `Debug` class have a property called `Listeners`, which holds a reference to a collection of listeners. The collection object is of type `TraceListenerCollection` and represents a collection of type `TraceListener`. That means trace information can be consumed by more than one listener and those listeners have the full control on where to direct the tracing information.

The `Trace` and `Debug` classes share the same `TraceListenerCollection` object. Therefore, if you add a listener to a `Trace` object, it will also be available to a `Debug` object and vice versa.

All trace listeners have the following functions. Their functionality is the same except that the target media for the tracing output is determined by the trace listener.

- ▶ `Fail`—Outputs the specified text with the call stack

- ▶ `Write`—Outputs the specified text

- ▶ `WriteLine`—Outputs the specified text and moves the cursor to the next line

- ▶ `Flush`—Flushes the output buffer to the target media

- ▶ `Close`—Closes the output stream in order not to receive the tracing/debugging output

The `DefaultTraceListener` is the default trace listener that is added to the `TraceListenerCollection` object of the `Trace` and `Debug` classes. You don't have to manually add this listener into the Listeners list in a configuration file. The `Fail` method displays a message box provided that the application is running in user-interface mode. This class redirects all output generated by `Trace` and `Debug` classes to the console of the .NET IDE. If it's necessary to use other target media, you must use another trace listener (predefined or your own).

`TextWriterTraceListener` redirects trace output to an instance of the `TextWriter` class or to any object that is a `Stream` class, such as a log file, network stream, or console.

The first step that should be done is adding an `App.config` (application configuration file) to your project. You can add it by choosing the File, Add New Item menu item and selecting the Application Configuration File item in the list that appears (see Figure 43.4).

Then add the XML fragment in Listing 43.3 into the `App.config` configuration XML file.

43

Debugging and Tracing Statements

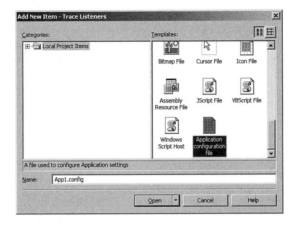

FIGURE 43.4   Adding a configuration file.

LISTING 43.3
Example of Registration of Listener in the Application's Configuration XML File

```
<system.diagnostics>
  <trace autoflush="true">
   <listeners>
    <remove name="Default"/>
    <add name="TextWriterListener"
       type="System.Diagnostics.TextWriterTraceListener"
initializeData="trace.log"/>
   </listeners>
  </trace>
 </system.diagnostics>
```

The following section briefly describes the tags used in the configuration section above. The definitions of the XML elements are as contained in the MSDN Library for the .NET Framework.

- ▸ <system.diagnostics>—Specifies trace listeners that collect, store, and route messages and the level where a trace switch is set.

- ▸ <trace>—Contains listeners that collect, store, and route tracing messages.

- ▸ <listeners>—Specifies a listener that collects, stores, and routes messages.

- ▸ <remove>—Removes a listener from the Listeners collection.

- ▸ <add>—Adds a listener to the Listeners collection. This tag has the following attributes:

  name—Specifies the name of the listener.

type—Specifies the type of the listener. When specifying the type string, you need to follow the rules set out for specifying fully qualified type names, such as specifying the assembly, version, and culture information. For more information on this, consult the MSDN Library.

initializeData—The string passed to the constructor for the specified class.

In the preceding XML, the default Trace Listener has been removed and the predefined TextWriterTraceListener (called TextWriterListener) has been added. Also we have initialized this listener with the name of the file (trace.log) to which information will be written.

After you've run the application, you can find the trace.log file in the folder where the application's execution file is located.

> **NOTE**
>
> You can define several similar listeners in the configuration file. If a developer defines several TextWriterTraceListeners, all log information will be written in all files that are mentioned in these listeners. For example, if you register another TextWriterTraceListener with the initializeData attribute set to the value "another.log", all output information will be written in both the trace.log and the another.log file. So, you could direct information to several targets simultaneously.

43

The generated content of trace.log is the following:

```
Some Trace information
  Indented Debug information
  Indented Trace information
Some Debug information
```

There is another way to use TextWriterTraceListener, which is discussed following the source code example in Listing 43.4.

LISTING 43.4
Using TextWriterTraceListener

```
using System;
using System.IO;
using System.Diagnostics;
namespace AnotherTraceListeners {
      class AnotherTraceListeners {
            [STAThread]
            static void Main(string[] args) {
                  FileStream someStream =
```

Debugging and Tracing Statements

LISTING 43.4
Continued

```
                              new FileStream("trace.log", FileMode.OpenOrCreate);
            TextWriterTraceListener traceListener =
                new TextWriterTraceListener(someStream);
            Trace.Listeners.Add(traceListener);
            Debug.WriteLine("Some Debug information");
            Trace.WriteLine("Some Trace information");
            Trace.Flush();
            someStream.Close();
        }
    }
}
```

This example explicitly creates an instance of TextWriterTraceListener and initializes it with an instance of the FileStream class. This listener is registered by using the Trace.Listeners.Add() method. As mentioned earlier, you could initialize TextWriterTraceListener with all stream classes. Our FileStream instance is initialized with the filename equal to trace.log (with open or create mode). So, after the calling of some write method of the Trace or Debug class, all log information will be redirected through the trace listener to the FileStream class's instance. It will write this information into the trace.log file (the location of this file is the same as the location of the application's execution file).

43

> **NOTE**
>
> You are allowed to register several trace listeners that are initialized with different target media. In that way, log information could be written in several destinations simultaneously.

EventLogTraceListener is used to redirect tracing and debug information to the Windows event log. One of the most important benefits of this class is that it can even output tracing and debugging information to the event log of a remote computer. This makes this class useful for machines that do not support the event log, such as Microsoft Windows Me, Microsoft Windows 98, and so forth.

Before using this class for writing tracing or debugging information to the event log, you must associate it with an event log. For that, you should use the third constructor of this class for passing the name of the event source. Doing so will automatically associate it to that event source. Listing 43.5 shows how to use EventLogTraceListener.

LISTING 43.5
Using `EventLogTraceListener`

```
using System;
using System.Diagnostics;
namespace EventLogTraceListenerSample {
        class EventLogTraceListenerSample {
                [STAThread]
                static void Main(string[] args) {
                        EventLogTraceListener traceListener =
                          new EventLogTraceListener("EventLogTraceListenerSample");
                        Trace.Listeners.Add(traceListener);
                        Debug.WriteLine("Some Debug information");
                        Trace.WriteLine("Some Trace information");
                        Trace.Flush();
                }
        }
}
```

After execution of this code, you could see two new records in the event log (see Figure 43.5).

43

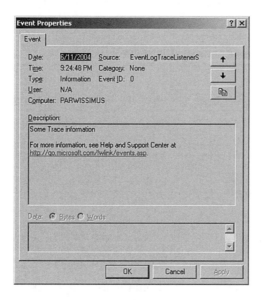

FIGURE 43.5   Two new records in the event log.

Trace Switches

You've reviewed how to use the `Trace` and `Debug` classes for outputting log information. Also, you've seen how to redirect this information into some persistence mechanism by using trace listeners. But you haven't yet seen how to manage the tracing behavior of an application after it is in production.

.NET enables us to manage the tracing behavior of an application with the help of trace switches. These objects can be controlled by an application's configuration file, eventually eliminating the need to change, compile, and distribute your code each time you want to change the tracing behavior. The main idea is to manage application tracing only at the configuration file level, without recompiling the source code.

Trace switches are always assigned a name and description. The name of the switch object is important because it is used to look up the corresponding entry in the `.config` file. There are two types of trace switches: `BooleanSwitch` and `TraceSwitch`. Both are explained in detail in the following sections.

`BooleanSwitch` supports just two modes: `true` (enabled or on) and `false` (disabled or off).

If you want to use `BooleanSwitch` in your code, you have to create an instance of it in the source code. You have to set the name of `BooleanSwitch` that is equal to one of the names of the switches that are registered in your `.config` file. If an instance of switch in your code has a name that is different from the name registered in the configuration file, this switch will be disabled by default. Listing 43.6 shows part of a configuration file that defines a trace switch.

LISTING 43.6

Example of Registration of Trace Switch in the Application's Configuration XML File

```xml
<system.diagnostics>
        <switches>
                <add name="SomeBooleanSwitch" value="1" />
        </switches>
</system.diagnostics>
```

The preceding XML code contains several predefined tags (some of them have already been discussed):

- `<switches>`—Specifies a set of switches are available in the application.

- `<remove>`—Removes a switch from the `switches` set.

- `<add>`—Adds a switch to the `switches` set. This tag has the following attributes:

  name—Specifies the name of the switch (this name should be used in your source code).

value—Specifies the value of the switch. This attribute should be an integer. If value is zero, the switch will be disabled; otherwise, the switch will be enabled.

After you've defined a switch in the configuration file, you can refer to it and query its status in the source code. Look over the example in Listing 43.7.

LISTING 43.7
BooleanSwitch Example

```
using System;
using System.Diagnostics;
namespace BooleanSwitchSample {
    class BooleanSwitchSample {
            [STAThread]
            static void Main(string[] args) {
                    BooleanSwitch booleanSwitch = new BooleanSwitch("SomeBooleanSwitch",
"BooleanSwitch example");
                    Trace.WriteLineIf(booleanSwitch.Enabled, "Some Trace information");
                    Debug.WriteLineIf(!booleanSwitch.Enabled, "Some Debug informa-
tion");
            }
    }
}
```

In Listing 43.7, we create an instance of the BooleanSwitch class by using a constructor with two parameters. The first parameter contains the name of the switch. As mentioned earlier, this name should match one of the names registered in the configuration file. The second parameter contains a description of the switch.

After the instantiation of the BooleanSwitch, we use the WriteLineIf method of the Trace and Debug classes. In the configuration file (refer to Listing 43.6), we registered the SomeBooleanSwitch switch with its value equal to 1. So, our switch is enabled. Because of this, only the Trace.WriteLineIf method will be performed. The Debug.WriteLineIf method's invocation will be ignored.

The following section explains how to use the second trace switch, called TraceSwitch.

The TraceSwitch class has more to offer than the simple BooleanSwitch class. TraceSwitch provides support for multiple levels instead of the simple on/off control offered by the BooleanSwitch class. TraceSwitch works with the following tracing levels:

43

Debugging and Tracing Statements

- Off (0)—Outputs no messages to trace listeners

- Error (1)—Outputs only error messages to trace listeners

- Warning (2)—Outputs error and warning messages to trace listeners

- Info (3)—Outputs informational, warning, and error messages to Trace Listeners

- Verbose (4)—Outputs all messages to trace listeners

An instance of the TraceSwitch class is constructed just like the BooleanSwitch object. Tracing is enabled for a TraceSwitch object through the Level property. When you set the Level property of a switch to a particular level (one of the values from the preceding list), it includes all levels from the indicated level down. For example, if you set a TraceSwitch's Level property to TraceLevel.Info, all the lower levels, from TraceLevel.Error to TraceLevel.Warning, will be included.

In addition, notice that the TraceSwitch class exposes several properties that give you the ability to determine the current level of the trace switch:

- TraceError—Gets a value indicating whether the Level is set to Error

- TraceWarning—Gets a value indicating whether the Level is set to Warning

- TraceInfo—Gets a value indicating whether the Level is set to Info

- TraceVerbose—Gets a value indicating whether the Level is set to Verbose

- Level—Gets or sets the trace level that specifies the messages to output for tracing and debugging

Before you review a code example that shows how to use TraceSwitch, you should see how to register TraceSwitch in the application's configuration file, as in Listing 43.8.

LISTING 43.8

Example of Registration of Trace Switch in the Application's Configuration XML File

```
<system.diagnostics>
      <switches>
            <add name="SomeTraceSwitch" value="2" />
      </switches>
</system.diagnostics>
```

In Listing 43.8, we have registered a trace switch called SomeTraceSwitch with a level of 2 (TraceLevel.Warning). So, all informational and verbose messages will be ignored by trace listeners using this trace switch.

43

Now examine the code in Listing 43.9, which instantiates TraceSwitch with name equal to SomeTraceSwitch (which is registered in the configuration file).

LISTING 43.9
TraceSwitch Example

```
using System;
using System.Diagnostics;
namespace TraceSwitchSample {
   class TraceSwitchSample {
        [STAThread]
        static void Main(string[] args) {
            TraceSwitch traceSwitch =
        new TraceSwitch("SomeTraceSwitch", "TraceSwitch example");
            Trace.WriteLineIf(traceSwitch.TraceWarning,
        "Some Warning message");
            Trace.WriteLineIf(traceSwitch.TraceError, "Some Error message");
            Trace.WriteLineIf(traceSwitch.TraceInfo, "Some Info message");
          }
        }
}
```

The preceding example uses a TraceSwitch called SomeTraceSwitch and Level (refer to the earlier configuration file) equal to 2 (Warning). To filter messages that should be passed to the trace listener, you should use WriteLineIf or WriteIf method of the Trace or Debug class. (You also could perform a simple if statement before calling Write statements of these classes.)

We are trying to output three message types: error, warning, and information. In each message, we check the level of the trace switch. Because we have registered the trace switch with the level equal to Warning, only the first two messages will be passed to the trace listener. The first message (with level checking equal to Info) will be ignored.

Custom Trace Listeners

Trace listeners provided by .NET are enough for most applications. But you might need to redirect output information to some other target media that is not supported by .NET's trace listeners. In such a situation, you should create your own trace listener.

.NET provides the ability to write your own trace listeners in the form of the TraceListener class. Every trace listener is inherited from this class. Therefore, to implement your own trace listener, you must inherit your trace listener's class from this class.

43

Debugging and Tracing Statements

The `TraceListener` class provides many virtual and abstract methods. An inheritor of this class should implement at least the `Write` and `WriteLine` methods. The `Write` and `WriteLine` methods are overloaded. The following is a list of all the overloaded versions of the `Write` method:

```
public override void Write(string message)
public override void Write(object o)
public override void Write(string message, string category)
public override void Write(object o, string category)
```

There is one-to-one mapping between the overloaded methods of `Write` and `WriteLine`. The `Write`, `WriteIf`, `WriteLine`, and `WriteLineIf` methods of the `Trace` and `Debug` classes are also overloaded and have the same four versions of each of these methods. Because methods of the `Trace` and `Debug` classes call `Write` and `WriteLine` methods on trace listeners, `TraceListener` has these overloaded methods.

So, to implement you own trace listener, you should just create a class that is inherited from the `TraceListener` class and implement the `Write` and `WriteLine` methods (and all overloaded versions of these methods). Listing 43.10 shows how to create a custom trace listener. This example creates a trace listener that displays all messages in the modal message box. Implementations of `Write` and `WriteLine` methods are the same.

43

LISTING 43.10
Example of Custom Trace Listener Creation

```
using System;
using System.Windows.Forms;
using System.Diagnostics;
namespace CustomTraceListener {
        public class MessageBoxTraceListener : TraceListener {
                public override void Write(string message) {
                        WriteMessage(message);
                }
                public override void Write(object o) {
                        WriteMessage(o);
                }
                public override void Write(string message, string category) {
                        WriteMessage(message, category);
                }
```

LISTING 43.10
Continued

```csharp
        public override void Write(object o, string category) {
                WriteMessage(o, category);
        }
        public override void WriteLine(string message) {
                WriteMessage(message);
        }
        public override void WriteLine(object o) {
                WriteMessage(o);
        }
        public override void WriteLine(string message, string category) {
                WriteMessage(message, category);
        }
        public override void WriteLine(object o, string category) {
                WriteMessage(o, category);
        }
        private void WriteMessage(object message) {
                WriteMessage(message.ToString(), "");
        }
        private void WriteMessage(object message, string category) {
                MessageBox.Show(message.ToString(), category);
        }
    }
    class CustomTraceListener {
        [STAThread]
        static void Main(string[] args) {
                MessageBoxTraceListener
    messageBoxTraceListener = new MessageBoxTraceListener();
                Trace.Listeners.Add(messageBoxTraceListener);
                Trace.Write("Some Trace information", "Some Category");
                Debug.Write("Some Debug information");
        }
    }
}
```

43

The preceding example declares the MessageBoxTraceListener class, which redirects all log information to message boxes. The example also contains a CustomTraceListener test class. If you run this application, you will see the results shown in Figure 43.6.

Debugging and Tracing Statements

FIGURE 43.6   Results of the sample application.

Summary

In this chapter, you have learned about debugging and tracing of applications in .NET and how to use them. We discussed .NET's main toolkit for working with debugging and tracing. Also, you learned how to redirect log information to different target media with help of a trace listener. The rules of trace listeners' configuration were also described.

You learned what trace switches are and how to configure debugging and tracing of an application with the help of trace switches without requiring recompilation of source code on the level of the application's configuration file.

43

44 Instrumenting Your Application

IN BRIEF

This chapter explains the reasons for and how to instrument a .NET application. In this chapter, you will learn why you instrument your application. You will learn the different methods of instrumentation that are provided in the Windows operating system. Finally, you will learn how to create an application that utilizes the Enterprise Instrumentation Framework (EIF) to enable your application to provide instrumentation services by utilizing the Windows event log, Windows event trace, and/or Windows Management Instrumentation (WMI).

WHAT YOU NEED

RECOMMENDED SOFTWARE	Windows XP Professional or Windows 2000 Professional SP3 or higher .NET Framework v1.0 or higher Visual Studio.NET Enterprise Architect, Enterprise Developer, or Professional Edition C# .NET environment Enterprise Instrumentation Framework WMI
RECOMMENDED HARDWARE	.NET-enabled desktop client
SKILLS REQUIRED	C# coding

INSTRUMENTING YOUR APPLICATION AT A GLANCE

Instrumenting Applications	**890**		
Introduction to Instrumenting an Application	891	Examining the Debug and Trace Classes	895
Methods of Instrumentation	892	Windows Management Instrumentation	897
Windows Event Log	892		
Enterprise Instrumentation Framework	**902**		
Introducing the EIF	902	Elements of the EIF	903
Enterprise Instrumentation Framework Requirements	903	Configuring EIF	906
Summary	**907**		
Further Reading	**907**		

Instrumenting Applications

Since the inception of computer programs, there have been bugs and performance-challenged applications. For developers, this is one of the reasons that they have jobs. For operations, this is a reason to blame developers. The problem is that each job category of the people responsible for the application seems to have a different language and interpretation of the events that led up to someone claiming that there is a bug or performance problem with the application. For some people, the response is always, "It just broke. I was sitting there minding my own business and it just broke." For others it is "I did A, B, and C and it started to perform very slowly." Unfortunately, when you start investigating the problem, you discover that they didn't do A, B, and C, but they did D, E, and F. Not only does this lead to a lot of frustration, but also to quite a bit of wasted time. Fortunately, you have an option. You can build in functionality to report on the health, performance, and events of a system. This is known as *instrumenting an application*.

Introduction to Instrumenting an Application

The phrase *instrumenting your application* refers to the act of modifying it to generate internal events and metrics. By instrumenting your application, you are adding the ability for people or processes outside the application to determine its health, performance, and events. This can be an important feature when attempting to debug your application; determining potential areas of improvement and performance bottlenecks; logging of transactions; and formulating the sequence of events of an application that is either in development or production. There are five basic reasons to instrument your application:

- ▶ Provide health-monitoring information

- ▶ Analyze potential performance problems

- ▶ Profile runtime operations

- ▶ Diagnose areas of opportunity or bugs

- ▶ Configure applications

44

Instrumenting Versus External Monitoring

There are two basic types of application monitoring that can be performed: external monitoring techniques and instrumenting. When using external monitoring techniques, you are essentially using some form of query to check the metrics of an application. For example, consider the Task Manager. In the Task Manager, you can check to see which processes are running, how much CPU time they are utilizing, how much memory they have allocated, and if they are still responding (application hang). On a basic level, this is useful. However, what if the Task Manager asserts that an application is using an exorbitant amount of memory and is utilizing 100% of the CPU? After seeing this information, the natural next questions are "What is the application doing? What steps were being executed?" The answer to both questions is that you can't determine an answer from the Task Manager. The information simply isn't available. When you rely on an external program to monitor your application, you are completely at its mercy.

Instrumenting Applications

When you instrument your application, you are taking control. You specify which metrics need to be reported and in what fashion. You can also specify specific tracing routines that should be executed and how they will be made available to the end user. Simply because you have more control over the content and method of reporting system health, performance problems, critical failures, and general metrics, instrumenting an application is superior to using external monitoring techniques.

Methods of Instrumentation

There are many methods with which to instrument your application. You can choose to use the Windows event log, the Windows trace log, Windows Management Instrumentation, or you could use a custom technique for relaying you metric information to the end user. With the exception of creating a custom instrumentation technique (which is beyond the scope of this book), the next section will focus on the three more common techniques of instrumentation: Windows event log, Windows trace log, and Windows Management Instrumentation.

Windows Event Log

The Windows event log, shown in Figure 44.1, is one of the easier ways to instrument your application. It enables you to write information to a log that is maintained by the Windows operating system. Users can retrieve and display the event log at a later date and time.

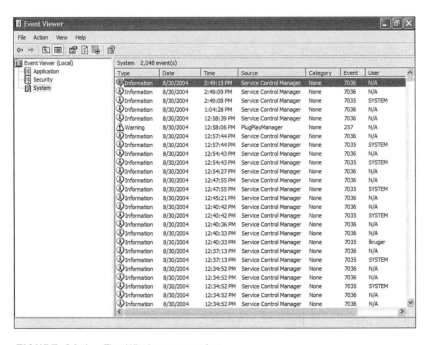

FIGURE 44.1   The Windows event log.

Using C#, it is easy to write information to the Windows event log. The .NET Framework provides an `EventLog` class that enables you to easily create and delete logs, add log entries, read entries, and respond to log entries. When writing to the event log, you must specify an event source. This registers your application as a valid provider of log entries for that log.

TIP

Because the Windows event log can store only a limited number of entries, it is recommended that the Windows event log be used only for lower-frequency events such as errors, warnings, and high-level audit information.

Listing 44.1 shows a simple application that checks to see whether a log exists. If a log doesn't already exist, the application creates one. If a log does exist, the application registers an entry and exits **1**. Although this application creates a log on the local machine, it can easily be modified to create and write to a machine at a different location by simply adding the machine name to the following lines:

```
if(!EventLog.SourceExists("EventLogDemo", "Enter Machine Name Here"))
```

and

```
EventLog.CreateEventSource("EventLogSource", "EventLogDemo", "Enter Machine Name
Here");
```

LISTING 44.1
Simple Event Log Demo

```csharp
using System;
using System.Diagnostics;

namespace Sams.VisualCSharpDotNetUnleashed.WindowsEventLogDemo
{
  /// <summary>
  /// Summary description for Class1.
  /// </summary>
  class EventLogDemo
  {
    /// <summary>
    /// The main entry point for the application.
    /// </summary>
    [STAThread]
    static void Main(string[] args)
    {
```

Instrumenting Applications

LISTING 44.1
Continued

```
// Check to see if the log already exists.
if(!EventLog.SourceExists("EventLogDemo"))
{
    // Create the eventlog on the local machine.  By specifying
    // a third parameter, you can create the log on a different machine.
    EventLog.CreateEventSource("EventLogSource", "EventLogDemo");
    Console.WriteLine("A new event log was created.");
}

// Create an instance of an EventLog.
EventLog eventLog = new EventLog();
// Assign the source to the event log.
eventLog.Source = "EventLogSource";

// Write a log entry.
eventLog.WriteEntry("This is a sample log entry", EventLogEntryType.
Information);
        }
    }
}
```

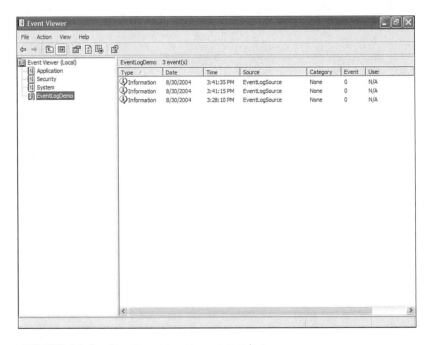

FIGURE 44.2   The EventLogDemo event log.

Examining the `Debug` and `Trace` Classes

As previously stated, the phrase *instrumenting an application* refers to modifying an application to monitor or measure the level of its performance and to diagnose errors. In the world of programming, this means that the application has the capability to incorporate code tracing, debugging, performance counters, and event logs. Provided in .NET are the `Trace` and `Debug` classes. These classes give you the means to monitor your application's performance during both development and after deployment.

Adding Debug and Trace Code to Your Application

Adding debug and trace code to your applications is simple. For a debug statement, you simply add the following:

```
System.Diagnositics.Debug.WriteLine("This is a Debug Statement!");
```

For a trace statement, there is a minor change:

```
System.Diagnositics.Trace.WriteLine("This is a Debug Statement!");
```

Of course, the previous statements are at a basic level. There are several overloaded methods of both the `Debug` and `Trace` classes that enable you to add variables and format them to their proper usage. When testing your application, you can build your application with the `DEBUG` and/or `TRACE` conditional attributes turned on. This enables you to view both `Debug` and `Trace` statements. When you deploy the application, simply recompile the application with the `DEBUG` and/or `TRACE` conditional attributes turned off. This instructs the compiler not to include the debug and trace code in the final executable.

44

> **TIP**
>
> To view debug and/or trace code, you must instruct the compiler to include this code in your executable. This is done by setting the `DEBUG` and/or `TRACE` conditional attributes to true. Visual Studio .NET includes both the `TRACE` and `DEBUG` conditional attributes. This enables you to specify whether to include `Debug`, `Trace`, or both in your executable.

Trace Switches

In addition to tracing of your code, it is sometimes desirable to filter out some of the messages. For example, if you have an application that is monitoring the status of a bit on an I/O port and you are polling the bit every millisecond, you might want to see the results of all the individual reads, or you might want to see the status only when the bit changes. After all, if you view the status every millisecond, you will have 1,000 statements every second. Fortunately, .NET provides trace switches to aid in filtering trace statements. With trace switches, you can enable, disable, and filter tracing output. The best part about trace switches is that they are configurable from the .config file. In .NET, there are two basic types of trace switches: BooleanSwitch and TraceSwitch.

BooleanSwitch

The BooleanSwitch acts as an on/off switch. To use the BooleanSwitch, simply instantiate a BooleanSwitch variable and check the Enabled property. For example, the following code snippet checks the enabled property and outputs the statement (if enabled) to the console:

```
static BooleanSwitch booleanSwitch = new BooleanSwitch(
"Some Category", "Some Module");

static public void SomeMethod(string location)
{
   // Code omitted for brevity.
   if(booleanSwitch.Enabled)
      Console.WriteLine("Error occurred at " + location);
}
```

TraceSwitch

The TraceSwitch class provides multilevel switching to control trace and debug output from your application. As previously stated, the TraceSwitch is configurable from the .config file. As a general rule, trace switching is generally deployed disabled. It is only when a problem occurs, or you need more information about what is happening in your application, that you would enable this functionality. Before you can use a switch, you must first create an instance of a switch from a BooleanSwitch, TraceSwitch, or a custom switch class.

The following code snippet demonstrates the basic use of TraceSwitch:

```
static TraceSwitch traceSwitch = new TraceSwitch("Some Category ",
"Some Application");

static public void TraceSwitchMethod()
{
  // Output this message if the TraceSwitch level is set to Error or higher.
  if(traceSwitch.TraceError)
    Console.WriteLine("A trace message.");

  // Output this message if the TraceSwitch level is set to Verbose.
  if(traceSwitch.TraceVerbose)
    Console.WriteLine("Another trace message.");
}
```

For detailed information about using debug statements, trace statements, and trace listeners to instrument your application, please see Chapter 43, "Monitoring Your Application."

Windows Management Instrumentation

Windows Management Instrumentation (WMI) is Microsoft's implementation of the Web-Based Enterprise Management (WBEM) initiative. Included in the .NET namespace `System.Management.Instrumentation`, WMI has interfaces to languages such as C++, HTML, ODBC, and Visual Basic. In the following section, you will learn the basics of instrumenting an application through WMI.

WMI Architecture

WMI uses the Common Information Model (CIM) to represent managed components such as applications, systems, devices, and networks. As shown in Figure 44.3, WMI consists of a management infrastructure (Common Information Model Object Manager [CIMOM] Repository and CIM Object Manager) and WMI providers. The CIMOM provides applications with uniform access to management functions and the WMI providers are components that serve as mediators between the CIMOM and managed objects.

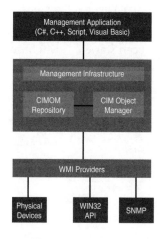

FIGURE 44.3   WMI architecture.

The WMI architecture provides two features that enable you to easily write powerful applications. The first is that the WMI is extensible. It allows you to seamlessly add providers to the architecture. The second helpful feature is that WMI hides the details of specific instrumentation sources from the CIMOM and the CIMOM in turn hides the capabilities of specific providers from a WMI-based client application. This

Instrumenting Applications

allows the CIMOM to present a uniform set of capabilities (queries, method execution, events, and updates).

Listing 44.2 shows a basic WMI-instrumented application. It demonstrates how to expose a class to a WMI client application and fire an event. To run and view the capabilities of the application follow these steps:

1. Compile and start the console application as in Figure 44.4.

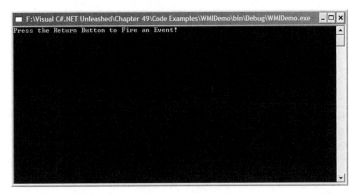

FIGURE 44.4   Run the console application, but don't press a key until later in the steps.

2. After the application has been started, it will be available to be viewed in the Visual Studio .NET Server Explorer Add-On.

3. Switch to the Server Explorer View, as shown in Figure 44.5.

FIGURE 44.5   The Server Explorer view.

4. Select and expand the Servers, *Your Computer name*, and Management Classes nodes.

5. Right-click on the Management Classes node and select the Add Classes menu item, as shown in Figure 44.6.

FIGURE 44.6   Select the Add Classes menu item.

6. In the Add Classes dialog shown in Figure 44.7, search for and add the `WMIDemoProvider` class and click the OK button.

FIGURE 44.7   Search for the `WMIDemoProvider` class in the Add Classes dialog.

Instrumenting Applications

7. In the Server Explorer, select the `WMIDemoProvider` class. This will enable you to view the properties of this class in the Properties inspector, as in Figure 44.8.

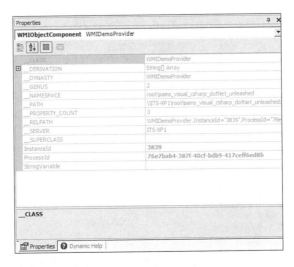

FIGURE 44.8   View the properties of the `WMIDemoProvider` class in the Properties inspector.

8. Add an event by right-clicking on the Management Events node in the Server Explorer and selecting the Add Event Query menu item.

9. In the Build Management Event Query dialog, search for and add the `WMIDemo_SampleEvent` event, as in Figure 44.9, and then click the OK button.

10. Next, return to the console application, as shown in Figure 44.10, and press any key. This will fire the sample event.

11. Open the Visual Studio .NET Output window and see the event that has been fired, Figure 44.11.

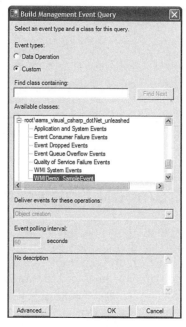

FIGURE 44.9   Add the
WMIDemo_
SampleEvent
event.

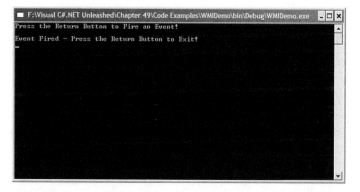

FIGURE 44.10   Fire the sample event.

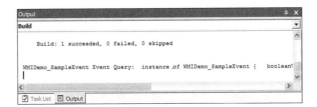

FIGURE 44.11   The sample event was fired. The event is now logged in the Output window of Visual Studio .NET.

Enterprise Instrumentation Framework

In previous sections, you explored three methods of instrumenting your application. Each method had both benefits and limitations. When employing any of those methods, you have to choose which one you think would work best and then code it into your application. In addition, you are forced to learn the different APIs for each method that you choose to deploy. Unfortunately, if you choose the wrong one, you would have to recode your instrumentation with your new choice. For most developers, this is a major drawback. Fortunately, Microsoft has provided this solution for you: the Enterprise Instrumentation Framework (EIF). Unfortunately, it is available only in the Visual Studio .NET Enterprise Architect edition.

Introducing the EIF

The Enterprise Instrumentation Framework is a simple yet extensible framework for instrumenting your application. It provides a unified API for instrumenting your application using the event log, WMI, or Windows Trace. More importantly, it enables you to tell the application at runtime, in a configuration file, which method to employ. As previously stated, this was a major drawback of using the individual method's API directly. By supporting the instrumentation of applications on one machine as well as applications that are distributed across multiple machines, the Enterprise Instrumentation Framework is suitable for all enterprise-class applications. Some important features of the Enterprise Instrumentation Framework are as follows:

▶ It provides a unified programming model that both enterprise developers and system developers alike can use.

▶ It uses a structured WMI event schema. This enables the development, test, and operations teams to work together to support the application.

▶ It implements a scriptable configuration layer. This enables the operations teams to configure how to raise or log events from an application.

44

- ▶ It supports raising or logging events through WMI, Windows event log, and Windows event tracing.

- ▶ It correlates events to business processes or operations using request tracing. This enables your operations staff to troubleshoot requests across a distributed application.

Enterprise Instrumentation Framework Requirements

Along with the benefits of using the Enterprise Instrumentation Framework come some limitations. These limitations come in the form of system requirements. Before embarking on the journey of using the EIF, make sure that your system meets the following requirements:

- ▶ The EIF is compatible with the .NET Framework 1.0 Service Pack 2 and above.

- ▶ Visual Studio .NET Enterprise Architect, Visual Studio .NET Enterprise Developer, or Visual Studio .NET Professional.

- ▶ Windows XP Professional or Windows 2000 Professional Service Pack 3 or later.

TIP

You can obtain the Enterprise Instrumentation Framework through MSDN Universal. Also, when using the EIF, you must include a reference to the framework in your projects.

Elements of the EIF

The EIF uses a number of elements that interact together to support application instrumentation. As shown in Figure 44.12, there are five main elements of the EIF architecture.

- ▶ Event schema—The event schema defines the set of events that an application can raise.

- ▶ Event sources—The event sources are the objects that the applications use to raise events.

- ▶ Event sinks—The event sinks are objects that represent event-reporting mechanisms.

- ▶ Instrumentation API—The instrumentation API is a unified API for providing application instrumenting to an application.

- ▶ Configuration File—The configuration file enables you to define which instrumentation to use and which events to filter out.

44

Enterprise Instrumentation Framework

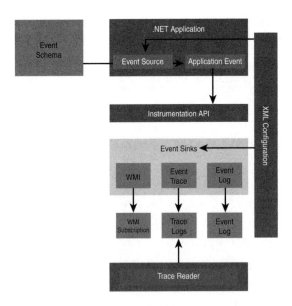

FIGURE 44.12   The EIF architecture.

Event Schema

The event schema is similar to an interface in C#. It is a contract between the development and operations team that states which events an application can raise. Applications that use the EIF publish well-known events to which the operations team can observe and respond.

TIP

In actuality, the EIF schema is a WMI event schema assembly. Because of this, the EIF relies on WMI and the `System.Management` namespace for its event schema implementation and support.

Event Sources

Although the enterprise instrumentation framework provides a default event source for each application, you can define additional event source objects. Event sources are the mechanism in the EIF to raise events. Using the configuration file, you can configure the event sources to determine which events are raised, the information they contain, and to which event sink (described in the next section) the events will be routed. The EIF supports two types of event sources: `SoftwareElement` and `Request`.

`SoftwareElement` Event Source

The `SoftwareElement` event source is a basic event source that provides simple events. They can be linked to classes, pages, or components in order to raise events.

The EIF creates a default `SoftwareElement` event source with the reserved name `Application`. If you do not specify an event source, the EIF assumes and assigns the default event source `Application` to the event. By enabling you to create many event sources, the EIF gives you greater flexibility in that it gives you the ability to filter out unwanted information assigned to different event sources.

`Request` Event Source

A `Request` event source provides events that include contextual information about an application or process. Closely linked to the business process of an application, the `Request` event source enables you to mark the beginning and end of a process such as a transaction or business logic.

For example, in an application that forces you to log on to the system before any additional functionality can be used, you can choose to use a `Request` event source to mark the beginning of the users attempt to log on, log the steps the user took such as entering the wrong password twice, and then mark the end of the process when the user finally enters the correct password. This enables the operations team to identify any problems that might occur when the user was attempting to log on to the system.

Event Sinks

An event sink represents the method of instrumentation, such as WMI, trace log, or event log. Event sinks are specified in your application's EIF configuration file (explained in a later section) and are not objects that you instantiate and use directly. The EIF enables you to use three standard event sinks: `TraceEventSink`, `LogEventSink`, and `WMIEventSink`. In addition to these three standard event sinks, you can develop your own custom event sink. If you choose to create your own event sink, you can use an existing log format and routing mechanism such as MSMQ.

TraceEventSink

The `TraceEventSink` writes events to a Windows event trace log file. The location of the log file is determined by looking at the settings for the trace session named in the event sink. The `TraceEventSink` is suitable for high frequency events. Although the tools for viewing the trace logs are limited, you can create a custom tool for reading and analyzing the trace logs by using the `TraceLogReader` API.

LogEventSink

The `LogEventSink` writes events to the Windows event log. The default severity of the entry and the computer to which the entry is written are determined by the event sink parameters. Because the event log has a limited capacity of events that it can store, it is suitable only for low frequency events such as high level logging of an application.

WMIEventSink

The `WMIEventSink` sends the events to WMI. In addition, WMI supports the greatest number of management tools. These tools enable you to easily analyze the instrumentation data from your application. However, because WMI is somewhat

44

performance-challenged, it should be used only for infrequent and high visibility events. Not withstanding the previous statement, the performance of WMI has been greatly improved and will likely be improved further in the future.

Request Tracing

Request tracing enables you to trace a business process through the course of its execution and is a key feature of EIF. Unlike any of the other tracing mechanisms, request tracing works between defined start and end points in your application's code. Any events that are raised between these points contain information that identifies them as being part of this request. Because the EIF implements request tracing using .NET's Remoting infrastructure, the LogicalCallContext class stores the information about the request. Unfortunately, there are three scenarios that do not currently support request tracing:

- Managed code calling into native code, which calls back into managed code

- Managed code sending an MSMQ message, triggering additional code on the listener

- Managed code invoking a SOAP web service, which then executes additional managed code

In each of these scenarios, the request does not include the execution path after the scenario.

Configuring EIF

The EIF configuration file enables you to define which instrumentation to use and which events to filter out in a production environment. Providing both configuration files and a configuration API, the EIF makes it possible for you to control event generation, tracing, and logging. In the EIF, there are two types of configuration files: application and Windows event trace session configuration files.

Application Configuration File
Every application that uses the Enterprise Instrumentation Framework has its own application configuration file. By default, the file is named Enterpriseinstrumentation.config. By using this file, you can configure event sources. This enables you to specify which instrumentation technique (WMI, event trace, or event log) and which events to allow or filter out. Although you specify most of the configuration information when you deploy the application, you can use this file to fine-tune the settings. The application configuration file enables you to define and control the following: event source registration and parameters, event sink configuration, event categories, event filters, and filter bindings.

Windows Event Trace Session Configuration File

The default Windows event trace session configuration file is named `TraceSessions.config`. This file can be edited manually or through the API. Each trace session corresponds to a trace log file on your computer. This enables you to have different log files for each trace session.

Summary

In this chapter, you explored the different methods of instrumenting your applications. In the first section, you learned both the benefits and limitations of using the Windows event log. Next you saw how to add debug and trace statements for a peek into how your application is performing. Then you saw the power and flexibility of instrumenting your application through the Windows Management Instrumentation API. Finally, you got a peek into the Enterprise Instrumentation Framework and how you could use it to leverage all three methods of instrumentation that you learned in this chapter.

Further Reading

WMI Essentials for Automating Windows Management by Marcin Policht, Sams Publishing. ISBN: 0672321440.

Developing WMI Solutions: A Guide to Windows Management Instrumentation by Craig Tunstall and Gwyn Cole, Addison-Wesley Professional. ISBN: 0201616130.

44

45 The Future of C#

IN BRIEF

This chapter will provide you with a brief preview of the features that will be available in the upcoming C# 2.0. At the time this book was being written, a beta version of the .NET Framework 2.0 was available for download from MSDN with the various Express editions of Visual Studio .NET 2005. Before that, a beta was made available to MSDN subscribers and PDC 2003 attendees for the "Whidbey" technology preview of Visual Studio. Before you attempt to use any of the code in this chapter, be sure that you consult the documentation from Microsoft concerning changes to C# 2.0 between the various betas. During the beta stage, Microsoft often takes feedback from testers and invariably renames various classes and name-spaces as well as changes some functionality and, of course, fixes bugs.

WHAT YOU NEED

REQUIRED SOFTWARE	.NET Framework 2.0 Beta (or newer if available)
RECOMMENDED HARDWARE	PC that meets .NET SDK minimum requirements
SKILLS REQUIRED	C# and .NET familiarity

THE FUTURE OF C# AT A GLANCE

The Future of C#	908		
Generics	909	List Management with Iterators	913
Anonymous Methods	912	Partial Types	914
Nullable Types at Last	913	Static Classes	915
Summary	**916**		
Further Reading	**916**		

The Future of C#

Since the first pre-beta versions of the original 1.0 release of the .NET Framework were placed into the eager hands of waiting developers, Microsoft has been actively listening to feedback from the development community.

Many times upgrades to developer tools are actually driven by marketing and other departments that have nothing to do with development. This isn't true for the next version of C#. Although countless new features are available in ASP.NET 2.0, Visual Studio .NET 2005, and the new Team System suite of Visual Studio projects, this chapter will focus on the improvements to the C# language itself.

These improvements have been seamlessly integrated to the core of the language and are not simple add-ons. In some cases (as with Generics), changes have been made to the Common Language Runtime in order to accommodate these language features. The syntax and features of C# 1.1 are completely compatible with C# 2.0, so no existing syntax will ever break any C# 2.0

code. What follows is a quick tour of some of the exciting new features that are waiting for you in the next evolution of Visual C# .NET 2005.

Generics

Generics provide a way for programmers to create classes that, at runtime, can be given types as parameters in order to more specifically control the behavior of the class.

The best way to understand generics is to take a look at a programming task that many programmers have to accomplish with the current version of C# and then illustrate how that task is no longer necessary with C# 2.0 and generics. Listing 45.1 shows a class that inherits from `CollectionBase` to provide a strongly typed collection.

LISTING 45.1
An Implementation of a Strongly Typed Collection

```
using System;
using System.Collections;
using System.Collections.Specialized;

namespace OldCollection
{
  /// <summary>
  /// Summary description for Class1.
  /// </summary>
  public class OrderCollection: CollectionBase
  {
    public OrderCollection(): base() { }

    public Order this[int index]
    {
      get
      {
        return (Order)this.List[index];
      }
      set
      {
        List[index] = value;
      }
    }

    public void Add( Order newOrder )
    {
```

46

The Future of C#

LISTING 45.1
Continued

```
      List.Add( newOrder );
    }

    public void IndexOf( Order order )
    {
      List.IndexOf( order );
    }

    public void Remove( Order order )
    {
      List.Remove( order );
    }
  }
}
```

If you need to create a collection of orders, it takes a decent amount of extra code.
Many times programmers decide to skip the strong typing and simply use the standard object-based collection classes because it's quicker and easier. With generics, all
of that becomes unnecessary. You can now parameterize types. Microsoft has
provided many generics-aware classes, such as `Collection`, that allow type arguments. Instead of writing an extra class just to get a collection of orders, you can now
use the following syntax:

```
Collection<Order> ordersCollection = new Collection<Order>();
```

To create a generic class, simply use the <> **1** notation to indicate a type parameter, as in the following code:

```
using System;
using System.Collections;
using System.Collections.Specialized;

namespace GenericSample
{
    class GenericClass<T>
    {
      void GenericClass() { }

      public void PerformStrongOperation()
      {
        T myVariable;

        // perform some operation on myVariable
```

```
    }
  }
}
```

Anywhere in the class definition that the type parameter `T` is used, C# considers it a type definition. So, at runtime, `T myVariable` might actually evaluate to `Order myVariable` or `LineItem myVariable`, depending on how the `Generic` class is instantiated.

You can supply constraints on the `Generic` class, requiring that the type being used as a parameter provide a default constructor, implement certain interfaces, or even be derived from certain classes. This is just a preview of C# 2.0, so this chapter won't go into too much depth on the syntax for advanced generics. *Visual C# .NET 2005 Unleashed* (upcoming) will provide all the detail on generics that you might need.

One thing to keep in mind is that generics are not the same as templates in C++ or generics in Java. Unlike other implementations that are compile-time substitutions, generics have been integrated completely into the Common Language Runtime. When the generic class is compiled by the JIT (Just-in-Time) compiler at runtime, the generic substitution is made. In other words, by using generics, the strong typing is available at compile time, so it is *faster* in some cases than providing your own strong typing at runtime, and it is completely IntelliSense-aware.

The next version of the .NET Framework contains dozens of classes that have been built from the ground up with generics in mind. The following is a list of some of the collection-style classes that can be used with C# 2.0:

- `List<T>`
- `Dictionary<K,V>`
- `Stack<T>`
- `Queue<T>`
- `Collection<T>`
- `KeyedCollection<T>`
- `Nullable<T>`
- `EventHandler<T>`

In addition to the preceding classes and many others, several interfaces also support generics. Some of the collection-related interfaces are as follows:

- `IList<T>`
- `IDictionary<K,V>`
- `IEnumerable<T>`

46

The Future of C#

Anonymous Methods

Regardless of what kind of application you're creating, you have more than likely encountered a situation in which you need an extremely simple event handler. It can be tedious and unnecessarily complex to create this kind of event handler.

To compensate for this, C# 2.0 provides support for anonymous (often referred to as *inline*) methods. An *anonymous* method is one that is defined within the context from which it is called.

In standard code, to declare a delegate for a method and then invoke that delegate, the code looks something like this:

```
class DelegateClass
{
   delegate void MessageShowDelegate(string message);

   public void InvokeMethod()
   {
      MessageShowDelegate dg = new MessageShowDelegate( ShowMessage );
      dg("Hello!");
   }

   void ShowMessage( string msg )
   {
      MessageBox.Show( msg );
   }
}
```

Delegates are a crucial part of the event-handling plumbing of the .NET Framework. Instead of writing an extra method and creating an instance of a new delegate, you can write an anonymous method as the delegate, as shown in this C# 2.0 code:

```
class DelegateClass
{
   delegate void MessageShowDelegate(string message);

   public void InvokeMethod()
   {
     MessageShowDelegate dlg = delegate(string message)
       {
         MessageBox.Show(message);
       };
     del(message);
   }
}
```

The preceding code demonstrates that you can create a method on the fly using anonymous methods. It's simple code, but it has a variety of applications for making things extremely easy. Another added benefit of anonymous methods is that you often don't even have to declare the delegate type; its type can be inferred from the signature when it is invoked.

Nullable Types at Last

Nullable types are a blessing that has been long awaited by database programmers everywhere. Programmers who spend a lot of their time interfacing with databases are often frustrated by the fact that the database allows scalar types (such as integer, double, float, bit, and so on) to contain a null value. Unlike the database, the current version of C# doesn't allow for nullable scalar types to match the features of the database.

With C# 2.0, that is no longer true. Through the use of generics, developers can create an instance of the `Nullable` class parameterized with a value type. This provides the ability to create nullable integers, doubles, floats, and so forth. The following code shows how to create a nullable type:

```
Nullable<int> x = new Nullable<int>();
x = 12;
if ( x == null ) { // perform action }
if (x.HasValue) { // perform some other action }
```

Just like C# has shortcuts for `System.String` and `System.Int32`, it also has shortcuts for the nullable types. Instead of declaring `Nullable<int>`, you can simply declare a variable as `int?`, `double?`, and so forth. Adding the question mark to the end of the value type changes the declaration from a simple value type to a nullable value type.

List Management with Iterators

If you've ever created a class that implemented an iterator, you are aware of how painful the process can be. It requires very certain code to be in place in a certain way, and is very prone to errors. Many people simply skip the process rather than deal with the headache of creating their own `IEnumerable` implementations.

To create your own custom list of elements, not only do you have to implement `IEnumerator`, but you must also provide a class that implements `IEnumerable`. In C# 2.0, there is a new keyword called `yield`. This keyword enables you to easily define what information is to be yielded during enumeration of instances of the class. It dramatically simplifies the task of creating a class that implements the `IEnumerable` interface.

46

The Future of C#

The following code shows how to create an enumerable class that uses the new `yield` keyword:

```
public class OrderCollection : IEnumerable<Order>
{
    Order[] orders;

    public OrderCollection()
    {
        // populate the orders array
    }

    public IEnumerator<Order> GetEnumerator()
    {
        for (int i=0; i<orders.Length; i++)
            yield return orders[i];
    }
}
```

With the preceding code, you can iterate through the collection of orders in a strongly typed fashion with no typecasting penalty and with a simple syntax:

```
foreach (Order order in Orders) { // process order }
```

Partial Types

Partial types are part of the new design philosophy with the entire Visual Studio .NET 2005 product offering. The main goal behind partial types was to separate the code generated by visual designers from the code written by programmers. Today, that code is somewhat obscured from the developer by hiding it behind a collapsible IDE text region.

With the new `partial` keyword, a C# 2.0 project can have multiple classes with the same name. The members of each partial definition become merged at compile time. Consider the following two partial classes:

```
public partial class Car
{
    private int mph;
    private bool AWD = false;

    public string GetColor()
    {
        return color.ToString();
```

```
    }
}

public partial class Car
{
    private Color color;

    public string GetAWD()
    {
     return AWD ? "All-Wheel Drive " : "Two-Wheel Drive";
    }
}
```

The interesting thing about the preceding two class definitions is that they refer to the same class. Each definition can have properties, fields, methods, and so on. What is new about this code is that either one of the partial class definitions can access members defined by the other. It is important to realize that even though the definitions are in different files and seemingly different classes, they contribute to the same class. There can even be more than two partial class definitions for the same class.

The main benefit of partial classes will be immediately obvious to you when you start working with Visual Studio .NET 2005 and the new designers for Windows and Web Forms programming. Your code will no longer be cluttered, disorganized, and covered with auto-generated designer output.

Static Classes

Static members of a class are those that are part of the class definition and not part of an individual instance of the class. Therefore, static members are retained in memory throughout the lifetime of the process in which the class resides. Such members are often used to store global data and configuration information in many different kinds of applications.

Currently, you must create a class that looks something like the following class in order to prevent other programmers from creating an instance of the class:

```
public class StaticClass
{
    static int intMember = 0;

    private StaticClass()
    {
        // private-only constructor ...
        // throws exception when instantiated
    }
```

46

The Future of C#

```
public static int IntMember
{
    get { return intMember; }
    set { intMember = value; }
}
}
```

Rather than have to rig up something like the preceding class with a private default constructor, C# 2.0 enables you to use the keyword `static` when defining classes. A *static class* is one that must define only static members. The compiler will enforce that rule, saving you the trouble. Static classes cannot be instantiated, and attempts to instantiate a static class will be flagged as errors at compile time.

Summary

Quite a few exciting new features are coming out with the release of the .NET Framework in 2005, especially in Visual Studio .NET. This chapter has given you a quick preview of some of the more notable language enhancements that are coming with the next version of C#.

Further Reading

For more details on features and enhancements coming up with the .NET Framework, check out MSDN's .NET Framework developer center (msdn.microsoft.com/ netframework) for news and technical information as it is released.

46

Index

Symbols

+ (addition) operator, 170

@ attribute, 170

. (group)s operation, 170

* (multiplication) operator, 170

: namespace separator, 170

!= operator, 171

/ operator, 170

// operator, 170

= operator, 171

- (subtraction) operator, 170

<%# %> syntax, 635

* wildcard, 170

A

Abort method (Thread class), 186

Abstract class polymorphism, 123

abstract classes, 123

abstract method, 123

access

code

security, 42-43

security. *See* CAS

enterprise templates, 844-845

Acme Stock Company License Provider Implementation, 761-762

AcquireRequestState event, 513

activation (JIT), 810, 817

Activation tab (Properties dialog), 817

ActivityId property, 821

Add Classes dialog, 899

Add Classes menu, 899

Add Project Output dialog box, 416

add tag, 878, 882

Add Web Reference dialog box, 397

Addr parameter, 539

AddRange method, 307

address operators, 55

Address parameter, 539

AddressList class, 107, 109

Adjust Zone Security task
(Runtime Security Policy
folder), 700

Adjust Zone Security
wizardWizard, 701-702

administration, CAS,
698-700

ADO.NET

DataAdapter binding,
548

associating
DataSets with
DataAdapters, 549

linking DataSets
with
DataAdapters,
549-551

data providers,
554-555

commands,
569-570, 575

connections,
565-566, 569

DataAdapters, 582,
587

DataReaders,
575-576, 581

implementation,
556

overview of remote
data provider,
557-558

parameters,
558-559, 563, 565

sample scenario,
556-557

when to create,
555-556

AdsUtil, 504

advanced COM+, 823

events, 823-826

queued components,
826

Advanced page, 321

AL.EXE, 248

algorithms

DES (Data Encryption
Standard), 711

hiding, 769-770

SHA1 (Secure Hash
Algorithm), 717

TripleDES encryption,
713

alignment, string
formatting, 76-77

all element, XSD complex
data types, 593

allocated objects,
Generation 0, 296

AllowDirectoryBrowsing
property, 525

AllowReadAccess property,
525

AllowScriptSourceAccess
property, 525

Amazon.com, connecting to
web service, 398-399

annotation

typed DataSets,
609-611

XML schemas, 593-594

anonymous methods, future
considerations, 912-913

Any attribute (Location
attribute), 486

ApartmentState property
(Thread class), 185

APIs

calling, 305-306

instrumentation, 903

Win32 APIs, 42

App.config (application
configuration files), 379,
382, 877

AppDomain class, 259

methods, 259-260

properties, 260

AppDomains, 42, 242,
259-260, 793-794

application plug-ins
example, 264-272

domain-neutral
assemblies, 794

global exception
handlers, 795

PluginLoader, 272

programming, 260,
263-264

Append method, 83

AppendFormat method, 83

Application Name
parameter, 539

Application.LoadFrom method, 393-394

ApplicationId property, 821

ApplicationQueuing attribute, 826

applications
ASP.NET, deployment, 520-533
debugging, 850, 854
Autos window, 855
breakpoints, 859-861
Breakpoints window, 857
Call Stack window, 856
Command window, 857
configurations, 850-851
Locals window, 855
Memory window, 857
Modules window, 857
navigation commands, 858-859
Output window, 857
Registers window, 857
syntax errors, 852-854
This window, 855
Threads window, 856

Visual Studio .NET, 861, 864, 867
Watch window, 855

Harness Console, 250-251

Hello World, creating with ASP.NET, 426-432

instrumenting, 890-892
compared to monitoring, 891-892
Debug class, 895
Event Log, 892-894
Trace class, 895-897

monitoring, 872
custom trace listeners, 885-887
debugging and tracing statements, 872-876
trace listeners, 876-881
trace switches, 882-885

plug-ins, creating, 264-272

PluginTester Console, 271-272

state, 480
creating ASP.NET applications in web farms, 503-504
storing data, 480
synchronizing, 480-481

Application_AuthenticateRequest event handler, 745-746

architecture
EIF, 903
configuration file, 903
event schemas, 903-904
event sinks, 903-906
event sources, 903-905
instrumentation API, 903
enterprise templates, 829-830, 835-836
WMI, 897-902

arithmetic operators, 54

ArrayList collection, 100-101

arrays, 93
jagged, 93-96, 307-308
multidimensional, 93
parsing, as parameters, 96-97
rectangular, 307-308
single-dimensional, 93-95
two-dimensional, 93-95
storing the months of year in, 95

ASP.NET

caching, 484-486

Cache object, 491-496

HttpCachePolicy class, 489-491

OutputCache directive, 486-488

controls. *See* controls

creating applications in web farms, 499

application state, 503-504

best practices, 505-506

configuration, 504-505

deployment, 504-505

session state maintenance, 501-503

ViewState, 499-500

creating Hello World application, 426-432

deploying applications, 520

advanced deployment, 529-533

automated deployment, 523-529

manual deployment, 521-523

event handling, 433-438

globalization, 506

displaying localized content, 507-511

localization functionality, 511-513

localized resources, 506-507

localization, 506

displaying localized content, 507-511

functionality, 511-513

localized resources, 506-507

security

data, 748-751

SSL, 751

user, 734-747

ViewState, 751-752

state management, 456

client-side, 456, 463-479

customizing ViewState, 462

customizing ViewState, 462

ViewState property, 456-461, 479-482

Web Forms, data binding, 635-657

ASP.NET State Service, session state maintenance, 503

ASP.NET web Service service project, 839

AspNetHostingPermission class, 696

assemblies, 242-243

application plug-ins example, 264-272

creating, 247-251, 405-409

delayed signing, 408-409

deployment, 403

domain-neutral, 794

dynamic, 244

embedding content in, 251-255

embedding resources in, 251-255

Manifest section, 245-246

metadata, 246

mscorlib, 264

MSIL code, 247

multifile, 244-245

placing in GAC, 404-409

primary Interop assembly. *See* PIA

resources, 247

embedding, 251-255

localization, 255-259

satellite, 256-259

single-file, 244

System.Data, 246

trusted, 695-696

Adjust Zone
Security
wizardWizard,
701-702

increasing trust
levels, 700

untrusted, 695-696

Adjust Zone
Security
wizardWizard,
701-702

increasing trust
levels, 700

verification, 409

Assembly class, 249

Assembly property,
System.Type class, 230

assembly resource files,
255

AssemblyInfo.cs, 248, 428

default
AssemblyInfo.cs file,
406-408

modifying, 406-408

AssemblyIntro project,
248-249, 252

AssemblyTool class,
248-249, 252, 254, 263

assertions, regular
expressions, 89

assigning handlers to
events, 225-226

assignment expressions, 53

assignment operators, 55

asymmetric encryption,
720-721

DSACryptoServiceProvi
der class, 721, 723

RSACryptoServiceProvi
der class, 723

asynchronous calls, web
services, 675-676

asynchronous consumption,
web services, 383-385

asynchronous I/O, 310

attachments, messaging
with, 690-691

Attachments collection, 690

attributes, 113, 234-235

ApplicationQueuing,
826

AutoCompleteAttri-
bute, 813

COM Interop, 282-283

custom, 236-241

customizing XML
serialization,
181-183

defined, 113

DllImportAttribute,
290

LicenseProvider,
757-759

.NET for COM Interop,
281

ObjectPooling, 817

OutputCache directive,
486-488

PrimaryInterOpAssem
bly, 287

SecurityRole, 823

Serializable, 143

SomeAttribute, 777

TransactionAttribute,
813

UML, 113-114

WebMethodAttribute,
235

XML, 162-163

XmlAttribute, 182

XmlConvert class,
167-168

XmlRoot, 182

XPath, 170

Attributes filter,
FileSystemWatcher class,
138

Attributes property,
System.Type class, 230

AttributeUsageAttribute
declaration, 237

Authenticate method, 738

AuthenticateRequest event,
513

authentication, 735

forms, 737-739

passport, 739-740

Windows, 735-736

AuthorizeRequest event,
513

authorizing users, roles, 740

Authorkey, 603

AutoCompleteAttribute, 813

autohiding windows, 12-14

automated deployment,
ASP.NET applications,
523-529

AutomationProxyAttribute attribute, 282

AutoResetEvent class, 194

Autos window, 17, 855

B

background threads, 185, 501

Backward navigation, Visual Studio .NET IDE, 20

BannerText property, 527

Base Class Library. *See* BCL

base classes, inheritance, 119-122

BaseDirectory property (AppDomain class), 260

BaseType property, System.Type class, 230

BCL (Base Class Library), 48

BeginHelloWithParameters method, 676

BeginRequest event, 513

BeginSlowHelloWorld method, 385

BeginTransaction method, IDbConnection interface, 566

BeginTransaction method (SqlConnection class), 538

best practices, visual inheritance, 358-359

BestFitMapping property, 290

binary files, editing, 30

Binary serialization, 142

binding data, 613

  Windows Forms, 613

    binding to a ComboBox, 622

    BindingContext class, 617

    cascading header/detail forms, 628, 631

    complex data binding, 616

    CurrencyManager class, 617-618, 620

    DataGrid binding, 622-625

    header/detail forms, 625, 628

    one-way data binding, 616

    PropertyManager class, 620-621

    simple data binding, 613-615, 621-622

    two-way data binding, 616

BindingContext class, 617

Bindings property

  CurrencyManager class, 618

  PropertyManager class, 621

bin\debug directory, 258

BitArray collection, 103-104

BLL (business logic layer), 835

BLLWebService project, 841

BluePlugin class, 266, 268

BODY tag, user controls, 449

BodyText property, 527

bookmarks, IDE, 20-23

BooleanSwitch (trace switch), 882-883, 896

BooleanSwitch trace switch, 896

boxing, 300-303

Breakpoint Properties dialog box, 859

breakpoints, debugging applications, 859-861

Breakpoints window, 17

  debugging applications, 857-859

Build Events page, 320

Build page, 321

business logic layer. *See* BLL

Button control, 330-331, 443

  Windows Forms Hello World, 324-329

ByValue method, 40

C

C#

  future issues, 908-909

    anonymous methods, 912-913

    generics, 909-911

    managing lists with iterators, 913-914

nullable types, 913

partial types, 914-915

static classes, 915-916

object-oriented features, 37

Cache object, 484, 491-496

CacheDependency class, 494

caches, 484

caching, 484-486

Cache object, 491-496

HttpCachePolicy class, 489-491

OutputCache directive, 486-488

Calendar control, 443

Call Stack window, 17

debugging applications, 856

CallingConvention property, 290

calls

API, chunky APIs, 305-306

asynchronous, 675-676

synchronous, 674-675

camel case, 113

Cancel method, IDbCommand interface, 570

card tables, 296

CAS (code access security), 694-695

administration, 698-700

assemblies, trust levels, 695-696, 700-702

deployment packages, creating, 703-704

permissions, 695-697

defined, 696

Evaluate Assembly task (Runtime Security Policy folder), 701-703

identity, 697-698

resolving, 695-696

role-based, 698

writing CAS-aware code, 704

blocking unwanted clients, 706-708

declarative security, 705-706

imperative security, 704-705

cascading header forms, 652-654, 657

data binding, 628, 631

case sensitivity, XPath operators, 171

case statement, 66

cases

camel, 113

strings, modifying, 82

CASLibrary class library, 700

CASPOL.EXE, CAS policy modification, 699

cast operators, 55

cbSize field (CRYPTPROTECT_PROMPTSTRUCT structure), 726

CCW (COM callable wrapper), 281-282

centralized servers, deploying smart clients from, 392

self-updating applications, 394-396

System.Reflection method, 393-394

URL-based executable deployments, 393

web server deployments, 393

certificates, X.509, 689

ChangeDatabase method, IDbConnection interface, 566

ChangeDatabase method (SqlConnection class), 538

Channel URI, 796

channels

Channel URI, 796

client-activated URLs, 797

HttpChannel, 796-797

selecting, 796-797

server-activated URLs, 797

TcpChannel, 796-797

characters
replacing, 84
strings
replacing, 81-82
trimming, 81
CharSet property, 290
CheckBox control, 443
CheckBoxList control, 443
choice element, XSD complex data types, 593
chunky API calls, 305-306
CIM (Common Information Model), 897-902
class libraries
CASLibrary, 700
SampleHttpModule, 514
Class View window, 14
Class1 class, 257-258
Class1.cs file, deleting, 248
classes, 112-113, 116-118
abstract, 123
AddressList, 107, 109
AppDomain, 259
methods, 259-260
properties, 260
AspNetHostingPermission, 696
Assembly, 249
AssemblyTool, 248-249, 252, 254, 263
attributes, 113
defined, 113
UML, 113-114
AutoResetEvent, 194

base, inheritance, 119-122
BindingContext, 617
BluePlugin, 266, 268
CacheDependency, 494
character classes (regular expressions), 87
Class1, 257-258
Collection, 910
CollectionBase, 107
COM+ serviced components, 808
ContextUtil, 811, 821
control, 640
CurrencyManager, 617
complex data binding, 618, 620
events, 618
public properties, 617
CustomIdentity, 741-742
CustomPrincipal, 743-745
CustomTraceListener test class, 887
DataBinder, 639-640
DataGrabber, 284
DataGrid, 640
DataList, 640
DbDataPermission, 697
Debug, 873, 895
Delegate constructors, 218-219

DESCryptoServiceProvider, 711-712
Directory, 131-132
DirectoryServicesPermission, 696
DnsPermission, 697
DSACryptoServiceProvider, 721, 723
EnvironmentPermission, 697
EventLog, 893
EventLogPermission, 697
File, 129
FileDialogPermission, 697
FileInfo, 130-131
FileIOPermission, 697
FileStream, 132-134, 880
FileSystemWatcher, 138-142
FormsAuthentication, 738-739
Generic, 911
generics, 909-911
HelloService, 668-673
HelloWorld, 278-279
HttpApplicationState, 480-481
HttpCachePolicy, 489-491
HttpHandlers, creating, 516-518
inheritance, 351-352
Interlocked, thread synchronization, 203

IsolatedStorageFilePer mission, 697

IsolatedStoragePermiss ion, 697

LicenseManager, 757-759

LicenseProvider, 760, 762, 764

LogicalCallContext, 906

MACTripleDES, 716-717

ManualResetEvent, 194

MD5CryptoServiceProv ider, 719-720

MemoryStream, 134-135

MessageBoxTraceListe ner, 887

MessageQueuePermissi on, 697

MessageReceiver, 681-682

MessagingSoapClient, 686-687

Mile, 59

Monitor, 198-201, 203

Mutex, 196-197

MyDataLayer, 47

Nullable, 913

OdbcPermission, 697

OleDbCommand, 545

OleDbConnection, 545

OleDbDataAdapter, 546

OleDbDataReader, 546

OleDbPermission, 697

OraclePermission, 697

PerformanceCounterPe rmission, 697

PluginLoader, 269-270

PluginTool, 268-269

PrintingPermission, 697

PropertyManager, 620-621

PublisherIdentityPermi ssion, 698

PublisherProtected, 707

RC2CryptoServiceProvi der, 712

RDPCommand, 570, 575

RDPConnection, 566, 569

RDPDataAdapter, 582, 587

RDPDataReader, 576, 581

RDPParameter, 559, 563

RDPParameterCollec- tion, 563, 565

ReaderWriterLock, 203

RedPlugin, 266, 268

ReflectionPermission, 697

RegistryPermission, 697

Repeater, 640

ResourceManager, 255

ResourcePermission Base, 697

RijndaelManaged, 713

RoleSecurity, 822

RSACryptoServiceProvi der, 723

SampleService, 803

SecurityPermission, 697

ServiceControllerPermi ssion, 697

ServicedComponent, 811, 813

SHA1Managed, 718-719

SharedPropertyGroup Manager, 818

SiteIdentityPermission, 698

SoapClient, 686-687

SoapReceiver, 680-684

SoapSender, 680-684

SoapService, 683-685

SocketPermission, 697

SomeDelegate, 211

SPMGetter 3, 818

SPMSetter 4, 818

SqlClientPermission, 697

SqlCommand, 540-542

SqlConnection, 537

   database connection strings, 539-540

   events, 539

   methods, 538-539

   properties, 538

SqlDataAdapter, 542-544

SqlDataReader, 542

static, 915-916

StreamReader, 136-138

StreamWriter, 136-138

String, 75, 80

StringBuilder, 75, 83, 303-305

StringReader, 135-136

StringWriter, 135-136

StrongNameIdentityPe rmission, 698, 706

System.Array, 93

System.Attribute, 237

System.MulticastDeleg ate, 220

System.Type, 229

   methods, 230

   properties, 230

SystemString class, 80

the System.Array, 94

ThreadPool, 206

   passing data to threads, 208-209

   ThreadPool.QueueU serWorkItem method, 207

   WaitCallback delegate, 206-207

TimeSpan, 197

Trace, 873, 895

   adding code to applications, 895

   trace switches, 895-897

TraceListener, 876, 886

TraceSwitch, 896-897

TripleDESCryptoService Provider, 713, 715

UIPermission, 697

UML, 116-117

URLIdentityPermission, 698

UsernameToken, 688-689

WebPermission, 697

WMIDemoProvider, 899-900

wrapper, 726-727, 732

XmlAttribute, 155, 161-162

XmlComment, 155

XmlConvert, 167-168

XmlDocument, 155, 161, 163

XmlElement, 155, 162

XmlNode, 155, 162-163

XmlNodeList, 155

XmlNodeReader, 164, 167

XmlReader, 163-164

   XmlNodeReader, 164, 167

   XmlTextReader, 164-166

   XmlValidatingRead er, 164, 166

XmlSchema, 595, 598

XmlSerializer, 181

XmlTextReader, 164-166

XmlValidatingReader, 164, 166

XPathDocument, 171-174

XPathNavigator, 172-174

XPathNodeIterator, 174

ZoneIdentityPermissio n, 698

ClassInterfaceAttribute attribute, 282

CLI (common language infrastructure), 44

Client attribute (Location attribute), 486

client-activated remote objects, 798-799

client-activated URLs, 797

client-side state management, 456

   cookies, 467-471

   customizing ViewState, 462

   hidden form fields, 463-467

   passing server control values between forms, 474-479

   query strings, 471-474

   ViewState property, 456-461

clients

   creating, 805-806

   proxies, 674

   reliability, 385-386

   smart, 391-392

      deploying updates from centralized servers, 392-396

design, 391

high fidelity, 391

intelligent connections, 391

offline functionalities, 400

offloading server processing with web services, 396-400

operations, 391

smart clients, 390-391

Close function (trace listeners), 877

Close method

IDataReader interface, 576

IDbConnection interface, 566

Close method (SqlConnection class), 538

CLR, . *See* Common Language Runtime

memory management, 300

boxing, 300-303

StringBuilder class, 303-305

unboxing, 300-302

CLS (common language specification), 42

CoClassAttribute attribute, 282

code

access security. *See* CAS

Debug class, 895

execution, 43

GCs, 296-297

interoperability, 278-280

outlining, 18-19

performance, 305

AddRange method, 307

asynchronous I/O, 310

chunky API calls, 305-306

exceptions, 305

for loop, 308-309

foreach loop, 308-309

jagged arrays, 307-308

rectangular arrays, 307-308

reference types, 306

value types, 306

replacing comments with, 50

spaghetti, 774

Trace class, 895

code access security. *See* **CAS**

code attributes, 234-235

Code Group Properties dialog, 703

code groups, 695, 701, 704

Code view

FirstForm.aspx, 476-477

SecondForm.aspx, 478-479

Code View window, Text property, 318

Collection class, 910

Collection interfaces, 98

CollectionBase class, 107

collections, 98

ArrayList, 100-101

Attachments, 690

BitArray, 103-104

boxing, 302-303

creating custom collections, 107

AddressList class, 107, 109

CollectionBase class, 107

Garbage Collector, 45

iterating through, 98-99

Queue, 104-105

SortedList, 106-107

Stack, 101-103

strongly typed, 909-910

collisions, 718

columns, DataSets, 599-600

COM (Component Object Model), 275

interoperability, 43-44

.NET, 281-282

objects, 279-280

RCW, 276

COM callable wrapper. *See* **CCW**

COM Interop, 275

code interoperability, 278-280

code utilizing .NET components, 283-285

data marshalling, 276-278

custom mar- shalling, 285-286

from COM to .NET, 282-283

.NET code attributes, 281

objects, COMtoDotNet, 285

PIA, 286

deployment, 287-288

producing, 287-288

programming code attributes, 282-283

RCW, 275-276

COM+, 809

advanced, 823

events, 823-826

queued compo- nents, 826

applications

Library mode, 809

Server mode, 809

construction strings, 811, 815-817

creating components, 813

events, 812-813

JIT (just-in-time), 810, 817

object pooling, 810-811, 817-818

queued components, 812

role-based security, 811-812

security, 820

object contexts, 820-821

role-based, 821-823

security contexts, 820-821

serviced components, 808

shared groups, 818-820

shared properties, 818-820

transactions, 809-810, 813-815

COM+ New Subscription Wizard, 825

Combine method, System.Delegate class, 220

ComboBoxes, data binding, 622

ComImportAttribute attribute, 282

Command window, 15

debugging applica- tions, 857

commands

AL.EXE, 248

data providers, 569

IDbCommand interface, 569-570

RDPCommand class, 570, 575

Debug menu, Windows, 16

debugging applications, 858-859

ILDASM, 245

Project menu

Copy Project, 521-522

New Project, 426

System.Console.ReadlL ine, 128

System.Console.WriteLi ne, 128

XCopy, 410

CommandText property, IDbCommand interface, 570

CommandTimeout property, IDbCommand interface, 570

CommandType property, IDbCommand interface, 570

comments

replacing with code, 50

reports, 24-25

common files, creating server applications, 804

Common Information Model. See CIM

common language infrastructure. See CLI

Common Language Runtime, 40

assembly deployment, locating assemblies to load, 403

benefits, 41

code access security, 42-43

code execution, 43

COM interoperability, 43-44

isolation, 42

JIT compiler, 43

just-in-time compilation, 40

memory management, 300

boxing, 300-303

StringBuilder class, 303-305

unboxing, 300-302

multiple languages, 41

PInvoke, 42

Rotor, 44

Common Language Runtime. See CLR

common language specification. See CLS

Common Type System. See CTS

common type systems

functions, 38

reference types, 39-40

value types, 38-39

versus reference types, 40

CompanyOKCancel Inherited Form, 354, 356

compiler behavior, events processing, 222

compiling Windows Forms applications, 322-323

complex data binding, 616, 638

CurrencyManager class, 618, 620

complex data types, XSD, 592-593

Component Object Model. See COM

components, .NET, 283-286

composite controls, 445

ComRegisterFunctionAttribute attribute, 282

COMtoDotNet object, 285

ComUnregisterFunctionAttribute attribute, 283

ComVisibleAttribute attribute, 283

condemned objects, 296

conditional operators, 55, 64-65

conditional statements, 60-61

if, 61

if/else, 61

configuration file

EIF, 903

registering remote objects, 802-803

Configuration Manager dialog box, 851

configurations

debugging applications, 850-851

EIF, 906

application configuration file, 906

trace session configuration file, 907

IIS in web farms, 504-505

sessionState, 481-482

InProc mode, 481

Off mode, 481

SQLServer mode, 482

StateServer mode, 482

web farms, 504-505

Connect Timeout parameter, 539

Connection Lifetime parameter, 540

Connection property, IDbCommand interface, 570

Connection Reset parameter, 540

Connection Timeout parameter, 539

connections

data providers, 565

IDbConnection interface, 566

RDPConnection class, 566, 569

strings, 539-540, 748

ConnectionString method, IDbConnection interface, 566

ConnectionString property
(SqlConnection class), 538

ConnectionTimeout
property, IDbConnection
interface, 566

ConnectionTimeout property
(SqlConnection class), 538

connectivity, network,
386-387

console applications, Hello
World, 49-50

Console.Write() statements,
872

Console.WriteLine method,
50, 188

Console.WriteLine()
statements, 872

constraints, defining
DataSets using XML
schema, 600

key constraints, 601

keyref constraints,
602-603

relationships, 601

unique constraints,
601

Construct method, 811,
815

construction strings, COM+,
811, 815-817

constructors

Delegate class,
218-219

Mutex class, 196

consuming

.NET components,
283-286

DLLs, 288-289

consumption

UDDI, 382-383

wWeb services, 674

asynchronous,
383-385

creating client
proxies, 674

Contains method,
IDataParameterCollection
interface, 559

content, enterprise
templates, 830-831

Contents window, 15

context, remotingRemoting,
795-796

context menus, dynamic,
359-360

pop-up context menu
event handler, 361

populating ListView,
362-363

ContextId property, 821

ContextMenu property, 360

ContextUtil class, 811, 821

methods, 821

properties, 821

continue statement, 72

contract-first programming,
674

control classes, 640

control structures, 53, 60

conditional state-
ments, 60-61

execution path, 60

if conditional
statements, 61

if/else conditional
statements, 61

short circuit
evaluations, 62-64

switch statement,
65-68

ternary operator, 64-65

controls

Button, 324-329

composite, 445

custom, creating,
445-455

Help, 454

HTML, 440-442

License-Protected
Label, 765, 767

licensed, 764, 767

ListBox, 653-654, 657

maintaining lists, 337

ListBox control, 337

ListView control,
338-342

TreeView control,
342-345

modifying values,
334-336

nesting controls within
controls, 345

GroupBox control,
345-346

Panel control, 346

TabControl control,
346

NET Framework, 330

Button, 330-331

Label, 334

ListBox, 337

ListView, 338-342

StatusBar, 336

TextBox, 335

ToolBar, 331-333

TreeView, 342-345

OwnerDraw, 368

Repeater, 641, 643-644

server. *See* server controls

StockLabel, 767

storing values, 334-336

user, 347-348, 444-455

Webweb, 768

web server, 443-444

Windows Forms, 768

CookieExample.aspx

Design view, 468-469

Source view, 469, 471

cookies, client-side state management, 467-471

Copy Project command (Project menu), 521-522

Copy Project dialog box, 521

CopyTo method, 98

Count property, 98

CurrencyManager class, 618

PropertyManager class, 621

Create Deployment Package task (Runtime Security Policy folder), 700

CreateAttribute method, 161-162

CreateCDataSection method, 162

CreateCommand method, 538

CreateComment method, 162

CreateDomain method, 259

CreateElement method, 162

CreateInstance method, 263

CreateInstanceFrom method, 259

CreateNode method, 162

CreateParameter property, 570

CreateWhitespace method, 162

CreationTime filter, FileSystemWatcher class, 138

critical sections, 198

CryptoStreams, 712

CryptProtectData function, 724

CRYPTPROTECT_AUDIT flag, 725

CRYPTPROTECT_CRED_SYNC flag, 725

CRYPTPROTECT_LOCALMACHINE flag, 725

CRYPTPROTECT_PROMPT STRUCT structure, 726

CRYPTPROTECT_SYSTEM flag, 725

CRYPTPROTECT_UI_FORBIDDEN flag, 725

CTS (Common Type System), 75, 210

currency, localized, 511-512

CurrencyManager class, 617

complex data binding, 618-20

events, 618

public properties, 617

Current Language parameter, 539

Current property, 99

CurrencyManager class, 618

PropertyManager class, 621

CurrentChanged event, CurrencyManager class, 618

CurrentDomain property (AppDomain class), 260

CurrentThread property (Thread class), 185

custom attributes, 236-241

custom collections, creating, 107-109

custom controls, creating, 445

custom data providers, 554-555

commands, 569

IDbCommand interface, 569-570

RDPCommand class, 570, 575

connections, 565

IdbConnection interface, 566

RDPConnection class, 566, 569

How can we make this index more useful? Email us at indexes@samspublishing.com

DataAdapters, 582

  IDbDataAdapter interface, 582

  RDPDataAdapter class, 582, 587

DataReaders, 575

  IDataReader interface, 575-576

  RDPDataReader class, 576, 581

  implementation, 556

  overview of remote data provider, 557-558

  parameters, 558

    IDataParameter interface, 558-559

    IDataParameterColl ection interface, 559

    RDPParameter class, 559, 563

    RDPParameterColle ction class, 563, 565

  sample scenario, 556-557

  when to create, 555-556

custom dates, formatting, 78-79

Custom dialog, 527

custom help, enterprise templates, 829

custom HttpHandlers, 516-518

custom HttpModules, 513-515

custom integer formatting, 77-78

custom licensing, 757

  creating licenses, 759-760

  licensed controls, 764, 767

  LicenseManager class, 757-759

  LicenseProvider attribute, 757-759

  LicenseProvider class, 760, 762, 764

  web controls compared to Windows Forms controls, 768

custom list elements, 363

  DrawMode property, 363

  ListBoxes, 363-365

  menu items, 365-367

custom trace listeners, 885-887

custom user controls, 445-455

custom wizards, enterprise templates, 831

CustomIdentity class, 741-742

customized interfaces, developer profiles, 7-8

customizing Visual Studio .NET, 7

  autohiding windows, 12-14

  developer profiles, 7

  dockable windows, 10-11

  keyboard shortcuts, 8

  maximizing viewable area, 9-10

CustomModule, 514

CustomPrincipal class, 743-745

CustomTraceListener test class, 887

D

DAL (data access layer), 835

data

  adapters, 543

  binding. *See* data binding

  localized

    displaying, 510-511

    queries, 510-511

  marshalling, 276-278

    custom marshalling, 285-286

    from COM to .NET, 282-283

    P/Invoke, 289-290

  protection. *See* data protection

  providers. *See* data providers

  security, 748

    connection strings, 748

    SSL, 751

    user passwords, 749-751

    ViewState, 751-752

sources, data adapters, 543

storage, application state, 480

structures, card tables, 296

types. *See* data types

validation, regular expressions, 89

data access layer. See DAL

data binding, 613

read-only, 635

Web Forms, 635

%# % syntax, 635

cascading header forms, 652-654, 657

complex, 638

DataBind method, 638-639

DataBinder class, 639-640

DataGrid, 647-653

DataItem property, 639

DataList, 645, 647

detail forms, 648-657

header forms, 648-52

ItemDataBound event, 640

repeater, 641-644

simple, 636-641

Windows Forms, 613

binding to a ComboBox, 622

BindingContext class, 617

cascading header/detail forms, 628, 631

complex data binding, 616

CurrencyManager class, 617-620

DataGrid binding, 622-625

header/detail forms, 625, 628

one-way data binding, 616

PropertyManager class, 620-621

simple data binding, 613-15, 621-622

two-way data binding, 616

Data Encryption Standard. See DES

Data mode (XPath), 168

data protection

DPAPI, 732-733

encryption. *See* encryption

hashes, 716

MACTripleDES class, 716-717

MD5CryptoServiceP rovider class, 719-720

SHA1Managed class, 718-719

data providers, 547, 554-555

commands, 569

IDbCommand interface, 569-570

RDPCommand class, 570, 575

connections, 565

IDbConnection interface, 566

RDPConnection class, 566, 569

DataAdapter binding, 548-549

associating DataSets with DataAdapters, 549

linking DataSets with DataAdapters, 549, 551

DataAdapters, 582

IDbDataAdapter interface, 582

RDPDataAdapter class, 582, 587

DataReaders, 575

IDataReader interface, 575-576

RDPDataReader class, 576, 581

defined, 536

implementation, 556

Microsoft .NET data
provider, 547

mySQL .NET, 548

.NET ODBC, 548

OLEDB, 544-546

Oracle .NET, 547

overview of remote
data provider,
557-558

parameters, 558

  IDataParameter
interface, 558-559

  IDataParameterColl
ection interface,
559

  RDPParameter
class, 559, 563

  RDPParameterColle
ction class, 563,
565

sample scenario,
556-557

SQL, 537

  SqlCommand class,
540-542

  SqlConnection class,
537-540

  SqlDataAdapter
class, 542-544

  SqlDataReader
class, 542

when to create,
555-556

Data Source parameter,
539

data types

  complex (XSD),
592-593

  derived (XSD), 591-592

  nullable types, 913

  partial types, 914-915

  primitive (XSD), 591

DataAdapters

  binding, 548-549

    associating
DataSets with
DataAdapters, 549

    linking DataSets
with
DataAdapters,
549-551

  data providers, 582

    IDbDataAdapter
interface, 582

    RDPDataAdapter
class, 582, 587

Database parameter, 539

Database property, 566

Database property, 538

databases, connection
strings, 539-540

DataBind method, 635,
638-639

DataBinder class, 639-640

DataGrabber class, 284

DataGrid binding, 622-625

DataGrid class, 640

DataGrid control, 444

DataGrid data binding,
647-653

DataItem property, 639

DataList class, 640

DataList control, 444

DataList data binding, 645,
647

DataReaders, data
providers, 575

  IDataReader interface,
575-576

  RDPDataReader class,
576, 581

DataSets

  data adapters, 543

  DataAdapter binding,
548-549

    associating
DataSets with
DataAdapters, 549

    linking DataSets
with
DataAdapters,
549, 551

  XSD, 599

    defining keys and
constraints,
600-603

    defining tables and
columns, 599-600

    typed DataSets,
603-611

DataSource property
(SqlConnection class), 538

DATA_BLOB struct, 724-725

dates

  formatting, 78

  localized, 511

DbDataPermission class,
697

DbType property,
IDataParameter interface,
559

DeactivateOnReturn
property, 821

deactivation (JIT), 810

Debug class, 873, 895

Debug menu commands,
Windows, 16

DEBUG symbol, 873

Debug.WriteLineIf method,
883

Debug/Step Over com-
mand, 875

debugging applications,
850, 854

Autos window, 855

breakpoints, 859-861

Breakpoints window,
857

Call Stack window, 856

Command window,
857

configurations,
850-851

Locals window, 855

Memory window, 857

Modules window, 857

navigation commands,
858-859

Output window, 857

Registers window, 857

syntax errors, 852-854

This window, 855

Threads window, 856

Visual Studio .NET,
861, 864, 867

Watch window, 855

Debugging page, 321

debugging statements,
monitoring applications,
872-876

debugging tool windows,
16-18

declarations

AttributeUsageAttri-
bute, 237

delegates, 211

events, 221

interfaces, 776

events, 778

explicitly, 784, 786

implicitly, 778-783

indexers, 778

methods, 777

practical declara-
tions, 776-777

properties, 777

declarative security,
705-706

decrement operators, 55

pre-operation, 60

prepost-operation, 60

default AssemblyInfo.cs file,
406-408

Default Web Application
template, 428

default.aspx, 739, 746-747

Default.aspx page, 512

DefaultDocument property,
525

DefaultTraceListener,
876-877

Delegate class,
constructors, 218-219

delegates, 210, 226, 912

declaration, 211

events, 221, 225-226

assigning handlers,
225-226

class declaration,
224

compiler behavior,
222

declaration, 221

defining delegates,
224

event handler
signatures, 224

handlers, 221

raising the event,
224

initialization, 212-213

invocation of methods,
213, 219

Method property, 219

multicast, 215-220

sample source code,
213

singlecast, 215-219

ThreadStart, 187

trace of, 214-215

WaitCallback, 206-208

DeleteCommand property,
582

deleting Class1.cs file, 248

deployment
    ASP.NET applications,
        520
        advanced
            deployment,
            529-533
        automated
            deployment,
            523-529
        manual deploy-
            ment, 521-523
    licensing, 768
    packages, creating,
        703-704
    PIAs (primary Interop
        assemblies), 287-288
    web farms, 504-505
Depth property,
    IDataReader interface,
    576
Depth property
    (SqlDataReader class),
    542
derived data types, XSD,
    591-592
DES (Data Encryption
    Standard) algorithm, 711
DESCryptoServiceProvider
    class, 711-712
Deserialize method, 181
design
    for deployment,
        531-532
    smart clients, 391
    web pages, 27

Design view, 425
    CookieExample.aspx,
        468-469
    Hello World
        application, 430
    ViewStateExampleFor
        m.aspx.cs, 460-461
Designer Defaults page,
    320
destructors, 297-300
detail forms, 648-654, 657
Details property, 339
dialog boxes
    Activation tab, 817
    Add Project Output,
        416
    Add Web Reference,
        397
    Breakpoint Properties,
        859
    Code Group Properties,
        703
    Configuration
        Manager, 851
    Copy Project, 521
    New Project, 415, 836
    Project Properties, 851
    WMIDemoProvider,
        899
    Zone Security
        Adjustment, 702
digital certificates, X.509,
    689
digital signatures, 720-723
DIME (Direct Internet
    Message Encapsulation),
    690

Direct Internet Message
    Encapsulation. See DIME
Direction property,
    IDataParameter interface,
    559
directives, OutputCache,
    484-488
directories, bin\debug, 258
Directory class, 131-132
DirectoryName filter,
    FileSystemWatcher class,
    138
DirectoryServicesPermission
    class, 696
DisableCommit method,
    821
Disabled option, 673
Disassembly window, 17
displaying
    localized content, 507
        data, 510-511
        images, 507-508
        text, 508-510
    Windows Forms appli-
        cations, 321
Dispose method, 47, 298,
    538
distributed transactions,
    673
Div (division) operator, 170
DllImportAttribute attribute,
    290
dllName property, 290
DLLs
    consuming, 288-289
    SimpleApplicationLibr
        ary.dll, 417

DMZs, advanced ASP.NET deployment, 530-532

DnsPermission class, 697

do..while loop, 72-73

do..while statement, 72-73

dockable windows, 10-11

Document Object Model. *See* DOM

Document Outline window, 15

documents (XML)

creating, 161-162

transformations, 175-178

DOM (Document Object Model), 155-161, 163

domain-neutral assemblies, 794

domains

AppDomains, 793-794

domain-neutral assemblies, 794

global exception handlers, 795

remotingRemoting, 793-794

domain-neutral assemblies, 794

global exception handlers, 795

Dotfuscator, 770

double-backslash (\\) character, 80

Downstream attribute (Location attribute), 487

DPAPI (Windows Data Protection API), 710, 723-726

creating wrapper classes, 726-727, 732

data protection in .NET, 732-733

drawing modes, 363

DrawItem event handler, 364-365

DrawMode property, 363

DrawMode.Normal mode, 363

DrawMode.OwnerDrawFixed mode, 363

DrawMode.OwnerDrawVaria ble mode, 363

DropDownList control, 444

DSACryptoServiceProvider class, 721, 723

dumb terminals, 390-391

Duration attribute (OutputCache directive), 486

dwFlags parameter, 725

dwPromptFlags field (CRYPTPROTECT_ PROMPTSTRUCT structure), 726

dynamic assemblies, 244

dynamic content, enterprise templates, 830-831

dynamic context menus, 359-360

pop-up context menu event handler, 361

populating ListView, 362-363

Dynamic Help, 23

Dynamic Help window, 15

dynamic URLs, 378

app.config file, 379

isolated storage, 379-380, 382

UDDI consumption, 382-383

E

Edit1Label property, 527

Edit1Property property, 527

Edit2Visible property, 527

Edit3Visible property, 527

Edit4Visible property, 527

editing

binary files, 30

HTML, 26-27

HTML editor, 28-29

HTML view window, 28

web page design, 27

XML, 29-30

editors

hex, 30

HTML, 28-29

EIF (Enterprise Instrumentation Framework), 890, 903

architecture, 903

configuration file, 903

event schemas, 903-904

event sinks, 903-906

event sources, 903-905

instrumentation API, 903

configuring, 906

application configuration file, 906

trace session configuration file, 907

request tracing, 906

System.Management namespace, 904

elements (XML), 162-163

EmbeddedData.xml, AssemblyIntro project, 252

embedding

content in assemblies, 251-255

resources in assemblies, 251-255

EnableCommit method, 821

Encrypt parameter, 539

encryption

asymmetric, 720-721

DSACryptoServicePr ovider class, 721, 723

RSACryptoServicePr ovider class, 723

public key, 720-721

DSACryptoServicePr ovider class, 721, 723

RSACryptoServicePr ovider class, 723

SSL, 751

symmetric, 711

DESCryptoServicePr ovider class, 711-712

RC2CryptoServicePr ovider class, 712

RijndaelManaged class, 713

TripleDESCryptoServ iceProvider class, 713, 715

ViewState, 751-752

EndRequest event, 513

EndSlowHelloWorld method, 385

EndsWith method, 80

Enlist parameter, 540

Enter method (Monitor class), 200

Enter Outlining Mode When Files Open check box, 19

Enterprise Instrumentation Framework. See EIF

Enterprise Template Definition Language. See TDL

enterprise templates, 828-829

accessibility, 844-845

architecture, 829-830, 835-836

assigning policies, 839-840

content, 830-831

custom wizards, 831

manual construction, 840

deletion of ancillary files, 841

modification of project files, 841, 843

policy files, 831-834

projects, 829

setting up prerequisites, 834

static prototypes, 831

structure, 836-839

subproject wizards, 831

testing, 845

Enterpriseinstrumentation.c onfig, 906

EntryPoint property, 290

enumerations

HttpCacheability.Publi c, 490

TransactionOption, 673

enumerators, 99

EnvironmentPermission class, 697

Error (1) tracing level (TraceSwitch), 884

errors

messages, debugging applications, 852-854

web services, 387

escape character (\), 79

escape sequences, strings, 79-80

Evaluate Assembly task (Runtime Security Policy folder), 700-703

evaluation expressions, 53

evaluations, short circuit, 62, 64

event handlers

  Application_Authentic ateRequest, 745-746

  DrawItem, 364-365

  MeasureItem, 364-365

  MouseDown, 369-370

  MouseMove, 369-370

  Page_Load, 511

  pop-up context menu, 361

event handling

  ASP.NET, 433-438

  delegates, 912

Event Log, instrumenting, 892-894

event logs, EventLogDemo, 894

EventLog class, 893

EventLogDemo event log, 894

EventLogPermission class, 697

EventLogTraceListener, 876, 880

events, 221, 225-226

  AcquireRequestState, 513

  advanced COM+, 823-826

  assigning handlers, 225-226

  AuthenticateRequest, 513

  AuthorizeRequest, 513

  BeginRequest, 513

  class declaration, 224

  COM+, 812-813

  compiler behavior, 222

  CurrencyManager class, 618

  declaration, 221

  declaring, 778

  defining delegates, 224

  EndRequest, 513

  event handler signatures, 224

  handlers, 221

  ItemDataBound, 640

  raising, thread synchronization, 194-196

  raising the event, 224

  schemas, 903-904

  sinks, 903-906

  sources, 903-904

    Request, 905

    SoftwareElement, 904

  SqlConnection class, 539

  WMIDemo_SampleEve nt, 900-901

Evidence property (AppDomain class), 260

evaluation variables, 60

ExactSpelling property, 290

exception handlers, 795

exceptions, 305, 493

ExecuteNonQuery method, 542

ExecuteNonQuery property, 570

ExecutePermissions proper ty, 525

ExecuteReader method, 542

ExecuteReader property, 570

ExecuteScalar method, 542

ExecuteScalar property, 570

execution

  code, 43

  path, 60

exitContext parameter, 201

explicit declarations, declar ing interfaces, 784-786

Explore Here tool, creating, 31

expressions, 53

  assignment, 53

  defined, 53

  evaluation, 53

  regular expressions, 85

    assertions, 89

    data validation, 89

    matching, 85-91

    syntax, 85

  short circuit evalua tions, 62-64

expressions (XPath), 168

ExtendingSerialization example, 149-152

Extensible Markup Language, See XML

eXtensible Extensible Stylesheet Language: Transformations. See XSLT

extern keyword, 288

external method, 288

external tools, 30-31

F

facets, XML schemas, 594-595

Fail function (trace listeners), 877

failover, 499

false mode (BooleanSwitch), 882

farms, web

best practices, 505-506

creating ASP.NET applications in, 499

application state, 503-504

configuration, 504-505

deployment, 504-505

session state maintenance, 501-503

ViewState, 499-500

Favorites window, 15

FCL (Framework Class Library), 38

namespaces, 48-49

value types, 38-39

FieldCount property (SqlDataReader class), 542

fields

DllImportAttribute attribute, 290

forms, hidden, 463-467

.vsdir files, 844

FIFO (first in, last out)

Queue, 104-105

SortedList, 106-107

File class, 129

FileDialogPermission class, 697

FileInfo class, 130-131

FileIOPermission class, 697

FileName filter, FileSystemWatcher class, 138

files

AssemblyInfo.cs, 248, 406-408

Class1.cs, 248

Default Web Application template, 428

Enterpriseinstrumentat ion.config, 906

I/O, 128-129

Directory class, 131-132

File class, 129

FileInfo class, 130-131

TraceSessions.config, 907

transferring, 691

Web.config, 735

XSD, 589-590

FileStream class, 132-134, 880

FileSystemWatcher class, 138-142

filtering

MSDN help, 9

nodes, 170-171

filters, notification, 138

finalizers, 297-300

Find Results window, 15

Find Symbol Results window, 15

firewalls, advanced ASP.NET deployment, 530-532

FirstForm.aspx

Code view, 476-477

HTML view, 475

flags, 725

flow (program)

control structures, 60

conditional statements, 60-61

execution path, 60

if conditional statements, 61

if/else conditional statements, 61

short circuit evaluations, 62, 64

switch statement, 65-68

ternary operator, 64-65

Flush function (trace listeners), 877

folders, Web Application, 524-525

for loops, 68-69, 308-309

for statement, 69

foreach loop, 308-309

foreach statement, 69

foreground threads, 185

Form1.cs, 326-329

formatting strings, 75-76

alignment, 76-77

custom dates, 78-79

custom integers, 77-78

dates, 78

escape sequences, 79-80

integers, 77

padding, 76-77, 80-81

forms

authentication, 737-739

fields, hidden, 463-467

passing server controls between, 474-479

shaped, 368-370

visual inheritance, 351-359

Web Forms, 634

data binding, 635-657

event handling, 433-438

Windows Forms, 314, 634

Button control, 324-329

compiling, 322-323

creating buttons on, 316-317

custom list elements, 363-367

Forms Designer, 316-318

Hello World, 318-321

licensing, 768

Main method, 315-316

running, 322-323

setting properties, 321-322

Forms Designer, 316-318

FormsAuthentication class, 738-739

Forward navigation, Visual Studio .NET IDE, 20

Framework Class Library

reference types, 39-40

value types, 38-40

free licenses, 756

FriendlyName property (AppDomain class), 260

full collections, 295

FullName property, System.Type class, 230

functions

common type systems, 38

CryptProtectData, 724

myFunction, 638

XPath, 169

future considerations (C#), 908-909

anonymous methods, 912-913

generics, 909-911

managing lists with iterators, 913-914

nullable types, 913

partial types, 914-915

static classes, 915-916

G

GAC (global assembly cache), 404-409

gacutil.exe, 404-405

Garbage Collector (GCs), 44

collections, 45

destructors, 297-300

finalizers, 297-300

full collections, 295

generations, 295-296

IDisposable interface, 46-48

managed heap, 295

memory management, 44

nondeterministic finalization, 45-46

programming, 296-297

Garbage Collectors. See GCs

GCs (Garbage Collectors), 295

collections, 45

destructors, 297-300

finalizers, 297-300

full collections, 295

generations, 295-296

IDisposable interface, 46-48

managed heap, 295

memory management, 44

nondeterministic finalization, 45-46

programming, 296-297

Gen0, 296

General property page, 320

Generation 0, 296

Generations, 44, 295-296

Generic class, 911

generics, 909-911

GetAppDomainInfo method, 263

GetArrayList method, 671

GetAssemblies method (AppDomain class), 260

GetConstructors method, System.Type class, 230

GetData method (AppDomain class), 260

GetDataNodeValue method, 252, 254

GetDataSet method, 672

GetEnumerator method, 98

GetEvents method, System.Type class, 230

GetInvocationList method (System.MulticastDelegate class), 220

GetLeastSmartest() method, debugging applications, 867

GetManifestResource Stream method, 254-255

GetMember method, System.Type class, 230

GetMembers method, System.Type class, 230

GetNamedProperty method, 821

GetPanelText method, 638

GetProperties method, 231, 234

GetProperty method, System.Type class, 231

GetRedirectUrl method, 738

GetSchemaTable method, IDataReader interface, 576

GetStrings method, 672

global assembly cache. See GAC

global exception handlers, 795

Global XML Web Services Architecture. See GXA

Global.asax file, 428

globalization, ASP.NET, 506

displaying localized content, 507-511

localization function-ality, 511-513

localized resources, 506-507

greater than or equal to operator, 171

group control attributes, XSD complex data types, 593

group element, XSD complex data types, 593

GroupBox control, 345-346

groups

collections. See collections

matches (regular expressions), 89-90

shared, COM+, 818-820

GuidAttribute attribute, 283

GXA (Global XML Web Services Architecture), 679

H

handlers, event, 221, 225-226

Harness application, 263

Harness project, 249

hashes, 716

MACTripleDES class, 716-717

MD5CryptoServiceProv ider class, 719-720

SHA1Managed class, 718-719

HashPasswordForStoringInC onfigFile method, 738

Hashtable collection, 102-103

HasRows property (SqlDataReader class), 542

header forms, 648-652

header/detail forms, data binding, 625, 628, 631

Hello World

creating, 426-432

web services, 665-669

Windows Forms, 318

Button control, 324-329

compiling, 322-323

running, 322-323

setting properties, 321-322

Windows Application Wizard, 319-321

Hello World application, C#, 49-50

HelloService class, 668-673

HelloWorld class, 278-279

help, 22

comment reports, 24-25

Dynamic Help, 23

Intellisense, 25-26

MSDN, filtering, 9

Help control, 454

hex editor, 30

hidden form fields, 463-467

HiddenVariableExample. aspx, 464

HiddenVariableExample.asp x.cs, 465

hiding

algorithms, 769-770

windows, 12-14

high fidelity, smart clients, 391

history, WSE, 679

hosted environments, advanced ASP.NET deployment, 532-533

HTML (HyperText Hypertext Markup Language)

controls

HtmlAnchor, 441

HtmlButton, 441

HtmlForm, 441

HtmlGenericControl, 441

HtmlImage, 441

HtmlInputButton, 442

HtmlInputCheckBox, 442

HtmlInputFile, 442

HtmlInputHidden, 442

HtmlInputImage, 442

HtmlInputRadioButt on, 442

HtmlInputText, 442

HtmlSelect, 442

HtmlTable, 442

HtmlTableCell, 442

HtmlTableRow, 442

HtmlTextArea, 442

server controls, 440-442

System.Web.UI.Html Controls name-space, 441

editing, 26-27

HTML editor, 28-29

HTML view window, 28

web page design, 27

View, 28, 425

FirstForm.aspx, 475

QueryStringExample .aspx, 472

SecondForm.aspx, 477-478

HtmlAnchor control, 441

HtmlButton control, 441

HtmlForm control, 441

HtmlGenericControl control, 441

HtmlImage control, 441

HtmlInputButton control, 442

HtmlInputCheckBox control, 442

HtmlInputFile control, 442

HtmlInputHidden control, 442

HtmlInputImage control, 442

HtmlInputRadioButton control, 442

HtmlInputText control, 442

HtmlSelect control, 442

HtmlTable control, 442

HtmlTableCell control, 442

HtmlTableRow control, 442

HtmlTextArea control, 442

HttpApplicationState class, 480-481

HttpApplicationState object, 480

HttpCache object, 485

HttpCacheability.Public enumeration, 490

HttpCachePolicy class, 489-491

HttpCachePolicy object, 484

HttpChannel, 796-797

HttpHandlers, creating, 516-518

HttpModules, creating, 513-515

hwndApp field (CRYPTPRO TECT_PROMPTSTRUCT structure), 726

HyperLink control, 444

I

I/O (input and output), 128

  asynchronous, 310

  file, 128-129

    Directory class, 131-132

    File class, 129

    FileInfo class, 130-131

  stream, 128-129, 132

    FileStream class, 132-134

    FileSystemWatcher class, 138-142

    MemoryStream class, 134-135

    StreamReader class, 136-138

    StreamWriter class, 136-138

    StringReader class, 135-136

    StringWriter class, 135-136

IAsyncComponent interface, 826

ICollection interface, 98

IComparer interface, 98

IDataParameter interface, 558-559

IDataParameterCollection interface, 559

IDataReader interface, 575-576

IDbCommand interface, 569-570

IDbConnection interface, 566

IDbDataAdapter interface, 582

IDE

  binary file edits, 30

  help, 22

    comment reports, 24-25

    Dynamic Help, 23

    Intellisense, 25-26

  HTML edits, 26-27

    HTML editor, 28-29

    HTML view window, 28

    web page design, 27

  text editors, 18

    bookmarks, 20-23

    navigation, 20

    outlining code, 18-19

  XML edits, 29-30

identity permissions, 697-698

IDictionary interface, 98

IDictionaryEnumerator interface, 98

IDisposable interface, 46-48, 298-299

IEnumerable interface, 98-99, 638, 913

if conditional statement, 61

if-else-if statement, 66-67

if/else conditional statement, 61

IIdentity interface, implementation, 740-747

IIS

  configuration in web farms, 504-505

  remotingRemoting, 806-807

IL (Intermediate Language), 40

ILDASM command, 245

IList interface, 98

Image control, 444

ImageButton control, 444

images, localized, 507-508

Immediate window, 17

immutability, strings, 75

imperative security, 704-705

implicit declarations, declaring interfaces, 778-783

ImplicitInterfaceImplementation, output, 781

InAttribute attribute, 283

Increase Assembly Trust task (Runtime Security Policy folder), 699

increment operators, 55, 60

Indent method, 874-875

Index property, 525

Index Results window, 15

Index window, 15

indexers, declaring, 778

indexing operators, 55

IndexOf method, 80, 559

IndexOfAny method, 80

indirection operators, 55

Info (3) tracing level (TraceSwitch), 884

InfoMessage event (SqlConnection class), 539

inheritance, base classes, 119-122

Inheritance polymorphism, 123

inheritance, visual, 351-352

  best practices, 358-359

  WinForms, 352-353, 356

    CompanyOKCancel, 354-356

    InheritedForm, 358

    InheritedOKCancel, 356-359

InheritedForm inherited form, 358

InheritedOKCancel inherited form, 356-358

InheritedOKCancel Windows form, 359

inheriting interfaces, 789-790

Initial Catalog parameter, 539

Initial Directory field, 31

initialization

  delegate instances, 212-213

  variables, 53

initializeData attribute (add tag), 879

InnerText property, 441

InProc mode, sessionState, 481

input and output. See I/O

input strings, parsing with while statement, 70, 72

Insert method, 83

  Cache object, 493

  creating SQL statements, 83-84

InsertCommand property, 582

installation projects, creating, 415-420

installing

  .NET applications, 402

    assembly deployment, 403

    placing assemblies in GAC, 404-406, 408-409

    private installations, 409

  web applications, 410

    smart client deployments, 412

    URL deployments, 410

InstallShield, 415

instance documents, 593

instrumentation API, 903

instrumenting, 890

  applications, 890-892

    compared to monitoring, 891-892

    Debug class, 895

    Event Log, 892-894

    Trace class, 895-897

  EIF (Enterprise Instrumentation Framework), 890, 903

    architecture, 903-906

    configuring, 906-907

    request tracing, 906

  WMI (Windows Management Instrumentation), 890, 897-902

integer formatting, strings, 77

Integrated Security parameter, 539

intellectual property, licensing and, 755, 769

  alternative back-ends, 770-771

  hiding algorithms, 769-770

  obfuscation, 770

intelligent connections, smart clients, 391

Intellisense, 25-26

interations, collections, 98-99

Interface interface polymorphism, 123

interface programming, 774-786

interfaces
  Collection, 98
  developer profiles, 7-8
  IAsyncComponent, 826
  ICollection, 98
  IComparer, 98
  IDictionary, 98
  IDictionaryEnumerator, 98
  IDisposable, 46-48, 298-299
  IEnumerable, 98-99, 638, 913
  IList, 98
  implementation of custom data providers
    IDataParameter interface, 558-559
    IDataParameterCollection interface, 559
    IDataReader interface, 575-576
    IDbCommand interface, 569-570
    IDbConnection interface, 566
    IDbDataAdapter interface, 582

inheriting, 789-790
IPlugin, 266
IPrincipal, 740, 812
ISomeInterface, 775
ISpeak, 783
mapping, 786-788

InterfaceTypeAttribute attribute, 283

Interlocked class, thread synchronization, 203

Intermediate Language. See IL

interoperability, COM, 43-44

interprocess communication (IPC), 793

Interrupt method (Thread class), 187

invocation, delegate methods, 213, 219

Invoke method, 385

IPC (interprocess communication), 793

IPlugin interface, 266

IPrincipal interface, 740-747, 812

is operator, 230

IsAbstract property, System.Type class, 230

IsAlive property (Thread class), 185

IsApplication property, 525

IsBackground property (Thread class), 185

IsCallerInRole method, 812, 821

IsClass property, System.Type class, 230

IsClosed property, IDataReader interface, 576

IsClosed property (SqlDataReader class), 542

ISerializable.GetObjectData method, 149

IsInRole method, 740, 812

IsInterface property, System.Type class, 230

IsInTransaction property, 821

IsNullable property, IDataParameter interface, 559

IsolatedStorageFilePermission class, 697

IsolatedStoragePermission class, 697

isolation
  Common Language Runtime, 42
  storage retrieval for XML documents, 380-382
  URL storage, 379-382

ISomeInterface interface, 775

isOwned property, 196

ISpeak interface, 783

IsSecurityEnabled property, 821

IsSynchronized property, 98

IsThreadPoolThread method (Thread class), 185

Item property, IDataParameterCollection interface, 559

Item property
(SqlDataReader class),
542

ItemChanged event,
CurrencyManager class,
618

ItemDataBound event, 640

iterations, collections, 98-99

iterators, managing lists,
913-914

J

jagged arrays, 93, 95-96,
307-308

JIT (just-in-time), 810

activation, 810, 817

compiler, Common
Language Runtime,
43

deactivation, 810

Join method (Thread class),
187

joining threads, 191

just-in-time. See JIT

K

key pairs, public/private,
405-406

keyboard shortcuts, 8

keypair.snk file, 406

keyref constraints, 602-603

keys

defining DataSets
using XML schema,
600

key constraints, 601

keyref constraints,
602-603

relationships, 601

unique constraints,
601

secret, 711

keywords

extern, 288

new, 39

partial, 914

struct, 38

using, 47

virtual, 123

L

Label control, 334, 444

languages

creating new lan-
guages, reasons for,
37

Language data type,
592

object-oriented, 37

projects, enterprise
template structure,
829, 837-839

LargeIcon property, 339

LastAccess filter,
FileSystemWatcher class,
138

LastIndexOf method, 80

LastIndexOfAny method, 80

LastWriteu filter,
FileSystemWatcher class,
138

layers, enterprise templates,
835-836

leastSmartest variable, 865

less than operator, 171

Less less than or equal to
operator, 171

Level property (TraceSwitch
class), 884

libraries

CASLibrary, 700

SampleHttpModule,
514

Library mode, 809

License-Protected Label
control, 765, 767

licensed controls, 764, 767

LicenseManager class,
757-759

LicenseProvider attribute,
757-759

LicenseProvider class, 760,
762, 764

licensing, 755-756

creating licenses,
759-760

custom, 757

LicenseManager
class, 757-759

LicenseProvider
attribute, 757-759

defined, 755

free, 756

implementation

deployment
methods, 768

licensing schemes,
769

purchase methods,
768

verification
methods, 768

intellectual property
protection, 755, 769

alternative back-
ends, 770-771

hiding algorithms,
769-770

obfuscation, 770

licensed controls, 764,
767

LicenseProvider class,
760, 762, 764

one-time, 756

per action, 756

per CPU, 756

per seat, 756

subscription, 756

verification, 756

web controls compared
to Windows Forms
controls, 768

LIFO (last in, first out)

BitArray collection,
103-104

Hashtable collection,
102-103

Stack collection,
101-102

LinkButton control, 444

List property

CurrencyManager
class, 618

ListView.View property,
339

ListBox control, 337, 444

ListBox controls, 337, 444

advanced data bind-
ing, 653-654, 657

ListBoxes, 363-365

Listeners property (Trace
and Debug classes), 877

listeners tag, 878

listings

Acme Stock Company
License Provider
Implementation,
761-762

AddressCollection,
107-109

annotated typed
DataSets, 609-611

Application_Authentic
ateRequest event
handler, 745-746

ArrayList example,
100

AssemblyTool class,
248-263

asynchronous web ser-
vice calls, 675-676

attributes for
customizing XML
serialization, 181-183

BitArray example, 104

bll.etp file after
modifications,
842-843

bll.etp file before
modifications, 842

BluePlugin class,
266-268

BooleanSwitch (trace
switch) sample, 883

boxing, 300-301

Cache object, 491-496

caching HTML pages
with HttpCachePolicy
class, 489-490

caching HTML pages
with OutputCache
directive, 485-486

Class1 class, 257-258

classes decorated with
custom attributes,
238

classes that read cur-
rent values of shared
properties, 818

classes that set values
of shared properties,
819-820

classes with methods
that utilize objects
and security, 822-823

client console applica-
tion, 805-806

code

attribute class,
236-237

C# console
application, 50

displaying authors
of methods,
240-241

web form utilizing
new resources,
509-510

collections, strongly typed, 909-910

common file, 804

configuration file defining a trace switch, 882

connecting to Amazon.com's web service, 398-399

console application code utilizing VB6 COM object, 279-280

CookieExample.aspx

Design view, 468-469

Source view, 469-471

creating .NET citizens, 47

creating XSD files, 595-598

CurrencyManager class and complex data, 618-620

custom trace listener creation, 886-887

custom UsernameToken processing class, 688-689

CustomIdentity class, 741-742

CustomPrincipal class, 743-745

data-bound repeater, 641-644

DataGrabber class, 284

DataGrid binding and CurrencyManager class, 622-624

DataGrid data binding, 648-650

Debug class sample, 874

declaration of delegates, 211

default AssemblyInfo.cs file, 406-408

default.aspx, 746-747

Directory example, 131

DPAPIWrapper class, 727-732

DrawItem event handler for ListBoxes, 364-365

DSACryptoServiceProvider class

verifying signatures with key pairs, 721-722

event class, subscriber class, and shared interface, 824-826

EventLogTraceListener, 880-881

ExtendingSerialization example, 149-152

File example, 129

FileInfo example, 130-131

FileStream class, 133-134

FileSystemWatcher, 139-142

FirstForm.aspx

Code view, 476-477

HTMl HTML view, 475

Form1.cs, 326-329

gacutil.exe output, 404-405

generated XML document, 180-181

global exception handler, 795

grid binding form with cascade parent/detail, 628-631

grouping regular expressions, 90

Hashtable example, 102-103

header/detail grid binding, 625-628

HeaderDetail.aspx Page, 650-652

Hello World web services code, 665-669

HelloService, 668-669

HelloService class, returning data to clients, 669-673

HelloWorld class, 278-279

HiddenVariableExample.aspx, 464

HiddenVariableExample.aspx.cs, 465

HTML code for custom user control, 448-449

HTML code for web page, 446

HttpHandler class, 516

identity-protected method, 707-708

IDisposable interface, 298-299

if-else-if statement, 66-67

implementing interfaces implicitly, 778-781

incorrectly redeclaring interface method, 781-783

inheritance, 119-122

inheriting interfaces, 789-790

Insert method, creating SQL statements, 83-84

IPlugin interface, 266

isolated storage for XML documents, 380-382

jagged arrays, 96

License Class Implementation, 759

License-Protected Label control, 765-767

linking DataSets with DataAdapters, 549-551

ListBox controls, 653-657

ListView control example, 339-342

Logon user control, 347-348

MACTripleDES hash algorithm, 716

main form of simple data binding, 614-615

manipulating typed DataSets, 608

mapping interfaces, 787-788

MD5 cryptographic service provider, 719-720

MeasureItem event handler for ListBoxes, 364-365

MemoryStream example, 135

MessageReceiver class derives from SoapReceiver class, 681-682

MessagingSoapClient class, 686-687

MessagingSoapClient class derives from SoapClient, 686-687

methods with same signatures, 784-786

Monitor class, Wait and PulseAll methods, 201-203

Monitor class application, 198-199

MouseDown event handler, 369-370

MouseMove event handler, 369-370

nested schema example, 603-604

overloading operators, 56-59

P/Invoke example, 291

padding and alignment in string formatting, 76-77

parsing input strings with while statement, 70-72

passing arrays as parameters, 97

passing data to a worker thread, 208-209

passing value types to methods, 40

PluginLoader class, 269-270

PluginTester Console application, 271-272

PluginTool, 268-269

polymorphism, 124-125

pop-up context menu event handler, 361

populating DataSets with SqlCommand/SqlDataAdapter, 543-544

populating ListView, 362-363

pseudo smart client application, 412

public information stored in keypair.snk, 406

Queue example, 105

ReaderWriterLock class application, 203-206

RedPlugin class, 266-268

reflection example, 231-234

Regex class, 87-89

registering remote objects, 803

registering single call and singleton methods, 800-801

registering TraceSwitch in App.config, 884

registration of listeners in App.config file, 877

remote data provider class, 560-563

remote data provider command class, 570-575

remote data provider connection, 566-569

remote data provider data adapter, 582-587

remote data provider DataReader class, 576-581

remote data provider parameter collection class, 563-565

resource leaks in .NET, 46

sample source code using delegates, 213

Sample Validation Web Service Used by the License Provider to Authenticate Client Controls, 762-764

SampleModule HttpModule Implementation, 514-515

SerializationDeSerializationExample, 143-149

server host application, 803-804

SHA-1 Managed Hash Algorithm Class, 718

short circuit evaluations, 62-64

simple data binding, 636-641

Simple Event Log demo, 893

simple string formatting example, 75-76

single instance application using Mutex class, 196

singlecast and multicast delegates, 215

Soap Message Sender, 682

SortedList example, 106-107

source code for user control, 450-451

source code for web page, 447-448

Source View, 467

SqlCommand instance, 540-541

Stack example, 101-102

StaticAndDynamicContent Project, 830

storing months of the year in single-dimensional arrays, 94-95

storing months of the year in two-dimensional arrays, 95

StringReaderWriter example, 136

stub applications using Application.LoadFrom method, 393-394

switch statement, 67-68

symmetric encryption, 713-715

synchronous web service calls, 675

syntax errors sample program (debugging applications), 861-867

Test Harness Console application, 250-251

TextWriterTraceListener, 879-880

thread application, 189-190

Thread class, 191

thread pool sample, 207-208

Trace class sample, 874

trace of delegates, 214-215

trace of singlecast and multicast delegates, 217

TraceSwitch example, 885

TreeView sample program, 343-345

utility classes, finding method authors using code attributes, 239

variable names, 54

VB client consuming .MET COM object, 285

verifying strongly names assemblies, 409

ViewStateExampleForm.aspx, 457-459

ViewStateExampleForm.aspx.cs, 458-461

Visual Studio .NET Auto-Generated Web Service Client Proxy, 374-376

waiting for events, 194-196

waiting for mutexes, 197

Web.config, 807

WebForm1.aspx, 431-437

WebForm1.aspx.cs, 432-438

while statement compared to do..while, 73

XML Document, 165-166

XML document transformations, 176

XML DOM, 156-161

XML generated after customization of XML serialization, 183

XML Sample, 161

XML serialization, 179-180

XmlTextReader source code, 165

XPath Document class and XPathNavigator, 172-174

XPathNodeIterator Using Sample, 174

XSD sample file, 589-590

XSL file containing transformation template, 176-177

XSL transformation sample source code, 177-178

lists
maintaining with controls, 337
ListBox control, 337
ListView control, 338-342
TreeView control, 342-345
managing with iterators, 913-914

ListView, populating, 362-363

ListView control, 338-342

live objects, 296

Load method (AppDomain class), 260

LoadEmbeddedDoc method, 254

LoadViewState method, overriding, 462

localization
ASP.NET, 506
displaying localized content, 507-511
functionality, 511-513
localized resources, 506-507
assembly resource file, 255-259

localized currency, 511-512

localized dates, 511

localized resources, 506-507

localized time zones, 512-513

Locals window, 17, 855

Location attribute (OutputCache directive), 486

Location paths (XPath), 168

lock keyword, thread synchronization, 193

Lock method, HttpApplicationState class, 481

LogEventSink event sink, 905

logging, 872-876

logical operators, 54

logical units. See assemblies

LogicalCallContext class, 906

LogVisits property, 525

loops, 68

  do..while, 72-73

  for, 68-69, 308-309

  foreach, 308-309

  foreach statement, 69

  while, 70, 72

loosely coupled events (COM+), 812

M

Macro Explorer window, 15

MACTripleDES class, 716-717

Main method, 50, 315-316

managed code, reflection, 228-231, 234

managed heap, 295

Manifest section, 245-246

manual construction, enterprise templates, 840-843

manual deployment, ASP.NET applications, 521-523

ManualResetEvent class, 194

mapping interfaces, 786-788

Marshal.BindToMoniker method, 826

MarshalAsAttribute attribute, 283

matching regular expressions, 85-87

  character classes, 87

  grouping matches, 89-90

  Regex class, 87, 89

  replacing matched strings, 90-91

  single-character escape sequences, 86

Max Pool Size parameter, 540

MD5CryptoServiceProvider class, 719-720

MeasureItem event handler, 364-365

members

  access operators, 55

  ICollection interface, 98

memory

  CLRCommon Language Runtime, 300

    boxing, 300-303

    StringBuilder class, 303-305

    unboxing, 300, 302

  management, 44

Memory window, 17, 857

MemoryStream class, 134-135

menus

  Add Classes, 899

  custom Windows Forms, 365-367

  dynamic context, 359-363

message digest, 721

message signatures, 690

MessageBoxes, web service invocation, 377

MessageBoxTraceListener class, 887

MessageQueuePermission class, 697

MessageReceiver class, SoapReceiver class, 681-682

messaging

  TCP, 679-680

    SOAP over TCP, 680

    SoapClient class, 686-687

    SoapReceiver class, 680-684

    SoapSender class, 680-684

    SoapService class, 683-685

    WSE 2.0 attachments, 690-691

MessagingSoapClient class, 686-687

metadata, 246

MetaDataChanged event, CurrencyManager class, 618

MetaEdit, 504

Method property, 219

methods

  abstract, 123

  AddRange, 307

  anonymous, 912-913

  app.config, 382

AppDomain class, 259-260

Append, 83

AppendFormat, 83

Authenticate, 738

BeginHelloWithParameters, 676

BeginSlowHelloWorld, 385

ByValue, 40

Console.WriteLine, 50

Construct, 811, 815

ContextUtil class, 821

CopyTo, 98

CreateAttribute, 161-162

CreateCDataSection, 162

CreateComment, 162

CreateElement, 162

CreateInstance, 263

CreateNode, 162

CreateWhitespace, 162

DataBind, 635, 638-639

declaring, 777

delegate management, 222

Deserialize, 181

Dispose, 47, 298

EndSlowHelloWorld, 385

EndsWith, 80

enumerators, 99

ExecuteNonQuery, 542

ExecuteReader, 542

ExecuteScalar, 542

external, 288

FormsAuthentication class, 738-739

GetAppDomainInfo, 263

GetArrayList, 671

GetDataNodeValue, 252, 254

GetDataSet, 672

GetEnumerator, 98

GetManifestResourceStream, 254-255

GetPanelText, 638

GetProperties, 234

GetRedirectUrl, 738

GetStrings, 672

HashPasswordForStoringInConfigFile, 738

IDataParameterCollection interface, 559

IDataReader interface, 575-576

IDbCommand interface, 569-570

IDbConnection interface, 566

IndexOf, 80

IndexOfAny, 80

Insert, 83
    Cache object, 493
    creating SQL statements, 83-84

Invoke, 385

IsCallerInRole, 812

ISerializable.GetObjectData, 149

IsInRole, 740, 812

LastIndexOf, 80

LastIndexOfAny, 80

LoadEmbeddedDoc, 254

LoadFrom, 393-394

LoadViewState, 462

Lock, 481

Main, 315-316

Marshal.BindToMoniker, 826

MoveNext, 99

passing value types to, 40

PerformAdministrativeAction, 823

PublishEvent, 825

RedirectFromLoginPage, 738

Remove, 84

RenewTicketIfOld, 738

Replace, 81, 84

Reset, 99

same signatures, 784, 786

SaveViewState, 462

Serialize, 181

SetAuthCookie, 739

SetCacheability, 490

SetExpires, 490

SignOut, 739

Split, 82

SqlConnection class, 538-539

StartsWith, 80

System.Array.GetUpperBound, 95

System.Delegate class, 220

System.MulticastDeleg ate class, 220

System.Reflection, 393-394

System.String class, 80

System.Type class, 230

threads, 186-187

ToUpper, 82

Trim, 81

TrimEnd, 81

TrimStart, 81

Unlock, 481

virtual, 123-125

WriteContentTo, 163

WriteLine, 40, 60

WriteTo, 163

XmlDocument.Save, 163

Microsoft .NET, 547

Microsoft Intermediate Language. *See* MSIL

Microsoft Jscript, 831

Microsoft Message Queuing. *See* MSMQ

Microsoft Transaction Services (MTS), 809

Mile class, 59

millisecondTimeout parameter (threads), 197

Min Pool Size parameter, 540

Mod operator, 170

Modules window, 17, 857

Monitor class, 198-203

Monitor.Enter / Monitor.Exit code block, 198

Monitor.TryEnter method, 200

monitoring applications, 872

    compared to instru-menting, 891-892

    custom trace listeners, 885-887

    debugging and tracing statements, 872-876

    trace listeners, 876-881

    trace switches, 882-885

MouseDown event handler, 369-370

MouseMove event handler, 369-370

MoveNext method, 99

mscorlib assembly, 264

MSDN help, filtering, 9

MSI (Windows Installer)

    creating setup projects, 523-529

    deploying setup pro-jects, 529

MSIL (Microsoft Intermediate Language), 247

MSMQ (Microsoft Message Queuing), 555

MTS (Microsoft Transaction Services), 809

multicast delegates, 215-220

multidimensional arrays, 93

multifile assemblies, 244-245

multithreaded program-ming, threads, 184-185

    creating, 188

    joining, 191

    methods, 186-187

    properties, 185

    running, 188

    sleeping, 191

    suspending, 191

    synchronization, 192-203

    terminating, 188-190

    ThreadPool class, 206-209

    ThreadStart delegate, 187

    ThreadState values, 186

multithreaded service consumption, 384-385

Mutex class, thread synchronization, 196-197

Mutex.WaitOne method, 197

MyDataLayer class, 47

MyDataLayer object, 47

myFunction function, 638

mySQL .NET data provider, 548

N

name attribute (add tag), 878, 882

Name property (Thread class), 185

names, variables, 53-54

Namespace property, System.Type class, 230

namespaces
FCL, 48-49
: separator, 170
System.Collections, 98
System.Management, 904
System.Text.RegularEx pressions, 85
System.Web.UI.HtmlCo ntrols, 441
System.Xml, 155, 168
System.Xml.XPath, 168-169

Navigate Backward button, 20

navigation
commands, debugging applications, 858-859
IDE, 20

nesting controls within controls, 345
GroupBox control, 345-346
Panel control, 346
TabControl control, 346

.NET
COM
CCW, 281-282
code attributes for COM Interop programming, 281
components, consuming, 283-286

data marshalling, from COM to .NET, 282-283
data protection with DPAPI, 732-733
resource leaks, 46

.NET applications
installing, 402
assembly deploy ment, 403
placing assemblies in GAC, 404-409
private installa tions, 409
instrumenting. See instrumenting

.NET Framework, 37
controls, 330
Button, 330-331
Label, 334
ListBox, 337
ListView, 338-342
StatusBar, 336
TextBox, 335
ToolBar, 331-333
TreeView, 342-345
XPath, 171-174

.NET remotingRemoting, 792-793
context, 795-796
creating clients, 805-806
creating server appli cations, 803-804

domains, 793-794
domain-neutral assemblies, 794
global exception handlers, 795
IIS, 806-807
remote objects, 797
client-activated, 798-799
registering, 800-803
single call, 797-798
singleton, 798-799
selecting channels, 796-797

Network Address parame ter, 539

Network Library parameter, 539

networks, connectivity, 386-387

new keyword, 39

New Project command (Project menu), 426

New Project dialog box, 415, 836

NextResult method, IDataReader interface, 576

nodes, 832
filtering, 170-171
Reference.map, 374

nodes (XML), 162-163

nondeterministic finaliza tion, 45-46

None attribute (Location attribute), 487

not operator, 171

notification filters,
FileSystemWatcher class,
138

NotSupported option, 673

nTierTemplate enterprise
template, 836

Nullable class, 913

nullable types, future
considerations, 913

NullReferenceException
exception, 493

nullValue annotation, typed
DataSets, 609

O

obfuscation, 770

Object Browser window, 15

object contexts, COM+,
820-821

object creation operators,
55

object pooling, 810-811,
817-818

Object URI, 796

object-oriented languages,
37

object-oriented program-
ming. See OOP

ObjectPooling attribute, 817

objects, 112-113, 117-118

  allocated, Generation
  0, 296

  Cache, 484, 491-496

  COMtoDotNet, 285

  condemned, 296

enumerators.
See enumerators

HttpApplicationState,
480

HttpCache, 485

HttpCachePolicy, 484

inheritance, base
classes, 119-122

live, 296

MyDataLayer, 47

persistence, 142-149,
152

polymorphism,
122-125

state maintenance,
118

UML, 117-118

WindowsIdentity,
735-736

WindowsPrincipal,
735-736

OdbcPermission class, 697

ODP.NET, 547

Off (0) tracing level
(TraceSwitch), 884

Off mode, sessionState,
481

offline actions, web service
support, 387

offline work, smart clients,
400

OLEDB data providers,
544-546

OleDbCommand class, 545

OleDbConnection class, 545

OleDbDataAdapter class,
546

OleDbDataReader class,
546

OleDbPermission class, 697

one-time licenses, 756

one-way data binding, 616

OOP (object-oriented pro-
gramming), 112-113

  inheriting from base
  classes, 119-122

  operations, 114-116

  polymorphism,
  122-125

Open method
(SqlConnection class), 538

operations, 114-115

  reflection, 254

  UML, 115-116

  XPath

    (.), 170

    [ ], 170

operators, 54-56

  address, 55

  arithmetic, 54

  assignment, 55

  case sensitivity, 171

  cast, 55

  conditional, 55, 64-65

  decrement, 55, 60

  increment, 55, 60

  indexing, 55

  indirection, 55

  is, 230

  logical, 54

  member access, 55

  object creation, 55

  overflow, 55

overloading, 56, 59

relational, 55

shift, 55

type information, 55

typeof, 230

XPath, 170-171

OptionalAttribute attribute, 283

or operator, 171

Oracle Microsoft .NET data provider, 547

Oracle .NET ODP.NET, 547

OraclePermission class, 697

out-of-process session state, 501

OutAttribute attribute, 283

outlining code, 18-19

output

    gacutil.exe, 404-405

    ImplicitInterfaceImplementation, 781

Output window, 15, 857

OutputCache directive, 484-488

overflow operators, 55

overloading operators, 56, 59

OwnerDraw control, 368

P

P/Invoke, 288

    consuming unmanaged DLLs, 288-289

    data marshalling, 289-290

    when to use, 292

    Win32 API, 290-291

PacketSize property (SqlConnection class), 538

padding, string formatting, 76-77, 80-81

Page_Load event handler, 511

Panel control, 346, 444

ParameterName property, IDataParameter interface, 559

parameters

    connection strings, 539-540

    data providers, 558

        IDataParameter interface, 558-559

        IDataParameterCollection interface, 559

        RDPParameter class, 559, 563

        RDPParameterCollection class, 563, 565

    dwFlags, 725

    parsing arrays as, 96-97

    pDataIn, 724

    pOptionalEntropy, 725

    pPromptStruct, 725

    pvReserved, 725

    szDataDescr, 724

    ToolTips, 26

Parameters property, IDbCommand interface, 570

parent/child relationship, header/detail forms (data binding), 628

parsing

    arrays as parameters, 96-97

    input strings with while statement, 70, 72

partial collections, Garbage Collector, 45

partial keyword, 914

partial types, future considerations, 914-915

passport authentication, 739-740

Password parameter, 540

passwords, user, 749-751

pDataIn parameter, 724

PE (portable executable) files, 244

Pending Checkins window, 15

per action licenses, 756

per CPU licenses, 756

per hit licensing, 756

per seat licenses, 756

perform, 305

PerformAdministrativeAction method, 823

performance, 305

    AddRange method, 307

    asynchronous I/O, 310

    chunky API calls, 305-306

    exceptions, 305

    for loop, 308-309

foreach loop, 308-309

jagged arrays, 307-308

rectangular arrays, 307-308

reference types, 306

value types, 306

Performance Monitor, 305

PerformanceCounterPermission class, 697

permissions, 695-697

defined, 696

Evaluate Assembly task (Runtime Security Policy folder), 701-703

identity, 697-698

policy modification, 698-700

resolving, 695-696

role-based, 698

persistence (objects), 142-149, 152

persisting DOM, 163

PIA (primary Interop assembly), 286

deployment, 287-288

producing, 287-288

PInvoke Common Language Runtime, 42

Platform Invoke. See P/Invoke

plug-ins, creating, 264-266, 268-272

PluginAPI project, 265-266

PluginLoader AppDomain, 272

PluginLoader class, 269-270

PluginTester Console application, 271-272

PluginTool class, 268-269

policies

assigning to enterprise templates, 839-840

CAS, 698-700

policy files, enterprise templates, 829-834

polymorphism, 122-125

pooling, 810-811, 817-818

Pooling parameter, 540

pop-up context menu event handler, 361

pOptionalEntropy parameter, 725

Port property, 525

portable executable (PE) files, 244

Position property

CurrencyManager class, 618

PropertyManager class, 621

PositionChanged event, CurrencyManager class, 618

post-operation evaluation, 60

pPromptStruct parameter, 725

pre-operation evaluation, 60

preemptive multitasking (threads), 192

prerequisites, enterprise templates, 834

PreserveSig property, 290

primary Interop assembly. See PIA

PrimaryInterOpAssembly attribute, 287

primitive data types, XSD, 591

PrintingPermission class, 697

Priority property (Thread class), 185

private installations, .NET applications, 409

processes, 793

profiles (developer), 7-8

ProgIdAttribute attribute, 283

program flow, control structures, 60

conditional statements, 60-61

execution path, 60

if conditional statements, 61

if/else conditional statements, 61

short circuit evaluations, 62, 64

switch statement, 65-68

ternary operator, 64-65

programmatically registering remote objects, 800-801

Project menu commands

Copy Project, 521-522

New Project, 426

Project Properties dialog box, 851

projects

AssemblyIntro, 248-252

enterprise templates, 829-830

Harness, 249

installation, 415-420

PluginAPI project, 265-266

properties

AppDomain class, 260

BestFitMapping, 290

CallingConvention, 290

CharSet, 290

ContextMenu, 360

ContextUtil class, 821

Count, 98

CurrencyManager class, 617

Current, 99

Custom dialog, 527

DataItem, 639

declaring, 777

delegates, 219

dllName, 290

DrawMode, 363

EntryPoint, 290

enumerators, 99

ExactSpelling, 290

IDataParameter interface, 558-559

IDataParameterCollect ion interface, 559

IDataReader interface, 575-576

IDbCommand interface, 569-570

IDbConnection interface, 566

IDbDataAdapter interface, 582

InnerText, 441

IsSynchronized, 98

PreserveSig, 290

PropertyManager class, 620-621

RequestSoapContext, 690

ResponseSoapContext, 690

SetLastError, 290

shared, COM+, 818-820

SqlConnection class, 538

SqlDataReader class, 542

SyncRoot, 98

System.Type class, 230

Tenths, 59

Text, Code View window, 318

threads, 185

ThrowOnUnmappable Char, 290

TraceSwitch, 884

TransparencyKey, 368

ViewState, client-side state management, 456-462

Web Application folder, 525

WholePart, 59

Windows Forms, 321-322

WMIDemoProvider class, 900

Properties menu, 320

Properties window, 16

PropertyManager class, 620-621

protecting data. *See security*

prototypes, enterprise templates, 829

proxies, clients, 674

public and private key pairs, creating, 405-406

public key encryption, 720-721

DSACryptoServiceProvi der class, 721, 723

RSACryptoServiceProvi der class, 723

public properties, CurrencyManager class, 617

PublisherIdentityPermission class, 698

PublisherProtected class, 707

PublishEvent method, 825

Pulse method (Monitor class), 199

PulseAll method (Monitor class), 199-203

purchasing methods, licensing, 768

pvReserved parameter, 725

Q

queries
  custom attributes,
    238-241
  localized content
    data, 510-511
query strings
  client-side state man-
    agement, 471-472,
    474
QueryStringExample.aspx
  HTML view, 472
  Source view, 472, 474
Queue collection, 104-105
queued components
  advanced COM+, 826
  COM+, 812

R

race conditions, 207
RadioButton control, 444
RadioButtonList control,
  444
raising events, 194, 196,
  224
RC2CryptoServiceProvider
  class, 712
RCW (runtime callable
  wrapper), 275-278
RDPCommand class, 570,
  575
RDPConnection class, 566,
  569
RDPDataAdapter class,
  582, 587

RDPDataReader class, 576,
  581
RDPParameter class, 559,
  563
RDPParameterCollection
  class, 563, 565
read-only data binding, 635
ReaderWriterLock class,
  thread synchronization,
  203
RecordsAffected property
  (SqlDataReader class),
  542, 576
rectangular arrays, 307-308
RedirectFromLoginPage
  method, 738
RedPlugin class, 266, 268
refactoring, 113
reference counting, 44
reference types, 300
  common type systems,
    39
  versus value types, 40,
    306
Reference.map node, 374
references
  adding, 373
    in Visual Studio
      .NET, 373-377
    WSDL, 377-378
    XSD, 601
References Path page, 320
reflection, 228-231, 234
reflection operations, 254
ReflectionPermission class,
  697
Regex class, matching,
  87-89
Registers window, 17, 857

registration, remote objects,
  800
  programmatically,
    800-801
  with configuration file,
    802-803
RegistryPermission class,
  697
regular expressions, 85
  assertions, 89
  data validation, 89
  matching, 85-87
    character classes, 87
    grouping matches,
      89-90
    Regex class, 87, 89
    replacing matched
      strings, 90-91
    single-character
      escape sequences,
      86
  syntax, 85
relational operators, 55
relationships, XSD, 601
remote objects, 797
  client-activated,
    798-799
  registering, 800
    programmatically,
      800-801
    with configuration
      file, 802-803
  single call, 797-798
  singleton, 798-799
remotingRemoting,
  792-793
  context, 795-796
  creating clients,
    805-806

creating server applications, 803-804

domains, 793-794

domain-neutral assemblies, 794

global exception handlers, 795

IIS, 806-807

remote objects, 797

client-activated, 798-799

registering, 800-803

single call, 797-798

singleton, 798-799

selecting channels, 796-797

Remove method, 84

remove tag, 878, 882

RemoveAt method, IDataParameterCollection interface, 559

removing substrings, 84

rendering data

%# % syntax, 635

complex data binding, 638

DataBind method, 638-639

simple data binding, 636-638, 641

RenewTicketIfOld method, 738

Repeater class, 640

Repeater control, 444, 641-644

repeater data binding, 641-644

Replace method, 81, 84

replacing

characters, 84

strings, 84

replacing characters (strings), 81-82

replacing matched strings, 90-91

reports, comments, 24-25

Request event source, 905

request tracing, EIF, 906

RequestSoapContext property, 690

Required option, 673

RequiresNew option, 673

Reset All Policy Levels task (Runtime Security Policy folder), 700

Reset method, 99

ResetAbort method (Thread class), 187

resource files, assembly, 255

Resource View window, 16

ResourceManager class, 255

ResourcePermissionBase class, 697

resources

assemblies, 247

embedding, 251-255

localization, 255-259

localized, 506-507

ResponseSoapContext property, 690

Resume method (Thread class), 187

reverse-engineering, 770-771

RijndaelManaged class, 713

role-based permissions, 698

role-based security, COM+, 811-812, 821-823

roles, authorizing users, 740

RoleSecurity class, 822

roots, 295

Rotor, 44

routers, advanced ASP.NET deployment, 530-532

RSACryptoServiceProvider class, 723

running

threads, 188

Windows Forms applications, 322-323

runtime callable wrapper. See RCW

Runtime Security Policy folder, tasks, 699-703

S

SampleHttpModule, 514

SampleService class, 803

satellite assemblies, 256-259

SaveViewState method, overriding, 462

schema documents, 593

schemas, event, 903-904

Search Results window, 16

SecondForm.aspx
    Code view, 478-479
    HTML view, 477-478
secret key, 711
secrets, 711
security
    CAS
        blocking unwanted
            clients, 706-708
        declarative, 705-706
        imperative, 704-705
    COM+, 820
        object contexts,
            820-821
        role-based, 821-823
        role-based security,
            811-812
        security contexts,
            820-821
    Common Language
        Runtime, 42-43
    contexts, COM+,
        820-821
    data, 748
        connection strings,
            748
        SSL, 751
        user passwords,
            749-751
        ViewState, 751-752
    digital signatures,
        720-721
        DSACryptoServicePr
            ovider class, 721,
            723
        RSACryptoServicePr
            ovider class, 723

encryption
    asymmetric,
        720-723
    public key, 720-721
    DSACryptoServiceProvi
        der class, 721, 723
    RSACryptoServiceProvi
        der class, 723
    symmetric encryption,
        711
        DESCryptoServicePr
            ovider class,
            711-712
        RC2CryptoServicePr
            ovider class, 712
        RijndaelManaged
            class, 713
        TripleDESCryptoServ
            iceProvider class,
            713, 715
user, 734, 747
    authenticating
        users, 735-740
    authorizing users
        with roles, 740
    IIdentity interface
        implementation,
        740-747
    IPrincipal interface
        implementation,
        740-747
WSE w2.0, 687
    signing messages,
        690
    UsernameToken
        class, 688-689
    X.509 digital
        certificates, 689

Security filter,
    FileSystemWatcher class,
    138
SecurityPermission class,
    697
SecurityRole attribute, 823
SelectCommand property,
    582
self-updating applications,
    creating, 394-396
sequence element, XSD
    complex data types, 593
Serializable attribute, 143
serialization
    web services,
        669-673
    XML, 179-183
SerializationDeSerialization
    Example, 143-149
Serialize method, 181
serializing objects, 143-149
    Binary serialization,
        142
    extending, 149, 152
    XML serialization, 142
Server parameter, 539
Server attribute (Location
    attribute), 487
Server Explorer view, 898
Server Explorer window, 16
Server mode, 809
server-activated URLs, 797
server-side state
    management, 479-480
    application state, 480
        storing data, 480
        synchronizing,
            480-481
    session state, 481-482

servers

controls

HTML, 440-442

passing between forms, 474-479

web server controls, 443-444

SQL Server, 501-503

ServerVersion property (SqlConnection class), 538

ServiceControllerPermission class, 697

serviced components, 808

ServicedComponent class, 811, 813

session state, 481-482

sessions

shared, 501

state

creating ASP.NET applications in, 501-503

out-of-process, 501

sessionState, configuring, 481-482

SetAbort method, 821

SetAuthCookie method, 739

SetCacheability method, 490

SetComplete method, 821

SetData method (AppDomain class), 260

SetExpires method, 490

SetLastError property, 290

Setup Project Wizard, 415-420

setup projects

creating, 523-529

default user interface, 526

deploying, 529

views, 525-526

SHA1 (Secure Hash Algorithm), 717

SHA1Managed class, 718-719

shaped forms, 368-370

ShapedForms application, 368

shared groups, COM+, 818-820

shared properties, COM+, 818-820.

shared secrets, 711

shared sessions, 501

SharedPropertyGroupManager class, 818

shift operators, 55

short circuit evaluations, 62-64

shortcuts

keys, 8

SimpleApplication.exe, 419

Show Next Statement command, 859

signatures, 720-721

DSACryptoServiceProvider class, 721, 723

event handlers, 224

methods, 784, 786

RSACryptoServiceProvider class, 723

signing

assemblies, delayed signing, 408-409

messages, 690

SignOut method, 739

simple data binding, 613, 615, 621-622, 636-638, 641

simple data types

derived, 591-592

primitive, 591

Simple Object Access Protocol. See **SOAP**

SimpleApplication.exe, 417

dependencies, 420

shortcut, 419

SimpleApplicationLibrary.dll, 417

SimpleWorkerThreadMethod method, 190

single call remote objects, 797-798

single-character escape sequences, 86

single-dimensional arrays, 93-95

single-file assemblies, 244

singlecast delegates, 215, 217-219

singleton remote objects, 798-799

sinks, event, 903-906

SiteIdentityPermission class, 698

Size filter, FileSystemWatcher class, 138

Sleep method (Thread class), 187

sleeping threads, 191

SmallIcon property, 339

smart clients, 390-392

  deploying updates from centralized servers, 392

    self-updating applications, 394-396

    System.Reflection method, 393-394

    URL-based executables, 393

    web server deployments, 393

  design, 391

  high fidelity, 391

  intelligent connections, 391

  offline functionalities, 400

  offloading server processing with web services, 396-400

  operations, 391

  web application deployments, 412

SOAP (Simple Object Access Protocol), 663-664, 678

  over TCP, 680

  SoapClient class, 686-687

  SoapReceiver class, 680-684

  SoapSender class, 680-684

  SoapService class, 683-685

SOAP Message Sender, 682

SoapClient class, 686-687

SoapReceiver class, 680-684

SoapSender class, 680-684

SoapService class, 683-685

SocketPermission class, 697

SoftwareElement event source, 904

Solution Explorer

  displaying Windows Forms applications, 321

  Hello World, 428

Solution Explorer window, 16

SomeAttribute, 777

SomeBooleanSwitch switch, 883

SomeDelegate class, 211

SortedList collection, 106-107

Source view

  CookieExample.aspx, 469, 471

  QueryStringExample.aspx, 472, 474

Source View listing, 467

SourceColumn property, IDataParameter interface, 559

sources, event, 903-904

  Request, 905

  SoftwareElement, 904

SourceVersion property, IDataParameter interface, 559

spaghetti code, 774

SpinWait method (Thread class), 187

Split method, 82

splitting strings, 82

SPMGetter class, 818

SPMSetter class, 818

SQL data providers, 537

  SqlCommand class, 540-542

  SqlConnection class, 537-540

  SqlDataAdapter class, 542-544

  SqlDataReader class, 542

SQL Server, session state maintenance, 501-503

SQL statements, creating with Insert method, 83-84

SqlClientPermission class, 697

SqlCommand class, 540-542

SqlConnection class, 537

  database connection strings, 539-540

  events, 539

  methods, 538-539

  properties, 538

SqlDataAdapter class, 542-544

SqlDataReader class, 542

SSL, 751

Stack collection, 101-102

Start command, debugging applications, 859

Start method (Thread class), 186-187

StartsWith method, 80

state

application, in web farms, 503-504

maintenance, 118

management, 456

client-side, 456-469, 471-472, 474-479

server-side, 479-482

sessions

creating ASP.NET applications in web farms, 501-503

out-of-process, 501

web services, 673

State property, IDbConnection interface, 566

State property, SqlConnection class, 538

State Service (ASP.NET), 503

StateChange event (SqlConnection class), 539

statements

case, 66

conditional, 60-61

continue, 72

do..while, 72-73

for, 69

foreach, 69

if-else-if, 66-67

switch, 65-68

while, 70-72

StateServer mode

sessionState, 482

SQLServer, 482

static classes, future considerations, 915-916

static content, enterprise templates, 830-831

static methods, 738-739

static prototypes, 831

StatusBar control, 336

Step Into command, 859

Step Out command, 859

Step Over command, 859

StockLabel control, 767

Stop command, 859

storage

data, 480

URLs

app.config file, 379

isolated storage, 379-382

values, 334-336

stream I/O, 128-129, 132

FileStream class, 132-134

FileSystemWatcher class, 138-142

MemoryStream class, 134-135

StreamReader class, 136-138

StreamWriter class, 136-138

StringReader class, 135-136

StringWriter class, 135-136

StreamReader class, 136-138

StreamReaderWriter example, 137-138

streams, 252

StreamWriter class, 136-138

String class, 75, 80

StringBuilder class, 75, 83, 303-305

StringReader class, 135-136

strings, 75

cases, modifying, 82

COM+, 811, 815-817

connection, 539-540, 748

formatting, 75-76

alignment, 76-77

custom dates, 78-79

custom integers, 77-78

dates, 78

escape sequences, 79-80

integers, 77

padding, 76-77, 80-81

immutability, 75

query, client-side state management, 471-474

regular expressions. See regular expressions

replacing, 84

replacing characters, 81-82

splitting, 82

StringBuilder class, 83

substrings

   locating, 80

   removing, 84

   trimming characters, 81

StringWriter class, 135-136

strongly named assemblies, creating, 405-409

StrongNameIdentityPermission class, 698, 706

struct keyword, 38

StructLayoutAttribute attribute, 283

structs

   CRYPTPROTECT_PROMPTSTRUCT, 726

   DATA_BLOB, 724-725

structure, enterprise templates, 836-839

subproject wizards, enterprise templates, 831

subscription licenses, 756

substrings

   locating, 80

   removing, 84

Supported option, 673

Suspend method (Thread class), 187

suspending threads, 191

switch statement, 65-68

switch tag, 882

switches, trace, 895-896

   BooleanSwitch, 896

   TraceSwitch class, 896-897

symmetric encryption, 711

   DESCryptoServiceProvider class, 711-712

   RC2CryptoServiceProvider class, 712

   RijndaelManaged class, 713

   TripleDESCryptoService Provider class, 713, 715

synchronization,

   application state, 480-481

   threads, 192-193

      Interlocked class, 203

      lock keyword, 193

      Monitor class, 198-203

      Mutex class, 196-197

      raising events, 194-196

      ReaderWriterLock class, 203

synchronous calls, web services, 674-675

synchronous HttpHandlers, creating, 516-518

SyncRoot property, 98

syntax

   errors, debugging applications, 852-854

   regular expressions, 85

   XPath, 169-170

System.Array class, 93

System.Array.GetUpperBound method, 95

System.Attribute class, 237

System.Collections namespace, 98

System.Console.ReadlLine command, 128

System.Console.WriteLine command, 128

System.Data assembly, 246

System.Delegate class, 220

System.Diagnostics namespace, 874

system.diagnostics tag, 878

System.Diagnostics.DefaultTraceListener, 874

System.Management namespace, 904

System.MulticastDelegate class, 220

System.Reflection method, 393-394

System.Text.RegularExpressions namespace, 85

System.Type class, 229-230

System.Web.UI.HtmlControls namespace, 441

System.Xml namespace, 155, 168

System.Xml.XPath namespace, 168-169

SystemString class, 80

szDataDescr parameter, 724

szPrompt field (CRYPTPROTECT_PROMPTSTRUCT structure), 726

T

TabControl control, 346

Table control, 444

TableCell control, 444

TableRow control, 444

tables

  card, 296

  DataSets, 599-600

Task List window, 16

Task Manager, 891

TCP (Transmission Control Protocol)

  messaging, 679-680

    SOAP over TCP, 680

    SoapClient class, 686-687

    SoapReceiver class, 680-684

    SoapSender class, 680-684

    SoapService class, 683-685

  SOAP over, 680

TcpChannel, 796-797

TDL (Enterprise Template Definition Language), 831-834

templates

  Default Web Application, 428

  enterprise templates, 828-829

    accessibility, 844-845

    architecture, 829-830, 835-836

    assigning policies, 839-840

    content, 830-831

    custom wizards, 831

    manual construction, 840-843

    policy files, 831-834

    setting up prerequisites, 834

    static prototypes, 831

    structure, 836-839

    subproject wizards, 831

    testing, 845

Tenths property, 59

terminals, dumb terminals, 391

terminating threads, 188-190

ternary operator, 64-65

Test Harness Console application, 250-251

testing

  enterprise templates, 845

  network connectivity, 386-387

text, localized, 508-510

text editors, 18

  bookmarks, 20-23

  navigation, 20

  outlining code, 18-19

Text property, Code View window, 318

TextBox control, 335, 444

TextWriterTraceListener, 876-877, 879

the System.Array class, 94

This window, 17, 855

Thread objects, Start method, 188

Thread.Abort method, terminating threads, 189

Thread.AbortReset method, 190

Thread.Join method, 191

Thread.Sleep method, 191

Thread.Suspend method, 191

ThreadAbortException exception, terminating threads, 188

ThreadPool class, 206

  passing data to threads, 208-209

  ThreadPool.QueueUser WorkItem method, 207

  WaitCallback delegate, 206-207

ThreadPool.QueueUserWorkItem method (thread pool), 207

threads, 184-185

  background, 185, 501

  creating, 188

  foreground, 185

  joining, 191

  methods, 186-187

  properties, 185

  running, 188

  sleeping, 191

  suspending, 191

synchronization, 192-193

Interlocked class, 203

lock keyword, 193

Monitor class, 198-203

Mutex class, 196-197

raising events, 194, 196

ReaderWriterLock class, 203

terminating, 188, 190

ThreadPool class, 206

passing data to threads, 208-209

ThreadPool.QueueU serWorkItem method, 207

WaitCallback delegate, 206-207

ThreadStart delegate, 187

ThreadState values, 186

Threads window, 17, 856

ThreadStart delegate, 187

ThreadState property (Thread class), 185

ThreadState values, 186

ThrowOnUnmappableChar property, 290

tightly coupled events (COM+), 812

time zones, localized, 512-513

TimeSpan class, 197

tokenxs:Token data type, 592

tool windows, 14-18

ToolBar control, 331-333

Toolbox window, 16

tools, debugging application windows, 854-857

Tools menu, external tools, 31

ToolTips, parameter lists, 26

ToUpper method, 82

Trace class, 873, 895

adding code to applications, 895

trace switches, 895-896

BooleanSwitch, 896

TraceSwitch class, 896-897

trace listeners, 873, 876-881, 885-887

trace switches, 874, 882-885, 895-896

BooleanSwitch, 896

TraceSwitch class, 896-897

TRACE symbol, 873

trace tag, 878

Trace.Listeners.Add() method, 880

Trace.WriteLineIf method, 883

TraceError property (TraceSwitch class), 884

TraceEventSink event sink, 905

TraceInfo property (TraceSwitch class), 884

TraceListener class, 876, 886

TraceListenerCollection objects, 877

TraceSessions.config, 907

TraceSwitch (trace switch), 882-885

properties, 884

registering in App.config, 884

tracing levels, 883-884

TraceSwitch class, 896-897

TraceVerbose property (TraceSwitch class), 884

TraceWarning property (TraceSwitch class), 884

tracing statements, debugging applications, 872, 874-876

Transaction property, 570, 821

TransactionAttribute, 813

TransactionId property, 821

TransactionOption enumeration, 673

transactions

COM+, 809-810, 813-815

distributed, 673

web services, 673

transformations, XML documents, 175-178

TransparencyKey property, 368

TreeView control, 342-345

Trim method, 81

TrimEnd method, 81

trimming characters (strings), 81

TrimStart method, 81

TripleDES encryption algorithm, 713

TripleDESCryptoService Provider class, 713, 715

troubleshooting web service errors, 387

true mode (BooleanSwitch), 882

trusted assemblies, 695-696

  Adjust Zone Security wizardWizard, 701-702

  increasing trust levels, 700

Trusted Connection parameter, 539

TryEnter method (Monitor class), 199

two-dimensional arrays, 93-95

two-way data binding, 616

type attribute (add tag), 879

type information operators, 55

typed DataSets, 603-606

  annotation, 609-611

  application, 607

  building with CSD.EXE, 607

  creating in Visual Studio .NET, 606-607

typedChildren annotation, typed DataSets, 609

typedName annotation, typed DataSets, 609

typedParent annotation, typed DataSets, 609

typedPlural annotation, typed DataSets, 609

typeof operator, 230

types, determining at runtime, 229-231, 234

U

UDDI (Universal Description, Discovery, and Integration), 382-383

UIL (user interface layer), 835

UIPermission class, 697

UML

  attributes, 113-114

  classes, 116-117

  objects, 117-118

  operations, 115-116

unboxing, 300-302

Unindent method, 874-875

uninitialized variables. See variables, initializing

unique constraints, 601

Universal Description, Discovery, and Integration. See UDDI

Unload method (AppDomain class), 260

Unlock method, HttpApplicationState class, 481

untrusted assemblies, 695-696

  Adjust Zone Security wizardWizard, 701-702

  increasing trust levels, 700

UpdateCommand property, 582

UpdatedRowSource property, 570

updates, smart clients, 392-396

URL-based executables, deploying, 393

URLIdentityPermission class, 698

URLs

  client-activated, 797

  dynamic, 378

    app.config file, 379

    isolated storage, 379-382

    UDDI consumption, 382-383

  server-activated, 797

  web application deployments, 410

user controls, 347-348, 444-455

User ID parameter, 540

user interface layer. See UIL

user interfaces, setup projects, 526

user passwords, 749-751

user security, 734, 747

   authenticating users, 735

      forms, 737-739

      passport, 739-740

      Windows, 735-736

   authorizing users with roles, 740

   IIdentity interface implementation, 740-747

   IPrincipal interface implementation, 740-747

UsernameToken class, 688-689

using keyword, 47

V

validation, data, 89

value attribute (add tag), 883

Value property, IDataParameter interface, 559

value types, 300

   common type systems, 38-40

   passing to methods, 40

   versus reference types, 306

values

   Location attribute, 486

   modifying, 334-336

   storing, 334-336

   ThreadState, 186

variables

   evaluation

      post-operation, 60

      pre-operation, 60

   initializing, 53

   names, 53-54

   operators. *See* operators

VaryByCustom attribute (OutputCache directive), 488

VaryByHeader attribute (OutputCache directive), 488

VaryByParam attribute (OutputCache directive), 487-488

Verbose (4) tracing level (TraceSwitch), 884

verification

   assemblies, 409

   licensing, 756, 768

views

   Code

      FirstForm.aspx, 476-477

      SecondForm.aspx, 478-479

   Design, 425, 430

   HTML, 425

      FirstForm.aspx, 475

      QueryStringExampl e.aspx, 472

      SecondForm.aspx, 477-478

Server Explorer, 898

setup projects, 525-526

Source, QueryStringExample. aspx, 472, 474

ViewState

   creating ASP.NET applications in web farms, 499-500

   data security, 751-752

ViewState property, 456-462

ViewStateExampleForm. aspx, 457-459

ViewStateExampleForm. aspx.cs, 458-461

virtual keyword, 123

virtual methods, 123-125

VirtualDirectory property, 525

Visual Basic 6

   client consumption of .NET components, 285

   COM objects, 279-280

Visual C# .NET 2005 Unleashed, 911

visual inheritance, 351-352

   best practices, 358-359

   WinForms, 352-353, 356

      CompanyOKCancel, 354-356

      InheritedForm, 358

      InheritedOKCancel, 356-359

Visual Studio .NET

adding web references in, 373-377

Auto-Generated Web Service Client Proxy, 374, 376

creating Hello World application, 427

creating typed DataSets, 606-607

customizing, 7

autohiding windows, 12-14

developer profiles, 7

dockable windows, 10-11

keyboard shortcuts, 8

maximizing viewable area, 9-10

debugging applications, 861, 864, 867

developer profiles, 7-8

Explore Here tool, creating, 31

external tools, 30-31

IDE, 18

binary files, 30

bookmarks, 20-23

help, 22-26

HTML edits, 26-29

navigation, 20

outlining code, 18-19

XML edits, 29-30

tool windows, 14-18

window management, 7

Visual Studio .NET 2005, 532

VolatileRead method (Thread class), 187

VolatileWrite method (Thread class), 187

W

Wait method (Monitor class), 199-203

WaitAll method, 194

WaitAny method, 194

WaitCallback delegate, 206-208

WaitOne method, 194

WaitSleepJoin state (threads), 191, 194

Warning (2) tracing level (TraceSwitch), 884

Watch window, 18, 855

Web Application folder, 524-525

web applications, installing, 410

smart client deployments, 412

URL deployments, 410

web controls, licensing, 768

web farms

advanced ASP.NET deployment, 530

best practices, 505-506

creating ASP.NET applications in, 499

application state, 503-504

configuration, 504-505

deployment, 504-505

session state maintenance, 501-503

ViewState, 499-500

Web Forms, 634

data binding, 635

%# % syntax, 635

cascading header forms, 652-654, 657

complex, 638

Container.DataItem property, 639

DataBind method, 638-639

DataBinder class, 639-640

DataGrid, 647-653

DataList, 645, 647

detail forms, 648-654, 657

header forms, 648-652

ItemDataBound event, 640

repeater, 641-644

simple, 636-638, 641

Designer, 424-425, 430

even handling, 433-438

web pages, design, 27

web references, adding, 373

   in Visual Studio .NET, 373-377

   WSDL, 377-378

web servers

   controls, 443-444

   deploying, 393

Web Service Enhancements. See WSE v2.0

web services, 663

   Amazon.com, connecting to, 398-399

   asynchronous calls, 675-676

   client reliability, 385-386

   consuming asynchronously, 383-385

   consumption, 674

   contract-first programming, 674

   creating

      Hello World, 665-669

      serialization, 669-673

   defined, 663

   errors, 387

   MessageBox, 377

   offline actions, 387

   offloading server processing with, 396-400

   SOAP, 663-664

   state maintenance, 673

   synchronous calls, 674-675

   testing network connectivity, 386-387

   transactions, 673

   WSDL, 665

Web Services Description Language. See WSDL

Web.config file, 428, 687, 735

WebForm1.aspx, 431, 436-437

WebForm1.aspx.cs, 432, 437-438

WebMethodAttribute attribute, 235

WebPermission class, 697

while loop, 70, 72

while statement, 70, 72

Whitehorse, 532

WholePart property, 59

wildcards, XPath, 170

Win32, P/Invoke, 290-291

Win32 APIs, 42

Windows, authentication, 735-736

windows

   Code View, Text property, 318

   debugging applications, 854

      Autos window, 855

      Breakpoints window, 857

      Call Stack window, 856

      Command window, 857

      Locals window, 855

      Memory window, 857

      Modules window, 857

      Output window, 857

      Registers window, 857

      This window, 855

      Threads window, 856

      Watch window, 855

   dockable, 10-11

   hiding, 12-14

   HTML view, 28

   management, 7

      developer profiles, 7

      maximizing viewable area, 9-10

   tool, 14-18

Windows Application Wizard

   Button control, 324-329

   compiling, 322-323

   creating applications, 319-321

   running, 322-323

   setting properties, 321-322

Windows command (Debug menu), 16

Windows Data Protection API. See DPAPI

Windows Forms, 314, 634

controls, licensing, 768

creating buttons on, 316-317

custom list elements, 363

DrawMode property, 363

ListBoxes, 363-365

menu items, 365-367

Forms Designer, 316-318

Hello World, 318

Button control, 324-329

compiling, 322-323

running, 322-323

setting properties, 321-322

Windows Application Wizard, 319-321

Main method, 315-316

Windows Forms data binding, 613

binding to a ComboBox, 622

BindingContext class, 617

cascading header/detail forms, 628, 631

complex data binding, 616

CurrencyManager class, 617

complex data binding, 618, 620

events, 618

public properties, 617

DataGrid binding, 622-625

header/detail forms, 625, 628

one-way data binding, 616

PropertyManager class, 620-621

simple data binding, 613, 615, 621-622

two-way data binding, 616

Windows Management Instrumentation. *See* WMI

WindowsIdentity object, 735-736

WindowsPrincipal object, 735-736

WinForms, 352-353, 356

CompanyOKCancel, 354, 356

InheritedForm, 358

InheritedOKCancel, 356, 358-359

WISE InstallMaster, 415

wizards

Adjust Zone Security, 701-702

COM+ New Subscription, 825

Setup Project, creating installation projects, 415, 417-420

Windows Application

compiling, 322-323

creating applications, 319-321

running, 322-323

setting properties, 321-322

WMI (Windows Management Instrumentation), 897-900, 902

WMIDemoProvider class, 899-900

WMIDemo_SampleEvent event, 900-901

WMIEventSink event sink, 905

workerThread, 191

Workstation ID parameter, 540

WorkstationId property (SqlConnection class), 538

wrapper classes, DPAPI, 726-727, 732

Write function (trace listeners), 877

Write method

log writing, 875

TraceListener class, 886

WriteContentTo method, 163

WriteIf method, log writing, 875

WriteLine function (trace listeners), 877

WriteLine method, 40, 60, 874, 886

WriteLineIf method, log writing, 875

WriteTo method, 163

WSDL (Web Services Description Language), 377-378, 665, 678

WSE v2.0 (Web Service Enhancements), 678-679

history, 679

messaging with attachments, 690

DIME, 690

file transfers, 691

security, 687

signing messages, 690

UsernameToken class, 688-689

X.509 digital certificates, 689

TCP messaging, 679-680

SOAP over TCP, 680

SoapClient class, 686-687

SoapReceiver class, 680-684

SoapSender class, 680-684

SoapService class, 683-685

X - Z

X.509 digital certificates, 689

XCopy

ASP.NET application deployment, 522-523

command, 410

XML (Extensible Markup Language), 29

attributes, 162-163

documents

creating, 161-162

isolated storage, 380, 382

transformations, 175-178

DOM (Document Object Model), 155-161, 163

editing, 29-30

elements, 162-163

nodes, 162-163

schemas

annotation, 593-594

facets, 594-595

programming, XmlSchema class, 595, 598

serialization, 142, 179-183

XSLT (eXtensible Extensible Stylesheet Language Transformations), 175

XML Path Language. See XPath

XML Schema Definition Language. See XSD

XML Schema Definition. See XSD

XML Spy tool, 594

XmlAttribute attribute, 182

XmlAttribute class, 155, 161-162

XmlComment class, 155

XmlConvert class, 167-168

XmlDocument class, 155, 161, 163

XmlDocument.Save method, 163

XmlElement class, 155, 162

XmlNode class, 155, 162-163

XmlNodeList class, 155

XmlNodeReader class, 164, 167

XmlReader classes, 163-164

XmlNodeReader, 164, 167

XmlTextReader, 164-166

XmlValidatingReader, 164, 166

XmlRoot attribute, 182

XmlSchema class, 595, 598

XmlSerializer class, 181

XmlTextReader class, 164-166

XmlValidatingReader class, 164, 166

XPath, 168-171

XPathDocument class, 171-174

XPathNavigator class, 172-174

XPathNodeIterator class, 174

xs:anyUri, 591

xs:base64Binary, 591

xs:Bool, 591

xs:date, 591

xs:dateTime, 591

xs:decimal, 591

xs:double, 591

xs:duration, 591

xs:float, 591

xs:hexBinary, 591

xs:integer data type, 592

xs:Name data type, 592

xs:nonPositiveInteger data type, 592

xs:normalizedString data type, 592

xs:positiveInteger data type, 592

xs:string, 591

xs:time, 591

xs:unsignedByte data type, 592

xs:unsignedInt data type, 592

xs:unsignedLong data type, 592

xs:unsignedShort data type, 592

XSD (XML Schema Definition Language), 588-589, 669

annotation of XML schemas, 593-594

complex data types, 592-593

derived data types, 591-592

files, 589-590

introduction, 589-590

primitive data types, 591

programming XML schemas, 595, 598

structuring DataSets, 599

defining keys and constraints, 600-603

defining tables and columns, 599-600

typed DataSets, 603, 605-606

annotation, 609-611

application, 607

building with CSD.EXE, 607

creating in Visual Studio .NET, 606-607

XML schema facets, 594-595

XSD.EXE, creating typed DataSets, 607

XSLT (eXtensible Extensible Stylesheet Language: Transformations), 175

Zone Security Adjustment dialog, 702

ZoneIdentityPermission class, 698

Your Guide to Computer Technology

www.informit.com